# Food and Drug Regulation

# Food and Drug Regulation: A Statutory Approach

Adam I. Muchmore
Professor of Law
Penn State Law
University Park, PA

Carolina Academic Press
Durham, North Carolina

ISBN 978-1-5310-0445-3
e-ISBN 978-1-5310-0446-0
LCCN 2020947321

Carolina Academic Press
700 Kent Street
Durham, North Carolina 27701
Telephone (919) 489-7486
Fax (919) 493-5668
www.cap-press.com

Printed in the United States of America

*To my parents*

# Summary of Contents

# Contents

# List of Tables

# Table of Cases

References are to pages. Bold numbers indicate the page on which an excerpt of a principal case begins.

# Table of Principal Cases

# Table of Principal Federal Register Documents

# Table of Principal Guidance Documents

# Acknowlegments

This project developed over many years, and I accordingly owe many thanks. The first set goes to the students who have taken my food and drug classes over the years. From them, I learned the importance of organizing course materials in an approachable manner—something I hope I have managed to do here.

I am grateful for many years of summer research funding from Penn State Law, which allowed the project to develop in response to each year's class. A Fall 2019 sabbatical provided by Penn State University gave me time to restructure the book in a manner that, I hope, makes it more useful to the reader.

For excellent research assistance, I am grateful to Penn State Law students Kelly Allenspach, Rachel Awan, Michael Bond, Justin Fiorilli, Doug Fogle, Megan Green, Megan Janowiak, Sean Jorgensen, Kirill Lavinski, Chiao May Lee, Brandon Merritt, Rachel Sanders, Mike Schmidt, Corinne (Cori) Smith, Shaya Rubenstein, Megan Wells, and Jacob Wonn. For helpful comments on Chapter 4, I am grateful to Katrice Bridges Copeland, Steve Ostroff, and Chen-Sen (Samson) Wu.

Finally, I am grateful for the love and support of my dear family—Julia, Aaron, Keira, and Lydia. My gratitude to them goes beyond what words can express.

# Preface—About This Book

This book is intended for a law school survey course on food and drug regulation. It covers the Food and Drug Administration's (FDA's) regulation of food, food additives, dietary supplements, drugs, animal drugs, medical devices, combination products, biologics, HCT/Ps (human cells, tissues, and cellular and tissue-based products), cosmetics, color additives, and tobacco products. It also covers administrative procedure, regulation of research, FDA enforcement, federal preemption, and regulation of imports. It presents more limited material on related areas regulated primarily by other agencies.[1] In addition to covering this substantive material, the book will introduce you to the process of understanding a complex statute, its implementing regulations, and related enforcement policies.

The book's coverage is not intended to be comprehensive. Several existing books present treatise-level coverage and even those cannot cover FDA's regulatory programs comprehensively. This book instead focuses on core aspects of selected FDA regulatory programs in the areas of food and medical products.[2]

Food and drug regulation is primarily a statutory and regulatory subject. Accordingly, this book relies on a different set of documents and a different style of presentation than a typical casebook. The book emphasizes guided reading of the Federal Food, Drug, and Cosmetic Act, related statutes, FDA regulations, and Federal Register documents. Cases are presented primarily when they involve major issues of statutory interpretation, are historically significant, or are in one of the areas—such as federal preemption—where case law plays a major role in the overall regulatory scheme. Cases are also included where they provide a concise discussion of a regulatory program or a useful illustration of a concept.

This book is designed to work as a set with the accompanying Statutory & Regulatory Supplement (Supplement). The Supplement is available free, in PDF format, on this book's page of the Carolina Academic Press website.[3] The statutes and regulations in the Supplement have been aggressively edited, like the cases in a typical

1. These include USDA-regulated foods (meat, eggs, poultry, and fish of the order siluriformes (catfish and related species)), agricultural biotechnology, alcohol, controlled substances, and veterinary biologics.

2. The main categories the book does not address are animal food and feed, radiation-emitting products, and medical gases.

3. *See* https://cap-press.com/books/isbn/9781531004453/Food-and-Drug-Regulation.

law school casebook, to emphasize those aspects that are most important to a general understanding of the subject.

## Structure of the Book

The book is organized around the structure of the Federal Food, Drug, and Cosmetic Act of 1938 (FFDCA) and the relevant portion of the Public Health Services Act (PHSA).[4] This means that Chapter IV products (food, food additives, and dietary supplements), Chapter V products (drugs, animal drugs, medical devices, and combination products), and PHSA products (biologics and HCT/Ps) are each grouped together. The single-product-category chapters—Chapter VI (cosmetics), Chapter VII (color additives), and Chapter IX (tobacco products)—are then included in a final, catch-all group. Parts I, II, and VII of the book address cross-cutting issues, while Parts III, IV, V, and VI address the four groups of individual product categories. Part VIII contains the appendices.

Part I of the book introduces the basic structure of FDA and the FFDCA. Within Part I, Chapter 1 addresses the structure of the agency and the product categories set out in the FFDCA. Chapter 2 addresses administrative procedure. It contains material on administrative procedure generally and on administrative procedure specific to FDA.

Part II of the book addresses regulation of research, marketing authorization, and background regulatory requirements associated with marketing authorization. This Part emphasizes those aspects of research, marketing authorization, and background requirements that are similar across multiple product categories. Within Part II, Chapter 3 addresses regulation of research. It focuses on FDA regulation of human-subject research. Chapter 4 addresses marketing authorization. It contains material on pathways to market, designations, and access before market authorization. Chapter 5 addresses background requirements associated with marketing authorization. It contains information on production-process requirements, labeling requirements, establishment registration requirements, user fees, and postmarket requirements.

Part III of the book addresses those products regulated primarily under Chapter IV of the FFDCA. Chapter 6 addresses food, Chapter 7 addresses food additives, and Chapter 8 addresses dietary supplements. Chapter 9 does not address a single product category. Instead, it contains material on label claims for the two Chapter IV categories—food and dietary supplements—for which label-claim

---

4. Please note that this book uses: Roman numerals when referring to *parts of this book* (Part V); Arabic numerals when referring to *parts of the CFR* (21 C.F.R. Part 5); Arabic numerals when referring to *chapters of this book* (Chapter 5); and roman numerals when referring to *chapters of the FFDCA* (Chapter V).

issues arise. Label claims receive a separate chapter to avoid presenting duplicative material in the earlier chapters on food and dietary supplements.

Part IV of the book addresses those products regulated primarily under Chapter V of the FFDCA. Chapter 10 addresses drugs, Chapter 11 addresses animal drugs, Chapter 12 addresses medical devices, and Chapter 13 addresses combination products.

Part V of the book addresses those products regulated primarily under the PHSA. Chapter 14 addresses those aspects of biological products regulated primarily by the PHSA.[5] Chapter 15 addresses HCT/Ps.

Part VI of the book addresses those products regulated under the FFDCA Chapters VI, VII, and IX. Chapter 16 addresses cosmetics, Chapter 17 addresses color additives, and Chapter 18 addresses tobacco products.

Part VII returns to cross-cutting issues of the type addressed in Parts I and II. Chapter 19 addresses FDA enforcement, Chapter 20 addresses federal preemption, and Chapter 21 addresses regulation of imports.

Part VIII is an appendix recommending further reading. Its focus is on books rather than academic articles, with a particular emphasis on items available as audiobooks (a wonderful help to the busy lawyer during commuting or exercise). It includes both law-specific reading and material on scientific, technological, and industrial developments relevant to food and drug regulation.

For a description of the structure of individual chapters, see "Introduction to this Book" in Chapter 1, Part A.

## Citation Format and Editorial Approach

I have aggressively edited the documents that I have excerpted in this book. My goal in doing this is to emphasize those aspects of the excerpted documents that are most relevant to basic goal of this book: presenting an approachable overview of the basic structure of food and drug regulation.

Citations in this book conform generally to the 20th edition of *The Bluebook: A Uniform System of Citation*. Significant exceptions are the following:

I have cited Federal Register documents in a format that emphasizes the date of publication and type of document, rather than document title. I have done this for two reasons. First, these documents frequently contain cumbersome multipart titles that—despite their length—are of only limited value in describing the document's

5. As you will see later, all products meeting the statutory definition of biological product, PHSA §351(i)(1), also meet the statutory definition of drug, FFDCA §201(g)(1). Accordingly, much of this chapter of the book is focused on the relationship between FDA's biologics division (transferred from the National Institute of Health to FDA in the 1970s) and FDA's drugs division.

content. Second, the administrative rulemaking process typically results in multiple documents with very similar titles. This book uses the format below, which I believe will help you distinguish more clearly between the different documents cited:

> *[date of publication in YYYY-MM-DD format] [abbreviated agency name (FDA, USDA, EPA, etc.)] [type of document (notice, proposed rule, final rule, etc.)], [title or shortened title] [FR volume #]* Fed. Reg. *[FR page #]*

Within quoted original sources, the original citation format is retained except where I have determined that a modification will increase clarity or make the document more readable.

Also within quoted original sources, I have made the following omissions without any indication in the text:

- omitted most citations and footnotes, retaining only those that I believe will be of use to the reader (retained footnotes have their original numbering);
- omitted most quotation marks in situations where courts are simply quoting the language of prior judicial opinions as part of their own sentences (in the standard style of judicial opinion-writing);[6]
- modified the format of some retained citations to conform to the style of this book;
- replaced the use of a series of asterisks (common in older documents) with the modern use of three-dot or four-dot ellipses, as appropriate;
- omitted text from the part of an excerpted document that precedes the quoted language.

Where I have omitted text from a quoted source, I have used three-dot ellipses to indicate omissions of less than a sentence and four-dot ellipses to indicate omissions of a full sentence or more.

Within quotations and excerpts referencing the FFDCA or the PHSA, I have replaced references to U.S. Code section numbers with references to the corresponding FFDCA section numbers, following the standard approach in this book. Where I have done this, I have used the notation "[FFDCA §]" to indicate the change.

One final editorial convention bears emphasis. Both the FFDCA and the PHSA are phrased in terms of authorities granted to, and obligations imposed upon, "the Secretary"—meaning the Secretary of Health and Human Services—rather than FDA. See FFDCA § 201(d). The Secretary of Health and Human Services, however, has delegated nearly all of the authority to administer these statutes to the Commissioner of Food and Drugs. See FDA STAFF MANUAL GUIDES, VOLUME

6. This is necessary to facilitate omission of citations to the quoted documents, with the aim of making those excerpts more readable. I have done this only in excerpts, not within the text of the book. Even within excerpts, I have never intentionally omitted quotation marks from sources other than judicial opinions.

II—Delegations of Authority § 1410.10 (Effective Date: August 26, 2016). To make textual descriptions of statutory language more readable, I have generally substituted "FDA" for "the Secretary" in describing the language of the statute. This means that:

- In places where the FFDCA grants "the Secretary" authority to take a particular action, I typically describe it as granting "FDA" such authority.
- In places where the FFDCA requires "the Secretary" to take some action, I typically describe it as requiring "FDA" to take such action.

# Part One

# Agency Structure, Product Categories, and Administrative Procedure

# Chapter 1

# Agency Structure and Product Categories

## A. Introduction

### 1. Introduction to This Casebook

As noted in the Preface, this book is designed to work as a set with the accompanying Statutory & Regulatory Supplement (Supplement).[1] The statutes and regulations in the Supplement have been aggressively edited, like the cases in a typical law school casebook, to emphasize those aspects that are most important to a general understanding of the subject.

#### *Primary Document Types*

The primary document types included in this book and its Supplement are: codified statutory materials, calendar-based statutory materials, codified regulatory materials, calendar-based regulatory materials, judicial decisions, formal agency guidance, and agency website materials. Each of these document types is explained below. Students new to regulatory work often wonder about the relationship between statutes and regulations, and between calendar-based and codified materials. That is addressed in more detail further below.

- *Codified statutory materials.* These are the U.S. statutes as collected and organized into the 54 Titles of the United States Code (USC). This book deals primarily with material from Title 21—Food and Drugs. It also addresses some material from other titles, including Title 5—Government Organization and Employees, Title 7—Agriculture, Title 15—Commerce and Trade, Title 18—Crimes and Criminal Procedure, Title 35—Patents, and Title 42—The Public Health and Welfare.

  The Federal Food, Drug, and Cosmetics Act of 1938 (FFDCA), as amended, is codified in Chapter 9 of Title 21. The Public Health Services Act (PHSA), as amended, is codified in Chapter 6A of Title 42. When referencing these two statutes, this book follows the standard practice among food-and-drug lawyers of referring to the section numbers of the amended statutes, rather than the numbers for the corresponding section of the U.S. Code. The FFDCA section

1. The Supplement is available free, in PDF format, on the Carolina Academic Press website.

numbers correspond to the relevant chapters of the statute and are much easier to remember than the section numbers in the U.S. Code.[2]

- *Calendar-based statutory materials.* These are the actual statutes as enacted through the process specified in Article I, Section 7 of the U.S. Constitution. These are published as Public Laws, with a number corresponding to the relevant session of Congress,[3] a hyphen, and a number assigned in ascending order from the beginning of that congressional session. They are also published in the U.S. Statutes at Large.
- *Codified regulatory materials.* These are the regulations (laws promulgated by executive branch agencies under delegated statutory authority) of the United States as collected and organized into the 50 titles of the U.S. Code of Federal Regulations (CFR). This book deals primarily with material from Title 21—Food and Drugs. It also references some materials from other titles, including Title 7—Agriculture, Title 9—Animals and Animal Products, and Title 16—Commercial Practices.[4]
- *Calendar-based regulatory materials.* These are the various documents published in the Federal Register (FR), the official, chronological record of the executive branch. These include, most importantly, proposed rules for comment and final rules that will be codified as part of the CFR. They also include notices of various matters, including the availability of guidance documents (which are not themselves published in the FR). Many proposed and final rules from recent decades include a preamble stating publicly the reasons for the relevant agency action. But older proposed and final rules rarely contain an explanatory preamble. Where an explanatory preamble is available, it can be helpful to read it much as you would read the reasoning of a court decision (and, at times, with the same healthy dose of skepticism).
- *Judicial decisions.* These are, of course, the core content of a traditional law school casebook in a common-law field. Because food and drug regulation is a statutory field, they play less of a role here. In most chapters of this book, judicial decisions are included when they resolve major issues of statutory

---

2. For example, when referring to the "Definitions; generally" provision of the statute, the book will refer to FFDCA § 201, rather than 21 U.S.C. § 321. To avoid overwhelming you with section numbers, parallel citations to the U.S. Code are included in the statutory supplement but not in the book itself.

3. The 1st Congress sat from March 1789 to March 1791; the 116th Congress sits from January 2019 to January 2021.

4. Note that title numbers in the CFR sometimes match title numbers in the USC, but sometimes do not. Title 21 carries the title "Food and Drugs" in both the USC and the CFR. However, CFR Title 21 includes some regulations based on statutes outside of USC Title 21 (such as the Public Health Services Act, codified in USC Title 42). In many other regulatory areas, the numbers do not match at all. For example, the primary statutes administered by the Securities and Exchange Commission are codified in Title 15 of the USC. However, the regulations of the Securities and Exchange Commission are codified in Title 17 of the CFR.

or constitutional interpretation. They are also occasionally included when they provide a concise summary of a particular aspect of food and drug regulation. They play a larger role in Chapter 20 on federal preemption.

- *Formal agency guidance.* These are the documents published by FDA under procedures set out in FFDCA § 701(h) and 21 C.F.R. § 10.115—Good Guidance Practices. They do not bind FDA or regulated parties, but nonetheless play a large role in communicating FDA's expectations to regulated parties.
- *Agency website materials.* These are simply materials from FDA's website that do not qualify as formal agency guidance. In general, this book prefers excerpts from the other above document types to agency website materials. However, there are some situations where website materials are available in an area where other document types are not. At other times, an agency website provides a more concise and approachable explanation than other document types. In those situations, website materials are included.

**The Relationship between Codified and Calendar-Based Materials**

| | Statutory materials | Regulatory materials |
|---|---|---|
| **Calendar-based** (organized by date) | Statutes promulgated (through Congress/president interaction) on a particular date; legislative history materials | Everything published in federal register; items that have their availability announced in federal register (but themselves made available online—guidance documents are the most prominent example) |
| **Codified** (organized by subject matter) | The 54 titles of the USC *Statutes, but not legislative history materials, are codified* | The 50 titles of the CFR *The regulations promulgated by a final rule (but not its preamble, and not other federal register documents) are codified* |

## *Where to Find the Different Document Types*

With rare exceptions, the text of codified statutory and regulatory materials is included only in the Supplement, and not in this casebook. This is done for two reasons. First, this will help you learn the structure of the statute and regulations, as you will always see them set out in the order in which they are codified. Second, you will find yourself referring repeatedly to the same statutory sections (but often different subsections) in different parts of the course. You will understand the interactions between these sections and subsections much better when you return to a page in the Supplement you have read—and ideally begun to mark up—previously.

In the book itself, you will find the remaining document types: excerpts of judicial decisions, calendar-based regulatory materials, formal agency guidance, and agency website materials.

### *Structure of Individual Chapters*

Most chapters begin by requesting that you read (or review, as appropriate) specific statutory and regulatory sections in the Supplement. The idea behind this is to allow you to become familiar with the language and structure of the statute itself, rather than simply reading out-of-context quotations.

Each chapter then contains, under the heading *Outline of Regulatory Regime*, several charts.[5] None of these is intended to be comprehensive, as comprehensive charts would provide too much detail to be useful. Instead, they are intended to give you a general sense of the statutory history, statutory structure, and regulatory structure relevant to the topics addressed in that chapter.

First, a "Timeline of Key Statutes" chart sets out, in chronological order, the key calendar-based statutory material. The idea is to give you a historical sense of the times that statutory change has occurred. How much you should focus on this depends on the style of your professor. If you have a historically minded professor, this chart will serve as a reference point for you as your professor discusses statutory changes over time. If your professor is focused more on current law, you should spend less time with this chart and more with those that follow.

Second, a "Key Statutory Provisions" chart sets out, in numerical order, the key sections and subsections of codified statutory material. This will usually be a longer (and at times, much longer) list of sections than those you are asked to read.[6] This is likely the most important of the charts included in each chapter. The idea is to give you an overview of the statutory structure in the relevant area. As your professor discusses current law, this chart should serve as a reference point for you on the major statutory provisions relevant to the regulatory area you are discussing. It should also serve as a starting point if you would like to learn more about some aspect of the area not covered in this book.

Third, a "Key Regulatory Provisions" chart sets out, in numerical order, the key parts and subparts (and occasionally sections and subsections) of codified regulatory material (in other words, CFR provisions).[7] The idea is to give you an overview of the regulatory structure in the relevant area. The Supplement includes excerpts from only a small number of these key regulatory provisions. Most are too long, and too technically detailed, to ask you to read their text in a one-semester course. What you should understand is that a large portion of the actual law relevant to food and drug regulation is contained in this codified regulatory material. Few practicing lawyers will have read large numbers of these provisions in their entirety. However, it is critical to know, for any particular regulatory area: (1) what codified provisions exist; (2) where to find them; and (3) what role they play (in relation to statutes and guidance) in the regulatory scheme.[8]

---

5. In addition to, or instead of, the outline at the beginning of the chapter, a few chapters contain a separate *Outline of Regulatory Regime* section for one or more subtopics.

6. Portions of many, but not all, key statutory provisions are excerpted in the Supplement.

7. This is sometimes a single chart and sometimes two or more charts grouped by subtopic.

8. The legal status of agency guidance is discussed in more detail in Chapter 2.

As you read each chapter for the first time, you should do no more than skim these charts to get a general sense of the structure of the laws and regulations relevant to the topic of the chapter. As you begin to review the material at the end of the semester (or perhaps work on a seminar paper), you may find it helpful to look back at these charts in more detail.

Following these charts, most chapters contain various additional parts, many of which contain excerpts from relevant documents. All chapters conclude with a "Key Points" section. This Key Points section is placed at the end of the chapter, as that is the point where it is likely to be most useful to you. However, you may also find it useful to skip to the relevant Key Points section, and review it briefly, before you begin reading each chapter—and then to review it again when you reach the chapter's end.

### *The Relationship Between Codified and Uncodified Material (and Why It Is Necessary to Study Both)*

Students often wonder why, when codified statutory and regulatory materials are available, it is nonetheless important to study non-codified materials as well. The answer is that non-codified materials provide information that is not available in the codified materials.

For statutory provisions, the U.S. Code is your best source of current law. But if you want to know when a particular provision was added to—or removed from—the codified law, the individual statutes passed by Congress are your best source of information. Additionally, individual statutes will be important to you as a practicing lawyer for a reason few students contemplate in law school. Once you begin practice, you will find that the codified law—as it existed at the time you began working in the field—is the baseline structure for your understanding of the way that field works. Changes made by Congress after you begin practicing in a field will, at least initially, seem like awkward additions to that initial baseline. And you are likely to refer to them not as part of the FFDCA, but by the name of the individual statute that made the relevant statutory changes. ("This is mandated by the 21st Century Cures Act," rather than "This is mandated by the FFDCA.")

The same applies, of course, to the senior lawyers for whom you are likely to work. Unless you are conversant with the names and general content of the individual statutes that have modified the FFDCA over time, you will not be able to communicate effectively with your colleagues.

For regulatory provisions, the CFR is your best source of current law.[9] Like with statutes, it is necessary to turn to calendar-based materials—in this case, the

9. For most purposes, the best way to access the CFR is the eCFR ("Electronic Code of Federal Regulations") website maintained by the U.S. Government Publishing Office. It is free, usually updated within a few days of any regulatory change, and—most importantly—formatted in a manner that allows you to view an entire regulatory "Part" rather than just an individual "Section." In other words, it permits you to view all of 21 C.F.R. Part 101—Food Labeling on a single page, rather than requiring you to click individually on each subsection (21 C.F.R. §§ 101.1, 101.2, 101.15,

Federal Register—to learn when a particular provision was added to, or removed from, the CFR. But, for regulations, calendar-based materials play an additional role. It is in these calendar-based materials—especially "Proposed Rules" and "Final Rules"—that agencies today set out the reasoning behind their rulemaking decisions.

### *The Relationship Between Food & Drug Regulation and Administrative Law*

Food & Drug Regulation is a course in a substantive regulatory field. In this manner, it is similar to law school courses in Securities Regulation or Environmental Law. The general course in Administrative Law is not a course in a substantive regulatory field. Instead, Administrative Law is a broad survey of the interactions among executive branch agencies, Congress, and the courts.

This book is designed to present Food & Drug Regulation in a manner that is accessible to students who have not yet taken Administrative Law. It is also designed to avoid duplicating the coverage of an Administrative Law course.[10] Past experience suggests two things. First, students find that an earlier course in Food & Drug Regulation makes the abstract concepts of Administrative Law easier to understand. Second, students find that an earlier course in Administrative Law gives them some additional perspective on a later course in a Food & Drug Regulation. In other words, whichever course you take first is likely to help you understand the course you take later (or concurrently). And you will learn more by taking both courses than by taking either course alone.

## 2. Introduction to This Chapter

This chapter introduces you to the history and structure of the U.S. Food and Drug Administration (FDA). The first part of the chapter focuses on the agency's current structure and the historical context for the agency as it exists today. The second part introduces a number of the product categories provided for in the Federal Food, Drug, and Cosmetic Act (FFDCA). It also introduces some of the difficulties involved in determining the category into which a particular product fits.

---

101.18, etc.). Unfortunately, there does not seem to be a single web link that has remained stable over time for the main eCFR landing page. Your best bet is to Google "eCFR gpo.gov" (including "gpo.gov" is important, as "ecfr" alone sometimes turns up strange results).

10. The necessary exception is the *Chevron* case and the provisions of the Administrative Procedure Act discussed in the first part of Chapter 2 of this casebook. *Chevron* and the APA provisions will have been covered in almost any Administrative Law course. But the remainder of Chapter 2, on FDA's administrative procedures, will be new material even to most alumni of a good Administrative Law course.

Food and drug regulation is based around a limited set of product categories. All of these are set out in just a few statutory and regulatory provisions: FFDCA § 201, FFDCA § 503(g)(1), PHSA § 351, 21 C.F.R. §§ 3.2 and 1271.3(d).

FFDCA § 201 will provide you with the statutory definitions for most—but not all—FDA-regulated product categories. You will want to bookmark that section, as you will refer to it repeatedly throughout this course. PHSA § 351(i) will provide you with the statutory definition of biological product (or biologic), which is not defined in FFDCA § 201. FFDCA § 503(g)(1)(A), together with 21 C.F.R. § 3.2, will provide you with the definition of combination product. Finally, 21 C.F.R. § 1271.3(d) will provide you with the regulatory definition of one product category that is not defined explicitly by statute—human cells, tissues, and cellular and tissue-based products (HCT/Ps).

At this point, please read (or review) the following excerpts in the statutory supplement:

- FFDCA § 201. Definitions; generally.
- FFDCA § 503. Exemptions and considerations for certain drugs, devices, and biological products. *Subsection (g)(1) only.* [statutory reference to combination products]
- PHSA § 351. Regulations of biological products. *Subsection (i) only.*
- 21 C.F.R. § 3.2. [regulatory definition of "combination product"]
- 21 C.F.R. § 1271.3(d). [definition of "Human cells, tissues, and cellular or tissue-based products" (HCT/Ps)]

Moving on from product categories, we turn to the core operational provision of the statute: FFDCA § 301. The first three subsections, FFDCA § 301(a)–(c), set out a general prohibition on adulteration and misbranding of FDA-regulated products. Much of the remainder of the FFDCA simply describes actions that will make one of these products adulterated or misbranded in violation of § 301. Other portions of FFDCA § 301 prohibit other, more specific actions.

At this point, please read (or review) the following excerpts in the statutory supplement:

- FFDCA § 301. Prohibited acts. *Subsections (a), (b),* and *(c).*

Finally, FFDCA § 1003(b) sets out FDA's statutory mission statement. As you read this, note that it has more significance than the mission statement developed internally by a private sector or public sector organization. Instead, this mission statement was prescribed in a major congressional effort to reform the agency, the FDA Modernization Act of 1997. Subsection (f)—also part of that same 1997 statute—explicitly sets out Congress's view that FDA was not then in compliance with its statutory obligations. It directed the agency to develop a plan to bring itself into statutory compliance, and to report annually on its progress toward such compliance.

At this point, please read (or review) the following excerpts in the statutory supplement:

- FFDCA § 1003. Food & Drug Administration. *Subsections (b) and (f) only.*

## B. Outline of Regulatory Regime

This is your first example of the "Outline of Regulatory Regime" described in the "Introduction to this Casebook" section, above. The first chart is a timeline of key statutes, listed in chronological order. The second chart is a list of key statutory provisions, listed in the order those provisions appear in the FFDCA and PHSA. The third chart is a list of key regulatory provisions, listed in the order those appear in the CFR. None of these charts is intended to be comprehensive, as comprehensive charts would provide too much detail to be useful. Instead, they are intended to give you a general sense of the statutory history, statutory structure, and regulatory structure relevant to this casebook chapter.

*As you read this chapter for the first time, you should do no more than skim these charts to get a general sense of the structure of the applicable statutes and regulations.* As you begin to review the material at the end of the semester (or perhaps work on a seminar paper), you may find it helpful to look back at these charts in more detail. You should follow this same approach (skimming first, returning to read in more detail later if necessary) in each "Outline of Regulatory Regimes" section of this book.

| Timeline of Key Statutes: FDA Structure | | | |
|---|---|---|---|
| **Year** | **PL** | **Stat** | **Name of Statute** |
| 1906 | 59-384 | 34 Stat. 768 | Pure Food and Drug Act |
| 1938 | 75-717 | 52 Stat. 1040 | FFDCA of 1938 |
| 1988 | 100-607 | 102 Stat. 3048, 3120 | Food and Drug Administration Act of 1988 |
| 1997 | 105-115 | 111 Stat. 2296 | FDA Modernization Act of 1997 |
| **Timeline of Key Statutes: Product Categories** | | | |
| **Year** | **PL** | **Stat** | **Name of Statute** |
| 1906 | 59-384 | 34 Stat. 768 | Pure Food and Drug Act |
| 1938 | 75-717 | 52 Stat. 1040 | FFDCA of 1938 |
| 1944 | 78-410 | 58 Stat. 682 | Public Health Services Act |
| 1968 | 90-399 | 82 Stat. 342 | Animal Drug Amendments of 1968 |
| 1976 | 94-295 | 90 Stat. 539 | Medical Devices Amendments of 1976 |
| 1994 | 103-417 | 108 Stat. 4325 | Dietary Supplement Health and Education Act of 1997 |

| Key Statutory Provisions: FDA Structure | | |
|---|---|---|
| **Statute Name or U.S.C. Title** | **§** | **Title of Section or Subsection** |
| FFDCA | 1001 | Separability clause |
| FFDCA | 1003 | Food and Drug Administration |
| FFDCA | 1003a | Office of Pediatric Therapeutics |
| FFDCA | 1004 | Scientific review groups |
| FFDCA | 1007 | Contracts for expert review |
| FFDCA | 1010 | Office of the Chief Scientist |
| FFDCA | 1011 | Office of Women's Health |
| 21 U.S.C. | 399g | Food and Drug Administration Intercenter Institutes |

| Key Statutory Provisions: Product Categories | | |
|---|---|---|
| **Statute Name or U.S.C. Title** | **§** | **Title of Section or Subsection** |
| FFDCA | 201 | Definitions |
| FFDCA | 503(g) | Regulation of combination products |
| FFDCA | 563 | Classification of products |

| Key Statutory Provisions: Adulteration and Misbranding | | |
|---|---|---|
| **Statute Name or U.S.C. Title** | **§** | **Title of Section or Subsection** |
| FFDCA | 201 | Definitions |
| FFDCA | 301 | Prohibited acts |
| FFDCA | 402, 501, 601, 902 | Chapter-specific *adulteration* provisions<br>402: food<br>501: drugs, devices, biologics, combination products<br>601: cosmetics<br>902: tobacco products |
| FFDCA | 403, 502, 602, 903 | Chapter-specific *misbranding* provisions<br>403: food<br>502: drugs, devices, biologics, combination products<br>602: cosmetics<br>903: tobacco products |

| Key Regulatory Provisions: FDA Structure | | |
|---|---|---|
| 21 C.F.R. Part | Subpart | Title of Part or Subpart |
| 5 | — | Organization |

| Key Regulatory Provisions: Product Categories | | |
|---|---|---|
| 21 C.F.R. Part | Subpart | Title of Part or Subpart |
| 3 | — | Product jurisdiction |
| 1270 | — | Human tissue intended for transplantation |
| 1271 | — | Human cells, tissues, and cellular and tissue-based products |

# C. Historical Context

## 1. Organizational History

The excerpt immediately below, from FDA's website, summarizes the organizational history of FDA and its predecessor entities.

### FDA Website, History of FDA's Internal Organization: Brief Organizational History*

In his 1837 annual report, Patent Commissioner Henry L. Ellsworth recommended a national agency for the encouragement of agriculture. Congress responded in 1839 by an appropriation of $1000 to the Commissioner of Patents for "the collection of agricultural statistics, and for other agricultural purposes." From then on, the Patent Office collected and reported agricultural statistics, sponsored or conducted chemical investigations on agricultural matters, monitored agricultural developments, and reported on all of these in its annual reports. Beginning in 1849, a separate report was made by the Patent Commissioner to Congress on agricultural matters. An Agricultural Division was established in the Patent Office and a chemical laboratory was created in that Division.

When the U.S. Department of Agriculture was created in 1862, the Patent Office's Agricultural Division was transferred to the new Department, becoming the Division of Chemistry in 1890 and the Bureau of Chemistry in 1901. In 1927, the Bureau of Chemistry became the United States Food, Drug and Insecticide Administration, and in 1930 the name was shortened to the U.S. Food and Drug Administration. Ten years later, in 1940, the FDA was transferred from the U.S. Department of Agriculture to the newly created Federal Security Agency, which was renamed

* From https://www.fda.gov/about-fda/history-fdas-fight-consumer-protection-and-public-health/history-fdas-internal-organization (last updated January 31, 2018).

the Department of Health Education and Welfare in 1953, and again renamed the Department of Health and Human Services in 1979.

## 2. FDA's "Milestones" List

For some time now, FDA's History Office has maintained a list of "Milestones in U.S. Food and Drug Law History." The most recent version at the time of this writing is excerpted below. Experience suggests that this is a useful document for those seeking to learn food and drug regulation. You may find it helpful to bookmark this list and refer to it later in the semester when you are trying to consolidate what you have learned. Many of the milestones on this list will be more meaningful to you after you have covered the relevant topics in more detail.

### FDA Website, Milestones in U.S. Food and Drug Law History*

From the beginnings of civilization people have been concerned about the quality and safety of foods and medicines. In 1202, King John of England proclaimed the first English food law, the Assize of Bread, which prohibited adulteration of bread with such ingredients as ground peas or beans. Regulation of food in the United States dates from early colonial times. Federal controls over the drug supply began with inspection of imported drugs in 1848, although the first federal biologics law, which addressed the provision of reliable smallpox vaccine to citizens, was passed in 1813. The following chronology describes some of the milestones in the history of food and drug regulation in the United States.

**1820**

Eleven physicians meet in Washington, D.C., to establish the **U.S. Pharmacopeia**, the first compendium of standard drugs for the United States.

**1848**

**Drug Importation Act** passed by Congress requires U.S. Customs Service inspection to stop entry of adulterated drugs from overseas.

**1862**

**President Lincoln** appoints a chemist, Charles M. Wetherill, to serve in the new Department of Agriculture. This was the beginning of the Bureau of Chemistry, the predecessor of the Food and Drug Administration.

**1880**

**Peter Collier**, chief chemist, U.S. Department of Agriculture, recommends passage of a national food and drug law, following his own food adulteration investigations. The bill was defeated, but during the next 25 years more than 100 food and drug bills were introduced in Congress.

---

* From: https://www.fda.gov/about-fda/fdas-evolving-regulatory-powers/milestones-us-food-and-drug-law-history (last updated January 31, 2018).

**1883**

Dr. Harvey W. Wiley becomes chief chemist, expanding the Bureau of Chemistry's food adulteration studies. Campaigning for a federal law, Dr. Wiley is called the "Crusading Chemist" and "Father of the Pure Food and Drugs Act." He retired from government service in 1912 and died in 1930.

**1897**

**Tea Importation Act** passed, providing for Customs inspection of all tea entering U.S. ports, at the expense of the importers.

**1898**

Association of Official Agricultural Chemists (now AOAC International) establishes a **Committee on Food Standards** headed by Dr. Wiley. States begin incorporating these standards into their food statutes.

**1902**

The **Biologics Control Act** is passed to ensure purity and safety of serums, vaccines, and similar products used to prevent or treat diseases in humans.

Congress appropriates $5,000 to the Bureau of Chemistry to study **chemical preservatives and colors** and their effects on digestion and health. Dr. Wiley's studies draw widespread attention to the problem of food adulteration. Public support for passage of a federal food and drug law grows.

**1906**

The original **Food and Drugs Act** is passed by Congress on June 30 and signed by President Theodore Roosevelt. It prohibits interstate commerce in misbranded and adulterated foods, drinks and drugs.

**The Meat Inspection Act** is passed the same day.

Shocking disclosures of insanitary conditions in meat-packing plants, the use of poisonous preservatives and dyes in foods, and cure-all claims for worthless and dangerous patent medicines were the major problems leading to the enactment of these laws.

**1907**

**First Certified Color Regulations**, requested by manufacturers and users, list seven colors found suitable for use in foods.

**1911**

In **U.S. v. Johnson**, the Supreme Court rules that the 1906 Food and Drugs Act does not prohibit false therapeutic claims but only false and misleading statements about the ingredients or identity of a drug.

**1912**

Congress enacts the **Sherley Amendment** to over come the ruling in U.S. v. Johnson. It prohibits labeling medicines with false therapeutic claims intended to defraud the purchaser, a standard difficult to prove.

Mrs. Winslow's Soothing Syrup for teething and colicky babies, unlabeled yet laced with morphine, killed many infants.

1913

**Gould Amendment** requires that food package contents be "plainly and conspicuously marked on the outside of the package in terms of weight, measure, or numerical count."

1914

In **U.S. v. Lexington Mill and Elevator Company**, the Supreme Court issues its first ruling on food additives. It ruled that in order for bleached flour with nitrite residues to be banned from foods, the government must show a relationship between the chemical additive and the harm it allegedly caused in humans. The court also noted that the mere presence of such an ingredient was not sufficient to render the food illegal.

**The Harrison Narcotic Act** requires prescriptions for products exceeding the allowable limit of narcotics and mandates increased record-keeping for physicians and pharmacists who dispense narcotics.

1924

In **U.S. v. 95 Barrels Alleged Apple Cider Vinegar**, the Supreme Court rules that the Food and Drugs Act condemns every statement, design, or device on a product's label that may mislead or deceive, even if technically true.

1927

The Bureau of Chemistry is reorganized into two separate entities. Regulatory functions are located in the **Food, Drug, and Insecticide Administration**, and nonregulatory research is located in the **Bureau of Chemistry and Soils**.

1930

**McNary-Mapes Amendment** authorizes FDA standards of quality and fill-of-container for canned food, excluding meat and milk products.

The name of the Food, Drug, and Insecticide Administration is shortened to **Food and Drug Administration (FDA)** under an agricultural appropriations act.

1933

FDA recommends a complete revision of the obsolete **1906 Food and Drugs Act**. The first bill is introduced into the Senate, launching a five-year legislative battle.

1935

U.S. Government begins publication of the **Federal Register**.

1937

Elixir of Sulfanilamide, containing the poisonous solvent diethylene glycol, kills 107 persons, many of whom are children, dramatizing the need to establish drug safety before marketing and to enact the pending food and drug law.

1938

**The Federal Food, Drug, and Cosmetic** (FDC) **Act of 1938** is passed by Congress, containing new provisions:

Extending control to cosmetics and therapeutic devices.

Requiring new drugs to be shown safe before marketing-starting a new system of drug regulation.

Eliminating the Sherley Amendment requirement to prove intent to defraud in drug misbranding cases.

Providing that safe tolerances be set for unavoidable poisonous substances.

Authorizing standards of identity, quality, and fill-of-container for foods.

Authorizing factory inspections.

Adding the remedy of court injunctions to the previous penalties of seizures and prosecutions.

Under the **Wheeler-Lea Act**, the Federal Trade Commission is charged with overseeing advertising associated with products otherwise regulated by FDA.

1939

**First Food Standards** issued (canned tomatoes, tomato purée, and tomato paste).

1940

**FDA transferred** from the Department of Agriculture to the Federal Security Agency, with Walter G. Campbell appointed as the first Commissioner of Food and Drugs.

1941

**Insulin Amendment** requires FDA to test and certify purity and potency of this lifesaving drug for diabetes

1943

In **U.S. v. Dotterweich**, the Supreme Court rules that the responsible officials of a corporation, as well as the corporation itself, may be prosecuted for violations. It need not be proven that the officials intended, or even knew of, the violations.

1944

**Public Health Service Act** is passed, covering a broad spectrum of health concerns, including regulation of biological products and control of communicable diseases.

1945

**Penicillin Amendment** requires FDA testing and certification of safety and effectiveness of all penicillin products. Later amendments extended this requirement to all antibiotics. In 1983 such control was found no longer needed and was abolished.

**1948**

**Miller Amendment** affirms that the [FFDCA] applies to goods regulated by the Agency that have been transported from one state to another and have reached the consumer.

**1949**

FDA publishes **guidance to industry** for the first time. This guidance, "Procedures for the Appraisal of the Toxicity of Chemicals in Food," came to be known as the "black book."

**1950**

In **Alberty Food Products Co. v. U.S.**, a court of appeals rules that the directions for use on a drug label must include the purpose for which the drug is offered. Therefore, a worthless remedy cannot escape the law by not stating the condition it is supposed to treat.

**Oleomargarine Act** requires prominent labeling of colored oleomargarine, to distinguish it from butter.

**Delaney Committee** starts congressional investigation of the safety of chemicals in foods and cosmetics, laying the foundation for the 1954 Miller Pesticide Amendment, the 1958 Food Additives Amendment, and the 1960 Color Additive Amendment.

**1951**

**Durham-Humphrey Amendment** defines the kinds of drugs that cannot be safely used without medical supervision and restricts their sale to prescription by a licensed practitioner.

**1952**

In **U.S. v. Cardiff**, the Supreme Court rules that the factory inspection provision of the 1938 FDC Act is too vague to be enforced as criminal law.

**FDA consumer consultants** are appointed in each field district to maintain communications with consumers and ensure that FDA considers their needs and problems.

**1953**

**Federal Security Agency** becomes the Department of Health, Education, and Welfare (HEW).

**Factory Inspection Amendment** clarifies previous law and requires FDA to give manufacturers written reports of conditions observed during inspections and analyses of factory samples.

**1954**

**Miller Pesticide Amendment** spells out procedures for setting safety limits for pesticide residues on raw agricultural commodities.

First large-scale **radiological examination of food** carried out by FDA when it received reports that tuna suspected of being radioactive was being imported from Japan following atomic blasts in the Pacific. FDA begins monitoring around the clock to meet the emergency.

1955

**HEW Secretary Oveta Culp Hobby** appoints a committee of 14 citizens to study the adequacy of FDA's facilities and programs. The committee recommends a substantial expansion of FDA staff and facilities, a new headquarters building, and more use of educational and informational programs.

**The Division of Biologics Control** became an independent entity within the National Institutes of Health, after polio vaccine thought to have been inactivated is associated with about 260 cases of polio.

1958

**Food Additives Amendment** enacted, requiring manufacturers of new food additives to establish safety. The Delaney proviso prohibits the approval of any food additive shown to induce cancer in humans or animals.

FDA publishes in the Federal Register the first list of **substances generally recognized as safe (GRAS)**. The list contains nearly 200 substances.

1959

**U.S. cranberry crop** recalled three weeks before Thanksgiving for FDA tests to check for aminotriazole, a weedkiller found to cause cancer in laboratory animals. Cleared berries were allowed a label stating that they had been tested and had passed FDA inspection, the only such endorsement ever allowed by FDA on a food product.

1960

**Color Additive Amendment** enacted, requiring manufacturers to establish the safety of color additives in foods, drugs and cosmetics. The Delaney proviso prohibits the approval of any color additive shown to induce cancer in humans or animals.

**Federal Hazardous Substances Labeling Act**, enforced by FDA, requires prominent label warnings on hazardous household chemical products.

1962

**Thalidomide**, a new sleeping pill, is found to have caused birth defects in thousands of babies born in western Europe. News reports on the role of Dr. Frances Kelsey, FDA medical officer, in keeping the drug off the U.S. market, arouse public support for stronger drug regulation.

**Kefauver-Harris Drug Amendments** passed to ensure drug efficacy and greater drug safety. For the first time, drug manufacturers are required to prove to FDA the effectiveness of their products before marketing them. The new law also exempts from the Delaney proviso animal drugs and animal feed additives shown to induce cancer but which leave no detectable levels of residue in the human food supply.

**Consumer Bill of Rights** is proclaimed by President John F. Kennedy in a message to Congress. Included are the right to safety, the right to be informed, the right to choose, and the right to be heard.

**1965**

**Drug Abuse Control Amendments** are enacted to deal with problems caused by abuse of depressants, stimulants and hallucinogens.

**1966**

FDA contracts with the National Academy of Sciences/National Research Council to evaluate the **effectiveness of 4,000 drugs** approved on the basis of safety alone between 1938 and 1962.

**Child Protection Act** enlarges the scope of the Federal Hazardous Substances Labeling Act to ban hazardous toys and other articles so hazardous that adequate label warnings could not be written.

**Fair Packaging and Labeling Act** requires all consumer products in interstate commerce to be honestly and informatively labeled, with FDA enforcing provisions on foods, drugs, cosmetics, and medical devices.

**1968**

**FDA Bureau of Drug Abuse Control** and Treasury Department Bureau of Narcotics are transferred to the Department of Justice to form the Bureau of Narcotics and Dangerous Drugs (BNDD), consolidating efforts to police traffic in abused drugs.

**Reorganization** of federal health programs places FDA in the Public Health Service.

FDA forms the **Drug Efficacy Study Implementation (DESI)** to implement recommendations of the National Academy of Sciences investigation of effectiveness of drugs first marketed between 1938 and 1962.

**Animal Drug Amendments** place all regulation of new animal drugs under one section of the Food, Drug, and Cosmetic Act—Section 512—making approval of animal drugs and medicated feeds more efficient.

**1969**

FDA begins administering **Sanitation Programs** for milk, shellfish, food service, and interstate travel facilities, and for preventing poisoning and accidents. These responsibilities were transferred from other units of the Public Health Service.

The **White House Conference on Food, Nutrition, and Health** recommends systematic review of GRAS substances in light of FDA's ban of the artificial sweetener cyclamate. President Nixon orders FDA to review its GRAS list.

**1970**

In **Upjohn v. Finch** the Court of Appeals upholds enforcement of the 1962 drug effectiveness amendments by ruling that commercial success alone does not constitute substantial evidence of drug safety and efficacy.

FDA requires the first **patient package insert:** oral contraceptives must contain information for the patient about specific risks and benefits.

**Drug Abuse Prevention and Control Act** replaces previous laws and categorizes drugs based on abuse and addiction potential compared to their therapeutic value.

**Environmental Protection Agency** established; takes over FDA program for setting pesticide tolerances.

**1971**

**PHS Bureau of Radiological Health** transferred to FDA. Its mission: protection against unnecessary human exposure to radiation from electronic products in the home, industry, and the healing arts.

**National Center for Toxicological Research** is established in the biological facilities of the Pine Bluff Arsenal in Arkansas. Its mission is to examine biological effects of chemicals in the environment, extrapolating data from experimental animals to human health.

Artificial sweetener **saccharin**, included in FDA's original GRAS list, is removed from the list pending new scientific study.

**1972**

**Over-the-Counter Drug Review** begun to enhance the safety, effectiveness and appropriate labeling of drugs sold without prescription.

**Regulation of Biologics**—including serums, vaccines, and blood products—is transferred from NIH to FDA.

**1973**

**The U.S. Supreme Court** upholds the 1962 drug effectiveness law and endorses FDA action to control entire classes of products by regulations rather than to rely only on time-consuming litigation.

**Low-acid food processing** regulations issued, after botulism outbreaks from canned foods, to ensure that low-acid packaged foods have adequate heat treatment and are not hazardous.

**Consumer Product Safety Commission** created by Congress; takes over programs pioneered by FDA under 1927 Caustic Poison Act, 1960 Federal Hazardous Substances Labeling Act, 1966 Child Protection Act, and PHS accident prevention activities for safety of toys, home appliances, etc.

**1976**

**Medical Device Amendments** passed to ensure safety and effectiveness of medical devices, including diagnostic products. The amendments require manufacturers to register with FDA and follow quality control procedures. Some products must have pre-market approval by FDA; others must meet performance standards before marketing.

**Vitamins and Minerals Amendments** ("Proxmire Amendments") stop FDA from establishing standards limiting potency of vitamins and minerals in food supplements or regulating them as drugs based solely on potency.

**1977**

**Saccharin Study and Labeling Act** passed by Congress to stop FDA from banning the chemical sweetener but requiring a label warning that it has been found to cause cancer in laboratory animals.

**1979**

Introduction of the **Bioresearch Monitoring Program** as an agency-wide initiative ensures the quality and integrity of data submitted to FDA and provides for the protection of human subjects in clinical trials by focusing on preclinical studies on animals, clinical investigations, and the work of institutional review boards.

In the hours following the **Three Mile Island** nuclear emergency of March 28, 1979, FDA contracted with firms in Missouri, Michigan, and New Jersey to prepare and package enough doses of potassium iodide to protect those threatened with thyroid cancer if exposed to radiation. Nearly one quarter of a million bottles—enough for every household in the area—were delivered to Harrisburg, Pennsylvania within 72 hours.

**1980**

**Infant Formula Act** establishes special FDA controls to ensure necessary nutritional content and safety

**1981**

FDA and the Department of Health and Human Services revise **regulations for human subject protections**, based on the 1979 Belmont Report, which had been issued by the National Commission for the Protection of Human Subjects of Biomedical and Behavioral Research. The revised rules provide for wider representation on institutional review boards and they detail elements of what constitutes informed consent, among other provisions.

**1982**

**Tamper-resistant Packing Regulations** issued by FDA to prevent poisonings such as deaths from cyanide placed in Tylenol capsules. The Federal Anti-Tampering Act passed in 1983 makes it a crime to tamper with packaged consumer products.

FDA publishes first **Red Book** (successor to 1949 "black book"), officially known as Toxicological Principles for the Safety Assessment of Direct Food Additives and Color Additives Used in Food.

**1983**

**Orphan Drug Act** passed, enabling FDA to promote research and marketing of drugs needed for treating rare diseases.

**1984**

**Fines Enhancement Laws** of 1984 and 1987 amend the U.S. Code to greatly increase penalties for all federal offenses. The maximum fine for individuals is now $100,000 for each offense and $250,000 if the violation is a felony or causes death. For corporations, the amounts are doubled.

**Drug Price Competition and Patent Term Restoration Act** expedites the availability of less costly generic drugs by permitting FDA to approve applications to market generic versions of brand-name drugs without repeating the research done to prove them safe and effective. At the same time, the brand-name companies can apply for up to five years additional patent protection for the new medicines they developed to make up for time lost while their products were going through FDA's approval process.

**1985**

**AIDS test for blood** approved by FDA in its first major action to protect patients from infected donors.

**1986**

**Childhood Vaccine Act** requires patient information on vaccines, gives FDA authority to recall biologics, and authorizes civil penalties.

**1987**

**Investigational drug regulations revised** to expand access to experimental drugs for patients with serious diseases with no alternative therapies.

**1988**

**Food and Drug Administration Act** of 1988 officially establishes FDA as an agency of the Department of Health and Human Services with a Commissioner of Food and Drugs appointed by the President with the advice and consent of the Senate, and broadly spells out the responsibilities of the Secretary and the Commissioner for research, enforcement, education, and information.

The **Prescription Drug Marketing Act** bans the diversion of prescription drugs from legitimate commercial channels. Congress finds that the resale of such drugs leads to the distribution of mislabeled, adulterated, subpotent, and counterfeit drugs to the public. The new law requires drug wholesalers to be licensed by the states; restricts reimportation from other countries; and bans sale, trade or purchase of drug samples, and traffic or counterfeiting of redeemable drug coupons.

**Generic Animal Drug and Patent Term Restoration Act** extends to veterinary products benefits given to human drugs under the 1984 Drug Price

Competition and Patent Term Restoration Act. Companies can produce and sell generic versions of animal drugs approved after October 1962 without duplicating research done to prove them safe and effective. The act also authorizes extension of animal drug patents.

**1989**

FDA issues a nationwide recall of all over-the-counter dietary supplements containing 100 milligrams or more of **L-Tryptophan**, due to a clear link between the consumption of L-tryptophan tablets and its association with a U.S. outbreak of Eosinophilia Myalgia Syndrome (EMS), characterized by fatigue, shortness of breath, and other symptoms. By 1990 the Centers for Disease Control and Prevention confirm over 1,500 cases of EMS, including 38 deaths, and FDA prohibits the importation of l-tryptophan.

**1990**

Responding to increasing illicit traffic, Congress passes the **Anabolic Steroid Act of 1990**, which identifies anabolic steroids as a class of drugs and specifies over two dozen items as controlled substances. In addition, a four-part definition of this class is established to permit new, black market compounds to be assigned to this category, and thus subject to regulation as controlled substances.

**Nutrition Labeling and Education Act** requires all packaged foods to bear nutrition labeling and all health claims for foods to be consistent with terms defined by the Secretary of Health and Human Services. The law preempts state requirements about food standards, nutrition labeling, and health claims and, for the first time, authorizes some health claims for foods. The food ingredient panel, serving sizes, and terms such as "low fat" and "light" are standardized.

**Safe Medical Devices Act** is passed, requiring nursing homes, hospitals, and other facilities that use medical devices to report to FDA incidents that suggest that a medical device probably caused or contributed to the death, serious illness, or serious injury of a patient. Manufacturers are required to conduct post-market surveillance on permanently implanted devices whose failure might cause serious harm or death, and to establish methods for tracing and locating patients depending on such devices. The act authorizes FDA to order device product recalls and other actions.

**1991**

Regulations published to **Accelerate the Review of Drugs** for life-threatening diseases.

The policy for protection of human subjects in research, promulgated in 1981 by FDA and the Department of Health and Human Services, is adopted by more than a dozen federal entities involved in human subject research and becomes known as the **Common Rule**. This rule issues requirements for researchers who obtain and document informed consent, secures special protection for children, women, and prisoners, elaborates on required procedures for institutional review boards, and ensures that research institutions comply with the regulations.

1992

**Generic Drug Enforcement Act** imposes debarment and other penalties for illegal acts involving abbreviated drug applications.

**Prescription Drug User Fee Act** requires drug and biologics manufacturers to pay fees for product applications and supplements, and other services. The act also requires FDA to use these funds to hire more reviewers to assess applications.

**Mammography Quality Standards Act** requires all mammography facilities in the United States to be accredited and federally certified as meeting quality standards effective Oct. 1, 1994. After initial certification, facilities must pass annual inspections by federal or state inspectors.

**Nutrition facts**, basic per-serving nutritional information, are required on foods under the Nutrition Labeling and Education Act of 1990. Based on the latest public health recommendations, FDA and the Food Safety and Inspection Service of the Department of Agriculture recreate the food label to list the most important nutrients in an easy-to-follow format.

1993

A consolidation of several adverse reaction reporting systems is launched as **MedWatch**, designed for voluntary reporting of problems associated with medical products to be filed with FDA by health professionals.

Revising a policy from 1977 that excluded women of childbearing potential from early drug studies, FDA issues guidelines calling for improved assessments of **medication responses as a function of gender**. Companies are encouraged to include patients of both sexes in their investigations of drugs and to analyze any gender-specific phenomena.

1994

**Dietary Supplement Health and Education Act** establishes specific labeling requirements, provides a regulatory framework, and authorizes FDA to promulgate good manufacturing practice regulations for dietary supplements. This act defines "dietary supplements" and "dietary ingredients" and classifies them as food. The act also establishes a commission to recommend how to regulate claims.

FDA announces it could consider **regulating nicotine** in cigarettes as a drug, in response to a Citizen's Petition by the Coalition on Smoking OR Health.

**Uruguay Round Agreements Act** extends the patent terms of U.S. drugs from 17 to 20 years.

**Animal Medicinal Drug Use Clarification Act** allows veterinarians to prescribe extra-label use of veterinary drugs for animals under specific circumstances. In addition, the legislation allows licensed veterinarians to prescribe human drugs for use in animals under certain conditions.

**1995**

FDA declares **cigarettes** to be "drug delivery devices." Restrictions are proposed on marketing and sales to reduce smoking by young people.

A series of **proposed reforms to reduce regulatory burden** on pharmaceutical manufacturers is announced, including an expansion of allowable promotional material on approved uses of drugs that firms can distribute to health professionals, streamlining certain elements in the documentation of investigational drug studies, and a reduction in both environmental impact filings and pre-approval requirements in tablet manufacture.

**1996**

**Federal Tea Tasters Repeal Act** repeals the Tea Importation Act of 1897 to eliminate the Board of Tea Experts and user fees for FDA's testing of all imported tea. Tea itself is still regulated by FDA.

**Saccharin Notice Repeal Act** repeals the saccharin notice requirements.

**Animal Drug Availability Act** adds flexibility to animal drug approval process, providing for flexible labeling and more direct communication between drug sponsors and FDA.

**Food Quality Protection Act** amends the Food, Drug, and Cosmetic Act, eliminating application of the Delaney proviso to pesticides.

**1997**

**Food and Drug Administration Modernization Act** reauthorizes the Prescription Drug User Fee Act of 1992 and mandates the most wide-ranging reforms in agency practices since 1938. Provisions include measures to accelerate review of devices, regulate advertising of unapproved uses of approved drugs and devices, and regulate health claims for foods.

**1998**

FDA promulgates the **Pediatric Rule**, a regulation that requires manufacturers of selected new and extant drug and biological products to conduct studies to assess their safety and efficacy in children.

**Mammography Quality Standards Reauthorization Act** continues 1992 Act until 2002.

First phase to consolidate FDA laboratories nationwide from 19 facilities to 9 by 2014 includes dedication of the first of five new regional laboratories.

**1999**

**ClinicalTrials.gov** is founded to provide the public with updated information on enrollment in federally and privately supported clinical research, thereby expanding patient access to studies of promising therapies.

A final rule mandates that all over-the-counter drug labels must contain data in a standardized format. These **drug facts** are designed to provide the patient with easy-to-find information, analogous to the nutrition facts label for foods.

**2000**

The U. S. Supreme Court, upholding an earlier decision in Food and Drug Administration v. Brown & Williamson Tobacco Corp. et al., ruled 5–4 that **FDA does not have authority to regulate tobacco as a drug**. Within weeks of this ruling, FDA revokes its final rule, issued in 1996, that restricted the sale and distribution of cigarettes and smokeless tobacco products to children and adolescents, and that determined that cigarettes and smokeless tobacco products are combination products consisting of a drug (nicotine) and device components intended to deliver nicotine to the body.

Federal agencies are required to issue guidelines to maximize the quality, objectivity, utility, and integrity of the information they generate, and to provide a mechanism whereby those affected can secure correction of information that does not meet these guidelines, under the **Data Quality Act**.

Publication of a **rule on dietary supplements** defines the type of statement that can be labeled regarding the effect of supplements on the structure or function of the body.

**2002**

**The Best Pharmaceuticals for Children Act** improves safety and efficacy of patented and off-patent medicines for children. It continues the exclusivity provisions for pediatric drugs as mandated under the Food and Drug Administration Modernization Act of 1997, in which market exclusivity of a drug is extended by six months, and in exchange the manufacturer carries out studies of the effects of drugs when taken by children. The provisions both clarify aspects of the exclusivity period and amend procedures for generic drug approval in cases when pediatric guidelines are added to the labeling.

In the wake of the events of September 11, 2001, the **Public Health Security and Bioterrorism Preparedness and Response Act of 2002** is designed to improve the country's ability to prevent and respond to public health emergencies, and provisions include a requirement that FDA issue regulations to enhance controls over imported and domestically produced commodities it regulates.

Under the **Medical Device User Fee and Modernization Act**, fees are assessed sponsors of medical device applications for evaluation, provisions are established for device establishment inspections by accredited third-parties, and new requirements emerge for reprocessed single-use devices.

The **Office of Combination Products** is formed within the Office of the Commissioner, as mandated under the Medical Device User Fee and Modernization Act, to oversee review of products that fall into multiple jurisdictions within FDA.

An effort to enhance and update the regulation of manufacturing processes and end-product quality of animal and human drugs and biological medicines is announced, the **current good manufacturing practice** (cGMP) **initiative.** The goals of the initiative are to focus on the greatest risks to public health in manufacturing procedures, to ensure that process and product quality standards do not impede innovation, and to apply a consistent approach to these issues across FDA.

2003

The **Medicare Prescription Drug Improvement and Modernization Act** requires, among other elements, that a study be made of how current and emerging technologies can be utilized to make essential information about prescription drugs available to the blind and visually impaired.

To help consumers choose heart-healthy foods, the Department of Health and Human Services announces that FDA will require **food labels to include trans fat content**, the first substantive change to the nutrition facts panel on foods since the label was changed in 1993.

An obesity working group is established by the Commissioner of Food and Drugs, charged to develop an action plan to deal with the nation's obesity epidemic from the perspective of FDA. In March 2004 the group releases **"Calories Count: Report of the Obesity Working Group,"** which addresses issues connected to the food label, obesity therapeutics, research needs, the role of education, and other topics.

The National Academy of Sciences releases **"Scientific Criteria to Ensure Safe Food,"** a report commissioned by FDA and the Department of Agriculture, which buttresses the value of the Hazard Analysis and Critical Control Point (HACCP) approach to food safety already in place at FDA and invokes the need for continued efforts to make food safety a vital part of our overall public health mission.

**The Animal Drug User Fee Act** permits FDA to collect subsidies for the review of certain animal drug applications from sponsors, analogous to laws passed for the evaluation of other products FDA regulates, ensuring the safety and effectiveness of drugs for animals and the safety of animals used as foodstuffs.

FDA is given clear authority under the **Pediatric Research Equity Act** to require that sponsors conduct clinical research into pediatric applications for new drugs and biological products.

2004

**Project BioShield Act of 2004** authorizes FDA to expedite its review procedures to enable rapid distribution of treatments as countermeasures to chemical, biological, and nuclear agents that may be used in a terrorist attack against the U. S., among other provisions.

Passage of the **Food Allergy Labeling and Consumer Protection Act** requires the labeling of any food that contains a protein derived from any one of the following foods that, as a group, account for the vast majority of food allergies: peanuts, soybeans, cow's milk, eggs, fish, crustacean shellfish, tree nuts, and wheat.

A ban on over-the-counter steroid precursors, increased penalties for making, selling, or possessing illegal steroids precursors, and funds for preventive education to children are features of the **Anabolic Steroid Control Act of 2004.**

FDA publishes "Innovation or Stagnation?—Challenge and Opportunity on the Critical Path to New Medical Products," which examines the **critical path** needed to bring therapeutic products to fruition, and how FDA can collaborate in the process, from laboratory to production to end use, to make medical breakthroughs available to those in need as quickly as possible.

Based on recent results from controlled clinical studies indicating that **Cox-2 selective agents** may be connected to an elevated risk of serious cardiovascular events, including heart attack and stroke, FDA issues a public health advisory urging health professionals to limit the use of these drugs.

To provide for the treatment of animal species other than cattle, horses, swine, chickens, turkeys, dogs, and cats, as well as other species that may be added at a later time, the **Minor Use and Minor Species Animal Health Act** is passed to encourage the development of treatments for species that would otherwise attract little interest in the development of veterinary therapies.

Deeming such products to present an unreasonable risk of harm, **FDA bans dietary supplements containing ephedrine alkaloids** based on an increasing number of adverse events linked to these products and the known pharmacology of these alkaloids.

**2005**

Formation of the **Drug Safety Board** is announced, consisting of FDA staff and representatives from the National Institutes of Health and the Veterans Administration. The Board will advise the Director, Center for Drug Evaluation and Research, FDA, on drug safety issues and work with the agency in communicating safety information to health professionals and patients.

**2009**

President Obama signs the **Family Smoking Prevention and Tobacco Control Act** into law. The Tobacco Control Act gives FDA authority to regulate the manufacture, distribution, and marketing of tobacco products to protect public health.

FDA **Center for Tobacco Products** established.

FDA announced a **ban on cigarettes with flavors characterizing fruit, candy, or clove.**

**2011**

**FDA Food Safety and Modernization Act (FSMA).** FSMA provides FDA with new enforcement authorities related to food safety standards, gives FDA tools to hold imported foods to the same standards as domestic foods, and directs FDA to build an integrated national food safety system in partnership with state and local authorities.

**2012**

**Food and Drug Administration Safety and Innovation Act (FDASIA).** Expands FDA authorities to collect user fees from industry to fund reviews of innovator drugs, medical devices, generic drugs and biosimilar biological products; promotes innovation to speed patient access to safe and effective products; increases stakeholder involvement in FDA processes, and enhances the safety of the drug supply chain.

**Medical Device User Fee and Modernization Act (MDUFMA III).** As part of FDASIA, reauthorizes user fees from industry to fund reviews of medical devices in exchange for FDA to meet certain performance goals.

In 2012, an outbreak of fungal meningitis linked to a contaminated **compounded drug product** resulted in the loss of 64 lives and caused more than 751 illnesses. In response, Congress enacted the 2013 Drug Quality and Security Act (DQSA) that insures greater regulatory oversight of facilities creating compounded drugs.

**2013**

**Pandemic and All-Hazards Preparedness Reauthorization Act (PAHPRA).** Establishes and reauthorizes certain programs under the Public Health Service Act and the Food, Drug, and Cosmetic Act with respect to public health security and all-hazards preparedness and response.

**Drug Quality and Security Act.** Following an outbreak in 2012 of an epidemic of fungal meningitis linked to a compounded steroid, Congress enacted the Drug Quality Safety and Security Act (DQSA). Among other provisions it outlines steps for an electronic and interoperable system to identify and trace certain prescription drugs throughout the U.S.

*[FDA's milestones list ends in 2013.]*

## D. Product Categories

The entire structure of food and drug regulation is based on the idea of product categories. To know the regulatory requirements that apply to a particular product, you must first know the category into which it falls.

Most categories are initially defined by Congress at the statutory level. These are found in the U.S. Code. Except for the provisions governing biologics, these are found in FFDCA § 201. The provisions governing biologics are found in § 351(i) of PHSA. One category, today known as HCT/Ps, is defined only by regulation, based on authority granted in § 361 of the PHSA. Another category, combination products, is referenced in FFDCA § 503(g)(1) and defined by regulation in 21 C.F.R. § 3.2.

Further definition of the product categories is done by FDA at the regulatory level. These are found in the Code of Federal Regulations. They are not consolidated in a few areas, as the statutory definitions are. Instead, they tend to be intermixed with the other provisions relating to the relevant product category.

## 1. Categorization Problems

New products do not always fit easily into existing product categories. Sometimes a new product is genuinely outside existing categories. Other times, a product potentially fits into two or more categories, but would be subject to heavier regulation in one category than the other.

One of the historically significant product-category disputes reached the U.S. Supreme Court in *United States v. An Article of Drug . . . Bacto-Unidisk* (1969). This case was a dispute over whether a particular product, an antibiotic sensitivity disk, should be regulated as a drug or a medical device. Under then-existing law, drugs were subject to marketing authorization for both safety and efficacy. Medical devices, by contrast, did not have to undergo any marketing authorization. (This would begin to change seven years later, with the passage of the Medical Device Amendments of 1976).

As you read, think about the problems associated with regulating industries where major innovations often involve previously nonexistent technology. We will return to *Bacto-Unidisk* when we discuss both drug and medical device regulation.

*Note: In the* Bacto-Unidisk *case, you will find several references to FFDCA § 507. This provision, specific to antibiotic drugs, was repealed by the Food and Drug Administration Modernization Act of 1997. Today, new antibiotic drugs are regulated, like other new drugs, under FFDCA § 505.*

### United States v. An Article of Drug . . . Bacto-Unidisk . . .

394 U.S. 784 (1969)

**Mr. Chief Justice WARREN delivered the opinion of the court.**

At issue here is the scope of the statutory definition of drug contained in the [FFDCA] and the extent of the Secretary of Health, Education, and Welfare's regulatory authority under that definition. The specific item involved in this definitional controversy is a laboratory aid known as an antibiotic sensitivity disc, used as a screening test for help in determining the proper antibiotic drug to administer to patients. If the article is a "drug" within the general definition of § 201 of the [FFDCA], then the Secretary can subject it to pre-market clearance regulations promulgated pursuant to § 507 of the [FFDCA]. Section 507 authorizes the Secretary to require batch certification of any antibiotic product which also meets the general drug definition of § 201. If, on the other hand, the article is merely a "device" under the [FFDCA], it is subject only to the misbranding and adulteration proscriptions of the [FFDCA] and does not have to be pre-tested before marketing; and, of course, if the disc does not fall under either definition, the [FFDCA] itself is totally inapplicable.

When the discs were marketed without complying with the certification regulations of the Secretary, the Government condemned them pursuant to § 334 of the [FFDCA] on the assumption that the discs were drugs and thus validly subject to pre-market regulation. In this action following the condemnation, however, the United States District Court for the Eastern District of Michigan held that the discs were not drugs within the meaning of the [FFDCA], suggesting that, if anything, they were devices. It therefore ruled that, since pre-market clearance was not required or authorized, the seizure was improper. The Court of Appeals for the Sixth Circuit affirmed on the same reasoning. We reverse.

I.

Some background information about the development of the discs and the controlling legislation is necessary for an understanding of the determinations made by the Secretary and the courts below. Various antibiotics, known more commonly as "wonder drugs" . . . have proved very useful since World War II in treating numerous infectious diseases. Produced biologically, however, these drugs tend to vary greatly in their quality and potency unless developed, and thereafter tested, under very carefully controlled conditions. Consequently, Congress enacted § 507 of the Food, Drug, and Cosmetic Act, directing the Secretary of Health, Education, and Welfare to promulgate regulations establishing such standards of identity, potency, quality, and purity as necessary to ensure the "safety" and "efficacy" of those antibiotics. . . .

With the proliferation of the various types of antibiotics, doctors found a need for a screening test to help choose which antibiotic to use in treating a particular infection. . . . In this test, a round paper disc, which has been impregnated with a specific antibiotic, is placed in contact with sample cultures, or isolates, of a patient's virus, grown in a special culture medium (agar) from a specimen of the patient's fluid (blood, spinal fluid, sputum, urine, etc.). In those places impregnated with an antibiotic to which the patient's infection is sensitive, no new isolate will grow, leaving a clear area (an "inhibition zone"); in those places impregnated with a drug to which the infection is resistant, the isolate will grow, leaving no clear area. . . .

After notice and an opportunity for public participation, the Commissioner of Food and Drugs, under authority delegated by the Secretary, promulgated regulations requiring pre-clearance, batch-testing, and certification of antibiotic sensitivity discs. The Commissioner's action, the regulations noted, followed "numerous complaints by the medical profession, hospitals, and laboratory technicians" and a resulting extensive survey of the use of the discs. That study found the discs unreliable in their statements of potency with resulting loss of safety and efficacy, and thus found it "vital for the protection of the public health" to adopt the regulations.

This case arose in May 1962 as an in rem seizure proceeding against an interstate shipment of a number of cases of sensitivity discs, manufactured by Difco

Laboratories, Inc., under the trade name of "Bacto-Unidisk." In condemning the product pursuant to § 301 et seq. of the Food, Drug, and Cosmetic Act, the United States claimed, inter alia, that the product, as a "drug" within the meaning of the [FFDCA], had not been certified nor exempted from certification as required by § 507 and the regulations thereunder and was therefore misbranded under § 502. . . . Since the scope of the Secretary's pre-market regulatory power over antibiotic drugs under § 507 depends ultimately on the [FFDCA]'s general definition of "drug" in § 201(g), the validity of the disc regulations allegedly violated turned on the coverage of the drug definition:

> For the purposes of this chapter—
>
> . . . .
>
> (g)(1) The term 'drug' means (A) articles recognized in the official United States Pharmacopoeia, official Homoeopathic Pharmacopoeia of the United States, or official National Formulary, or any supplement to any of them; and (B) articles intended for use in the diagnosis, cure, mitigation, treatment, or prevention of disease in man or other animals; and (C) articles (other than food) intended to affect the structure or any function of the body of man or other animals; and (D) articles intended for use as a component of any article specified in clauses (A), (B), or (C) of this paragraph; but does not include devices or their components, parts, or accessories.

If, on the other hand, the product was a "device," only the misbranding, adulteration, and labeling provisions of §§ 501 and 502 applied, and the Secretary's disc certification regulations were invalidly promulgated. Although a "device" expressly cannot be a "drug" under the last phrase of the drug definition above, a device is given almost a parallel definition in § 201(h):

> The term 'device' . . . means instruments, apparatus, and contrivances, including their components, parts, and accessories, intended (1) for use in the diagnosis, cure, mitigation, treatment, or prevention of disease in man or other animals; or (2) to affect the structure or any function of the body of man or other animals.

Finally, it was established at trial that of the various definitions given above, the operative ones in this case were § 201(g)(1)(B) of the drug provision and § 201(h)(1) of the parallel device definition; the essential question underlying the validity of the regulations, then, was whether the Bacto-Unidisks were "articles intended for use in the diagnosis, cure, mitigation, treatment, or prevention of disease in man or other animals."

. . . . The District Court pointed out that although a "literal reading" of § 201(g)(1)(B) "clearly has application to the article libeled herein," enforcing such an application would be "ridiculous and contrary to common sense." The court therefore held that the Bacto-Unidisk did not fall within the purview of the [FFDCA] for the reason that it was not medically a drug, and suggested, without deciding, that the discs would be more appropriately classified as "devices" under the [FFDCA].

On appeal, the Court of Appeals for the Sixth Circuit affirmed, accepting the District Court's conclusions that the Bacto-Unidisk was not a "drug" in the medical sense of the term and that Congress did not intend the statutory definition of "drug" to be any broader than the medical one.... We granted the Government's petition for certiorari because this interpretation of the [FFDCA] raised issues of importance in the administration of the [FFDCA].

II.

.... The courts below quite properly confined the inquiry to an examination of whether the disc regulations, even if medically unwise, were authorized by the [FFDCA], and more specifically, by the [FFDCA]'s definition of "drug." ... Our sole concern is whether the statute's definition of "drug" authorizes the disc regulations contested here; and while we agree with the lower courts' limited conception of the issue, for reasons outlined below, we reverse their disposition of it.

Respondent's primary contention here is that the sensitivity discs are not subject to any of the provisions of the [FFDCA] because Congress did not intend it to cover articles used so indirectly in the "cure, mitigation, [and] treatment" of disease. Respondent uses the same two-step analysis relied on by the courts below: (1) Congress did not intend to write the drug definition more broadly than does the medical profession, and (2) the medical concept of drug is limited to articles that are administered to man either internally or externally. Alternatively, respondent argues, even if the [FFDCA]'s "in-tended for use" language does cover the discs, they must clearly be classified as devices....

We need not stop to parse the language of the [FFDCA]'s definition of drug, for the District Court found, and the parties do not disagree here, that a literal reading of the words "intended for use in the ... cure, mitigation, [or] treatment" of disease "clearly has application" to the Bacto-Unidisk. Although respondent again urges that the disc itself does not "treat" a patient in the same way an antibiotic does in terms of personal application, the disc plays at least some role in the selection of the appropriate drug. Thus, the essential question for our determination is whether Congress intended the definition of drug to have the broad coverage the courts below and the parties agree its words allow. Viewing the structure, the legislative history, and the remedial nature of the [FFDCA], we think it plain that Congress intended to define "drug" far more broadly than does the medical profession. The reason for including a separate, almost parallel, definition of "devices" in the [FFDCA] is, as the legislative history shows, relevant to congressional intent. It is therefore helpful to consider both the question of the [FFDCA]'s initial application and the question of the drug-device dichotomy at the same time.

III.

At the outset, it is clear from § 201 that the word "drug" is a term of art for the purposes of the [FFDCA], encompassing far more than the strict medical definition of that word. If Congress had intended to limit the statutory definition to the medical one, it could have so stated explicitly, or simply have made reference to the official United States Pharmacopoeia (or the National Formulary), as it did in the first of the three subsections of § 201(g)(1), and let the definition rest there. The historical expansion of the statute's definition, furthermore, clearly points out Congress' intention of going beyond the medical usage. The 1906 Food and Drug Act, for instance, defined "drug" in a rather limited way to include "all medicines and preparations recognized in the United States Pharmacopoeia or National Formulary for internal or external use, and any substance or mixture of substances intended to be used for the cure, mitigation, or prevention of disease of either man or other animals." As subsequent congressional action clearly indicates, however, the scope of that original definition has since been greatly enlarged.

The enactment of the [FFDCA] illustrates the expansion of the definition of drug. One of the changes contemplated in S. 2800, an early version of the [FFDCA], defined "drug" to include:

> (1) all substances and preparations recognized in the United States Pharmacopoeia, Homoeopathic Pharmacopoeia of the United States, or National Formulary or supplements thereto; and (2) all substances, preparations, and *devices* intended for use in the cure, mitigation, treatment, or prevention of disease in man or other animals; and (3) all substances and preparations, other than food, and all devices intended to affect the structure or any function of the body. *[Emphasis on "devices" added by Court.]*

Senator Copeland of New York, who sponsored the [FFDCA], remarked about the inclusion of the word "devices" in his prepared statement introducing S. 2800 as follows:

> The present law defines drugs as substances or mixtures of substances intended to be used for the cure, mitigation, or prevention of disease. This narrow definition permits escape from legal control of all therapeutic or curative devices like electric belts, for example. It also permits the escape of preparations which are intended to alter the structure or some function of the body, as, for example, preparations intended to reduce excessive weight. There are many worthless and some dangerous devices and preparations falling within these classifications. S. 2800 contains ample authority to control them.

The definition was revised in S. 5, 74th Cong., 1st Sess. (1935), to include substances, preparations, and devices in-tended for diagnostic purposes, as well as for cure, mitigation, treatment, or prevention of disease. As the inclusion of the word "diagnosis" came before the Senate for consideration, a controversy developed on the floor, aimed more at the word "devices," which was not then before the Senate, than at the word "diagnosis." Senator Clark contended that it was not proper to classify devices as drugs, and that diagnostic devices were so broadly defined as to make even a bathroom scale a drug:

> If the devices ought to be outlawed, they ought to be outlawed, and I have no objection to that; but to maintain that a purely mechanical device is a drug and to be treated as a drug in law and in logic and in lexicography is a palpable absurdity, in my opinion.

In answer to Senator Clark's remark that a bathroom scale would be classified as a drug, Senator Copeland made the following comment:

> Mr. President, I desire to state the effect of this amendment. There are on the market certain electrical devices. A man takes hold of the handles of the machine, and the indicator spins around. It stops at 'appendicitis,' or it stops at 'meningitis' .... Such a device is manifestly a fraud upon society. That is what the amendment is designed to deal with.

As a result of the criticism on the Senate floor, Senator Copeland proposed an amendment to add a definition of "device" to parallel that of drug, an amendment which was included when the bill was returned to the Senate Committee on Commerce and later agreed to by the Senate without debate. The ultimate effect of the various amendments, of course, was still to include devices under the control of the [FFDCA] for the first time, the goal Senator Copeland had originally set out to achieve.... According to the Chief of the Food and Drug Administration, the reason for providing a separate definition of devices, instead of using Senator Copeland's original drug definition, was simply to avoid "the incongruity of classifying certain devices, such as the electric belt, therapeutic lamps, and so forth, as drugs...." (Testimony given during hearings held on S. 5 by a subcommittee of the House Committee on Interstate and Foreign Commerce, 74th Cong., 1st Sess. (1935).) .... No practical significance to the distinction between the two words arose until the pre-market clearance provisions.... The excepting clause of § 201(g)(1), stating clearly that a drug cannot be a device, was also added in 1938.

The historical expansion of the definition of drug, and the creation of a parallel concept of devices, clearly show, we think, that Congress fully intended that the [FFDCA]'s coverage be as broad as its literal language indicates—and equally clearly, broader than any strict medical definition might otherwise allow. Strong indications from legislative history that Congress intended the broad coverage the District Court thought "ridiculous" should satisfy us that the lower courts erred in refusing to apply the [FFDCA]'s language as written. But we are all the more convinced that we must give effect to congressional intent in view of the well-accepted principle that remedial legislation such as the Food, Drug, and Cosmetic Act is to be given a liberal construction consistent with the [FFDCA]'s overriding purpose to protect the public health, and specifically, § 507's purpose to ensure that antibiotic products marketed serve the public with "efficacy" and "safety." *Cf. United States v. Sullivan*, 332 U.S. 689 (1948); *United States v. Dotterweich*, 320 U.S. 277 (1943).

**IV.**

Respondent's alternative contention, that even if its product does fall within the purview of the [FFDCA], it is plainly a "device" and therefore by definition necessarily not a "drug," must also be rejected, we believe, in light of the foregoing analysis. At the outset, it must be conceded that the language of the statute is of little assistance in determining precisely what differentiates a "drug" from a "device": to the extent that both are intended for use in the treatment, mitigation and cure of disease, the former is an "article" and the latter includes "instruments," "apparatus," and "contrivances." Despite the obvious areas of overlap in definition, we are not entirely without guidance in determining the propriety of the Secretary's decision below, given the overall goals of the [FFDCA] and its legislative history.

More specifically, as we have previously held in an analogous situation where the statute's language seemed insufficiently precise, the "natural way" to draw the line "is in light of the statutory purpose." Since the patient will tend to derive less benefit and perhaps some harm from a particular antibiotic if, though the drug itself was properly batch-tested, it was not the proper antibiotic to use, it was entirely reasonable for the Secretary to determine that the discs, like the antibiotics they serve, are drugs and similarly subject to pre-clearance certification under § 507. An opposite conclusion might undercut the value of testing the antibiotics themselves, for such testing would be a useless exercise if the wrong drug were ultimately administered, even partially as the result of an unreliable disc.

Furthermore, the legislative history, read in light of the statute's remedial purpose, directs us to read the classification "drug" broadly, and to confine the device exception as nearly as is possible to the types of items Congress suggested in the debates, such as electric belts, quack diagnostic scales, and therapeutic lamps, as well as bathroom weight scales, shoulder braces, air conditioning units, and crutches. . . . Finally, we are supported in the decision to uphold the FDA's determination that the sensitivity discs fall under the coverage of the [FFDCA] and specifically under the drug provision thereof by the knowledge that the classification of these discs as drugs may not be as contrary to common medical usage as the District Court and respondent would have us believe.

In upholding the Secretary's construction of the [FFDCA], we are not unmindful of our warning that "in our anxiety to effectuate the congressional purpose of protecting the public, we must take care not to extend the scope of the statute beyond the point where Congress indicated it would stop." *62 Cases of Jam v. United States*, 340 U.S. 593 (1951). Our holding here simply involves an obvious corollary to that principle, that we must take care not to narrow the coverage of a statute short of the point where Congress indicated it should extend.

Reversed.

**Mr. Justice DOUGLAS**, being of the view that an antibiotic sensitivity disc used by physicians to aid them in determining what antibiotic drug, if any, to give to a patient, is a "device" as defined in § 201(h) of the [FFDCA], not a "drug" as defined in § 201(g), would affirm the judgment.

## E. Key Points

- FDA is currently based in the Department of Health and Human Services. However, it has a complex organizational history. It has previously been housed in other Cabinet-level departments. It has at times acquired new responsibilities from other agencies and it has at times had some of its responsibilities transferred to other agencies.
- Product categories are the basis of almost all FDA regulation. The basic categories addressed in this book are food, food additives, dietary supplements, drugs, animal drugs, medical devices, combination products, biologics, HCT/Ps (human cells, tissues, and cellular and tissue-based products), cosmetics, color additives, and tobacco products. There are other categories, but these are less critical to a basic understanding of food and drug regulation.
- There are inevitable disputes about which product category is the correct fit for a particular product. These disputes can be tremendously important, as the regulatory requirements differ dramatically among the different product categories.
    - The different regulatory requirements are most significant with respect to marketing authorization (see Chapter 4).
        - Products in some categories must undergo rigorous FDA review before they can be marketed in the United States.
        - Products in other categories can be marketed without any requirement for FDA authorization before marketing begins.

Chapter 2

# Administrative Procedure

## A. Introduction

Please read (or review) the following excerpts in the statutory supplement:

- FFDCA § 701. Regulations and hearings.
- 5 U.S.C. § 553. Rule making.
- 5 U.S.C. § 556. Hearings; presiding employees; powers and duties; burden of proof; evidence; record as basis of decision.
- 5 U.S.C. § 557. Initial decisions; conclusiveness; review by agency; submissions by parties; contents of decisions; record.

The first item, FFDCA § 701, is the basic administrative procedure provision specific to FDA. Section 701 was originally passed in 1938, as part of the FFDCA (though it has since been updated).

The next three items, 5 U.S.C. §§ 553, 556, and 557, are from the Administrative Procedure Act. This statute was originally passed in 1946 (though it, too, has since been updated). They apply to agencies generally, but do not abrogate the more specific provisions of FFDCA § 701.

Section 553 sets out what is known as the informal, or notice and comment, rulemaking process. The "informal" term can be confusing to students first encountering this statute, as the informal rulemaking process is quite rigorous. It is only "informal" when compared to formal rulemaking. Today, the vast majority of federal rulemaking is done through the § 553 informal rulemaking process.

Section 556 and 557 set out the formal rulemaking process. The formal rulemaking process involves rulemaking through trial-type procedures.

## B. Outline of Regulatory Regime

As in other chapters of this book, this chapter begins with a set of charts. As you read this chapter for the first time, you should do no more than skim these charts to get a general sense of the structure of the applicable statutes and regulations. (For more information on the role of the charts in this casebook, see Chapter 1, Parts A.1 and B).

| Timeline of Key Statutes: Administrative Procedure | | | |
|---|---|---|---|
| Year | PL | Stat | Name of Statute |
| 1906 | 59-384 | 34 Stat. 768 | Pure Food and Drug Act |
| 1938 | 75-717 | 52 Stat. 1040 | FFDCA of 1938 |
| 1946 | 79-404 | 60 Stat. 237 | Administrative Procedure Act |
| 1997 | 105-115 | 111 Stat. 2296 | FDA Modernization Act of 1997 |

| Key Statutory Provisions: Administrative Procedure Generally | | |
|---|---|---|
| Statute Name or U.S.C. Title | § | Title of Section or Subsection |
| 5 U.S.C. | 551 | Definitions |
| 5 U.S.C. | 552 | Public information; agency rules, opinions, orders, records, and proceedings |
| 5 U.S.C. | 553 | Rule making |
| 5 U.S.C. | 554 | Adjudications |
| 5 U.S.C. | 555 | Ancillary matters |
| 5 U.S.C. | 556 | Hearings; presiding employees; powers and duties; burden of proof; evidence; record as basis of decision |
| 5 U.S.C. | 557 | Initial decisions; conclusiveness; review by agency; submissions by parties; contents of decisions; record |
| 5 U.S.C. | 558 | Imposition of sanctions; determination of applications for licenses; suspension, revocation, and expiration of licenses |
| 5 U.S.C. | 559 | Effect on other laws; effect of subsequent statute |
| 5 U.S.C. App 2 | 9 | Establishment and purpose of advisory committees; publication in Federal Register; charter: filing, contents, copy |

| Key Statutory Provisions: Administrative Procedure at FDA | | |
|---|---|---|
| Statute Name or U.S.C. Title | § | Title of Section or Subsection |
| FFDCA | 701 | Regulations and hearings |
| FFDCA | 702 | Examinations and investigations |
| FFDCA | 703 | Records |
| FFDCA | 704 | Inspection |
| FFDCA | 705 | Publicity |
| FFDCA | 708 | Confidential information |
| FFDCA | 709 | Presumption of existence of jurisdiction |
| FFDCA | 710 | Consolidated administrative and laboratory facility |
| FFDCA | 712 | Conflicts of interest |

| Key Regulatory Provisions: Administrative Procedure at FDA | | |
|---|---|---|
| 21 C.F.R. Part | Subpart | Title of Part or Subpart |
| 2 | — | General administrative rulings and decisions |
| 3 | — | Product jurisdiction |
| 10 | — | Administrative practices and procedures |
| 11 | — | Electronic records; electronic signatures |
| 12 | — | Formal evidentiary public hearing |
| 13 | — | Public hearing before a public board of inquiry |
| 15 | — | Public hearing before the commissioner |
| 16 | — | Regulatory hearing before the Food and Drug Administration |
| 17 | — | Civil money penalties hearings |
| 19 | — | Standards of conduct and conflicts of interest |
| 20 | — | Public information |
| 21 | — | Protection of privacy |
| 25 | — | Environmental impact considerations |

## C. Agency Statutory Interpretation — Generally

Before moving to FDA-specific administrative procedure, you need a general introduction to one of the core issues in administrative law more generally— agency statutory interpretation. The case below, involving judicial review of an EPA statutory-interpretation decision, remains the leading case on this issue.

As you read the case, focus less on the EPA-specific issues and more on two general questions. First, how much discretion do agencies have when they interpret, through notice-and-comment rulemaking, the statutes they administer? Second, to what extent does a change in presidential administrations (especially one involving a change of political parties) justify a change in an agency's view of the proper interpretation of a statute?

## Chevron, U.S.A., Inc. v. Natural Res. Def. Council, Inc.

467 U.S. 837 (1984)

**Justice STEVENS delivered the opinion of the Court.**

In the Clean Air Act Amendments of 1977, Congress enacted certain requirements applicable to States that had not achieved the national air quality standards established by the Environmental Protection Agency (EPA) pursuant to earlier legislation. The amended Clean Air Act required these "nonattainment" States to establish a permit program regulating "new or modified major stationary sources" of air pollution. Generally, a permit may not be issued for a new or modified major stationary source unless several stringent conditions are met. The EPA regulation promulgated to implement this permit requirement allows a State to adopt a plantwide definition of the term "stationary source." Under this definition, an existing plant that contains several pollution-emitting devices may install or modify one piece of equipment without meeting the permit conditions if the alteration will not increase the total emissions from the plant. The question presented by these cases is whether EPA's decision to allow States to treat all of the pollution-emitting devices within the same industrial grouping as though they were encased within a single "bubble" is based on a reasonable construction of the statutory term "stationary source."

### I

The EPA regulations containing the plantwide definition of the term stationary source were promulgated on October 14, 1981. Respondents filed a timely petition for review in the United States Court of Appeals for the District of Columbia Circuit. . . . The Court of Appeals set aside the regulations.

The court observed that the relevant part of the amended Clean Air Act "does not explicitly define what Congress envisioned as a 'stationary source, to which the permit program . . . should apply," and further stated that the precise issue was not "squarely addressed in the legislative history." In light of its conclusion that the legislative history bearing on the question was "at best contradictory," it reasoned that "the purposes of the nonattainment program should guide our decision here." Based on two of its precedents concerning the applicability of the bubble concept to certain Clean Air Act programs, the court stated that the bubble concept was "mandatory" in programs designed merely to maintain existing air quality, but held that it was "inappropriate" in programs enacted to improve air quality. Since the purpose of the permit program—its "raison d'être," in the court's view—was to improve air quality, the court held that the bubble concept was inapplicable in these cases under its prior precedents. It therefore set aside the regulations embodying the bubble concept as contrary to law. We granted certiorari to review that judgment, and we now reverse.

The basic legal error of the Court of Appeals was to adopt a static judicial definition of the term "stationary source" when it had decided that Congress itself had not commanded that definition. Respondents do not defend the legal reasoning of the Court of Appeals. Nevertheless, since this Court reviews judgments, not opinions, we must determine whether the Court of Appeals' legal error resulted in an erroneous judgment on the validity of the regulations.

II

When a court reviews an agency's construction of the statute which it administers, it is confronted with two questions. First, always, is the question whether Congress has directly spoken to the precise question at issue. If the intent of Congress is clear, that is the end of the matter; for the court, as well as the agency, must give effect to the unambiguously expressed intent of Congress.[9] If, however, the court determines Congress has not directly addressed the precise question at issue, the court does not simply impose its own construction on the statute, as would be necessary in the absence of an administrative interpretation. Rather, if the statute is silent or ambiguous with respect to the specific issue, the question for the court is whether the agency's answer is based on a permissible construction of the statute.[11]

"The power of an administrative agency to administer a congressionally created ... program necessarily requires the formulation of policy and the making of rules to fill any gap left, implicitly or explicitly, by Congress." *Morton v. Ruiz*, 415 U.S. 199, 231 (1974). If Congress has explicitly left a gap for the agency to fill, there is an express delegation of authority to the agency to elucidate a specific provision of the statute by regulation. Such legislative regulations are given controlling weight unless they are arbitrary, capricious, or manifestly contrary to the statute. Sometimes the legislative delegation to an agency on a particular question is implicit rather than explicit. In such a case, a court may not substitute its own construction of a statutory provision for a reasonable interpretation made by the administrator of an agency.

We have long recognized that considerable weight should be accorded to an executive department's construction of a statutory scheme it is entrusted to administer, and the principle of deference to administrative interpretations

> has been consistently followed by this Court whenever decision as to the meaning or reach of a statute has involved reconciling conflicting policies, and a full understanding of the force of the statutory policy in the given situation has depended upon more than ordinary knowledge respecting the matters subjected to agency regulations.
>
> .... *United States v. Shimer*, 367 U.S. 374, 382, 383 (1961).

---

9. The judiciary is the final authority on issues of statutory construction and must reject administrative constructions which are contrary to clear congressional intent. If a court, employing traditional tools of statutory construction, ascertains that Congress had an intention on the precise question at issue, that intention is the law and must be given effect.

11. The court need not conclude that the agency construction was the only one it permissibly could have adopted to uphold the construction, or even the reading the court would have reached if the question initially had arisen in a judicial proceeding.

In light of these well-settled principles it is clear that the Court of Appeals misconceived the nature of its role in reviewing the regulations at issue. Once it determined, after its own examination of the legislation, that Congress did not actually have an intent regarding the applicability of the bubble concept to the permit program, the question before it was not whether in its view the concept is "inappropriate" in the general context of a program designed to improve air quality, but whether the Administrator's view that it is appropriate in the context of this particular program is a reasonable one. Based on the examination of the legislation and its history which follows, we agree with the Court of Appeals that Congress did not have a specific intention on the applicability of the bubble concept in these cases, and conclude that the EPA's use of that concept here is a reasonable policy choice for the agency to make.

### III

. . . .

### VII

In this Court respondents expressly reject the basic rationale of the Court of Appeals' decision. That court viewed the statutory definition of the term "source" as sufficiently flexible to cover either a plantwide definition, a narrower definition covering each unit within a plant, or a dual definition that could apply to both the entire "bubble" and its components. It interpreted the policies of the statute, however, to mandate the plantwide definition in programs designed to maintain clean air and to forbid it in programs designed to improve air quality. Respondents place a fundamentally different construction on the statute. They contend that the text of the [Clean Air Act Amendments of 1977] requires the EPA to use a dual definition—if either a component of a plant, or the plant as a whole, emits over 100 tons of pollutant, it is a major stationary source. They thus contend that the EPA rules adopted in 1980, insofar as they apply to the maintenance of the quality of clean air, as well as the 1981 rules which apply to nonattainment areas, violate the statute.

#### Statutory Language

The definition of the term "stationary source" in § 111(a)(3) refers to "any building, structure, facility, or installation" which emits air pollution. This definition is applicable only to the NSPS program by the express terms of the statute; the text of the statute does not make this definition applicable to the permit program. Petitioners therefore maintain that there is no statutory language even relevant to ascertaining the meaning of stationary source in the permit program aside from § 302(j), which defines the term "major stationary source." We disagree with petitioners on this point.

The definition in § 302(j) tells us what the word "major" means—a source must emit at least 100 tons of pollution to qualify—but it sheds virtually no light on the meaning of the term "stationary source." It does equate a source with a facility—a "major emitting facility" and a "major stationary source" are synonymous under

§ 302(j). The ordinary meaning of the term "facility" is some collection of integrated elements which has been designed and constructed to achieve some purpose. Moreover, it is certainly no affront to common English usage to take a reference to a major facility or a major source to connote an entire plant as opposed to its constituent parts. Basically, however, the language of § 302(j) simply does not compel any given interpretation of the term "source."

Respondents recognize that, and hence point to § 111(a)(3). Although the definition in that section is not literally applicable to the permit program, it sheds as much light on the meaning of the word "source" as anything in the statute. As respondents point out, use of the words "building, structure, facility, or installation," as the definition of source, could be read to impose the permit conditions on an individual building that is a part of a plant. On the other hand, the meaning of a word must be ascertained in the context of achieving particular objectives, and the words associated with it may indicate that the true meaning of the series is to convey a common idea. The language may reasonably be interpreted to impose the requirement on any discrete, but integrated, operation which pollutes. This gives meaning to all of the terms—a single building, not part of a larger operation, would be covered if it emits more than 100 tons of pollution, as would any facility, structure, or installation. Indeed, the language itself implies a "bubble concept" of sorts: each enumerated item would seem to be treated as if it were encased in a bubble. While respondents insist that each of these terms must be given a discrete meaning, they also argue that § 111(a)(3) defines "source" as that term is used in § 302(j). The latter section, however, equates a source with a facility, whereas the former defines "source" as a facility, among other items.

We are not persuaded that parsing of general terms in the text of the statute will reveal an actual intent of Congress. We know full well that this language is not dispositive; the terms are overlapping and the language is not precisely directed to the question of the applicability of a given term in the context of a larger operation. To the extent any congressional "intent" can be discerned from this language, it would appear that the listing of overlapping, illustrative terms was intended to enlarge, rather than to confine, the scope of the agency's power to regulate particular sources in order to effectuate the policies of the [Clean Air Act Amendments of 1977].

**Legislative History**

In addition, respondents argue that the legislative history and policies of the [Clean Air Act Amendments of 1977] foreclose the plantwide definition, and that the EPA's interpretation is not entitled to deference because it represents a sharp break with prior interpretations of the [Clean Air Act Amendments of 1977].

Based on our examination of the legislative history, we agree with the Court of Appeals that it is unilluminating. . . .

Our review of the EPA's varying interpretations of the word "source"—both before and after the 1977 Amendments—convinces us that the agency primarily responsible for administering this important legislation has consistently interpreted it flexibly—not in a sterile textual vacuum, but in the context of implementing policy decisions in a technical and complex arena. The fact that the agency has from time to time changed its interpretation of the term "source" does not, as respondents argue, lead us to conclude that no deference should be accorded the agency's interpretation of the statute. An initial agency interpretation is not instantly carved in stone. On the contrary, the agency, to engage in informed rulemaking, must consider varying interpretations and the wisdom of its policy on a continuing basis. Moreover, the fact that the agency has adopted different definitions in different contexts adds force to the argument that the definition itself is flexible, particularly since Congress has never indicated any disapproval of a flexible reading of the statute.

Significantly, it was not the agency in 1980, but rather the Court of Appeals that read the statute inflexibly to command a plantwide definition for programs designed to maintain clean air and to forbid such a definition for programs designed to improve air quality. The distinction the court drew may well be a sensible one, but our labored review of the problem has surely disclosed that it is not a distinction that Congress ever articulated itself, or one that the EPA found in the statute before the courts began to review the legislative work product. We conclude that it was the Court of Appeals, rather than Congress or any of the decisionmakers who are authorized by Congress to administer this legislation, that was primarily responsible for the 1980 position taken by the agency.

### Policy

The arguments over policy that are advanced in the parties' briefs create the impression that respondents are now waging in a judicial forum a specific policy battle which they ultimately lost in the agency and in the 32 jurisdictions opting for the "bubble concept," but one which was never waged in the Congress. Such policy arguments are more properly addressed to legislators or administrators, not to judges.

In these cases, the Administrator's interpretation represents a reasonable accommodation of manifestly competing interests and is entitled to deference: the regulatory scheme is technical and complex, the agency considered the matter in a detailed and reasoned fashion, and the decision involves reconciling conflicting policies. Congress intended to accommodate both interests, but did not do so itself on the level of specificity presented by these cases. Perhaps that body consciously desired the Administrator to strike the balance at this level, thinking that those with great expertise and charged with responsibility for administering the provision would be in a better position to do so; perhaps it simply did not consider the question at this level; and perhaps Congress was unable to forge a coalition on either side of the question, and those on each side decided to take their chances with the scheme devised by the agency. For judicial purposes, it matters not which of these things occurred.

Judges are not experts in the field, and are not part of either political branch of the Government. Courts must, in some cases, reconcile competing political interests, but not on the basis of the judges' personal policy preferences. In contrast, an agency to which Congress has delegated policy-making responsibilities may, within the limits of that delegation, properly rely upon the incumbent administration's views of wise policy to inform its judgments. While agencies are not directly accountable to the people, the Chief Executive is, and it is entirely appropriate for this political branch of the Government to make such policy choices—resolving the competing interests which Congress itself either inadvertently did not resolve, or intentionally left to be resolved by the agency charged with the administration of the statute in light of everyday realities.

When a challenge to an agency construction of a statutory provision, fairly conceptualized, really centers on the wisdom of the agency's policy, rather than whether it is a reasonable choice within a gap left open by Congress, the challenge must fail. In such a case, federal judges—who have no constituency—have a duty to respect legitimate policy choices made by those who do. The responsibilities for assessing the wisdom of such policy choices and resolving the struggle between competing views of the public interest are not judicial ones: "Our Constitution vests such responsibilities in the political branches." *TVA v. Hill*, 437 U.S. 153 (1978).

We hold that the EPA's definition of the term "source" is a permissible construction of the statute which seeks to accommodate progress in reducing air pollution with economic growth. . . .

The judgment of the Court of Appeals is reversed.

It is so ordered.

## D. FDA's Rulemaking Authority

The *Chevron* case immediately above introduced you to the rulemaking process in administrative law more generally. The next two cases focus specifically on FDA's rulemaking authority. The case immediately below, *Abbott Laboratories v. Gardner*, is part of a trilogy of FDA-related U.S. Supreme Court cases decided on the same day. It is often taught in administrative law courses as a leading case on the ripeness doctrine.

For purposes of this course, however, you should focus instead on the FDA-specific portions of the case. Before you begin reading, review FFDCA § 701(a) and 701(e) in the Supplement. As you read *Abbott Laboratories*, focus on two things. First, focus on FDA's decision to proceed under FFDCA § 701(a) rather than FFDCA § 701(e). Second, focus on the court's discussion of whether the challenged regulations are binding or advisory.

## Abbott Labs. v. Gardner

387 U.S. 136 (1967)

**Mr. Justice HARLAN delivered the opinion of the Court.**

In 1962 Congress amended the [FFDCA] to require manufacturers of prescription drugs to print the "established name" of the drug "prominently and in type at least half as large as that used thereon for any proprietary name or designation for such drug," on labels and other printed material, § 502(e)(1)(B). . . . The Commissioner of Food and Drugs, exercising authority delegated to him by the Secretary, published proposed regulations designed to implement the statute. After inviting and considering comments submitted by interested parties the Commissioner promulgated the following regulation for the "efficient enforcement" of the [FFDCA], § 701(a):

> If the label or labeling of a prescription drug bears a proprietary name or designation for the drug or any ingredient thereof, the established name, if such there be, corresponding to such proprietary name or designation, shall accompany each appearance of such proprietary name or designation.
>
> 21 C.F.R. § 1.104 (g)(1).

. . . .

The present action was brought by a group of 37 individual drug manufacturers and by the Pharmaceutical Manufacturers Association . . . challenging the regulations on the ground that the Commissioner exceeded his authority under the statute by promulgating an order requiring labels, advertisements, and other printed matter relating to prescription drugs to designate the established name of the particular drug involved every time its trade name is used anywhere in such material.

The District Court . . . granted the declaratory and injunctive relief sought, finding that the statute did not sweep so broadly as to permit the Commissioner's "every time" interpretation. The Court of Appeals for the Third Circuit reversed without reaching the merits of the case. . . . We granted certiorari.

### I.

The first question we consider is whether Congress by the [FFDCA] intended to forbid pre-enforcement review of this sort of regulation promulgated by the Commissioner. . . . The Administrative Procedure Act provides specifically not only for review of "agency action made reviewable by statute" but also for review of "final agency action for which there is no other adequate remedy in a court," 5 U. S. C. § 704. . . . In *Rusk v. Cort* [369 U.S. 367 (1962)], the Court held that only upon a showing of "clear and convincing evidence" of a contrary legislative intent should the courts restrict access to judicial review.

Given this standard, we are wholly unpersuaded that the statutory scheme in the food and drug area excludes this type of action. The Government relies on no explicit statutory authority for its argument that pre-enforcement review is unavailable, but insists instead that because the statute includes a specific procedure for such review of certain enumerated kinds of regulations, not encompassing those of the kind involved here, other types were necessarily meant to be excluded from any pre-enforcement review. The issue, however, is not so readily resolved; we must go further and inquire whether in the context of the entire legislative scheme the existence of that circumscribed remedy evinces a congressional purpose to bar agency action not within its purview from judicial review....

In this case the Government has not demonstrated such a purpose; indeed, a study of the legislative history shows rather conclusively that the specific review provisions were designed to give an additional remedy and not to cut down more traditional channels of review. At the time the Food, Drug, and Cosmetic Act was under consideration, in the late 1930's, the Administrative Procedure Act had not yet been enacted, the Declaratory Judgment Act was in its infancy, and the scope of judicial review of administrative decisions under the equity power was unclear. It was these factors that led to the form the statute ultimately took. There is no evidence at all that members of Congress meant to preclude traditional avenues of judicial relief.... It was specifically brought to the attention of Congress that such methods had in fact been used in the food and drug area, and the Department of Justice, in opposing the enactment of the special-review procedures of § 701, submitted a memorandum which was read on the floor of the House stating: "As a matter of fact, the entire subsection is really unnecessary, because even without any express provision in the bill for court review, any citizen aggrieved by any order of the Secretary, who contends that the order is invalid, may test the legality of the order by bringing an injunction suit against the Secretary, or the head of the Bureau, under the general equity powers of the court."

The main issue in contention was whether these methods of review were satisfactory... The supporters of the special-review section sought to include it in the [FFDCA] primarily as a method of reviewing agency factual determinations....

A second reason for the special procedure was to provide broader venue to litigants challenging such technical agency determinations....

Against this background we think it quite apparent that the special-review procedures provided in § 701(f), applying to regulations embodying technical factual determinations,[11] were simply intended to assure adequate judicial review of such agency decisions, and that their enactment does not manifest a congressional purpose to eliminate judicial review of other kinds of agency action.

11. See Toilet Goods Assn. v. Gardner, 360 F.2d 677, 683, where the court noted that "The agency determinations specifically reviewable under § 701(e) relate to such technical subjects as chemical properties of particular products and the formulation and application of safety standards for protecting public health; Congress naturally did not wish courts to consider such matters without the benefit of the agency's views after an evidentiary hearing before it."

This conclusion is strongly buttressed by the fact that the [FFDCA] itself, in § 701(f)(6), states, "The remedies provided for in this subsection shall be in addition to and not in substitution for any other remedies provided by law...." The Government deals with the clause by arguing that it should be read as applying only to review of regulations under the sections specifically enumerated in § 701(e). This is a conceivable reading, but it requires a considerable straining both of language and of common understanding. The saving clause itself contains no limitations, and it requires an artificial statutory construction to read a general grant of a right to judicial review begrudgingly, so as to cut out agency actions that a literal reading would cover.

....

The only other argument of the Government requiring attention on the preclusive effect of the [FFDCA] is that *Ewing v. Mytinger & Casselberry, Inc.*, 339 U.S. 594 [(1950)], counsels a restrictive view of judicial review in the food and drug area. In that case the Food and Drug Administrator found that there was probable cause that a drug was "adulterated" because it was misbranded in such a way as to be "fraudulent" or "misleading to the injury or damage of the purchaser or consumer." § 304(a). Multiple seizures were ordered through libel actions. The manufacturer of the drug brought an action to challenge directly the Administrator's finding of probable cause. This Court held that the owner could raise his constitutional, statutory, and factual claims in the libel actions themselves, and that the mere finding of probable cause by the Administrator could not be challenged in a separate action. That decision was quite clearly correct, but nothing in its reasoning or holding has any bearing on this declaratory judgment action challenging a promulgated regulation.

.... To equate a finding of probable cause for proceeding against a particular drug manufacturer with the promulgation of a self-operative industry-wide regulation, such as we have here, would immunize nearly all agency rulemaking activities from the coverage of the Administrative Procedure Act.

Second, the determination of probable cause in Ewing has "no effect in and of itself"; only some action consequent upon such a finding could give it legal life. As the Court there noted, like a determination by a grand jury that there is probable cause to proceed against an accused, it is a finding which only has vitality once a proceeding is commenced, at which time appropriate challenges can be made....

We conclude that nothing in the Food, Drug, and Cosmetic Act itself precludes this action.

II.

A further inquiry must, however, be made. The injunctive and declaratory judgment remedies are discretionary, and courts traditionally have been reluctant to apply them to administrative determinations unless these arise in the context of a controversy "ripe" for judicial resolution.... The problem is best seen in a twofold aspect, requiring us to evaluate both the fitness of the issues for judicial decision and the hardship to the parties of withholding court consideration.

As to the former factor, we believe the issues presented are appropriate for judicial resolution at this time. First, all parties agree that the issue tendered is a purely legal one: whether the statute was properly construed by the Commissioner to require the established name of the drug to be used every time the proprietary name is employed. Both sides moved for summary judgment in the District Court, and no claim is made here that further administrative proceedings are contemplated....

Second, the regulations in issue we find to be "final agency action" within the meaning of § 10 of the Administrative Procedure Act, as construed in judicial decisions. An "agency action" includes any "rule," defined by the [Administrative Procedure Act] as "an agency statement of general or particular applicability and future effect designed to implement, interpret, or prescribe law or policy," §§ 2 (c), 2 (g).... When, as here, [regulations] are promulgated by order of the Commission and the expected conformity to them causes injury cognizable by a court of equity, they are appropriately the subject of attack...."

....

The regulation challenged here, promulgated in a formal manner after announcement in the Federal Register and consideration of comments by interested parties is quite clearly definitive. There is no hint that this regulation is informal, or only the ruling of a subordinate official, or tentative.* It was made effective upon publication, and the Assistant General Counsel for Food and Drugs stated in the District Court that compliance was expected.

The Government argues, however, that the present case can be distinguished from [previous cases where the court found final action] on the ground that in those instances the agency involved could implement its policy directly, while here the Attorney General must authorize criminal and seizure actions for violations of the statute. In the context of this case, we do not find this argument persuasive. These regulations are not meant to advise the Attorney General, but purport to be directly authorized by the statute. Thus, if within the Commissioner's authority, they have the status of law and violations of them carry heavy criminal and civil sanctions. Also, there is no representation that the Attorney General and the Commissioner disagree in this area; the Justice Department is defending this very suit. It would be adherence to a mere technicality to give any credence to this contention. Moreover, the agency does have direct authority to enforce this regulation in the

* *[The Court's language in this paragraph can be confusing. The established-name regulations at issue in this case were promulgated through informal rulemaking under FFDCA § 701(a), not formal rulemaking under FFDCA § 701(e). Do not be confused by the court's reference to rules "promulgated in a formal manner" and its statement that "no hint that this regulation is informal." The court is using these terms in their more casual sense, not as a reference to the technical distinction between formal and informal rulemaking.]*

context of passing upon applications for clearance of new drugs, [FFDCA] § 505, or certification of certain antibiotics, [FFDCA] § 507.

This is also a case in which the impact of the regulations upon the petitioners is sufficiently direct and immediate as to render the issue appropriate for judicial review at this stage. These regulations purport to give an authoritative interpretation of a statutory provision that has a direct effect on the day-to-day business of all prescription drug companies . . . As the District Court found on the basis of uncontested allegations, "Either they must comply with the every time requirement and incur the costs of changing over their promotional material and labeling or they must follow their present course and risk prosecution." . . . If petitioners wish to comply they must change all their labels, advertisements, and promotional materials; they must destroy stocks of printed matter; and they must invest heavily in new printing type and new supplies. The alternative to compliance—continued use of material which they believe in good faith meets the statutory requirements, but which clearly does not meet the regulation of the Commissioner—may be even more costly. That course would risk serious criminal and civil penalties for the unlawful distribution of "misbranded" drugs.[19]

. . . . The Government does not dispute the very real dilemma in which petitioners are placed by the regulation, but contends that "mere financial expense" is not a justification for pre-enforcement judicial review. . . . But there is no question in the present case that petitioners have sufficient standing as plaintiffs: the regulation is directed at them in particular; it requires them to make significant changes in their everyday business practices; if they fail to observe the Commissioner's rule they are quite clearly exposed to the imposition of strong sanctions.

The Government further contends that the threat of criminal sanctions for noncompliance with a judicially untested regulation is unrealistic; the Solicitor General has represented that if court enforcement becomes necessary, "the Department of Justice will proceed only civilly for an injunction . . . or by condemnation." We cannot accept this argument as a sufficient answer to petitioners' petition. This action at its inception was properly brought and this subsequent representation of the Department of Justice should not suffice to defeat it.

Finally, the Government urges that to permit resort to the courts in this type of case may delay or impede effective enforcement of the [FFDCA]. We . . . do not find the Government's argument convincing. First, in this particular case, a pre-enforcement challenge by nearly all prescription drug manufacturers is calculated to speed enforcement. If the Government prevails, a large part of the industry is bound by the decree; if the Government loses, it can more quickly revise its regulation.

---

19. Section 502(e)(1)(B) declares a drug not complying with this labeling requirement to be "misbranded." Section 301 designates as "prohibited acts" the misbranding of drugs in interstate commerce. Such prohibited acts are subject to injunction § 302, criminal penalties § 303, and seizure § 304 (a).

. . . .

Further, the declaratory judgment and injunctive remedies are equitable in nature, and other equitable defenses may be interposed. If a multiplicity of suits are undertaken in order to harass the Government or to delay enforcement, relief can be denied on this ground alone. The defense of laches could be asserted if the Government is prejudiced by a delay. And courts may even refuse declaratory relief for the nonjoinder of interested parties who are not, technically speaking, indispensable.

In addition to all these safeguards against what the Government fears, it is important to note that the institution of this type of action does not by itself stay the effectiveness of the challenged regulation. There is nothing in the record to indicate that petitioners have sought to stay enforcement of the "every time" regulation pending judicial review. *See* 5 U. S. C. § 705. If the agency believes that a suit of this type will significantly impede enforcement or will harm the public interest, it need not postpone enforcement of the regulation and may oppose any motion for a judicial stay on the part of those challenging the regulation. It is scarcely to be doubted that a court would refuse to postpone the effective date of an agency action if the Government could show, as it made no effort to do here, that delay would be detrimental to the public health or safety.

We . . . remand the case to the Court of Appeals for the Third Circuit to review the District Court's decision that the regulation was beyond the power of the Commissioner.

Reversed and remanded.

---

Before you begin reading the next excerpt, *NAPM v. FDA*, please look back at the *Timeline of Key Statutes* earlier in this chapter. The basic issue in this case arises from the following sequence of events. First, Congress enacted the FFDCA in 1938, which granted FDA some type of rulemaking authority in FFDCA § 701. In 1946, Congress enacted the APA, which transformed the field of administrative law across the entire federal government. Then, in 1962, Congress enacted the Kefauver-Harris Amendments to the FFDCA. (This last statute is not on this chapter's *Timeline of Key Statutes* because it was focused on drug regulation rather than administrative procedure). The Kefauver-Harris Amendments referenced FFDCA § 701 without making any changes to that provision. However, as you will see, the Kefauver-Harris Amendments nonetheless play an important role in the court's analysis.

As you read this case, focus on three things. First, focus on the relationships among the FFDCA of 1938, the APA, and the Kefauver-Harris Amendments. Second, focus on the court's discussion of whether FDA can promulgate binding regulations through the informal rulemaking procedures of FFDCA § 701(a), rather than the formal rulemaking procedures of FFDCA § 701(e). Third, focus on the key role that the U.S. Supreme Court's *Abbott Laboratories* decision (the excerpt immediately above) plays in Judge Friendly's analysis.

## Nat'l Ass'n of Pharm. Mfrs. v. FDA

637 F.2d 877 (2d Cir. 1981)

**FRIENDLY, Circuit Judge:**

In 1962 Congress enacted various amendments to the [FFDCA] .... Among the amendments was a section by which a drug is deemed adulterated if its packaging, processing, holding or manufacturing fail to conform to "current good manufacturing practice ((CGMP)) to assure that such drug meets the requirements of this chapter as to safety and has the identity and strength, and meets the quality and purity characteristics, which it purports or is represented to possess." § 501(a)(2)(B). The Food and Drug Administration (FDA) issued its first regulations under this section in 1963. In February, 1976, FDA announced a proposal to revise and update the then current CGMP regulations. This proposal, which provided for the notice and comment procedures contemplated by 5 U.S.C. § 553, announced:

> The Commissioner intends for CGMP regulations to become binding specific requirements that must be complied with; failure to do so shall render a drug product adulterated under section 501(a)(2)(B) of the [FFDCA] .... Binding regulations will ... serve to inform courts of FDA's expert judgments regarding current good manufacturing practice for drugs in the United States; this will expedite and assist enforcement proceedings to assure compliance with section 501(a)(2)(B) of the [FFDCA].

The FDA received numerous comments both upon the substance of its requirements and upon its proposal that the new CGMP regulations should have the force of law. In an extensive preamble to the new regulations it set forth a legal analysis supporting its view that it had power to issue binding regulations, and the reasons why it believed binding rather than merely interpretive regulations would be in the public interest. The regulations ... cover a broad spectrum of affairs, including requirements for personnel practices, record keeping, building design, and procedures for the control of drug production, packaging and labeling.

In this action in the District Court for the Southern District of New York ... the National Association of Pharmaceutical Manufacturers and the National Pharmaceutical Alliance ... sought a declaration that FDA's attempt to give binding effect to the new CGMP Regulations was beyond its authority. The FDA moved to dismiss the complaint for failure to state a claim upon which relief can be granted. Chief Judge MacMahon granted the motion in a brief opinion, this appeal followed, and we now affirm.

Two different subsections of [FFDCA] § 701 confer rulemaking authority upon the FDA. [FFDCA] 701(a) provides:

> The authority to promulgate regulations for the efficient enforcement of this chapter, except as otherwise provided in this section, is vested in the Secretary (of Health and Human Services).

The effect of § 4 of the Administrative Procedure Act of 1946 (APA), now 5 U.S.C. § 553, is to require that rulemaking under [FFDCA] § 701(a), with certain exceptions, including "interpretative rules", follow an informal notice and comment procedure, which was done here. [FFDCA] 701(e) provides that "(any) action for the issuance, amendment, or repeal of any regulation" under various sections of the [FFDCA] of which § 501(a)(2)(B) is not one, shall follow a complex procedure which has been read to include a trial-type hearing; § 701(f) provides that review of any order resulting from such rulemaking lies in a court of appeals. *See National Nutritional Foods Ass'n v. FDA*, 504 F.2d 761 (2 Cir. 1974). Admittedly § 701(e) procedures were not followed here and the FDA's authority to give binding effect to the CGMP regulations at issue must rest on § 701(a).

Reading the language of that subsection, which comes from the [FFDCA] of 1938, with the eyes of 1980, one would have little difficulty in concluding that the words suffice to empower the Commissioner of the FDA . . . to issue regulations, substantive as well as procedural, having the force of law. . . .

In 1953 . . . the Court decided *American Trucking Ass'ns v. United States*, in which the issue was whether the Interstate Commerce Commission, under the Motor Carrier Act of 1935, had the authority to promulgate rules restricting leasing and interchange practices in the trucking industry. In an outstanding opinion by Justice Reed, the Court expressly rejected the arguments that the Commission had exceeded its authority because the statute lacked an express delegation of power to regulate the practices in question, and because the general rulemaking power the statute did confer was intended only for rules governing agency procedure:

> As a matter of principle, we might agree with appellants' contentions if we thought it a reasonable canon of interpretation that the draftsmen of acts delegating agency powers, as a practical and realistic matter, can or do include specific consideration of every evil to be corrected. But no great acquaintance with practical affairs is required to know that such prescience, either in fact or in the minds of Congress, does not exist. . . .

As documented by Judge Wright in *National Petroleum Refiners*, this generous construction of agency rulemaking authority has become firmly entrenched.

Beyond this there is formidable authority to the effect that § 701(a) itself is a grant of power to issue binding regulations. The first is the statement in *Abbott Laboratories*, 387 U.S. at 151–52, adverting to certain drug labeling regulations issued pursuant to § 701(a):

> These regulations are not meant to advise the Attorney General, but purport to be directly authorized by the statute. Thus, if within the Commissioner's authority, they have the status of law and violations of them carry heavy criminal and civil sanctions.

The Court also spoke of the regulations as "self-operative" rules "that must be followed by an entire industry."

Next came the quartet of cases decided by the Supreme Court in 1973: *Weinberger v. Hynson, Westcott & Dunning, Inc.*, 412 U.S. 609; *CIBA Corp. v. Weinberger*, 412 U.S. 640; *Weinberger v. Bentex Pharmaceuticals, Inc.*, 412 U.S. 645; and *USV Pharmaceutical Corp. v. Weinberger*, 412 U.S. 655. Although Professor Kenneth Culp Davis cites these, along with the passage just quoted from *Abbott Laboratories*, for the proposition that "(rules) issued under § 701(a) are legislative rules and not merely interpretive," plaintiffs emphasize his remark that "the four cases are weak authority because the regulation rested only in part on § 701(a) and because the Court did not address itself to the question whether § 701(a) was sufficient support for the rules." Examination of the briefs confirms that discussion of § 701(a) and the legislative-interpretive distinction was meager, the only instance being in the briefs in the *Bentex* case. Still we find it difficult not to see in the passage of Mr. Justice Douglas' opinion quoted in the margin[7] an endorsement of the Government's position that § 701(a) authorized the FDA to issue substantive regulations having the force of law.

In any event this court, in *National Nutritional Foods Ass'n v. Weinberger*, characterized the 1973 quartet of Supreme Court decisions as having dispelled "(whatever) doubts might have been entertained regarding the FDA's power under § 701(a) to promulgate binding regulations". . . .

Appellants' claim is that, whether or not the FDA may generally issue binding substantive regulations under § 701(a), although they obviously think it may not, it cannot do so with respect to the CGMP Regulations. In support of this position they rely on the legislative history of the portion of the 1962 amendments that added § 501(a)(2)(B). . . .

On July 19, 1962, the Senate Judiciary Committee reported out S. 1552, the Senate version of what ultimately became the Drug Amendments of 1962. Section 5 of the bill, after making the substantive amendment adding the current good manufacturing practices requirement, added:

> The Secretary is authorized to issue interpretative regulations, upon notice and in accordance with the procedures set forth in section 4 of the Administrative Procedure Act (5 U.S.C. 1003), which shall in any proceeding involving this paragraph, be prima facie evidence of what constitutes current good manufacturing practice.

. . . .

---

7.

> We think that it is implicit in the regulatory scheme, not spelled out in haec verba, that FDA has jurisdiction to decide with administrative finality, subject to the types of judicial review provided, the "new drug" status of individual drugs or classes of drugs. The deluge of litigation that would follow if "me-too" drugs and OTC drugs had to receive de novo hearings in the courts would inure to the interests of manufacturers and merchants in drugs, but not to the interests of the public that Congress was anxious to protect. . . .

*Weinberger v. Bentex Pharmaceuticals, Inc.*, supra, 412 U.S. at 653.

On August 21, 1962, the Senate Committee reported out a revised version of the bill. The reworded § 501(a)(2)(B) omitted any reference to regulations. The Committee explained this as follows:

> The President, in the recommendations submitted for the consideration of the committee with his letter of August 3, 1962, proposed a revised version which included the following principal amendments to the reported bill:
>
> > (1) It proposed to replace the provisions on regulations with prima facie evidentiary effect with a provision that the adequacy of the quality controls be determined "in accordance with regulations promulgated by the Secretary on the basis of good manufacturing practice" after formal rule-making procedures, i.e., after affording an opportunity for hearing, and for judicial review on the basis of the hearing record, with respect to such regulations.
>
> The explanation accompanying the recommendations of the President expressed concern lest the language as to interpretative regulations with prima facie evidentiary effect invite endless de novo litigation on the question of what constitutes good manufacturing practice each time there is enforcement action under the new quality control provisions. The committee acceded to the President's request for elimination of the "prima facie" regulatory authority in the bill. It felt, however, on balance, that there was no need for inserting provisions for regulations through formal rulemaking on the subject of what is good manufacturing practice. Section 701(a) now vests in the Secretary "authority to promulgate regulations for the efficient enforcement of this Act." This permits the Department to issue such regulations as it desires and their scope and effect will be the same as that of other regulations issued under such general authority. Numerous regulations have been issued under section 701(a) and have been the subject of consideration and application in the courts in actions arising under the various provisions of the [FFDCA] not now subject to formal rulemaking procedures.

During the floor debate on August 23, Senator Eastland, Chairman of the Judiciary Committee, said on the subject of rulemaking:

> The Secretary could use his general rulemaking authority under section 701(a) of the [FFDCA] to announce what he, in the administration of the [FFDCA], considers to be good manufacturing practice insofar as methods and administration are concerned. As in the case of other regulations, the court in the final analysis will pass upon the scope and effect of such regulations.

A month later the House Interstate and Foreign Commerce Committee reported ... its version of the Drug Amendments.... It ... would have amended § 701(e) to include CGMP Regulations among the categories requiring "formal" rulemaking procedures. The accompanying report accurately paraphrased the bill and expressly stated:

> The promulgation of these regulations would be subject to opportunity for hearing and judicial review. Thus, legal action could be brought against firms failing to abide by these standards and against the products they ship.

The House debated the bill on September 27, 1962. Representative Schenck offered an amendment to delete the parenthetical clause in § 501(a)(2) and the amendment to § 701(e). His explanation, so far as here pertinent, was as follows:

> My amendment to section 101 of the bill, which was approved by the committee, provides simply that the drug will be deemed to be adulterated and subject to seizure if the methods, facilities, or controls used in the manufacture of the drug do not conform with current good manufacturing practice, as determined in accordance with regulations promulgated by the Secretary.
>
> . . . .
>
> The committee adopted an amendment which would make the formal rulemaking procedures of section 701(e) of the [FFDCA] applicable to regulations referred to which may be made pursuant to the above amendment.
>
> I am opposed to the amendment in section 101(b) of the bill which would require the Secretary to hold a formal hearing under section 701(e) of the [FFDCA] in order to issue regulations as to what constitutes current good manufacturing practice. I favor the approach adopted by the Senate under which this determination is made pursuant to section 701(a) of the [FFDCA]. This procedure permits the Secretary to issue such regulations as he desires and their scope and effect will be the same as that of other regulations issued under such general authority. This procedure is more flexible. Numerous regulations have been issued under this section and they have been the subject of consideration and application in the courts in actions arising under the various provisions of the [FFDCA] not now subject to formal rulemaking procedures.

. . . . The House thereupon adopted the section which, as revised by the Schenck amendment, was the same as the Senate bill and made no mention of regulations.

. . . . So far as concerns the precise issue here before us, plaintiffs' resort to the legislative history of the 1962 Amendments works against rather than for them. It is clear the 1962 Congress intended to do something in response to President Kennedy's request and also that the something was not compulsory resort to the procedure required by § 701(e). Yet there is no substantial difference between the "prima facie " evidence standard in the original Senate bill and the "interpretive" limitation urged by plaintiffs.

Plaintiffs' other argument is more impressive, although not sufficiently so. This is that when the 1962 Congress decided to rely on the Secretary's rulemaking authority under § 701(a), it was to that authority as then understood; that the pre-1962 case law established that any substantive regulations issued under § 701(a) could be interpretive only; that the legislative history of the 1938 Act strongly corroborates this; and that the Supreme Court's statements in *Abbott Laboratories* in 1967 and the *Hynson* quartet in 1973 and our own still later decisions are thus not dispositive of the problem in hand. . . .

We do not find the pre-1962 decisions with respect to the extent of the Secretary's power under § 701(a) to be so conclusive as plaintiffs assert. Weighing in the Government's favor is *United States v. Sullivan*, 332 U.S. 689 (1948), in which the Supreme Court remarked that an inscription on a label appeared to constitute adequate directions for use in compliance with § 502(f)(1) of the [FFDCA] since the wording of the label was "required by regulation issued by the Administrator pursuant to authority of the [FFDCA], 21 C.F.R. Cum.Supp. § 2.106(b)(3)" (1944), a regulation promulgated under § 701(a). . . . In addition, the plaintiffs rely on *United States v. Various Articles of Drugs,* 83 F. Supp. 882 (D.D.C.1949), and *United States v. 38 Dozen Bottles,* 114 F. Supp. 461 (D.Minn.1953), district court cases which did indeed speak of § 701(a) regulations as interpretive. In none of the cases we have cited, however, was the issue sharply posed.

. . . .

On the other hand plaintiffs seem on solid ground when they contend that if the 1962 Congress had made the detailed examination of the legislative history and contemporary understanding of the 1938 Act, which plaintiffs' counsel have now made at long last, it might well have concluded that § 701(a) in fact very likely was not intended to confer power to issue binding substantive rules. We shall give only an abbreviated version of what is spelled out in plaintiffs' brief. The story begins in 1933 with the introduction of a bill, S.1944, 73d Cong. 1st Sess. . . . At the next session Senator Copeland of the Senate Commerce Committee substituted a different bill, S. 2800, 73d Cong., 2d Sess., proposing the establishment of committees on public health and food standards with the power to veto any regulations proposed by the Secretary of Agriculture. Senator Copeland explained that "the first bill placed in the hands of the Secretary of Agriculture what personally I regard as too great arbitrary power". In the next Congress, the Senate passed a similar bill, denominated S. 5, 74th Cong., 1st Sess. The accompanying report submitted by Senator Copeland listed seven areas in which regulations were contemplated, later catalogued in § 701(e), and said:

> While other regulations are authorized for the purpose of making exemptions or for purely administrative operations, the only regulations imposing positive requirements are those listed above.

In the House, the attempt to control the Secretary's discretion by the committee structure was abandoned, and the dichotomy later to become §§ 701(a) and (e) was proposed instead. The bill to be finally enacted, with §§ 701(a) and (e) in place, was reported out by the House Committee on Interstate and Foreign Commerce in April, 1938. The end of the story is in House Report No. 2139, 75th Cong., 3d Sess. 9-10 (1938):

> Section 701 relates generally to regulations. In the case of regulations, the violation of which constitutes an offense, it is required that appropriate notice of a public hearing be given and that adequate time shall be given after the promulgation of a regulation before it becomes effective.
>
> . . .
>
> Section 701(e), (f), and (g) of the committee amendment set forth the procedure governing the formulation and judicial review of certain regulations to be issued by the Secretary. . . .
>
> Such regulations are not merely interpretive. They have the force and effect of law and must be observed. Their violation may result in the imposition of criminal penalties, or in the confiscation of the goods involved if shipped in interstate commerce, or in their exclusion from the country if imported.

. . . .

A principal difficulty with plaintiffs' argument is that there is no evidence that these arcana concerning the legislative history of the 1938 Act were known to the 1962 Congress. Much water had flowed under the bridge since 1938. The principal consideration in 1938 against permitting the FDA to issue binding substantive rules except by following the complex procedures of § 701(e), namely the absence of any statutorily prescribed procedures under § 701(a), was radically changed when Congress enacted the APA in 1946. Pursuant to § 4 of that Act, now 5 U.S.C. § 553, the FDA, as previously indicated, cannot issue a binding substantive rule under § 701(a) without complying with notice and comment procedures that give affected parties an adequate opportunity to be heard. While the [FFDCA] has not been completely reenacted since 1946, it has been repeatedly amended to give the Secretary new powers. Many of these provisions have expressly authorized him to make implementing regulations, e.g., Color Additive Amendments of 1960; Animal Drug Amendments of 1968; Medical Device Amendments of 1976; Infant Formula Act of 1980; when Congress has wished this to be done only by following § 701(e) procedures, it has said so, e.g., Color Additive Amendments of 1960; Drug Amendments of 1962. When it has provided for regulations but has not required this or, as in the case of the current good manufacturing practice provisions, it has said nothing about regulations, it is more reasonable to believe that Congress meant the FDA to have the same power to issue binding substantive regulations as the Supreme Court had recognized for other agencies beginning with the National Broadcasting decision in 1943.

Plaintiffs' argument also goes astray in asking that we disregard subsequent decisions on the effect of § 701(a) regulations for the purpose of determining the intent of the 1962 Congress. It is true, of course, that decisions dating from 1967 to the present concerning the meaning of the 1938 Act afford no key to what Congress was thinking in 1962.[13] But since there is no evidence that the 1962 Congress was

---

13. *Abbott Laboratories* and the *Hyson* quartet, like the instant case, concerned regulations issued to enforce provisions added to the [FFDCA] by the Drug Amendments of 1962. It could

familiar with the legislative history of the 1938 Act, plaintiffs' argument is really nothing more than an invitation to reconsider the question of the power originally conferred by § 701(a) in 1938. We decline to do so. . . . Moreover, the FDA, since the decision in *Abbott Laboratories*, has issued a substantial number of binding substantive regulations under § 701(a). A decision at this late date denying such power to it would thus create turmoil throughout numerous areas subject to regulation by the FDA.

It remains to be considered whether, as plaintiffs strongly urge, a different result is required by *Chrysler Corp. v. Brown*, 441 U.S. 281. We shall not endeavor to state the case in detail; the part of interest for us is that portion of the opinion holding that disclosure regulations issued pursuant to the general grant of rulemaking power to the Secretary of Labor provided in § 201 of Executive Order 11246, did not have the force and effect of law, and thus did not lift the prohibition on certain kinds of disclosures of agency information contained in the Trade Secrets Act, 18 U.S.C. § 1905. . . .

The Court moved swiftly from this holding to put to rest any argument that the Chrysler decision cast doubt on the ability of agencies to make binding substantive regulations where Congress had authorized this in general terms . . . :

> This is not to say that any grant of legislative authority to a federal agency must be specific before regulations promulgated pursuant to them can be binding on courts in a manner akin to statutes. What is important is that the reviewing court reasonably be able to conclude that the grant of authority contemplates the regulations issued.

The Court thought the "best illustration" of this process to be Justice Frankfurter's opinion in *National Broadcasting Co. v. United States*, cited above as one of the pre-1962 decisions holding that a general grant of rulemaking authority similar to § 701(a) empowered an agency to issue regulations which "had the force of law and were binding on the courts unless they were arbitrary or not promulgated pursuant to prescribed procedures."

In these passages of the Chrysler opinion we find no indication that the Court meant to overrule the principle that a Congressional delegation of power to make regulations for the efficient enforcement of a statute confers power to make substantive regulations that are binding. That principle was essentially adopted in the National Broadcasting case, was established beyond doubt in American Trucking Ass'ns v. United States, and was recently reaffirmed in *Mourning v. Family Publications Service, Inc.*, 411 U.S. 356 (1973), where the Court declared it "well established" that the validity of a regulation promulgated under a general grant of rulemaking

---

thus be argued that insofar as those cases upheld the power of the Commissioner to issue binding regulations under § 701(a), they accept a Congressional understanding of that provision in 1962 at odds with the result desired by the plaintiffs and would preclude our ruling in their favor even if we were otherwise disposed to do so.

authority will be sustained so long as it is " "reasonably related to the purposes of the enabling legislation.'" Here the legislative history of the Drug Amendments of 1962 demonstrates, if this were needed, that Congress intended its broad language to be fleshed out by regulations issued by the FDA under § 701(a).

The judgment of the district court is affirmed.

## E. The Role of Guidance Documents

Guidance documents do not purport to bind either regulated parties or FDA. They simply purport to set out the agency's current thinking on a particular topic. A regulated party is not required to comply with anything set out in a guidance document. It can instead determine on its own how to comply with the applicable statutes and regulations. It can even take actions that flatly contradict the recommendations in a guidance document, so long as those actions comply with the applicable statutes and regulations. Moreover, compliance with applicable guidance documents is not sufficient to prevent adverse agency action if the agency determines that a party, despite following the letter of relevant guidance documents, has contravened some aspect of an applicable statute or regulation.[1]

Despite their nonbinding nature, most regulated parties make sincere efforts to comply with guidance documents most of the time. This is because it is usually easier to comply with existing guidance than to convince FDA that some other course of action also meets statutory and regulatory requirements. In fact, regulated parties frequently urge FDA to develop additional and more specific guidance documents in the regulatory areas in which they operate.

All current FDA guidance documents are available through a single online portal.[2] The chart below documents the results of a series of searches of this online portal conducted on September 6, 2020.[3] It provides a snapshot of current FDA guidance on that date. The number of draft and final guidance documents for each FDA office is listed; the total number of current draft and final guidance documents at FDA is listed at the bottom.

---

1. An important qualification is that FDA employees may not deviate from a guidance document without "appropriate justification and supervisory concurrence." 21 C.F.R. § 10.115(d)(3).

2. FDA Website, Search for FDA Guidance Documents, https://www.fda.gov/regulatory-information/search-fda-guidance-documents#guidancesearch.

3. The portal gives an option to search for all FDA guidance (by leaving the "Document Type" field blank), or to choose from the following list of document types: "Guidance Document," "Compliance Policy Guide (CPG)," "Small Entity Compliance Guide," "Information Sheet," "Good Review Practices," "Special Controls Document," "Industry Letter," "Concept Paper," "Manual," and "Memorandum." The presence of "Guidance Document" can be confusing, as most—and perhaps all—of the other document types also qualify as guidance. *See* 21 C.F.R. § 10.115(b)(2) (defining guidance broadly); *id.* § 10.115(b)(3) (providing a list of document types excluded from the definition of guidance). To capture this broad range of document types, the numbers in this chart are the result of searches with the "Document Type" field left blank.

| FDA Guidance Documents as of September 6, 2020 | | |
|---|---|---|
| | Final Guidance | Draft Guidance |
| Center for Biologics Evaluation and Research (CBER) | 450 | 110 |
| Center for Devices and Radiological Health (CDRH) | 560 | 64 |
| Center for Drug Evaluation and Research (CDER) | 683 | 241 |
| Center for Food Safety and Applied Nutrition (CFSAN) | 494 | 59 |
| Center for Tobacco Products (CTP) | 37 | 11 |
| Center for Veterinary Medicine (CVM) | 264 | 46 |
| National Center for Toxicology Research (NCTR) | 0 | 1 |
| Office of Regulatory Affairs (ORA) | 421 | 14 |
| Office of the Commissioner | 89 | 20 |
| Total current FDA guidance documents[4] | 2,225 | 378 |

As this chart suggests, FDA offers a substantial amount of guidance on compliance with its regulatory programs. To keep the total reading material manageable, this book presents you primarily with statutory text, regulatory text, and case law.[5] However, you should be aware that the agency publishes substantial amounts of guidance—and that FDA guidance documents are a major source of information for the practicing food and drug lawyer.

At this point, please read (or review) the following excerpts in the statutory supplement:

- FFDCA § 701. Regulations and hearings. *Subpart (h) only.*
- 21 C.F.R. § 10.115. Good guidance practices.

---

4. This total is the result of a search of the online portal without choosing an individual FDA office. It is a smaller number than the sum of the numbers for each individual office (which comes to 2,998 final documents and 566 draft documents). The differing numbers appear to result, at least in part, from the fact that FDA lists a number of these documents under multiple FDA offices. This listing under multiple offices can be seen by exporting search results from the online portal in spreadsheet format.

5. You will, however, see excerpts from some guidance documents later in this book. In particular, guidance may be presented in situations where FDA has not promulgated regulations on the relevant topic. In these situations, the relevant regulatory program is administered by FDA through a combination of statutory language and guidance documents, rather than statutory language and regulations.

## F. Key Points

- FFDCA § 701, promulgated as part of the FFDCA of 1938, is still the main statutory provision governing administrative procedure at FDA (though it has been amended). Section 701 was passed eight years before the passage of the Administrative Procedure Act (APA) of 1946.
- Courts have been repeatedly been forced to reconcile the language of FFDCA § 701 with the more general case law that has developed under the APA.
- Today, it is accepted that FDA can, in most areas subject to its jurisdiction, promulgate binding regulations through the informal, notice-and-comment rulemaking process of FFDCA § 701(a) and APA § 553. However, this informal rulemaking is still an involved and extensive process.
- Agency guidance, while not formally binding, plays a major role in communicating FDA's expectations to regulated parties.

# Part Two

# Research, Marketing Authorization, and Background Requirements

# Chapter 3

# Regulation of Research

## A. Introduction

Please read (or review) the following excerpts in the statutory supplement:

- 21 C.F.R. Part 50—Protection of human subjects.
- 21 C.F.R. Part 56—Institutional review boards.
- 21 C.F.R. Part 58—Good laboratory practice for nonclinical laboratory studies.

These three C.F.R. parts will provide you with a basic overview of regulations applicable to FDA regulated research today.

The broad division in research regulation is between clinical research and nonclinical research. Clinical research is a term of art used to refer to all research involving human subjects (whether conducted in a "clinical" setting or not). Nonclinical research is all research not involving human subjects. Nonclinical research includes both *in vivo* research using nonhuman animals and *in vitro* laboratory research.

FDA's authority over research is both broad and narrow. FDA has no general authority over research itself. The agency's authority over both clinical and nonclinical research rests on the prospect that the results of that research may might eventually be submitted to "support applications for research or marketing permits for [certain] products regulated by the Food and Drug Administration" 21 C.F.R. §§ 50.1(a) (clinical research); 58.1(a) (nonclinical laboratory research). Failure to comply with FDA research regulations can result in FDA declining to credit that research, and—accordingly—declining to grant marketing authorization for the relevant product.[1]

FDA-regulated clinical research must comply with the requirements set out in 21 C.F.R. Part 50—Protection of Human Subjects. With limited exceptions, FDA-regulated clinical research must also comply with 21 C.F.R. Part 56—Institutional

1. For color additives, food additives, drugs, animal drugs, biologics, and medical devices, those submitting marketing authorization applications must certify compliance with FDA research regulations (or include explanations for noncompliance) as part of those applications. *See* 21 C.F.R. § 71.1(g), (i) (color additives); 21 C.F.R. § 171.1(k)(m) (food additives); 21 C.F.R. § 314.50.(d)(2)(v), (d)(5)(ix) (drugs); 21 C.F.R. § 514.1(b)(8)(12)(iii) (animal drugs); 21 C.F.R. § 601.2(a) (biologics); 21 C.F.R. § 814.20(b)(6) (medical devices). For drugs, animal drugs, and medical devices, regulations explicitly list failure to comply with research regulations as a reason the agency can decline to grant marketing authorization. *See* 21 C.F.R. 314.125(b)(15)-(16) (human drugs); 21 C.F.R. § 514.111(b)(11) (animal drugs); 21 C.F.R. § 814.45(a)(4)–(5) (medical devices).

Review Boards.[2] Those involved in clinical research are also subject to extensive financial disclosure requirements set out in 21 C.F.R. Part 54—Financial Disclosure by Clinical Investigators. Nonclinical laboratory research intended to determine the safety of a potential product must comply with 21 C.F.R. Part 58—Good Laboratory Practice for Nonclinical Laboratory Studies.[3]

## B. Outline of Regulatory Regime

As in other chapters of this book, this chapter begins with a set of charts. As you read this chapter for the first time, you should do no more than skim these charts to get a general sense of the structure of the applicable statutes and regulations. (For more information on the role of the charts in this casebook, see Chapter 1, Parts A.1 and B).

| Timeline of Key Statutes: Regulation of Research | | | |
|---|---|---|---|
| Year | PL | Stat | Name of Statute |
| 1902 | 57-244 | 32 Stat. 728 | Biologics Control Act of 1902 |
| 1944 | 78-410 | 58 Stat. 682 | Public Health Services Act |
| 1938 | 75-717 | 52 Stat. 1040 | FFDCA of 1938 |
| 1962 | 87-781 | 76 Stat. 780 | Kefauver-Harris Amendments of 1962 |
| 1974 | 93-348 | 88 Stat. 342 | National Research Act |
| 1976 | 94-295 | 90 Stat. 539 | Medical Device Amendments of 1976 |
| 2003 | 108-155 | 117 Stat. 1936 | Pediatric Research Equity Act of 2003 |
| 2004 | 108-267 | 118 Stat. 835 | Project BioShield Act of 2004 |
| 2006 | 109-147 | 120 Stat. 2831 | Pandemic and All-Hazards Preparedness Act |
| 2013 | 113-5 | 127 Stat. 161 | Pandemic and All-Hazards Preparedness Reauthorization Act of 2013 |

| Key Statutory Provisions: Regulation of Research | | |
|---|---|---|
| Statute Name or U.S.C. Title | § | Title of Section or Subsection |
| FFDCA | 409(j) | Exemptions for investigational use [of food additives] |
| FFDCA | 505(i) | Exemptions of drugs for research; discretionary and mandatory conditions; direct reports to Secretary |

2. The exceptions to this requirement are set out in 21 C.F.R. §§ 56.104–105.

3. This regulation limits the definition of covered "nonclinical laboratory study" to "in vivo or in vitro experiments in which test articles are studied prospectively in test systems under laboratory conditions to determine their safety." 21 C.F.R. § 58.3(d). It explicitly excludes "field trials in animals" and "basic exploratory studies carried out to determine whether a test article has any potential utility or to determine physical or chemical characteristics of a test article."

| Statute Name or U.S.C. Title | § | Title of Section or Subsection |
|---|---|---|
| FFDCA | 520(g) | Exemption for devices for investigational use |
| FFDCA | 721(f) | Exemptions [for investigational use of color additives] |
| FFDCA | 910(g) | Investigational tobacco product exemption for investigational use |
| FFDCA | 569A | Optimizing global clinical trials |
| FFDCA | 539B | Use of clinical investigation data from outside the United States |
| FFDCA | 569C | Patient participation in medical product discussion |
| 21 U.S.C. | § 399e | Nanotechnology |
| 21 U.S.C. | § 399f | Ensuring adequate information regarding pharmaceuticals for all populations, particularly underrepresented subpopulations, including racial subgroups |
| 21 U.S.C. | § 399g | Food and Drug Administration Intercenter Institutes |

**Key Regulatory Provisions: Regulation of Research**

| 21 C.F.R. Part | Subpart or Section | Title of Part or Subpart |
|---|---|---|
| 50 | — | Protection of human subjects |
| 54 | — | Financial disclosure by clinical investigators |
| 56 | — | Institutional review boards |
| 58 | — | Good laboratory practice for nonclinical laboratory studies |

# C. Research on Human Subjects

## 1. The Belmont Report

### 1979-04-18 Dept. of Health, Education, and Welfare Notice, Protection of Human Subjects

44 Fed. Reg. 23,192

ACTION: Notice of Report for Public Comment

SUMMARY: On July 12, 1974, the National Research Act was signed into law, there-by creating the National Commission for the Protection of Human Subjects of Biomedical and Behavioral Research. One of the charges to the Commission was to identify the basic ethical principles that should underlie the conduct of biomedical and behavioral research involving human subjects and to develop guidelines which should be followed to assure that such research is conducted in accordance with those principles. In carrying out the above, the Commission was directed to consider: (i) the boundaries between biomedical and behavioral research and the accepted and routine practice of medicine, (ii) the role of assessment of risk-benefit criteria in the determination of the appropriateness of research involving human subjects, (iii) appropriate guidelines for the selection of human subjects for participation in such research and (iv) the nature and definition of informed consent in various research settings.

The Belmont Report attempts to summarize the basic ethical principles identified by the Commission in the course of its deliberations. It is the outgrowth of an intensive four-day period of discussions that were held in February 1976 at the Smithsonian Institution's Belmont Conference Center supplemented by the monthly deliberations of the Commission that were held over a period of nearly four years. It is a statement of basic ethical principles and guidelines that should assist in resolving the ethical problems that surround the conduct of research with human subjects. By publishing the Report in the Federal Register, and providing reprints upon request, the Secretary intends that it may be made readily available to scientists, members of Institutional Review Boards, and Federal employees ....

Unlike most other reports of the Commission, the Belmont Report does not make specific recommendations for administrative action by the Secretary of Health, Education, and Welfare. Rather, the Commission recommended that the Belmont Report be adopted in its entirety, as a statement of the Department's policy. The Department requests public comment on this recommendation.

....

**Ethical Principles & Guidelines for Research Involving Human Subjects**

Scientific research has produced substantial social benefits. It has also posed some troubling ethical questions. Public attention was drawn to these questions by reported abuses of human subjects in biomedical experiments, especially during the Second World War. During the Nuremberg War Crime Trials, the Nuremberg code was drafted as a set of standards for judging physicians and scientists who had conducted biomedical experiments on concentration camp prisoners. This code became the prototype of many later codes intended to assure that research involving human subjects would be carried out in an ethical manner.

The codes consist of rules, some general, others specific, that guide the investigators or the reviewers of research in their work. Such rules often are inadequate to cover complex situations; at times they come into conflict, and they are frequently difficult to interpret or apply. Broader ethical principles will provide a basis on which specific rules may be formulated, criticized and interpreted.

Three principles, or general prescriptive judgments, that are relevant to research involving human subjects are identified in this statement. Other principles may also be relevant. These three are comprehensive, however, and are stated at a level of generalization that should assist scientists, subjects, reviewers and interested citizens to understand the ethical issues inherent in research involving human subjects. These principles cannot always be applied so as to resolve beyond dispute particular ethical problems. The objective is to provide an analytical framework that will guide the resolution of ethical problems arising from research involving human subjects.

This statement consists of a distinction between research and practice, a discussion of the three basic ethical principles, and remarks about the application of these principles.

### A. Boundaries Between Practice and Research

It is important to distinguish between biomedical and behavioral research, on the one hand, and the practice of accepted therapy on the other, in order to know what activities ought to undergo review for the protection of human subjects of research. The distinction between research and practice is blurred partly because both often occur together (as in research designed to evaluate a therapy) and partly because notable departures from standard practice are often called "experimental" when the terms "experimental" and "research" are not carefully defined.

For the most part, the term "practice" refers to interventions that are designed solely to enhance the well-being of an individual patient or client and that have a reasonable expectation of success. The purpose of medical or behavioral practice is to provide diagnosis, preventive treatment or therapy to particular individuals. By contrast, the term "research' designates an activity designed to test an hypothesis, permit conclusions to be drawn, and thereby to develop or contribute to generalizable knowledge (expressed, for example, in theories, principles, and statements of relationships). Research is usually described in a formal protocol that sets forth an objective and a set of procedures designed to reach that objective.

When a clinician departs in a significant way from standard or accepted practice, the innovation does not, in and of itself, constitute research. The fact that a procedure is "experimental," in the sense of new, untested or different, does not automatically place it in the category of research. Radically new procedures of this description should, however, be made the object of formal research at an early stage in order to determine whether they are safe and effective. Thus, it is the responsibility of medical practice committees, for example, to insist that a major innovation be incorporated into a formal research project.

Research and practice may be carried on together when research is designed to evaluate the safety and efficacy of a therapy. This need not cause any confusion regarding whether or not the activity requires review; the general rule is that if there is any element of research in an activity, that activity should undergo review for the protection of human subjects.

### B. Basic Ethical Principles

The expression "basic ethical principles" refers to those general judgments that serve as a basic justification for the many particular ethical prescriptions and evaluations of human actions. Three basic principles, among those generally accepted in our cultural tradition, are particularly relevant to the ethics of research involving human subjects: the principles of respect of persons, beneficence and justice.

*1. Respect for Persons.*—Respect for persons incorporates at least two ethical convictions: first, that individuals should be treated as autonomous agents, and second, that persons with diminished autonomy are entitled to protection. The principle of respect for persons thus divides into two separate moral requirements: the requirement to acknowledge autonomy and the requirement to protect those with diminished autonomy.

. . . .

2. *Beneficence.*—Persons are treated in an ethical manner not only by respecting their decisions and protecting them from harm, but also by making efforts to secure their well-being. Such treatment falls under the principle of beneficence. The term "beneficence" is often understood to cover acts of kindness or charity that go beyond strict obligation. In this document, beneficence is understood in a stronger sense, as an obligation. Two general rules have been formulated as complementary expressions of beneficent actions in this sense: (1) do not harm and (2) maximize possible benefits and minimize possible harms.

. . . .

3. *Justice.*—Who ought to receive the benefits of research and bear its burdens? This is a question of justice, in the sense of "fairness in distribution" or "what is deserved." An injustice occurs when some benefit to which a person is entitled is denied without good reason or when some burden is imposed unduly. Another way of conceiving the principle of justice is that equals ought to be treated equally. . . .

Questions of justice have long been associated with social practices such as punishment, taxation and political representation. Until recently these questions have not generally been associated with scientific research. However, they are foreshadowed even in the earliest reflections on the ethics of research involving human subjects. For example, during the 19th and early 20th centuries the burdens of serving as research subjects fell largely upon poor ward patients, while the benefits of improved medical care flowed primarily to private patients. Subsequently, the exploitation of unwilling prisoners as research subjects in Nazi concentration camps was condemned as a particularly flagrant injustice. In this country, in the 1940's, the Tuskegee syphilis study used disadvantaged, rural black men to study the untreated course of a disease that is by no means confined to that population. These subjects were deprived of demonstrably effective treatment in order not to interrupt the project, long after such treatment became generally available.

Against this historical background, it can be seen how conceptions of justice are relevant to research involving human subjects. For example, the selection of research subjects needs to be scrutinized in order to determine whether some classes (e.g., welfare patients, particular racial and ethnic minorities, or persons confined to institutions) are being systematically selected simply because of their easy availability, their compromised position, or their manipulability, rather than for reasons directly related to the problem being studied. . . .

### C. Applications

Applications of the general principles to the conduct of research leads to consideration of the following requirements: informed consent, risk/benefit assessment, and the selection of subjects of research.

. . . .

*1. Informed Consent.*—Respect for persons requires that subjects, to the degree that they are capable, be given the opportunity to choose what shall or shall not happen to them. This opportunity is provided when adequate standards for informed consent are satisfied.

. . . .

*2. Assessment of Risks and Benefits.*—The assessment of risks and benefits requires a careful arrayal of relevant data, including, in some cases, alternative ways of obtaining the benefits sought in the research. Thus, the assessment presents both an opportunity and a responsibility to gather systematic and comprehensive information about proposed research. For the investigator, it is a means to examine whether the proposed research is properly designed. For a review committee, it is a method for determining whether the risks that will be presented to subjects are justified. For prospective subjects, the assessment will assist the determination whether or not to participate.

. . . .

*3. Selection of Subjects.*—Just as the principle of respect for persons finds expression in the requirements for consent, and the principle of beneficence in risk/benefit assessment, the principle of justice gives rise to moral requirements that there be fair procedures and outcomes in the selection of research subjects.

. . . .

One special instance of injustice results from the involvement of vulnerable subjects. Certain groups, such as racial minorities, the economically disadvantaged, the very sick, and the institutionalized may continually be sought as research subjects, owing to their ready availability in settings where research is conducted. Given their dependent status and their frequently compromised capacity for free consent, they should be protected against the danger of being involved in research solely for administrative convenience, or because they are easy to manipulate as a result of their illness or socioeconomic condition.

## 2. FDA Implementation of the Belmont Report

### *a. Informed Consent*

On January 27, 1981, FDA promulgated a final rule adopting major changes to its informed-consent regulations. The general background of this revision is set out in an earlier proposed rule on which that final rule was based. A portion of this

August 14, 1979, proposed rule is set out below. (The final rule, which goes into less detail on the background, is not excerpted here).

## 1979-08-14 FDA Proposed Rule, Informed Consent

44 Fed. Reg. 47,713

The agency believes that a complete revision of FDA requirements relating to informed consent is needed because (1) current regulations have not been comprehensively reviewed in 12 years; (2) actions by the Department of Health, Education, and Welfare (HEW) and the Congress suggest the need for, and desirability of, strengthening and clarifying informed consent requirements as they apply to research that involves human subjects and is intended for submission to FDA; (3) when possible, informed consent requirements adopted by FDA should be identical to, or compatible with, HEW regulations; (4) the General Accounting Office (GAO) has recommended changes in current FDA regulations; (5) Congress, in enacting the Medical Device Amendments of 1976, required that informed consent be obtained before an investigational device is used on a human subject; (6) the new FDA Bioresearch Monitoring Program, designed to ensure compliance with FDA requirements to protect human research subjects and reinforce the validity and reliability of clinical data submitted to FDA, can be more efficiently and effectively conducted with uniform, agency-wide requirements for informed consent; and (7) the National Commission for the Protection of Human Subjects of Biomedical and Behavioral Research (National Commission) has issued its report and recommendations regarding Institutional Review Boards and informed consent, published in the Federal Register of November 30, 1978.

Because the agency finds that informed consent is a concept that has grown more complex as it has evolved, and because the standards for informed consent reflected by the Medical Device Amendments of 1976 are more stringent than the standards reflected by the Drug Amendments of 1962, there is included in this preamble an extensive discussion of the background and history of informed consent as it applies to experimentation with human subjects.

....

*Background*

*The Federal Food, Drug, and Cosmetic Act of 1938*

In 1938, Congress for the first time required that a manufacturer demonstrate the safety of a new drug before introducing the drug into interstate commerce. This requirement was not intended, however, to apply to shipments to clinical investigators who were testing drugs to determine toxicity or other safety problems.... Between 1938 and 1962, FDA regulations were silent on the matter of informed consent.

*Nuremberg Code of Ethics in Medical Practice*

Following World War II, disclosure of brutal experiments conducted in Nazi concentration camps forced a reevaluation of the moral, ethical, and legal principles applied to research involving human subjects. The war crimes trial of physicians at Nuremberg produced a set of ten basic principles, which has since been termed the "Nuremberg Code of Ethics in Medical Research." First on the list was informed consent, which was described in terms of the information to be provided and the ability of the subject to consent. . . .

*The Drug Amendments of 1962*

In late July 1962, during the deliberations leading to the Drug Amendments of 1962, reports of the thalidomide drug disaster appeared in print. One of the many unfortunate aspects of that tragedy was that many of the pregnant women in the United States to whom thalidomide was given were not informed that the drug was experimental, that they were research subjects, or that the safety of the drug had not been established. As a result of the thalidomide reports, a revised and strengthened bill, substitute S. 1552, was reported out of the Senate Committee on the Judiciary.

. . . .

*Implementation of the Drug Amendments of 1962 (1962–1976).*

On August 10, 1962, before enactment of the Drug Amendments, the FDA proposed in the Federal Register an extensive revision and expansion of its regulations under section 505(i) of the [FFDCA] as enacted in 1938. These proposals did not refer to informed consent; nevertheless, when made final on January 8, 1963, the regulations included a requirement . . . that each clinical investigator certify to the sponsor of the drug research that informed consent would be obtained in accordance with the newly revised section 505(i) of the [FFDCA], except where not required by that statute.

The FDA did not attempt to define specifically the content or form of informed consent, or the circumstances under which the law did not require consent of the research subject, until 1966. In the Federal Register of August 30, 1966, the Commissioner issued § 130.37 (21 CFR 130.37) that required consent in all nontherapeutic drug studies and in all but exceptional cases of therapeutic application of an experimental drug. The exceptions were allowed (a) when communication with the patient or the patient's legal representative was not possible and it was imperative to administer the drug without delay, and (b) when communication of the necessary information would seriously affect the disease state of the patient and the physician had made a professional judgment that the patient's best interests would suffer if consent were sought. The regulation also spelled out the types of information that were to be conveyed to the subject: (a) the nature, duration, and purpose of the administration of the investigational drug; (b) the method and means by which the drug was to be administered; (c) all inconveniences and hazards reasonably to be expected, including the fact (when applicable) that the person might be used as a control; (d) the existence of alternative forms of therapy, if any; and (e) the effects upon the subject's health or person that might possibly come from the administration of the investigational drug. Finally, the 1968 order established an absolute rule that consent was always to be obtained in writing.

In 1967, the FDA reconsidered the new regulation in light of the Declaration of Helsinki, adopted by the World Health Organization in 1964, and the "Ethical Guidelines for Clinical Investigation," adopted by the House of Delegates of the American Medical Association (AMA) in 1966. . . .

*The Medical Device Amendments*

The Medical Device Amendments of 1976 became law on May 28, 1976. Section 520(g) of the [FFDCA], which was added by those amendments, concerns investigational devices and contains provisions similar to those governing the investigational use of new drugs, biologics, and antibiotic drugs that are found in sections 505(i) and 507(d)(3) of the [FFDCA]. . . .

The informed consent provisions contained in this proposal would be uniform agency-wide requirements. . . .

*Evolution of the Concept of Informed Consent*

Although the statutory history detailed above does demonstrate that, as the concept of informed consent has evolved, the requirements for subject protection have become more complex, it does not fully explain the changes in attitude that have resulted in this increased complexity. The statutory standards established for the use of investigational drugs by Congress in 1962 are inconsistent with the standards established by Congress for the use of investigational devices in 1976. FDA believes that the standards expressed through the regulations now being proposed should be consistent with current thinking. Therefore, FDA is including a brief discussion of how and why the concept has changed.

. . . .

*The Need for Revision of FDA Regulations*

The concept of informed consent has changed as outlined above. For several years, FDA has been planning to revise substantially the regulations governing drug research under sections 505(i) and 507(d) of the [FFDCA]. Many of the current regulations were, as noted previously, first issued in 1963 under the Drug Amendments of 1962. Current FDA policy regarding consent for use of investigational new drugs on humans was adopted in 1967 and is set forth in § 310.102, although significant discrepancies exist between the regulation and the statements in [two FDA forms]. Until now, however, there has been no comprehensive review or update of these regulations. The actions of the Congress, the National Commission, and the Department in the area of human experimentation all demonstrate the need for a uniform FDA regulation that covers the investigational use of drugs, devices, and other test articles subject to FDA jurisdiction.

The concept of "informed consent" is not a narrow or technical concept, limited in application to this or that particular kind of research on human subjects. Rather, the concept has a broad sweep; and, like the concepts of "due process of law" and "equal protection of the laws," it reflects fundamental social value judgments about how people should be treated.

Like those other concepts, too, the concept of "informed consent" changes and grows in light of increasing experience in its application and more precise identification of problems to be addressed in its articulation.

In principle, there is no reason for requirements of informed consent to differ depending on whether the article administered to the human subjects of research is a drug, an antibiotic, or a medical device. The basic notions of autonomy and fairness that undergird the concept of "informed consent" apply in the same way to all categories of human biomedical research.

Indeed, on the basis of FDA's experience with the regulation of human biomedical research, the agency strongly believes that maintenance of separate and different systems for informed consent in different categories of research would promote confusion among investigators and institutional review boards, and would frustrate the congressional purpose, reflected in both the Drug Amendments of 1962 and the Medical Device Amendments of 1976, to require that biomedical research be conducted in accordance with the highest contemporary ethical standards.

The same investigators may from time to time do research on drugs and devices. One investigation may include one treatment group receiving a drug and another receiving a device. The concept of "informed consent" has developed only in the last quarter century. As the history of its development described above makes plain, the concept has changed over the years; most likely, it will continue to change.

The agency recognizes that the language, interpreted literally, of sections 505(i) and 507(d)(3) of the [FFDCA] allows an investigator using experimental drugs greater freedom to dispense with informed consent when, in the exercise of professional judgment, the investigator concludes that obtaining such consent is "not feasible" or is "contrary to the best interests of the patient." This language, as discussed above, does not appear in the informed consent provisions of the Medical Device Amendments. The informed consent regulations adopted by FDA in 1967, and now codified under § 310.102, provide that the exception to the requirement that Informed consent be obtained be carefully limited to those situations in which either communications with the patient is not possible and it is imperative to employ the drug without delay, or in which communication of the necessary information would seriously affect the disease state of the patient. Both of these exceptions assume situations in which the patient subject is seriously ill; and, when read in light of the context in which they would actually apply, the exceptions do not differ greatly from the emergency exemptions contained in section 520(g)(3)(D) of the Medical Device Amendments. Thus, the actual policy, which has been followed by the agency since 1967 regarding the investigational use of drugs, is quite similar to the policy that the agency is now proposing.

To the extent that the informed consent provisions of the Drug Amendments differ from those of the Medical Device Amendments, however, FDA is proposing to make the latter applicable to both. In light of the nature of the concept of "informed consent" and its anchorage in ethical values basic to our society, FDA believes that the particular language of the Drug Amendments should not be interpreted literally or strictly or as preventing progress in the evolution of informed consent requirements. Amendments to the [FFDCA] have occurred historically on a product-by-product basis, and Congress, in enacting the informed consent requirements of the Medical Device Amendments, did not address the fact that the exemption requirements for investigational devices being proposed were different from those previously enacted for investigational drugs. The agency finds that the informed consent requirements contained in section 520(g)(3)(D) of the [FFDCA] represent the most recent congressional thinking regarding the standards required of clinical investigators of FDA-regulated products and, as such, should be the standards applied to all FDA-regulated research, regardless of the regulated product involved. It is fair to assume that each time Congress addressed the issue of informed consent, it intended to adopt the most highly developed and practical informed consent requirements then available. In 1962 there was ample reason to expect that the concept would evolve; and, as discussed above, it has done so. In proposing a uniform system of informed consent applicable to research on all articles regulated by FDA, the agency is seeking to administer the informed consent provisions of the law in the manner that will most effectively carry out the congressional purpose and facilitate the obtaining of informed consent.

### *b. Prisoners as Research Subjects*

## 1980-05-30 FDA Final Rule, Protection of Human Subjects; Prisoners Used as Subjects in Research

45 Fed. Reg. 36,386

SUMMARY: This document establishes regulations to provide protection for prisoners involved in research activities that fall within the jurisdiction of the Food and Drug Administration (FDA). These regulations implement the recommendations of the National Commission for the Protection of Human Subjects in Biomedical and Behavioral Research (National Commission) *[the Belmont Report, excerpted earlier in this chapter]* on research involving prisoners. These regulations restrict the use of prisoners in research within the jurisdiction of FDA and establish requirements for the composition of and additional duties for institutional review boards when prisoners are involved in the research.

. . . .

SUPPLEMENTARY INFORMATION: Under the National Research Act (Pub. L. 93-348), the National Commission was charged with, among other duties, identifying the requirements for informed consent by prisoners for participation in biomedical and behavioral research. On the basis of its investigation and study of this issue (see paragraph 7), the National Commission identified the requirements for informed consent and made recommendations to the Secretary of Health and Human Services (HHS) about appropriate administrative actions to ensure that those requirements would be met in research subject to the Department's jurisdiction. The National Commission's recommendations covered research conducted or supported under programs administered by the Secretary and research reported to the Secretary in fulfillment of regulatory requirements. Section 205 of the National Research Act, however, only required the Secretary to determine whether the National Commission's recommendations were appropriate to assure the protection of prisoners as subjects of biomedical or behavioral research conducted or supported under the programs the Secretary administered. Section 205 did not explicitly impose an obligation on the Secretary to respond to the National Commission's recommendations with regard to research reported in fulfillment of regulatory requirements. Nevertheless, the Secretary believed that a determination should be made as to whether the National Commission's recommendations should be adopted for non-HHS supported research that is submitted to FDA to satisfy its regulatory requirements. Because rulemaking authority with respect to FDA activities has been delegated to the Commissioner of Food and Drugs, the Secretary directed the Commissioner to take appropriate action on these recommendations.

In the Federal Register of May 5, 1978, ·the Commissioner announced the tentative decision to adopt the findings of both the National Commission and the Secretary regarding the inherently coercive nature of the prison environment and the need for special protections for prisoners involved as subjects of clinical research. Therefore, on the basis of the authority granted under the [FFDCA], the Commissioner proposed these regulations to establish those special protections.

. . . .

## D. Key Points

- FDA's authority over research is derived from, and limited by, its authority over marketing authorization.
- The history of clinical research is rife with experiments that we would today consider abusive. This abuse was concentrated among (but not limited to) those with less power in society—especially the poor, racial minorities, persons with disabilities, and institutionalized persons.
- The basic division in FDA-regulated research is between clinical research and nonclinical research (sometimes referred to as "preclinical" research). Clinical research involves human subjects, nonclinical research does not.
- For all FDA-regulated research, one primary goal is ensuring that research is designed and implemented in a manner that can produce valid, reproducible results. For clinical research, a second primary goal—protection of human subjects—can at times override the first.

- There is often a trade-off between ideal research design (for the purposes of obtaining valid, reproducible results) and protection of human subjects. Current law manages this trade-off—a necessarily imperfect process—through the evolving concept of informed consent.

# Chapter 4

# Marketing Authorization

## A. Introduction

This book adopts the term *marketing authorization* to refer generally to all processes by which FDA permits products to be marketed in the United States.[1] This chapter addresses marketing authorization, as a whole, for all FDA-regulated products. Presenting marketing authorization in this consolidated manner shortens each of the chapters on the individual product categories. This necessarily requires coverage of a large range of material, and you will probably find this to be the most difficult chapter in the book. However, there are two advantages to presenting the material in this manner.

First, there are a sufficient number of similarities between the many varieties of marketing authorization that they can be grouped broadly into a set of types and subtypes. This makes them easier to learn, and remember, than if they are presented individually within the chapters covering each product category. Second, it is difficult to understand what makes each individual product category distinct until you understand the way they fit together in food and drug regulation as a whole.

You have already had an initial introduction to each product category in Chapter 1. Chapter 1 focused on the most basic issue—the statutory or regulatory definition of each product category. In this chapter, you will encounter each product category a second time, but in a different manner. This time, you will see each product category within a discussion of the applicable marketing authorization standard. As you read, note that the applicable marketing authorization standard is one of the reasons the product-category definitions you encountered Chapter 1 are so important. A small change in intended use can move a product from a category that requires no marketing authorization (such as food or cosmetics) to a category that requires an extraordinarily expensive marketing authorization process, such as that for new drugs.

1. "[M]arketing authorization" is the term used in FFDCA §802 to refer generally to the processes other countries use to permit drugs or devices to be marketed in their own territories. The term is also used by FDA in its combination-product regulations, 21 C.F.R. Part 4, to refer generally to the various processes by which drugs, devices, and biologics are permitted on the market. Marketing authorization is not a perfect term to refer generally to highly varied processes by which FDA permits marketing of a product. However, given its existing uses, this book adopts it rather than coining a new term.

*A Note on Terminology*

FDA uses a variety of terms to describe the processes by which it permits a particular product to be marketed in the United States. These terms have developed over time and are not always used consistently.[2] Roughly speaking, however, FDA's current use of these terms is set out below.

Some products are formally *approved* (new drugs), *listed* (color additives), or *licensed* (biologics). These terms denote a finding by FDA that the relevant product meets an applicable standard of safety and (where relevant) efficacy. Medical devices can be either *approved* or *cleared*—with the former reserved for products that undergo a more rigorous review process (premarket approval), and the latter used for products that undergo a less rigorous review process (premarket notification). Tobacco products receive *marketing orders*. Other products, such as many substances added to food, are permitted on the market based on a determination that they are exempt from the FFDCA's definition of "food additive." Some animal drugs are *conditionally approved*, and some animal drugs are *indexed* as explicitly unapproved products that are nonetheless permitted to be marketed.

As you read this chapter, you will encounter these terms in more detail. Keep two things in mind. First, each of these terms denotes an authorization by FDA for a particular product to be marketed. Second, do not fall into the habit of referring to all marketing authorization decisions as FDA "approval." You should be careful to reserve this term for the more limited subset of situations where it applies.

*Organization of This Chapter*

This chapter proceeds as follows. Following this introduction, Part B presents this book's standard outline of the regulatory regime. Part C introduces the relevant policy issues with a case highlighting the trade-offs involved in marketing authorization decisions for drugs.

Parts D through H are the core of the chapter. Part D introduces the various standards for marketing authorization. Part E introduces pathways to market, and divides these into two broad sets: paradigm pathways and alternate pathways. Part F presents pathways for therapeutic products, Part G presents pathways for non-therapeutic products, and Part H presents situations where no marketing authorization is required (and, thus, no pathway to market is necessary).

Part I presents the designations. These are not pathways to market, but methods developed by Congress and FDA to designate certain products for faster review, for assistance with review, or for extra incentives for successful marketing

---

2. FDA is a large organization. Its written materials develop gradually over time, with different officials choosing to emphasize different distinctions between the various marketing authorization processes. For some materials, such as those produced through notice-and-comment rulemaking, the agency cannot easily change them—even to clarify terminology—without undergoing a fairly extensive legal process. Moreover, the fact that some products are regulated in more than one category creates additional terminological complications.

authorization. Part J provides a short overview of medical countermeasures, an area related to both the designations and the later topic of emergency use.

Part K presents four mechanisms for obtaining access to FDA-regulated products before marketing authorization. These are standard investigational use, expanded access, emergency use, and the "Right to Try" Act. Part L concludes with key points on marketing authorization.

*Role of This Chapter in the Course*

This chapter covers what is, in many ways, the single most important aspect of each product category—whether (and, if so, what type of) marketing authorization is required. Chapters 6–18 then cover other aspects of each product category, without repeating the marketing authorization material covered here. Before you begin reading each of those later chapters, it would be a good idea to look back at this chapter and review the information in Parts D (on standards for marketing authorization) and Parts E through G (on the various pathways to market) for the product category you are about to cover.

It would also be a good idea to reread this full chapter after you have covered each of the individual product categories in Chapters 6–18. This chapter contains a large amount of information, and you will likely retain only a portion of it in your initial reading. It should make more sense to you, and be easier to remember, on a rereading after you have covered each of the individual product categories.

## B. Outline of Regulatory Regime

As in other chapters of this book, this chapter begins with a set of charts. As you read this chapter for the first time, you should do no more than skim these charts to get a general sense of the structure of the applicable statutes and regulations. (For more information on the role of the charts in this casebook, see Chapter 1, Parts A.1 and B).

| Timeline of Key Statutes: Marketing Authorization | | | |
|---|---|---|---|
| Year | PL | Stat | Name of Statute |
| 1938 | 75-717 | 52 Stat. 1040 | FFDCA of 1938 |
| 1944 | 78-410 | 58 Stat. 682 | Public Health Services Act |
| 1962 | 87-781 | 76 Stat. 780 | Kefauver-Harris Amendments of 1962 |
| 1968 | 90-399 | 82 Stat. 342 | Animal Drug Amendments of 1968 |
| 1976 | 94-295 | 90 Stat. 539 | Medical Devices Amendments of 1976 |
| 1983 | 97-414 | 96 Stat. 2049 | Orphan Drug Act |
| 1984 | 98-417 | 98 Stat. 1585 | Hatch-Waxman Act |
| 1990 | 101-629 | 104 Stat. 4511 | Safe Medical Devices Act |

| Year | PL | Stat | Name of Statute |
|---|---|---|---|
| 1992 | 102-282 | 106 Stat. 149 | Generic Drug Enforcement Act of 1992 |
| 1992 | 102-300 | 106 Stat. 238 | Medical Device Amendments of 1992 |
| 1994 | 103-417 | 108 Stat. 4325 | Dietary Supplement Health and Education Act |
| 1997 | 105-115 | 111 Stat. 2296 | FDA Modernization Act of 1997 |
| 2002 | 107-188 | 116 Stat. 595 | Public Health Security and Bioterrorism Preparedness and Response Act of 2002 |
| 2012 | 112-144 | 126 Stat. 993 | FDA Safety and Innovation Act |
| 2013 | 113-54 | 127 Stat. 587 | Drug Quality and Security Act |
| 2014 | 113-195 | 128 Stat. 2035 | Sunscreen Innovation Act |
| 2016 | 114-255 | 130 Stat. 1033 | 21st Century Cures Act |
| 2017 | 115-52 | 131 Stat. 1005 | FDA Reauthorization Act of 2017 |
| 2017 | 115-92 | 131 Stat. 2023 | An Act To amend the Federal Food, Drug, and Cosmetic Act to authorize additional emergency uses for medical products to reduce deaths and severity of injuries caused by agents of war, and for other purposes. |
| 2020 | 116-136 | 134 Stat. 281 | Coronavirus Aid, Relief, and Economic Security (CARES) Act |

| Key Statutory Provisions: Marketing Authorization | | |
|---|---|---|
| **Statute Name or U.S.C. Title** | **§** | **Title of Section or Subsection** |
| FFDCA | 409 | Food additives |
| FFDCA | 505 | New drugs |
| FFDCA | 505H | Regulation of certain nonprescription drugs that are marketed without an approved drug application. |
| FFDCA | 506 | Expedited approval of drugs for serious or life-threatening diseases or conditions |
| FFDCA | 506H | Competitive generic therapies |
| FFDCA | 510 | Registration of producers of drugs and devices. |
| FFDCA | 512 | New animal drugs. |
| FFDCA | 513 | Classification of devices intended for human use. |
| FFDCA | 515 | Premarket approval [for medical devices] |
| FFDCA | 586F | Nonsunscreen time and extent applications |
| FFDCA | 571 | Conditional approval of new animal drugs for minor use and minor species |

| Statute Name or U.S.C. Title | § | Title of Section or Subsection |
|---|---|---|
| FFDCA | 572 | Index of legally marketed unapproved new animal drugs for minor species |
| FFDCA | 721 | Color additives |
| FFDCA | 905 | Annual registration [of tobacco products] |
| FFDCA | 910 | Application for review of certain tobacco products |
| PHSA | 351 | Regulation of biological products |
| PHSA | 361 | Regulations to control communicable diseases |

**Key Regulatory Provisions: Marketing Authorization**

| 21 C.F.R. Part | Subpart | Title of Part or Subpart |
|---|---|---|
| 3 | — | Product jurisdiction |
| 71 | — | Color additive petitions |
| 171 | — | Food additive petitions |
| 190 | — | Dietary supplements |
| 310 | — | New drugs |
| 314 | — | Applications for FDA approval to market a new drug |
| | B | Applications |
| | C | Abbreviated applications |
| | D | FDA action on applications and abbreviated applications |
| | H | Accelerated approval of new drugs for serious or life-threatening illnesses |
| | I | Approval of new drugs when human efficacy studies are not ethical or feasible |
| 316 | — | Orphan drugs |
| 320 | — | Bioavailability and bioequivalence requirements |
| 510 | — | New animal drugs |
| 514 | — | New animal drug applications |
| 516 | — | New animal drugs for minor use and minor species |
| 601 | — | Licensing [of biological products] |
| | C | Biologics licensing |
| | E | Accelerated approval of biological products for serious or life-threatening illnesses |
| | H | Approval of biological products when human efficacy studies are not ethical or feasible |

| 21 C.F.R. Part | Subpart | Title of Part or Subpart |
|---|---|---|
| 807 | — | Establishment registration and device listing for manufacturers and initial importers of devices |
| 814 | — | Premarket approval of medical devices |
| | B | Premarket approval application |
| | C | FDA action on a PMA |
| | H | Humanitarian use devices |
| 860 | — | Medical device classification procedures |
| 1107 | — | Establishment registration, product listing, and substantial equivalence reports [for tobacco products] |

## C. The Trade-Off Between Rigorous Marketing Authorization Requirements and Availability of Useful Products

The case below illustrates the tension between rigorous marketing authorization requirements and the resulting restrictions on access to potentially useful products. It also introduces one particularly significant marketing authorization regime: the new drug approval process. The new drug approval process is discussed in more detail later in this chapter.

### Abigail Alliance v. Von Eschenbach

495 F.3d 695 (D.C. Cir. 2007)

**GRIFFITH, Circuit Judge:**

This case presents the question whether the Constitution provides terminally ill patients a right of access to experimental drugs that have passed limited safety trials but have not been proven safe and effective. The district court held there is no such right. A divided panel of this Court held there is. Because we conclude that there is no fundamental right "deeply rooted in this Nation's history and tradition" of access to experimental drugs for the terminally ill, *see Washington v. Glucksberg,* 521 U.S. 702 (1997) (quoting *Moore v. East Cleveland,* 431 U.S. 494 (1977), we affirm the judgment of the district court.

I.

A.

The Abigail Alliance for Better Access to Developmental Drugs (the "Alliance") is an organization of terminally ill patients and their supporters that seeks expanded access to experimental drugs for the terminally ill. The Food, Drug, and Cosmetic

Act ("FDCA" or "Act"), however, generally prohibits access to new drugs unless and until they have been approved by the Food and Drug Administration ("FDA"). Gaining FDA approval can be a long process. First, an experimental drug's sponsor (*e.g.*, a drug company) must submit an application for approval. Because no drug may be approved without a finding of "substantial evidence that the drug will have the effect it purports or is represented to have," an application must contain "full reports of investigations which have been made to show whether or not such drug is safe for use and whether such drug is effective in use." Such reports rely in large measure on clinical trials with human subjects.

But before a sponsor can even begin human testing, it must submit for the FDA's approval an investigational new drug application ("IND"), containing detailed information establishing that human testing is appropriate. Once the application for human testing has been approved, several phases of clinical testing begin. The Alliance's amended complaint alleges that this testing process is an extremely lengthy one, requiring nearly seven years for the average experimental drug.[1]

Clinical testing for safety and effectiveness requires three or sometimes four phases. Phase I involves the initial introduction of a new drug into human subjects. A Phase I study usually consists of twenty to eighty subjects and is "designed to determine the metabolism and pharmacologic actions of the [new] drug in humans, the side effects associated with increasing doses, and, if possible, to gain early evidence on effectiveness." Although gathering data on effectiveness may be part of Phase I, its primary focus is to determine whether the drug is safe enough for continued human testing. Phase II studies are "well controlled" and "closely monitored" clinical trials of no more than several hundred subjects, used to evaluate both the "effectiveness of the drug for a particular indication" and its "common short-term side effects and risks."

Phase III studies are expanded clinical trials of several hundred to several thousand subjects designed to "gather ... additional information about effectiveness and safety that is needed to evaluate the overall benefit-risk relationship of the drug and to provide an adequate basis for physician labeling." At any time during the clinical trials, a drug sponsor is required to notify the FDA of "[a]ny adverse experience associated with the use of the drug that is both serious and unexpected," and the FDA may order a "clinical hold" halting the trials if it determines that safety concerns so warrant. To guide the clinical testing process, Congress has directed the FDA to establish "[s]cientific advisory panels" to "provid[e] expert scientific advice and recommendations to the Secretary regarding a clinical investigation of a drug or the approval for marketing of a drug." These panels must include scientists from a variety of disciplines.

1. In FDA parlance, experimental drugs that have not yet been approved for public use are deemed "investigational drug[s]." *See* 21 C.F.R. § 312.3(b).

Terminally ill patients need not, however, always await the results of the clinical testing process. The FDA and Congress have created several programs designed to provide early access to promising experimental drugs when warranted. For example, under the "treatment IND" program, the FDA may approve use of an investigational drug by patients not part of the clinical trials for the treatment of "serious or immediately life-threatening disease[s]" if there exists "no comparable or satisfactory alternative drug or other therapy,"; if "[t]he drug is under investigation in a controlled clinical trial,"; and if the drug's sponsor "is actively pursuing marketing approval of the investigational drug with due diligence." The FDA reserves the right, however, to deny any treatment IND request if (1) the agency believes there is no "reasonable basis" to conclude that the drug is effective; or (2) granting the request "[w]ould . . . expose the patient[] . . . to an unreasonable and significant additional risk of illness or injury." Sponsors may not profit from any approved treatment IND program and may only "recover costs of manufacture, research, development, and handling of the investigational drug."[4]

### B.

Concluding that the FDA's current process for early access to new drugs was inadequate to meet the needs of its terminally ill members, the Alliance submitted its own proposals to the FDA. Those proposals culminated in a "citizen petition" to the FDA, arguing that there is a "different risk-benefit tradeoff facing patients who are terminally ill and who have no other treatment options." Although the Alliance agreed that "[e]xtensive marshalling of evidence regarding drug interactions, dose optimization, and the like" is "appropriate for new drugs to treat patients with other alternatives . . . [,] these steps may well entail a delay that is fatal" for terminally ill patients. The Alliance contended that these patients "should have the ability to opt for a new treatment that has met a lower evidentiary hurdle with respect to safety and efficacy." The Alliance's proposal suggested that the FDA allow early access based upon "the risk of illness, injury, or death from the disease in the absence of the drug." Accordingly, the Alliance requested that the FDA promulgate new regulations that would allow sponsors to market experimental drugs, under some circumstances, after the completion of Phase I trials.

The FDA never responded to the Alliance's citizen petition, but did respond to the Alliance's earlier submissions. After noting that a number of senior FDA officials had reviewed those submissions, the agency concluded that the Alliance "raised several important questions about expanded access that we believe deserve further consideration," but questioned whether the specific proposal put forward by the Alliance "would have the intended desirable effects for patients." The officials concluded that the early access proposed by the Alliance "points to an area of

---

4. The FDA has several other regulatory programs designed to hasten research of the safety and effectiveness of drugs for terminally or severely ill patients and allow early access where scientifically and medically warranted . . . .

significant range of opinion within the patient and provider communities about the standards that should be met before a drug is marketed." Although "some members of the cancer community have suggested that [the] FDA needs to maintain a strong clinical trial system as the basis of the approval of cancer drugs, . . . others, like [the Alliance], have criticized [the FDA] for relying too heavily on completing certain trials before approval." The FDA noted that "[i]n the realm of reviewing medical products to treat serious and life-threatening diseases, there is inevitable tension between early availability of products to patients, especially patients with refractory disease, and the need to obtain sufficient data to provide a reasonable expectation of benefit and lack of excessive harm."

Relying upon its experience exercising its scientific and medical judgment in creating its regulations for experimental drugs and, in certain circumstances, exceptions to those regulations for the terminally ill, the FDA noted that "a reasonably precise estimate of response rate" and "enough experience to detect serious adverse effects" are "critical" in determining when experimental drugs should be made available. For example, most experimental cancer drugs "have potentially lethal toxicity, with potentially large effects on a patient's remaining quality of life." Accordingly, "it does not serve patients well to make drugs too widely available before there is a reasonable assessment of such risks to guide patient decisions, and experience in managing them." The FDA concluded that accepting the Alliance's proposal "would upset the appropriate balance that [it is] seeking to maintain, by giving almost total weight to the goal of early availability and giving little recognition to the importance of marketing drugs with reasonable knowledge for patients and physicians of their likely clinical benefit and their toxicity."

Having thus been rejected by the FDA, the Alliance turned to the courts, arguing that the United States Constitution provides a right of access to experimental drugs for its members. In a complaint that mirrored much of its earlier submissions to the FDA, the Alliance argued that the FDA's lengthy clinical trials, combined with the "FDA's restrictions on pre-approval availability[,] amount to a death sentence for these [terminally ill] patients." Nor, the Alliance argues, are the FDA's exceptions to the clinical testing process sufficient to provide the terminally ill the access they need because they "are small, when they exist at all," and the ban on profits prevents many drug sponsors from participating.

"Terminally ill patients," in the Alliance's view, "are typically willing to assume risks. . . ." Before the district court, the Alliance argued that the Constitution guarantees them the right to do so. The district court rejected that argument, holding that "there is no constitutional right of access to unapproved drugs." A divided panel of this Court reversed, concluding that "where there are no alternative government-approved treatment options, a terminally ill, mentally competent adult patient's informed access to potentially life-saving investigational new drugs determined by the FDA after Phase I trials to be sufficiently safe for expanded human trials warrants protection under the Due Process Clause." We vacated that decision and granted rehearing *en banc*.

As framed by the Alliance, we now consider:

> Whether the liberty protected by the Due Process Clause embraces the right of a terminally ill patient with no remaining approved treatment options to decide, in consultation with his or her own doctor, whether to seek access to investigational medications that the [FDA] concedes are safe and promising enough for substantial human testing.

That is, we must determine whether terminally ill patients have a fundamental right to experimental drugs that have passed Phase I clinical testing. If such a right exists, the Alliance argues that both 21 C.F.R. § 312.34(b)(3) (preventing access to experimental drugs for terminally ill patients where there is insufficient evidence of effectiveness or where there is an unreasonable risk of injury) and 21 C.F.R. § 312.7 (prohibiting drug manufacturers from profiting on the sale of experimental drugs) must be subjected to strict scrutiny because they interfere with a fundamental constitutional right. We do not address the broader question of whether access to medicine might ever implicate fundamental rights.

. . . .

### IV.

Because the Alliance's claimed right is not fundamental, the Alliance's claim of a right of access to experimental drugs is subject only to rational basis scrutiny. See *Glucksberg*, 521 U.S. at 722 (noting that "a challenged state action [must] implicate a fundamental right" to avoid rational basis review). The rational basis test requires that the Alliance prove that the government's restrictions bear no rational relationship to a legitimate state interest. The challenged policy "need not be in every respect logically consistent with its aims to be constitutional. It is enough that there is an evil at hand for correction, and that it might be thought that the particular legislative measure was a rational way to correct it." *Williamson v. Lee Optical of Okla., Inc.*, 348 U.S. 483 (1955).

The Alliance acknowledges the risk inherent in taking experimental drugs. The Alliance would rather that individual patients make decisions about this risk than have the FDA decide which drugs are safe enough for limited access to the terminally ill. The FDA counters that "[w]ithout a requirement of FDA approval, patients could be exposed to unreasonable risks from investigational drugs that may be neither safe nor effective."

Applying the rational basis standard to the Alliance's complaint, we cannot say that the government's interest does not bear a rational relation to a legitimate state interest. That conclusion is compelled by the Supreme Court's decision in *United States v. Rutherford*, 442 U.S. 544 (1979). In that case, terminally ill patients sought to prevent the FDA from prohibiting access to the drug laetrile, even though the drug had not been approved for public use. In rejecting a challenge by terminally ill patients claiming that the [FFDCA]'s safety requirement did not apply to them, the Supreme Court held that "[f]or the terminally ill, as for anyone else, a drug is unsafe if its potential for inflicting death or physical injury is not offset by the possibility of therapeutic benefit." Id. at 555–56; see also id. at 558 (noting that history has demonstrated that numerous "resourceful entrepreneurs" might try to take advantage of an unregulated market, which "suggest[s] why Congress could reasonably have determined to protect the terminally ill, no less than other patients, from the vast range of self-styled panaceas that inventive minds can devise").

Although terminally ill patients desperately need curative treatments, as *Rutherford* holds, their deaths can certainly be hastened by the use of a potentially toxic drug with no proven therapeutic benefit. Thus, we must conclude that, prior to distribution of a drug outside of controlled studies, the Government has a rational basis for ensuring that there is a scientifically and medically acceptable level of knowledge about the risks and benefits of such a drug. We therefore hold that the FDA's policy of limiting access to investigational drugs is rationally related to the legitimate state interest of protecting patients, including the terminally ill, from potentially unsafe drugs with unknown therapeutic effects.

Although in the Alliance's view the FDA has unjustly erred on the side of safety in balancing the risks and benefits of experimental drugs, this is not to say that the FDA's balance can never be changed. The Alliance's arguments about morality, quality of life, and acceptable levels of medical risk are certainly ones that can be aired in the democratic branches, without injecting the courts into unknown questions of science and medicine. Our Nation's history and traditions have consistently demonstrated that the democratic branches are better suited to decide the proper balance between the uncertain risks and benefits of medical technology, and are entitled to deference in doing so. As the Supreme Court has held:

> We must assume that, when the statute in question was passed, the legislature . . . was not unaware of these opposing theories, and was compelled, of necessity, to choose between them. It was not compelled to commit a matter involving the public health and safety to the final decision of a court or jury. It is no part of the function of a court or a jury to determine which one of two modes was likely to be the most effective for the protection of the public against disease.

*Jacobson v. Massachusetts,* 197 U.S. 11 (1905); *see also Gonzales v. Carhart,* 127 S. Ct. 1610, 1636 (2007) ("The Court has given state and federal legislatures wide discretion to pass legislation in areas where there is medical and scientific uncertainty."); *cf. Greenwood v. United States,* 350 U.S. 366 (1956) ("The only certain thing that can be said about the present state of knowledge and therapy . . . is that science has not reached finality of judgment. . . . Certainly, denial of constitutional power . . . to Congress in dealing with a situation like this ought not to rest on dogmatic adherence to one view or another on controversial psychiatric issues."). Consistent with that precedent, our holding today ensures that this debate among the Alliance, the FDA, the scientific and medical communities, and the public may continue through the democratic process. *See Glucksberg,* 521 U.S. at 735.

V.

For the foregoing reasons, the judgment of the district court is affirmed.

*So ordered.*

**ROGERS, Circuit Judge . . . dissenting:**

Today, the court rejects the claim that terminally ill patients who have exhausted all government-approved treatment options have a fundamental right to access investigational new drugs. The court's opinion reflects a flawed conception of the right claimed by the Abigail Alliance for Better Access to Developmental Drugs and a stunning misunderstanding of the stakes. The court shifts the inquiry required by *Washington v. Glucksberg,* 521 U.S. 702 (1997), by changing the nature of the right, by conflating the right with the deprivation, and by prematurely advancing countervailing government interests. The court fails to come to grips with the Nation's history and traditions, which reflect deep respect and protection for the right to preserve life, a corollary to the right to life enshrined in the Constitution. The court confuses this liberty interest with the manner in which the Alliance alleges that the liberty has been deprived, namely by denying terminally ill patients access to investigational medications under the narrow conditions described by the Alliance. The court conflates the inquiry as to whether a fundamental right exists at all with whether the government has demonstrated a compelling interest, when strictly scrutinized, rendering its restrictive policy constitutional.

. . . .

For these reasons, I have serious disagreements with the court's assessment of the Alliance's claim to a fundamental right protected by the Fifth Amendment to the Constitution. It is no more than tragic wordplay to suggest that the Alliance's liberty claim to potentially life prolonging medications, when no other government approved alternatives exist, does not involve a corollary to the right to life enshrined in the Fifth Amendment to the Constitution. Denying a terminally ill patient her only chance to survive without even a strict showing of governmental necessity presupposes a dangerous brand of paternalism. As the court phrases it, because " [w]e . . . cannot know until the clinical testing process has been completed that these drugs are necessary," the terminally ill patient, informed by her physician, is denied a right to decide whether to bear those risks in an attempt to preserve her life. Such intervention is directly at odds with this Nation's history and traditions giving recognition to individual self-determination and autonomy where one's own life is at stake and should extend no further than the result in this case. Because the right of a terminally ill patient to access potentially life-saving investigational medications satisfies the *Glucksberg* test, I would remand this case for the district court to assess in the first instance whether there exists a compelling governmental interest, narrowly tailored, to overcome the Alliance's interest. Accordingly, I respectfully dissent.

## D. Standards for Marketing Authorization

The *Abigail Alliance* case involved the most prominent of FDA's marketing authorization standards—the safety and efficacy standard applicable to the new drug approval process. However, this is not the only marketing authorization standard enforced by FDA. At a broad level, it is useful to think of five basic marketing authorization standards enforced by FDA: *safety only*; *safety and efficacy*; *safe, pure, and potent*; *protection of the public health;* and *no marketing authorization required.* At this broad level, the standard for food and color additives is safety; the standard for drugs is safety and efficacy; the standard for biologics is safety, purity, and potency; and the standard for tobacco products is consistency with protection of the public health.

However, these broad distinctions break down when looking closely at the actual statutory language and implementing regulatory requirements. As set out in more detail in the next section, most product categories involve more than one potential pathway to marketing authorization, with only one of those pathways involving a determination that the most rigorous version of the relevant standard is satisfied.

There are also some FDA-regulated products for which no marketing authorization is required. The product categories for which marketing authorization is generally not required are food, dietary supplements, cosmetics, and those HCT/Ps that are not also regulated in another product category. Additionally, there is a subset of drugs and medical devices that FDA has determined by regulation not to be subject to marketing authorization. These are certain over-the-counter drugs and certain low-risk medical devices.

Part E, below, addresses these pathways to market generally. Parts F through H then address pathways to market under each of these marketing authorization standards. Part F addresses therapeutic products; Part G addresses nontherapeutic products, and Part H addresses those products for which no marketing authorization is required.

## E. Pathways to Market: Generally

A *pathway to market* is a process by which FDA grants marketing authorization. This book divides pathways to market for FDA-regulated products into two broad sets: *paradigm pathways* and *alternate pathways.* Paradigm pathways are the paradigm for the relevant product category. Each paradigm pathway requires a determination by FDA that the product meets the most rigorous version of the requirement the applicable statutes and regulations set for marketing authorization. They are not necessarily the typical pathway used. For some product categories, marketing authorization is done far more frequently through one or more alternate pathways. Each pathway (paradigm and alternate) is addressed in more detail in the following sections of this chapter.

Alternate pathways are processes by which a product can receive marketing authorization without following the paradigm pathway. Most alternate pathways do not formally alter the requirement applicable to the relevant product category. Instead, they permit the requirement to be satisfied in one of five ways. First, an alternate pathway may permit marketing authorization based on data held by FDA that the applicant neither owns nor has a right to reference.[3] Second, an alternate pathway may permit marketing authorization based on establishing some specified degree of similarity to a product already on the market (through either marketing authorization or grandfathering).[4] Third, an alternate pathway may permit marketing authorization based on some endpoint (roughly speaking, a measurable study target) other than the ultimate clinical outcome in the full population of potential users.[5] Fourth, an alternate pathway may permit marketing authorization by exempting a product from regulation under the seemingly applicable category, or from the portion of the category for which marketing authorization is otherwise required.[6] Fifth, an alternate pathway may formally alter the marketing authorization standard applicable to the paradigm pathway, usually based on the limited size of the product's potential market.[7]

---

3. This type of alternate pathway is available for drugs and is known as a § 505(b)(2) application. *See infra* Part F.2.a.

4. The type of alternate pathway, involving similarity to a product already on the market, is available for generic drugs, generic animal drugs, biosimilar biological products, interchangeable biological products, substantially equivalent medical devices, and substantially equivalent tobacco products. *See infra* Parts F.2.a, F.2.d, and G.2.b.

5. This type of alternate pathway is, of course, only relevant to product categories for which the paradigm pathway requires proof of efficacy in humans. These stand-ins include proof of efficacy at satisfying a surrogate endpoint (an endpoint other than clinical efficacy, but reasonably likely to predict clinical efficacy) in humans, proof of efficacy on some clinical endpoint other than irreversible morbidity or mortality, proof of efficacy in animals, or proof of safety and efficacy (via a favorable risk-benefit ratio) in a limited subpopulation of potential users. *See infra* Parts F.2.b, F.2.c, and F.2.f.

6. The first form of this type of alternate pathway, exemption from the product category itself, is available for certain substances added to food. This pathway leads to exemption from the food additive definition. It is used for substances generally recognized as safe (GRAS) and substances in food-contact articles that fall below the threshold of regulation. *See infra* Part G.1.b. This second form of this type of alternative pathway is available for OTC drugs subject to a monograph and for medical devices exempted from premarket notification requirements. *See infra* Part F.2.e.

7. This type of alternate pathway is available for medical devices, *see infra* Part F.2.g, and animal drugs, *see infra* Parts F.2.h and F.2.i.

In addition to products that receive marketing authorization through existing paradigm and alternate pathways, there are also products that received marketing authorization either through a *former pathway* or a *grandfathering provision.* A former pathway is a pathway that once existed but is no longer available. In many cases, some products approved through these former pathways (when they were available) continue to have marketing authorization, even though those former pathways no longer exist. An example is the *GRAS affirmation process* for food additives. This pathway has been replaced by the *GRAS notification process,* but—unless explicitly withdrawn by FDA—individual affirmations made through the former pathway remain valid.

A grandfathering provision is a statutory or regulatory provision providing that certain existing products can continue to be marketed—despite a significant change in the applicable regulatory regime—unless or until that product's authorization is explicitly revoked by statute or regulation. Typically, these provisions are structured to be a temporary part of a transition to a new regulatory regime. They generally apply either to products explicitly approved under a prior regulatory regime or to products lawfully marketed in the United States prior to a particular date. Despite their structure as transitional provisions, many products remain on the market under a grandfathering provision for decades. Product categories with important grandfathering provisions still relevant today include food additives (prior-sanctioned substances), medical devices (products on market prior to May 28, 1976), HCT/Ps (human tissue recovered prior to May 25, 2005), and tobacco products (products on market prior to February 15, 2007).

The chart below summarizes the pathways addressed in Parts F, G, and H, which follow.[8]

8. An additional note on terminology. Some of the pathways mentioned themselves have pathway in the title, and some do not. This is an artifact of the way these pathways are typically described in FDA documents; this book adds "pathway" at the end in situations where it appears FDA typically does so. However, there is no formal significance to the presence or absence of the word "pathway" in the name used for it.

| Marketing Authorization: Standards and Pathways | | | | |
|---|---|---|---|---|
| Where Addressed in This Chapter | Standard of Review | Product Category | Paradigm Pathways | Alternate Pathways |
| Part F | Substantial evidence of safety and efficacy | Drugs (not including biologics) | NDA under FFDCA § 505 (b)(1) | 505(b)(2) application<br>ANDA under FFDCA § 505(j)<br>Accelerated approval under FFDCA § 506(c)<br>Animal rule under 21 CFR 314.610<br>LPAD under FFDCA § 506(c)(1)(A)<br>Request for inclusion in OTC monograph under FFDCA § 505H(b) |
| Part F | Substantial evidence of safety and efficacy | Animal drugs | NADA under FFDCA § 512 (b)(1) | ANADA under FFDCA § 512(b)(2)<br>Conditional approval under FFDCA § 571<br>Indexing under FFDCA § 572 |
| Part F | Safe, pure, and potent (plus substantial evidence of safety and efficacy) | Biologics | Biologics license application under PHSA § 351(a)(2)(C) | Biosimilar or interchangeable application under PHSA 351(k) |
| Part F | Reasonable assurance of safety and efficacy | Medical devices | PMA under FFDCA § 515(c) | PMN under FFDCA § 510(k)<br>Reclassification, under FFDCA § 513(e) or FFDCA § 513(f), to exempt from PMN<br>*De novo* classification, under FFDCA § 513(f)(2), to exempt from PMN<br>HDE under FFDCA § 520(m) |

| Where Addressed in This Chapter | Standard of Review | Product Category | Paradigm Pathways | Alternate Pathways |
|---|---|---|---|---|
| Part G | Safety only | Food additives | FFDCA § 409 food additives petition | GRAS process resulting in exemption from food additive definition under FFDCA § 201(s)<br>FFDCA § 409(h) notification for certain food-contact substances<br>Exemption for food contact substance as below threshold of regulation under 21 C.F.R. § 170.39 |
| Part G | Safety only | Color additives | Color additive petition under FFDCA § 721(b) | N/A |
| Part H | No marketing authorization required | Food; dietary supplements; cosmetics; medical devices exempt from premarket notification; over-the-counter drugs subject to monograph | N/A | N/A |

# F. Pathways to Market: Therapeutic Products

## 1. Paradigm Pathways

For drugs, animal drugs, devices, and biologics, the paradigm pathway to marketing authorization requires demonstration of safety and efficacy. However, the precise marketing-authorization requirements—and the type of evidence required to satisfy those requirements—vary among the different products.[9] Before moving to the content of these requirements, recall that FDA takes the position that all products qualifying as biologics under PHSA § 351(i) also qualify as drugs under

9. For drugs, animal drugs, and medical devices, the marketing-authorization standards are generally set out in statutory language indicating when FDA should decline to grant the relevant application. For biologics, the marketing-authorization standard is set out in language indicating when FDA should approve a biologics license application.

FFDCA § 201(g). Accordingly, biologics are subject to regulation under both the drug requirement and the biologics requirement.

Drugs, animal drugs, devices, and biologics must all be shown to be safe for their intended conditions of use. This requirement is in FFDCA §§ 505(d) for drugs, 512(d) for animal drugs, 515(d)(2)(A) for medical devices, and PHSA § 351(a)(2)(C) for biologics. One important difference is that, for animal drugs, the safety requirement also includes a requirement of safety in humans who may consume the animal or its products.

Additional differences among these products come in the phrasing—and content—of the relevant efficacy requirements. For drugs, FFDCA § 505(d)(5) requires "substantial evidence" that it "will have the effect it purports or is represented to have" under its labeled conditions of use. It then defines "substantial evidence" to require, among other things, "adequate and well-controlled investigations, including clinical investigations," to make the required showing of efficacy. FDA sets out its famously rigorous interpretation of the adequate and well-controlled investigations requirement in 21 C.F.R. § 314.126.

For animal drugs, FFDCA § 512(d)(1)(E) similarly requires "substantial evidence" that it "will have the effect it purports or is represented to have" under its labeled conditions of use. It also defines "substantial evidence" to require "adequate and well controlled investigations," but—unlike for drugs generally—it does not require clinical (i.e., human-subject) investigations. FDA sets out its interpretation of adequate and well-controlled investigations for animal drugs in 21 C.F.R. § 514.117.

For devices, FFDCA § 515(d)(2)(A) requires "reasonable assurance that the device is effective" under its labeled conditions of use. Procedures for satisfying this reasonable-assurance requirement are set out in 21 C.F.R. Part 814.

For biologics, the situation is more complicated, given that both drug and biologic rules apply. PHSA § 351(a)(2)(C) requires that biologics be "safe, pure, and potent." In 21 C.F.R. § 600.3, FDA defines these terms in a manner that overlaps to some degree with the FFDCA drug requirements. In particular, it defines "potency" as "ability or capacity . . . to effect a given result." However, for this potency standard, either "appropriate laboratory tests" or "adequately controlled clinical data" can be used to satisfy the § 600.3 potency requirement. Additionally, PHSA § 351(a)(2)(C) also requires that all relevant facilities "meet[] standards designed to assure that the biological product continues to be safe, pure, and potent." This was once interpreted to require separate licenses for biologics establishments and individual biological products. However, the two separate licenses have more recently been merged into a single *biologics license* covering both products and facilities.

At this point, please read (or review) the following excerpts in the statutory supplement:

- FFDCA § 505. New drugs. *Subsection (d) only.*
- FFDCA § 512. New animal drugs. *Subsection (d) only.*

- FFDCA § 515. Premarket approval [of medical devices]. *Subsection (d) only.*
- PHSA § 351. Regulation of biological products. *Subsection (a) only.*

## 2. Alternate Pathways

The paradigm pathways discussed above, however, are not the only pathways available for these products. The tensions you saw highlighted in the *Abigail Alliance* case—the more rigorous the premarket review, the fewer potentially life-saving products on the market—long pre-date that individual case. These tensions have led both Congress and FDA to develop new pathways that make it easier for FDA to approve certain categories of drugs, animal drugs, devices, and biological products.

### *a. Abbreviated Pathways*

For drugs, animal drugs, and biologics, Congress has established a set of abbreviated pathways. One of these involves reliance on a different data source than the paradigm pathway. The others involve a showing that the relevant product is sufficiently similar to an approved product that it can be expected to have roughly the same effect on the human body.

For small-molecule drugs, there are two abbreviated pathways—the *505(b)(2) pathway* and the *Abbreviated New Drug Application (ANDA)*.[10] Both were promulgated as part of the 1984 Hatch-Waxman Act. The 505(b)(2) pathway involves submission of a standard (rather than abbreviated) new drug application. It differs from the paradigm pathway because it involves reliance on studies the applicant does not own, and for which the applicant has not obtained a right of reference.[11] However, with 505(b)(2) application, FDA makes the same safety and efficacy determination as under the paradigm pathway.

An ANDA, by contrast, does not involve the type of safety and efficacy determination as involved in the paradigm pathway. To approve an ANDA, FDA must conclude that the product is bioequivalent to the reference product. Procedures are set out in 21 C.F.R. Part 314, Subpart C, and success results in the approval of a *generic drug.*

For animal drugs, the abbreviated pathway is the *Abbreviated New Animal Drug Application* (ANADA) under FFDCA § 512(c)(2). Procedures are set out 21 C.F.R. Part 514, and success results in the approval of a *generic animal drug.* For biologics, the abbreviated pathway is a *Biologics License Application* submitted for a biosimilar or interchangeable product under PHSA § 351(k) and 21 C.F.R. Part 601. Procedures

---

10. The 505(b)(2) pathway is an application under FFDCA§ 505(b)(2). The Abbreviated New Drug Application is an application under FFDCA § 505(j). FDA refers to both as types of "Abbreviated Approval Pathways." *See* FDA, Guidance for Industry: Determining Whether to Submit an ANDA or a 505(b)(2) Application 1 (May 2019).

11. FDA, Guidance for Industry: Determining Whether to Submit an ANDA or a 505(b)(2) Application 2 (May 2019).

are currently set in in guidance documents, and success results in approval of a *biosimilar product* or an *interchangeable product.*[12]

For all three, the key difference from the paradigm pathway is that the required showing is not one of safety and effectiveness. Instead, applicants must show that their product is absorbed by the body, and functions in the body, with the required degree of similarity to the previously approved drug, animal drug, or biological product to which it is being compared. For generic drugs, the standard is bioequivalence under FFDCA § 505(j)(2)(A)(iv) and 21 C.F.R. Parts 314 and 320.[13] For generic animal drugs, the standard is bioequivalence under FFDCA § 512(c) and 21 C.F.R. Part 514.

For biosimilar biological products, the standard is biosimilarity under PHSA § 351(k)(2). Roughly speaking, biosimilarity is designed as a concept analogous to the bioequivalence concept for generic drugs. However, it is structured differently—and given a separate name—to reflect the additional complexity of biological products. For interchangeable biological products, the standard is interchangeability under PHSA § 351(k)(4). This requires, roughly speaking, an even higher showing of similarity between the proposed interchangeable product and the reference product. These two additional demonstrations relate to a real-world difference in how biosimilar and interchangeable products can be used. A pharmacy can dispense a biosimilar product, instead of the reference product, only with the explicit approval of the prescribing health-care provider. But, under PHSA 351(i)(3), a pharmacist may substitute an interchangeable product for the reference product "without the intervention of the health care provider who prescribed the reference product."

At this point, please read (or review) the following excerpts in the statutory supplement:

- FFDCA § 505. New drugs. *Subsection (j) only.*
- FFDCA § 351. Regulation of biological products. *Subsection (k) only.*

### *b. Accelerated Pathways*

For drugs and biologics intended to treat a "serious or life-threatening disease or condition," FFDCA § 506(c) provides for an *accelerated approval* pathway. This pathway permits approval of a drug or biologic based an endpoint—roughly speaking, a measurable study target—other than the long-term clinical outcome. FFDCA § 506(c)(1)(A) permits accelerated approval based on two alternative endpoints. The first is a "a surrogate endpoint that is reasonably likely to predict clinical benefit,"

12. These are the two biologics analogues of "generic" drugs. However, the term "generic" is not used in relation to biologics.

13. 21 C.F.R. § 314.3 defines bioequivalence as "absence of a significant difference in the rate and extent to which the active ingredient or active moiety . . . becomes available at the site of drug action when administered at the same molar dose under similar conditions in an appropriately designed study." 21 C.F.R. Part 320 sets out, in detail, procedures for determining bioequivalence.

and the second is "clinical endpoint that can be measured earlier than irreversible morbidity or mortality." As part of a decision to grant accelerated approval, FFDCA § 506(c)(2) provides that approval can be made subject to post-approval study requirements and requirements for submission of promotional materials to FDA. After an accelerated approval has been granted, FFDCA § 506(c)(3) provides for several circumstances permitting FDA to withdraw the approval using "expedited procedures."

Procedures for accelerated approval of drugs are set out in 21 C.F.R. Part 314, Subpart H. Procedures for accelerated approval of biologics are set out in 21 C.F.R. Part 601, Subpart E.

At this point, please read (or review) the following excerpts in the statutory supplement:

- FFDCA § 506. Expedited approval of drugs for serious or life-threatening diseases or conditions. *Subsection (c) only.*

### *c. Human Efficacy Studies Not Ethical or Feasible (Animal Rule)*

FDA has established special procedures applicable to proof of efficacy for drugs and biologics intended to treat certain conditions for which *human efficacy studies are not ethical or feasible.* These are set out in 21 C.F.R. Part 314, Subpart I, for drugs and in 21 C.F.R. Part 601, Subpart H, for biologics. These two sets of procedures have come to be known, collectively, as the *animal rule.*[14] These procedures permit proof of efficacy (but not safety) based on "evidence of effectiveness from studies in animals." 21 C.F.R. Part 314.610 (drugs); 21 C.F.R. Part 601.91 (biologics).

Both sets of regulations apply only to products intended to treat "serious or life-threatening conditions caused by exposure to lethal or permanently disabling toxic biological, chemical, radiological, or nuclear substance." 21 C.F.R. § 314.600 (drugs); 21 C.F.R. § 601.90 (biologics). Both sets of regulations are limited to situations where three conditions apply. First, FDA must conclude that human-volunteer trials would not ethical because they would require "deliberately expos[ing] human volunteers to a lethal or permanently disabling toxic biological, chemical, radiological, or nuclear substance." 21 C.F.R. § 314.600 (drugs); 21 C.F.R. § 601.90 (biologics). Second, FDA must conclude that "field trials to study the product's efficacy after an accidental or hostile exposure have not been feasible." 21 C.F.R. § 314.600 (drugs); 21 C.F.R. § 601.90 (biologics). Third, FDA must conclude that it would not be possible to approve the product based on "efficacy standards described elsewhere in FDA's regulations (e.g., accelerated approval based on surrogate markers or clinical endpoints other than survival or irreversible morbidity)." 21 C.F.R. § 314.600 (drugs); 21 C.F.R. § 601.90 (biologics).

---

14. *See generally* FDA, Guidance for Industry: Product Development under the Animal Rule (Oct. 2015).

Both sets of procedures contain requirements for postmarketing studies if an "exigency arises" in which they become feasible. 21 C.F.R. § 314.610(b)(1) (drugs); 21 C.F.R. § 601.91(b)(1) (biologics). Both require patient labeling disclosing that the product was approved "based on efficacy studies conducted in animals alone." 21 C.F.R. § 314.610(b)(3) (drugs); 21 C.F.R. § 601.91(b)(3). And both require FDA to determine whether the products "can be safely used only if distribution or use is restricted," and—if so—require FDA to impose such restrictions. 21 C.F.R. § 314.610(b)(2) (drugs); 21 C.F.R. § 601.91(b)(2).

At this point, please read (or review) the following excerpts in the statutory supplement:

- FFDCA § 505. New drugs. *Subsection (d) only.*
- 21 C.F.R. §§ 314.600, 314.610, 314.650 (all are from Part 314, Subpart I, referenced above).
- 21 C.F.R. §§ 601.90, 601.91, 601.95 (all are from Part 601, Subpart H, referenced above).

### *d. Premarket Notification/510(k) Pathway*

For medical devices, Congress and FDA have established a pathway that provides access to products deemed to be *substantially equivalent* to a *predicate device.*[15] This pathway is of particular importance. Most medical devices on the market today have been authorized either through this substantial equivalence process or through an exemption from this process (and, thus, from any marketing authorization requirement).[16] The process is often described as either *premarket notification (PMN)* or the *510(k) pathway.*

This pathway is set out most directly in 21 C.F.R. Part 807, Subpart E. The notification requirement is based on statutory authority set out in FFDCA § 510(k). This provision requires that those seeking to introduce a medical device to the U.S. market report certain information to FDA at least 90 days beforehand. The content of the substantial equivalence requirement is based on statutory authority in FFDCA § 513(i).

Section 513(i) sets out the circumstances when a device will be substantially equivalent to a predicate device. To qualify as substantially equivalent, a device must first have "the same intended use as the predicate device." If it has the same intended use, the question of substantial equivalence turns on the relationship between the device's "technological characteristics" and those of the predicate device.

---

15. A predicate device is a device that is already on the market. A predicate device can be one that reached the market through the paradigm pathway (premarket approval), through this alternate pathway (premarket notification), through another alternate pathway (de novo classification), or through grandfathering.

16. *See* Part G, *infra.*

FFDCA § 513(i)(1)(A)(i) provides that if the device has the "same intended use" and the "same technological characteristics" as the predicate device, this is sufficient for substantial equivalence. However, if the device has "difference technological characteristics," FFDCA § 513(i)(1)(A)(ii) sets out a more complicated test.[17] For a device with different technological characteristics, the person making the submission must demonstrate both that the device is "as safe and effective as a legally marketed device" and that it "does not raise different questions of safety and effectiveness than the predicate device." In evaluating devices with different technological characteristics, FDA is permitted to require "appropriate clinical or scientific data" to demonstrate substantial equivalence.[18]

We will encounter a substantial-equivalence-based premarket notification process again shortly.[19] When Congress gave FDA authority over tobacco products in 2009, it adopted a combination of a premarket approval and premarket notification processes similar to those applicable to tobacco products. The key difference, however, is the substantive approval standard. Tobacco products are not granted marketing authorization on grounds of safety (a requirement that perhaps all would fail) or efficacy. Instead, FFDCA § 910(c)(2)(A) sets the paradigm standard for tobacco products as a showing that "permitting such tobacco product to be marketed would be appropriate for the protection of the public health."

At this point, please read (or review) the following excerpts in the statutory supplement:

- FFDCA § 510. Registration of producers of drugs or devices. *Subsection (k) only.*
- FFDCA § 513. Classification of devices intended for human use. *Subsection (i) only.*

### *e. Determination That a Drug or Device Falls into a Subset for Which No Marketing Authorization Is Required*

As set out in Part H, below, there are certain subsets of drugs and devices for which no marketing authorization is required. This means that, for certain drugs and devices, one pathway to market is to request that FDA determine that the drug or device in question falls within one of these subsets. For drugs, the most significant subset is those over-the-counter (OTC) drugs that comply with an *OTC drug monograph*—a regulation setting out the conditions under which particular drugs

---

17. FFDCA § 513(i)(1)(B) defines "different technological characteristics" quite broadly as "a significant change in the materials, design, energy source, or other features of the device from those of the predicate device."

18. FDA has also issued guidance suggesting that it is open to premarket notification submissions that seek to demonstrate something closer to what is required in the paradigm pathway—a reasonable assurance of overall safety and effectiveness (rather than demonstrating equivalence to a predicate device). *See, e.g.*, FDA, Guidance for Industry and the Food & Drug Administration: Safety and Performance Based Pathway (Sep 20, 2019).

19. *See infra* Part G.2.b.

are generally recognized as safe and effective (GRASE). For devices, the most significant subset is those devices FDA has classified as devices *exempt from premarket notification requirements.*

*OTC Drugs Subject to Monograph*

A process is available for requesting inclusion of a drug in an OTC drug monograph. Products meeting the criteria set out in an OTC drug monograph are GRASE and not misbranded. They are accordingly, once included in a monograph, no longer subject to marketing authorization.

The OTC monograph process was, until recently, a cumbersome process requiring FDA to engage in notice-and-comment rulemaking. In March 2020, Congress included a major revision of the OTC drug monograph system as part of the Coronavirus Aid, Relief, and Economic Security (CARES) Act.[20] This created a new FFDCA section, FFDCA § 505H, which sets out a new statutory structure for FDA regulation of over-the-counter drugs.[21]

FFDCA § 505H(a) retains the existing monograph system. However, FFDCA §§ 505H(b) and 505H(p) make monograph revision much easier for FDA by permitting the agency to promulgate, revise, or repeal monographs through administrative orders rather than traditional notice-and-comment rulemaking.[22] FFDCA 505H(b) provides for a process by which companies can request that FDA determine that that a particular combination of active and inactive drug ingredients is GRASE. Once FDA makes such a GRASE determination, and incorporates it into a monograph, numerous drugs based on that combination of ingredients (and meeting the other conditions of the monograph) may be marketed without any further marketing authorization.

At this point, please read (or review) the following excerpts in the statutory supplement:

- FFDCA § 505H. Regulation of certain nonprescription drugs that are marketed without an approved drug application. *Subsections (a), (b), and (f) only.*

*Medical Devices Exempt from Premarket Notification*

Medical devices are divided into three classes: Class I, Class II, and Class III.[23] Class III devices are generally subject to the paradigm pathway for medical devices, premarket approval. But Class I and Class II devices can either be subject to

---

20. CARES Act, Pub. L. No. 116-136, 134 Stat. 281 (March 27, 2020), §§ 3851–3855.

21. To fund this new approach to OTC drug regulation, a separate portion of the CARES Act established a new user fee program for over-the-counter drugs. *See* CARES Act §§ 3861–3862.

22. FFDCA 505H(b) includes its own system for public comment on proposed monograph revisions, but it appears designed to be much less extensive than traditional notice-and-comment rulemaking. *See generally* FFDCA § 505H(b).

23. Medical device classification is addressed in more detail in Chapter 12, Part D, Medical Device Classification and Review.

premarket notification (the pathway discussed in Part F.2.d, *supra*) or exempt from premarket notification.

The decision on exemption from premarket notification is made as part of the device classification process. This means that convincing FDA to reclassify a device type to the exempt version of Class I or Class II is, in effect, a pathway to market. The primary FFDCA provision on medical device classification is FFDCA § 513, "Classification of devices intended for human use."

Within this statutory provision, FFDCA § 513(g) provides for an FDA determination as to whether such an exemption applies. FFDCA § 513(e) provides for reclassification "[b]ased on new information respecting a device." FFDCA § 513(f) provides for "[i]nitial classification and reclassification" of devices introduced into the market after the effective date of the Medical Device Amendments of 1976. And FFDCA § 513(f)(2) permits *de novo classification*[24] of a device type in a situation where there is "no legally marketed device upon which to base a determination of substantial equivalence."

At this point, please read (or review) the following excerpts in the statutory supplement:

- FFDCA § 513. Classification of devices intended for human use. *Subsections (e), (f), and (g) only.*

### *f. Limited Population Pathway for Antibacterial and Antifungal Drugs (LPAD)*

For certain antibacterial and antifungal drugs and biologics, FFDCA § 506(h) permits FDA to approve a product based on a "favorable risk-benefit profile" in a limited population. This is known as the *limited population pathway for antibacterial and antifungal drugs* (LPAD).

FFDCA § 506(h)(1)(A) makes this limited population pathway available only for drugs intended to treat "a serious or life-threatening infection in a limited population of patients with unmet needs." It requires that the drug meet the safety and effectiveness standard applicable in the paradigm pathway (FFDCA 505(d) for drugs; FFDCA § 351(a) for biologics). However, it permits that assessment to be based on a smaller group of potential users, "notwithstanding a lack of evidence to fully establish a favorable benefit-risk profile in a population that is broader than the intended limited population." FFDCA § 506(h)(2).

In August 2020, FDA issued final guidance implementing the LPAD pathway (the "LPAD Guidance").[25] In the LPAD Guidance, FDA set out its view that the LPAD

---

24. *See* FDA, Guidance for Industry and FDA Staff: De Novo Classification Process (Evaluation of Automatic Class III Designation) (Oct. 30, 2017).

25. FDA, Guidance for Industry: Limited Population Pathway for Antibacterial and Antifungal Drugs (August 2020).

Pathway is available only for situations where the relevant tests are designed to show safety and efficacy in a subset of the broader population of patients who suffer from the relevant disease. The Agency generally does not view the LPAD Pathway as appropriate for situations where the disease itself is rare, and the relevant limited population would be the full set of patients who suffer from the disease. In other words, the key to eligibility for the LPAD pathway is the ability to demonstrate safety and efficacy in a limited subset of users, but not in the larger population.

### *g. Exemption from Efficacy Requirement (Humanitarian Device Exemption)*

For medical devices for use in diagnosing or treating rare diseases or conditions, FFDCA § 520(m) provides for the *humanitarian device exemption* (HDE). This pathway entirely exempts qualifying devices from the statute's efficacy requirements. However, devices that receive this exemption—known as *humanitarian use devices*—may only be used in facilities with an Institutional Review Board (IRB), and generally only with advance IRB approval. FFDCA § 520(m)(4). Except in certain situations involving pediatric patients, they may not be sold for more than "the costs of research and development, fabrication, and distribution." FFDCA § 520(m)(3).

For the HDE to apply, three conditions must be met. First, the relevant device must be "designed to treat or diagnose a disease or condition that affects not more than 8,000 individuals in the United States." FFDCA § 520(m)(2)(A). Second, FDA must determine that the relevant device would not be available without an exemption and that "no comparable device" is currently available. FFDCA § 520(m)(2)(B). Third, FDA must determine that "the device will not expose patients to an unreasonable or significant risk of illness or injury" and that the benefits of device use outweigh its risks. FFDCA § 520(m)(2)(C).

Procedures for the HDE are set out in 21 C.F.R. Part 814, Subpart H.

At this point, please read (or review) the following excerpts in the statutory supplement:

- FFDCA § 520. General provisions respecting control of devices intended for human use. *Subsection (m) only.*

### *h. Conditional Approval (Animal Drugs Only)*

FFDCA § 571 sets out a pathway permitting the agency to *conditionally approve* certain animal drugs. Conditional approval is applicable to new animal drugs for minor species, for minor uses in major species, and for certain uses in major species.[26] Conditional approval permits marketing based on a finding of safety, along

26. The terms "major use," "minor species," and "minor use" are defined in FFDCA § 201(nn), (oo), and (pp), respectively. For major uses in major species, two additional requirements must be met. First, the animal drug must either be "intended to treat a serious or life-threatening disease or condition" or be for a use that that "addresses an unmet animal or human health need."

with a "reasonable expectation" of efficacy, FFDCA § 571(c). This one-year period is renewable up to five times. FFDCA § 571(d). During this limited marketing period, the holder of the approval is expected to "conduct additional investigations to meet the requirements for the full demonstration of effectiveness." FFDCA § 571(a)(2).

Procedures for conditional approval are set out in 21 C.F.R. Part 516, Subpart B.

At this point, please read (or review) the following excerpts in the statutory supplement:

- FFDCA § 571. Conditional approval of new animal drugs for minor use and minor species and certain new animal drugs.

### *i. Indexing (Animal Drugs Only)*

FFDCA § 572 provides for legal marketing of certain explicitly unapproved, but *indexed*, animal drugs. This form of marketing authorization is limited to two types of drugs. First, FFDCA § 572(a)(1)(A) permits indexing for certain "minor species" unlikely to be "consumed by humans or food-producing animals." Second, FFDCA § 572(a)(1)(B) permits indexing—after a demonstration of safety for humans—for intended uses in "early, non-food life stage of a food-producing minor species" in a "hatchery, tank, pond, or other similar contained man-made structure."

At this point, please read (or review) the following excerpts in the statutory supplement:

- FFDCA § 572. Index of legally marketed unapproved new animal drugs for minor species.

## G. Pathways to Market: Nontherapeutic Products

### 1. Safety Only

*Food and Color Additives*

Two product categories require marketing authorization based only on a finding of safety. These are food and color additives. There are many similarities between these two categories, but also some important differences.

First, note some important similarities. Both are categories of products intended for addition to other FDA-regulated products. Both are subject to a *Delaney Clause*, imposing rigorous anti-carcinogen requirements in the marketing authorization process. FDA approves both based on a requirement of safety, and indicates approval by publication of a regulation in the Federal Register amending the relevant provisions of the C.F.R. This last similarity means that existing approvals for both can

FFDCA § 571(a)(1)(ii)(I). Second, FDA must determine that, for this intended use, "demonstration of effectiveness would require a complex or particularly difficult study or studies." FFDCA § 571(a)(1)(ii)(II).

be found through the simple process of checking the relevant portion of the C.F.R., portions of which are detailed lists of existing approvals.

However, there are also important differences between food and color additives. The two most important are these: First, food additives and color additives are governed by different statutory authorities located in different "chapters" of the statute. FFDCA § 409, located in Chapter IV of the statutes, governs food additives. FFDCA § 721, located in chapter VII of the statute, governs color additives.[27] Second, food additives can only be used in food, while color additives can be used in food, drugs, cosmetics, and medical devices. FDA approves color additives separately for use in each of these categories.

### *a. Paradigm Pathways*

*Food Additives*

For food additives, there is a single paradigm pathway that leads to marketing authorization. This takes place through formal approval of a food additive as safe for its intended use. There are also three alternate pathways: a notification process for substances generally recognized as safe (leading to exemption from the FFDCA § 201(s) definition of a food additive); a notification process for certain food-contact substances under FFDCA § 409(h); and a process for requesting exemption from regulation as a food additive for certain food contact substances used at levels below the threshold of regulation under 21 C.F.R. § 170.39.

The paradigm pathway for food additives is the food additive petition, set out in FFDCA § 409(b). Procedures for the food additive petition are set out in FFDCA § 409(c), 21 C.F.R. Part 171 (for food additives generally) and 21 C.F.R. Part 571 (for animal food additives). This is a regulatory process that culminates in the issuance or denial of a final rule in the Federal Register. The rule either amends, or declines to amend, the relevant C.F.R. provisions. A similar proceeding can also be commenced on FDA's initiative under FFDCA § 409(d).

27. As a consequence, different adulteration and misbranding provisions apply to food additives and color additives. Food additives are subject to the adulteration and misbranding provisions of Chapter IV—FFDCA §§ 402 and 403. Products containing color additives are subject to the adulteration and misbranding provisions relevant to the product category in which they are used—FFDCA §§ 402 and 403 for food; FFDCA §§ 501 and 502 for drugs and devices; and FFDCA §§ 601 and 602 for cosmetics.

*Color Additives*

For color additives, there is a single paradigm pathway to marketing authorization. This takes place through formal approval, or "listing," of a color additive as safe for its intended use pursuant to FFDCA § 721(b). FDA lists color additives separately for use on food, drugs, cosmetics, and medical devices. Listing procedures, which can be initiated by a person, entity, or FDA, are set out in FFDCA §§ 721(b) and 721(d), and in 21 C.F.R. Part 71.

Listed color additives are set out in 21 C.F.R. Parts 73–74. A relatively small number of color additives that were in use prior to the Color Additives Amendment of 1960 remain provisionally listed (another type of grandfathering provision) in 21 C.F.R. Parts 81–82.

### *b. Alternate Pathways*

*Food Additives*

There are three alternate pathways for food additives. The first, and most substantively important, alternate pathway derives from the definition of "food additive" in FFDCA § 201(s). This definition explicitly excludes substances "generally recognized . . . as . . . safe" (GRAS) from the definition of food additive. Procedures for notifying FDA of a GRAS determination are set out in 21 C.F.R. Part 170, Subpart E (for food additives generally) and 21 C.F.R. Part 570, Subpart E (for animal food additives).

The second alternate pathway is notification of a determination that a food-contact substance is safe under FFDCA § 409(h). Procedures for the FFDCA § 409(h) notification process are set out in 21 C.F.R. Part 170, Subpart D.

The third alternate pathway is a process for requesting that FDA determine that potential dietary exposure resulting from a food-contact substance migrating to food is at such a low level that it is below the threshold of regulation. Procedures for this process are set out in 21 C.F.R. § 170.39.

In addition to food additives permitted under current procedures, there are two other categories of substances that can be used in food without marketing authorization. These are substances explicitly affirmed by the agency as GRAS (under a former pathway that has since been withdrawn in favor of GRAS notification) and substances excluded from the § 201(s) definition as *prior-sanctioned substances.* Prior-sanctioned substances—authorized through a grandfathering provision—are substances approved for food use by either USDA or FDA prior to the 1958 Food Additives Amendments. There are also some food additives approved on an interim basis.

These various pathways have resulted in the following regulations listing substances that can be used in food. Approved food additives are listed in 21 C.F.R. Parts 172–179 (for food additives generally) and Parts 573 and 579 (for animal food additives). Food additives approved on an interim basis are listed in 21 C.F.R.

Part 180. Substances that FDA has explicitly determined to be GRAS are set out in 21 C.F.R. Parts 182, 184, and 186 (for food additives generally) and Parts 582 and 584 (for animal food additives). Prior-sanctioned substances are set out in 21 C.F.R. Part 171. Substances explicitly prohibited from use in food are set out in 21 C.F.R. Part 189 (for food additives generally) and Part 589 (for animal food additives).

*Color Additives*

There are no alternate pathways for color additives

---

At this point, please read (or review) the following excerpts in the statutory supplement with respect to food additives:

- FFDCA § 201. Definitions; generally. *Subsection (s) only.*
- FFDCA § 409. Food additives. *Subsections (a)(2), (b), (c)(1), (c)(3), (d), and (h) only.*

At this point, please read (or review) the following excerpts in the statutory supplement with respect to color additives:

- FFDCA § 201. Definitions; generally. *Subsection (t) only.*
- FFDCA § 721. Color additives. *Subsections (a)(1)(A) and (b)(1), (b)(2), (b)(5)(A) only.*

## 2. Protection of the Public Health

For tobacco products, marketing authorization requirements apply only to products not covered by the grandfathering provision of FFDCA § 910(a)(1). This provision explicitly exempts products commercially marketed in the United States "as of February 15, 2007," and unmodified since that time, from its definition of "new tobacco product."[28]

Accordingly, a tobacco product meeting one of two criteria qualifies as a *new tobacco product*. First, FFDCA § 910(a)(1)(A) provides that it is a new tobacco product if it was "not commercially marketed in the United States as of February 15, 2007." Second, FFDCA § 910(a)(1)(B) provides that it is a new tobacco product if it is "any modification" of a tobacco product that was commercially marketed in the United States on that date. FFDCA § 910(a)(1)(B) explicitly provides that "any modification" includes "a change in design, any component, any part, or any constituent,

---

28. FDA has set out, in guidance, its view that only products commercially marketed in the United States *on that precise date* are covered by this grandfathering provision. FDA, Guidance for Industry: Establishing That a Tobacco Product Was Commercially Marketed in the United States as of February 15, 2007 (Sep. 2014) ("If your tobacco product had been commercially marketed in the United States before February 15, 2007, but was not commercially marketed on that date, it is not a grandfathered product . . . .").

including a smoke constituent, or in the content, delivery or form of nicotine, or any other additive or ingredient."

For new tobacco products, there is one paradigm pathway, the *premarket tobacco product application* (PMTA). There is also a related, paradigm-style process for modified risk claims. This must be filed for modified risk products in addition to the PMTA. There are two alternate pathways, the *substantial equivalence pathway* and a pathway providing for *exemption from substantial equivalence.*

### a. Paradigm Pathway

For a *new tobacco product*, the paradigm pathway is the PMTA. This pathway requires neither a showing of safety nor a showing of efficacy. Instead, FFDCA § 910(c)(2) requires FDA to conclude that permitting marketing of the tobacco product at issue would be "appropriate for the protection of the public health." In assessing whether this standard is met, FFDCA § 910(c)(4) requires FDA to consider "risks and benefits to the population as a whole, including users and nonusers of the tobacco product." FFDCA § 910(c)(4). This risk-benefit calculation must "tak[e] into account" the effect it will have on both the possibility that "existing users . . . will stop using" and that "those who do not use . . . will start using" tobacco products. FFDCA § 910(c)(4).

A similar paradigm process applies to *modified-risk tobacco products*. However, this is less a traditional pathway to market than a means for obtaining approval to make risk-reduction claims for the product. A modified-risk tobacco product must also receive general marketing authorization (i.e., of the product without the modified-risk claim) through one of the other pathways. A modified-risk application may be filed concurrently with a PMTA or substantial equivalence application.

FFDCA § 911(b) defines "modified risk tobacco product" as "any tobacco product that is sold or distributed for use to reduce harm or the risk of tobacco-related disease associated with commercially marketed tobacco products." FFDCA § 911(g) provides that FDA may issue a marketing order for an MRTP if it determines that the product, "as it is actually used by consumers," will do two things. First, it must "significantly reduce harm and the risk of tobacco-related disease to individual tobacco users." FFDCA § 911(g)(1)(A). Second, it must "benefit the health of the population as a whole taking into account both users of tobacco products and persons who do not currently use tobacco products." FFDCA § 911(g)(1)(B).

At this point, please read (or review) the following excerpts in the statutory supplement:

- FFDCA § 910. Application for review of certain tobacco products. *Subsections (a)–(c) only.*
- FFDCA § 911. Modified risk tobacco products.

### *b. Alternate Pathways*

There are two alternate pathways for tobacco products. The first is a substantial equivalence pathway; the second is a pathway providing for exemption from substantial equivalence requirements.

*Substantial Equivalence Pathway*

FFDCA § 910(a)(2)(A)(i) provides that premarket review is not required for a tobacco product that is "substantially equivalent" to a tobacco product marketed in the United States as of February 15, 2007. FFDCA § 910(a)(3)(A) provides for two types of tobacco products that qualify as substantially equivalent. First, FFDCA § 910(a)(3)(A)(i) provides that a tobacco product with "the same characteristics as the predicate tobacco product" qualifies as substantially equivalent. Second, FFDCA § 910(a)(3)(A)(ii) provides that a tobacco product with "different characteristics" can qualify as substantially equivalent if "the information submitted contains information ... that demonstrates that it is not appropriate to regulate the product under this section because the product does not raise different questions of public health."[29] For purposes of the substantial equivalence process, FFDCA § 910(a)(3)(B) defines "characteristics" as "materials, ingredients, design, composition, heating source, or other features of a tobacco product."

*Exemption from Substantial Equivalence (and Premarket Review)*

FFDCA § 910(a)(2)(A)(ii) provides that neither premarket review, nor substantial equivalence, is required for certain products explicitly exempted by FDA from the FFDCA § 910(a)(2)(A)(i) substantial equivalence requirement. However, this exemption is strictly limited. FFDCA § 905(j)(3) provides that it applies only to relatively minor minification of existing products. It can be used only for "products that are modified by adding or deleting a tobacco additive, or increasing or decreasing the quantity of an existing tobacco additive." FFDCA § 905(j)(3). To grant this exemption, FDA must conclude that it is only a "minor modification," that a substantial equivalence report "is not necessary" to ensure appropriate "protection of the public health," and that the proposed exemption is "otherwise appropriate."

FDA has not yet promulgated detailed regulations setting out procedures for the premarket tobacco product application, substantial equivalence application, or modified risk tobacco product application. However, 21 C.F.R. § 1107 sets out procedures for requesting exemption from the substantial equivalence requirements, and 21 C.F.R. § 1105.10 sets out the circumstances under which FDA will refuse to accept the various tobacco product applications for review.

At this point, please read (or review) the following excerpts in the statutory supplement:

---

29. This can include a requirement for "clinical data if deemed necessary" by FDA. FFDCA § 910(a)(3)(A)(ii).

- FFDCA § 905. Annual registration. *Subsection (j) only.*
- FFDCA § 910. Application for review of certain tobacco products. *Subsection (a)(3) only.*

## H. No Marketing Authorization Required: Therapeutic and Nontherapeutic Products

Finally, there are some product categories, and some subsets within product categories, for which no marketing authorization is required. First, three product categories and one subset within a product category are simply not subject to any marketing authorization requirement. The three product categories are food, dietary supplements, and cosmetics; the subset within a product category consists of those HCT/Ps regulated solely as HCT/Ps (and not also regulated as drugs, devices, biologics, or combination products). Second, important subsets within two product categories are exempted from otherwise-applicable marketing authorization requirements. These are over-the-counter (OTC) drugs subject to an OTC drug monograph and medical devices FDA has determined to be exempt from premarket notification.

For the first group, those not subject to any marketing authorization requirement, pathways to market are not relevant. Products in these categories must simply comply with the background regulatory requirements applicable to the relevant product category. These background requirements are addressed in the next chapter of this casebook.

For the second group, those that are subsets within product categories otherwise subject to marketing authorization requirements, pathways still retain some relevance. In these circumstances, no pathway is necessary for products that fall into an existing exemption. A pathway is necessary only for products that are candidates for (but not yet included in) the relevant exemption.[30]

### 1. Products Not Subject to Any Marketing Authorization Requirement

*Food*

No marketing authorization is required for food. However, some label claims for food do require authorization by FDA. These are addressed in Chapter 9—Label Claims for Food and Dietary Supplements.

30. The OTC monograph process plays this role for OTC drugs and the device classification process plays this role for medical devices. *See* Part F.2.e., *supra*.

*Dietary Supplements*

No marketing authorization is required for dietary supplements. However, for supplements containing a new dietary ingredient (one not marketed in the United States prior to October 15, 1994), FFDCA § 413(a)(2) requires notification to FDA of the reasons the manufacturer or distributor has concluded that the new dietary ingredient is safe. This notification must be made 75 days before marketing is expected to begin. Procedures for this notification are set out in 21 C.F.R. Part 190.

*Cosmetics*

No marketing authorization is required for cosmetics. However, many components of cosmetics—but not the finished cosmetics themselves—are regulated as color additives.

*Products Regulated Solely As HCT/Ps*

No marketing authorization is required for products regulated solely as HCT/Ps under PHSA § 361, such as traditional human tissues harvested for use in surgical procedures. However, some products regulated as HCT/Ps are also are also regulated as drugs, biologics, devices, or combination products. For HCT/Ps also regulated under one or more of those other product categories, the marketing authorization requirements of the relevant other categories apply.

## 2. Products Exempted from Otherwise-Applicable Marketing Authorization Requirements

*Over-the-Counter Drugs Subject to an OTC Drug Monograph*

FDA has determined that OTC drugs prepared using particular combinations of active and inactive ingredients are GRASE (and, accordingly, do not meet the FFDCA § 201(p) definition of "new drug" that triggers marketing authorization requirements). These combinations of ingredients qualifying as GRASE are found in a series of regulations known as *OTC drug monographs* and set out in 21 C.F.R. Parts 331–358. You will find a chart of these OTC drug monographs in the "Outline of Regulatory Regime" section of Chapter 10 of this book.

*Certain Low-Risk Medical Devices*

FDA has exempted many low-risk medical device types from premarket notification requirements. These exemptions are set out in individual device classification regulations, 21 C.F.R. Parts 862–892.[31] You will find a chart of these device classification regulations in the "Outline of Regulatory Regime" section of Chapter 12 of this book.

---

31. Examples of such low-risk devices include the "manual toothbrush," 21 C.F.R. § 872.6855, "tongue depressor," 21 C.F.R. § 880.6230, and "cane," 21 C.F.R. § 890.3075.

# I. The Designations

## 1. Description

Now that you are familiar with the pathways to marketing authorization, we will turn to a separate topic: the "designations."

FDA now has numerous "designations" to speed the approval process or provide development incentives for medical products that are intended to treat a serious condition and meet certain other considerations. *None of these designations is a pathway to marketing authorization.* Instead, you can think of these as flags that can be attached to a particular application to have it treated more advantageously by FDA either during or after its trip along the relevant marketing authorization pathway.

This book divides these designations into three types: *review clock designations, review assistance designations*, and *market exclusivity designations.* The first type, review clock designations, provide for a commitment by FDA to try to issue a complete response to a marketing authorization request more rapidly than it would for a typical product. The second type, review assistance designations, provide for FDA assistance in navigating the relevant marketing authorization pathway. The third type, market exclusivity designations, provide for an award—a period of market exclusivity for the approved product—as an incentive for a successful application.

There is currently only one review-clock designation: *priority review.* There are four review assistance designations: *fast track, breakthrough therapy, breakthrough device*, and *regenerative medicine advanced therapy* (RMAT). There are three market exclusivity designations: *orphan drug designation, qualified infectious disease product (QIDP) designation*, and *competitive generic therapy (CGT) designation.*[32]

### *a. Review Clock Designations*

As noted above, priority review is currently the only review clock designation. The priority review process developed in negotiations between Congress and FDA, but is now referenced by statute in various provisions providing for transferable priority review vouchers.

On its website, FDA describes the priority review process as follows:[33]

> Prior to approval, each drug marketed in the United States must go through a detailed FDA review process. In 1992, under the Prescription Drug User Fee Act (PDUFA), FDA agreed to specific goals for improving the drug review time and created a two-tiered system of review times—*Standard Review* and *Priority Review.* A Priority Review designation means FDA's

32. As discussed further below, QIDP designation also includes both review-clock and review-assistance elements.

33. FDA Website, Priority Review, https://www.fda.gov/patients/fast-track-breakthrough-therapy-accelerated-approval-priority-review/priority-review (last visited June 12, 2020).

goal is to take action on an application within 6 months (compared to 10 months under standard review).

A *Priority Review* designation will direct overall attention and resources to the evaluation of applications for drugs that, if approved, would be significant improvements in the safety or effectiveness of the treatment, diagnosis, or prevention of serious conditions when compared to standard applications.

Significant improvement may be demonstrated by the following examples:

- evidence of increased effectiveness in treatment, prevention, or diagnosis of condition;
- elimination or substantial reduction of a treatment-limiting drug reaction;
- documented enhancement of patient compliance that is expected to lead to an improvement in serious outcomes; or
- evidence of safety and effectiveness in a new subpopulation.

FDA decides on the review designation for every application. However, an applicant may expressly request priority review as described in the *Guidance for Industry Expedited Programs for Serious Conditions—Drugs and Biologics.* It does not affect the length of the clinical trial period. FDA informs the applicant of a Priority Review designation within 60 days of the receipt of the original BLA, NDA, or efficacy supplement. Designation of a drug as "Priority" does not alter the scientific/medical standard for approval or the quality of evidence necessary.

Since FDA's initial development of priority review, Congress has added numerous provisions to the FFDCA that address eligibility for priority review.[34] Congress has also established a number of programs that provide a *priority review voucher* for use in a future application for approval of new drug or biologic.[35] These vouchers may be transferred or sold.

34. *See, e.g.*, FFDCA § 506(g)(6)(A) (stating that RMATs may be "eligible for priority review"); 21 U.S.C. 356-1 (indicating that a drug or biologic designated as a "priority countermeasure" will be "considered a priority drug or biological product for purposes of performance goals for priority drugs or biological products agreed to by the Commissioner of Food and Drugs"); FFDCA § 515C (permitting designation of devices for "expedited development and priority review," and setting out some of the benefits of that designation).

35. *See, e.g.*, FFDCA § 524 (voucher granted in return for successful application for new drug to treat certain tropical diseases); FFDCA § 524A (voucher granted in return for successful application for drug designated as "qualified infectious disease product"); FFDCA § 529 (voucher granted in return for successful application for a drug to treat a "rare pediatric disease"); FFDCA § 565A (voucher granted in return for successful application for "material threat medical countermeasure").

### *b. Review Assistance Designations*

Four review assistance designations provide FDA assistance with various aspects of the marketing authorization process. These are fast track, breakthrough therapy, breakthrough device, priority review, and regenerative medicine advanced therapy.

FDA has not yet promulgated regulations implementing any of these programs. However, it has issued guidance describing the content of the various programs. The programs are, accordingly, administered through a combination of statutory language and guidance documents.

*Fast Track Designation*

FFDCA § 506(b) provides that "fast track" designation is available for a drug (including a biologic) that meets two conditions. First, the drug must be intended "for the treatment of a serious or life-threatening disease or condition." Second, the drug must "demonstrate[] the potential to address unmet medical needs."

If FDA designates a drug as a fast-track product, FFDCA § 506(b)(3) provides that the agency "shall take such actions as are appropriate to expedite the development and review of the application for approval of such product."

FDA guidance describes the benefits of fast track designation as follows:[36]

> **B. Features of Fast Track Designation**
>
> *1. Actions to Expedite Development and Review*
>
> There are opportunities for frequent interactions with the review team for a fast track product. These include meetings with FDA, including pre-IND meetings, end-of-phase 1 meetings, and end-of-phase 2 meetings to discuss study design, extent of safety data required to support approval, dose-response concerns, and use of biomarkers. Other meetings may be scheduled as appropriate (e.g., to discuss accelerated approval, the structure and content of an NDA, and other critical issues).
>
> In addition, such a product could be eligible for priority review if supported by clinical data at the time of BLA, NDA, or efficacy supplement submission
>
> *2. Submission of Portions of an Application (Rolling Review)*
>
> If FDA determines, after preliminary evaluation of clinical data submitted by a sponsor, that a fast track product may be effective, the Agency may consider reviewing portions of a marketing application before the sponsor submits the complete application.

---

36. FDA, Guidance for Industry: Expedited Programs for Serious Conditions—Drugs and Biologics (May 2014).

At this point, please read (or review) the following excerpts in the statutory supplement:

- FFDCA § 506. Expedited approval of drugs for serious or life-threatening diseases or conditions. *Subsection (b) only.*

*Breakthrough Therapy*

FFDCA § 506(a) provides that "breakthrough therapy" designation is available for a drug that meets two conditions. First, it must be intended "to treat a serious or life-threatening disease or condition." Second, FDA must determine that "preliminary clinical evidence indicates that the drug may demonstrate substantial improvement over existing therapies on 1 or more clinically significant endpoints." An example of an appropriate, clinically significant endpoint is "substantial treatment effects observed early in clinical development." FFDCA § 506(a)(3) specifies a number of specific actions FDA may take in response to a breakthrough therapy designation. These primarily involve additional communications with the agency, earlier and more active involvement with senior FDA staff, rolling review of the application, and help with trial design.

At this point, please read (or review) the following excerpts in the statutory supplement:

- FFDCA § 506. Expedited approval of drugs for serious or life-threatening diseases or conditions. *Subsection (a) only.*

*Breakthrough Device Designation*

FFDCA § 515C provides that "breakthrough device" designation is available for certain devices "that provide for more effective treatment or diagnosis of life-threatening or irreversibly debilitating human disease or conditions." To qualify for breakthrough device designation, the devices must meet four additional conditions. First, they must "represent breakthrough technologies." Second, these must be devices "for which no approved or cleared alternatives exist." Third, they must "offer significant advantages over existing approved or cleared alternatives." Fourth, availability of the breakthrough device must be "in the best interest of patients."

If FDA designates a device as a breakthrough device, FFDCA § 515C(e)(1) sets out numerous actions FDA "shall" take to speed the development of the device. FFDCA § 515C(e)(2) sets out additional actions FDA "may" take to speed development of the device. Like with fast-track products and breakthrough therapies, FDA can take these actions to assist with—and increase the speed of—the product review process.

At this point, please read (or review) the following excerpts in the statutory supplement:

- FFDCA § 515C. Breakthrough devices.

*Regenerative Medicine Advanced Therapy (RMAT) Designation*

FFDCA § 506(g) provides that "regenerative advanced therapy" designation is available for certain drugs that meet three conditions. First, FFDCA § 506(g)

(2)(A) provides that it must be a "regenerative medicine therapy," which FFDCA § 506(g)(8) defines as including "cell therapy, therapeutic tissue engineering products, human cell and tissue products, and combination products using any such therapies or products." Second, FFDCA § 506(g)(2)(B) provides that it must be "intended to treat, modify, reverse, or cure a serious or life-threatening disease or condition." Third, FFDCA § 506(g)(2)(C) provides that FDA must conclude that "preliminary clinical evidence indicates that the drug has the potential to address unmet medical needs for such a disease or condition."

FFDCA § 506(g)(5)–(6) sets out several benefits of RMAT designation. First, FFDCA § 506(g)(5) makes RMAT products eligible for the benefits associated with breakthrough therapy designation. Second, FFDCA § 506(g)(6)(A) provides that RMAT-designated applications can be eligible for priority review. Third, FFDCA § 506(g)(6)(B) provides that RMAT-designated applications can be eligible for the accelerated approval pathway.

At this point, please read (or review) the following excerpts in the statutory supplement:

- FFDCA § 506. Expedited approval of drugs for serious or life-threatening diseases or conditions. *Subsection (g) only.*

### *c. Market Exclusivity Designations*

Three market exclusivity designations—orphan drug, qualified infectious disease product (QIDP), and competitive generic therapy (CGT)—provide an incentive for development of a drug by granting a period of market exclusivity.[37] The excerpt immediately below will introduce you to the relationship between patents (the subject of a separate course) and market exclusivity periods. We will then look briefly at each of the three market exclusivity designations.

## FDA Website, Frequently Asked Questions on Patents and Exclusivity*

. . . .

**1. What is the difference between patents and exclusivity?**

Patents and exclusivity work in a similar fashion but are distinct from one another and governed by different statutes. Patents are a property right granted by the United States Patent and Trademark Office anytime during the development of a drug and can encompass a wide range of claims. Exclusivity refers to certain delays and prohibitions on approval of competitor drugs available under the statute that attach upon approval of a drug or of certain supplements. A new drug application

37. Designations, however, are not the only way to qualify for market exclusivity. Other market exclusivity periods are associated with the abbreviated drug pathways and with pediatric testing.

* From https://www.fda.gov/drugs/development-approval-process-drugs/frequently-asked-questions-patents-and-exclusivity (last updated 2019-12-08).

(NDA) or abbreviated new drug application (ANDA) holder is eligible for exclusivity if statutory requirements are met. See 21 C.F.R. 314.108, 316.31, 316.34 and sections 505A, 505E, and 505(j)(5)(B)(iv) of the [FFDCA]. Periods of exclusivity and patent terms may or may not run concurrently. Exclusivity was designed to promote a balance between new drug innovation and greater public access to drugs that result from generic drug competition.

**2. How long is a patent term?**

Patent terms are set by statute. Currently, the term of a new patent is 20 years from the date on which the application for the patent was filed in the United States. Many other factors can affect the duration of a patent.

**3. How long does an exclusivity period last?**

It depends on what type of exclusivity is at issue.

Orphan Drug Exclusivity (ODE)—7 years

New Chemical Entity Exclusivity (NCE)—5 years

Generating Antibiotic Incentives Now (GAIN) Exclusivity—5 years added to certain exclusivities

New Clinical Investigation Exclusivity—3 years

Pediatric Exclusivity (PED)—6 months added to existing Patents/Exclusivity

Patent Challenge (PC)—180 days (this exclusivity is for ANDAs only)

Competitive Generic Therapy (CGT)—180 days (this exclusivity is for ANDAs only)

*See* 21 C.F.R. 314.108, 316.31, 316.34 and sections 505A, 505E, 505(j)(5)(B)(iv), and Section 505(j)(5)(B)(v) of the [FFDCA].

. . . .

**4. Why does the exclusivity expire before the patent? Patent before exclusivity? Why does a particular drug product only have patents? Only have exclusivity? Have neither?**

Patents and exclusivity apply to drugs in different ways. Patents can be issued or expire at any time regardless of the drug's approval status. Exclusivity attaches upon approval of a drug product if the statutory requirements are met. Some drugs have both patent and exclusivity protection while others have just one or neither. Patents and exclusivity may or may not run concurrently and may or may not cover the same aspects of the drug product. Patents and exclusivities that have expired are removed from the Orange Book.

**5. What information related to pediatric exclusivity is listed in the Orange Book?**

When pediatric exclusivity is obtained, a 6-month period of exclusivity is added to all existing patents and exclusivity on all applications held by the sponsor for that active moiety. Pediatric exclusivity does not stand alone, but attaches to existing exclusivity. When pediatric exclusivity attaches, in the patent column of the Orange Book, the patent is shown twice—once with the original patent expiration date and a second time reflecting the six month period of pediatric exclusivity linked to that particular patent.

. . . .

**7. How is an NDA holder notified if their application has received a period of exclusivity?**

No letters are sent to the application holder to indicate that a period of exclusivity has attached to their application. The posting of exclusivity information in the Orange Book is the official vehicle for dissemination of this information.

---

As noted earlier, three of the market exclusivity periods referenced in the excerpt immediately above are market exclusivity designations. These are orphan drug designation, QIDP designation (referenced in the above excerpt as GAIN exclusivity),[38] and CGT designation. Orphan drug designation is available for a drug "intended for use in a rare disease or condition." 21 C.F.R. § 316.3(b)(10). When FDA approves an application with an orphan drug designation, the successful applicant receives a seven-year exclusivity period. FFDCA § 527(a).

QIDP designation is available for "an antibacterial or antifungal drug for human use intended to treat serious or life-threatening infections." FFDCA § 505E(g). When FDA approves an application for a drug with a QIPD designation, the successful applicant receives a five-year extension of other existing exclusivity periods. FFDCA § 505E(a). QIDP designation also includes review-clock and review-assistance elements.[39]

Competitive generic therapy (CGT) designation is available for a drug for which FDA "determines that there is inadequate generic competition." FFDCA § 506H(b)(3). There is inadequate generic competition when there is either no actively marketed competitor to a reference listed drug, or when the reference listed drug is no longer marketed and only a single generic drug is actively marketed. See FFDCA § 506H(e)(2). As CGT designation is relevant only to generic drugs, it is available only for Abbreviated New Drug Applications (ANDAs). See FFDCA § 505H(a). The first CGT-designated drug FDA approves to compete with a given already-marketed

---

38. QIDP designation originated in Title VII, Generating Antibiotic Incentives Now (GAIN), of the Food and Drug Administration Safety and Innovation Act (2012). 126 Stat. 993, 1077–1082. It is, accordingly, sometimes described by FDA as GAIN exclusivity, rather than QIDP exclusivity.

39. FDA must give priority review to the first application submitted for a particular QIDP-designated drug. FFDCA § 524A(a). A QIDP-designated drug is also eligible for fast track designation. See FFDCA § 506(b)(1).

drug is entitled to a 180-day exclusivity period. FFDCA § 505(j)(5)(B)(v). CGT designation also includes some review-assistance elements.[40]

## 2. Example: Use of the Designations

### 2019-12-19 FDA News Release, First FDA-Approved Vaccine for the Prevention of Ebola Virus Disease, Marking a Critical Milestone in Public Health Preparedness and Response

The U.S. Food and Drug Administration announced today the approval of Ervebo, the first FDA-approved vaccine for the prevention of Ebola virus disease (EVD), caused by Zaire ebolavirus in individuals 18 years of age and older. Cases of EVD are very rare in the U.S., and those that have occurred have been the result of infections acquired by individuals in other countries who then traveled to the U.S., or health care workers who became ill after treating patients with EVD.

....

EVD is contagious and is transmitted through direct contact with blood, body fluids and tissues of infected wild animals or people, as well as with surfaces and materials, such as bedding and clothing, contaminated with these fluids. Onset of symptoms of EVD can be sudden and can include fever, fatigue, muscle pain, headache and sore throat. This is followed by vomiting, diarrhea, rash, impaired kidney and liver function and in some cases internal and external bleeding. EVD has an incubation period that ranges from 2 to 21 days. Individuals who provide care for people with EVD, including health care workers who do not use correct infection control precautions, are at the highest risk for infection.

Confirmed outbreaks of EVD have been documented since the 1970s, primarily in areas of sub-Saharan Africa, where scientists believe the virus is always present at low levels in certain infected wild animals. On rare occasions, people become sick with EVD after coming into direct contact with infected animals, which can then lead to EVD outbreaks when the virus spreads between people.

An outbreak in three West African countries (Guinea, Liberia and Sierra Leone) from 2014 to 2016 resulted in more than 28,000 cases of EVD and more than 11,000 deaths that were caused by Zaire ebolavirus.

The Democratic Republic of the Congo (DRC) is currently experiencing the world's second largest EVD outbreak. In 2018, the World Health Organization (WHO) and the DRC began to use Ervebo as an investigational vaccine under an expanded access program to help mitigate this outbreak. With or without vaccination, it is critical to implement appropriate infection control and prevention measures as part of efforts to prevent the spread of EVD.

---

40. These are set out in FFDCA § 505H(c).

"Ebola virus disease is a rare but severe and often deadly disease that knows no borders. Vaccination is essential to help prevent outbreaks and to stop the Ebola virus from spreading when outbreaks do occur," said Peter Marks, M.D., Ph.D., director of the FDA's Center for Biologics Evaluation and Research. "The FDA's approval of Ervebo is a major advance in helping to protect against the Zaire ebolavirus as well as advancing U.S. government preparedness efforts. The research approach used to study the effectiveness and safety of this vaccine was precedent-setting during a public health emergency and may help create a model for future studies under similar circumstances. The FDA is committed to continuing our work across the U.S. government and with our international partners to prevent future Ebola outbreaks and mitigate the current outbreak in the DRC, reflecting our nation's commitment to preparing for and responding to biological threats, like Ebola."

The approval of Ervebo is supported by a study conducted in Guinea during the 2014–2016 outbreak in individuals 18 years of age and older. The study was a randomized cluster (ring) vaccination study in which 3,537 contacts, and contacts of contacts, of individuals with laboratory confirmed EVD received either "immediate" or 21-day "delayed" vaccination with Ervebo. This noteworthy design was intended to capture a social network of individuals and locations that might include dwellings or workplaces where a patient spent time while symptomatic, or the households of individuals who had contact with the patient during that person's illness or death. In a comparison of cases of EVD among 2,108 individuals in the "immediate" vaccination arm and 1,429 individuals in the "delayed" vaccination arm, Ervebo was determined to be 100% effective in preventing Ebola cases with symptom onset greater than 10 days after vaccination. No cases of EVD with symptom onset greater than 10 days after vaccination were observed in the "immediate" cluster group, compared with 10 cases of EVD in the 21-day "delayed" cluster group.

In additional studies, antibody responses to Ervebo were assessed in 477 individuals in Liberia, approximately 500 individuals in Sierra Leone and approximately 900 individuals in Canada, Spain and the U.S. The antibody responses among those in the study conducted in Canada, Spain and the U.S. were similar to those among individuals in the studies conducted in Liberia and Sierra Leone.

The safety of Ervebo was assessed in approximately 15,000 individuals in Africa, Europe and North America. The most commonly reported side effects were pain, swelling and redness at the injection site, as well as headache, fever, joint and muscle aches and fatigue.

Ervebo is administered as a single-dose injection, and is a live, attenuated vaccine that has been genetically engineered to contain a protein from the Zaire ebolavirus.

The FDA granted this application Priority Review and a Tropical Disease Priority Review Voucher under a program intended to encourage development of new drugs and biologics for the prevention and treatment of certain tropical diseases. The FDA also granted Breakthrough Therapy designation for Ervebo to facilitate the development and scientific evaluation of the vaccine. Because of the public health importance of a vaccine to prevent EVD, the FDA worked closely with the company and completed its evaluation of the safety and effectiveness of Ervebo in less than six months.

The approval was granted to Merck & Co., Inc.

. . . .

## J. Related Area Involving Extensive Interaction with Other Agencies: Medical Countermeasures

*Medical countermeasures* is a general term used by the U.S. federal government to refer to FDA-regulated medical products "that can be used to diagnose, prevent, protect from, or treat conditions associated with chemical, biological, radiological, or nuclear (CBRN) threats, emerging infectious diseases, or a natural disaster."[41]

Medical countermeasures activities are based in the Department of Health and Human Services (HHS) and coordinated by the HHS Assistant Secretary for Preparedness and Response (ASPR). ASPR directs the Public Health Emergency Medical Countermeasures Enterprise (PHEMCE). PHEMCE "coordinates the full spectrum of federal medical countermeasure activities" in the United States.[42] Partner agencies include the Biomedical Advanced Research and Development Authority (BARDA), the National Institute of Health (NIH), FDA, the Centers for Disease Control and Prevention (CDC), the Department of Defense (DOD), and the Department of Homeland Security.

Medical countermeasures are a complex and rapidly developing area that go, in many ways, beyond the scope of this book. For now, however, you should be aware of a few key points.

First, 21 U.S.C. § 306bbb-3c permits the Secretary of Defense to request that FDA "take actions to expedite the development of a medical product" in certain situations where the relevant medical product "would be reasonably likely to diagnose, prevent, treat, or mitigate" a "specific and imminently life-threatening risk to United States military forces." Second, FFDCA § 565 directs the Secretary of HHS to take specific steps to ensure active FDA cooperation in efforts to develop and review certain medical countermeasures. Third, FFDCA 565A provides for the award of transferable priority review vouchers in return for successful applications for certain "material threat medical countermeasures."

---

41. CDC, Medical Countermeasures Readiness, https://www.cdc.gov/cpr/readiness/mcm.html (last visited 2020-06-12).

42. PHEMCE, https://www.medicalcountermeasures.gov/phemce/aspr/ (last visited 2020-06-12).).

## K. Access Before Marketing Authorization

The FFDCA sets out four primary ways to access investigational products prior to marketing authorization. The first, *standard investigational use*, applies to all product categories requiring marketing authorization. The second, *expanded access*, applies to drugs (including biologic drugs) and medical devices; the third, *emergency use*, applies to drugs (including biologic drugs), animal drugs, and medical devices; the fourth, the *Right to Try Act*, applies to drugs (including biologic drugs).

First, for all products requiring marketing authorization, the FFDCA provides for investigational use exemptions from its marketing authorization requirements. As described in the section immediately below, these exemptions are set out in subsections of the various FFDCA provisions relating to the individual product categories. Second, for drugs, biologics, and medical devices, FFDCA § 561 sets out mechanisms for providing expanded access to investigational medical products to patients outside of the relevant clinical trial. Third, FFDCA §§ 564 and 564A provide for emergency use of unapproved drugs, animal drugs, biologics, or medical devices during certain declared emergencies. Fourth, in certain circumstances, the Right to Try Act provides some liability protections for companies and health-care providers involved in providing an investigational drug to a patient.

### 1. Standard Investigational Use

For each product category where testing is sometimes required for marketing authorization, the FFDCA largely bars any distribution in interstate commerce (not just sale of the product). Because of this, the FFDCA provides for various exemptions for investigational use of these products. These are FFDCA §§ 409(j) (investigational food additives), 505(i) (investigational new drugs), 512(i) (investigational new animal drugs), 520(g) (investigational devices), 721(f) (investigational color additives), and 910(g) (investigational tobacco products). For all except tobacco products, FDA has promulgated regulations setting out procedures for these investigational exemptions in more detail. For food additives, this is 21 C.F.R. § 107.17 (for food additives generally) and 21 C.F.R. § 570.17 (for animal food additives). For new drugs and biologics, this is 21 C.F.R. Part 312. For new animal drugs, this is 21 C.F.R. Part 511. For devices, this is 21 C.F.R. Part 512. For color additives, this is 21 C.F.R. Part 71. FDA has not yet promulgated regulations for investigational tobacco products.

At this point, please read (or review) the following excerpts in the statutory supplement:

- FFDCA 409. Food additives. *Subsection (j) only.*
- FFDCA 505. New drugs. *Subsection (i) only.*
- FFDCA 512. New animal drugs. *Subsection (a)(3) only.*

- FFDCA 520. General provisions respecting control of devices for human use. *Subsection (g) only.*
- FFDCA 721. Color additives. *Subsection (f) only.*
- FFDCA 910. Application for review of certain tobacco products. *Subsection (g) only.*

These are the statutory provisions exempting, for investigational use, products in their respective categories.

The excerpt immediately below is from the preamble to FDA's late 1980s rewrite of its investigational new drug (IND) regulations. It is intended to highlight for you some of the policy concerns that arise in the regulation of investigational products.

## 1987-03-19 FDA Final Rule, New Drug, Antibiotic, and Biologic Drug Product Regulations

52 Fed. Reg. 8798

### I. Introduction

This final rule continues the rulemaking efforts by the Department of Health and Human Services and FDA to revise Federal regulations governing the new drug approval process. This phase of the regulations (called the IND Rewrite) makes final new procedures in 21 CFR Part 312 for FDA review of investigational new drug applications and for monitoring the progress of investigational drug use. . . . The first phase of these regulatory revision efforts (called the NDA Rewrite) covers FDA procedures in 21 CFR Part 314 for FDA review of new drug and antibiotic applications for marketing. This first phase was completed with publication of final regulations in the Federal Register of February 22, 1985 . . . . These regulations are promulgated under the [FFDCA].

The objectives of the IND Rewrite final rule are to establish an efficient investigational drug process in order both: (a) To focus FDA's attention during the early phase of clinical research on protecting the safety of human test subjects and to give sponsors greater freedom to design, revise, and implement clinical research studies; and (b) to facilitate consultation between FDA and drug sponsors, once the preliminary human studies have been completed and a drug appears to have marketing potential, to help ensure that the design of major clinical trials is acceptable and will support marketing approval if the test results are favorable. These regulations are also intended to encourage innovation and drug development while continuing to assure the safety of test subjects. In addition, through better planning and closer consultation, FDA's later review of applications for marketing should proceed more efficiently. These changes will benefit the consumer by enhancing the prompt marketing availability of safe and effective therapies.

. . . .

FDA's IND Rewrite final rule complements the revised NDA regulations. For example, one of the themes of the IND/NDA Rewrites is to establish a continuing dialogue between FDA staff and drug sponsors/applicants. Accordingly, the regulations codify a sequence of four standard conferences targeted at key stages of the drug approval process. These are (in the IND regulations) the "end-of-Phase 2 conference" and the "pre-NDA conference" and (in the NDA regulations) the "ninety-day conference" and the "end-of-review conference." In addition, both the IND and NDA regulations provide for other communication between FDA staff and sponsors/applicants on an as needed basis, as well as a strong commitment to resolve any disputes in a timely manner.

. . . .

In connection with issuance of the IND and NDA Rewrites, FDA has significantly expanded the use of guidelines. FDA has recently issued guidelines on how to fulfill certain technical requirements in order to provide applicants with greater guidance in these areas. These guidelines, which apply to regulatory requirements for both NDA and IND applications, should materially assist implementation of the new regulations.

. . . .

### II. Highlights of the Final Rule

The guiding principle in the IND Rewrite final rule is that different stages of the IND process will be regulated differently. Safety concerns will predominate at the beginning of the process to ensure that research subjects are not exposed to unreasonable risks. In the later phases of drug investigation, FDA will also evaluate the scientific merit of study protocols to ensure that planned clinical studies are capable of producing valid information on safety and effectiveness necessary to obtain marketing approval. In response to comments and further internal deliberations, the final rule has modified certain provisions of the proposal to meet these objectives better. The major provisions of the final rule are summarized as follows:

1. *Regulation of the early phase of human research.* The final rule incorporates the proposed revisions designed to give drug sponsors greater freedom during the early phase of human research (Phase 1) by permitting such research to proceed unless it presents an unreasonable and significant risk to test subjects. Thus, the final rule narrows the scope of FDA's review of Phase 1 studies to focus on the safety of human test subjects and permit clinical investigators in Phase 1 to modify protocols on the basis of experience gained during the investigation without prior notification to FDA. Moreover, the final rule emphasizes to drug sponsors that the amount of toxicology and chemistry information required in the initial IND submission depends on the nature and extent of the proposed clinical studies. These changes are intended to encourage innovation in drug development while continuing current safeguards governing the safety of test subjects.

   In the proposed rule, FDA solicited comments on the merits of adopting a dual track system for Phase 1 studies in which drug firms would have the option of submitting IND's either to FDA or to nongovernmental "Outside

Review Boards" (ORBs). As discussed later in this preamble, FDA has decided to solicit further comment on the feasibility of ORB's, focusing in particular on the possible establishment of a pilot program.

2. *Format for IND submission.* The final rule establishes a new format for IND submissions, similar to that in the proposal, that will result in better organized applications and thus facilitate agency review. The revised format focuses on the proposed human studies so that supporting toxicology and chemistry information can be reviewed in light of the proposed clinical investigations. The new IND will consist of a greatly simplified IND form that serves as a cover sheet, a brief overview of the investigational plan, and the protocols and supporting technical information on the drug's chemistry, pharmacology, and toxicology.
3. *IND safety reports.* The final rule specifies a drug company's obligations in reviewing and reporting adverse drug reaction information, clarifying the proposal in several respects. The rule requires that sponsors promptly review and evaluate all safety information received by the sponsor and that the sponsor report to FDA within 10 working days all adverse drug reactions that are both serious and unexpected. In addition, the final rule requires the sponsor to notify FDA by telephone of any unexpected death or life-threatening experience no later than 3 working days after the sponsor first learns of the experience. This telephone call will provide an early warning of the most serious kinds of adverse experiences and will enable FDA to discuss with the sponsor the need, if any, to modify or discontinue the study. These safety report provisions should significantly improve FDA's ability to monitor the safety of clinical studies.
4. *Amendment procedures.* Like the proposal, the final rule divides the IND amendment procedures into three distinct categories: (i) Protocol amendments, for new protocols and changes in existing protocols; (ii) information amendments, for additional data as they develop; and (iii) IND safety reports, as described above. Appropriate reporting intervals apply to each category depending upon the need for prompt agency review. The final rule also clarifies the scope of the annual reports, which are intended to provide an overview of the progress to date and future plans for the IND.
5. *Meetings between FDA and drug sponsors.* The final rule codifies FDA's proposal to extend to the sponsor of any IND an opportunity for an "end-of-Phase 2" conference with FDA to obtain concurrence on an overall plan for the conduct of Phase 3 trials and the design of specific studies. The final rule also codifies the policy that gives IND sponsors and opportunity to meet with FDA for a "pre-NDA" conference to discuss appropriate formats for data presentation in a marketing application.
6. *"Clinical hold" procedures.* The final rule adopts procedures essentially the same as those contained in the proposal pertaining to FDA's instituting a

"clinical hold." A clinical hold is an order either not to begin or not to continue a clinical study. The final rule limits clinical holds in Phase 1 studies to situations where there is an unreasonable and significant risk to human subjects. In Phases 2 and 3, FDA's authority to issue a clinical hold would exten[d] to serious defects in study design that would render the study incapable of producing valid evidence of safety and effectiveness. All clinical holds must be approved by the director of the division in FDA's Center for Drugs and Biologics with responsibility for review of the IND.

7. Exemptions for certain studies on marketed drugs. The final rule exempts from most IND requirements certain investigations conducted with drugs already approved for marketing. The exemption applies where safety is not an issue (because of a similarity in dose, route of administration, and patient population with the approved labeling) and where the investigation is not being conducted for the purpose of changing the drug labeling (for example, where the study is not for purposes of adding a new indication or comparative safety claim). The agency expects that this exemption will apply primarily to researchers in academic or other institutions. This exemption is intended to reduce burdens on researchers while permitting FDA resources to be devoted to monitoring clinical investigations requiring FDA oversight and to reviewing marketing applications. Although exempt from most IND requirements, the investigations would nonetheless be subject to the general prohibition against promotion of investigational drugs (§ 312.7), and to the other regulations designed to protect the rights and safety of patients, such as the institutional review board (21 CFR Part 56) and informed consent (21 CFR Part 50) regulations.

8. *Dispute resolution.* The final rule has been significantly revised to emphasize, similar to the NDA final rule, the use of informal meetings and other informal communications as the means for resolving differences between FDA and sponsors. For administrative and procedural issues, the final rule establishes an ombudsman whose function will be to facilitate timely and equitable resolutions of administrative and managerial disagreements about IND's. For scientific and medical disputes, the final rule encourages applicants to seek resolution through informal meetings with appropriate agency staff and management representatives as the need may arise. The final rule also provides for the participation of outside experts at these informal meetings when feasible. This procedure supersedes the appeals process described in the IND Rewrite proposal.

. . . .

### III. Economic Analysis

FDA has examined the economic consequences of the changes implemented by the final rule in accordance with Executive Order 12291 and the Regulatory Flexibility Act. The agency concludes that these revisions will have favorable economic impacts on the health care system, drug sponsors, and the agency without compromising the safety of human subjects. Although some of these favorable impacts are quantifiable, others with greater potential for savings can only be characterized in a very generalized, nonquantitative manner at this time.

Quantifiable impacts include an estimated net annual savings of $4.9 million to sponsors, arising from a simplified IND format; reduced and/or staged submission of manufacturing and controls data; a reduction in the number of amendments that are submitted during the first year that an IND is active; savings in start-up expenses associated with studies that would no longer be placed on clinical hold under the revised criteria; and savings of sponsor-investigator resources currently used to prepare IND's that will no longer be necessary. The only projected cost increase is modest by comparison and arises from requirements to improve the quality of annual reports. These revisions will also produce some savings in agency review resources.

A potential for substantially larger savings is presented by the provisions for increased use of guidelines, meetings, and informal advice to aid commercial IND sponsors in assembling the data for those IND's that lead to the submission of a marketing application. These initiatives, taken together, could result in substantial savings from fewer deficiencies being noted in the NDA review process due to better designed clinical trials, as well as further savings from the elimination of some unnecessary or poorly designed clinical studies. For example, gaining advice on the proper protocol for a major clinical study could save a year or more in the process if it prevents the need to redo certain key research as a result of faulty study design.

....

The revisions to the IND regulations have a significance well beyond the specific cost reductions summarized above. As noted earlier, these regulations are part of a comprehensive review of the new drug approval process designed to accelerate the development and marketing of new drug therapies without compromising the safety and effectiveness of new drugs. Collectively, FDA's new regulations, guidelines, procedures, and policies should produce considerable benefits. A quicker, more efficient drug development process means that the American public will have more safe and effective drugs sooner. A less costly drug development process means that the pharmaceutical industry will be able to develop more new drugs with the same number of research dollars, or alternatively to market less costly drugs. Either outcome will be of direct benefit to the American public. Most importantly, the prompt availability of safe and effective drug therapies has enormous potential benefit to patients and the public in terms of improving the length and quality of life and in reducing health care and hospital costs.

....

## 2. Expanded Access

As you saw in the *Abigail Alliance* case presented earlier in this chapter, there are potential costs to rigorous requirements for marketing authorization. The traditional form of access before marketing authorization is the standard investigational use process addressed immediately above. Under these standard investigational provisions, individual patient access to an investigational medical product is available only through participation in a clinical trial. Some patients, however, are not able to participate in clinical trials.[43] And trial design frequently dictates that some participating patients are randomly assigned between groups that receive the relevant product and groups that receive a placebo.

In 1987, FDA published regulations providing for what came to be known as the *treatment investigational new drug application,* or *treatment IND.* Those regulations set out certain circumstances under which drugs still in the investigational phase could be made available for treatment use. In 2009, FDA replaced its treatment IND regulations with new regulations based on FFDCA § 561.[44]

FFDCA § 561(a) provides that FDA may, "under appropriate conditions," permit investigational drugs or devices to be shipped for "the diagnosis, monitoring, or treatment of a serious disease or condition in emergency situations." FFDCA § 561(b) sets out the circumstances for expanded access by individual patients. Under FFDCA § 561(b), an "[i]ndividual patient," through his or her physician, "may request" that a "manufacturer or distributor" provide "an investigational drug or investigational device for the diagnosis, monitoring, or treatment of a serious disease." FFDCA § 561(c) sets out the circumstances under which expanded access to an investigational drug can be provided for a group broader than an individual patient. Under FFDCA § 561(c), FDA can approve "widespread access" to an investigational drug or device under "treatment investigational new drug application" or a "treatment investigational device exemption." However, FDA may only approve such widespread expanded access under limited conditions, including those set out in FFDCA § 561(c)(1) through FFDCA § 561(c)(7). FDA has promulgated regulations implementing FFDCA § 561 at 21 C.F.R. Part 314, Subpart I. The preamble to the rule setting out these *expanded access* regulations is excerpted below.

At this point, please read (or review) the following excerpts in the statutory supplement:

- FFDCA 561. Expanded access to unapproved therapies and diagnostics.

---

43. Common reasons for being unable to participate include living too far from the study location to make participation practical and not meeting medical criteria for inclusion in the relevant clinical trial.

44. The first version of this provision did not become law until 1997. Accordingly, FFDCA § 561 was not available to FDA when it promulgated the treatment IND regulations.

## 2009-08-13 FDA Final Rule, Expanded Access to Investigational Drugs for Treatment Use

74 Fed. Reg. 40,900

The Food and Drug Administration (FDA) is amending its regulations on access to investigational new drugs for the treatment of patients. The final rule clarifies existing regulations and adds new types of expanded access for treatment use. Under the final rule, expanded access to investigational drugs for treatment use is available to individual patients, including in emergencies; intermediate-size patient populations; and larger populations under a treatment protocol or treatment investigational new drug application (IND). The final rule is intended to improve access to investigational drugs for patients with serious or immediately life-threatening diseases or conditions who lack other therapeutic options and who may benefit from such therapies....

I. Background

In the Federal Register of December 14, 2006, FDA proposed to amend its regulations permitting access to investigational drugs to treat patients with serious or immediately life-threatening diseases or conditions when there is no comparable or satisfactory alternative therapy to diagnose, monitor, or treat the patient's disease or condition.

As discussed in greater detail in the preamble to the proposed rule, there have been several statutory and regulatory efforts to expand access to investigational drugs for treatment use. Before 1987, there was no formal recognition of treatment use in FDA's regulations concerning INDs, but investigational drugs were made available for treatment use informally. In 1987, FDA revised the IND regulations in part 312 to explicitly provide for one specific kind of treatment use of investigational drugs. Section 312.34 authorized access to investigational drugs for a broad population under a treatment protocol or treatment IND when certain criteria were met. Section 312.35 described the submission requirements for such treatment use. The 1987 IND regulations also implicitly acknowledged the existence of other kinds of treatment use, notably use in individual patients, by adding a provision for obtaining an investigational drug for treatment use in an emergency situation (§312.36). However, §312.36 did not describe criteria or requirements that must be met to authorize individual patient treatment use.

In response to criticisms that this lack of criteria and submission requirements resulted in inconsistent policies, inequitable access, and preferential access for certain categories of patients, Congress included in the Food and Drug Administration Modernization Act of 1997 (FDAMA), which amended the [FFDCA], specific provisions concerning expanded access to investigational drugs for treatment use (Expanded Access to Unapproved Therapies and Diagnostics, section 561 of the [FFDCA]).

FDA proposed this rule in December 2006 to further address the concerns that motivated the FDAMA changes, including problems of inconsistent application of access policies and programs and inequities in access based on the relative sophistication of the setting in which a patient is treated or on the patient's disease or condition. By describing in detail in the final rule the criteria, submission requirements, and safeguards for the different types of expanded access for treatment use of investigational drugs, FDA hopes to increase awareness and knowledge of expanded access programs and the procedures for obtaining investigational drugs for treatment use. The agency believes that the final rule appropriately authorizes access to promising drugs for treatment use, while protecting patient safety and avoiding interference with the development of investigational drugs for marketing under approved applications.

. . . .

This final rule applies both to drug products that are subject to section 505 of the [FFDCA] and biological products subject to the licensing provisions of the Public Health Service Act and 21 CFR part 601. This is consistent with the previous regulations on treatment use, which applied to both drug and biological products.

. . . .

## 3. Emergency Use

The novel coronavirus, SARS-CoV-2, that arose in early 2019 has highlighted the role of FDA's authority to authorize emergency use of medical products. FFDCA § 564(a)(1) provides that, "[n]otwithstanding any provision of this [FFDCA Chapter V] and section 351 of the Public Health Service Act," FDA may "authorize the introduction into interstate commerce," during the period of a declared emergency, "of a drug, device, or biological product intended for use in an actual or potential emergency."

FFDCA § 564(b) provides that the HHS Secretary can "make a declaration that the circumstances exist justifying the authorization under this subsection for a product" on the basis of one of four types of determinations by the appropriate authorities. These are a "domestic emergency" pursuant to § 564(b)(1)(A), a "military emergency" pursuant to § 564(b)(1)(B), a "public health emergency" pursuant to § 564(b)(1)(C), or an "identification of a material threat" pursuant to 21 U.S.C. § 247d-6b.

Once the FFDCA § 564(b) declaration is made, FFDCA § 564(c) sets out the criteria under which FDA can issue an emergency use authorization (EUA). There are numerous criteria, but a core aspect of the emergency-use test is set out in FFDCA § 564(c)(2).[45] Under FFDCA § 564(c)(2), the agency must conclude that "it is reasonable to believe" two things. First, under FFDCA § 564(c)(2)(A) it must be "reasonable to believe" that the relevant product "may be effective in diagnosing, treating, or preventing" the relevant disease or condition. Second, under FFDCA § 564(c)(2)(B), it must be "reasonable to believe" that the "known and potential benefits

45. Other criteria include a requirement that the disease or condition subject to the declaration "can cause a serious or life-threatening condition" under FFDCA § 564(c)(1) and "there is no adequate, approved, and available alternative to the product" under FFDCA § 564(c)(3).

of the product . . . outweigh the known and potential risks of the product." In making these § 564(c)(2) determinations, FDA must act "based on the totality of scientific evidence available" to the agency, "including data from adequate and well-controlled clinical trials, if available."

FFDCA § 564A sets out additional authorities available to FDA once a § 564(b) emergency has been declared. FFDCA § 564B sets out certain circumstances under which "a government entity (including a Federal, State, local, or tribal government entity)" may "introduce" FDA-regulated products "into interstate commerce" without marketing authorization. To do this, the product must satisfy three criteria. First, FFDCA § 564B requires that it be "intended for emergency use." Second, FFDCA § 564B(1) requires that it be "intended to be held and not used." Third, FFDCA § 564B(2) requires that "it is held and not used, unless and until" it receives an appropriate marketing authorization, investigational use authorization, or EUA.

At this point, please read (or review) the following excerpts in the statutory supplement:

- FFDCA 564. Authorization for medical products for use in emergencies.
- FFDCA 564A. Emergency use of medical products.
- FFDCA 564B. Products held for emergency use.

Now read the two excerpts below. The first grants, and the second revokes, a high-profile EUA issued early in the COVID-19 pandemic.

The letter immediately below was sent by FDA's Chief Scientist to the Director of the Medical Countermeasures Program at HHS's Biomedical Advanced Research and Development Authority (BARDA). The letter grants an EUA for certain uses of chloroquine phosphate and hydroxychloroquine sulfate supplied from the Strategic National Stockpile.[46] This EUA, and its later revocation, made national headlines. This is because the EUA was issued during a period when President Donald Trump was aggressively promoting these two drugs for use in the treatment of COVID-19.

## 2020-03-28 Emergency Use Authorization for Use of Chloroquine Phosphate or Hydroxychloroquine Sulfate Supplied from the Strategic National Stockpile for Treatment of 2019 Coronavirus Disease

This letter is in response to your request that the Food and Drug Administration (FDA) issue an Emergency Use Authorization (EUA) for emergency use of oral formulations of chloroquine phosphate and hydroxychloroquine sulfate for the treatment of 2019 coronavirus disease (COVID-19) when administered by a health-care provider (HCP) pursuant to a valid prescription of a licensed practitioner as

46. The connection to the Strategic National Stockpile is significant. No EUA was necessary for simple, off-label use of this already approved drug. For further discussion of off-label use of approved drugs, see the *Caronia* case in Chapter 10.

described in the Scope of Authorization (section II) of this letter. The authorized chloroquine phosphate and hydroxychloroquine sulfate are limited to product supplied from the Strategic National Stockpile (SNS) to public health authorities, pursuant to Section 564 of the [FFDCA]. On February 4, 2020, pursuant to Section 564(b)(1)(C) of the [FFDCA], the Secretary of the Department of Health and Human Services (HHS) determined that there is a public health emergency that has a significant potential to affect national security or the health and security of United States citizens living abroad, and that involves the virus that causes COVID-19. Pursuant to Section 564 of the [FFDCA], and on the basis of such determination, the Secretary of HHS then declared that circumstances exist justifying the authorization of emergency use of drugs and biologics during the COVID-19 outbreak, pursuant to section 564 of the [FFDCA], subject to terms of any authorization issued under that section.

Chloroquine phosphate and hydroxychloroquine sulfate are not FDA-approved for treatment of COVID-19. Some versions of chloroquine phosphate are approved by FDA for other indications—for prophylaxis and acute attacks of certain strains of malaria and for the treatment of extraintestinal amebiasis, but the chloroquine phosphate drug product covered by this letter has not been approved. Several versions of hydroxychloroquine sulfate are approved by FDA for prophylaxis of and treatment of malaria, treatment of lupus erythematosus, and treatment of rheumatoid arthritis. The safety profile of these drugs has only been studied for FDA approved indications, not COVID-19.

Based upon limited in-vitro and anecdotal clinical data in case series, chloroquine phosphate and hydroxychloroquine sulfate are currently recommended for treatment of hospitalized COVID-19 patients in several countries, and a number of national guidelines report incorporating recommendations regarding use of chloroquine phosphate or hydroxychloroquine sulfate in the setting of COVID-19. FDA encourages the conduct and participation in randomized controlled clinical trials that may produce evidence concerning the effectiveness of these products in treating COVID-19. FDA is issuing this EUA to facilitate the availability of chloroquine phosphate and hydroxychloroquine sulfate during the COVID-19 pandemic to treat patients for whom a clinical trial is not available, or participation is not feasible.

Having concluded that the criteria for issuance of this authorization under 564(c) of the [FFDCA] are met, I am authorizing the emergency use of chloroquine phosphate and hydroxychloroquine sulfate, as described in the Scope of Authorization section of this letter (Section II) for treatment of COVID-19 when clinical trials are not available, or participation is not feasible, subject to the terms of this authorization.

Clinical trial data results, and any information derived from clinical trials, as well as clinical trial results from studies of other investigational medical products to treat COVID-19, will continue to inform this risk benefit assessment.

I. Criteria for Issuance of Authorization

I have concluded that the emergency use of chloroquine phosphate and hydroxychloroquine sulfate for the treatment of COVID-19 when administered as described in the Scope of Authorization (section II) meet the criteria for issuance of an authorization under Section 564(c) of the [FFDCA], because:

1. The SARS-CoV-2 can cause a serious or life-threatening disease or condition, including severe respiratory illness, to humans infected by this virus;

2. Based on the totality of scientific evidence available to FDA, it is reasonable to believe that chloroquine phosphate and hydroxychloroquine sulfate may be effective in treating COVID-19, and that, when used under the conditions described in this authorization, the known and potential benefits of chloroquine phosphate and hydroxychloroquine sulfate when used to treat COVID-19 outweigh the known and potential risks of such products; and

3. There is no adequate, approved, and available alternative to the emergency use of chloroquine phosphate and hydroxychloroquine sulfate for the treatment of COVID-19.

II. Scope of Authorization

I have concluded, pursuant to Section 564(d)(1) of the [FFDCA], that the scope of this authorization is limited to chloroquine phosphate and hydroxychloroquine sulfate for the treatment of COVID-19, as described in this section.

. . . .

III. Waiver of Certain Requirements

Pursuant to Section 564(e)(3) of the [FFDCA], with respect to the emergency use of a product for which an authorization under this section is issued, FDA may waive or limit, to the extent appropriate given the circumstances of the emergency, requirements regarding current good manufacturing practice otherwise applicable to the manufacture, processing, packing, or holding of products subject to regulation under this Act, including such requirements established under Section 501. FDA grants that waiver with respect to the products covered by this authorization.

. . . .

V. Duration of Authorization

This EUA will be effective until the declaration that circumstances exist justifying the authorization of the emergency use of drugs and biologics for prevention and treatment of COVID-19 is terminated under Section 564(b)(2) of the [FFDCA] or the EUA is revoked under Section 564(g) of the [FFDCA].

---

The letter immediately below was sent by FDA's Chief Scientist to the Director of the Medical Countermeasures Program at HHS's Biomedical Advanced Research and Development Authority. The letter revokes the EUA granted in the excerpt immediately above.

## 2020-06-15 FDA Letter Revoking Emergency Use Authorization for Chloroquine Phosphate and Hydroxychloroquine Sulfate

This letter is in response to your request, dated today, that the Food and Drug Administration (FDA) revoke the Emergency Use Authorization (EUA) for emergency use of oral formulations of chloroquine phosphate (CQ) and hydroxychloroquine sulfate (HCQ) to be distributed from the Strategic National Stockpile (SNS) issued on March 28, 2020. Like BARDA's earlier request to FDA to issue the EUA, BARDA's request to revoke the EUA is part of a collaborative, USG-interagency effort to rapidly respond to this continuously evolving public health emergency. Today's request to revoke is based on new information, including clinical trial data results, that have led BARDA to conclude that this drug may not be effective to treat COVID-19 [Coronavirus Disease 2019] and that the drug's potential benefits for such use do not outweigh its known and potential risks.

The authorization of a product for emergency use under section 564 of the [FFDCA] may, pursuant to section 564(g)(2) of the [FFDCA], be revised or revoked when the criteria under section 564(b)(1) of the [FFDCA] no longer exist, the criteria under section 564(c) of the [FFDCA] for issuance of such authorization are no longer met, or other circumstances make such revision or revocation appropriate to protect the public health or safety.

FDA has determined that the criteria under section 564(c) of the [FFDCA] for issuance of the EUA referenced above are no longer met. Under section 564(c)(2) of the [FFDCA], an EUA may be issued only if FDA concludes "that, based on the totality of scientific evidence available to the Secretary, including data from adequate and well-controlled clinical trials, if available, it is reasonable to believe that: (A) the product may be effective in diagnosing, treating, or preventing—(i) such disease or condition [. . . .]; and (B) the known and potential benefits of the product, when used to diagnose, prevent, or treat such disease or condition, outweigh the known and potential risks of the product [. . .]."

As explained in the attached memorandum, based on a review of new information and a reevaluation of information available at the time the EUA was issued, FDA now concludes that these criteria are no longer met. The bases for this decision include the following:

- We now believe that the suggested dosing regimens for CQ and HCQ as detailed in the Fact Sheets are unlikely to produce an antiviral effect.
- Earlier observations of decreased viral shedding with HCQ or CQ treatment have not been consistently replicated and recent data from a randomized controlled trial assessing probability of negative conversion showed no difference between HCQ and standard of care alone.

- Current U.S. treatment guidelines do not recommend the use of CQ or HCQ in hospitalized patients with COVID-19 outside of a clinical trial, and the NIH guidelines now recommend against such use outside of a clinical trial.
- Recent data from a large randomized controlled trial showed no evidence of benefit for mortality or other outcomes such as hospital length of stay or need for mechanical ventilation of HCQ treatment in hospitalized patients with COVID-19.

FDA has concluded that, based on this new information and other information discussed in the attached memorandum, it is no longer reasonable to believe that oral formulations of HCQ and CQ may be effective in treating COVID-19, nor is it reasonable to believe that the known and potential benefits of these products outweigh their known and potential risks. Accordingly, FDA revokes the EUA for emergency use of HCQ and CQ to treat COVID-19, pursuant to section 564(g)(2) of the [FFDCA]. As of the date of this letter, the oral formulations of HCQ and CQ are no longer authorized by FDA to treat COVID-19. While HCQ that has been distributed from SNS is no longer authorized under the EUA for the authorized use to treat hospitalized patients for COVID-19, FDA-approved HCQ can be distributed in interstate commerce. The CQ products covered by the EUA are not approved by FDA for any indication and therefore cannot be legally introduced into interstate commerce. In addition, under section 564(f)(2) of the [FFDCA], HCQ and CQ that were distributed from the SNS under this EUA remain authorized for emergency use to continue to treat any hospitalized patient to whom the authorized product has already been administered during the COVID-19 public health emergency, to the extent found necessary by such patient's attending physician.

Notice of this revocation will be published in the Federal Register, pursuant to section 564(h)(1) of the [FFDCA].

## 4. The "Right to Try" Act

FFDCA §561B is the codified version of the statute commonly known as the *Right to Try Act*. This statute permits drug sponsors to provide certain patients with access to investigational drugs "for which a Phase 1 clinical trial has been completed." FFDCA §561B(a)(2)(A). To qualify for this access, the patient must meet three conditions.

First, the patient must have been "diagnosed with a life-threatening disease or condition." FFDCA §561B(a)(1)(A). Second, the patient must be certified by a physician as having "exhausted approved treatment options" and being "unable to participate in a clinical trial" involving the investigational drug they seek to obtain. FFDCA §561B(a)(1)(B). Third, the patient must have provided "informed consent regarding the eligible investigational drug." FFDCA §561B(a)(1)(C).

If those circumstances are met, FFDCA §561B(b) provides that an "eligible investigational drug" provided to an "eligible patient" is "exempt" from various sections of the FFDCA, and its implementing regulations, that would otherwise bar provision of this unapproved drug to the patient.

The statute does not provide the patient with any right to access investigational drugs and does not require drug sponsors to provide the relevant drug. It does, however, provide significant protections from liability for those involved in providing a drug under the FFDCA § 561B. A drug "sponsor or manufacturer" receives full protection from liability, and a "prescriber, dispenser, or other individual entity" receives protection from liability "unless the relevant conduct constitutes reckless or willful misconduct, gross negligence, or an intentional tort." 21 U.S.C. § 360bbb-0a *note.*

## L. Key Points

- FDA administers five marketing authorization standards: safety only; safety and efficacy; safe, pure, and potent; protection of the public health; and no marketing authorization required.
- Pathways to market can be divided into paradigm pathways and alternate pathways.
  - For each product category, there is a single paradigm pathway that involves the most rigorous version of the applicable marketing authorization standard.
  - For most product categories, one or more alternate pathways exist. These alternate pathways permit marketing authorization without meeting the most rigorous version of the applicable marketing authorization standard.
  - These standards and pathways are summarized in the chart in Part E, *supra.*
- Designations are not pathways to market. You can think of these as flags that can be attached to a particular application to have it treated more advantageously by FDA, either during or after its trip along the relevant marketing authorization pathway.
  - Review clock designations provide for faster action by FDA once an application is submitted.
  - Review assistance designations provide for FDA assistance in navigating the relevant marketing authorization pathway.
  - Market exclusivity designations provide for an award—a period of market exclusivity for the approved product—as an incentive for a successful application.
- The FFDCA sets out four primary ways to access investigational products prior to marketing authorization.
  - Standard investigational use is a means for authorizing preclinical and clinical testing.

- Expanded access is a way of providing access to investigational medical products to patients who are unable to participate in clinical trials.
- Emergency use is a way of authorizing use of an unapproved medical product in response to an emergency.
- The Right to Try Act provides some liability protections to encourage the provision of certain drugs under expanded access programs.

# Chapter 5

# Background Requirements

## A. Introduction

This chapter presents five sets of background requirements that apply throughout many of FDA's regulatory programs. They are connected to marketing authorization in the sense that compliance with these requirements is required for lawful marketing of the relevant products. The five sets of background requirements are prohibition of adulteration, prohibition of misbranding, establishment registration requirements, user fees, and postmarket requirements.

For each of these five sets of requirements, the details vary substantially among the different product categories. To understand their role in food and drug regulation generally, however, you do not need to know the details—you can look those up when you need to know them in law practice. What you need to know, instead, is the more general role they play in FDA's regulatory programs.

## B. Outline of Regulatory Regime

As you know, most chapters in this casebook begin with an outline of the applicable regulatory regime. For this chapter, however, a single set of charts would be too long to be useful. Instead, this chapter presents a separate set of charts for each of the five sets of background requirements addressed in the chapter. Those charts are included within each of the relevant subparts of this chapter.

As you read this chapter for the first time, you should do no more than skim these charts to get a general sense of the structure of the applicable statutes and regulations. (For more information on the role of the charts in this casebook, see Chapter 1, Parts A.1 and B).

## C. The Five Sets of Background Requirements

### 1. Prohibition of Adulteration: Production-Process Requirements (Good Manufacturing Practices, Hazard Analysis, and Related Product Standards)

#### *a. Overview*

Please read (or review) the following excerpts in the statutory supplement:

- FFDCA § 402. Adulterated food. *Subsections (a) and (f) only.*
- FFDCA § 406. Tolerances for poisonous or deleterious substances in food, regulations.
- FFDCA § 418. Hazard analysis and risk-based preventative controls.
- FFDCA § 501. Adulterated drugs and devices. *Subsections (a), (h), and (j) only.*
- FFDCA § 601. Adulterated cosmetics.
- FFDCA § 902. Adulterated tobacco products.
- PHSA § 361. Regulations to control communicable diseases. *Subsection (a) only.*

This book uses the term "production-process requirements" to refer generally to various sets of requirements FDA has imposed on the general process of producing or harvesting FDA-regulated products. These derive both from the FFDCA's adulteration provisions and from other statutory provisions. Some production-process requirements apply broadly to a product category. These include: *current good manufacturing practices* (cGMP) for food, dietary supplements, medicated feed, drugs, devices, and tobacco; *hazard analysis and risk-based preventive controls* for food; *general biological product standards* for biological products, *quality system regulation* for medical devices; *current good tissue practices* (cGTP) for HCT/Ps; and *mitigation strategies to protect against intentional adulteration* for food.

Others apply to a more narrow subset within a product category. These include: *standards* for produce for human consumption, blood and blood products, diagnostic substances for laboratory tests, and allergenic products; *specialized cGMP* for infant formula, thermally processed low-acid foods in hermetically sealed containers, acidified food, bottled drinking water, positron emission tomography drugs, type A medicated articles (a type of new animal drug intended for use in producing either another type A medicated article or a medicated animal feed), blood and blood components, *hazard analysis and critical control points* (HACCP) for seafood and juices; and *refrigeration and transportation requirements* for shell eggs.

The different names for these requirements are probably less significant than they may seem. As you will see in the statutory provisions assigned above, some sections explicitly use the term "good manufacturing practice," others refer to the idea in more general terms, and § 418 explicitly requires "hazard analysis" and "risk-based preventive controls." FDA's view of the difference between cGMPs and hazard-analysis requirements is probably best seen in 21 C.F.R. Part 117, *Current good manufacturing practice, hazard analysis, and risk-based preventive controls for human food*. This was one of the major rules the agency promulgated to implement the Food Safety Modernization Act. As set out in the two charts below, Subpart B sets out cGMPs and Subpart C sets out hazard-analysis requirements.

| 21 C.F.R. Part 117, Subpart B—Current Good Manufacturing Practice | |
|---|---|
| 21 C.F.R. § | Title of Part |
| § 117.10 | Personnel. |
| § 117.20 | Plant and grounds. |
| § 117.35 | Sanitary operations. |
| § 117.37 | Sanitary facilities and controls. |
| § 117.40 | Equipment and utensils. |
| § 117.80 | Processes and controls. |
| § 117.93 | Warehousing and distribution. |
| § 117.95 | Holding and distribution of human food by-products for use as animal food. |
| § 117.110 | Defect action levels. |

| 21 C.F.R. Part 117, Subpart C—Hazard Analysis and Risk-Based Preventive Controls | |
|---|---|
| 21 C.F.R. § | Title of Part |
| § 117.126 | Food safety plan. |
| § 117.130 | Hazard analysis. |
| § 117.135 | Preventive controls. |
| § 117.136 | Circumstances in which the owner, operator, or agent in charge of a manufacturing/processing facility is not required to implement a preventive control. |
| § 117.137 | Provision of assurances required under § 117.136(a)(2), (3), and (4). |
| § 117.139 | Recall plan. |
| § 117.140 | Preventive control management components. |
| § 117.145 | Monitoring. |
| § 117.150 | Corrective actions and corrections. |
| § 117.155 | Verification. |
| § 117.160 | Validation. |
| § 117.165 | Verification of implementation and effectiveness. |
| § 117.170 | Reanalysis. |
| § 117.180 | Requirements applicable to a preventive controls qualified individual and a qualified auditor. |
| § 117.190 | Implementation records required for this subpart. |

As these charts suggest, the cGMP requirements focus more on the actual conditions in the facility. They tend to be the type of requirements that are best enforced by in-person inspection of the facility's operations. The hazard-analysis requirements, by contrast, focus more on the preparation of a written plan to identify, and focus on preventing, the most significant hazards to which the facility is exposed. They can be enforced in part simply by reviewing the facility's written plan (though onsite inspection may of course be necessary to determine whether the facility is complying with the plan).

Beyond this rough distinction, it is probably not useful to rely too extensively on the different terms used to describe the various production-process requirements. Production-process requirements promulgated in different regulatory eras, or based on different statutory language, often use different terms. However, the general idea of all production-process requirements is the same. Each sets out a basic set of requirements applicable to all producers of the relevant type of product. These requirements have the force and effect of law,[1] and FDA has the power to sanction those who fail to comply.

### *b. Outline of Regulatory Regime*

As noted above, this chapter contains separate outline-of-regulatory-regime sections for each set of background requirements. This is the outline for prohibitions on adulteration, including through production-process requirements.

| Timeline of Key Statutes: Production-Process Requirements | | | |
|---|---|---|---|
| Year | PL | Stat | Name of Statute |
| 1906 | 59-384 | 34 Stat. 768 | Pure Food and Drug Act |
| 1938 | 75-717 | 52 Stat. 1040 | FFDCA of 1938 |
| 1976 | 94-295 | 90 Stat. 539 | Medical Devices Amendments of 1976 |
| 1994 | 103-417 | 108 Stat. 4325 | Dietary Supplement Health and Education Act |
| 2011 | 111-353 | 124 Stat. 3885 | FDA Food Safety Modernization Act |

| Key Statutory Provisions: Production-Process Requirements | | |
|---|---|---|
| Statute Name or U.S.C. Title | § | Title of Section or Subsection |
| FFDCA | 402(a)(4) | [adulteration of food prepared, packed, or held under insanitary conditions] |
| FFDCA | 402(g) | [adulteration of dietary supplements that do not comply with cGMP] |

1. See *Nat'l Ass'n of Pharmaceutical Mfrs. v. FDA*, 637 F.2d 877 (2d Cir. 1991), excerpted in Chapter 2.

| Statute Name or U.S.C. Title | § | Title of Section or Subsection |
|---|---|---|
| FFDCA | 406 | Tolerances for poisonous or deleterious substances in food; regulations |
| FFDCA | 418 | Hazard analysis and risk-based preventative controls |
| FFDCA | 501(a)(2)(b), 501(j) | [Drugs that fail to comply with cGMP are adulterated] |
| FFDCA | 520(f) | Good manufacturing practice requirements [for devices] |
| FFDCA | 564(e)(3) | [Waiver or limitation of GMP requirements in certain emergencies] |
| FFDCA | 564A(c) | [Waiver or limitation of GMP requirements in certain emergencies] |
| FFDCA | 802(f) | [GMP compliance required even for export of drugs and devices that lack U.S. marketing authorization] |
| FFDCA | 802(b) | Agreements with foreign countries [for mutual recognition of medical device GMP requirements] |
| FFDCA | 906(e) | Good manufacturing practice requirements for tobacco |

## Key Regulatory Provisions: Broadly Applicable Production-Process Requirements

| 21 C.F.R. Part | Subpart | Title of Part or Subpart |
|---|---|---|
| 26 | — | Mutual recognition of pharmaceutical good manufacturing practice reports, medical device quality system audit reports, and certain medical device product evaluation reports: united states and the european community |
| 110 | — | Current good manufacturing practice in manufacturing, packing, or holding human food *[currently in phase-out]* |
| 111 | — | Current good manufacturing practice in manufacturing, packaging, labeling, or holding operations for dietary supplements |
| 117 | — | Current good manufacturing practice, hazard analysis, and risk-based preventive controls for human food |
| 121 | — | Mitigation strategies to protect food against intentional adulteration |
| 210 | — | Current good manufacturing practice in manufacturing, processing, packing, or holding of drugs; general |
| 211 | — | Current good manufacturing practice for finished pharmaceuticals |
| 225 | — | Current good manufacturing practice for medicated feeds |
| 507 | — | Current good manufacturing practice, hazard analysis, and risk-based preventive controls for food for animals |
| 610 | — | General biological products standards |

| 21 C.F.R. Part | Subpart | Title of Part or Subpart |
|---|---|---|
| 820 | — | Quality system regulation [medical device cGMP requirements] |
| 1271 | D | [Good tissue practices] |

**Key Regulatory Provisions: Subcategory-Specific Production-Process Requirements**

| 21 C.F.R. Part | Subpart | Title of Part or Subpart |
|---|---|---|
| 106 | — | Infant formula requirements pertaining to current good manufacturing practice, quality control procedures, quality factors, records and reports, and notifications |
| 112 | — | Standards for the growing, harvesting, packing, and holding of produce for human consumption |
| 113 | — | Thermally processed low-acid foods packaged in hermetically sealed containers |
| 114 | — | Acidified foods |
| 115 | — | Shell eggs |
| 118 | — | Production, storage, and transportation of shell eggs |
| 120 | — | Hazard Analysis and Critical Control Point (HACCP) systems [for juices] |
| 123 | — | Fish and fishery products |
| 129 | — | Processing and bottling of bottled drinking water |
| 212 | — | Current good manufacturing practice for positron emission tomography drugs |
| 226 | — | Current good manufacturing practice for type a medicated articles |
| 606 | — | Current good manufacturing practice for blood and blood components |
| 630 | — | Requirements for blood and blood components intended for transfusion or for further manufacturing use |
| 640 | — | Additional standards for human blood and blood products |
| 660 | — | Additional standards for diagnostic substances for laboratory tests |
| 680 | — | Additional standards for miscellaneous products |

## 2015-09-17 FDA Final Rule, Current Good Manufacturing Practice, Hazard Analysis, and Risk-Based Preventive Controls for Human Food

80 Fed. Reg. 55,908

### Purpose and Coverage of the Rule

This rule is part of FDA's implementation of the FDA Food Safety Modernization Act (FSMA), which intends to better protect public health by, among other things, adopting a modern, preventive, and risk-based approach to food safety regulation. This rule creates certain new requirements for the production of human food by registered food facilities, and revises previous requirements, in three key ways.

First, this rule creates new requirements for certain domestic and foreign facilities to establish and implement hazard analysis and risk-based preventive controls for human food. In general, these requirements apply to establishments that are required to register with FDA as a food "facility." This portion of the rule requires registered food facilities to maintain a food safety plan, perform a hazard analysis, and institute preventive controls for the mitigation of those hazards, unless an exemption applies. Facilities must also monitor their controls, conduct verification activities to ensure the controls are effective, take appropriate corrective actions, and maintain records documenting these actions.

Second, this rule modernizes FDA's long-standing current good manufacturing practice (CGMP) regulations regarding the manufacturing, processing, packing, or holding of human food. We have updated, revised, and otherwise clarified certain requirements within the CGMP regulations, which were last updated in 1986.

Third, this rule clarifies the scope of the exemption for "farms" in FDA's current food facility registration regulations and makes corresponding revisions to FDA's current regulations for the establishment, maintenance, and availability of records. These revisions affect who is subject to the existing regulations for registration and recordkeeping, as well as the new requirements for hazard analysis and risk-based preventive controls requirements established here.

This final rule is the result of significant stakeholder engagement, beginning before the proposed rule. In response to extensive stakeholder input on the proposed rule, we revised key provisions in a supplemental notice of proposed rulemaking. After the supplemental notice of proposed rulemaking, we conducted even more outreach to the stakeholder community to ensure that the risk-based, preventive requirements in this final rule are practical and protective of public health.

### Summary of the Major Provisions of the Rule

The final rule implements the requirements of FSMA for covered facilities to establish and implement a food safety system that includes a hazard analysis and risk-based preventive controls. Specifically, the rule establishes requirements for:

- A written food safety plan;
- Hazard analysis;

- Preventive controls;
- Monitoring;
- Corrective actions and corrections;
- Verification;
- Supply-chain program;
- Recall plan; and
- Associated records.

We have added flexibility and clarity to these provisions in response to comments. Although there are similarities between these requirements of FSMA and the requirements of food safety systems known as Hazard Analysis and Critical Control Point (HACCP) systems, not every provision in FSMA is identical to the provisions of HACCP systems, and we have revised much of our terminology to distinguish FSMA's requirements for hazard analysis and risk-based preventive controls from HACCP requirements. A facility subject to the rule must conduct a hazard analysis to identify and evaluate known or reasonably foreseeable hazards for each type of food manufactured, processed, packed, or held at the facility to determine whether there are any hazards requiring preventive controls. The first step of a hazard analysis is hazard identification, which must consider known or reasonably foreseeable hazards, including biological, chemical, and physical hazards. The hazard analysis must consider hazards that may be present in the food because they occur naturally, are unintentionally introduced, or are intentionally introduced for purposes of economic gain. We continue to believe that hazards that may be intentionally introduced for economic gain will need preventive controls in rare circumstances, usually in cases where there has been a pattern of economically motivated adulteration in the past. Economically motivated adulteration that affects product integrity or quality, for example, but not food safety, is out of the scope of this rule.

A facility subject to the rule must identify and implement preventive controls to provide assurances that any hazards requiring a preventive control will be significantly minimized or prevented and the food manufactured, processed, packed, or held by the facility will not be adulterated. The rule establishes preventive control management components (monitoring, corrective actions and corrections, and verification) as appropriate to ensure the effectiveness of the preventive controls. One way we have clarified the risk-based flexibility of these requirements is by clearly stating in the final rule that a facility must take into account the nature of the preventive control and the facility's food safety system when considering which activities are appropriate for that facility.

We have also added flexibility and made risk-based modifications for specific preventive control management components. For example, the final rule allows flexibility for the specific records required to document monitoring of refrigeration controls during storage of a food that requires time/temperature control for safety. These records can be either affirmative records demonstrating temperature is controlled or "exception records" demonstrating loss of temperature control. As another example, the rule includes tailored, less burdensome requirements for corrections. A correction is defined in this rule as an action to identify and correct a problem that occurred during the production of food, without other actions associated with a corrective action procedure (such as actions to reduce the likelihood that the problem will recur, evaluate all affected food for safety, and prevent affected food from entering commerce). The final rule clarifies that corrections must be taken in a timely manner and must be recorded when appropriate, but they do not, for example, need to be included in a written plan or accompanied by a reanalysis of the written food safety plan.

As a third example, the final rule provides flexibility for which verification activities must occur. In general, a facility is required to conduct verification activities, as appropriate to the nature of the preventive control and its role in the facility's food safety system, including validation, verification of monitoring, verification of corrective actions, verification of implementation and effectiveness, and reanalysis. Validation is not required for all controls. For example, the rule specifies that validation is not required for certain types of preventive controls (i.e., food allergen controls, sanitation controls, supply-chain controls, and the recall plan) and provides flexibility for the facility to not validate other preventive controls with a written justification based on factors such as the nature of the hazard, and the nature of the preventive control and its role in the facility's food safety system. Product testing and environmental monitoring are listed as possible verification activities, but, like other preventive control management components in general, they are only required as appropriate to the food, facility, the nature of the preventive control, and the preventive control's role in the facility's food safety system. In many cases, neither product testing nor environmental monitoring will be appropriate. For example, there would be little or no benefit to product testing or environmental monitoring in facilities that pack or hold produce raw agricultural commodities that are rarely consumed raw, such as potatoes.

A facility must reanalyze the food safety plan as a whole at least once every three years. The final rule provides the flexibility for a facility to only reanalyze the applicable portion of the food safety plan under certain other circumstances, such as when a facility becomes aware of new information about potential hazards associated with a food.

The final rule also adds flexibility to the preventive controls requirements and recognizes the reality of modern distribution chains by not requiring a manufacturing/processing facility to implement a preventive control in certain circumstances when the hazard requiring a preventive control will be controlled by another entity in the distribution chain. For example, if a facility's customer (or another entity in the distribution chain) will control the hazard, then that facility can rely on its customer to provide written assurance that the identified hazard will be controlled by an entity in the distribution chain, with flexibility for how the customer provides that written assurance depending on whether the customer, or an entity subsequent to the customer, will control the hazard. We have identified four specific circumstances in which a manufacturing/processing facility can rely on another entity in the distribution chain to control a hazard, with practical solutions explained further in section XXVII. We also have provided flexibility for a facility to establish, document, and implement an alternative system that ensures adequate control, at a later distribution step, of the hazards in the food product distributed by a manufacturing/processing facility such that the facility would not need to implement a preventive control.

We revised the proposed provisions for a supplier program to add flexibility, recognizing that the receiving facility and the supplier may be separated by several entities in a supply chain. We are allowing entities such as distributors, brokers, and aggregators to determine, conduct, and document appropriate supplier verification activities as a service to the receiving facility, provided that the receiving facility reviews and assesses applicable documentation provided by the other entity and documents that review and assessment. However, because the approval of suppliers is ultimately the responsibility of the receiving facility, the rule specifies that only a receiving facility can approve suppliers. To improve clarity and readability we redesignated the proposed provisions into eight distinct sections of regulatory text in a newly established subpart G (Supply-Chain Program).

Each facility subject to the rule must have a recall plan for a food with a hazard requiring a preventive control.

Many activities required by the final rule must be conducted (or overseen) by a preventive controls qualified individual, a new term we are coining here. A preventive controls qualified individual is a qualified individual who has successfully completed certain training in the development and application of risk-based preventive controls or is otherwise qualified through job experience to develop and apply a food safety system.

The rule establishes several exemptions (including modified requirements in some cases) from the requirements for hazard analysis and risk-based preventive controls. All of these exemptions are expressly authorized by FSMA. A facility that manufactures, processes, packs, or holds food and that is required to register with FDA would be required to comply with the requirements for hazard analysis and risk-based preventive controls unless it is covered by an exemption, as shown in the following table.

. . . .

The rule includes procedures for withdrawing a qualified facility exemption, in the event of an active investigation of a foodborne illness outbreak that is directly linked to the facility, or if FDA determines that it is necessary to protect the public health and prevent or mitigate a foodborne illness outbreak based on relevant conditions or conduct associated with the qualified facility. The final rule provides procedures for a facility to appeal an order to withdraw a qualified facility exemption, for a facility to request an informal hearing, for the conduct of an informal hearing, for an appeal, for revoking an order to withdraw a qualified facility exemption, and for reinstating an exemption that was withdrawn.

The rule finalizes recordkeeping provisions associated with the new provisions for hazard analysis and risk-based preventive controls. These records allow facilities to show, and FDA to determine, compliance with the new requirements. To meet these requirements, a facility may use existing records as appropriate.

In addition to finalizing new requirements for hazard analysis and risk-based preventive controls as required by FSMA, the rule does two more key things. First, it modernizes the existing CGMPs. Second, it revises the "farm" definition.

The rule makes several revisions to the CGMPs to update and clarify them. For example, the final CGMPs do not include nonbinding provisions, because it is no longer FDA's practice to include guidance in the regulatory text. The rule finalizes some of the previously nonbinding provisions in the CGMPs as binding requirements, including a requirement for education and training, but deletes other nonbinding provisions. We have revised some key terms for consistency and clarity. And we have clarified FDA's long-standing position that the CGMPs address allergen cross-contact by making that explicit in the regulatory text. Finally, the rule revises a long-standing exemption from the CGMP requirements regarding specific activities conducted on raw agricultural commodities to reflect the contemporary regulatory framework associated with the "farm" definition. In addition, elsewhere in this issue of the Federal Register, in a final rule that establishes requirements for hazard analysis and risk-based preventive controls for food for animals, FDA is establishing an additional revision to the human food CGMPs to address comments about the practice of human food manufacturers sending by-products to local farmers or animal food manufacturers for use as animal food. Because we proposed these requirements as part of the rulemaking for the animal preventive controls rule, we are finalizing these provisions in the final animal preventive controls rule rather than in this rule.

Finally, the rule clarifies the "farm" definition that is central to the determination of whether certain entities must register as a food facility and, thus, become subject to the new requirements for hazard analysis and risk-based preventive controls. The final "farm" definition reflects current farming practices, differentiates between two types of farm operations (i.e., a "primary production farm" and a "secondary activities farm"), and allows for a consistent—although not identical—regulatory approach across similar operations, to the extent possible. In general, a "primary production farm" is an operation under one management in one general (but not necessarily contiguous) physical location devoted to the growing of crops, the harvesting of crops, the raising of animals (including seafood), or any combination of these activities. A farm packs and holds raw agricultural commodities and may conduct certain manufacturing/processing activities (i.e., drying/dehydrating raw agricultural commodities to create a distinct commodity (such as drying/dehydrating grapes to produce raisins), treatment to manipulate the ripening of raw agricultural commodities (such as by treating produce with ethylene gas), and packaging and labeling). The term farm also now includes a "secondary activities farm," which is an operation, not located on a primary production farm, devoted to the key farming operations of harvesting, packing, and/or holding of raw agricultural commodities, provided that the primary production farm(s) that grow, harvest, and/or raise the majority of the raw agricultural commodities harvested, packed, and/or held by the secondary activities farm owns, or jointly owns, a majority interest in the secondary activities farm. A secondary activities farm may also conduct those additional activities allowed on a primary production farm.

## 2. Prohibition of Misbranding: Labeling Requirements

### *a. Overview*

Labeling requirements are based, to a significant degree, on the FFDCA's misbranding provisions. At a basic level, FDA has promulgated detailed requirements for product identity, quality, ingredient content, and fill of container in many regulatory areas. At a deeper level—that of the structure of FDA's regulatory regime—claims made or implied in product labeling are often determinative of the product category, or categories, into which the relevant product falls.

Please read (or review) the following excerpts in the statutory supplement:

- FFDCA 201. Definitions; generally. *Subsections (k), (l), and (m).*
- FFDCA 301. Prohibited acts. *Subsection (k) only.*
- FFDCA 403. Misbranded food.
- FFDCA 502. Misbranded drugs and devices.
- FFDCA 602. Misbranded cosmetics.
- FFDCA 903. Misbranded tobacco products.

The three subsections of FFDCA 201 provide statutory definitions for *label*, *labeling*, and *immediate container*. FFDCA 301(k) prohibits various acts relating to alteration or removal of labeling. FFDCA §§403, 502, 602, and 903 are the act's chapter-specific misbranding provisions.

### *b. Outline of Regulatory Regime*

As noted above, this chapter contains separates outline-of-regulatory-regime sections for each set of background requirements. This is the outline for prohibitions on misbranding, including through labeling requirements.

| Timeline of Key Statutes: Labeling | | | |
|---|---|---|---|
| Year | PL | Stat | Name of Statute |
| 1906 | 59-384 | 34 Stat. 768 | Pure Food and Drug Act |
| 1912 | 62-419 | 37 Stat. 732 | Gould Amendment |
| 1938 | 75-717 | 52 Stat. 1040 | FFDCA of 1938 |
| 1944 | 78-410 | 58 Stat. 682 | Public Health Services Act |
| 1950 | 81-459 | 64 Stat. 20 | Oleomargarine Act |
| 1966 | 89-755 | 80 Stat. 1296 | Fair Packaging and Labeling Act |
| 1968 | 90-398 | 82 Stat. 342 | Animal Drug Amendments of 1968 |
| 1976 | 94-295 | 90 Stat. 539 | Medical Devices Amendments of 1976 |
| 1990 | 101-535 | 104 Stat. 2353 | Nutrition Labeling and Education Act |
| 1993 | 103-80 | 107 Stat. 773 | Nutrition Labeling and Education Amendments of 1992 |
| 1994 | 103-417 | 108 Stat. 4325 | Dietary Supplement Health and Education Act of 1994 |

| Key Statutory Provisions: Labeling | | |
|---|---|---|
| Statute Name or U.S.C. Title | § | Title of Section or Subsection |
| FFDCA | 201(g)(2) | [Definition of "counterfeit drug"] |
| FFDCA | 201(k) | [Definition of "label"] |
| FFDCA | 201(m) | [Definition of "immediate container"] |
| FFDCA | 201(m) | [Definition of "labeling"] |
| FFDCA | 301(i) | [Prohibition on various acts relating to creation of counterfeit drugs] |
| FFDCA | 301(k) | [Prohibition of alteration, removal, etc. of labeling] |
| FFDCA | 301(qq) | [Prohibition on various acts relating to creation of counterfeit tobacco products] |
| FFDCA | 403 | Misbranded food |
| FFDCA | 403B | Dietary supplement labeling exemptions |
| FFDCA | 411 | Vitamins and minerals |
| FFDCA | 502 | Misbranded drugs and devices |
| FFDCA | 503 | Exemptions and consideration for certain drugs, devices, and biological products |
| FFDCA | 602 | Misbranded cosmetics |
| FFDCA | 903 | Misbranded tobacco products |
| FFDCA | 920 | Labeling, recordkeeping, records inspection |

| Key Regulatory Provisions: Labeling | | |
|---|---|---|
| 21 C.F.R. Part | Subpart | Title of Part or Subpart |
| 70 | B | Packaging and labeling [of color additives] |
| 99 | — | Dissemination of information on unapproved/new uses for marketed drugs, biologics, and devices |
| 101 | — | Food labeling |
| 102 | — | Common or usual names for nonstandardized food |
| 105 | B | Label statements [for foods for special dietary uses] |
| 107 | B | Labeling [of infant formula] |
| 111 | L | Production and process control system: requirements for packaging and labeling operations [for dietary supplements] |
| 190 | — | Dietary supplements |
| 201 | — | Labeling [for drugs] |
| 208 | — | Medication guides for prescription drug products |
| 299 | — | Drugs; official names and established names |
| 310 | — | New drugs |
| 312 | — | Investigational new drug application |
| 314 | — | Applications for FDA approval to market a new drug |
| 369 | — | Interpretative statements re warnings on drugs and devices for over-the-counter sale |
| 501 | — | Animal food labeling |
| 502 | — | Common or usual names for nonstandardized animal foods |
| 510 | — | New animal drugs |
| 511 | — | New animal drugs |
| 530 | — | Extralabel drug use in animals |
| 511 | — | New animal drugs for investigational use |
| 516 | — | New animal drugs for minor use and minor species |
| 601 | — | Licensing [of biologics] |
| 701 | — | Cosmetic labeling |
| 740 | — | Cosmetic product warning statements |
| 801 | — | Labeling [of devices] |
| 812 | — | Investigational device exemptions |
| 814 | — | Premarket approval of medical devices |
| 820 | — | Quality system regulation |

| 21 C.F.R. Part | Subpart | Title of Part or Subpart |
|---|---|---|
| 821 | — | Medical device tracking requirements |
| 830 | — | Unique device identification |
| 895 | — | Banned devices |
| 1140 | D | Labeling and advertising [of tobacco products] |
| 1141 | — | Cigarette package and advertising warnings |
| 1143 | — | Minimum required warning statements [for tobacco products] |
| 1271 | — | Human cells, tissues, and cellular and tissue-based products |

## 3. Establishment Registration

### *a. Overview*

Please read (or review) the following excerpts in the statutory supplement:

- FFDCA § 415. Registration of food facilities.
- FFDCA § 510. Registration of producers of drugs and devices. *Subsections (a)–(j) only.*
- FFDCA § 905. Annual registration. *Subsections (a)–(i) only.*

These are the establishment registration requirements for food, medical products, and tobacco. FFDCA § 415 governs food establishment; FFDCA § 510 governs drug (including biologic and animal drug), device, and combination-product establishments; and FFDCA § 905 governs tobacco-product establishments.

### *b. Outline of Regulatory Regime*

As noted above, this chapter contains separates outline-of-regulatory-regime sections for each set of background requirements. This is the outline for establishment-registration requirements.

| Timeline of Key Statutes: Establishment Registration | | | |
|---|---|---|---|
| Year | PL | Stat | Name of Statute |
| 1962 | 87-781 | 76 Stat. 780 | Kefauver-Harris Amendments of 1962 |
| 1965 | 89-74 | 79 Stat. 226 | Drug Abuse Control Amendments of 1965 |
| 1970 | 91-513 | 84 Stat. 1236 | Comprehensive Drug Abuse Prevention and Control Act of 1970 |
| 1972 | 92-387 | 86 Stat. 559 | Drug Listing Act of 1972 |
| 1976 | 94-295 | 90 Stat. 539 | Medical Devices Amendments of 1976 |
| 2002 | 107-188 | 116 Stat. 594 | Public Health Security and Bioterrorism Preparedness and Response Act of 2002 |

| Year | PL | Stat | Name of Statute |
|---|---|---|---|
| 2007 | 110-85 | 121 Stat. 823 | FDA Amendments Act of 2007 |
| 2009 | 111-31 | 123 Stat. 1776 | Family Smoking Prevention and Tobacco Control Act |
| 2011 | 111-353 | 124 Stat. 3885 | FDA Food Safety Modernization Act |
| 2012 | 112-144 | 126 Stat. 993 | FDA Safety and Innovation Act |

| Key Statutory Provisions: Establishment Registration | | |
|---|---|---|
| **Statute Name or U.S.C. Title** | **§** | **Title of Section or Subsection** |
| FFDCA | 415 | Registration of food facilities |
| FFDCA | 510 | Registration of producers of drugs and devices |
| FFDCA | 905 | Annual registration [of producers of tobacco products] |

| Key Regulatory Provisions: Establishment Registration | | |
|---|---|---|
| **21 C.F.R. Part** | **Subpart** | **Title of Part or Subpart** |
| 207 | — | Requirements for foreign and domestic establishment registration and listing for human drugs, including drugs that are regulated under a biologics license application, and animal drugs, and the national drug code |
| 515 | — | Medicated feed mill license |
| 607 | — | Establishment registration and product listing for manufacturers of human blood and blood products and licensed devices |
| 710 | — | Voluntary registration of cosmetic product establishments |
| 807 | A through D | Establishment registration and device listing for manufacturers and initial importers of devices<br>*[Note: Subpart E contains device premarket notification procedures. For a variety of reasons that will be addressed in the medical device chapter of this book, those requirements are tied to the establishment registration provision of the statute.]* |
| 1107 | — | Establishment registration, product listing, and substantial equivalence reports<br>*[Note: This section does not currently contain any establishment registration requirements (though such requirements exist in the statute). However, the title of the section suggests it is the location where future establishment registration regulations will be located].* |
| 1271 | B | Procedures for registration and listing [of HCT/P establishments] |

## 4. User Fees

### *a. Overview*

The details of FFDCA user-free provisions are complex and beyond the scope of this book. For a general understanding of food and drug regulation, you should know that these programs exist, that they require regular renewal by Congress, and they play a significant role in the funding many of FDA's marketing authorization programs.

### *b. Outline of Regulatory Regime*

As noted above, this chapter contains separate outline-of-regulatory-regime sections for each set of background requirements. This is the outline for user fees, but it includes only a timeline of key statutes. Because this casebook does not address user fees in detail, no "Key Statutory Provisions" or "Key Regulatory Provisions" charts are included.

**Timeline of Key Statutes: User Fees**

| Year | PL | Stat | Name of Statute |
|---|---|---|---|
| 1992 | 102-571 | 106 Stat. 4491 | Prescription Drug User Fee Act of 1992 |
| 2002 | 107-250 | 116 Stat. 1588 | Medical Device User Fee and Modernization Act of 2002 |
| 2007 | 110-85 | 121 Stat. 823 | FDA Amendments Act of 2007, *which includes, as separate titles:*<br>• Prescription Drug User Fee Amendments of 2007<br>• Medical Device User Fee Amendments of 2007 |
| 2008 | 110-316 | 122 Stat. 3509 | Animal Drug User Fee Amendments of 2008 |
| 2008 | 110-316 | 122 Stat. 3509 | Generic Animal Drug User Fee Act |
| 2012 | 112-144 | 126 Stat. 993 | Food & Drug Administration Safety and Innovation Act, *which includes, as separate titles:*<br>• Prescription Drug User Fee Amendments of 2012<br>• Medical Device User Fee Amendments of 2012<br>• Generic Drug User Fee Amendments of 2012<br>• Biosimilar User Fee Act of 2012 |
| 2013 | 113-14 | 127 Stat. 451 | Animal Drug and Animal Generic Drug User Fee Reauthorization Act of 2013 |
| 2017 | 115-52 | 131 Stat. 1005 | FDA Reauthorization Act of 2017, *which includes, as separate titles:*<br>• Prescription Drug User Fee Amendments of 2017<br>• Medical Device User Fee Amendments of 2017<br>• Generic Drug User Fee Amendments of 2017<br>• Biosimilar User Fee Amendments of 2017 |

| Year | PL | Stat | Name of Statute |
|---|---|---|---|
| 2018 | 115-234 | 132 Stat. 2427 | Animal Drug and Animal Generic Drug User Fee Amendments of 2018 |
| 2020 | 116-136 | 134 Stat. 281 | Coronavirus Aid, Relief, and Economic Security Act (CARES Act) |

## Congressional Research Service, FDA Human Medical Product User Fee Programs: In Brief

Nov. 21, 2017

The Food and Drug Administration (FDA) regulates human medical products to ensure they are safe and effective for their intended use in patients. Medical products include prescription and nonprescription (over the counter) drugs, biologics, and medical devices. FDA regulation of these products involves both premarket and postmarket regulatory requirements. Premarket requirements, which use a significant portion of the agency's resources, include the review of products and product applications for FDA approval or clearance prior to marketing. Postmarket requirements are varied, but may include passive surveillance mechanisms used to monitor the performance of medical products once they are marketed and certain postmarket studies and reporting.

To support these premarket and postmarket activities, the agency relies on (1) discretionary appropriations provided through the annual appropriations process, and (2) user fees paid by each regulated industry. The primary purpose of the user fee programs is to reduce the time necessary to review and make decisions on medical product marketing applications. Lengthy review times affect the industry, which waits to market its products, and patients, who wait to use these products. Some critics of the current scope of the user fee programs are concerned that FDA's mission to protect public health may be compromised if reliance on these fees affects the impartiality of FDA's scientists.

User fees are authorized in legislation on a five year cycle, with authority for their actual collection and expenditure provided each year through the annual appropriations process, The four user fee programs discussed in this report are prescription drugs, medical devices, generic drugs, and biosimilars....

A shared element of all four user fee programs is that the user fees are to supplement congressional appropriations, not replace them. The laws include limiting conditions, known as "triggers," to enforce this goal. FDA may collect and use fees only if the direct appropriations for specified activities involved in the review of products remains at a level at least equal (adjusted for inflation) to an amount or benchmark specified in each law. Originally the fees were authorized to be used to support only premarket review activities, allowing FDA to hire additional staff to review premarket applications with the goal of reducing review time. Over time, Congress added preclinical drug development and certain postmarket activities to the allowable activities that may be paid for with user fee revenue.

In exchange for paying user fees, industry receives from FDA a commitment to meet performance goals, such as completing premarket review within a specified timeframe. Prior to each five year reauthorization cycle, FDA and industry negotiate the performance goals, which are finalized in a written agreement. The reauthorization process allows for input from other relevant stakeholders, including academic experts and representatives of patient and consumer advocacy groups, and provides opportunity for public comment on the agreement. For the next reauthorization cycle, the [FFDCA] requires the Health and Human Services (HHS) Secretary to submit the four user fee agreements to Congress by January 15, 2022. In each previous reauthorization, Congress has accepted unchanged the terms and conditions as negotiated between FDA and the industry. The four performance goal documents for FY2018 through FY2022 are provided on the FDA website.

Due to the importance of user fees to FDA's budget, reauthorization of the user fee programs has been considered to be "must pass" legislation. Congress generally uses the reauthorization bill to address related FDA regulatory concerns; it therefore serves as an important driver for the ongoing modification of overall agency regulatory policy.

## 5. Postmarket Requirements

### *a. Overview*

This section addresses postmarket study, surveillance, reporting, and tracking requirements that go beyond FDA's traditional authority to proceed against a product that is adulterated or misbranded. Some of these programs are highly detailed, others more general—and most are specific to a single product category. For a general understanding of food and drug regulation, it is sufficient to note a few things.

First, as a matter of public policy, premarket authorization and postmarket surveillance are alternative ways to address product safety. They are not, however, mutually exclusive. A regulatory regime with weak premarket requirements may seek to compensate for that through rigorous postmarket requirements. Alternatively, a regulatory regime with strong premarket requirements may see less need to invest in postmarket requirements.

Second, adverse events that occur in only a small proportion of users are difficult to detect through standard clinical trials. For example, an adverse event that occurs in one out of 100,000 product users is unlikely to be detected in a clinical trial of a few thousand individuals. A prospective clinical trial large enough to detect such an event would be prohibitively expensive. Accordingly, postmarket methods are generally the only ones available for detecting relatively rare adverse events.

Third, when bad things do happen, FDA needs to be able to determine when—in the path from production to consumption—things went wrong. Accordingly, large-scale, long-distance trade in FDA-regulated products has led to an increased focus on methods for tracing the source of an individual product associated with an adverse event. Tracing tends to be more difficult for high-volume, low-cost products produced at multiple facilities (such as food), and less difficult for low-volume, higher-cost products produced at a small number of facilities (such as many drugs and devices). Accordingly, tracing requirements vary substantially across the different product categories.

### *b. Outline of Regulatory Regime*

As noted above, this chapter contains separates outline-of-regulatory-regime sections for each set of background requirements. This is the outline for postmarket registration requirements.

| Timeline of Key Statutes: Postmarket Requirements | | | |
|---|---|---|---|
| **Year** | **PL** | **Stat** | **Name of Statute** |
| 2007 | 110-85 | 121 Stat. 823 | FDA Amendments Act of 2007 |
| 2011 | 111-353 | 124 Stat. 3885 | FDA Food Safety Modernization Act |
| 2012 | 112-144 | 126 Stat. 993 | FDA Safety and Innovation Act |
| 2013 | 113-5 | 127 Stat. 161 | Pandemic and All-Hazards Preparedness Reauthorization Act of 2013 |
| 2016 | 114-255 | 130 Stat. 1033 | 21st Century Cures Act |
| 2017 | 115-52 | 131 Stat. 1005 | FDA Reauthorization Act of 2017 |
| 2018 | 115-271 | 132 stat. 3894 | SUPPORT for Patients and Communities Act |

| Key Statutory Provisions: Postmarket Requirements | | |
|---|---|---|
| **Statute Name or U.S.C. Title** | **§** | **Title of Section or Subsection** |
| FFDCA | 417 | Reportable food registry |
| FFDCA | 502(z) | Postmarket studies and clinical trials; new safety information in labeling |
| FFDCA | 505(k)(3) | Active postmarket risk identification [for new drugs] |
| FFDCA | 505(o) | Postmarket studies and clinical trials; labeling [for new drugs] |
| FFDCA | 505-1 | Risk evaluation and mitigation strategy [for new drugs] |
| FFDCA | 505F(a)(1) | [Potential use of real-world evidence to satisfy postapproval study requirements] |
| FFDCA | 506 | Expedited approval of drugs for serious or life-threatening diseases or conditions |
| FFDCA | 506B | Reports of postmarketing studies |
| FFDCA | 513(a)(1)(B) | [Including postmarket surveillance as possible "special control"] |

| Statute Name or U.S.C. Title | § | Title of Section or Subsection |
|---|---|---|
| FFDCA | 513(a)(3)(C) | [Requiring considering of postmarket controls as one way of reducing the extent of data required in a premarket approval application under § 515] |
| FFDCA | 519(d) | Inclusion of devices in the postmarket risk identification and analysis system |
| FFDCA | 522 | Postmarket surveillance |
| FFDCA | 567 | Risk communication [for prescription-drug supply chain] |
| FFDCA | 581 | Definitions [for prescription-drug supply chain] |
| FFDCA | 582 | Requirements [for prescription-drug supply chain] |
| FFDCA | 583 | National standards for prescription drug wholesale distributors |
| FFDCA | 584 | National standards for third-party logistics providers *[for prescription-drug supply chain]* |
| FFDCA | 585 | Uniform national policy [for prescription-drug supply chain] |
| FFDCA | 1003(f)(2) | [Requiring "agency plan for statutory compliance" to include discussion of implementing "postmarket monitoring provisions"] |
| FFDCA | 1010 | [Requiring chief scientist to "develop postmarket safety performance measures that are as measurable and rigorous as the ones already developed for premarket review"] |
| 21 U.S.C. | 2223 | Enhancing tracking and tracing of food and recordkeeping |
| 21 U.S.C. | 2224 | Surveillance [for foodborne illness outbreaks] |

## Key Regulatory Provisions: Postmarket Requirements

| 21 C.F.R. Part | Subpart, Section, or Subsection | Title of Part, Subpart, Section, or Subsection |
|---|---|---|
| 201 | 201.57(c)7)(II)(B) | [Requiring listing, on prescription drug and biologic labels, of adverse reactions from postmarketing experience) |
| 310 | 310.305 | Records and reports concerning adverse drug experiences on marketed prescription drugs for human use without approved new drug applications. |
| 314 | 314.80 | Postmarketing reporting of adverse drug experiences [after standard new-drug applications] |
| 314 | 314.81 | Other postmarketing reports [after standard new-drug applications] |
| 314 | 314.98 | Postmarketing reports [after abbreviated new-drug applications] |
| 314 | 314.540 | Postmarketing safety reporting [after accelerated-approval new-drug application] |

| 21 C.F.R. Part | Subpart, Section, or Subsection | Title of Part, Subpart, Section, or Subsection |
|---|---|---|
| 314 | 314.630 | Postmarketing safety reporting [after approval of new drug when human efficacy studies not ethical or feasible] |
| 329 | — | Nonprescription human drug products subject to [serious-event reporting requirements of] section 760 of the Federal Food, Drug, and Cosmetic Act |
| 514 | 514.80(b)(4)(iv)(C) | [Requiring reports of adverse animal drug experiences that occur in post-approval studies] |
| 516 | 516.165 | Records and reports [relating to indexed animal drugs] |
| 600 | D | Reporting of adverse experiences [with biologics] |
| 803 | — | Medical device reporting |
| 804 | — | Medical devices; reports of corrections and removals |
| 821 | — | Medical device tracking requirements |
| 822 | — | Postmarket surveillance [for medical devices] |

## D. Key Points

- Production-process requirements
  - Production-process requirements now exist for most product categories. They are based on a combination of the FFDCA's chapter-specific adulteration provisions, the PHSA's communicable diseases provision, and some category-specific provisions.
  - These can broadly be divided into good manufacturing practice requirements and hazard-analysis requirements, but there is some overlap between them—and different terms are used in different product categories.
  - Production-process requirements tend to be highly detailed and make unusually boring reading. However, they play a major role in FDA's regulatory programs and should not be overlooked.
- Labels and Labeling
  - Labeling requirements apply throughout FDA's regulatory programs. They are based on a combination of the FFDCA's chapter-specific misbranding prohibitions and some category-specific statutory provisions.
  - For many product categories, FDA has promulgated highly detailed regulations implementing the more general statutory requirements.
- Establishment Registration
  - Establishment registration requirements serve as the basis for many of FDA's regulatory programs.

    - At their most basic level, they give FDA information on where to look for potential problems.
    - However, additional substantive requirements are also embedded in some establishment registration programs.
        - The most prominent of these is the substantial equivalence process (a form of marketing authorization) for medical devices and tobacco products. (Discussed in Chapters 4, 12, and in 18 of this casebook.)
- User fees
    - User fees now fund a substantial portion of FDA's product-review programs for drugs, medical devices, animal drugs, and biologics.
    - Up to this point, user fee programs have been authorized by Congress only for limited time periods. Each time a program comes up for renewal, Congress has an opportunity to use a threat not to renew the program as a way to influence the agency's operations more generally.
- Postmarket requirements
    - Postmarket requirements have become increasingly significant to FDA's regulatory programs.
    - Premarket and postmarket requirements can serve as alternative ways to meet the same regulatory objective.

# Part Three

# FFDCA Chapter IV Products—Food, Food Additives, and Dietary Supplements

Chapter 6

# Food

## A. Introduction

Please read (or review) the following excerpts in the statutory supplement:

- FFDCA 201. Definitions; generally. *Subsection (f) only.*

## B. Outline of Regulatory Regime

As in other chapters of this book, this chapter begins with a set of charts. As you read this chapter for the first time, you should do no more than skim these charts to get a general sense of the structure of the applicable statutes and regulations. (For more information on the role of the charts in this casebook, see Chapter 1, Parts A.1 and B).

This chapter also includes three additional sets of charts for *Related Areas Not Regulated Primarily by FDA:* (1) meat, eggs, poultry, and fish of the order Siluriformes; (2) alcohol; and (3) agricultural biotechnology. Those charts are included within the relevant subparts of this chapter.

| Timeline of Key Statutes: Food | | | |
|---|---|---|---|
| Year | PL | Stat | Name of Statute |
| 1906 | 59-384 | 34 Stat. 768 | Pure Food and Drug Act |
| 1906 | 59-242 | 34 Stat. 1256 | Meat Inspection Act |
| 1913 | 62-419 | 37 Stat. 732 | Gould Amendment |
| 1930 | 71-538 | 46 Stat. 1019 | McNary-Mapes Amendment |
| 1938 | 75-717 | 52 Stat. 1040 | FFDCA of 1938 |
| 1954 | 83-518 | 68 Stat. 511 | Miller Pesticide Amendment |
| 1980 | 96-359 | 94 Stat. 1190 | Infant Formula Act of 1980 |
| 1990 | 101-535 | 104 Stat. 2353 | Nutrition Labeling and Education Act of 1990 |
| 1993 | 103-80 | 107 Stat. 773 | Nutrition Labeling and Education Act Amendments of 1993 |
| 1996 | 104-170 | 110 Stat. 1489 | Food Quality Protection Act of 1996 |
| 1997 | 105-115 | 111 Stat. 2296 | FDA Modernization Act |

| Year | PL | Stat | Name of Statute |
|---|---|---|---|
| 2004 | 108-282 | 118 Stat. 891 | Food Allergy Labeling and Consumer Protection Act of 2004 |
| 2005 | 109-59 | 114 Stat 1144, 1911–1914 | Sanitary Food Transportation Act of 2005 |
| 2011 | 111-353 | 124 Stat. 3885 | FDA Food Safety Modernization Act |

| Key Statutory Provisions: Food | | |
|---|---|---|
| Statute Name or U.S.C. Title | § | Title of Section or Subsection |
| FFDCA | 401 | Definitions and standards for food |
| FFDCA | 402 | Adulterated food |
| FFDCA | 403 | Misbranded food |
| FFDCA | 404 | Emergency permit control |
| FFDCA | 406 | Tolerances for poisonous or deleterious substances in food; regulations |
| FFDCA | 408 | Tolerances and exemptions for pesticide chemical residues |
| FFDCA | 414 | Maintenance and inspection of records |
| FFDCA | 415 | Registration of food facilities |
| FFDCA | 416 | Sanitary transportation practices |
| FFDCA | 417 | Reportable food registry |
| FFDCA | 418 | Hazard analysis and risk-based preventative controls |
| FFDCA | 419 | Standards for produce safety |
| FFDCA | 420 | Protection against intentional adulteration |
| FFDCA | 421 | Targeting of inspection resources for domestic facilities, foreign facilities, and ports of entry; annual report |
| FFDCA | 422 | Library accreditation for analyses of foods |
| FFDCA | 706 | Examination of sea food on request of packer; marking food with results; fees; penalties |
| FFDCA | 707 | Advertising of foods |
| FFDCA | 1002 | Exemption of meats and meat food products |
| FFDCA | 1008 | Notices to States regarding imported food |
| FFDCA | 1009 | Grants to enhance food safety |
| FFDCA | 1012 | Improving the training of State, local, territorial, and tribal food safety officials |
| FFDCA | 1013 | Employee protections [from retaliation by food industry companies] |

| Key Regulatory Provisions: Food Generally | | |
|---|---|---|
| 21 C.F.R. Part | Subpart | Title of Part or Subpart |
| 101 | — | Food labeling |
| 102 | — | Common or usual name for nonstandardized foods |
| 104 | | Nutritional quality guidelines for foods |
| 105 | — | Foods for special dietary use |
| 106 | — | Infant formula requirements pertaining to current good manufacturing practice, quality control procedures, quality factors, records and reports, and notifications |
| 107 | — | Infant formula |
| 108 | — | Emergency permit control |
| 109 | — | Unavoidable contaminants in food for human consumption and food-packaging material |
| 110 | — | Current good manufacturing practice in manufacturing, packing, or holding human food |
| 112 | — | Standards for the growing, harvesting, packing, and holding of produce for human consumption |
| 113 | — | Thermally processed low-acid foods packaged in hermetically sealed containers |
| 502 | — | Common or usual names for nonstandardized animal foods |

| Key Regulatory Provisions: Food Standards | | |
|---|---|---|
| 21 C.F.R. Part | Subpart | Title of Part or Subpart |
| 130 | — | Food standards: general |
| 131 | — | Milk and cream |
| 133 | | Cheeses and related cheese products |
| 135 | — | Frozen desserts |
| 136 | — | Bakery products |
| 137 | — | Cereal flours and related products |
| 139 | — | Macaroni and noodle products |
| 145 | — | Canned fruits |
| 155 | — | Canned vegetables |
| 156 | — | Vegetable juices |
| 158 | — | Frozen vegetables |
| 160 | — | Eggs and egg products |

| 21 C.F.R. Part | Subpart | Title of Part or Subpart |
|---|---|---|
| 161 | — | Fish and shellfish |
| 163 | — | Cacao products |
| 164 | — | Tree nut and peanut products |
| 165 | — | Beverages |
| 166 | — | Margarine |
| 168 | — | Sweeteners and table syrups |
| 169 | — | Food dressings and flavorings |

# C. Adulteration

Please read (or review) the following excerpts in the statutory supplement:

- FFDCA 402. Adulterated food.

## United States v. 298 Cases, etc., Ski Slide Brand Asparagus, etc.

88 F. Supp. 450 (D. Or. 1949)

**McCOLLOCH, District Judge.**

Defendant is an asparagus packer. One of his products is the center cut of the asparagus. This retails for 20 cents per can (1 lb. 3 oz.) containing 95 to 100 cuts, as compared with 40 to 45 cents per can for the choicier tips.

The Government contends that defendant's center cuts are fibrous and woody beyond the permissible limits set up by the Federal Food, Drug and Cosmetic Administration. Three witnesses for the Government said that they had each eaten a can (or attempted to) of defendant's cuts. The composite of their testimony was that 25% or more of the cuts were inedible and the Government's witnesses condemned them as a food product.

On the other hand, the Director of Mary Cullen's Cottage found only 5 or 6 pieces out of 100 that she had to lay aside. Confronted with this conflict in testimony, I obtained counsels' consent to eat a can. This I have done, although I confess had I understood all the difficulties of the undertaking, I might not have been so bold.

To eat a can of asparagus, hand-running, as the saying is, is quite a chore. I took three days to eat the can. That, I can now state, is as much as an old protein user should attempt on his first venture into herbalism. I suspect the Government witnesses tried to eat their cans all at one time, and that may explain the severity of their judgment about defendant's asparagus. I can see where after 50 or 60 cuts, eaten without spelling oneself, one might become very particular.

My test more than confirmed Miss Laughton's good opinion of the cuts. She found 5 or 6 per cent. inedible, whereas I ate all of my can, and felt that I was helped by it. There was one runty, tough piece and two or three slivers, but I treated them as de minimis.

I agree with the Director of Mary Cullen's Cottage that this is an excellent product, particularly considering its low price. Not everybody in this country can 'keep up with the Joneses' and eat only asparagus tips. Indeed it seems strange to me that the Government should be interested in keeping from the market a moderately priced, wholly nutritious food product. I should think in this period of declining income the Government's interest would be the other way. If Mr. Prendergast will prepare appropriate findings, I will give his client's center cuts a clean bill of health. They deserve it.

## D. Misbranding

Please read (or review) the following excerpts in the statutory supplement:

- FFDCA § 403. Misbranded food.

### United States v. Ninety-five Barrels (More or Less) Alleged Apple Cider Vinegar

265 U.S. 438 (1924)

**Mr. Justice BUTLER delivered the opinion of the Court.**

This case arises under the Food and Drugs Act of June 30, 1906. The United States filed information in the District Court for the Northern District of Ohio, Eastern Division, for the condemnation of 95 barrels of vinegar. Every barrel seized was labeled:

> "Douglas Packing Company, Excelsior Brand Apple Cider Vinegar made, from Selected Apples, Reduced to 4 Percentum, Rochester, N.Y."

The information alleged that the vinegar was adulterated, in violation of § 7 of the [Pure Food & Drug] act. It also alleged that the vinegar was made from dried or evaporated apples, and was misbranded in violation of § 8, in that the statements on the label were false and misleading, and in that it was an imitation of and offered for sale under the distinctive name of another article, namely apple cider vinegar.

The Douglas Packing Company . . . admitted that the vinegar was labeled as alleged, and that evaporated apples had been used in its manufacture. It averred that nevertheless it was pure cider vinegar and denied adulteration and misbranding. . . . The court found that the charge of adulteration was not sustained, but held that the vinegar was misbranded. Claimant appealed, and the Circuit Court of Appeals reversed the judgment.

The question for decision is whether the vinegar was misbranded.

The substance of the agreed statement of facts may be set forth briefly. Claimant . . . from about September 25 to December 15, makes apple cider and apple cider vinegar from fresh or unevaporated apples. During the balance of the year, it makes products which it designates as "apple cider" and "apple cider vinegar" from evaporated apples. The most approved process for dehydrating apples is used, and, in applying it, small quantities of sulphur fumes are employed to prevent rot, fermentation, and consequent discoloration. The principal result of dehydration is the removal of about 80 per cent. of the water. . . . Only mature fruit, free from rot and ferment, can be used economically and advantageously.

In manufacturing. . . . claimant employs the same receptacles, equipment and process of manufacturing for evaporated as for unevaporated apples, except that in the case of evaporated apples, pure water is added [to rehydrate], and in the process of fining and filtration, an additional chemical is used to precipitate any sulphur compounds present and resulting from dehydration.

The resulting liquid, upon chemical analysis, gives results similar to those obtained from an analysis of apple cider made from unevaporated apples, except that it contains a trace of barium incident to the process to manufacture. . . . There is no claim by libellant that this trace of barium renders it deleterious or injurious to health. It was conceded that the vinegar involved in these proceedings was vinegar made from dried or evaporated apples by substantially the process above described. There is no claim by the libellant that the vinegar was inferior to that made from fresh or unevaporated apples.

. . . . Before and since the passage of the Food and Drugs Act, vinegar in large quantities, and to a certain extent a beverage, made from evaporated apples, were sold in various parts of the United States as "apple cider vinegar" and "apple cider," respectively, by many manufacturers. Claimant, in manufacturing and selling such products so labeled, acted in good faith. The Department of Agriculture has never sanctioned this labeling, and its attitude with reference thereto is evidenced by the definition of "apple cider vinegar" set forth in Circulars 13, 17, 19 and 136, and Food Inspection Decision 140. It is stipulated that the juice of unevaporated apples when subjected to alcoholic and subsequent acetous fermentation is entitled to the name "apple cider vinegar."

Section 6 of the [Pure Food & Drug] act provides that, ". . . The term 'food', as used herein, shall include all articles used for food, drink, confectionery, or condiment by man or other animals, whether simple, mixed, or compound." Section 8 provides, "That the term 'misbranded', as used herein, shall apply to all . . . articles of food, or articles which enter into the composition of food, the package or label of which shall bear any statement, design, or device regarding such article, or the ingredients or substances contained therein which shall be false or misleading in any particular, . . . That for the purposes of this Act an article shall also be deemed to be misbranded: . . . In the case of food: First. If it be an imitation of or offered for sale under the distinctive name of another article. Second. If it be labeled or branded so as to deceive or mislead the purchaser, . . . Fourth. If the package containing it or its label shall bear any statement, design, or device regarding the ingredients or the substances contained therein, which statement, design, or device shall be false or misleading in any particular. . . ."

The statute is plain and direct. Its comprehensive terms condemn every statement, design and device which may mislead or deceive. Deception may result from the use of statements not technically false or which may be literally true. The aim of the statute is to prevent that resulting from indirection and ambiguity, as well as from statements which are false. It is not difficult to choose statements, designs and devices which will not deceive. Those which are ambiguous and liable to mislead should be read favorably to the accomplishment of the purpose of the [Pure Food & Drug] act. The statute applies to food, and the ingredients and substances contained therein. It was enacted to enable purchasers to buy food for what it really is.

The vinegar made from dried apples was not the same as that which would have been produced from the apples without dehydration. The dehydration took from them about 80 per cent. of their water content,—an amount in excess of two-thirds of the total of their constituent elements. The substance removed was a part of their juice from which cider and vinegar would have been made if the apples had been used in their natural state. That element was not replaced. The substance extracted from dried apples is different from the pressed out juice of apples. Samples of cider fermented and unfermented made from fresh and evaporated apples, and vinegar made from both kinds of cider were submitted to and examined by the District Judge who tried the case. He found that there were slight differences in appearance and taste, but that all had the appearance and taste of cider and vinegar. While the vinegar in question made from dried apples was like or similar to that which would have been produced by the use of fresh apples, it was not the identical product. The added water, constituting an element amounting to more than one-half of the total of all ingredients of the vinegar, never was a constituent element or part of the apples. The use of dried apples necessarily results in a different product.

If an article is not the identical thing that the brand indicates it to be, it is misbranded. The vinegar in question was not the identical thing that the statement "Excelsior Brand Apple Cider Vinegar made from selected apples", indicated it to be. These words are to be considered in view of the admitted facts and others of which the court may take judicial notice. The words "Excelsior Brand", calculated to give the impression of superiority, may be put to one side as not liable to mislead. But the words, "apple cider vinegar made from selected apples" are misleading. Apple cider vinegar is made from apple cider. Cider is the expressed juice of apples and is so popularly and generally known. It was stipulated that the juice of unevaporated apples when subjected to alcoholic and subsequent acetous fermentation is entitled to the name "apple cider vinegar". The vinegar in question was not the same as if made from apples without dehydration. The name "apple cider vinegar" included in the brand did not represent the article to be what it really was; and, in effect, did represent it to be what it was not,—vinegar made from fresh or unevaporated apples. The words "made from selected apples" indicate that the apples used were chosen with special regard to their fitness for the purpose of making apple cider vinegar. They give no hint that the vinegar was made from dried apples, or that the larger part of the moisture content of the apples was eliminated and water substituted therefore. As used on the label, they aid the misrepresentation made by the words "apple cider vinegar".

The misrepresentation was in respect of the vinegar itself, and did not relate to the method of production merely. When considered independently of the product, the method of manufacture is not material. The act requires no disclosure concerning it. And it makes no difference whether vinegar made from dried apples is or is not inferior to apple cider vinegar.

The label was misleading as to the vinegar, its substance and ingredients. The facts admitted sustain the charge of misbranding.

Judgment reversed.

## United States v. 24 Bottles . . . Sterling Vinegar and Honey

338 F.2d 157 (2d Cir. 1964)

**LUMBARD, Chief Judge.**

The sole question on this appeal is whether the display and sale of books in the same shop as an article which the books misleadingly recommend as a remedy for various ailments constitutes misbranding in violation of § 301(a) of the Food Drug and Cosmetic Act . . .

. . . . The books and Vinegar and Honey were seized in its warehouse in New York City and condemned as misbranded drugs under § 304 of the Federal Food, Drug and Cosmetic Act, on the ground that the books were 'labeling' for the Vinegar and Honey and are misleading. We find that the former conclusion is not supported by the record, and we reverse the judgment of the district court.

Vinegar and Honey seems to have been one of the minor ephemera characteristic of the health and diet food trade. That it gained shelf space among boxes of sunflower seed, wheat germ and healing grasses can be attributed to the wide reading of Dr. D. C. Jarvis' first book, 'Folk Medicine,' subtitled 'A Vermont Doctor's Guide to Good Health.' Its publisher, Henry Holt & Company, sold nearly half a million copies of the book, and a considerable number of its readers at least sampled from Dr. Jarvis' pharmacopoeia.

Prominent among Dr. Jarvis' remedies is a mixture of cider vinegar and honey, which is prescribed for a wide variety of maladies. Inevitably some people found it burdensome to mix the vinegar with the honey, and, true to the traditions of free enterprise, several companies responded by producing a pre-mixed product. Among them was Sterling.

'Folk Medicine' and its sequel, 'Arthritis and Folk Medicine,' mention Sterling cider vinegar by name as suitable for medicinal use, and the two books certainly have promoted the sale of Sterling's Honey and Vinegar. In addition, Balanced

Foods stocked both and sold both to a number of retailers. The question is whether the sum of these relationships constitutes labeling. We do not think that it does.

The Vinegar and Honey bottles bear a label, which claims no more than that they contain one pint of 'aged in wood cider vinegar blended with finest honey.' The labeling subject to the [FFDCA] is not limited to this common form of label, however; it includes not only the written matter 'upon any article or any of its containers or wrappers,' but also written matter 'accompanying such article.' § 301(m). On the other hand, labeling does not include every writing which bears some relation to the product. There is a line to be drawn and, if the statutory purpose is to be served, it must be drawn in terms of the function served by the writing.

....

The distinguishing characteristic of a label is that, in some manner or another, it is presented to the customer in immediate connection with his view and his purchase of the product. Such a connection existed at both wholesale and retail levels in *Kordel [v. United States,* 225 U.S. 345 (1948)]: Although the pamphlets and drugs were mailed to retailers separately, they were mailed in 'integrated transactions'; the vendors in turn gave the pamphlets away with the sale of the drugs in some cases.

.... Balanced Foods sold both [the book and the mixture], and the government presented some evidence that it took special steps to promote 'Folk Medicine.' There was no evidence of any joint promotion of either book with Vinegar and Honey, however. It perhaps could be inferred that the officers of Balanced Foods realized that sale of the books would tend to promote sale of Vinegar and Honey. But there can be no inference that it sold the books for that purpose. It first ordered 'Folk Medicine' almost two years before it began carrying Vinegar and Honey; it sold over 7,000 copies of 'Folk Medicine' at $ 2.00 each wholesale and fewer than 2,000 pint bottles of Vinegar and Honey. There was, in sum, no basis for finding that Balanced Foods did more than carry two related products.... Nor was there any evidence of displays featuring both Vinegar and Honey and the books, and the five-foot distance between the books and the bottles in one shop supplies little basis for inference when the entire store was estimated by the government's witness to be only 20 by 25 feet.

'Folk Medicine' was a bestselling book which Balanced Foods and health food shops could be expected to carry without regard to Vinegar and Honey, as they did prior to introduction of the latter product. The book made broad claims for a vinegar and honey mixture, which led ultimately to Sterling's marketing Vinegar and Honey. It is not disputed that these claims were misleading, but the Federal Food, Drug and Cosmetic Act was not intended to deal generally with misleading claims; much more general proscriptions may be found in §§ 12–15 of the Federal Trade Commission Act, 15 U.S.C. §§ 52–55. In our view, the Food and Drug Act was intended to deal with such claims only when made in immediate connection with sale of the product. This was not the use to which 'Folk Medicine' and 'Arthritis and Folk Medicine' were put by Balanced Foods or its retailers.

The judgment of the district court is reversed.

# E. Standardized, Imitation, and Nonstandardized Food

Please read (or review) the following excerpts in the statutory supplement:

- FFDCA § 401. Definitions and standards for food.
- FFDCA § 403. Misbranded food. *Subsection (c) only.*
- 21 C.F.R. Part 101. Food labeling. *Sections 101.1, 101.2, 101.4, 101.9, and 101.18 only.*
- 21 C.F.R. Part 102. Common or usual name for nonstandardized foods.

## Federal Security Adm'r v. Quaker Oats Co.

318 U.S. 218 (1943)

**Mr. Chief Justice STONE delivered the opinion of the Court.**

The Federal Security Administrator,* acting under §§ 401 and 701(e), of the Federal Food, Drug and Cosmetic Act, promulgated regulations establishing 'standards of identity' for various milled wheat products, excluding vitamin D from the defined standard of 'farina' and permitting it only in 'enriched farina', which was required to contain vitamin B1, riboflavin, nicotinic acid and iron. The question is whether the regulations are valid as applied to respondent. The answer turns upon (a) whether there is substantial evidence in support of the Administrator's finding that indiscriminate enrichment of farina with vitamin and mineral contents would tend to confuse and mislead consumers; (b) if so, whether, upon such a finding, the Administrator has statutory authority to adopt a standard of identity, which excludes a disclosed nondeleterious ingredient, in order to promote honesty and fair dealing in the interest of consumers; and (c) whether the Administrator's treatment, by the challenged regulations, of the use of vitamin D as an ingredient of a product sold as 'farina' is within his statutory authority to prescribe 'a reasonable definition and standard of identity.'

Section 401 of the [FFDCA] provides that 'Whenever in the judgment of the Administrator such action will promote honesty and fair dealing in the interest of consumers, he shall promulgate regulations fixing and establishing for any food, under its common or usual name so far as practicable, a reasonable definition and standard of identity.... In prescribing a definition and standard of identity for any food or class of food in which optional ingredients are permitted, the Administrator shall, for the purpose of promoting honesty and fair dealing in the interest of consumers, designate the optional ingredients which shall be named on the label.' By § 701(e) the Administrator, on his own initiative or upon application of any

* *[During the relevant period, FDA was housed within the Federal Security Agency, led by the Federal Security Administrator. For more information on various administrative locations where FDA has been housed over time, see the section on Organizational History in Chapter 1 of this casebook.]*

interested industry or a substantial part of it, is required to 'hold a public hearing upon a proposal to issue, amend, or repeal any regulation contemplated by' § 401. At the hearing 'any interested person may be heard.' The Administrator is required to promulgate by order any regulation he may issue, to 'base his order only on substantial evidence of record at the hearing,' and to 'set forth as part of the order detailed findings of fact on which the order is based.'

Any food which 'purports to be or is represented as a food for which a definition and standard of identity has been prescribed' pursuant to § 401 is declared by § 403(g) to be misbranded 'unless (1) it conforms to such definition and standard, and (2) its label bears the name of the food specified in the definition and standard, and, insofar as may be required by such regulations, the common names of optional ingredients . . . present in such food'. The shipment in interstate commerce of 'misbranded' food is made a penal offense by §§ 301 and 303. 'In a case of actual controversy as to the validity' of an order issuing regulations under §§ 401 and person 'adversely affected' by it may secure its review on appeal to the Circuit Court of Appeals for the circuit of his residence or principal place of business. On such review the findings of the Administrator 'as to the facts, if supported by substantial evidence, shall be conclusive.' § 701(f)(1), (f)(3).

After due notice and a hearing in which respondent participated, the Administrator by order promulgated regulations establishing definitions and standards of identity for sixteen milled wheat products, including 'farina' and 'enriched farina.' Regulation 15.130 defined 'farina' as a food prepared by grinding and bolting cleaned wheat, other than certain specified kinds, to a prescribed fineness with the bran coat and germ of the wheat berry removed to a prescribed extent. The regulation made no provision for the addition of any ingredients to 'farina.' Regulation 15.140 defined 'enriched farina' as conforming to the regulation defining 'farina', but with added prescribed minimum quantities of vitamin B1, riboflavin, nicotinic acid (or nicotinic acid amide) and iron. The regulation also provided that minimum quantities of vitamin D, calcium, wheat germ or disodium phosphate might be added as optional ingredients of 'enriched farina', and required that ingredients so added be specified on the label. In support of the regulations the Administrator found that 'unless a standard' for milled wheat products 'is promulgated which limits the kinds and amounts of enrichment, the manufacturers' selection of the various nutritive elements and combinations of elements on the basis of economic and merchandising considerations is likely to lead to a great increase in the diversity, both qualitative and quantitative, in enriched flours offered to the public. Such diversity would tend to confuse and mislead consumers as to the relative value of the need for the several nutritional elements, and would impede rather than promote honesty and fair dealing in the interest of consumers.'

On respondent's appeal from this order the Court of Appeals for the Seventh Circuit set it aside, holding that the regulations did not conform to the statutory standards of reasonableness, that the Administrator's findings as to probable consumer confusion in the absence of the prescribed standards of identity were without support in the evidence and were 'entirely speculative and conjectural,' and that in any case such a finding would not justify the conclusion that the regulations would 'promote honesty and fair dealing in the interest of consumers.' We granted certiorari.

Respondent asserts, and the Government agrees, that the [FFDCA] as supplemented by the Administrator's standards will prevent the marketing of its product as 'farina' since, by reason of the presence of vitamin D as an ingredient, it does not conform to the standard of identity prescribed for 'farina' and that respondent cannot market its product as 'enriched farina' unless it adds the prescribed minimum quantities of vitamin B1, riboflavin, nicotinic acid and iron. Respondent challenges the validity of the regulations on the grounds sustained below and others so closely related to them as not to require separate consideration.

As appears from the evidence and the findings, the products of milled wheat are among the principal items of the American diet, particularly among low-income groups. Farina, which is a highly refined wheat product resembling flour but with larger particles[,] is used in macaroni, as a breakfast food, and extensively as a cereal food for children. It is in many cases the only cereal consumed by them during a period of their growth. Both farina and flour are manufactured by grinding the whole wheat and discarding its bran coat and germ. This process removes from the milled product that part of the wheat which is richest in vitamins and minerals, particularly vitamin B1, riboflavin, nicotinic acid and iron[—]valuable food elements which are often lacking in the diet of low income groups. In their diet, especially in the case of children, there is also frequently a deficiency of calcium and vitamin D, which are elements not present in wheat in significant quantities. Vitamin D, whose chief dietary value is as an aid to the metabolism of calcium, is developed in the body by exposure to sunlight. It is derived principally from cod liver and other fish oils. Milk is the most satisfactory source of calcium in digestible form, and milk enriched by vitamin D is now on the market.

In recent years millers of wheat have placed on the market flours and farinas which have been enriched by the addition of various vitamins and minerals. The composition of these enriched products varies widely. There was testimony of weight before the Administrator, principally by expert nutritionists, that such products, because of the variety and combination of added ingredients, are widely variable in nutritional value; and that consumers generally lack knowledge of the relative value of such ingredients and combinations of them.

These witnesses also testified, as did representatives of consumer organizations which had made special studies of the problems of food standardization, that the number, variety and varying combinations of the added ingredients tend to confuse the large number of consumers who desire to purchase vitamin-enriched wheat food products but who lack the knowledge essential to discriminating purchase of them; that because of this lack of knowledge and discrimination they are subject to exploitation by the sale of foods described as 'enriched', but of whose inferior or unsuitable quality they are not informed. Accordingly a large number of witnesses recommended the adoption of definitions and standards for 'enriched' wheat products which would ensure fairly complete satisfaction of dietary needs, and a somewhat lesser number recommended the disallowance, as optional ingredients in the standards for unenriched wheat products, of individual vitamins and minerals whose addition would suggest to consumers an adequacy for dietary needs not in fact supplied.

The court below characterized this evidence as speculative and conjectural, and held that because there was no evidence that respondent's product had in fact confused or misled anyone, the Administrator's finding as to consumer confusion was without substantial support in the evidence. It thought that, if anything, consumer confusion was more likely to be created, and the interest of consumers harmed, by the sale of farinas conforming to the standard for 'enriched farina', whose labels were not required to disclose their ingredients, than by the sale of respondent's product under an accurate and informative label such as that respondent was using.

The Act does not contemplate that courts should thus substitute their own judgment for that of the Administrator. As passed by the House it appears to have provided for a judicial review in which the court could take additional evidence, weigh the evidence, and direct the Administrator 'to take such further action as justice may require.' But before enactment, the Conference Committee substituted for these provisions those which became § 701(f) of the [FFDCA]. While under that section the Administrator's regulations must be supported by findings based upon 'substantial evidence' adduced at the hearing, the Administrator's findings as to the facts if based on substantial evidence are conclusive. In explaining these changes the chairman of the House conferees stated on the floor of the House that 'there is no purpose that the court shall exercise the functions that belong to the executive or the legislative branches'.

The review provisions were patterned after those by which Congress has provided for the review of 'quasi-judicial' orders of the Federal Trade Commission and other agencies, which we have many times had occasion to construe. Under such provisions we have repeatedly emphasized the scope that must be allowed to the discretion and informed judgment of an expert administrative body. These considerations are especially appropriate where the review is of regulations of general application adopted by an administrative agency under its rule-making power in carrying out the policy of a statute with whose enforcement it is charged. Section 401 calls for the exercise of the 'judgment of the Administrator'. That judgment, if based on substantial evidence of record, and if within statutory and constitutional limitations, is controlling even though the reviewing court might on the same record have arrived at a different conclusion.

None of the testimony which we have detailed can be said to be speculative or conjectural unless it be the conclusion of numerous witnesses, adopted by the Administrator, that the labeling and marketing of vitamin-enriched foods, not conforming to any standards of identity, tend to confuse and mislead consumers. The exercise of the administrative rule-making power necessarily looks to the future.

The statute requires the Administrator to adopt standards of identity which in his judgment 'will' promote honesty and fair dealing in the interest of consumers. Acting within his statutory authority he is required to establish standards which will guard against the probable future effects of present trends. Taking into account the evidence of public demand for vitamin-enriched foods, their increasing sale, their variable vitamin composition and dietary value, and the general lack of consumer knowledge of such values, there was sufficient evidence of 'rational probative force', to support the Administrator's judgment that, in the absence of appropriate standards of identity, consumer confusion would ensue.

Respondent insists, as the court below held, that the consumer confusion found by the Administrator affords no basis for his conclusion that the standards of identity adopted by the Administrator will promote honesty and fair dealing. But this is tantamount to saying, despite the Administrator's findings to the contrary, either that in the circumstances of this case there could be no such consumer confusion or that the confusion could not be deemed to facilitate unfair dealing contrary to the interest of consumers. For reasons already indicated we think that the evidence of the desire of consumers to purchase vitamin-enriched foods, their general ignorance of the composition and value of the vitamin content of those foods, and their consequent inability to guard against the purchase of products of inferior or unsuitable vitamin content, sufficiently supports the Administrator's conclusions.

Both the text and legislative history of the present statute plainly show that its purpose was not confined to a requirement of truthful and informative labeling. False and misleading labeling had been prohibited by the Pure Food and Drug Act of 1906. But it was found that such a prohibition was inadequate to protect the consumer from 'economic adulteration', by which less expensive ingredients were substituted, or the proportion of more expensive ingredients diminished, so as to make the product, although not in itself deleterious, inferior to that which the consumer expected to receive when purchasing a product with the name under which it was sold. The remedy chosen was not a requirement of informative labeling. Rather it was the purpose to authorize the Administrator to promulgate definitions and standards of identity 'under which the integrity of food products can be effectively maintained' (H.R.Rep. 2139, 75th Cong., 3d Sess., p. 2); and to require informative labeling only where no such standard had been promulgated, where the food did not purport to comply with a standard, or where the regulations permitted optional ingredients and required their mention on the label. §§ 403(g), 403(i).

The provisions for standards of identity thus reflect a recognition by Congress of the inability of consumers in some cases to determine, solely on the basis of informative labeling, the relative merits of a variety of products superficially resembling each other. We cannot say that such a standard of identity, designed to eliminate a source of confusion to purchasers—which otherwise would be likely to facilitate unfair dealing and make protection of the consumer difficult—will not 'promote honesty and fair dealing' within the meaning of the statute.

Respondent's final and most vigorous attack on the regulations is that they fail to establish reasonable definitions and standards of identity, as §401 requires, in that they prohibit the marketing, under the name 'farina', of a wholesome and honestly labeled product consisting of farina with vitamin D added, and that they prevent the addition of vitamin D to products marketed as 'enriched farina' unless accompanied by the other prescribed vitamin ingredients which do not co-act with or have any dietary relationship to vitamin D. Stated in another form, the argument is that it is unreasonable to prohibit the addition to farina of vitamin D as an optional ingredient while permitting its addition as an optional ingredient to enriched farina, to the detriment of respondent's business.

The standards of reasonableness to which the Administrator's action must conform are to be found in the terms of the [FFDCA] construed and applied in the light of its purpose. Its declared purpose is the administrative promulgation of standards of both identity and quality in the interest of consumers. Those standards are to be prescribed and applied, so far as is practicable, to food under its common or usual name, and the regulations adopted after a hearing must have the support of substantial evidence. We must reject at the outset the argument earnestly pressed upon us that the statute does not contemplate a regulation excluding a wholesome and beneficial ingredient from the definition and standard of identity of a food. The statutory purpose to fix a definition of identity of an article of food sold under its common or usual name would be defeated if producers were free to add ingredients, however wholesome, which are not within the definition. As we have seen, the legislative history of the statute manifests the purpose of Congress to substitute, for informative labeling, standards of identity of a food, sold under a common or usual name, so as to give to consumers who purchase it under that name assurance that they will get what they may reasonably expect to receive. In many instances, like the present, that purpose could be achieved only if the definition of identity specified the number, names and proportions of ingredients, however wholesome other combinations might be. The statute accomplished that purpose by authorizing the Administrator to adopt a definition of identity by prescribing some ingredients, including some which are optional, and excluding others, and by requiring the designation on the label of the optional ingredients permitted.

Since the definition of identity of a vitamin-treated food, marketed under its common or usual name, involves the inclusion of some vitamin ingredients and the exclusion of others, the Administrator necessarily has a large range of choice in determining what may be included and what excluded. It is not necessarily a valid objection to his choice that another could reasonably have been made. The judicial is not to be substituted for the legislative judgment. It is enough that the Administrator has acted within the statutory bounds of his authority, and that his choice among possible alternative standards adapted to the statutory end is one which a rational person could have made.

The evidence discloses that it is well known that the milling process for producing flours and farinas removes from the wheat a substantial part of its health-giving vitamin contents, which are concededly essential to the maintenance of health, and that many consumers desire to purchase wheat products which have been enriched by the restoration of some of the original vitamin content of the wheat. In fixing definitions and standards of identity in conformity with the statutory purpose the Administrator was thus confronted with two related problems. One was the choice of a standard which would appropriately identify unenriched wheat products which had long been on the market. The other was the selection of a standard for enriched wheat products which would both assure to consumers of vitamin-enriched products some of the benefits to health which they sought, and protect them from exploitation through the marketing of vitamin-enriched foods of whose dietary value they were ignorant. In finding the solution the Administrator could take into account the facts that whole wheat is a natural and common source of the valuable dietary ingredients which he prescribed for enriched farina; that wheat is not a source of vitamin D; that milk, a common article of diet, is a satisfactory source of an admissible form of calcium; that the principal function of vitamin D is to aid in the metabolism of calcium; and that milk enriched with vitamin D was already on the market.

We cannot say that the Administrator made an unreasonable choice of standards when he adopted one which defined the familiar farina of commerce without permitting addition of vitamin enrichment, and at the same time prescribed for 'enriched farina' the restoration of those vitamins which had been removed from the whole wheat by milling, and allowed the optional addition of vitamin D, commonly found in milk but not present in wheat. Consumers who buy farina will have no reason to believe that it is enriched. Those who buy enriched farina are assured of receiving a wheat product containing those vitamins naturally present in wheat, and, if so stated on the label, an additional vitamin D, not found in wheat.

Respondent speaks of the high cost of vitamin B1 ($700 per pound), but there was evidence that the cost of adding to flour the minute quantities of the four ingredients required for enriched farina would be about 75 cents per barrel, and respondent concedes that the cost to it may be but a fraction of a cent per pound. The record is otherwise silent as to the probable effect of the increased cost on the marketing of respondent's product. On this record it does not appear that the increased cost has any substantial bearing on the reasonableness of the regulation.

We conclude that the Administrator did not depart from statutory requirements in choosing these standards of identity for the purpose of promoting fair dealing in the interest of consumers, that the standards which he selected are adapted to that end, and that they are adequately supported by findings and evidence.

Reversed.

## 62 Cases, More or Less, Each Containing 6 Jars of Jam v. United States

340 U.S. 593 (1951)

**Mr. Justice FRANKFURTER delivered the opinion of the Court.**

The [FFDCA] authorizes the United States to bring a libel against any article of food which is 'misbranded' when using the channels of interstate commerce. The Act defines 'misbranded' in the eleven paragraphs of § 403. The question before us is raised by two apparently conflicting paragraphs.

One of them, subsection (c), comes from the original Pure Food and Drugs Act of 1906. It directs that a food shall be deemed 'misbranded' if it 'is an imitation of another food, unless its label bears, in type of uniform size and prominence, the word 'imitation' and, immediately thereafter, the name of the food imitated.' The other, subsection (g), was added to the enlargement of the statute in 1938. It condemns as 'misbranded' a product which 'purports to be or is represented as a food', the ingredients of which the Administrator has standardized, if the product does not conform in all respects to the standards prescribed. The Administrator has authority to promulgate standards when in his judgment 'such action will promote honesty and fair dealing in the interest of consumers'. [FFDCA] § 401.

The proceeding before us was commenced in 1949 in the District Court for the District of New Mexico. By it the United States seeks to condemn 62 cases of 'Delicious Brand Imitation Jam,' manufactured in Colorado and shipped to New Mexico. The Government claims that this product 'purports' to be fruit jam, a food for which the Federal Security Administrator has promulgated a 'definition and standard of identity.' The regulation specifies that a fruit jam must contain 'not less than 45 parts by weight' of the fruit ingredient. The product in question is composed of 55% sugar, 25% fruit, 20% pectin, and small amounts of citric acid and soda. These specifications show that pectin, a gelatinized solution consisting largely of water, has been substituted for a substantial proportion of the fruit required. The Government contends that the product is therefore to be deemed 'misbranded' under § 403(g).

On the basis of stipulated testimony the District Judge found that although the product seized did not meet the prescribed standards for fruit jam, it was 'wholesome' and 'in every way fit for human consumption.' It was found to have the appearance and taste of standardized jam, and to be used as a less expensive substitute for the standard product. In some instances, products similar to those seized were sold at retail to the public in response to telephone orders for jams, and were served to patrons of restaurants, ranches and similar establishments, who had no opportunity to learn the quality of what they received. But there is no suggestion of misrepresentation. The judge found that the labels on the seized jars were substantially accurate; and he concluded that since the product purported to be only an imitation fruit preserve and complied in all respects with subsection (c) of § 403 of the [FFDCA], it could not be deemed 'misbranded.'

The Court of Appeals for the Tenth Circuit, one judge dissenting, reversed this judgment. It held that since the product seized closely resembled fruit jam in appearance and taste, and was used as a substitute for the standardized food, it 'purported' to be fruit jam, and must be deemed 'misbranded' notwithstanding that it was duly labeled an 'imitation.' The court therefore remanded the cause with instructions to enter a judgment for condemnation. We granted certiorari.

By the [Pure Food & Drugs] Act of 1906, as successively strengthened, Congress exerted its power to keep impure and adulterated foods and drugs out of the channels of commerce. The purposes of this legislation, we have said, 'touch phases of the lives and health of people which, in the circumstances of modern industrialism, are largely beyond self-protection. Regard for these purposes should infuse construction of the legislation if it is to be treated as a working instrument of government and not merely as a collection of English words.' This is the attitude with which we should approach the problem of statutory construction now presented. But our problem is to construe what Congress has written. After all, Congress expresses its purpose by words. It is for us to ascertain—neither to add nor to subtract, neither to delete nor to distort.

Misbranding was one of the chief evils Congress sought to stop. It was both within the right and the wisdom of Congress not to trust to the colloquial or the dictionary meaning of misbranding, but to write its own. Concededly we are not dealing here with misbranding in its crude manifestations, what would colloquially be deemed a false representation. Our concern is whether the article of food sold as 'Delicious Brand Imitation Jam' is 'deemed to be misbranded' according to § 403(c) and (g) of the [FFDCA].

The controlling provisions of the [FFDCA] are as follows:

> Sec. 304. (a) Any article of food, drug, device, or cosmetic that is adulterated or misbranded when introduced into or while in interstate commerce or while held for sale (whether or not the first sale) after shipment in interstate commerce, . . . shall be liable to be proceeded against while in interstate commerce, or at any time thereafter, on libel of information and condemned in any district court of the United States within the jurisdiction of which the article is found: . . . .
>
> Sec. 401. Whenever in the judgment of the (Administrator) such action will promote honesty and fair dealing in the interest of consumers, he shall promulgate regulations fixing and establishing for any food, under its common or usual name so far as practicable, a reasonable definition and standard of identity, a reasonable standard of quality, and/or reasonable standards of fill of container: . . . . In prescribing a definition and standard of identity for any food or class of food in which optional ingredients are permitted, the (Administrator) shall, for the purpose of promoting honesty and fair dealing in the interest of consumers, designate the optional ingredients which shall be named on the label. . . .

Sec. 403. A food shall be deemed to be misbranded . . .

> (c) If it is an imitation of another food, unless its label bears, in type of uniform size and prominence, the word 'imitation' and, immediately thereafter, the name of the food imitated.
>
> (g) If it purports to be or is represented as a food for which a definition and standard of identity has been prescribed by regulations as provided by section 401, unless (1) it conforms to such definition and standard, and (2) its label bears the name of the food specified in the definition and standard, and, insofar as may be required by such regulations, the common names of optional ingredients (other than spices, flavoring, and coloring) present in such food.

By §§401 and 403(g), Congress vested in the Administrator the far-reaching power of fixing for any species of food 'a reasonable definition and standard of identity'. In *Federal Security Administrator v. Quaker Oats Co.*, 318 U.S. 218, we held that this means that the Administrator may, by regulation, fix the ingredients of any food, and that thereafter a commodity cannot be introduced into interstate commerce which 'purports to be or is represented as' the food which has been thus defined unless it is composed of the required ingredients. The Administrator had prescribed the ingredients of two different species of food—'farina' and 'enriched farina.' The former was an exclusively milled wheat product; the latter included certain additional ingredients, one of which optionally could be vitamin D. The Quaker Oats Company marketed a product it called 'Quaker Farina Wheat Cereal Enriched with Vitamin D,' which did not conform to either standard. Because it contained an additional vitamin it was not 'farina'; because it lacked certain of the essential ingredients it could not be called 'enriched farina.' It was concededly a wholesome product, accurately labeled; but under the Administrator's regulations it could not be sold. We sustained the regulations, holding that Congress had constitutionally empowered the Administrator to define a food and had thereby precluded manufacturers—or courts—from determining for themselves whether some other ingredients would not produce as nutritious a product. 'The statutory purpose to fix a definition of identity of an article of food sold under its common or usual name would be defeated if producers were free to add ingredients, however wholesome, which are not within the definition.'

Our decision in the *Quaker Oats* case does not touch the problem now before us. In that case it was conceded that although the Quaker product did not have the standard ingredients, it 'purported' to be a standardized food. We did not there consider the legality of marketing properly labeled 'imitation farina.' That would be the comparable question to the one now here.

According to the [FFDCA], nothing can be legally 'jam' after the Administrator promulgated his regulation in 1940, unless it contains the specified ingredients in prescribed proportion. Hence the product in controversy is not 'jam.' It cannot lawfully be labeled 'jam' and introduced into interstate commerce, for to do so would 'represent' as a standardized food a product which does not meet prescribed specifications.

But the product with which we are concerned is sold as 'imitation jam.' Imitation foods are dealt with in § 403(c) of the [FFDCA]. In that section Congress did not give an esoteric meaning to 'imitation.' It left it to the understanding of ordinary English speech. And it directed that a product should be deemed 'misbranded' if it imitated another food 'unless its label bears, in type of uniform size and prominence, the word 'imitation' and, immediately thereafter, the name of the food imitated.'

In ordinary speech there can be no doubt that the product which the United States here seeks to condemn is an 'imitation' jam. It looks and tastes like jam; it is unequivocally labeled 'imitation jam.' The Government does not argue that its label in any way falls short of the requirements of § 403(c). Its distribution in interstate commerce would therefore clearly seem to be authorized by that section. We could hold it to be 'misbranded' only if we held that a practice Congress authorized by § 403(c) Congress impliedly prohibited by § 403(g).

We see no justification so to distort the ordinary meaning of the statute. Nothing in the text or history of the legislation points to such a reading of what Congress wrote. In § 403(g) Congress used the words 'purport' and 'represent'—terms suggesting the idea of counterfeit. But the name 'imitation jam' at once connotes precisely what the product is: a different, an inferior preserve, not meeting the defined specifications. Section 403(g) was designed to protect the public from inferior foods resembling standard products but marketed under distinctive names. Congress may well have supposed that similar confusion would not result from the marketing of a product candidly and flagrantly labeled as an 'imitation' food. A product so labeled is described with precise accuracy. It neither conveys any ambiguity nor emanates any untrue innuendo. It purports and is represented to be only what it is—an imitation. It does not purport nor represent to be what it is not—the Administrator's genuine 'jam.'

In our anxiety to effectuate the congressional purpose of protecting the public, we must take care not to extend the scope of the statute beyond the point where Congress indicated it would stop. The Government would have us hold that when the Administrator standardizes the ingredients of a food, no imitation of that food can be marketed which contains an ingredient of the original and serves a similar purpose. If Congress wishes to say that nothing shall be marked in likeness to a food as defined by the Administrator, though it is accurately labeled, entirely wholesome, and perhaps more within the reach of the meager purse, our decisions indicate that Congress may well do so. But Congress has not said so. It indicated the contrary. Indeed, the Administrator's contemporaneous construction concededly is contrary to what he now contends. We must assume his present misconception results from a misreading of what was written in the Quaker Oats case.

Reversed.

# F. Related Areas Not Regulated Primarily by FDA

## 1. Meat, Eggs, Poultry, and Fish of the Order Siluriformes

Please read (or review) the following excerpts in the statutory supplement:

Poultry Product Inspection Act:

- 21 U.S.C. § 451. Congressional statement of findings.
- 21 U.S.C. § 452. Congressional declaration of policy.
- 21 U.S.C. § 458. Prohibited acts.

Federal Meat Inspection Act:

- 21 U.S.C. § 601. Definitions.
- 21 U.S.C. § 602. Congressional statement of findings.
- 21 U.S.C. § 603. Examination of animal prior to slaughter; use of humane methods.
- 21 U.S.C. § 604. Post mortem examination of carcasses and marking or labeling; destruction of carcasses condemned; reinspection.
- 21 U.S.C. § 610. Prohibited acts.
- 21 U.S.C. § 661. Federal and state cooperation.

Egg Products Inspection Act:

- 21 U.S.C. § 1031. Congressional statement of findings.
- 21 U.S.C. § 1032. Congressional declaration of policy.
- 21 U.S.C. § 1033. Definitions.
- 21 U.S.C. § 1037. Prohibited acts.

### *a. Outline of Regulatory Regime*

As noted earlier, this chapter contains separate outline-of-regulatory-regime sections for three related areas not regulated primarily by FDA. This is the outline for meat, eggs, poultry, and fish of the order Siluriformes. As with all such outlines in this book, you should do no more than skim this on your first reading of the chapter.

**Timeline of Key Statutes: USDA Inspection of Meat, Eggs, Poultry, and Fish of the Order Siluriformes**

| Year | PL | Stat. | Name of Statute |
|---|---|---|---|
| 1907 | 59-242 | 34 Stat. 1256 | Meat Inspection Act |
| 1957 | 85-172 | 71 Stat. 441 | Poultry Products Inspection Act |
| 1958 | 85-765 | 72 Stat. 862 | An Act to Establish the Use of Humane Methods of Slaughter of Livestock as a Policy of the United States, and for other purposes. |

| Year | PL | Stat. | Name of Statute |
|---|---|---|---|
| 1970 | 91-597 | 84 Stat. 1620 | Egg Products Inspection Act |
| 2008 | 110-234 | 122 Stat. 923 | 2008 Farm Bill |
| 2014 | 113-79 | 128 Stat. 649 | 2014 Farm Bill |

| Key Statutory Provisions: Federal Meat Inspection Act | | |
|---|---|---|
| Statute Name or U.S.C. Title | § | Title of Section or Subsection |
| Subchapter I—Inspection Requirements; Adulteration & Misbranding | | |
| 21 U.S.C. | 601 | Definitions |
| 21 U.S.C. | 602 | Congressional statement of findings |
| 21 U.S.C. | 603 | Inspection of meat and meat food products |
| 21 U.S.C. | 604 | Post mortem examination of carcasses and marking or labeling; destruction of carcasses condemned; reinspection |
| 21 U.S.C. | 605 | Examination of carcasses brought into slaughtering or packing establishments, and of meat food products issued from and returned thereto; conditions for entry |
| 21 U.S.C. | 606 | Inspectors of meat food products; marks of inspection; destruction of condemned products; products for export |
| 21 U.S.C. | 607 | Labeling, marking, and container requirements |
| 21 U.S.C. | 608 | Sanitary inspection and regulation of slaughtering and packing establishments; rejection of adulterated meat or meat food products |
| 21 U.S.C. | 609 | Examination of animals and food products thereof, slaughtered and prepared during nighttime |
| 21 U.S.C. | 610 | Prohibited acts |
| 21 U.S.C. | 611 | Devices, marks, labels, and certificates; simulations |
| 21 U.S.C. | 612 | Notification |
| 21 U.S.C. | 613 | Plans and reassessments |
| 21 U.S.C. | 615 | Inspection of carcasses, meat of which is intended for export |
| 21 U.S.C. | 616 | Inspectors of carcasses, etc., meat of which is intended for export; certificates of condition |
| 21 U.S.C. | 617 | Clearance prohibited to vessel carrying meat for export without inspector's certificate |
| 21 U.S.C. | 618 | Delivery of inspectors' certificates, and of copies |
| 21 U.S.C. | 619 | Marking, labeling, or other identification of kinds of animals of articles' derivation; separate establishments for preparation and slaughtering activities |

| Statute Name or U.S.C. Title | § | Title of Section or Subsection |
|---|---|---|
| 21 U.S.C. | 620 | Imports |
| 21 U.S.C. | 621 | Inspectors to make examinations provided for; appointment; duties; regulations |
| 21 U.S.C. | 622 | Bribery of or gifts to inspectors or other officers and acceptance of gifts |
| 21 U.S.C. | 623 | Exemptions from inspection requirements |
| 21 U.S.C. | 624 | Storage and handling regulations; violations; exemption of establishments subject to non-federal jurisdiction |
| 21 U.S.C. | 625 | Inapplicability of certain requirements to catfish |
| Subchapter II—Meat Processors & Related Industries | | |
| 21 U.S.C. | 641 | Prohibition of subchapter I inspection of articles not intended for use as human food; denaturation or other identification prior to distribution in commerce; inedible articles |
| 21 U.S.C. | 642 | Recordkeeping requirements |
| 21 U.S.C. | 643 | Registration of business, name of person, and trade names |
| 21 U.S.C. | 644 | Regulation of transactions, transportation, or importation of 4-D animals to prevent use as human food |
| 21 U.S.C. | 645 | Federal provisions applicable to state or territorial business transactions of a local nature and not subject to local authority |
| Subchapter III—Federal & State Cooperation | | |
| 21 U.S.C. | 661 | Federal and state cooperation |
| Subchapter IV—Auxiliary Provisions | | |
| 21 U.S.C. | 671 | Inspection services; refusal or withdrawal; hearing; business unfitness based upon certain convictions; other provisions for withdrawal of services unaffected; responsible connection with business; finality of Secretary's actions; judicial review; record |
| 21 U.S.C. | 672 | Administrative detention; duration; pending judicial proceedings; notification of governmental authorities; release |
| 21 U.S.C. | 673 | Seizure and condemnation |
| 21 U.S.C. | 674 | Federal court jurisdiction of enforcement and injunction proceedings and other kinds of cases; limitations of section 607(e) of this title |
| 21 U.S.C. | 675 | Assaulting, resisting, or impeding certain persons; murder; protection of such persons |
| 21 U.S.C. | 676 | Violations |
| 21 U.S.C. | 677 | Other federal laws applicable for administration and enforcement of chapter; location of inquiries; jurisdiction of Federal courts |

| Statute Name or U.S.C. Title | § | Title of Section or Subsection |
|---|---|---|
| 21 U.S.C. | 678 | Non-federal jurisdiction of federally regulated matters; prohibition of additional or different requirements for establishments with inspection services and as to marking, labeling, packaging, and ingredients; recordkeeping and related requirements; concurrent jurisdiction over distribution for human food purposes of adulterated or misbranded and imported articles; other matters |
| 21 U.S.C. | 679 | Application of Federal Food, Drug, and Cosmetic Act |
| 21 U.S.C. | 679a | Safe meat and poultry inspection panel |
| 21 U.S.C. | 679b | Pasteurization of meat and poultry |
| 21 U.S.C. | 679c. | Expansion of Food Safety Inspection Service activities |
| 21 U.S.C. | 680. | Authorization of appropriations |
| Subchapter IV-A—Inspections by Federal and State Agencies | | |
| 21 U.S.C. | 683. | Interstate shipment of meat inspected by federal and state agencies for certain small establishments |
| Subchapter V—Inspections by Federal and State Agencies | | |
| 21 U.S.C. | 692 | Inspection extended to reindeer |
| 21 U.S.C. | 693 | Inspection of dairy products for export |
| 21 U.S.C. | 694 | Authorization of appropriations |
| 21 U.S.C. | 695 | Payment of cost of meat-inspection service; exception |

| Key Statutory Provisions: Poultry Products Inspection Act | | |
|---|---|---|
| Statute Name or U.S.C. Title | § | Title of Section or Subsection |
| 21 U.S.C. | 451 | Congressional statement of findings |
| 21 U.S.C. | 452 | Congressional declaration of policy |
| 21 U.S.C. | 453 | Definitions. |
| 21 U.S.C. | 454 | Federal and state cooperation in development and administration of State poultry product inspection programs |
| 21 U.S.C. | 455 | Inspection in official establishments |
| 21 U.S.C. | 456 | Operation of premises, facilities and equipment |
| 21 U.S.C. | 457 | Labeling and container standards |
| 21 U.S.C. | 458 | Prohibited acts |
| 21 U.S.C. | 459 | Compliance by all establishments |
| 21 U.S.C. | 460 | Miscellaneous activities subject to regulation |

| Statute Name or U.S.C. Title | § | Title of Section or Subsection |
|---|---|---|
| 21 U.S.C. | 461 | Offenses and punishment |
| 21 U.S.C. | 462 | Reporting of violations; notice; opportunity to present views |
| 21 U.S.C. | 463 | Rules and regulations |
| 21 U.S.C. | 464 | Exemptions |
| 21 U.S.C. | 465 | Limitations upon entry of poultry products and other materials into official establishments |
| 21 U.S.C. | 466 | Imports |
| 21 U.S.C. | 467 | Inspection services |
| 21 U.S.C. | 467a | Administrative detention; duration; pending judicial proceedings; notification of government authorities; release; removal of official marks |
| 21 U.S.C. | 467b | Seizure and condemnation |
| 21 U.S.C. | 467c | Federal court jurisdiction of enforcement and injunction proceedings and other kinds of cases; limitations; United States as plaintiff; subpoenas |
| 21 U.S.C. | 467d | Administration and enforcement; applicability of penalty provisions; conduct of inquiries; power and jurisdiction of courts |
| 21 U.S.C. | 467e | Non-federal jurisdiction of federally regulated matters; prohibition of additional or different requirements for establishments with inspection services and as to marking, labeling, packaging, and ingredients; recordkeeping and related requirements; concurrent jurisdiction over distribution for human food purposes of adulterated or misbranded and imported articles; other matters |
| 21 U.S.C. | 467f | Federal Food, Drug, and Cosmetic Act applications |
| 21 U.S.C. | 471 | Safe meat and poultry inspection panel |
| 21 U.S.C. | 472 | Interstate shipment of poultry inspected by Federal and State agencies for certain small establishments |

**Key Statutory Provisions: Egg Products Inspection Act**

| Statute Name or U.S.C. Title | § | Title of Section or Subsection |
|---|---|---|
| 21 U.S.C | 1031 | Congressional statement of findings. |
| 21 U.S.C | 1032 | Congressional declaration of policy |
| 21 U.S.C | 1033 | Definitions |
| 21 U.S.C | 1034 | Inspection of egg products |
| 21 U.S.C | 1035 | Sanitary operating practices in official plants |
| 21 U.S.C | 1036 | Pasteurization and labeling of egg products at official plants |

| Statute Name or U.S.C. Title | § | Title of Section or Subsection |
|---|---|---|
| 21 U.S.C | 1037 | Prohibited acts |
| 21 U.S.C | 1038 | Cooperation with appropriate state and other governmental agencies; utilization of employees; reimbursement |
| 21 U.S.C | 1039 | Eggs and egg products not intended for use as human food; inspection; denaturing or otherwise identifying |
| 21 U.S.C | 1040 | Recordkeeping requirements; persons required to maintain records; scope of disclosure; access to records |
| 21 U.S.C | 1041 | Enforcement provisions |
| 21 U.S.C | 1042 | Reporting of violation to United States attorney for institution of criminal proceedings; procedure; presentation of views |
| 21 U.S.C | 1043 | Rules and regulations; administration and enforcement |
| 21 U.S.C | 1044 | Exemption of certain activities |
| 21 U.S.C | 1045 | Limitation on entry of eggs and egg products and other materials into official plants |
| 21 U.S.C | 1046 | Imports |
| 21 U.S.C | 1047 | Refusal or withdrawal of inspection services; hearing; grounds; person deemed to have responsible connection with business; finality of order of Secretary; judicial review; other provisions for refusal of services unaffected |
| 21 U.S.C | 1048 | Administrative detention of violative articles; duration; release; removal of official marks |
| 21 U.S.C | 1049 | Seizure and condemnation proceedings |
| 21 U.S.C | 1050 | Jurisdiction of district courts; United States as plaintiff in enforcement and restraining proceedings; subpoenas for witnesses |
| 21 U.S.C | 1051 | Other federal laws applicable for administration and enforcement of chapter; prosecution of inquiries; exercise of jurisdiction |
| 21 U.S.C | 1052 | State or local regulation |

**Key Regulatory Provisions: Meat and Poultry Inspection**

| 9 C.F.R. Part | Subpart | Title of Part or Subpart |
|---|---|---|
| 301 | — | Terminology; adulteration and misbranding standards |
| 302 | — | Application of inspection and other requirements |
| 303 | — | Exemptions |
| 309 | — | Ante-mortem inspection |
| 310 | — | Post-mortem inspection |
| 311 | — | Disposal of diseased or otherwise adulterated carcasses and parts |

| 9 C.F.R. Part | Subpart | Title of Part or Subpart |
|---|---|---|
| 312 | — | Official marks, devices and certificates |
| 313 | — | Humane slaughter of livestock |
| 314 | — | Handling and disposal of condemned or other inedible products at official establishments |
| 315 | — | Rendering or other disposal of carcasses and parts passed for cooking |
| 316 | — | Marking products and their containers |
| 317 | — | Labeling, marking devices, and containers |
| 318 | — | Entry into official establishments; reinspection and preparation of products |
| 319 | — | Definitions and standards of identity or composition |
| 320 | — | Records, registration, and reports |
| 321 | — | Cooperation with states and territories |
| 322 | — | Exports |
| 325 | — | Transportation |
| 327 | — | Imported products |
| 329 | — | Detention; seizure and condemnation; criminal offenses |
| 331 | — | Special provisions for designated states and territories; and for designation of establishments which endanger public health and for such designated establishments |
| 332 | — | Selected establishments; cooperative program for interstate shipment of carcasses, parts of carcasses, meat, and meat food products |
| 335 | — | Rules of practice governing proceedings under the federal meat inspection act |
| 350 | — | Special services relating to meat and other products |
| 351 | — | Certification of technical animal fats for export |
| 352 | — | Exotic animals and horses; voluntary inspection |
| 354 | — | Voluntary inspection of rabbits and edible products thereof |
| 355 | — | Certified products for dogs, cats, and other carnivora; inspection, certification, and identification as to class, quality, quantity, and condition |

**Key Regulatory Provisions: Meat and Poultry Regulatory Requirements**

| 9 C.F.R. Part | Subpart | Title of Part or Subpart |
|---|---|---|
| 412 | — | Label approval |
| 416 | — | Sanitation |

| 9 C.F.R. Part | Subpart | Title of Part or Subpart |
|---|---|---|
| 417 | — | Hazard analysis and critical control point (HACCP) systems |
| 418 | — | Recalls |
| 424 | — | Preparation and processing operations |
| 430 | — | Requirements for specific classes of product |
| 431 | — | Thermally processed, commercially sterile products |
| 439 | — | Accreditation of non-federal chemistry laboratories |
| 441 | — | Consumer protection standards: raw products |
| 442 | — | Quantity of contents labeling and procedures and requirements for accurate weights |

**Key Regulatory Provisions: Fish of the Order Siluriformes**

| 9 C.F.R. Part | Subpart | Title of Part or Subpart |
|---|---|---|
| 530 | — | General requirements; definitions |
| 531 | — | Definitions |
| 532 | — | Requirements for inspection |
| 533 | — | Separation of establishment; facilities for inspection; facilities for program employees; other required facilities |
| 534 | — | Pre-harvest standards and transportation to processing establishment |
| 537 | — | Sanitation requirements and hazard analysis and critical control points systems; notification regarding adulterated or misbranded products |
| 539 | — | Mandatory dispositions; performance standards respecting physical, chemical, or biological contaminants |
| 540 | — | Handling and disposal of condemned and other inedible materials |
| 541 | — | Marks, marking and labeling of products and containers |
| 544 | — | Food ingredients permitted |
| 548 | — | Preparation of products |
| 550 | — | Records required to be kept |
| 552 | — | Exports |
| 555 | — | Transportation of fish products in commerce |
| 557 | — | Importation |
| 559 | — | Detention, seizure, condemnation |
| 560 | — | State-federal, federal-state cooperative agreements; state designations |

| Key Regulatory Provisions: Poultry Products Inspection | | |
|---|---|---|
| 9 C.F.R. Part | Subpart | Title of Part or Subpart |
| 362 | — | Voluntary poultry inspection regulations |
| 381 | — | Poultry products inspection regulations |

| Key Regulatory Provisions: Egg Products Inspection | | |
|---|---|---|
| 9 C.F.R. Part | Subpart | Title of Part or Subpart |
| 590 | — | Inspection of eggs and egg products (Egg Products Inspection Act) |
| 592 | — | Voluntary inspection of egg products |

## 2015-12-02 USDA FSIS Final Rule, Mandatory Inspection of Fish of the Order Siluriformes and Products Derived from Such Fish

80 Fed. Reg. 75,590

SUMMARY: The Food Safety and Inspection Service (FSIS) is amending its regulations to establish a mandatory inspection program for fish of the order Siluriformes and products derived from these fish. These final regulations implement the provisions of the 2008 and 2014 Farm Bills, which amended the Federal Meat Inspection Act, mandating FSIS inspection of Siluriformes.

....

On the effective date (March 1, 2016), Siluriformes fish and fish products are under FSIS jurisdiction. By March 1, 2016, foreign countries seeking to continue exporting Siluriformes fish and fish products to the United States during the transitional period are required to submit lists of establishments (with the establishment name and number) that currently export and will continue to export Siluriformes fish and fish products to the United States. Foreign countries are also required to submit documentation showing that they currently have laws or other legal measures in place that provide authority to regulate the growing and processing of fish for human food and to assure compliance with the Food and Drug Administration's (FDA) regulatory requirements in 21 CFR part 123, Fish and Fishery Products.

....

SUPPLEMENTARY INFORMATION:

### Executive Summary

The 2008 Farm Bill amended the Federal Meat Inspection Act (FMIA), to make "catfish" a species amenable to the FMIA and, therefore, subject to FSIS inspection. In addition, the 2008 Farm Bill gave FSIS the authority to define the term "catfish."

On February 24, 2011, FSIS published a proposed rule that outlined a mandatory catfish inspection program and presented two options for defining "catfish": One option was to define catfish narrowly as those fish belonging to the family Ictaluridae. The other option was a broader definition, all fish of the order Siluriformes. FSIS sought public comments on the scope of the definition in the proposed rule. The Agency proposed regulatory requirements for mandatory catfish inspection that were adapted from the meat inspection regulations.

The 2014 Farm Bill, enacted on February 7, 2014, amended the FMIA to remove the term "catfish" and to make "all fish of the order Siluriformes" subject to FSIS jurisdiction and inspection. As a result, FSIS inspection of Siluriformes is mandated by law. This final rule adopts all the regulatory requirements outlined in the February 2011 proposal, with the following changes:

- The term "catfish" defined in proposed 9 CFR part 531 and used throughout the proposed regulatory text, is replaced in this final rule by the term "fish of the order Siluriformes," "Siluriformes fish," or simply "fish," understood to mean, for purposes of the final regulations, any fish of the order Siluriformes.
- The retail store exemption includes, as an exempt retail operation, the slaughter of fish at retail stores or restaurants for consumers who purchase the fish at those facilities, and in accordance with the consumers' request.
- Fish with unusual gross deformities caused by disease or chemical contamination (rather than merely with gross deformities) are not to be used for human food (9 CFR 539.1(d)).
- The labeling regulations (9 CFR 541.7) permit the use of the term "catfish" only on labels of fish classified within the family Ictaluridae, consistent with provisions of the Federal Food, Drug, and Cosmetic (FD&C) Act (21 U.S.C. 321d (a) and 343(t)). Fish of the order Siluriformes, from families other than Ictaluridae, must be labeled with an appropriate common or usual name.
- The labeling regulations (9 CFR 541.7) require packages of Siluriformes fish and fish products that are not ready-to-eat to bear safe-handling instructions to include "fish" in the rationale statement, i.e., "This product was prepared from inspected and passed fish, "and in the labeling statements, i.e., "Keep raw fish from other foods. Wash working surfaces (including cutting boards), utensils, and hands after touching raw fish."
- The labeling regulations (9 CFR 541.7) to clarify that the labeling of fish covered commodities sold by a retailer bear country of origin and method of production information, in compliance with the requirements in 7 CFR part 60, subpart A, Country of Origin Labeling for Fish and Shellfish.
- The import inspection regulations for Siluriformes fish and fish products (9 CFR part 557) to make them consistent with the September 19, 2014, rule amending the FSIS regulations for imported meat, poultry, and egg products (79 FR 56220).

. . . .

## 2. Alcohol

The Twenty-First Amendment delegated the decision of whether to permit the sale of alcohol to each of the individual states. However, it did not—and does not—prevent extensive federal regulation of the alcohol industry. There are two primary regulators of the alcohol industry. The first is the Alcohol and Tobacco Tax and Trade Bureau (TTB) of the U.S. Department of the Treasury. The second is the Bureau of Alcohol, Tobacco, Firearms, and Explosives (ATF) of the U.S. Department of Justice. Alcohol remains subject to FDA's adulteration and misbranding provisions. However, a memorandum of understanding between FDA and ATF delegates most enforcement responsibilities to ATF.

Please read (or review) the following excerpts in the statutory supplement:

- U.S. Constitution, Amendment XVIII.
- U.S. Constitution, Amendment XXI.

### *a. Outline of Regulatory Regime*

As noted ealier, this chapter contains separate outline-of-regulatory-regime sections for three related areas not regulated primarilty by FDA. This is the outline for alcohol. As with all such outlines in this book, you should do no more than skim this on your first reading of the chapter.

| Timeline of Key Statutes: Alcohol Regulation | | | |
|---|---|---|---|
| **Year** | **PL** | **Stat** | **Name of Statute** |
| 1890 | 51-736 | 26 Stat. 313 | Wilson Act |
| 1913 | 62-398 | 37 Stat. 699 | Webb-Kenyon Act |
| 1919 | 66-66 | 41 Stat. 305 | National Prohibition Act |
| 1935 | 74-401 | 49 Stat. 977 | Federal Alcohol Administration Act |

| Key Statutory Provisions: Alcohol Regulation | | |
|---|---|---|
| **Statute Name or U.S.C. Title** | **§** | **Title of Section or Subsection** |
| 27 U.S.C. | 121 | State statutes as operative on termination of transportation; original packages |
| 27 U.S.C. | 122 | Shipments into states for possession or sale in violation of state law |
| 27 U.S.C. | 122a. | Injunctive relief in federal district court |
| 27 U.S.C. | 124. | Direct shipment of wine |
| 27 U.S.C. | 202 | General provisions |
| 27 U.S.C. | 203 | Unlawful businesses without permit; application to state agency |
| 27 U.S.C. | 204 | Permits |

| Statute Name or U.S.C. Title | § | Title of Section or Subsection |
|---|---|---|
| 27 U.S.C. | 205 | Unfair competition and unlawful practices |
| 27 U.S.C. | 206 | Bulk sales and bottling |
| 27 U.S.C. | 207 | Penalties; jurisdiction; compromise of liability |
| 27 U.S.C. | 208 | Interlocking directorates |
| 27 U.S.C. | 211 | Miscellaneous provisions |
| 27 U.S.C. | 213 | Declaration of policy and purpose |
| 27 U.S.C. | 214 | Definitions |
| 27 U.S.C. | 215 | Labeling requirement |
| 27 U.S.C. | 216 | Preemption |
| 27 U.S.C. | 217 | Report to Congress |
| 27 U.S.C. | 218 | Civil penalties |
| 27 U.S.C. | 219 | Injunction proceedings; compromise of liability |

**Key Regulatory Provisions: Alcohol Regulations Administered by Treasury**

| 27 C.F.R. Part | Subpart | Title of Part or Subpart |
|---|---|---|
| 1 | — | Basic permit requirements under the federal alcohol administration act, nonindustrial use of distilled spirits and wine, bulk sales and bottling of distilled spirits |
| 4 | — | Labeling and advertising of wine |
| 5 | — | Labeling and advertising of distilled spirits |
| 6 | — | "Tied-house" |
| 7 | — | Labeling and advertising of malt beverages |
| 8 | — | Exclusive outlets |
| 9 | — | American viticultural areas |
| 10 | — | Commercial bribery |
| 11 | — | Consignment sales |
| 12 | — | Foreign nongeneric names of geographic significance used in the designation of wines |
| 13 | — | Labeling proceedings |
| 16 | — | Alcoholic beverage health warning statement |
| 17 | — | Drawback on taxpaid distilled spirits used in manufacturing nonbeverage products |
| 18 | — | Production of volatile fruit-flavor concentrate |

| 27 C.F.R. Part | Subpart | Title of Part or Subpart |
|---|---|---|
| 19 | — | Distilled spirits plants |
| 20 | — | Distribution and use of denatured alcohol and rum |
| 21 | — | Formulas for denatured alcohol and rum |
| 22 | — | Distribution and use of tax-free alcohol |
| 24 | — | Wine |
| 25 | — | Beer |
| 26 | — | Liquors and articles from Puerto Rico and the Virgin Islands |
| 27 | — | Importation of distilled spirits, wines, and beer |
| 28 | — | Exportation of alcohol |
| 29 | — | Stills and miscellaneous regulations |
| 30 | — | Gauging manual |
| 31 | — | Alcohol beverage dealers |

## FDA-ATF, Memorandum of Understanding between the Food and Drug Administration and the Bureau of Alcohol, Tobacco and Firearms

Nov 20, 1987

I. PURPOSE

This agreement between the Food and Drug Administration (FDA) and the Bureau of Alcohol, Tobacco and Firearms (ATF) is to clarify and to delineate the enforcement responsibilities of each agency with respect to alcoholic beverages considered adulterated under the [FFDCA], and for other related purposes. Specifically, this Memorandum of Understanding will:

(A) Effect a more efficient system of communication and exchange between FDA and ATF;

(B) Confirm ATF policy with respect to the labeling of ingredients and substances in alcoholic beverages that pose a public health problem; and

(C) Clarify and coordinate the responsibilities of each agency with respect to the identification, testing, and recall of adulterated alcoholic beverages.

II. BACKGROUND

A. Pursuant to the Federal Food, Drug and Cosmetic Act of 1938, as amended ([FFDCA]), 21 U.S.C. §§ 301, et seq., FDA has authority, inter alia, to take action with respect to adulterated food products, including alcoholic beverages, both domestic and imported. Among other things, a food is adulterated under section 402 of the [FFDCA] if it was produced, packed, or held under insanitary conditions; if it contains any poisonous or deleterious substance which may render the food injurious to health; or if it contains an unapproved food additive. FDA has authority to initiate seizure of adulterated foods, including alcoholic beverages, and to seek to enjoin the introduction of such products into interstate commerce. The [FFDCA] also authorizes FDA to refuse entry of imported products that appear to be adulterated and misbranded.

B. Pursuant to the Federal Alcohol Administration Act (FAA Act), 27 U.S.C. §§ 201, et seq. and the Internal Revenue Code of 1986 (IRC), Title 26, U.S.C., ATF has authority over distilled spirits, wines, and malt beverage products, both domestic and imported. In particular, section 5 of the FAA Act (27 U.S.C. § 205) vests ATF with the authority to promulgate regulations regarding the labeling and advertising of alcoholic beverages to insure that they provide the consumer with adequate information concerning the identity and quality of such products. Section 5(e) also makes it unlawful to sell or ship or deliver for sale or shipment, or otherwise introduce into interstate or foreign commerce, or to receive therein, or to remove from customs custody for consumption, any distilled spirits, wine, or malt beverages in bottles, unless such products are bottled, packaged, and labeled in conformity with regulations prescribed by the Secretary of the Treasury. ATF is charged with the administration and enforcement of the FAA Act and does this through, inter alia, the issuance of permits and through procedures that require the prior approval of all labels. In addition, ATF is charged with the administration and enforcement of Chapter 51 of the IRC, relating to Distilled Spirits, Wines and Beer. This chapter in conjunction with the FAA Act establishes a comprehensive system of controls of alcoholic beverages, including on-site inspections and procedures that require the advance approval of statements of process and of formulas showing each ingredient to be used in the product. The IRC also vests authority in ATF to detain any container that will be removed in violation of law (26 U.S.C. § 5311) and vests ATF with seizure and forfeiture authority (26 U.S.C. § 7302).

III. AGREEMENT

It is understood and agreed between the parties, as follows:

(A) ATF will be responsible for the promulgation and enforcement of regulations with respect to the labeling of distilled spirits, wine, and malt beverages pursuant to the FAA Act. When FDA has determined that the presence of an ingredient in food products, including alcoholic beverages, poses a recognized public health problem, and that the ingredient or substance must be identified on a food product label, ATF will initiate rulemaking proceedings to promulgate labeling regulations for alcoholic beverages consistent with ATF's health policy with respect to alcoholic beverages. ATF and FDA will consult on a regular basis concerning the propriety of promulgating regulations concerning the labeling of other ingredients and substances for alcoholic beverages.

(B) FDA will, upon ATF's request, provide ATF with a health hazard evaluation with respect to any substance found in alcoholic beverages. ATF agrees to provide FDA with any data or analyses it may have with respect to the substance in question.

(C) ATF will be responsible for testing alcoholic beverages to determine the extent of an adulteration problem. To the extent practicable, FDA will provide laboratory assistance at the request of ATF.

(D) ATF will prepare, in consultation with FDA, comprehensive formal procedures and guidelines for implementing voluntary recalls of adulterated alcoholic beverages. These procedures and guidelines will be developed in light of the FDA procedures and guidelines for such recalls and shall be implemented by ATF after review and comment by FDA.

(E) ATF, as the agency with a system of specific statutory and regulatory controls over alcoholic beverages, will have primary responsibility for issuing recall notices and monitoring voluntary recalls of alcoholic beverages that are adulterated under FDA law or mislabeled under the FAA Act by reason of being adulterated. This agreement does not affect or otherwise attempt to restrict the seizure or other statutory and regulatory authorities of the respective agencies.

(F) When FDA learns or is advised that an alcoholic beverage is or may be adulterated, FDA will contact ATF.

(G) When ATF learns or is advised that an alcoholic beverage is or may be adulterated, ATF will consult with FDA before it takes any action with respect to a notice of recall for the product. FDA, in turn, will expeditiously provide ATF with a written health hazard evaluation of each product involved in a recall situation or potential recall situation. ATF will provide FDA with any data or analyses it may have with respect to the product in question to assist FDA in undertaking a health hazard evaluation. Upon receipt of a FDA health hazard evaluation indicating a definitive hazard, ATF will advise the responsible firm as to an appropriate course of action which might include a voluntary recall.

(H) In situations involving a recall notice of an adulterated alcoholic beverage, ATF will advise FDA of how ATF intends to proceed and will keep FDA apprised of developments with respect to such recall.

(I) In situations involving a recall of an adulterated alcoholic beverage that poses a significant risk to the public health, ATF will consult with FDA before issuing any press release. Press releases will be issued in accordance with established ATF procedures and guidelines.

(J) FDA and ATF laboratories will continue to exchange information concerning methodologies and techniques for testing alcoholic beverages.

(K) FDA and ATF will continue to exchange a wide variety of information, including relevant consumer complaints concerning the adulteration of alcoholic beverages.

....

V. DURATION OF AGREEMENT

This agreement becomes effective upon acceptance by both parties and shall remain in effect indefinitely. This agreement may be modified by mutual consent or terminated by either party upon a thirty (30) day advance written notice to the other.

....

## Granholm v. Heald

544 U.S. 460 (2005)

**Justice KENNEDY delivered the opinion of the Court.**

These consolidated cases present challenges to state laws regulating the sale of wine from out-of-state wineries to consumers in Michigan and New York. The details and mechanics of the two regulatory schemes differ, but the object and effect of the laws are the same: to allow in-state wineries to sell wine directly to consumers in that State but to prohibit out-of-state wineries from doing so, or, at the least, to make direct sales impractical from an economic standpoint. It is evident that the object and design of the Michigan and New York statutes is to grant in-state wineries a competitive advantage over wineries located beyond the States' borders.

We hold that the laws in both States discriminate against interstate commerce in violation of the Commerce Clause, Art. I, § 8, cl. 3, and that the discrimination is neither authorized nor permitted by the Twenty-first Amendment. Accordingly, we affirm the judgment of the Court of Appeals for the Sixth Circuit, which invalidated the Michigan laws; and we reverse the judgment of the Court of Appeals for the Second Circuit, which upheld the New York laws.

### I

Like many other States, Michigan and New York regulate the sale and importation of alcoholic beverages, including wine, through a three-tier distribution system. Separate licenses are required for producers, wholesalers, and retailers. The three-tier scheme is preserved by a complex set of overlapping state and federal regulations. For example, both state and federal laws limit vertical integration between tiers. We have held previously that States can mandate a three-tier distribution scheme in the exercise of their authority under the Twenty-first Amendment. As relevant to today's cases, though, the three-tier system is, in broad terms and with refinements to be discussed, mandated by Michigan and New York only for sales from out-of-state wineries. In-state wineries, by contrast, can obtain a license for direct sales to consumers. The differential treatment between in-state and out-of-state wineries constitutes explicit discrimination against interstate commerce.

This discrimination substantially limits the direct sale of wine to consumers, an otherwise emerging and significant business. From 1994 to 1999, consumer spending on direct wine shipments doubled, reaching $500 million per year, or three percent of all wine sales. The expansion has been influenced by several related trends. First, the number of small wineries in the United States has significantly increased. By some estimates there are over 3,000 wineries in the country, more than three times the number 30 years ago. At the same time, the wholesale market has consolidated. Between 1984 and 2002, the number of licensed wholesalers dropped from 1,600 to 600. The increasing winery-to-wholesaler ratio means that many small wineries do not produce enough wine or have sufficient consumer demand for their wine to make it economical for wholesalers to carry their products. This has led many small wineries to rely on direct shipping to reach new markets. Technological improvements, in particular the ability of wineries to sell wine over the Internet, have helped make direct shipments an attractive sales channel.

Approximately 26 States allow some direct shipping of wine, with various restrictions. Thirteen of these States have reciprocity laws, which allow direct shipment from wineries outside the State, provided the State of origin affords similar nondiscriminatory treatment. In many parts of the country, however, state laws that prohibit or severely restrict direct shipments deprive consumers of access to the direct market. According to the Federal Trade Commission (FTC), "[s]tate bans on interstate direct shipping represent the single largest regulatory barrier to expanded e-commerce in wine."

The wine producers in the cases before us are small wineries that rely on direct consumer sales as an important part of their businesses. Domaine Alfred, one of the plaintiffs in the Michigan suit, is a small winery located in San Luis Obispo, California. It produces 3,000 cases of wine per year. Domaine Alfred has received requests for its wine from Michigan consumers but cannot fill the orders because of the State's direct-shipment ban. Even if the winery could find a Michigan wholesaler to distribute its wine, the wholesaler's markup would render shipment through the three-tier system economically infeasible.

Similarly, Juanita Swedenburg and David Lucas, two of the plaintiffs in the New York suit, operate small wineries in Virginia (the Swedenburg Estate Vineyard) and California (the Lucas Winery). Some of their customers are tourists, from other States, who purchase wine while visiting the wineries. If these customers wish to obtain Swedenburg or Lucas wines after they return home, they will be unable to do so if they reside in a State with restrictive direct-shipment laws. For example, Swedenburg and Lucas are unable to fill orders from New York, the Nation's second-largest wine market, because of the limits that State imposes on direct wine shipments.

### A

We first address the background of the suit challenging the Michigan direct-shipment law. Most alcoholic beverages in Michigan are distributed through the

State's three-tier system. Producers or distillers of alcoholic beverages, whether located in state or out of state, generally may sell only to licensed in-state wholesalers. Wholesalers, in turn, may sell only to in-state retailers. Licensed retailers are the final link in the chain, selling alcoholic beverages to consumers at retail locations and, subject to certain restrictions, through home delivery.

Under Michigan law, wine producers, as a general matter, must distribute their wine through wholesalers. There is, however, an exception for Michigan's approximately 40 in-state wineries, which are eligible for "wine maker" licenses that allow direct shipment to in-state consumers. The cost of the license varies with the size of the winery. For a small winery, the license is $25. Out-of-state wineries can apply for a $300 "outside seller of wine" license, but this license only allows them to sell to in-state wholesalers.

Some Michigan residents brought suit against various state officials in the United States District Court for the Eastern District of Michigan. Domaine Alfred, the San Luis Obispo winery, joined in the suit. The plaintiffs contended that Michigan's direct-shipment laws discriminated against interstate commerce in violation of the Commerce Clause. The trade association Michigan Beer & Wine Wholesalers intervened as a defendant. Both the State and the wholesalers argued that the ban on direct shipment from out-of-state wineries is a valid exercise of Michigan's power under § 2 of the Twenty-first Amendment.

On cross-motions for summary judgment the District Court sustained the Michigan scheme. The Court of Appeals for the Sixth Circuit reversed. Relying on *Bacchus Imports, Ltd. v. Dias*, 468 U.S. 263 (1984), the court rejected the argument that the Twenty-first Amendment immunizes all state liquor laws from the strictures of the Commerce Clause, and held the Michigan scheme was unconstitutional because the defendants failed to demonstrate the State could not meet its proffered policy objectives through nondiscriminatory means.

### B

New York's licensing scheme is somewhat different. It channels most wine sales through the three-tier system, but it too makes exceptions for in-state wineries. As in Michigan, the result is to allow local wineries to make direct sales to consumers in New York on terms not available to out-of-state wineries. Wineries that produce wine only from New York grapes can apply for a license that allows direct shipment to in-state consumers. These licensees are authorized to deliver the wines of other wineries as well, but only if the wine is made from grapes "at least seventy-five percent the volume of which were grown in New York state." An out-of-state winery may ship directly to New York consumers only if it becomes a licensed New York winery, which requires the establishment of "a branch factory, office or storeroom within the state of New York."

Juanita Swedenburg and David Lucas, joined by three of their New York customers, brought suit in the Southern District of New York against the officials responsible for administering New York's Alcoholic Beverage Control Law seeking, inter alia, a declaration that the State's limitations on the direct shipment of out-of-state wine violate the Commerce Clause. New York liquor wholesalers and representatives of New York liquor retailers intervened in support of the State.

The District Court granted summary judgment to the plaintiffs. The court first determined that, under established Commerce Clause principles, the New York direct-shipment scheme discriminates against out-of-state wineries. The court then rejected the State's Twenty-first Amendment argument, finding that the "[d]efendants have not shown that New York's ban on the direct shipment of out-of-state wine, and particularly the in-state exceptions to the ban, implicate the State's core concerns under the Twenty-first Amendment."

The Court of Appeals for the Second Circuit reversed. The court "recognize[d] that the physical presence requirement could create substantial dormant Commerce Clause problems if this licensing scheme regulated a commodity other than alcohol." The court nevertheless sustained the New York statutory scheme because, in the court's view, "New York's desire to ensure accountability through presence is aimed at the regulatory interests directly tied to the importation and transportation of alcohol for use in New York." As such, the New York direct-shipment laws were "within the ambit of the powers granted to states by the Twenty-first Amendment."

C

We consolidated these cases and granted certiorari on the following question: "'Does a State's regulatory scheme that permits in-state wineries directly to ship alcohol to consumers but restricts the ability of out-of-state wineries to do so violate the dormant Commerce Clause in light of § 2 of the Twenty-first Amendment?'"

For ease of exposition, we refer to the respondents from the Michigan challenge and the petitioners in the New York challenge collectively as the wineries. We refer to their opposing parties—Michigan, New York, and the wholesalers and retailers—simply as the States.

II

A

Time and again this Court has held that, in all but the narrowest circumstances, state laws violate the Commerce Clause if they mandate "differential treatment of in-state and out-of-state economic interests that benefits the former and burdens the latter." This rule is essential to the foundations of the Union. The mere fact of nonresidence should not foreclose a producer in one State from access to markets in other States. States may not enact laws that burden out-of-state producers or shippers simply to give a competitive advantage to in-state businesses. This mandate "reflect[s] a central concern of the Framers that was an immediate reason for calling the Constitutional Convention: the conviction that in order to succeed, the new Union would have to avoid the tendencies toward economic Balkanization that had plagued relations among the Colonies and later among the States under the Articles of Confederation."

The rule prohibiting state discrimination against interstate commerce follows also from the principle that States should not be compelled to negotiate with each other regarding favored or disfavored status for their own citizens. States do not need, and may not attempt, to negotiate with other States regarding their mutual economic interests. Rivalries among the States are thus kept to a minimum, and a proliferation of trade zones is prevented.

Laws of the type at issue in the instant cases contradict these principles. They deprive citizens of their right to have access to the markets of other States on equal terms. The perceived necessity for reciprocal sale privileges risks generating the trade rivalries and animosities, the alliances and exclusivity, that the Constitution and, in particular, the Commerce Clause were designed to avoid. State laws that protect local wineries have led to the enactment of statutes under which some States condition the right of out-of-state wineries to make direct wine sales to in-state consumers on a reciprocal right in the shipping State. California, for example, passed a reciprocity law in 1986, retreating from the State's previous regime that allowed unfettered direct shipments from out-of-state wineries. Prior to 1986, all but three States prohibited direct shipments of wine. The obvious aim of the California statute was to open the interstate direct-shipping market for the State's many wineries. The current patchwork of laws—with some States banning direct shipments altogether, others doing so only for out-of-state wines, and still others requiring reciprocity—is essentially the product of an ongoing, low-level trade war. Allowing States to discriminate against out-of-state wine "invite[s] a multiplication of preferential trade areas destructive of the very purpose of the Commerce Clause."

### B

The discriminatory character of the Michigan system is obvious. Michigan allows in-state wineries to ship directly to consumers, subject only to a licensing requirement. Out-of-state wineries, whether licensed or not, face a complete ban on direct shipment. The differential treatment requires all out-of-state wine, but not all in-state wine, to pass through an in-state wholesaler and retailer before reaching consumers. These two extra layers of overhead increase the cost of out-of-state wines to Michigan consumers. The cost differential, and in some cases the inability to secure a wholesaler for small shipments, can effectively bar small wineries from the Michigan market.

The New York regulatory scheme differs from Michigan's in that it does not ban direct shipments altogether. Out-of-state wineries are instead required to establish a distribution operation in New York in order to gain the privilege of direct shipment. This, though, is just an indirect way of subjecting out-of-state wineries, but not local ones, to the three-tier system. New York and those allied with its interests defend the scheme by arguing that an out-of-state winery has the same access to the State's consumers as in-state wineries: All wine must be sold through a licensee fully accountable to New York; it just so happens that in order to become a licensee, a winery must have a physical presence in the State. There is some confusion over the precise steps out-of-state wineries must take to gain access to the New York market, in part because no winery has run the State's regulatory gauntlet. New York's argument, in any event, is unconvincing.

The New York scheme grants in-state wineries access to the State's consumers on preferential terms. The suggestion of a limited exception for direct shipment from out-of-state wineries does nothing to eliminate the discriminatory nature of New York's regulations. In-state producers, with the applicable licenses, can ship directly to consumers from their wineries. Out-of-state wineries must open a branch office and warehouse in New York, additional steps that drive up the cost of their wine. For most wineries, the expense of establishing a bricks-and-mortar distribution operation in 1 State, let alone all 50, is prohibitive. It comes as no surprise that not a single out-of-state winery has availed itself of New York's direct-shipping privilege. We have "viewed with particular suspicion state statutes requiring business operations to be performed in the home State that could more efficiently be performed elsewhere." *Pike v. Bruce Church*, Inc., 397 U.S. 137, 145 (1970). New York's in-state presence requirement runs contrary to our admonition that States cannot require an out-of-state firm "to become a resident in order to compete on equal terms."

In addition to its restrictive in-state presence requirement, New York discriminates against out-of-state wineries in other ways. Out-of-state wineries that establish the requisite branch office and warehouse in New York are still ineligible for a "farm winery" license, the license that provides the most direct means of shipping to New York consumers. Out-of-state wineries may apply only for a commercial winery license. Unlike farm wineries, however, commercial wineries must obtain a separate certificate from the state liquor authority authorizing direct shipments to consumers; and, of course, for out-of-state wineries there is the additional requirement of maintaining a distribution operation in New York. New York law also allows in-state wineries without direct-shipping licenses to distribute their wine through other wineries that have the applicable licenses. This is another privilege not afforded out-of-state wineries.

We have no difficulty concluding that New York, like Michigan, discriminates against interstate commerce through its direct-shipping laws.

### III

State laws that discriminate against interstate commerce face "a virtually per se rule of invalidity." *Philadelphia v. New Jersey*, 437 U.S. 617, 624 (1978). The Michigan and New York laws by their own terms violate this proscription. The two States, however, contend their statutes are saved by § 2 of the Twenty-first Amendment, which provides:

> "The transportation or importation into any State, Territory, or possession of the United States for delivery or use therein of intoxicating liquors, in violation of the laws thereof, is hereby prohibited."

The States' position is inconsistent with our precedents and with the Twenty-first Amendment's history. Section 2 does not allow States to regulate the direct shipment of wine on terms that discriminate in favor of in-state producers.

A

Before 1919, the temperance movement fought to curb the sale of alcoholic beverages one State at a time. The movement made progress, and many States passed laws restricting or prohibiting the sale of alcohol. This Court upheld state laws banning the production and sale of alcoholic beverages, but was less solicitous of laws aimed at imports. In a series of cases before ratification of the Eighteenth Amendment the Court, relying on the Commerce Clause, invalidated a number of state liquor regulations.

These cases advanced two distinct principles. First, the Court held that the Commerce Clause prevented States from discriminating against imported liquor. . . .

Second, the Court held that the Commerce Clause prevented States from passing facially neutral laws that placed an impermissible burden on interstate commerce. . . .

The Wilson Act reaffirmed, and the Webb-Kenyon Act did not displace, the Court's line of Commerce Clause cases striking down state laws that discriminated against liquor produced out of state. The rule [of a set of cases whose discussion is omitted, above] remained in effect: States were required to regulate domestic and imported liquor on equal terms. . . .

B

The ratification of the Eighteenth Amendment in 1919 provided a brief respite from the legal battles over the validity of state liquor regulations. With the ratification of the Twenty-first Amendment 14 years later, however, nationwide Prohibition came to an end. Section 1 of the Twenty-first Amendment repealed the Eighteenth Amendment. Section 2 of the Twenty-first Amendment is at issue here.

Michigan and New York say the provision grants to the States the authority to discriminate against out-of-state goods. The history we have recited does not support this position. To the contrary, it provides strong support for the view that § 2 restored to the States the powers they had under the Wilson and Webb-Kenyon Acts. "The wording of § 2 of the Twenty-first Amendment closely follows the Webb-Kenyon and Wilson Acts, expressing the framers' clear intention of constitutionalizing the Commerce Clause framework established under those statutes." *Craig v. Boren*, 429 U.S. 190, 205–206 (1976) (footnote omitted).

The aim of the Twenty-first Amendment was to allow States to maintain an effective and uniform system for controlling liquor by regulating its transportation, importation, and use. The Amendment did not give States the authority to pass nonuniform laws in order to discriminate against out-of-state goods, a privilege they had not enjoyed at any earlier time.

Some of the cases decided soon after ratification of the Twenty-first Amendment did not take account of this history and were inconsistent with this view....

Our more recent cases, furthermore, confirm that the Twenty-first Amendment does not supersede other provisions of the Constitution and, in particular, does not displace the rule that States may not give a discriminatory preference to their own producers.

C

....

State policies are protected under the Twenty-first Amendment when they treat liquor produced out of state the same as its domestic equivalent. The instant cases, in contrast, involve straightforward attempts to discriminate in favor of local producers. The discrimination is contrary to the Commerce Clause and is not saved by the Twenty-first Amendment.

IV

Our determination that the Michigan and New York direct-shipment laws are not authorized by the Twenty-first Amendment does not end the inquiry. We still must consider whether either state regime "advances a legitimate local purpose that cannot be adequately served by reasonable nondiscriminatory alternatives." The States offer two primary justifications for restricting direct shipments from out-of-state wineries: keeping alcohol out of the hands of minors and facilitating tax collection. We consider each in turn.

The States, aided by several amici, claim that allowing direct shipment from out-of-state wineries undermines their ability to police underage drinking. Minors, the States argue, have easy access to credit cards and the Internet and are likely to take advantage of direct wine shipments as a means of obtaining alcohol illegally.

The States provide little evidence that the purchase of wine over the Internet by minors is a problem. Indeed, there is some evidence to the contrary. A recent study by the staff of the FTC found that the 26 States currently allowing direct shipments report no problems with minors' increased access to wine. This is not surprising for several reasons. First, minors are less likely to consume wine, as opposed to beer, wine coolers, and hard liquor. Second, minors who decide to disobey the law have more direct means of doing so. Third, direct shipping is an imperfect avenue of obtaining alcohol for minors who, in the words of the past president of the National Conference of State Liquor Administrators, "'want instant gratification.'" (explaining why minors rarely buy alcohol via the mail or the Internet). Without concrete evidence that direct shipping of wine is likely to increase alcohol consumption by minors, we are left with the States' unsupported assertions. Under our precedents, which require the "clearest showing" to justify discriminatory state regulation, this is not enough.

Even were we to credit the States' largely unsupported claim that direct shipping of wine increases the risk of underage drinking, this would not justify regulations limiting only out-of-state direct shipments. As the wineries point out, minors are just as likely to order wine from in-state producers as from out-of-state ones. Michigan, for example, already allows its licensed retailers (over 7,000 of them) to deliver alcohol directly to consumers. Michigan counters that it has greater regulatory control over in-state producers than over out-of-state wineries. This does not justify Michigan's discriminatory ban on direct shipping. Out-of-state wineries face the loss of state and federal licenses if they fail to comply with state law. This provides strong incentives not to sell alcohol to minors. In addition, the States can take less restrictive steps to minimize the risk that minors will order wine by mail. For example, the Model Direct Shipping Bill developed by the National Conference of State Legislatures requires an adult signature on delivery and a label so instructing on each package.

The States' tax-collection justification is also insufficient. Increased direct shipping, whether originating in state or out of state, brings with it the potential for tax evasion. With regard to Michigan, however, the tax-collection argument is a diversion. That is because Michigan, unlike many other States, does not rely on wholesalers to collect taxes on wines imported from out of state. Instead, Michigan collects taxes directly from out-of-state wineries on all wine shipped to in-state wholesalers. If licensing and self-reporting provide adequate safeguards for wine distributed through the three-tier system, there is no reason to believe they will not suffice for direct shipments.

New York and its supporting parties also advance a tax-collection justification for the State's direct-shipment laws. While their concerns are not wholly illusory, their regulatory objectives can be achieved without discriminating against interstate commerce. In particular, New York could protect itself against lost tax revenue by requiring a permit as a condition of direct shipping. This is the approach taken by New York for in-state wineries. The State offers no reason to believe the system would prove ineffective for out-of-state wineries. Licensees could be required to submit regular sales reports and to remit taxes. Indeed, various States use this approach for taxing direct interstate wine shipments, and report no problems with tax collection. This is also the procedure sanctioned by the National Conference of State Legislatures in their Model Direct Shipping Bill.

Michigan and New York benefit, furthermore, from provisions of federal law that supply incentives for wineries to comply with state regulations. The Tax and Trade Bureau (formerly the Bureau of Alcohol, Tobacco and Firearms) has authority to revoke a winery's federal license if it violates state law. Without a federal license, a winery cannot operate in any State. In addition the Twenty-first Amendment Enforcement Act gives state attorneys general the power to sue wineries in federal court to enjoin violations of state law.

These federal remedies, when combined with state licensing regimes, adequately protect States from lost tax revenue. The States have not shown that tax evasion from out-of-state wineries poses such a unique threat that it justifies their discriminatory regimes.

Michigan and New York offer a handful of other rationales, such as facilitating orderly market conditions, protecting public health and safety, and ensuring regulatory accountability. These objectives can also be achieved through the alternative of an evenhanded licensing requirement. Finally, it should be noted that improvements in technology have eased the burden of monitoring out-of-state wineries. Background checks can be done electronically. Financial records and sales data can be mailed, faxed, or submitted via e-mail.

In summary, the States provide little concrete evidence for the sweeping assertion that they cannot police direct shipments by out-of-state wineries. Our Commerce Clause cases demand more than mere speculation to support discrimination against out-of-state goods. The "burden is on the State to show that 'the discrimination is demonstrably justified.'" The Court has upheld state regulations that discriminate against interstate commerce only after finding, based on concrete record evidence, that a State's nondiscriminatory alternatives will prove unworkable. Michigan and New York have not satisfied this exacting standard.

V

States have broad power to regulate liquor under § 2 of the Twenty-first Amendment. This power, however, does not allow States to ban, or severely limit, the direct shipment of out-of-state wine while simultaneously authorizing direct shipment by in-state producers. If a State chooses to allow direct shipment of wine, it must do so on evenhanded terms. Without demonstrating the need for discrimination, New York and Michigan have enacted regulations that disadvantage out-of-state wine producers. Under our Commerce Clause jurisprudence, these regulations cannot stand.

We affirm the judgment of the Court of Appeals for the Sixth Circuit; and we reverse the judgment of the Court of Appeals for the Second Circuit and remand the case for further proceedings consistent with our opinion.

It is so ordered.

**Justice STEVENS, . . . dissenting.**

Congress' power to regulate commerce among the States includes the power to authorize the States to place burdens on interstate commerce. Absent such congressional approval, a state law may violate the unwritten rules described as the "dormant Commerce Clause" either by imposing an undue burden on both out-of-state and local producers engaged in interstate activities or by treating out-of-state producers less favorably than their local competitors. See, e.g., *Pike v. Bruce Church, Inc.*, 397 U.S. 137 (1970); *Philadelphia v. New Jersey*, 437 U.S. 617(1978). A state law totally prohibiting the sale of an ordinary article of commerce might impose an even more serious burden on interstate commerce. If Congress may nevertheless authorize the States to enact such laws, surely the people may do so through the process of amending our Constitution.

The New York and Michigan laws challenged in these cases would be patently invalid under well-settled dormant Commerce Clause principles if they regulated sales of an ordinary article of commerce rather than wine. But ever since the adoption of the Eighteenth Amendment and the Twenty-first Amendment, our Constitution has placed commerce in alcoholic beverages in a special category. Section 2 of the Twenty-first Amendment expressly provides that "[t]he transportation or importation into any State, Territory, or possession of the United States for delivery or use therein of intoxicating liquors, in violation of the laws thereof, is hereby prohibited."

Today many Americans, particularly those members of the younger generations who make policy decisions, regard alcohol as an ordinary article of commerce, subject to substantially the same market and legal controls as other consumer products. That was definitely not the view of the generations that made policy in 1919 when the Eighteenth Amendment was ratified or in 1933 when it was repealed by the Twenty-first Amendment.[1] On the contrary, the moral condemnation of the use of alcohol as a beverage represented not merely the convictions of our religious leaders, but the views of a sufficiently large majority of the population to warrant the rare exercise of the power to amend the Constitution on two occasions. The Eighteenth Amendment entirely prohibited commerce in "intoxicating liquors" for beverage purposes throughout the United States and the territories subject to its jurisdiction. While § 1 of the Twenty-first Amendment repealed the nationwide prohibition, § 2 gave the States the option to maintain equally comprehensive prohibitions in their respective jurisdictions.

The views of judges who lived through the debates that led to the ratification of those Amendments are entitled to special deference. Foremost among them was Justice Brandeis, whose understanding of a State's right to discriminate in its regulation of out-of-state alcohol could not have been clearer:

> The plaintiffs ask us to limit [§ 2's] broad command. They request us to construe the Amendment as saying, in effect: The State may prohibit the importation of intoxicating liquors provided it prohibits the manufacture and sale within its borders; but if it permits such manufacture and sale, it must let imported liquors compete with the domestic on equal terms. To say that, would involve not a construction of the Amendment, but a rewriting of it.... Can it be doubted that a State might establish a state monopoly of the manufacture and sale of beer, and either prohibit all competing importations, or discourage importation by laying a heavy impost, or channelize

1. In the words of Justice Jackson: "The people of the United States knew that liquor is a lawlessness unto itself. They determined that it should be governed by a specific and particular Constitutional provision. They did not leave it to the courts to devise special distortions of the general rules as to interstate commerce to curb liquor's 'tendency to get out of legal bounds.' It was their unsatisfactory experience with that method that resulted in giving liquor an exclusive place in constitutional law as a commodity whose transportation is governed by a special, constitutional provision." Duckworth v. Arkansas, 314 U.S. 390, 398–399 (1941) (opinion concurring in result).

desired importations by confining them to a single consignee?" *State Bd. of Equalization of Cal. v. Young's Market Co.*, 299 U.S. 59 (1936).[2]

In the years following the ratification of the Twenty-first Amendment, States adopted manifold laws regulating commerce in alcohol, and many of these laws were discriminatory. So-called "dry states" entirely prohibited such commerce; others prohibited the sale of alcohol on Sundays; others permitted the sale of beer and wine but not hard liquor; most created either state monopolies or distribution systems that gave discriminatory preferences to local retailers and distributors. The notion that discriminatory state laws violated the unwritten prohibition against balkanizing the American economy—while persuasive in contemporary times when alcohol is viewed as an ordinary article of commerce—would have seemed strange indeed to the millions of Americans who condemned the use of the "demon rum" in the 1920's and 1930's. Indeed, they expressly authorized the "balkanization" that today's decision condemns. Today's decision may represent sound economic policy and may be consistent with the policy choices of the contemporaries of Adam Smith who drafted our original Constitution; it is not, however, consistent with the policy choices made by those who amended our Constitution in 1919 and 1933.

My understanding (and recollection) of the historical context reinforces my conviction that the text of § 2 should be "broadly and colloquially interpreted." Indeed, the fact that the Twenty-first Amendment was the only Amendment in our history to have been ratified by the people in state conventions, rather than by state legislatures, provides further reason to give its terms their ordinary meaning. Because the New York and Michigan laws regulate the "transportation or importation" of "intoxicating liquors" for "delivery or use therein," they are exempt from dormant Commerce Clause scrutiny.

As Justice THOMAS has demonstrated, the text of the Twenty-first Amendment is a far more reliable guide to its meaning than the unwritten rules that the majority enforces today. I therefore join his persuasive and comprehensive dissenting opinion.

**Justice THOMAS, . . . dissenting.**

A century ago, this Court repeatedly invalidated, as inconsistent with the negative Commerce Clause, state liquor legislation that prevented out-of-state businesses from shipping liquor directly to a State's residents. The Webb-Kenyon Act and the Twenty-first Amendment cut off this intrusive review, as their text and

2. According to Justice Black, who participated in the passage of the Twenty-first Amendment in the Senate, § 2 was intended to return "'absolute control' of liquor traffic to the States, free of all restrictions which the Commerce Clause might before that time have imposed." Hostetter v. Idlewild Bon Voyage Liquor Corp., 377 U.S. 324, 338 (1964) (dissenting opinion).

history make clear and as this Court's early cases on the Twenty-first Amendment recognized. The Court today seizes back this power, based primarily on a historical argument that this Court decisively rejected long ago in *State Bd. of Equalization of Cal. v. Young's Market Co.*, 299 U.S. 59, 64 (1936). Because I would follow *Young's Market* and the language of both the statute that Congress enacted and the Amendment that the Nation ratified, rather than the Court's questionable reading of history and the "negative implications" of the Commerce Clause, I respectfully dissent.

I

The Court devotes much attention to the Twenty-first Amendment, yet little to the terms of the Webb-Kenyon Act. This is a mistake, because that Act's language displaces any negative Commerce Clause barrier to state regulation of liquor sales to in-state consumers.

A

The Webb-Kenyon Act immunizes from negative Commerce Clause review the state liquor laws that the Court holds are unconstitutional. The Act "prohibit[s]" any "shipment or transportation" of alcoholic beverages "into any State" when those beverages are "intended, by any person interested therein, to be received, possessed, sold, or in any manner used . . . in violation of any law of such State."[1] State laws that regulate liquor imports in the manner described by the [FFDCA] are exempt from judicial scrutiny under the negative Commerce Clause, as this Court has long held. The Webb-Kenyon Act's language, in other words, "prevent[s] the immunity characteristic of interstate commerce from being used to permit the receipt of liquor through such commerce in States contrary to their laws."

The Michigan and New York direct-shipment laws are within the Webb-Kenyon Act's terms and therefore do not run afoul of the negative Commerce Clause. . . .

*[A detailed analysis of the Webb-Kenyon Act is here omitted].*

---

1. The Webb-Kenyon Act provides:

"The shipment or transportation, in any manner or by any means whatsoever, of any spirituous, vinous, malted, fermented, or other intoxicating liquor of any kind from one State, Territory, or District of the United States, or place noncontiguous to but subject to the jurisdiction thereof, into any other State, Territory, or District of the United States, or place noncontiguous to but subject to the jurisdiction thereof, or from any foreign country into any State, Territory, or District of the United States, or place noncontiguous to but subject to the jurisdiction thereof, which said spirituous, vinous, malted, fermented, or other intoxicating liquor is intended, by any person interested therein, to be received, possessed, sold, or in any manner used, either in the original package or otherwise, in violation of any law of such State, Territory, or District of the United States, or place noncontiguous to but subject to the jurisdiction thereof, is prohibited."

27 U.S.C. § 122.

In sum, the Webb-Kenyon Act authorizes the discriminatory state laws before the Court today.

II

There is no need to interpret the Twenty-first Amendment, because the Webb-Kenyon Act resolves these cases. However, the state laws the Court strikes down are lawful under the plain meaning of § 2 of the Twenty-first Amendment, as this Court's case law in the wake of the Amendment and the contemporaneous practice of the States reinforce.

*[A detailed analysis of the Twenty-First Amendment and early post-amendment case law is here omitted].*

....

III

Though the majority dismisses this Court's early Twenty-first Amendment case law, it relies on the reasoning, if not the holdings, of our more recent Twenty-first Amendment cases. But the Court's later cases do not require the result the majority reaches. Moreover, I would resolve any conflict in this Court's precedents in favor of those cases most contemporaneous with the ratification of the Twenty-first Amendment.

....

IV

The Court begins its opinion by detailing the evils of state laws that restrict the direct shipment of wine. It stresses, for example, the Federal Trade Commission's opinion that allowing the direct shipment of wine would enhance consumer welfare. The Court's focus on these effects suggests that it believes that its decision serves this Nation well. I am sure that the judges who repeatedly invalidated state liquor legislation, even in the face of clear congressional direction to the contrary, thought the same. The Twenty-first Amendment and the Webb-Kenyon Act took those policy choices away from judges and returned them to the States. Whatever the wisdom of that choice, the Court does this Nation no service by ignoring the textual commands of the Constitution and Acts of Congress. The Twenty-first Amendment and the Webb-Kenyon Act displaced the negative Commerce Clause as applied to regulation of liquor imports into a State. They require sustaining the constitutionality of Michigan's and New York's direct-shipment laws. I respectfully dissent.

## 3. Agricultural Biotechnology

As noted earlier, this chapter contains separate outline-of-regulatory-regime sections for three related areas not regulated primarily by the FDA. This is the outline for agricultural biotechnology. As with all such outlines in this book, you should do no more than skim this on your first reading of the chapter.

## *a. Outline of Regulatory Regime*

| Timeline of Key Statutes: Agricultural Biotechnology | | | |
|---|---|---|---|
| Year | PL | Stat | Name of Statute |
| 1912 | 62-275 | 37 Stat. 315 | Plant Quarantine Act |
| 1938 | 75-717 | 52 Stat. 1040 | FFDCA of 1938 |
| 1957 | 85-36 | 71 Stat. 31 | Federal Plant Pest Act |
| 1958 | 85-929 | 72 Stat. 1784 | Food Additives Amendment of 1958 |
| 2000 | 106-224 | 114 Stat. 358 | Plant Protection Act |

| Key Statutory Provisions: Agricultural Biotechnology | | |
|---|---|---|
| Statute Name or U.S.C. Title | § | Title of Section or Subsection |
| FFDCA | 201(q) | [Definition of "pesticide chemical"] |
| FFDCA | 201(s) | [Definition of "food additive"] |
| FFDCA | 408 | Tolerances and exemptions for pesticide chemical residues |
| FFDCA | 409 | Food additives |
| 7 U.S.C. | 136a | Registration of pesticides |
| 7 U.S.C. | 7711 | Regulation of movement of plant pests |
| 7 U.S.C. | 7712 | Regulation of movement of plants, plant products, biological control organisms, noxious weeds, articles, and means of conveyance |
| 7 U.S.C. | 7714 | General remedial measures for new plant pests and noxious weeds |

| Key Regulatory Provisions: Agricultural Biotechnology | | |
|---|---|---|
| C.F.R. Vol. | C.F.R. Part | Title of Part or Subpart |
| 7 | 340 | Introduction of organisms and products altered or produced through genetic engineering which are plant pests or which there is reason to believe are plant pests |
| 40 | 152 | Pesticide registration and classification procedures |
| 40 | 174 | Procedures and requirements for plant-incorporated protectants |

## 1986-06-26 OSTP Policy Announcement, Coordinated Framework for the Regulation of Biotechnology

51 Fed. Reg. 23302

AGENCY: Executive Office of the President, Office of Science and Technology Policy.

ACTION: Announcement of policy; notice for public comment.

SUMMARY: This Federal Register notice announces the policy of the federal agencies involved with the review of biotechnology research and products. . . .

It is the intention of the Domestic Policy Council Working Group on Biotechnology, the Biotechnology Science Coordinating Committee (BSCC), the Department of Agriculture (USDA), the Environmental Protection Agency (EPA), the Food and Drug Administration (FDA), the National Institutes of Health (NIH), the National Science Foundation (NSF), and the Occupational Safety and Health Administration (OSHA) that the policies contained herein be effective immediately. In consideration of comments, modifications, if any, may be published either in a separate notice or as part of proposed rulemaking by the involved agencies.

. . . .

A. Introduction

This notice describes the comprehensive federal regulatory policy for ensuring the safety of biotechnology research and products. Specifically addressed are agency policies that formed part of the previously proposed Coordinated Framework for the Regulation of Biotechnology, published in the Federal Register December 31, 1984 (hereinafter "the December 84 Notice"). These agency policies build upon experience with agricultural, pharmaceutical, and other commercial products developed by traditional genetic modification techniques.

Existing statutes provide a basic network of agency jurisdiction over both research and products; this network forms the basis of this coordinated framework and helps assure reasonable safeguards for the public. This framework is expected to evolve in accord with the experiences of the industry and the agencies, and, thus, modifications may need to be made through administrative or legislative actions.

The application of traditional genetic modification techniques is relied upon broadly for enhanced characteristics of food (e.g., hybrid corn, selective breeding), manufactured food (e.g., bread, cheese, yogurt), waste disposal (e.g., bacterial sewage treatment), medicine (e.g., vaccines, hormones), pesticides (e.g., Bacillus thuringiensis) and other uses. Federal agencies implement an array of laws which seek to ensure the safety of these products. . . . These laws are product-specific because they regulate certain product uses, such as foods or pesticides. This approach provides the opportunity for similar products to be treated similarly by particular regulatory agencies.

Biotechnology also includes recently developed and newly emerging genetic manipulation technologies, such as recombinant DNA (rDNA), recombinant RNA (rRNA) and cell fusion, that are sometimes referred to as genetic engineering. While the recently developed methods are an extension of traditional manipulations that can produce similar or identical products, they enable more precise genetic modifications, and therefore hold the promise for exciting innovation and new areas of commercial opportunity.

Concerns were raised as to whether products resulting from the recently developed techniques would pose greater risks than those achieved through traditional manipulation techniques. For example, what might be the possible environmental consequences of the many anticipated agricultural and environmental applications that will take place outside the physical constraints of a contained facility? In particular, the environmental application of genetically engineered microorganisms may elicit concern because they are of microscopic size, and some may be able to reproduce, proliferate, and become established.

The underlying policy question was whether the regulatory framework that pertained to products developed by traditional genetic manipulation techniques was adequate for products obtained with the new techniques. A similar question arose regarding the sufficiency of the review process for research conducted for agricultural and environmental applications.

The Administration, recognizing its responsibility to confront these concerns, formed an interagency working group under the former White House Cabinet Council on Natural Resources and the Environment in the spring of 1984. The working group sought to achieve a balance between regulation adequate to ensure health and environmental safety while maintaining sufficient regulatory flexibility to avoid impeding the growth of an infant industry.

Upon examination of the existing laws available for the regulation of products developed by traditional genetic manipulation techniques, the working group concluded that, for the most part these laws as currently implemented would address regulatory needs adequately. For certain microbial products, however, additional regulatory requirements, available under existing statutory authority, needed to be established.

The existing health and safety laws had the advantage that they could provide more immediate regulatory protection and certainty for the industry than possible with the implementation of new legislation. Moreover, there did not appear to be an alternative, unitary, statutory approach since the very broad spectrum of products obtained with genetic engineering cut across many product uses regulated by different agencies.

Because of the rapid growth in the scientific knowledge base, the working group felt strongly that the federal agencies needed to have an interagency mechanism for sharing scientific information related to biotechnology, particularly information on research and product applications submitted to the agencies.

The December 1984 Notice described the regulatory framework envisioned by the working group, and recognizing the evolutionary nature of its development, asked for comments. In summary, the Notice stated that the Food and Drug Administration (FDA) would regulate genetic engineering products no differently that those achieved through traditional techniques. The Environmental Protection Agency (EPA) described existing and proposed new policies for regulating pesticidal and nonpesticidal microorganisms. The Department of Agriculture (USDA) stated that under its different legislative authorities it could broadly regulate genetically engineered plants and animals, and plant and animal pathogens. The Notice also proposed an interagency science coordinating mechanism.

. . . .

---

We will return to FDA's role in agricultural biotechnology in Chapter 7, during our discussion of on food additives.

### *b. Biotechnology Labeling and Required Speech*

## Int'l Dairy Foods Ass'n v. Amestoy

92 F.3d 67 (2d Cir. 1996)

**ALTIMARI, Circuit Judge:**

**Background**

. . . .

In 1993, the federal Food and Drug Administration ("FDA") approved the use of recombinant Bovine Somatotropin ("rBST") (also known as recombinant Bovine Growth Hormone ("rGBH")), a synthetic growth hormone that increases milk production by cows. It is undisputed that the dairy products derived from herds treated with rBST are indistinguishable from products derived from untreated herds; consequently, the FDA declined to require the labeling of products derived from cows receiving the supplemental hormone.

In April 1994, defendant-appellee the State of Vermont ("Vermont") enacted a statute requiring that "if rBST has been used in the production of milk or a milk product for retail sale in this state, the retail milk or milk product shall be labeled as such." Vt. Stat. Ann. tit. 6, § 2754(c). . . .

Appellants filed suit in April 1994, asserting that the statute was unconstitutional. In June 1995, the dairy manufacturers moved for preliminary injunctive relief, seeking to enjoin enforcement of the statute. The dairy manufacturers alleged that the Vermont statute (1) infringed their protected rights under the First Amendment to the Constitution and (2) violated the Constitution's Commerce Clause, U.S. Const., Art. 1, § 8. Following an extensive hearing, the United States District Court for the District of Vermont, denied appellants' motion. The dairy manufacturers now appeal.

Because we find that the dairy manufacturers are entitled to an injunction on First Amendment grounds, we do not reach their claims made pursuant to the Commerce Clause.

### Discussion

Generally, preliminary injunctive relief is appropriate when the movant shows "(a) irreparable harm and (b) either (1) likelihood of success on the merits or (2) sufficiently serious questions going to the merits to make them a fair ground for litigation and a balance of hardships tipping decidedly toward the party requesting the preliminary relief." However, because the injunction at issue stays "government action taken in the public interest pursuant to a statutory . . . scheme," this Court has determined that the movant must satisfy the more rigorous "likelihood of success prong."

We review the district court's denial of a preliminary injunction for an abuse of discretion, and will reverse the district court only if it relied on clearly erroneous findings of fact, misapprehended the law, or erred in formulating the injunction.

### 1. Irreparable Harm

Focusing principally on the economic impact of the labeling regulation, the district court found that appellants had not demonstrated irreparable harm to any right protected by the First Amendment. We disagree.

Irreparable harm is "injury for which a monetary award cannot be adequate compensation." It is established that "the loss of *First Amendment* freedoms, for even minimal periods of time, unquestionably constitutes irreparable injury." Because the statute at issue requires appellants to make an involuntary statement whenever they offer their products for sale, we find that the statute causes the dairy manufacturers irreparable harm.

. . . .

We conclude . . . that the manufacturers have carried their burden of establishing irreparable harm. The wrong done by the labeling law to the dairy manufacturers' constitutional right *not* to speak is a serious one that was not given proper weight by the district court. The right not to speak inheres in political and commercial speech alike, and extends to statements of fact as well as statements of opinion. If, however, as Vermont maintains, its labeling law compels appellants to engage in purely commercial speech, the statute must meet a less rigorous test. *See Central Hudson Gas & Elec. Corp. v. Public Serv. Comm'r,* 447 U.S. 557, 562–63 (1980) ("The Constitution . . . accords a lesser protection to commercial speech than to other constitutionally guaranteed expression."). The dairy manufacturers insist that the speech is not purely commercial because it compels them "to convey a message regarding the significance of rBST use that is 'expressly contrary to' their views." Agreeing with Vermont, the district court found that the speech was commercial in nature.

We need not resolve this controversy at this point; even assuming that the compelled disclosure is purely commercial speech, appellants have amply demonstrated that the First Amendment is sufficiently implicated to cause irreparable harm. The dairy manufacturers have clearly done more than simply "assert" their First Amendment rights: The statute in question indisputably requires them to speak when they would rather not. Because compelled speech "contravenes core First Amendment values," appellants have "satisfied the initial requirement for securing injunctive relief."

....

---

Because the statute at hand unquestionably implicates the dairy manufacturers' speech rights, we reject the district court's conclusion that the disclosure compelled by Vt. Stat. Ann. tit. 6, § 2754(c), is not a "loss of First Amendment freedoms," amounting to irreparable harm.

**2. Likelihood of Success on the Merits**

It is not enough for appellants to show, as they have, that they were irreparably harmed by the statute; because the dairy manufacturers challenge government action taken in the public interest, they must also show a likelihood of success on the merits. We find that such success is likely.

In *Central Hudson*, the Supreme Court articulated a four-part analysis for determining whether a government restriction on commercial speech is permissible. *447 U.S. at 566*. We need not address the controversy concerning the nature of the speech in question—commercial or political—because we find that Vermont fails to meet the less stringent constitutional requirements applicable to compelled commercial speech.

Under *Central Hudson*, we must determine: (1) whether the expression concerns lawful activity and is not misleading; (2) whether the government's interest is substantial; (3) whether the labeling law directly serves the asserted interest; and (4) whether the labeling law is no more extensive than necessary. Furthermore, the State of Vermont bears the burden of justifying its labeling law. As the Supreme Court has made clear, "this burden is not satisfied by mere speculation or conjecture; rather, a governmental body seeking to sustain a restriction on commercial speech must demonstrate that the harms it recites are real and that its restriction will in fact alleviate them to a material degree."

In our view, Vermont has failed to establish the second prong of the *Central Hudson* test, namely that its interest is substantial. In making this determination, we rely only upon those interests set forth by Vermont before the district court. As the district court made clear, Vermont "does not claim that health or safety concerns prompted the passage of the Vermont Labeling Law," but instead defends the statute on the basis of "strong consumer interest and the public's 'right to know' ...."

These interests are insufficient to justify compromising protected constitutional rights.

Vermont's failure to defend its constitutional intrusion on the ground that it negatively impacts public health is easily understood. After exhaustive studies, the FDA has "concluded that rBST has no appreciable effect on the composition of milk produced by treated cows, and that there are no human safety or health concerns associated with food products derived from cows treated with rBST." Because bovine somatotropin ("BST") appears naturally in cows, and because there are no BST receptors in a cow's mammary glands, only trace amounts of BST can be detected in milk, whether or not the cows received the supplement. Moreover, it is undisputed that neither consumers nor scientists can distinguish rBST-derived milk from milk produced by an untreated cow. Indeed, the already extensive record in this case contains no scientific evidence from which an objective observer could conclude that rBST has any impact at all on dairy products. It is thus plain that Vermont could not justify the statute on the basis of "real" harms.

We do not doubt that Vermont's asserted interest, the demand of its citizenry for such information, is genuine; reluctantly, however, we conclude that it is inadequate. We are aware of no case in which consumer interest alone was sufficient to justify requiring a product's manufacturers to publish the functional equivalent of a warning about a production method that has no discernible impact on a final product.

Although the Court is sympathetic to the Vermont consumers who wish to know which products may derive from rBST-treated herds, their desire is insufficient to permit the State of Vermont to compel the dairy manufacturers to speak against their will. Were consumer interest alone sufficient, there is no end to the information that states could require manufacturers to disclose about their production methods. For instance, with respect to cattle, consumers might reasonably evince an interest in knowing which grains herds were fed, with which medicines they were treated, or the age at which they were slaughtered. Absent, however, some indication that this information bears on a reasonable concern for human health or safety or some other sufficiently substantial governmental concern, the manufacturers cannot be compelled to disclose it. Instead, those consumers interested in such information should exercise the power of their purses by buying products from manufacturers who voluntarily reveal it.

Accordingly, we hold that consumer curiosity alone is not a strong enough state interest to sustain the compulsion of even an accurate, factual statement, in a commercial context. Because Vermont has demonstrated no cognizable harms, its statute is likely to be held unconstitutional.

### Conclusion

Because appellants have demonstrated both irreparable harm and a likelihood of success on the merits, the judgment of the district court is reversed, and the case is remanded for entry of an appropriate injunction.

## USDA Website, How the Federal Government Regulates Biotech Plants*

The Federal government has a coordinated, risk-based system to ensure that new biotechnology products are safe for the environment and human and animal health. Established as a formal policy in 1986, the Coordinated Framework for Regulation of Biotechnology describes the Federal system for evaluating products developed using modern biotechnology. The Coordinated Framework is based upon existing laws designed to protect public health and the environment. The U.S. government has written new regulations, policies, and guidance to apply these laws to biotechnology-derived products.

The U.S. Government agencies responsible for oversight of the products of agricultural modern biotechnology are the USDA's Animal and Plant Health Inspection Service (USDA-APHIS), the U.S. Environmental Protection Agency (EPA), and the Department of Health and Human Services' Food and Drug Administration (FDA). Depending on its characteristics, a product may be subject to the jurisdiction of one or more of these agencies. Regulatory officials from the three agencies regularly communicate and exchange information to ensure that any safety or regulatory issues that may arise are appropriately resolved.

### Roles of U.S. Regulatory Agencies

*USDA's Animal and Plant Health Inspection Service (APHIS)*

Within USDA, the Animal and Plant Health Inspection Service (APHIS) is responsible for protecting agriculture from pests and diseases. Under the Plant Protection Act, USDA-APHIS has regulatory oversight over products of modern biotechnology that could pose such a risk. Accordingly, USDA-APHIS regulates organisms and products that are known or suspected to be plant pests or to pose a plant pest risk, including those that have been altered or produced through genetic engineering. These are called "regulated articles." USDA-APHIS regulates the import, handling, interstate movement, and release into the environment of regulated organisms that are products of biotechnology, including organisms undergoing confined experimental use or field trials. Regulated articles are reviewed to ensure that, under the proposed conditions of use, they do not present a plant pest risk through ensuring appropriate handling, confinement and disposal.

USDA-APHIS regulations provide a petition process for the determination of nonregulated status. If a petition is granted, that organism will no longer be considered a "regulated article" and will no longer be subject to oversight by USDA-APHIS. The petitioner must supply information such as the biology of the recipient plant, experimental data and publications, genotypic and phenotypic descriptions of the genetically engineered organism, and field test reports. The agency evaluates

* From https://www.aphis.usda.gov/aphis/ourfocus/biotechnology/sa_regulations/ct_agency_framework_roles (last modified Oct 28, 2019).

a variety of issues including the potential for plant pest risk; disease and pest susceptibilities; the expression of gene products, new enzymes, or changes to plant metabolism; weediness and impact on sexually compatible plants; agricultural or cultivation practices; effects on non-target organisms; and the potential for gene transfer to other types of organisms. A notice is filed in the Federal Register and public comments are considered on the environmental assessment and determination written for the decision on granting the petition. Copies of the USDA-APHIS documents are available to the public.

. . . .

*U.S. Environmental Protection Agency (EPA)*

The EPA through a registration process regulates the sale, distribution and use of pesticides in order to protect health, and the environment, regardless of how the pesticide was made or its mode of action. This includes regulation of those pesticides that are produced by an organism through techniques of modern biotechnology. The Biopesticides and Pollution Prevention Division of the Office of Pesticide Programs, under the Federal Insecticide, Fungicide and Rodenticide Act (FIFRA), regulates the distribution, sale, use and testing of pesticidal substances produced in plants and microbes. Generally, Experimental Use Permits are issued for field testing. Applicants must register pesticidal products prior to their sale and distribution, and the EPA may establish conditions for use as part of the registration. The EPA also sets tolerance limits for residues of pesticides on and in food and animal feed, or establishes an exemption from the requirement for a tolerance, under the Federal Food, Drug and Cosmetic Act.

. . . .

*U.S. Food and Drug Administration (FDA)*

The FDA is responsible for ensuring the safety and proper labeling of all plant-derived food and feed, including those developed through genetic engineering. All food and feed, whether imported or domestic and whether derived from crops modified by conventional breeding techniques or by genetic engineering techniques, must meet the same rigorous safety standards. Under the [FFDCA], it is the responsibility of food and feed manufacturers to ensure that the products they market are safe and properly labeled. In addition, any food additive, including one introduced into food or feed by way of plant breeding, must receive FDA approval before marketing. (The term "food additive" refers to substances introduced into food that are not pesticides and are not generally recognized as safe by qualified scientific experts.)

The FDA ensures that food and feed manufacturers meet their obligations through its enforcement authority under the [FFDCA]. To help sponsors of food and feed derived from genetically engineered crops meet their legal obligations, the FDA encourages manufacturers to participate in its voluntary consultation process. Developers routinely consult with FDA prior to marketing. The goal of the consultation process is to ensure that human food and animal feed safety issues or other regulatory issues are resolved prior to commercial distribution.

# G. Key Points

- Many foods are "standardized," with recipe-style definitions set out in the Code of Federal Regulations.
  - "Imitation" foods resemble standardized food, but do not meet the requirements of the relevant standard—and must accordingly be labeled as "imitation."
  - Nonstandardized foods are identified through their "common or usual name."
- Production-process requirements, including both cGMP and hazard-analysis requirements (as discussed in Chapter 5, Part D, of this book), play a major role in food regulation.
- USDA is the primary regulatory for eggs, poultry, fish of the order siluriformes, and traditional meats. USDA's regulatory programs are very different from, and far more intrusive than, FDA's regulatory programs.
- Under the Twenty-First Amendment, alcohol regulation is left primarily to the states. However, FDA, the Department of Justice, and the U.S. Treasury continue to play a role in alcohol regulation.
- USDA, FDA, and EPA are collectively responsible for regulation of agricultural biotechnology in the United States. FDA's role is discussed in more detail in Chapter 7, Food Additives.

Chapter 7

# Food Additives

## A. Introduction

Please read (or review) the following excerpts in the statutory supplement:

- FFDCA 201. Definitions; generally. *Subsection* (s) *only.*
- FFDCA 409. Food additives.

The first item is the statutory definition of Food Additive. The second is the single statutory provision focused specifically on Food Additives. One subsection of that statute, FFDCA § 409(c)(3)(A), is commonly referred to as the "Food Additives Delaney Clause." (There are two other "Delaney Clauses" in the statute, one for color additives and one for animal drugs).

## B. Outline of Regulatory Regime

As in other chapters of this book, this chapter begins with a set of charts. As you read this chapter for the first time, you should do no more than skim these charts to get a general sense of the structure of the applicable statutes and regulations. (For more information on the role of the charts in this casebook, see Chapter 1, Parts A.1 and B).

| Timeline of Key Statutes: Food Additives | | | |
|---|---|---|---|
| Year | PL | Stat. | Name of Statute |
| 1958 | 85-929 | 72 Stat. 1784 | Food Additives Amendment of 1958 |
| 1977 | 95-203 | 91 Stat. 1451 | Saccharin Study and Labeling Act |

| Key Statutory Provisions: Food Additives | | |
|---|---|---|
| Statute Name or U.S.C. Title | § | Title of Section or Subsection |
| FFDCA | 201(s) | [Definition of "food additive"] |
| FFDCA | 409 | Food additives |

| Key Regulatory Provisions: Food Additives (Other Than Regulations Authorizing Particular Substances) | | |
|---|---|---|
| 21 C.F.R. Part | Subpart | Title of Part or Subpart |
| 170 | — | Food additives |
| 171 | — | Food additive petitions |
| 189 | — | Substances prohibited from use in human food |
| 570 | — | Food additives [for animal food] |
| 571 | — | Food additive petitions [for animal food] |
| 589 | — | Substances prohibited from use in animal food or feed |

| Key Regulatory Provisions: Regulations Authorizing Addition of Particular Substances to Food Generally | | |
|---|---|---|
| 21 C.F.R. Part | Subpart | Title of Part or Subpart |
| 172 | — | Food additives permitted for direct addition to food for human consumption |
| 173 | — | Secondary direct food additives permitted in food for human consumption |
| 174 | — | Indirect food additives: general |
| 175 | — | Indirect food additives: adhesives and components of coatings |
| 176 | — | Indirect food additives: paper and paperboard components |
| 177 | — | Indirect food additives: polymers |
| 178 | — | Indirect food additives: adjuvants, production aids, and sanitizers |
| 179 | — | Irradiation in the production, processing and handling of food |
| 180 | — | Food additives permitted in food or in contact with food on an interim basis pending additional study |
| 181 | — | Prior-sanctioned food ingredients |
| 182 | — | Substances generally recognized as safe |
| 184 | — | Direct food substances affirmed as generally recognized as safe |
| 186 | — | Indirect food substances affirmed as generally recognized as safe |

| Key Regulatory Provisions: Regulations Authorizing Addition of Particular Substances to Animal Food | | |
|---|---|---|
| 21 C.F.R. Part | Subpart | Title of Part or Subpart |
| 573 | — | Food additives permitted in feed and drinking water of animals |
| 579 | — | Irradiation in the production, processing, and handling of animal feed and pet food |
| 582 | — | Substances generally recognized as safe |
| 584 | — | Food substances affirmed as generally recognized as safe in feed and drinking water of animals |

## C. The Food Additives Delaney Clause

As you read the following case, note that the agency involved is EPA rather than FDA. However, the decision nonetheless involves agency interpretation of the FFDCA.

### Les v. Reilly

968 F.2d 985 (9th Cir. 1992)

**SCHROEDER, Circuit Judge:**

Petitioners seek review of a final order of the Environmental Protection Agency permitting the use of four pesticides as food additives although they have been found to induce cancer. Petitioners challenge the final order on the ground that it violates the provisions of the Delaney clause, [FFDCA § 409](c)(3), which prohibits the use of any food additive that is found to induce cancer.

Prior to 1988, EPA regulations promulgated in the absence of evidence of carcinogenicity permitted use of the four pesticides at issue here as food additives. In 1988, however, the EPA found these pesticides to be carcinogens. Notwithstanding the Delaney clause, the EPA refused to revoke the earlier regulations, reasoning that, although the chemicals posed a measurable risk of causing cancer, that risk was "de minimis."

We set aside the EPA's order because we agree with the petitioners that the language of the Delaney clause, its history and purpose all reflect that Congress intended the EPA to prohibit all additives that are carcinogens, regardless of the degree of risk involved.

#### Background

The [FFDCA] is designed to ensure the safety of the food we eat by prohibiting the sale of food that is "adulterated." Adulterated food is in turn defined as food containing any unsafe food "additive." A food "additive" is defined broadly as "any substance the intended use of which results or may reasonably be expected to result . . . in its becoming a component . . . of any food." [FFDCA § 201(s)]. A food additive is considered unsafe unless there is a specific exemption for the substance or a regulation prescribing the conditions under which it may be used safely.

Before 1988, the four pesticide chemicals with which we are here concerned—benomyl, mancozeb, phosmet and trifluralin—were all the subject of regulations issued by the EPA permitting their use. In October 1988, however, the EPA published a list of substances, including the pesticides at issue here, that had been found to induce cancer. As known carcinogens, the four pesticides ran afoul of a special provision of the FFDCA known as the Delaney clause, which prescribes that additives found to induce cancer can never be deemed "safe" for purposes of the FFDCA. The Delaney clause is found in FFDCA section 409. That section limits the conditions under which the Secretary may issue regulations allowing a substance to be used as a food additive:

> No such regulation shall issue if a fair evaluation of the data before the Secretary—(A) fails to establish that the proposed use of the food additive, under the conditions of use to be specified in the regulation, will be safe: Provided, That no additive shall be deemed to be safe if it is found to induce cancer when ingested by man or animal, or if it is found, after tests which are appropriate for the evaluation of the safety of food additives, to induce cancer in man or animal....

[FFDCA § 409](c)(3).

The FFDCA also contains special provisions which regulate the occurrence of pesticide residues on raw agricultural commodities. Section 402 of the FFDCA provides that a raw food containing a pesticide residue is deemed adulterated unless the residue is authorized under section 408 of the FFDCA, which allows tolerance regulations setting maximum permissible levels and also provides for exemption from tolerances under certain circumstances. When a tolerance or an exemption has been established for use of a pesticide on a raw agricultural commodity, then the FFDCA allows for the "flow-through" of such pesticide residue to processed foods, even when the pesticide may be a carcinogen. This flow-through is allowed, however, only to the extent that the concentration of the pesticide in the processed food does not exceed the concentration allowed in the raw food. The flow-through provisions are contained in section 402 which provides:

> That where a pesticide chemical has been used in or on a raw agricultural commodity in conformity with an exemption granted or a tolerance prescribed under section 346a of this title [FFDCA section 408] and such raw agricultural commodity has been subjected to processing such as canning, cooking, freezing, dehydrating, or milling, the residue of such pesticide chemical remaining in or on such processed food shall, notwithstanding the provisions of sections 346 and 348 of this title [FFDCA sections 406 and 409], not be deemed unsafe if such residue in or on the raw agricultural commodity has been removed to the extent possible in good manufacturing practice and the concentration of such residue in the processed food when ready to eat is not greater than the tolerance prescribed for the raw agricultural commodity.

It is undisputed that the EPA regulations at issue in this case allow for the concentration of cancer-causing pesticides during processing to levels in excess of those permitted in the raw foods.

The proceedings in this case had their genesis in October 1988 when the EPA published a list of substances, including these pesticides, that were found to induce cancer. Simultaneously, the EPA announced a new interpretation of the Delaney clause: the EPA proposed to permit concentrations of cancer-causing pesticide residues greater than that tolerated for raw foods so long as the particular substances posed only a "de minimis" risk of actually causing cancer. Finding that benomyl, mancozeb, phosmet and trifluralin (among others) posed only such a de minimis risk, the Agency announced that it would not immediately revoke its previous regulations authorizing use of these substances as food additives.

Petitioners filed an administrative petition in May 1989 requesting the EPA to revoke those food additive regulations. Following public comment, the EPA issued a Notice of Response refusing to revoke the regulations. After the petitioners filed objections to that response, the EPA published its final order denying the petition to revoke the food additive regulations. This petition for review . . . followed.

**Discussion**

The issue before us is whether the EPA has violated section 409 of the FFDCA, the Delaney clause, by permitting the use of carcinogenic food additives which it finds to present only a de minimis or negligible risk of causing cancer. The Agency acknowledges that its interpretation of the law is a new and changed one. From the initial enactment of the Delaney clause in 1958 to the time of the rulings here in issue, the statute had been strictly and literally enforced. The EPA also acknowledges that the language of the statute itself appears, at first glance, to be clear on its face. ("[S]ection 409 mandates a zero risk standard for carcinogenic pesticides in processed foods in those instances where the pesticide concentrates during processing or is applied during or after processing.").

The language is clear and mandatory. The Delaney clause provides that no additive shall be deemed safe if it induces cancer. The EPA states in its final order that appropriate tests have established that the pesticides at issue here induce cancer in humans or animals. The statute provides that once the finding of carcinogenicity is made, the EPA has no discretion. As a leading work on food and drug regulation notes:

> [T]he Delaney Clause leaves the FDA room for scientific judgment in deciding whether its conditions are met by a food additive. But the clause affords no flexibility once FDA scientists determine that these conditions are satisfied. A food additive that has been found in an appropriate test to induce cancer in laboratory animals may not be approved for use in food for any purpose, at any level, regardless of any "benefits" that it might provide.

Richard A. Merrill and Peter B. Hutt, Food and Drug Law 78 (1980).

This issue was litigated before the D.C. Circuit in connection with the virtually identical "color additive" prohibition. . . . The D.C. Circuit concluded that "[t]he natural—almost inescapable—reading of this language is that if the Secretary finds the additive to 'induce' cancer in animals, he must deny listing." *Public Citizen v. Young*, 831 F.2d 1108, 1112 (D.C.Cir. 1987). The court concluded that the EPA's de minimis interpretation of the [color additives] Delaney clause in . . . was "contrary to law." The *Public Citizen* decision reserved comment on whether the result would be the same under the food additive provisions as it was under the food color provisions, but its reasoning with respect to the language of the statute is equally applicable to both.

The Agency asks us to look behind the language of the Delaney clause to the overall statutory scheme governing pesticides, which permits the use of carcinogenic pesticides on raw food without regard to the Delaney clause. Yet section 402 of the FFDCA expressly harmonizes that scheme with the Delaney clause by providing that residues on processed foods may not exceed the tolerance level established for the raw food. The statute unambiguously provides that pesticides which concentrate in processed food are to be treated as food additives, and these are governed by the Delaney food additive provision contained in section 409. If pesticides which concentrate in processed foods induce cancer in humans or animals, they render the food adulterated and must be prohibited.

The legislative history, too, reflects that Congress intended the very rigidity that the language it chose commands. The food additive Delaney clause was enacted in response to increasing public concern about cancer. It was initially part of a bill, introduced in the House of Representatives in 1958 by Congressman Delaney, to amend the FFDCA. The bill, intended to ensure that no carcinogens, no matter how small the amount, would be introduced into food, was at least in part a response to a decision by the FDA to allow a known carcinogen, the pesticide Aramite, as an approved food additive. Of the FDA's approval for sale of foods containing small quantities of Aramite, Congressman Delaney stated:

> The part that chemical additives play in the cancer picture may not yet be completely understood, but enough is known to put us on our guard. The safety of the public health demands that chemical additives should be specifically pretested for carcinogenicity, and this should be spelled out in the law. The precedent established by the Aramite decision has opened the door, even if only a little, to the use of carcinogens in our foods. That door should be slammed shut and locked. That is the purpose of my anticarcinogen provision.

The scientific witnesses who testified before Congress stressed that because current scientific techniques could not determine a safe level for carcinogens, all carcinogens should be prohibited. While Congressman Delaney's bill was not ultimately passed, the crucial anticancer language from the bill was incorporated into the Food Additives Amendment of 1958 which enacted section 409 of the FFDCA into law. Thus, the legislative history supports the conclusion that Congress intended to ban all carcinogenic food additives, regardless of amount or significance of risk, as the only safe alternative.

Throughout its 30-year history, the Delaney clause has been interpreted as an absolute bar to all carcinogenic food additives. See 53 Fed.Reg. at 41,104 (announcing a shift in the EPA's position, away from reading section 409's Delaney clause "literally"). In 1958, the Department of Health, Education, and Welfare (which would be charged with administering the food additive provisions of the newly enacted Delaney clause) interpreted the clause as removing all agency discretion regarding carcinogens. As a contemporaneous agency construction of the statute, this interpretation is entitled to great weight. Further, Congress has repeatedly ratified a strict interpretation of the Delaney clause by reenacting all three FFDCA provisions which contain Delaney clauses without changing the Agency's interpretation. See [FFDCA §409] (amended 1960, 1962, 1984); [what is today FFDCA §721; FFDCA 706 at the time of this opinion] (amended 1988, 1991); 21 U.S.C. §376 [FFDCA §512] (amended 1960, 1962, 1970, 1976). "When the statute giving rise to the long-standing interpretation has been reenacted without pertinent change, the congressional failure to revise or repeal the agency's interpretation is persuasive evidence that the interpretation is the one intended by Congress."

The EPA contends that the legislative history shows that Congress never intended to regulate pesticides, as opposed to other additives, with extraordinary rigidity under the food additives provision. The Agency is indeed correct that the legislative history of the food additive provision does not focus on pesticides, and that pesticides are regulated more comprehensively under the Federal Insecticide, Fungicide, and Rodenticide Act (FIFRA). Nevertheless, the EPA's contention that Congress never intended the food additive provision to encompass pesticide residues is belied by the events prompting passage of the provision into law: FDA approval of Aramite was the principal impetus for the food additive Delaney clause and Aramite was itself a regulated pesticide. Thus, Congress intended to regulate pesticides as food additives under section 409 of the FFDCA, at least to the extent that pesticide residues concentrate in processed foods and exceed the tolerances for raw foods.

Finally, the EPA argues that a de minimis exception to the Delaney clause is necessary in order to bring about a more sensible application of the regulatory scheme. It relies particularly on a recent study suggesting that the criterion of concentration level in processed foods may bear little or no relation to actual risk of cancer, and that some pesticides might be barred by rigid enforcement of the Delaney clause while others, with greater cancer-causing risk, may be permitted through the flow-through provisions because they do not concentrate in processed foods. See National Academy of Sciences, Regulating Pesticides in Food: The Delaney Paradox (1987). The EPA in effect asks us to approve what it deems to be a more enlightened system than that which Congress established. The EPA is not alone in criticizing the scheme established by the Delaney clause. See, e.g., Richard A. Merrill, FDA's Implementation of the Delaney Clause: Repudiation of Congressional Choice or Reasoned Adaptation to Scientific Progress, 5 Yale J. on Reg. 1, 87 (1988) (concluding that the Delaney clause is both unambiguous and unwise: "at once an explicit and imprudent expression of legislative will"). Revising the existing statutory scheme, however, is neither our function nor the function of the EPA. There are currently bills pending before the House and the Senate which would amend the food additive provision to allow the Secretary to establish tolerance levels for carcinogens, including pesticide residues in processed foods, which impose a negligible risk. If there is to be a change, it is for Congress to direct.

The EPA's refusal to revoke regulations permitting the use of benomyl, mancozeb, phosmet and trifluralin as food additives on the ground the cancer risk they pose is de minimis is contrary to the provisions of the Delaney clause prohibiting food additives that induce cancer. The EPA's final order is set aside.

## D. GRAS Presumption for Proteins Produced through Genetic Engineering

The following case returns to a topic presented initially in Chapter 6—FDA's role in the regulation of agricultural biotechnology. As you will see in this case, FDA has determined that it will exercise its role in agricultural biotechnology regulation primarily through its authority over food additives.

### Alliance for Bio-Integrity v. Shalala

116 F. Supp. 2d 166 (D.D.C. 2000)

**KELLAR-KATELLY, District Judge.**

Technological advances have dramatically increased our ability to manipulate our environment, including the foods we consume. One of these advances, recombinant deoxyribonucleic acid (rDNA) technology, has enabled scientists to alter the genetic composition of organisms by mixing genes on the cellular and molecular level in order to create new breeds of plants for human and animal consumption. These new breeds may be designed to repel pests, retain their freshness for a longer period of time, or contain more intense flavor and/or nutritional value. Much controversy has attended such developments in biotechnology, and in particular the production, sale, and trade of genetically modified organisms and foods ...

Among Plaintiffs, some fear that these new breeds of genetically modified food could contain unexpected toxins or allergens, and others believe that their religion forbids consumption of foods produced through rDNA technology. Plaintiffs ... have brought this action to protest the Food and Drug Administration's ("FDA") policy on such foods in general, and in particular on various genetically modified foods that already have entered the marketplace. The parties have filed cross-motions for summary judgment on plaintiffs' multiple claims. Upon careful consideration of the parties' briefs and the entire record, the Court shall grant Defendants' motion as to all counts of Plaintiffs' Complaint.

#### I. Background

On May 29, 1992, the FDA published a "Statement of Policy: Foods Derived From New Plant Varieties" (Statement of Policy). In the Statement of Policy, FDA announced that the agency would presume that foods produced through the rDNA process were "generally recognized as safe" (GRAS) under [FFDCA] § 201(s), and therefore not subject to regulation as food additives. While FDA recommended that food producers consult with it before marketing rDNA-produced foods, the agency did not mandate such consultation. In addition, FDA reserved the right to regulate any particular rDNA-developed food that FDA believed was unsafe on a case-by-case basis, just as FDA would regulate unsafe foods produced through conventional means.

The Statement of Policy also indicated that rDNA modification was not a "material fact" under the [FFDCA], § 201(n), and that therefore labeling of rDNA-produced foods was not necessarily required. FDA did not engage in a formal notice-and-comment process on the Statement of Policy, nor did it prepare an Environmental Impact Statement or Environmental Assessment. At least thirty-six foods, genetically altered through rDNA technology, have been marketed since the Statement of Policy was issued.

Plaintiffs filed a Complaint in this Court challenging the FDA's policy on six different grounds: (1) the Statement was not properly subjected to notice-and-comment procedures; (2) the FDA did not comply with the National Environmental Protection Act (NEPA) by compiling an Environmental Assessment or Environmental Impact Statement; (3) the FDA's presumption that rDNA-developed foods are GRAS and therefore do not require food additive petitions under § 201(s) is arbitrary and capricious; (4) the FDA's decision not to require labeling for rDNA-developed foods is arbitrary and capricious . . .

### II. Discussion

. . . .

#### A. Subject Matter Jurisdiction

Defendants contend that Court lacks jurisdiction to hear plaintiffs' claims. . . . In particular, Defendants argue that the Statement of Policy functioned as a way for the agency to "set its own enforcement agenda," and therefore, that this enforcement action belongs to agency discretion by Congressional mandate and is not subject to judicial review. . . .

In the instant case, even without actual notice and comment procedures, the FDA's formal publication of the Statement of Policy provides a focal point for this Court's review of the agency's action. . . . Although the Court may not review FDA's policy-laden individual enforcement decisions, the Court has jurisdiction to review whether or not FDA's Statement of Policy comports with Congressional directives.

#### B. Notice and Comment

Plaintiffs argue that the Statement of Policy should be set aside because it was not subjected to notice and comment proceedings, as required under the Administrative Procedure Act ("APA"), 5 U.S.C. § 553. While conceding that the Statement of Policy did not undergo a formal notice and comment process, Defendants maintain that the Statement of Policy is a policy statement or an interpretive rule not subject to notice and comment requirements. Plaintiffs contend instead that the Statement of Policy is a substantive rule, and that therefore it was improperly exempted from a formal notice and comment process.

A substantive rule, which must undergo a formal notice-and-comment process, is a rule that "implement[s]" a statute and has "the force and effect of law." Policy statements, on the other hand, are "statements issued by an agency to advise the public prospectively of the manner in which the agency proposes to exercise a discretionary power." Although the distinction between these two categories is not entirely clear, in *American Bus. Ass'n v. United States*, 627 F.2d 525 (D.C. Cir. 1980), the Court of Appeals articulated a two-part test for determining when an agency action is a policy statement. Policy statements (1) must not impose any new rights or obligations, and (2) must "genuinely leave the agency and its decision-makers free to exercise discretion." In weighing these criteria, "the ultimate issue is the agency's intent to be bound." *Public Citizen v. United States Nuclear Regulatory Comm'n*, 940 F.2d 679, 682 (D.C. Cir. 1991). An agency's own characterization of its statement deserves some weight, but it is not dispositive. Rather, courts will look to the actual language of the statement.

By its very name, the Statement of Policy announces itself as a policy statement. More importantly, the plain language of the Statement suggests that it does not have a binding effect. For example, the Statement does not declare that transferred genetic material will be considered GRAS; rather, it announces that "such material is *presumed* to be GRAS." This presumption of safety is rebuttable, because FDA will "require food additive petitions in cases where safety questions exist sufficient to warrant formal premarket review by FDA to ensure public health protection." Rebuttable presumptions leave an agency free to exercise its discretion and may therefore properly be announced in policy statements.

In response to the argument that the Policy Statement vests broad discretion with the agency, Plaintiffs contend that the FDA's application of the Statement has given it a "practical effect" that has effectively bound the agency's discretion, as evidenced by the thirty-six genetically engineered foods that are currently on the market and not regulated by the FDA. Although courts will look to the "agency's actual applications" to determine the nature of an agency statement, such an inquiry occurs "where the language and context of a statement are inconclusive." Here, the plain language of the Statement clearly indicates that it is a policy statement that merely creates a presumption and does not ultimately bind the agency's discretion....

Because the Statement is a policy statement merely announcing a GRAS presumption, the omission of formal notice-and-comment procedures does not violate the Administrative Procedure Act.

### C. NEPA

Plaintiffs have also alleged that FDA violated the National Environmental Protection Act (NEPA) by not performing an Environmental Assessment (EA) or an Environmental Impact Statement (EIS) in conjunction with the Statement of Policy. NEPA requires "all agencies of the Federal Government ... [to] include in every recommendation or report on proposals for legislation and other major Federal actions significantly affecting the quality of the human environment, a detailed statement . . . on the environmental impact of the proposed action."

. . . .

In sum, because FDA's Statement of Policy is reversible, maintains the substantive status quo, and takes no overt action, the Statement of Policy does not constitute a major federal action under NEPA. FDA was not required to compile an Environmental Assessment or an Environmental Impact Statement in conjunction with the Statement of Policy, and therefore its failure to do so does not violate NEPA.

**D. GRAS Presumption**

In their challenge to the FDA's Statement of Policy, Plaintiffs further claim that the Statement of Policy's presumption that rDNA-engineered foods are GRAS violates the [FFDCA] § 201(s), and is therefore arbitrary and capricious. The [FFDCA] provides that any substance which may "become a component or otherwise affect[] the characteristics of any food" shall be deemed a food additive. A producer of a food additive must submit a food additive petition to FDA for approval unless FDA determines that the additive is "generally recognized [by qualified experts] . . . as having been adequately shown through scientific procedures . . . to be safe under the conditions of its intended use."

. . . . Accordingly, FDA reasoned that the only substances added to rDNA engineered foods are nucleic acid proteins, generally recognized as not only safe but also necessary for survival. Therefore, FDA concluded that rDNA engineered foods should be presumed to be GRAS unless evidence arises to the contrary. The Statement of Policy does acknowledge, however, that certain genetically modified substances might trigger application of the food additives petitioning process. In that vein, FDA recognized that "the intended expression product in a food could be a protein, carbohydrate, fat or oil, or other substance that differs significantly in structure, function, or composition from substances found currently in food. Such substances may not be GRAS and may require regulation as a food additive."

This Court's evaluation of the FDA's interpretation of § 201(s) is framed by *Chevron, U.S.A. v. Natural Resources Defense Council*, 467 U.S. 837 (1984). Since "'statutory interpretation begins with the language of the statute itself,'" as a general matter the Court first must determine whether Congress has spoken directly to the issue at hand, a line of analysis that has become known as *Chevron* step one. If, using "traditional tools of statutory construction," the Court answers this inquiry in the affirmative, then "that is the end of the matter; for the court, as well as the agency, must give effect to the unambiguously expressed intent of Congress." *Chevron*, 467 U.S. at 842–43.

But *Chevron* review also concerns itself with the extent and application of agency discretion in interpreting the statute at issue. In other words, "a reviewing court's inquiry under *Chevron* is rooted in statutory analysis and is focused on discerning the boundaries of Congress' delegation of authority to the agency." To resolve the issue, "the question for the reviewing court is whether the agency's construction of the statute is faithful to its plain meaning, or, if the statute has no plain meaning, whether the agency's interpretation 'is based on a permissible construction of the statute.'" If this interpretation is "reasonable and consistent with the statutory scheme and legislative history"), then the Court must defer to the agency. This inquiry into the agency's interpretation constitutes *Chevron* step two.

When Congress passed the Food Additives Amendment in 1958, it obviously could not account for the late twentieth-century technologies that would permit the genetic modification of food.... The plain language of [FFDCA] § 201(s) fosters a broad reading of "food additive" and includes "any substance intended for use in producing, manufacturing, packing, processing, preparing, treating, packaging, transporting, or holding food; and ... any source of radiation intended for any such use."

.... Plaintiffs have not disputed FDA's claim that nucleic acid proteins are generally recognized to be safe. Plaintiffs have argued, however, that significant disagreement exists among scientific experts as to whether or not nucleic acid proteins are generally recognized to be safe when they are used to alter organisms genetically. Having examined the record in this case, the Court cannot say that FDA's decision to accord genetically modified foods a presumption of GRAS status is arbitrary and capricious. "The rationale for deference is particularly strong when the [agency] is evaluating scientific data within its technical expertise." "In an area characterized by scientific and technological uncertainty[,] ... this court must proceed with particular caution, avoiding all temptation to direct the agency in a choice between rational alternatives."

To be generally recognized as safe, a substance must meet two criteria: (1) it must have technical evidence of safety, usually in published scientific studies, and (2) this technical evidence must be generally known and accepted in the scientific community. Although unanimity among scientists is not required, "a severe conflict among experts ... precludes a finding of general recognition." Plaintiffs have produced several documents showing significant disagreements among scientific experts. However, this Court's review is confined to the record before the agency at the time it made its decision. Therefore, the affidavits submitted by Plaintiffs that are not part of the administrative record will not be considered.

.... Plaintiffs have failed to convince the Court that the GRAS presumption is inconsistent with the statutory requirements.

### E. Labeling

Plaintiffs have also challenged the Statement of Policy's failure to require labeling for genetically engineered foods, for which FDA relied on the presumption that most genetically modified food ingredients would be GRAS. Plaintiffs claim that FDA should have considered the widespread consumer interest in having genetically engineered foods labeled, as well as the special concerns of religious groups and persons with allergies in having these foods labeled.

The [FFDCA], § 201(n), grants the FDA limited authority to require labeling. In general, foods shall be deemed misbranded if their labeling "fails to reveal facts . . . material with respect to consequences which may result from the use of the article to which the labeling . . . relates under the conditions of use prescribed in the labeling . . . or under such conditions of use as are customary or usual." § 201(n). Plaintiffs challenge the FDA's interpretation of the term "material." Thus, the question is again one of statutory interpretation. . . . Interpretation of the § 201(n)'s broad language is left to the agency.

. . . This Court must determine whether the agency's interpretation of the statute is reasonable. See *Chevron*, 467 U.S. at 864. Agency interpretations receive substantial deference, particularly when the agency is interpreting a statute that it is charged with administering. *See Rust v. Sullivan*, 500 U.S. 173 (1991). Even if the agency's interpretation is not "the best or most natural by grammatical or other standards," if the interpretation is reasonable, then it is entitled to deference.

The FDA takes the position that no "material change," under § 201(n), has occurred in the rDNA derived foods at issue here. Absent unique risks to consumer health or uniform changes to food derived through rDNA technology, the FDA does not read § 201(n) to authorize an agency imposed food labeling requirement. More specifically irksome to the Plaintiffs, the FDA does not read § 201(n) to authorize labeling requirements solely because of consumer demand. The FDA's exclusion of consumer interest from the factors which determine whether a change is "material" constitutes a reasonable interpretation of the statute. . . .

Plaintiffs fail to understand the limitation on the FDA's power to consider consumer demand when making labeling decisions because they fail to recognize that the determination that a product differs materially from the type of product it purports to be is a factual predicate to the requirement of labeling. Only once materiality has been established may the FDA consider consumer opinion to determine whether a label is required to disclose a material fact. Thus, "if there is a [material] difference, and consumers would likely want to know about the difference, then labeling is appropriate. If, however, the product does not differ in any significant way from what it purports to be, then it would be misbranding to label the product as different, even if consumers misperceived the product as different." The FDA has already determined that, in general, rDNA modification does not "materially" alter foods, and as discussed in Section II.E, supra, this determination is entitled to deference. Given these facts, the FDA lacks a basis upon which it can legally mandate labeling, regardless of the level of consumer demand.

Plaintiffs also contend that the *process* of genetic modification is a "material fact" under § 201(n) which mandates special labeling, implying that there are new risks posed to the consumer. However, the FDA has determined that foods produced through rDNA techniques do not "present any different or greater safety concern than foods developed by traditional plant breeding," and concluded that labeling was not warranted. That determination, unless irrational, is entitled to deference.

Accordingly, there is little basis upon which this Court could find that the FDA's interpretation of § 321(n) is arbitrary and capricious.

. . . .

*[The court's discussion of the Free Exercise Clause and the Religious Freedom Restoration Act Claims brought by the plaintiffs are omitted. Both claims were found to lack merit.]*

**Conclusion**

For the foregoing reasons. . . . the Court denies Plaintiffs' motion for summary judgment and grants Defendant's motion for same. An appropriate order accompanies this memorandum opinion.

## E. Cannabidiol (CBD)

The following press release is an early step in FDA's effort to determine how to regulate cannabidiol (CBD), a product derived from the marijuana plant (but that does not itself cause the "high" traditionally associated with marijuana). Note, as you read: (1) FDA's comments on the status of CBD under FFDCA § 409; and (2) FDA's comments on the various ways products containing CBD might violate the FFDCA.

### 2019-11-25 FDA Press Release re: Cannabidiol (CBD)

Today, the U.S. Food and Drug Administration issued warning letters to 15 companies for illegally selling products containing cannabidiol (CBD) in ways that violate the [FFDCA]. The FDA also published a revised Consumer Update detailing safety concerns about CBD products more broadly. Based on the lack of scientific information supporting the safety of CBD in food, the FDA is also indicating today that it cannot conclude that CBD is generally recognized as safe (GRAS) among qualified experts for its use in human or animal food.

Today's actions come as the FDA continues to explore potential pathways for various types of CBD products to be lawfully marketed. This includes ongoing work to obtain and evaluate information to address outstanding questions related to the safety of CBD products, while maintaining the agency's rigorous public health standards. The FDA plans to provide an update on its progress regarding the agency's approach to these products in the coming weeks.

"As we work quickly to further clarify our regulatory approach for products containing cannabis and cannabis-derived compounds like CBD, we'll continue to monitor the marketplace and take action as needed against companies that violate the law in ways that raise a variety of public health concerns. In line with our mission to protect the public, foster innovation, and promote consumer confidence, this overarching approach regarding CBD is the same as the FDA would take for any other substance that we regulate," said FDA Principal Deputy Commissioner Amy Abernethy, M.D., Ph.D. "We remain concerned that some people wrongly think that the myriad of CBD products on the market, many of which are illegal, have been evaluated by the FDA and determined to be safe, or that trying CBD 'can't hurt.' Aside from one prescription drug approved to treat two pediatric epilepsy disorders, these products have not been approved by the FDA and we want to be clear that a number of questions remain regarding CBD's safety—including reports of products containing contaminants, such as pesticides and heavy metals—and there are real risks that need to be considered. We recognize the significant public interest in CBD and we must work together with stakeholders and industry to fill in the knowledge gaps about the science, safety and quality of many of these products."

Many unanswered questions and data gaps about CBD toxicity exist, and some of the available data raise serious concerns about potential harm from CBD. The revised Consumer Update outlines specific safety concerns related to CBD products, including potential liver injury, interactions with other drugs, drowsiness, diarrhea, and changes in mood. In addition, studies in animals have shown that CBD can interfere with the development and function of testes and sperm, decrease testosterone levels and impair sexual behavior in males. Questions also remain about cumulative use of CBD and about CBD's impacts on vulnerable populations such as children and pregnant or breastfeeding women.

CBD is marketed in a variety of product types, such as oil drops, capsules, syrups, food products such as chocolate bars and teas, and topical lotions and creams. As outlined in the warning letters issued today, these particular companies are using product webpages, online stores and social media to market CBD products in interstate commerce in ways that violate the [FFDCA], including marketing CBD products to treat diseases or for other therapeutic uses for humans and/or animals. Other violations include marketing CBD products as dietary supplements and adding CBD to human and animal foods.

. . . .

The FDA has previously sent warning letters to other companies illegally selling CBD products in interstate commerce that claimed to prevent, diagnose, mitigate, treat or cure serious diseases, such as cancer, or otherwise violated the [FFDCA]. Some of these products were in further violation because CBD was added to food, and some of the products were also marketed as dietary supplements despite products which contain CBD not meeting the definition of a dietary supplement.

Under the [FFDCA], any product intended to treat a disease or otherwise have a therapeutic or medical use, and any product (other than a food) that is intended to affect the structure or function of the body of humans or animals, is a drug. The FDA has not approved any CBD products other than one prescription human drug product to treat rare, severe forms of epilepsy. There is very limited information for other marketed CBD products, which likely differ in composition from the

FDA-approved product and have not been evaluated for potential adverse effects on the body.

Unlike drugs approved by the FDA, there has been no FDA evaluation of whether these unapproved products are effective for their intended use, what the proper dosage might be, how they could interact with FDA-approved drugs, or whether they have dangerous side effects or other safety concerns. In addition, the manufacturing process of unapproved CBD drug products has not been subject to FDA review as part of the human or animal drug approval processes. Consumers may also put off getting important medical care, such as proper diagnosis, treatment and supportive care due to unsubstantiated claims associated with CBD products. For that reason, it's important that consumers talk to a health care professional about the best way to treat diseases or conditions with existing, approved treatment options.

Additionally, some of the products outlined in the warning letters issued today raise other legal and public health concerns:

- Some of the products are marketed for infants and children—a vulnerable population that may be at greater risk for adverse reactions due to differences in the ability to absorb, metabolize, distribute or excrete a substance such as CBD.
- Some of the products are foods to which CBD has been added. Under the [FFDCA], it is illegal to introduce into interstate commerce any human or animal food to which certain drug ingredients, such as CBD, have been added. In addition, the FDA is not aware of any basis to conclude that CBD is GRAS among qualified experts for its use in human or animal food. There also is no food additive regulation which authorizes the use of CBD as an ingredient in human food or animal food, and the agency is not aware of any other exemption from the food additive definition that would apply to CBD. CBD is therefore an unapproved food additive, and its use in human or animal food violates the [FFDCA] for reasons that are independent of its status as a drug ingredient.
- Some of the products are marketed as dietary supplements. However, CBD products cannot be dietary supplements because they do not meet the definition of a dietary supplement under the [FFDCA].
- One product outlined in a warning letter to Apex Hemp Oil LLC is intended for food-producing animals. The agency remains concerned about the safety of human food products (e.g. meat, milk, and eggs) from animals that consume CBD, as there is a lack of data establishing safe CBD residue levels.

The FDA has requested responses from the companies within 15 working days stating how the companies will correct the violations. Failure to correct the violations promptly may result in legal action, including product seizure and/or injunction.

. . . .

## F. Key Points

- Many substances routinely added to food do not meet the definition of food additive under FFDCA § 201(s). In particular, GRAS substances, prior-sanctioned substances, color additives, and pesticides are explicitly excluded from the food-additive definition.
  - The exclusion of GRAS substances means that a tremendous number of the substances added to food are not, for purposes of the FFDCA, food additives.
- Direct food additives are substances directly added to food. Indirect food additives are substances that may migrate to food from its packaging material.
- FDA has established a rebuttable presumption that proteins produced through genetic engineering are GRAS.
- FDA has promulgated two sets of regulations for substances added to food.
  - One set applies to substances added to food for human consumption. It is found in 21 C.F.R. Parts 170–189.
  - The second set applies to substances added to animal food. It is found in 21 C.F.R. Parts 570–589.
- Color additives should not be confused with food additives. Color additives are addressed separately in Chapter 17 of this casebook.
  - Color additives are based on entirely different statutory authority (in Chapter VII, instead of Chapter IV, of the FFDCA).
  - Color additives are used not only in food, but also in other product categories (including drugs, animal drugs, medical devices, and biologics).

Chapter 8

# Dietary Supplements

## A. Introduction

Please read (or review) the following excerpts in the statutory supplement:

- FFDCA § 201. Definitions, generally. *Subsections (g)(1), (s), and (ff) only.*
- FFDCA § 402. Adulterated food. *Subsections (f), (g), (r), and (s) only.*
- FFDCA § 403. Misbranded food. *Subsections (r) and (s) only.*
- FFDCA § 403B. Dietary supplement labeling exemptions.
- FFDCA § 411. Vitamins and minerals.
- FFDCA § 413. New dietary ingredients.
- 21 C.F.R. Part 105. Foods for special dietary use.
- 21 C.F.R. Part 190. Dietary supplements.

## B. Outline of Regulatory Regime

As in other chapters of this book, this chapter begins with a set of charts. As you read this chapter for the first time, you should do no more than skim these charts to get a general sense of the structure of the applicable statutes and regulations. (For more information on the role of the charts in this casebook, see Chapter 1, Parts A.1 and B).

| Timeline of Key Statutes: Dietary Supplements | | | |
|---|---|---|---|
| Year | PL | Stat | Name of Statute |
| 1938 | 75-717 | 52 Stat. 1040 | FFDCA of 1938 |
| 1976 | 94-278 | 90 Stat. 401, 410 | Proxmire Amendment |
| 1992 | 102-571 | 106 Stat. 4491, 4500 | Dietary Supplement Act of 1992 |
| 1994 | 103-417 | 108 Stat. 4325 | Dietary Supplement Health and Education Act of 1994 |

| Key Statutory Provisions: Dietary Supplements | | |
|---|---|---|
| Statute Name or U.S.C. Title | § | Title of Section or Subsection |
| FFDCA | 201(g)(1) | [Exclusion of foods and dietary supplements making certain claims, under FFDCA § 403(r), from "drug" definition] |
| FFDCA | 201(s) | [Exclusion of dietary supplements from "food additive" definition] |
| FFDCA | 201(ff) | [Definition of "dietary supplement"] |
| FFDCA | 402(f) | [Dietary supplement adulteration] |
| FFDCA | 402(g) | [Dietary supplement cGMP] |
| FFDCA | 403(r) | [Label claims for food and dietary supplements] |
| FFDCA | 403(s) | [Misbranding of dietary supplements] |
| FFDCA | 403B | Dietary supplement labeling exemptions |
| FFDCA | 411 | Vitamins and minerals |
| FFDCA | 413 | New dietary ingredients |

| Key Regulatory Provisions: Dietary Supplements | | |
|---|---|---|
| 21 C.F.R. Part | Subpart | Title of Part or Subpart |
| 105 | — | Foods for special dietary use |
| 111 | — | Current good manufacturing practice in manufacturing, packaging, labeling, or holding operations for dietary supplements |
| 119 | — | Dietary supplements that present a significant or unreasonable risk |
| 190 | — | Dietary supplements |

## C. FDA's Pre-DSHEA Effort to Regulate Vitamin and Mineral Supplements

As you read the next two cases, focus on understanding the complex history of FDA's dispute with the vitamin and mineral industry. The first case involves an FDA effort to regulate certain dosages of vitamins as drugs; the second involves the effect of the 1976 Proxmire Amendment on a long-running rulemaking proceeding.

## Nat'l Nutr. Foods Ass'n v. Mathews

557 F.2d 325 (2d Cir. 1977)

**ANDERSON, Circuit Judge:**

Plaintiffs-appellants, producers and vendors of vitamin preparations, appeal the dismissal of their action seeking declaratory and injunctive relief against regulations promulgated by the Food and Drug Administration (FDA) which classified preparations of Vitamins A and D in excess of 10,000 IU (international units) per dosage unit and 400 IU per dosage unit, respectively, as "drugs" under § 201(g)(1) of the Federal Food, Drug and Cosmetic Act, and which restricted them to prescription sale under § 503(b)(1) of the [FFDCA]. The district court upheld the regulations as not "arbitrary, capricious, an abuse of discretion or otherwise not in accordance with law" under the standard of review prescribed by 5 U.S.C. § 706(2)(A).

. . . .

On this appeal from the district court's dismissal following remand, plaintiffs contend that the district court . . . erred in upholding the classification of the regulated levels of Vitamins A and D, as drugs.

. . . .

As part of the FDA's regulatory scheme for the sale of vitamin and mineral dietary supplements, the Commissioner promulgated new U.S. Recommended Daily Allowances for the vitamins and minerals considered essential to human nutrition and for which there was available scientific evidence to show the level of ingestion nutritionally necessary. 21 C.F.R. § 80.1(f)(1). The U.S. RDA upper limits for Vitamin A is 2,500 IU for children under four years of age, 5,000 IU for adults, and 8,000 IU for pregnant and lactating women. The upper limit for Vitamin D is 400 IU for all age groups. As part of the general Dietary Supplement regulations, the FDA determined that all preparations containing more than the upper limit of the U.S. RDA per serving for any vitamin or mineral on the list is a "drug," 21 C.F.R. § 125.1(h), thus subjecting such products to the rigorous provisions of subchapter V of the [FFDCA].

. . . .

When the Commissioner adopted the Vitamins A and D regulations, he concluded that the available evidence showed that the U.S. RDA upper limits were adequate for all known nutritional needs; and, in view of the fact that there was no evidence to establish a food value or nutritional use for Vitamins A and D at higher levels, the ingestion of these vitamins at the regulated levels is "appropriate only for therapeutic uses and thus are properly classed as drugs." 38 Fed. Reg. 2073 (Aug. 2, 1973). The Commissioner based the drug classification for all vitamin and mineral preparations in excess of the U.S. RDA contained in 21 C.F.R. § 125.1(h) solely upon lack of nutritional usefulness for most people. This court, however, held in the course of invalidating the general drug classification in § 125.1(h), that "demonstrated uselessness as a food for most people" is an insufficient basis upon which to establish a drug classification under § 201(g)(1)(B) of the [FFDCA]. *National Nutritional Foods Ass'n v. FDA*, 504 F.2d [761, 789 (2d Cir. 1974)].

....

In determining whether an article is a "drug" because of an intended therapeutic use, the FDA is not bound by the manufacturer's subjective claims of intent but can find actual therapeutic intent on the basis of objective evidence. Such intent also may be derived or inferred from labeling, promotional material, advertising, and "any other relevant source." In remanding this case, this court expressly indicated that evidence that Vitamins A and D at the regulated levels were used "almost exclusively for therapeutic purposes" when coupled with lack of a recognized nutritional use, would be sufficient to show that high dosage Vitamins A and D products were intended for use in the treatment of disease.

....

There is no evidence in the administrative record that the manufacturers and vendors of Vitamins A and D preparations, at the regulated dosages, represent through labeling, promotional materials, or advertising that these products are effective in the cure or treatment of disease. They are sold as "dietary supplements."

....

The main issue on this appeal is whether the evidence of the extensive use of large doses of Vitamins A and D to treat or prevent diseases and the promotion of such usage by persons not associated with the manufacturers or vendors establishes such widespread therapeutic use at the regulated levels as to overcome the plaintiffs' claim of the lack of an intended use to cure or prevent disease and thus justifies the Commissioner's determination.

The Commissioner admits that below the stated levels of potency, Vitamins A and D are foods. The evidence relied upon to show therapeutic intent, therefore, must be related to the potency level chosen to differentiate between the use of Vitamins A and D as foods and the use of these vitamins as drugs. The administrative record clearly establishes that the factors involved in choosing the levels at which Vitamins A and D become drugs were solely related to the Commissioner's fear of potential toxic effect and his belief that the ingestion of vitamins at levels above the U.S. RDA is not nutritionally useful. No further record evidence has been produced on the remand to show that the 10,000 IU and 400 IU levels were chosen because at those potencies, consumption of them is almost exclusively for therapeutic purposes. A sampling of the comments submitted to the FDA after publication of the proposed regulations reveals that people believe that a wide range of doses of these vitamins are therapeutically useful. A large group of individuals indicated that they ingested these vitamins at various dosages solely to supplement their daily diet in the belief that more Vitamins A and D were needed to maintain optimal health than the upper limits in the U.S. RDA.

....

The Commissioner also seeks to justify the Vitamins A and D regulations on the basis of § 201(g)(1)(A), 21 U.S.C. § 321(g)(1)(A), which defines as drugs, articles "recognized" in the United States Pharmacopoeia (USP) or National Formulary (NF). Both Vitamins A and D are included in the USP and NF. The Eighteenth Revision of the USP, official from September 1, 1970, listed the usual daily dosage of Vitamin A for prophylactic uses at 5,000 U.S.P. vitamin A units 10 and for therapeutic uses at 25,000 U.S.P. vitamin A units. For Vitamin D, the respective daily dosages were 400 U.S.P. vitamin D units for prophylactic uses and 1,200 U.S.P. vitamin D units for therapeutic uses. Olive oil and salt are also included within the pages of these compendia. To construe § 201(g)(1)(A) so as to grant the Commissioner the power to regulate as drugs every item mentioned in the USP and NF solely on the basis of such inclusion would give the FDA virtually unlimited discretion to regulate as drugs a vast range of items. In *National Nutritional Foods Ass'n v. FDA*, the court concluded that a claim that a vitamin is a drug solely because of a listing in the USP and NF "would prove too much, for it would lead to the conclusion that all vitamin and mineral preparations even within the [U.S. RDA] limits are drugs—a position that would run counter to the regulations." An administrator's decision under a regulatory statute, such as the Food, Drug, and Cosmetic Act, must be governed by an intelligible statutory principle. If § 201(g)(1)(A) defines as drugs every item included in the USP and NF, the FDA is not being consistent in its treatment of other items similarly recognized. The Commissioner, therefore, has not applied the § 201(g)(1)(A) definition to every item in the compendia. Rather he has singled out for drug classification items included in the USP and NF on the basis of factors, such as toxicity in this case, that are not relevant to the statutory criteria in § 201(g).

....

The district court's dismissal of this action is reversed and the case is remanded with directions to enter an order granting summary judgment in plaintiffs' favor declaring 21 C.F.R. §§ 250.09 and 250.10 invalid as arbitrary and capricious and not in accordance with law.

It is so ordered.

## Nat'l Nutr. Foods Ass'n v. Kennedy

572 F.2d 377 (2d Cir. 1978)

**FRIENDLY, Circuit Judge:**

This is the latest but, unfortunately, probably not the last chapter in the bitter battle between the Food and Drug Administration (FDA) and manufacturers and vendors of pills and liquids containing vitamins and minerals and citizens allied with the latter. While the manufacturers and vendors have obvious private interests as well, the battle reflects what appears to be a sincere sentiment on the part of many citizens that daily ingestion of a substantial quantity and variety of vitamins and minerals in the form of pills or liquids, in addition to those furnished by ordinary diet, is needed for good health, especially because of the increasing consumption of "the modern food fads sweet drinks, junk foods, heavy sugar diets" and "wheat germ-free bread and nutritionally inadequate breakfast foods," and the FDA's equally sincere belief that the promotion of what, on a previous review, this court called a "dazzling array" of recommended daily dosages and combinations, *National Nutritional Foods Ass'n v. Food & Drug Administration*, 504 F.2d 761, 776 (2 Cir. 1974), is causing consumers to waste millions of dollars annually in the purchase of vitamin and mineral preparations which they either do not need at all or do not need in the potencies or combinations that are being bought. The battle began nearly a generation ago with the FDA's publication of a Proposal to Revise Regulations in the Federal Register of June 20, 1962; the proposal included the establishment of standards of identity for "food for special dietary uses" and revised label standards for them. Because the FDA's establishment of a standard of identity under §401 and its prescription of labels for foods for special dietary use under §403(j) are among the few instances on the statute books where an evidentiary hearing is required for rulemaking, §701(e), over twenty-two months were devoted to such a hearing, which developed a transcript of 32,405 pages and hundreds of exhibits. The Commissioner published final regulations on August 2, 1973.

Fifteen petitions to review were filed; their disposition by this court required a 47-page opinion, 504 F.2d 761 (1974), familiarity with which is assumed. Although "broadly sustaining the regulations," we stayed them and remanded the case for the FDA to carry out a number of directives.

.... After the Supreme Court had denied petitions for certiorari by those who had been petitioners here, the Commissioner published in the Federal Register of May 28, 1975, a paper bearing the three-headed title "Opportunity for Filing Applications for Additional Formulations of Dietary Supplements of Vitamins and Minerals; Preliminary Notice of Reopening of Hearing; Tentative Amendments to Final Orders." ....

Meanwhile the scene of action had shifted. On April 22, 1976, the President signed Public Law 94-278, extensively amending the Food, Drug and Cosmetic Act. Section 501(a) added to the [FFDCA] §411, which we reproduce in the margin.[5]

---

5. *[Note: the statute that added this provision to the FFDCA is often called the "Proxmire Amendment"]*

(a)

(1) Except as provided in paragraph (2)

(A) the Secretary may not establish, under section 201(n), 401, or 403, maximum limits on the potency of any synthetic or natural vitamin or mineral within a food to which this section applies;

(B) the Secretary may not classify any natural or synthetic vitamin or mineral (or combination thereof) as a drug solely because it exceeds the level of potency which the Secretary determines is nutritionally rational or useful;

(C) the Secretary may not limit, under section 201(n), 401, or 403, the combination or number of any synthetic or natural

(i) vitamin,

(ii) mineral, or

Broadly speaking subsection (a) put an end to the FDA's efforts to limit the potency of any vitamin or mineral included in "a food for special dietary use," as defined in

---

(iii) other ingredient of food,

within a food to which this section applies.

(2) Paragraph (1) shall not apply in the case of a vitamin, mineral, other ingredient of food, or food, which is represented for use by individuals in the treatment or management of specific diseases or disorders, by children, or by pregnant or lactating women. For purposes of this subparagraph, the term 'children' means individuals who are under the age of twelve years.

(b)

(1) A food to which this section applies shall not be deemed under section 403 to be misbranded solely because its label bears, in accordance with section 403(i)(2), all the ingredients in the food or its advertising contains references to ingredients in the food which are not vitamins or minerals.

(2)

(A) The labeling for any food to which this section applies may not list its ingredients which are not vitamins or minerals (i) except as a part of a list of all the ingredients of such food, and (ii) unless such ingredients are listed in accordance with applicable regulations under section 403. To the extent that compliance with clause (i) of this subparagraph is impracticable or results in deception or unfair competition, exemptions shall be established by regulations promulgated by the Secretary.

(B) Notwithstanding the provisions of subparagraph (A), the labeling and advertising for any food to which this section applies may not give prominence to or emphasize ingredients which are not

(i) vitamins,

(ii) minerals, or

(iii) represented as a source of vitamins or minerals.

(c)

(1) For purposes of this section, the term 'food to which this section applies' means a food for humans which is a food for special dietary use

(A) which is or contains any natural or synthetic vitamin or mineral, and

(B) which

(i) is intended for ingestion in tablet, capsule, or liquid form, or

(ii) if not intended for ingestion in such a form, does not simulate and is not represented as conventional food and is not represented for use as a sole item of a meal or of the diet.

(2) For purposes of paragraph (1)(B)(i), a food shall be considered as intended for ingestion in liquid form only if it is formulated in a fluid carrier and it is intended for ingestion in daily quantities measured in drops or similar small units of measure.

(3) For purposes of paragraph (1) and of section 403(j) insofar as that section is applicable to food to which this section applies, the term 'special dietary use' as applied to food used by man means a particular use for which a food purports or is represented to be used, including but not limited to the following:

(A) Supplying a special dietary need that exists by reason of a physical, physiological, pathological, or other condition, including but not limited to the condition of disease, convalescence, pregnancy, lactation, infancy, allergic hypersensitivity to food, underweight, overweight, or the need to control the intake of sodium.

(B) Supplying a vitamin, mineral, or other ingredient for use by man to supplement his diet by increasing the total dietary intake.

(C) Supplying a special dietary need by reason of being a food for use as the sole item of the diet.

subsection (c), or the number or combination of vitamins, minerals or other food ingredients included therein except when the vitamin, mineral, other ingredient of food, or food, . . . is represented for use by (1) individuals in the treatment or management of specific diseases or disorders, (2) children under the age of twelve, or (3) pregnant or lactating women. . . . Section 501(b) [of the Proxmire Amendment], which is of special importance to our decision, provided:

> The Secretary of Health, Education, and Welfare shall amend any regulation promulgated under the [FFDCA] which is inconsistent with section 411 of such Act (as added by subsection (a)) and such amendments shall be promulgated in accordance with section 553 of title 5, United States Code.

Without engaging in any further proceeding, the Commissioner published final regulations in the Federal Register of October 19, 1976. The Commissioner believed that almost all the applications for new formulations had been mooted by the 1976 amendment. He approved a new combination of vitamins A, D and C with provision for optional inclusion of vitamin E and/or iron, as a dietary supplement for infants and young children, denied an application for a preparation containing a higher level of vitamin $B_6$ for pregnant and lactating women, and determined to treat as drugs multinutrient supplements for women taking oral contraceptives which contained estrogen. He overruled the exceptions to the ALJ's report concerning the examination of Dr. Harper, to other evidentiary rulings at the reopened hearing, and to FDA's continued reliance on the NAS-RDA's. He passed upon and largely rejected the exceptions to the amendments proposed in the notice of May 28, 1975, noting that many exceptions were mooted as a result of the 1976 legislation. The Commissioner's technique was essentially to readopt the 1973 regulations with reorganization "to improve clarity," modifications designed to meet our directions, addition of a section classifying dietary supplements not "generally recognized as safe" as "food additives," and a further modification, § 80.1(e), "which provides that products subject to the new vitamin/mineral legislation are not subject to the maximum potency limits and the limits on inclusion of ingredients otherwise imposed on dietary supplements by §§ 80.1 and 125.2(b)(5)."

This action by the Commissioner evoked an "urgent petition" dated November 30, 1976, by the attorneys for National Nutritional Foods Association, National Association of Pharmaceutical Manufacturers and Solgar Co., Inc., who constitute one group of petitioners on this second round of review. While the petition advised that the details of the new regulations were being evaluated its emphasis was directed at the FDA's procedure in promulgating the final regulations without having "requested from the public any input as to what changes would be necessary in the regulations in light of the newly enacted vitamin and mineral legislation." The petition asked the Commissioner to "withdraw the final order published in Federal Register of October 19, 1976 and substitute therefor a republished proposed order which gives the public the full right to submit comments and objections in accordance with the requirements of § 701(e) of the Federal Food, Drug and Cosmetic Act." A prompt ruling was requested.

The Commissioner made no answer for four and a half months.[6] In the Federal Register for April 19, 1977, he published his response to the petition of November 30, 1976 . . . . On the procedural issue, the Commissioner now took note of § 501(b) of the 1976 legislation, as he had not previously done. He concluded that he was nevertheless empowered to issue final regulations "without prior notice of proposed rulemaking and public procedure" because of the provision in 5 U.S.C. § 553(b) that "Except when notice of hearing is required by statute," the requirement of publishing notice of proposed rulemaking does not apply

> (B) when the agency for good cause finds (and incorporates the finding and a brief statement of reasons therefor in the rules issued) that notice and public procedure thereon are impracticable, unnecessary, or contrary to the public interest.

The Commissioner reviewed the provisions of the final regulation "that were prompted by the new legislation," and concluded in each case that public rulemaking procedures would be "impracticable" and "unnecessary" because he was simply bowing to the will of the legislature. The Commissioner further rejected the contention that he should have followed the "hearing on the record" procedure described in § 701(e). These petitions for review followed.

**Discussion**

**(1) The procedural questions.**

We conclude that the Commissioner committed procedural error and that this requires a further remand. We reach this conclusion with regret in light of the fifteen and a half years that have elapsed since the FDA began its efforts to achieve better control of the identity and labelling of vitamin and mineral preparations. However, we are convinced that in failing to give notice of proposed rulemaking and to accord an opportunity for public participation in the process, as provided in 5 U.S.C. § 553(b) and (c), the Commissioner violated the mandate of Congress.

. . . .

In view of the important political interests served by public participation in rulemaking, it would be arguable that even in the absence of a specific direction, this unusual situation where Congress effected a profound alteration in an agency's

6. Meanwhile the regulations had been recodified into 21 C.F.R. Part 105, with s 105.3 containing definitions, §§ 105.77 and .79 containing labelling requirements and § 105.85 the standard of identity.

powers while rulemaking was in progress[10] would have called for a new issuance of proposed rules and public participation in rulemaking, as the Commissioner had accorded on his own motion after he had redrafted the 1973 regulations in light of our remand. We need not address that question, however, since Congress did give explicit directions in § 501(b) quoted above.

It is true that, if read literally, § 501(b) applies only to regulations amending "any regulation promulgated" under the [FFDCA] which is inconsistent with the new § 411 and the standard of identity regulations for vitamin and mineral food were not regulations amending a regulation that had been promulgated but rather regulations that were awaiting promulgation, since the previous opinion of this court stayed the regulations and remanded them to the FDA. However, the Commissioner properly did not attempt to read § 501(b) so literally; [11] clearly what Congress had in mind in enacting § 501(b) was the Commissioner's much debated proposed vitamin and mineral regulations, which Congress was aiming to restrict. Rather the Commissioner sought to justify his decision not to engage in public rulemaking on the basis, sound enough as an abstract proposition, that when Congress referred to 5 U.S.C. § 553(b), it included the exceptions therein contained. In effect the Commissioner reads § 501(b) as meaning only that if he decided that further procedures were needed, these could be of the notice and comment type prescribed by 5 U.S.C. § 553(b) and (c) rather than the trial type procedure prescribed by § 701(e) of the Food, Drug and Cosmetic Act in cases where it applies.

. . . .

The legislative history of the Administrative Procedure Act demonstrates that Congress intended the exceptions in § 553(b)(B) to be narrow ones. The Senate Report, No. 752, 79th Cong. 1st Sess. (1945), reprinted in the Legislative History of the [Administrative Procedure] Act at 200, stated:

> The exemption of situations of emergency or necessity is not an "escape clause" in the sense that any agency has discretion to disregard its terms or the facts. A true and supported or supportable finding of necessity or emergency must be made and published. "Impracticable" means a situation in which the due and required execution of the agency functions would be unavoidably prevented by its undertaking public rule-making proceedings. "Unnecessary" means unnecessary so far as the public is concerned, as would be the case if a minor or merely technical amendment in which the public is not particularly interested were involved. "Public interest" supplements the terms "impracticable" or "unnecessary"; it requires that public

10. Description of the changes required 8 pages in the House Conference Report, H.R.Rep. No. 94-1005, 94th Cong., 2d Sess. (1976).

11. In any event the proposed labelling regulations constituted an amendment of a 1955 regulation, 21 C.F.R. part 25.

> rule-making procedures shall not prevent an agency from operating and that, on the other hand, lack of public interest in rule making warrants an agency to dispense with public procedure.

The final regulations do not meet this strict standard. The exception for impracticability is plainly unavailable. "The due and required execution of the functions" of the FDA would hardly have been "unavoidably prevented" by further public rule-making in the fall of 1976 with respect to regulations which already were 14 years in the making and which the agency now has stayed on its own motion until July 1, 1979. Likewise, the Commissioner cannot resort to the exception invoking the "public interest" since requiring public rulemaking proceedings would not have prevented the FDA from operating or otherwise have harmed the public weal. In fact the Commissioner relies much more heavily on the claim that public participation was unnecessary; he argues that since Congress had spoken, there was nothing more for the public to say and the agency's duty was simply to excise portions of the proposed regulations that Congress had placed beyond its power. But the agency's task went beyond a mere wielding of scissors. While the 1976 legislation withdrew old powers, it also imposed new duties, notably with respect to labelling, see § 411(b)(2). Indeed in the preamble to the October 19, 1976 regulations, the Commissioner had noted that the new legislation "requires extensive labelling revisions even in the absence of the new FDA regulations." In view of the history of the administrative proceedings and the legislative struggle, there was no basis for the Commissioner's believing that the public would not be "particularly interested" in his next move; if he ever entertained such a belief, the "urgent petition" of November 30, 1976 must have disabused him of it. Moreover, the problem created by the 1976 amendment went deeper than the Commissioner would have it. His promulgation of a standard of identity for vitamin and mineral preparations had rested primarily not on considerations of safety but on the need to lessen confusion among consumers. As had been said in the Commissioner's finding 22, which we cited in our [earlier] opinion:

> The establishment of qualitative and quantitative limits on the composition of dietary supplements will reduce consumer confusion concerning choice of dietary supplements by ensuring a basically rational formula for all products.

By the 1976 legislation Congress pronounced that it was not concerned about this for the public in general or, at least, that it considered the costs incident to reducing consumer confusion for the entire public by the FDA's proposed standard of identity to be too high in relation to the benefits to be achieved. While Congress permitted the agency to impose a standard of identity in the three instances cited in § 411(a)(2), it did not require this. Presumably it wished the agency to consider whether to impose a standard and, if so, what standard for the three permitted cases. The record which we found to have furnished substantial evidence to support the standard of identity previously prescribed thus might not serve the same office with respect to the limited applications now permitted. At least those who did not believe so were entitled to an opportunity to present their views, with the agency and other opposing interests, if unpersuaded, then having an opportunity to show why these were wrong. In short the FDA's task was not simply to grant an exemption from provisions in the proposed regulations which the 1976 legislation had rendered illegal but to promulgate regulations which it deemed suitable in the light of what Congress had done. Performance of so major a task did not come within the limited exceptions of 5 U.S.C. § 553(b)(B).

On the other hand the Commissioner properly rejected the petitioners' claim that further trial type procedures under § 701(e) were required. The 1976 statute specifically directed that further procedures should be of the sort prescribed by § 553 and not by § 556 of Title V. Congress, which must have been fully aware of the snail-like pace and the Gargantuan record which compliance with § 701(e) had entailed, had had enough, so far as these regulations were concerned. In bringing these proceedings to an end, the FDA was relieved of the need of engaging in the trial type procedures that had been required when they began. . . .

The regulations are vacated and the cause is remanded to the Commissioner for further proceedings consistent with this opinion.

---

Following the Second Circuit's decision in the case immediately above, FDA published an order revoking the Vitamin-Mineral Regulations that had been challenged in that case. That order is excerpted immediately below.

### 1979-03-16 FDA Final Order, Vitamin and Mineral Products; Revocation of Regulations

44 Fed. Reg. 16,005

The Food and Drug Administration(FDA) revokes regulations that the United States Court of Appeals for the Second Circuit has ruled are invalid. The regulations had established definitions and a standard of identity and labeling requirements for dietary supplements of vitamins and minerals.

. . . .

## D. The Dietary Supplement Health and Education Act (DSHEA) of 1994

FDA's disputes with the vitamin and mineral industry—which became part of the broader dietary supplement industry—continued. By the mid-1990s, FDA's actions led to the Senate report excerpted immediately below. It would soon lead to a statute stripping FDA of much of the authority the agency thought it had over the dietary supplement industry.

## Senate Report No. 103-410, Oct. 8, 1994

The Committee on Labor and Human Resources, to which was referred the bill (S. 784) to amend the Federal Food, Drug and Cosmetic Act with respect to the regulation of dietary supplements, and for other purposes, having considered the same, reports favorably thereon with an amendment in the nature of a substitute and recommends that the bill as amended do pass.

. . . .

### THE HISTORY OF FOOD AND DRUG ADMINISTRATION EFFORTS RESTRICTING DIETARY SUPPLEMENTS

Despite a voluminous scientific record indicating the potential health benefits of dietary supplements, the Food and Drug Administration has pursued a heavy-handed enforcement agenda against dietary supplements for over 30 years. The agency's approach has forced the Congress to intervene on two previous occasions, and yet again with adoption of S. 784.

In 1962, the FDA published regulations setting minimum and maximum levels for supplements. These regulations were withdrawn in the face of strong citizen protest.

Between 1966 and 1973, the agency issued proposed regulations on the labeling and content of dietary food products. FDA tried to classify vitamins as over-the-counter drugs if the product exceeded 150 percent of the Recommended Daily Allowance (RDA). Vitamins A and D would have been considered prescription drugs. Combinations of vitamins and minerals would have been prohibited under most circumstances. Congress negated this action in 1976 when it approved the Proxmire/Rogers amendment to the Federal Food, Drug and Cosmetic Act.

Blocked by the Proxmire amendment, later in the 1970s, FDA tried to regulate vitamins by claiming they were toxic, and therefore their potencies could be regulated. The Federal Courts rejected . . . this attempt to end-run the Proxmire Amendment.

In 1980, the FDA issued a proposed over-the-counter drug monograph for vitamins and minerals. The document supposedly dealt only with potencies above the RDA, thereby implicitly placing a potency limit on vitamins and minerals. The proposal was withdrawn after strong opposition.

Beginning in the late 1970s, FDA turned from drug potency arguments to enforcement attempts utilizing the "food additive theory" to prohibit the sale of supplements which bore no claims. Essentially, the theory was that any ingredient added to a capsule or tablet rendered the resulting dietary supplement a food additive because the ingredient was added to the capsule or tablet. Under this theory, FDA could not lose, as it needed only to furnish an affidavit from one of its scientists stating that experts generally did not regard the product as safe. The actual safety of the product was never at issue.

Between 1986 and 1990, the FDA issued four "health messages" documents for food products. This reflected FDA's initial policy with respect to the ability of food manufacturers to make limited claims about how a nutrient might prevent certain chronic diseases (such as fiber and cancer) without rendering those drugs products unapproved drugs. FDA left a very narrow area for dietary supplement health messages. The level of proof required for dietary supplement claims was unrealistic in that the degree of scientific consensus and clinical data required eliminated almost all existing supplement claims.

With enactment of the Nutrition Labeling and Education Act (NLEA) of 1990, Congress directed the FDA to use the "significant scientific agreement" standard when deciding if foods could make claims about the relationship of the nutrient to a disease, so-called "health claims." The statute specifically said that the FDA could recommend a different standard and approval procedure for supplements.

In December, 1991, FDA proposed rules implementing the NLEA, but rejected all but one claim for supplements (for calcium/osteoporosis in White and Asian Women). Only one other claim has been approved since that time, the claim for folic acid and neural tube defects, and that claim was only approved after intense public pressure on the FDA.

Twice since 1991, FDA has proposed that it use the same standard and procedure for health claims for foods as on dietary supplements. In 1992, the Congress imposed a 1-year moratorium barring FDA from implementing the rule changes for 1 year. In 1993, the Senate unanimously adopted a second moratorium, but the House did not act on that legislation.

. . . .

The preceding examples show the need for congressional action to assure citizens have continued access to dietary supplements and information about their benefits.

## E. The Congressional Findings of Fact

The legal changes brought about by the Dietary Supplement Health and Education Act of 1994 will be addressed in the next section. First, however, take a moment to read the congressional findings of fact included in DSHEA. Consider, as you read this material, the potential implications these findings of fact have for FDA's ability to exercise discretion—based on its own factual findings—when administering the FFDCA as modified by DSHEA.

## Dietary Supplement Health and Education Act of 1994

PL 103-417, 108 Stat. 4325

Oct 25, 1994

SEC. 2. FINDINGS.

Congress finds that—

(1) improving the health status of United States citizens ranks at the top of the national priorities of the Federal Government;

(2) the importance of nutrition and the benefits of dietary supplements to health promotion and disease prevention have been documented increasingly in scientific studies;

(3)

(A) there is a link between the ingestion of certain nutrients or dietary supplements and the prevention of chronic diseases such as cancer, heart disease, and osteoporosis; and

(B) clinical research has shown that several chronic diseases can be prevented simply with a healthful diet, such as a diet that is low in fat, saturated fat, cholesterol, and sodium, with a high proportion of plant-based foods;

(4) healthful diets may mitigate the need for expensive medical procedures, such as coronary bypass surgery or angioplasty;

(5) preventive health measures, including education, good nutrition, and appropriate use of safe nutritional supplements will limit the incidence of chronic diseases, and reduce long-term health care expenditures;

(6)

(A) promotion of good health and healthy lifestyles improves and extends lives while reducing health care expenditures; and

(B) reduction in health care expenditures is of paramount importance to the future of the country and the economic well-being of the country;

(7) there is a growing need for emphasis on the dissemination of information linking nutrition and long-term good health;

(8) consumers should be empowered to make choices about preventive health care programs based on data from scientific studies of health benefits related to particular dietary supplements;

(9) national surveys have revealed that almost 50 percent of the 260,000,000 Americans regularly consume dietary supplements of vitamins, minerals, or herbs as a means of improving their nutrition;

(10) studies indicate that consumers are placing increased reliance on the use of nontraditional health care providers to avoid the excessive costs of

traditional medical services and to obtain more holistic consideration of their needs;

(11) the United States will spend over $1,000,000,000,000 on health care in 1994, which is about 12 percent of the Gross National Product of the United States, and this amount and percentage will continue to increase unless significant efforts are undertaken to reverse the increase;

(12)

(A) the nutritional supplement industry is an integral part of the economy of the United States;

(B) the industry consistently projects a positive trade balance; and

(C) the estimated 600 dietary supplement manufacturers in the United States produce approximately 4,000 products, with total annual sales of such products alone reaching at least $4,000,000,000;

(13) although the Federal Government should take swift action against products that are unsafe or adulterated, the Federal Government should not take any actions to impose unreasonable regulatory barriers limiting or slowing the flow of safe products and accurate information to consumers;

(14) dietary supplements are safe within a broad range of intake, and safety problems with the supplements are relatively rare; and

(15)

(A) legislative action that protects the right of access of consumers to safe dietary supplements is necessary in order to promote wellness; and

(B) a rational Federal framework must be established to supersede the current ad hoc, patchwork regulatory policy on dietary supplements.

## F. The Statutory Changes Brought About by DSHEA

Prior to the 1990s, the FFDCA did not contain a separate product category for dietary supplements. Products that fall into that category today would have been regulated as either food or drugs under the prior versions of the statute. The development of a separate product category for dietary supplements began with the Nutritional Labeling and Education Act of 1990 (NLEA), continued with the Dietary Supplement Act of 1992 (DSA), and came to fruition with the Dietary Supplement Health and Education Act of 1994.[1]

1. The NELA set out one procedure for claims that could be made for conventional food, and delegated FDA discretion to establish a separate procedure for "a dietary supplement of vitamins, minerals, herbs, or other similar nutritional substances." NELA § 3. The DSA then imposed a

In 1994, Congress created a new product category, "dietary supplement." The statute that created that category was the Dietary Supplement Health and Education Act (DSHEA). Among other things, DSHEA: (1) excluded dietary supplements from regulation as food additives, and (2) provided that dietary supplements would be permitted to make claims relating to "the structure or function" of the human body.

This statute created substantial upheaval in the world of food and drug regulation. To understand dietary supplement regulation today, it is necessary to understand why DSHEA created such an upheaval. Prior to DSHEA, two types of claims were sufficient to result in regulation of a particular product as a drug. The first was a disease claim, the second was a structure/function claim. A disease claim is a claim—using the current statutory text of the drug definition—that an "article" is "for use in the diagnosis, cure, mitigation, treatment, or prevention of disease in man or other animals." A structure/function claim—again using the current statutory text of the drug definition—is a claim that a substance is "intended to affect the structure or any function of the body of man or other animals." The most significant change DSHEA made was to exempt dietary supplements making certain types of structure/function claims from the otherwise-applicable drug definition.

There are several things that make dietary supplements a difficult product category to understand. First, Congress created the "dietary supplement" category for deregulatory purposes. Its goal was to reduce, rather than increase, FDA's regulatory authority over dietary supplements. Second, Congress did this by deeming dietary supplements to be food, excluding them from the definition of drugs, and subjecting them to requirements partway between those of food and drugs. This basic structure remains the law today.

Third, Congress chose to accomplish this change through a less-than-straightforward statutory structure. The key element was a complicated change in the legal implications of an intended use "to affect the structure or any function of the body of man or other animals." Prior to NELA and DSHEA, an intended use to affect the structure of function of the body (other than through the normal, nutritive mechanisms associated with consumption of conventional food) would turn a food-type product into a drug. After NELA and DSHEA, both conventional foods and dietary supplements could, under some but not all circumstances, make such claims without becoming drugs. However, the requirements for making these non-drug structure/function claims are different for conventional foods and dietary supplements. Moreover, if these specific requirements are not satisfied, a structure/function claim can still turn a conventional food or a dietary supplement into an illegally marked drug.

---

temporary delay on FDA's ability to issue the NELA-mandated dietary supplement procedures. DSHEA then expanded this idea of dietary supplements into a separate product category.

# G. FDA Implementation of DSHEA

## 1. New Dietary Ingredient Notification

Excerpted below is one of the few regulations FDA has promulgated relating to dietary supplements.

### 1997-09-23 FDA Final Rule, Premarket Notification for New Dietary Ingredients

62 Fed. Reg. 49886

ACTION: Final rule.

SUMMARY: The Food and Drug Administration (FDA) is establishing the procedure by which a manufacturer or distributor of dietary supplements or of a new dietary ingredient is to submit under the [FFDCA] the information on which it has concluded that a dietary supplement containing a new dietary ingredient will reasonably be expected to be safe. FDA is issuing this regulation to enable industry to comply with the requirements of the Dietary Supplement Health and Education Act of 1994 (the DSHEA).

. . . .

SUPPLEMENTARY INFORMATION:

I. Background

In the Federal Register of September 27, 1996, FDA published a proposed rule, entitled "Premarket Notification for a New Dietary Ingredient" (hereinafter referred to as "the September 1996 proposal"). FDA issued this proposal in response to section 8 of the DSHEA. This section of the DSHEA amended the act by adding, among other provisions, section 201(ff), which defines a dietary supplement, and by adding section 413(a), which provides, among other things, for the notification of the Secretary of Health and Human Services (the Secretary) (and by delegation FDA) at least 75 days before the introduction or delivery for introduction into interstate commerce of a dietary supplement that contains a new dietary ingredient. Section 413(a) of the [FFDCA] states that a dietary supplement that contains a new dietary ingredient shall be deemed adulterated unless it meets one of two requirements. One requirement is that "the dietary supplement contains only dietary ingredients which have been present in the food supply as an article used for food in a form in which the food has not been chemically altered." The alternative requirement is that:

> [T]here is a history of use or other evidence of safety establishing that the dietary ingredient when used under the conditions recommended or suggested in the labeling of the dietary supplement will reasonably be expected to be safe and, at least 75 days before being introduced or delivered for introduction into interstate commerce, the manufacturer or distributor of the dietary ingredient or dietary supplement provides the Secretary with information, including any citation to published articles, which is the basis

on which the manufacturer or distributor has concluded that a dietary supplement containing such dietary ingredient will reasonably be expected to be safe.

FDA published the September 1996 proposal to establish a procedure that would enable industry to comply with this notification requirement in an efficient manner. Adoption of this procedure will help to facilitate compliance with the notification required by section 413(a)(2) of the [FFDCA]. Interested persons were given until December 26, 1996, to comment on the proposal.

FDA received four letters each containing one or more comments from consumer groups, a trade association, and industry in response to the proposal. All of the comments generally supported the proposal. Several comments suggested modifications or revisions of various aspects of the proposal. A summary of the comments and the agency's responses follows. *[Discussions of comments 1, 2, and 4 are omitted from the discussion below, which addresses Comment 3 only.]*

. . . .

3. One comment stated that FDA's proposed rule on the notification for a new dietary ingredient is a procedural regulation when what is needed is a substantive regulation that provides adequate guidance to the manufacturer as to the quality and quantity of the information necessary to meet the requirements of section 413(a)(2) of the [FFDCA]. The comment disagreed with FDA's assertion that the manufacturer is only required to provide the basis on which it has concluded that the dietary supplement will reasonably to expected to be safe and that the manufacturer or distributor is not required to do a complete search of all available sources of information on the new dietary ingredient. The comment maintained that under the proposed regulation, manufacturers could knowingly market products with documented deleterious effects as long as they provide FDA with articles citing only a product's benefits.

The comment requested that FDA examine how the DSHEA amended section 402 of the [FFDCA] as well as section 413 of the [FFDCA]. Section 402(f)(1)(B) of the [FFDCA] states that a "food shall be deemed to be adulterated if it is a dietary supplement or contains a dietary ingredient that is a new dietary ingredient for which there is inadequate information to provide reasonable assurance that such ingredient does not present a significant or unreasonable risk of illness or injury." The comment argued that without a minimal safety data requirement, FDA risks that its interpretation of the DSHEA could cause a manufacturer to challenge the validity of the DSHEA on the grounds that the statute is void for vagueness because it does not provide fair warning to the manufacturer of what is expected. The comment requested that FDA issue regulations that elaborate on omissions in the statute by Congress.

The comment further suggested that FDA should require that a new dietary ingredient, when used under the conditions recommended or suggested in the labeling of the dietary supplement, be generally recognized as safe (GRAS); that is, that FDA apply to a new dietary ingredient the standard that there is general recognition that a dietary supplement containing the new dietary ingredient "will reasonably be expected to be safe." The comment further suggested that FDA should provide industry with examples of publications that are acceptable as evidence of safety and a list of sources to search for evidence of adverse effects associated with a new dietary ingredient. Further, the comment maintained that manufacturers should be required to provide FDA with a summary of studies and scientific data, including known adverse effects. The comment stated that, in the absence of an appropriate scientific standard of evidence, manufacturers would be free to submit articles from questionable publications or unpublished materials to establish the safety of the new dietary ingredient. The comment argued that reliance on a GRAS standard would not be contrary to the statute or to congressional intent because it would still permit the marketing of dietary supplements without prior approval.

FDA disagrees with the comment that a substantive, rather than a procedural, regulation is necessary to respond to section 413(a)(2) of the [FFDCA]. The comment appears to be opposed to proposed § 190.6(b)(4), which sets out the substantive information that the notification must include. Significantly, § 190.6(b)(4) simply tracks the language of section 413(a)(2) of the [FFDCA]. It is appropriate that the regulation do so because, contrary to what the comment asserts, the manufacturer or distributor is not required to do a complete literature search. It is required only to provide "the basis on which [it] has concluded that a dietary supplement containing such dietary ingredient will reasonably be expected to be safe" (section 413(a)(2) of the [FFDCA]). That is all that the regulation requires.

FDA agrees with the comment that sections 402(f)(1)(B) and 413 of the [FFDCA] are related in that they both relate to new dietary ingredients. FDA also acknowledges that Congress has provided in section 413(a) of the [FFDCA] that a failure to provide the information under section 413(a) of the [FFDCA] would render the dietary supplement adulterated under section 402(f) of the [FFDCA]. The agency, however, in deciding what information needs to be provided, is bound by the standard in the [FFDCA]. It is not free to rewrite the law, as the comment appears to suggest.

The fact that Congress did not create a minimal safety data requirement in section 413(a)(2) of the [FFDCA] does not render the DSHEA void for vagueness. The manufacturer's or distributor's obligation under section 413(a)(2) of the [FFDCA] is clear. It must make a showing as to why it considers that consumption of a new dietary ingredient will be safe.

FDA also does not agree that the GRAS concept has relevance here. The concept of GRAS was adopted by Congress in 1958, as a limitation on the scope of the "food additive" definition (section 201(s) of the [FFDCA]). Congress excluded from the definition of "food additive" substances that are generally recognized, among experts qualified by scientific training and experience to evaluate their safety, as having been adequately shown through scientific procedures (or, in the case of a substance used in food prior to January 1, 1958, through experience based on common use in food) to be safe under the conditions of their intended use. However, dietary ingredients, which are used in dietary supplements, are not food additives.

Congress excluded them from the definition of a "food additive" in the DSHEA (section 201(s)(6) of the [FFDCA], which was added by section 3(b) of the DSHEA). Thus, the concept of GRAS is not relevant to how dietary ingredients are regulated.

Furthermore, there is a fundamental difference between who is to make at least the initial judgment as to the safety of an ingredient under section 413(a)(2) of the [FFDCA] and whose judgment is relevant to a determination that an ingredient is GRAS. Whether an ingredient is GRAS is based on the judgment of "experts qualified by scientific training and experience to evaluate" the ingredient's safety. In contrast, the requirement in section 413(a)(2) of the [FFDCA] that a notification be made for a new dietary ingredient provides that the manufacturer or distributor is to determine whether a dietary supplement containing such dietary ingredient will reasonably be expected to be safe. While this determination is subject to review by FDA, section 413(a) of the [FFDCA] does not specify that the manufacturer or distributor must rely on any specified third party in making its judgment. For these reasons, FDA is not requiring in § 190.6(b)(4) that the notification for a new dietary ingredient include information establishing that the new dietary ingredient is GRAS or the subject of any other type of general recognition.

Furthermore, FDA is not persuaded that it is necessary for the agency to provide examples of scientific publications that are adequate to provide the information that can be the basis on which the manufacturer or distributor has concluded that a dietary supplement containing the new dietary ingredient will reasonably be expected to be safe. The agency also is not persuaded that the [FFDCA] requires that a manufacturer or distributor provide to FDA information on all known adverse effects attributable to the new dietary ingredient that is the subject of the submission. Section 413(a)(2) of the [FFDCA] requires only that the notification provide information "which is the basis on which the manufacturer or distributor has concluded that a dietary supplement containing such dietary ingredient will reasonably be expected to be safe when used under the conditions recommended or suggested in the labeling." Thus, the statute does not specify or limit what evidence a manufacturer or distributor may rely on in determining whether the use of the ingredient will reasonably be expected to be safe. Nonetheless, FDA expects that, in making a determination that a new dietary ingredient is reasonably expected to be safe and does not present a significant or unreasonable risk of illness or injury, a manufacturer or distributor will consider the evidence of safety that is available in the scientific literature and from examination of reports of adverse effects associated with the use of a new dietary ingredient.

FDA does not find that the statute requires that the agency determine the relative merit of different types of evidence of safety, and therefore, the agency is not modifying § 190.6 to specify specific safety requirements for new dietary ingredients or to establish standards that the evidence of safety must meet.

....

---

The statement below is from a 1999 appearance by FDA Commissioner Jane Henney before the House Committee on Government Reform. The portion excerpted below focuses on Commissioner Henney's description of the challenges presented by DSHEA.

## Statement by Jane E. Henney, M.D., Commissioner Food and Drug Administration, Before the Committee on Government Reform, U.S. House of Representatives

March 25, 1999

### I. Introduction

Mr. Chairman, and Members of the Committee, my name is Jane Henney. I am honored to address you as the Commissioner of Food and Drugs and pleased to be here today to discuss implementation of the Dietary Supplement Health and Education Act (DSHEA) of 1994.

. . . .

### V. Challenges

#### A. Boundaries

Before Congress passed DSHEA, dietary supplements (including vitamins and minerals) were regulated either as foods or as drugs, depending on their intended use. If a product was used primarily for its taste, aroma, or nutritive value, it was regulated as a food. This meant that the ingredients used in such dietary supplements were subject to the food additive provisions of the [FFDCA], which require the safety of an ingredient to be demonstrated before it can be marketed. The supplement was subject to regulation as a drug if therapeutic claims were made, i.e., claims to treat or prevent disease; if claims were made to affect the structure or function of the body through a non-nutritive mechanism; or if there was other evidence that the intended use of the product was as a drug. The supplement, with such claims, would have to meet the rigorous drug safety and efficacy requirements of the [FFDCA], including, in the great majority of cases, premarket approval.

When Congress passed DSHEA, it created a regulatory framework for dietary supplements that previously did not exist. The purpose of creating this new framework was to strike the right balance between providing consumers access to both products and truthful information about the products while retaining authority for FDA to take action against products that present safety problems or are improperly labeled. We are now engaged in the difficult task of delineating boundaries between drugs, dietary supplements, and conventional foods. This is a task that requires great care if the Agency is to fulfill Congressional intent with regard to the availability of dietary supplements while preserving the established food additive and drug regulatory frameworks for products that fall outside the dietary supplement boundaries.

For example, Congress has permitted dietary supplements to be intended to affect the structure or function of the body, but it has not permitted dietary supplements to be intended to treat, prevent, mitigate, cure, or diagnose disease, except that dietary supplements may bear authorized health claims. DSHEA required FDA to draw a line between two types of intended use that the Agency never needed to distinguish previously. Congress also drew a line between conventional foods and dietary supplements by saying that a dietary supplement may not be represented for use as a conventional food. This boundary, too, raises many complex issues that the Agency is responsible for clarifying.

Aspects of DSHEA's dietary supplement definition that have proven especially problematic to implement are the statute's limitation of dietary supplements to products that are intended to supplement the diet and its inclusion of dietary substance[s] for use by man to supplement the diet as dietary ingredients that may be used in dietary supplements. It is clear that the dietary ingredients specifically listed in DSHEA (vitamins, minerals, herbs or other botanicals, and amino acids) were intended by Congress to be broadly available under DSHEA, and many of these have a long history of safe use. Products are now being positioned as dietary supplements, however, by purporting to fall within the "dietary substance" language. The terms "dietary substance" and "intended to supplement the diet" are broad, but they must not allow the inclusion of ingredients never intended to fit within the universe of dietary supplements. Now, products that contain substances similar to those found in prescription drugs are marketed for children as dietary supplements. Likewise, products with ingredients that simulate illicit street drugs are marketed as dietary supplements to adolescents via the Internet and shops specializing in drug paraphernalia. FDA is working toward a solution that will be consistent with the intent of DSHEA.

**B. Claims**

DSHEA also amended the [FFDCA] to permit certain types of claims for dietary supplements that formerly would have made them drugs, including claims to affect the structure or function of the body through a non-nutritive mechanism. Congress recognized that if foods and dietary supplements were permitted to make disease treatment and prevention claims without premarket review, the burden would have been on consumers to evaluate the validity of a myriad of claims about products marketed for serious and life-threatening conditions. In addition, dietary supplements would be given an unfair advantage over prescription and over-the-counter drugs in the marketplace.

Thus, as I have noted above, the Agency issued a proposed rule intended to provide direction to the industry as to the types of statements that can be made concerning the effect of a dietary supplement on the structure or function of the body and to clarify the line between disease and structure/function claims. This is important because disease claims for drugs as well as for conventional foods and dietary supplements continue to require pre-market authorization by FDA.

For foods, including dietary supplements, disease claims are "health claims." These claims describe the relationship between a food substance and a disease. The claim is usually in the context of risk reduction of the disease. Any person or firm may petition FDA to authorize a health claim. FDA then reviews the scientific evidence for or against the claim. If the Agency finds that the claim is supported by significant scientific agreement among qualified experts, it will issue a regulation authorizing the claim. Recently, FDAMA authorized a second method for streamlined review of health claims. This involves the use of authoritative statements made by certain federal scientific bodies and the National Academy of Sciences in their publications. With this latter method, an interested party notifies FDA of its intent to make a health claim based on an authoritative statement and provides information as to the source of the statement.

**C. Safety**

With the passage of DSHEA, dietary supplements are deemed to be foods, except for purposes of the drug definition. In addition, Congress specifically excluded "dietary ingredients" in dietary supplements from the definition of "food additive." As a result, dietary ingredients used in dietary supplements no longer require premarket documentation of safety for submission to FDA unless they are new dietary ingredients subject to the notification requirement in Section 413(a)(2) of the [FFDCA]. The notification requirement stipulates that the manufacturer or distributor of the dietary supplement submit to FDA information which is the basis on which the manufacturer or distributor has concluded that a dietary supplement containing such dietary ingredient will reasonably be expected to be safe at least 75 days before marketing.

Because in most cases dietary supplement manufacturers are not required to provide safety information to FDA before marketing a product, FDA has the responsibility for gathering information before the Agency can take action to restrict the sale of a dietary supplement product for safety reasons. This means that the Agency must rely on adverse event reports, product sampling, information in the scientific literature, and other sources of evidence. The Agency's scientists have to determine whether a safety problem exists, and evidence adequate to support a regulatory action has to be gathered and assembled. As is the case whenever the Agency considers regulatory action against a product, it must take care to ensure that statutory requirements for an action against a dietary supplement are met. This process is often complex and warrants being thoughtful but timely.

## H. Key Points

- From the 1960s through the early 1990s, FDA made several efforts to regulate substances taken to supplement the diet (especially vitamins and minerals) more strictly. Both the Proxmire Amendment (1976) and DSHEA (1994) were congressional responses to these FDA efforts. Both statutes placed substantial limits on FDA authority.

- The statutory category "dietary supplement" did not exist until the passage of DSHEA in 1994.
- To qualify as a dietary supplement under FFDCA § 201(ff), a product must:
  - be something "intended to supplement the diet."
  - "bear or contain[]" one or more of the items on this list: "a vitamin," "a mineral," "an herb or other botanical," "an amino acid," "a dietary substance for use by man to supplement the diet by increasing the total dietary intake," or "a concentrate, metabolite, constituent, extract, or combination" of the items listed earlier.
  - not be either tobacco or (with some very limited exceptions) a new drug as defined in FFDCA § 201(p).
- The dietary supplement definition (FFDCA § 201(ff)) expressly "deem[s]" dietary supplements to be food for purposes of the FFDCA, except for purposes of the drug definition (FFDCA § 201(g)) and the reportable food registry (FFDCA § 417).
  - Despite being deemed to be food, FDA treats dietary supplements very differently from other foods.
  - Accordingly, this book treats dietary supplements as a separate product category. However, it is also possible to view dietary supplements as a subcategory of food.
  - FDA uses the term "conventional food" when it intends to explicitly refer only to foods that are not also dietary supplements.
- Dietary supplements are today permitted to make certain label claims that were historically permitted only for drugs. These claims, as well as related claims now permitted for conventional food, are discussed in the next chapter.

Chapter 9

# Label Claims for Food and Dietary Supplements

## A. Introduction

This chapter is both an extension of the earlier chapters on food (Chapter 6) and dietary supplements (Chapter 8), and a transition to the upcoming chapter on drugs (Chapter 10). At first glance, label claims may seem relatively innocuous—scarcely meriting the intense regulatory regime that limits their use.

The intense regime exists because at least some of these label claims blur the distinction between food and drugs. As you will recall from Chapter 1, drugs are defined not by their composition, but by their intended use. An intended use "in the diagnosis, cure, mitigation, treatment, or prevention of disease in man or other animals," leads to categorization as a drug. FFDCA § 201(g)(1)(B). For products "other than food," an intended use "to affect the structure or any function of the body of man or other animals," FFDCA 201(g)(1)(C), also leads to categorization as a drug.

The blurring of the food/drug distinction comes from language added in three statutes in the early 1990s.[1] Following these statutes, FFDCA §§ 201(g)(1) and 403(r) together carve out a set of exceptions from the drug definition for food and dietary supplements making certain claims that might otherwise meet the drug definition.

As you read the material below, focus on the tension between § 201(g)(1)(B) and 201(g)(1)(C), on one hand, and the exception carved out by the last paragraph of § 201(g)(1)—in combination with § 403(r)—on the other.

Please read (or review) the following excerpts in the statutory supplement:

- FFDCA § 201. Definitions; generally. *Subsections (g)(1) and (ff) only.*
- FFDCA § 403. Misbranded food. *Subsection (r) only.*
- 21 C.F.R. § 101.13 Nutrient content claims—general principles.
- 21 C.F.R. § 101.14 Health claims: general requirements.
- 21 C.F.R. § 101.93. Certain types of statements for dietary supplements.

1. These are the Nutrition Labeling and Education Act of 1990, the Dietary Supplement Act of 1992, and the Dietary Supplement Health and Education Act of 1994.

## B. Outline of Regulatory Regime

As in other chapters of this book, this chapter begins with a set of charts. As you read this chapter for the first time, you should do no more than skim these charts to get a general sense of the structure of the applicable statutes and regulations. (For more information on the role of the charts in this casebook, see Chapter 1, Parts A.1 and B).

| Timeline of Key Statutes: Label Claims | | | |
|---|---|---|---|
| **Year** | **PL** | **Stat** | **Name of Statute** |
| 1938 | 75-717 | 52 Stat. 1040 | FFDCA of 1938 |
| 1976 | 94-278 | 90 Stat. 401, 410 | Proxmire Amendment |
| 1990 | 101-535 | 104 Stat. 2353 | Nutrition Labeling and Education Act of 1990 |
| 1992 | 102-571 | 106 Stat. 4491, 4500 | Dietary Supplement Act of 1992 |
| 1994 | 103-417 | 108 Stat. 4325 | Dietary Supplement Health and Education Act of 1994 |

| Key Statutory Provisions: Label Claims | | |
|---|---|---|
| **Statute Name or U.S.C. Title** | **§** | **Title of Section or Subsection** |
| FFDCA | 201(g)(1) | [Exclusion of foods and dietary supplements making certain claims, under FFDCA § 403(r), from "drug" definition] |
| FFDCA | 201(s) | [Exclusion of dietary supplements from "food additive" definition] |
| FFDCA | 201(ff) | [Definition of "dietary supplement"] |
| FFDCA | 403(r) | [Label claims for food and dietary supplements] |
| FFDCA | 403(s) | [Misbranding of dietary supplements] |
| FFDCA | 403B | Dietary supplement labeling exemptions |

| Key Regulatory Provisions: Label Claims | | |
|---|---|---|
| **21 C.F.R. Part** | **Subpart** | **Title of Part or Subpart** |
| 101 | D | Specific requirements for nutrient content claims |
| 101 | E | Specific requirements for health claims |
| 101 | F | Specific requirements for descriptive claims that are neither nutrient content claims nor health claims |

| 21 C.F.R. 101, Subpart D. Specific Requirements for Nutrient Content Claims | |
|---|---|
| § | Section Title |
| § 101.54 | Nutrient content claims for "good source," "high," "more," and "high potency" |
| § 101.56 | Nutrient content claims for "light" or "lite" |
| § 101.60 | Nutrient content claims for the calorie content of foods |
| § 101.61 | Nutrient content claims for the sodium content of foods |
| § 101.62 | Nutrient content claims for fat, fatty acid, and cholesterol content of foods |
| § 101.65 | Implied nutrient content claims and related label statements |
| § 101.67 | Use of nutrient content claims for butter |
| § 101.69 | Petitions for nutrient content claims |
| **21 C.F.R. 101, Subpart E. Specific Requirements for Health Claims** | |
| § | Section Title |
| § 101.70 | Petitions for health claims |
| § 101.71 | Health claims: claims not authorized |
| § 101.72 | Health claims: calcium, vitamin D, and osteoporosis |
| § 101.73 | Health claims: dietary lipids and cancer |
| § 101.74 | Health claims: sodium and hypertension |
| § 101.75 | Health claims: dietary saturated fat and cholesterol and risk of coronary heart disease |
| § 101.76 | Health claims: fiber-containing grain products, fruits, and vegetables and cancer |
| § 101.77 | Health claims: fruits, vegetables, and grain products that contain fiber, particularly soluble fiber, and risk of coronary heart disease |
| § 101.78 | Health claims: fruits and vegetables and cancer |
| § 101.79 | Health claims: Folate and neural tube defects |
| § 101.80 | Health claims: dietary noncariogenic carbohydrate sweeteners and dental caries |
| § 101.81 | Health claims: Soluble fiber from certain foods and risk of coronary heart disease (CHD) |
| § 101.82 | Health claims: Soy protein and risk of coronary heart disease (CHD) |
| § 101.83 | Health claims: plant sterol/stanol esters and risk of coronary heart disease (CHD) |
| **21 C.F.R. 101, Subpart F. Specific Requirements for Descriptive Claims That Are Neither Nutrient Content Claims nor Health Claims** | |
| § | Section Title |
| § 101.91 | Gluten-free labeling of food |
| § 101.93 | Certain types of statements for dietary supplements |
| § 101.95 | "Fresh," "freshly frozen," "fresh frozen," "frozen fresh |

## C. The Five Primary Types of Label Claims

There are five primary types of health claims available for both conventional foods and dietary supplements: SSA health claims (sometimes described as "unqualified" health claims or simply "health claims"); qualified health claims; structure/function claims; nutrient content claims; and dietary guidance. Dietary supplements can also, under certain conditions, claim a benefit relating to a classical nutrient deficiency disease.

These tend to be confusing to students for several reasons. First, FDA has promulgated highly detailed regulations relating to some, but not all, of these claims. Second, there are both similarities and differences between the way these claims apply to conventional food and dietary supplements. Third, the structure/function claim—as a concept—borders closely on both the health claim and the type of disease-related claim that would turn the relevant product into a drug.

The chart below summarizes the five primary types of claims. Claims for conventional food are presented on a white background, with the similar dietary supplement claim presented immediately below on a gray background.

As you review the chart, note the following:

- For both conventional foods and dietary supplements, FDA has promulgated regulations for both *SSA health claims* and for *nutrient content claims.*
- For both conventional foods and dietary supplements, FDA has developed an interim process for requesting that the agency use its enforcement discretion to allow certain *qualified health claims.*
- Structure/function claims
    - For dietary supplements, FDA has promulgated regulations requiring advance notification to the agency of the intention to make a structure/function claim.
    - For conventional foods, FDA has promulgated neither regulations nor interim procedures for *structure/function claims.* FDA does not require advance notification of the intention to make a structure/function claim for conventional food.
- For both conventional foods and dietary supplements, FDA has promulgated neither regulations nor interim procedures for *dietary guidance.* Dietary guidance is simply a term the agency uses for claims that include only one of the two elements of a health claim. FDA does not require advance notification of the intention to make a statement that qualifies as dietary guidance.

You may find it helpful to return to this chart after finishing the remainder of this chapter.

| The Five Primary Types of Label Claims for Conventional Foods and Dietary Supplements | | | | | | |
|---|---|---|---|---|---|---|
| **Type of claim** | **What it does** | **Key FFDCA provisions** | **Where to find FDA requirements** | **Whether premarket approval required** | **Where to find list of approved claims** | **Whether notification required** |
| *SSA health claim*—conventional food | Characterize relationship between a substance and a disease or health-related condition | § 201(g)(1); § 403(r)(1)(B); § 403(r)(3) | 21 C.F.R. Part 101, Subpart E: "Specific requirements for health claims" (§§ 101.70–101.83) | Yes; through notice and comment rulemaking | 21 C.F.R. Part 101, Subpart E: "Specific requirements for health claims" (§§ 101.70–101.83) | N/A |
| *SSA health claim*—dietary supplement | Characterize relationship between a substance and a disease or health-related condition | § 201(g)(1); § 403(r)(1)(B); § 403(r)(5)(D); § 403(r)(6) | 21 C.F.R. Part 101, Subpart E: "Specific requirements for health claims" (§§ 101.70–101.83) | Yes; through notice and comment rulemaking | 21 C.F.R. Part 101, Subpart E: "Specific requirements for health claims" (§§ 101.70–101.83) | N/A |
| *Qualified health claim*—conventional food | Same as SSA health claim, but with less scientific support | § 201(g)(1); § 403(r)(1)(B); § 403(r)(3) | May 2006 and Jan 2009 FDA guidance documents | Yes in practice, though not termed "approval" | Letters of enforcement discretion (including appropriate qualifying statements) posted on FDA website | N/A |
| *Qualified health claim*—dietary supplement | Same as SSA health claim, but with less scientific support | § 201(g)(1); § 403(r)(1)(B); § 403(r)(5)(D); § 403(r)(6) | May 2006 and Jan 2009 FDA guidance documents | Yes in practice, though not termed "approval" | Letters of enforcement discretion (including appropriate qualifying statements) posted on FDA website | N/A |

| The Five Primary Types of Label Claims for Conventional Foods and Dietary Supplements | | | | | | |
|---|---|---|---|---|---|---|
| **Type of claim** | **What it does** | **Key FFDCA provisions** | **Where to find FDA requirements** | **Whether premarket approval required** | **Where to find list of approved claims** | **Whether notification required** |
| *Structure/function claim*—conventional food | Describes the effect of a substance on the structure or function of the body | § 201(g)(1)(C) | Not defined in codified regulations; described in various preambles and guidance documents, including FDA Food Labeling Guide (Jan 2013), p. 84–86. | No | N/A | No |
| *Structure/function claim*—dietary supplement | Describes the effect of a substance on the structure or function of the body | § 201(g)(1); § 403(r)(1)(B); § 403(r)(5)(D); § 403(r)(6) | 21 C.F.R. § 101.93 | No | N/A | Yes |
| *Nutrient content claim*—conventional food | Expressly or implicitly characterizes the level of a nutrient | § 403(r)(1)(A); § 403(r)(2) | 21 C.F.R. Part 101, Subpart D (§§ 101.54–101.69) | Yes; through notice and comment rulemaking | 21 C.F.R. Part 101, Subpart D (§§ 101.54–101.69) | N/A |
| *Nutrient content claim*—dietary supplement | Expressly or implicitly characterizes the level of a nutrient | § 403(r)(1)(A); § 403(r)(2) | 21 C.F.R. Part 101, Subpart D (§§ 101.54–101.69) | Yes; through notice and comment rulemaking | 21 C.F.R. Part 101, Subpart D (§§ 101.54–101.69) | N/A |
| *Dietary guidance*—conventional food | Term used by FDA to describe claim that contains one, but not both, elements of a health claim (substance; disease or health-related condition) | § 201(g)(1); § 403(r)(1)(B); § 403(r)(3) | Not defined in codified regulations; described in various preambles and guidance documents, including 58 FR 2478 (1993-01-06), 68 FR 66040 (2003-11-25), and FDA Food Labeling Guide (Jan 2013), p. 84–86. | No | N/A | No |

| The Five Primary Types of Label Claims for Conventional Foods and Dietary Supplements | | | | | | |
|---|---|---|---|---|---|---|
| Type of claim | What it does | Key FFDCA provisions | Where to find FDA requirements | Whether premarket approval required | Where to find list of approved claims | Whether notification required |
| *Dietary guidance—dietary supplement* | Term used by FDA to describe claim that contains one, but not both, elements of a health claim (substance; disease or health-related condition) | § 201(g)(1); § 403(r)(1)(B); § 403(r)(5)(D); § 403(r)(6) | Not defined in codified regulations; described in various preambles and guidance documents, including 59 FR 395 (1994-01-04), 68 FR 66040 (2003-11-25), and FDA Food Labeling Guide (Jan 2013), p. 81. | No | N/A | No |

# D. Label Claims and Commercial Speech

## 1. The Commercial Speech Doctrine Generally

The case below, which involves a First Amendment challenge to an advertising ban imposed by a New York state agency, remains the leading U.S. Supreme Court case on the *commercial speech doctrine*. As you will see both in this chapter and Chapter 10 (on drugs), the commercial speech doctrine doctrine has come to play a significant role in food and drug regulation.

### Cent. Hudson Gas & Electric Co. v. Pub. Serv. Comm'n of N.Y.

447 U.S. 557 (1980)

**Mr. Justice Powell delivered the opinion of the Court.**

This case presents the question whether a regulation of the Public Service Commission of the State of New York violates the First and Fourteenth Amendments because it completely bans promotional advertising by an electrical utility.

I

In December 1973, the Commission, appellee here, ordered electric utilities in New York State to cease all advertising that "promot[es] the use of electricity." The order was based on the Commission's finding that "the interconnected utility system in New York State does not have sufficient fuel stocks or sources of supply to continue furnishing all customer demands for the 1973–1974 winter."

Three years later, when the fuel shortage had eased, the Commission requested comments from the public on its proposal to continue the ban on promotional advertising. Central Hudson Gas & Electric Corp., the appellant in this case, opposed the ban on First Amendment grounds. After reviewing the public comments, the Commission extended the prohibition in a Policy Statement issued on February 25, 1977.

The Policy Statement divided advertising expenses "into two broad categories: promotional-advertising intended to stimulate the purchase of utility services-and institutional and informational, a broad category inclusive of all advertising not clearly intended to promote sales." The Commission declared all promotional advertising contrary to the national policy of conserving energy. It acknowledged that the ban is not a perfect vehicle for conserving energy. For example, the Commission's order prohibits promotional advertising to develop consumption during periods when demand for electricity is low. By limiting growth in "off-peak" consumption, the ban limits the "beneficial side effects" of such growth in terms of more efficient use of existing power-plants. And since oil dealers are not under the Commission's jurisdiction and thus remain free to advertise, it was recognized that the ban can achieve only "piecemeal conservationism." Still, the Commission adopted the restriction because it was deemed likely to "result in some dampening of unnecessary growth" in energy consumption.

The Commission's order explicitly permitted "informational" advertising designed to encourage "shifts of consumption" from peak demand times to periods of low electricity demand. Informational advertising would not seek to increase aggregate consumption, but would invite a leveling of demand throughout any given 24-hour period. The agency offered to review "specific proposals by the companies for specifically described [advertising] programs that meet these criteria."

When it rejected requests for rehearing on the Policy Statement, the Commission supplemented its rationale for the advertising ban. The agency observed that additional electricity probably would be more expensive to produce than existing output. Because electricity rates in New York were not then based on marginal cost, the Commission feared that additional power would be priced below the actual cost of generation. This additional electricity would be subsidized by all consumers through generally higher rates. The state agency also thought that promotional advertising would give "misleading signals" to the public by appearing to encourage energy consumption at a time when conservation is needed.

Appellant challenged the order in state court, arguing that the Commission had restrained commercial speech in violation of the First and Fourteenth Amendments. The Commission's order was upheld by the trial court and at the intermediate appellate level. The New York Court of Appeals affirmed. It found little value to advertising in "the noncompetitive market in which electric corporations operate." *Consolidated Edison Co. v. Public Service Comm'n*, 47 N.Y.2d 94, 110 (1979). Since consumers "have no choice regarding the source of their electric power," the court denied that "promotional advertising of electricity might contribute to society's interest in 'informed and reliable' economic decisionmaking." The court also observed that by encouraging consumption, promotional advertising would only exacerbate the current energy situation. The court concluded that the governmental interest in the prohibition outweighed the limited constitutional value of the commercial speech at issue. We noted probable jurisdiction and now reverse.

## II

The Commission's order restricts only commercial speech, that is, expression related solely to the economic interests of the speaker and its audience. *Virginia Pharmacy Board v. Virginia Citizens Consumer Council*, 425 U.S. 748 (1976); *Bates v. State Bar of Arizona*, 433 U.S 350, 363–364 (1977); *Friedman v. Rogers*, 440 U.S. 1, 11 (1979). The First Amendment, as applied to the States through the Fourteenth Amendment, protects commercial speech from unwarranted governmental regulation. *Virginia Pharmacy Board*, 425 U.S., at 761–762. Commercial expression not only serves the economic interest of the speaker, but also assists consumers and furthers the societal interest in the fullest possible dissemination of information. In applying the First Amendment to this area, we have rejected the "highly paternalistic" view that government has complete power to suppress or regulate commercial speech. "[P]eople will perceive their own best interests if only they are well enough informed, and . . . the best means to that end is to open the channels of communication rather than to close them. . . ." Even when advertising communicates only an incomplete version of the relevant facts, the First Amendment presumes that some accurate information is better than no information at all.

Nevertheless, our decisions have recognized "the 'commonsense' distinction between speech proposing a commercial transaction, which occurs in an area traditionally subject to government regulation, and other varieties of speech." The Constitution therefore accords a lesser protection to commercial speech than to other constitutionally guaranteed expression. The protection available for particular commercial expression turns on the nature both of the expression and of the governmental interests served by its regulation.

The First Amendment's concern for commercial speech is based on the informational function of advertising. See *First National Bank of Boston v. Bellotti*, 435 U.S. 765, 783 (1978). Consequently, there can be no constitutional objection to the suppression of commercial messages that do not accurately inform the public about lawful activity. The government may ban forms of communication more likely to deceive the public than to inform it or commercial speech related to illegal activity.

If the communication is neither misleading nor related to unlawful activity, the government's power is more circumscribed. The State must assert a substantial interest to be achieved by restrictions on commercial speech. Moreover, the regulatory technique must be in proportion to that interest. The limitation on expression must be designed carefully to achieve the State's goal. Compliance with this requirement may be measured by two criteria. First, the restriction must directly advance the state interest involved; the regulation may not be sustained if it provides only ineffective or remote support for the government's purpose. Second, if the governmental interest could be served as well by a more limited restriction on commercial speech, the excessive restrictions cannot survive.

Under the first criterion, the Court has declined to uphold regulations that only indirectly advance the state interest involved. In both *Bates* and *Virginia Pharmacy Board*, the Court concluded that an advertising ban could not be imposed to protect the ethical or performance standards of a profession. The Court noted in *Virginia Pharmacy Board* that "[t]he advertising ban does not directly affect professional standards one way or the other." In *Bates*, the Court overturned an advertising prohibition that was designed to protect the "quality" of a lawyer's work. "Restraints on advertising . . . are an ineffective way of deterring shoddy work."

The second criterion recognizes that the First Amendment mandates that speech restrictions be "narrowly drawn." *In re Primus*, 436 U.S. 412, 438 (1978). The regulatory technique may extend only as far as the interest it serves. The State cannot regulate speech that poses no danger to the asserted state interest, nor can it completely suppress information when narrower restrictions on expression would serve its interest as well. For example, in Bates the Court explicitly did not "foreclose the possibility that some limited supplementation, by way of warning or disclaimer or the like, might be required" in promotional materials. And in *Carey v. Population Services International*, 431 U.S. 678, 701–702 (1977), we held that the State's "arguments . . . do not justify the total suppression of advertising concerning contraceptives." This holding left open the possibility that the State could implement more carefully drawn restrictions.

In commercial speech cases, then, a four-part analysis has developed. At the outset, we must determine whether the expression is protected by the First Amendment. For commercial speech to come within that provision, it at least must concern lawful activity and not be misleading. Next, we ask whether the asserted governmental interest is substantial. If both inquiries yield positive answers, we must determine whether the regulation directly advances the governmental interest asserted, and whether it is not more extensive than is necessary to serve that interest.

### III

We now apply this four-step analysis for commercial speech to the Commission's arguments in support of its ban on promotional advertising.

*[In parts III.A through III.C, omitted here, the Court concluded that the first three prongs of the above test were satisfied.]*

### D

We come finally to the critical inquiry in this case: whether the Commission's complete suppression of speech ordinarily protected by the First Amendment is no more extensive than necessary to further the State's interest in energy conservation. . . .

The Commission also has not demonstrated that its interest in conservation cannot be protected adequately by more limited regulation of appellant's commercial expression. To further its policy of conservation, the Commission could attempt to restrict the format and content of Central Hudson's advertising. It might, for example, require that the advertisements include information about the relative efficiency and expense of the offered service, both under current conditions and for the foreseeable future. In the absence of a showing that more limited speech regulation would be ineffective, we cannot approve the complete suppression of Central Hudson's advertising.

IV

Our decision today in no way disparages the national interest in energy conservation. We accept without reservation the argument that conservation, as well as the development of alternative energy sources, is an imperative national goal. Administrative bodies empowered to regulate electric utilities have the authority—and indeed the duty—to take appropriate action to further this goal. When, however, such action involves the suppression of speech, the First and Fourteenth Amendments require that the restriction be no more extensive than is necessary to serve the state interest. In this case, the record before us fails to show that the total ban on promotional advertising meets this requirement.

Accordingly, the judgment of the New York Court of Appeals is

Reversed.

## 2. Litigation Over Dietary Supplement Label Claims

The next two cases are First Amendment commercial-speech-doctrine challenges to FDA's efforts to severely limit label claims on dietary supplements. Pay attention to the relationship between these two cases and the two label claim guidance documents excerpted in Part E, below. If you become confused by the label-claim terminology, you may want to refer back to the chart in Part C, above.

### Pearson v. Shalala

164 F.3d 650 (D.C. Cir. 1999)

**SILBERMAN, Circuit Judge, delivered the opinion of the Court.**

Marketers of dietary supplements must, before including on their labels a claim characterizing the relationship of the supplement to a disease or health-related condition, submit the claim to the Food and Drug Administration for preapproval. The FDA authorizes a claim only if it finds "significant scientific agreement" among experts that the claim is supported by the available evidence. Appellants failed to persuade the FDA to authorize four such claims and sought relief in the district court, where their various constitutional and statutory challenges were rejected. We reverse.

I.

Dietary supplement marketers Durk Pearson and Sandy Shaw, presumably hoping to bolster sales by increasing the allure of their supplements' labels, asked the FDA to authorize four separate health claims. A "health claim" is a "claim made on the label or in labeling of . . . a dietary supplement that expressly or by implication . . . characterizes the relationship of any substance to a disease or health-related condition." 21 C.F.R. § 101.14(a) (1) (1998). Each of appellants four claims links the consumption of a particular supplement to the reduction in risk of a particular disease:

(1) "Consumption of antioxidant vitamins may reduce the risk of certain kinds of cancers.

(2) "Consumption of fiber may reduce the risk of colorectal cancer."

(3) "Consumption of omega-3 fatty acids may reduce the risk of coronary heart disease."

(4) ".8 mg of folic acid in a dietary supplement is more effective in reducing the risk of neural tube defects than a lower amount in foods in common form."

Understanding the preapproval requirement for health claims on dietary supplements requires a brief excursus on the broader regulatory framework applicable to dietary supplements, foods, and drugs. A "dietary supplement" is a "product (other than tobacco) intended to supplement the diet" that contains one or more of certain dietary ingredients, including a vitamin, a mineral, an herb or other botanical, or an amino acid, [FFDCA § 201] (ff)(1)(A)–(D), "is not represented for use as a conventional food or as a sole item of a meal or the diet," [FFDCA § 201](ff)(2)(B), and "is labeled as a dietary supplement," [FFDCA § 201](ff)(2)(C). A "drug" includes, inter alia, "articles intended for use in the diagnosis, cure, mitigation, treatment, or prevention of disease." [FFDCA § 201](g)(1)(B). If the product is a "new drug," the product must survive the arduous drug approval process, see [FFDCA § 505], before the manufacturer may introduce it into interstate commerce [FFDCA § 505](a).

Although there is apparently some definitional overlap between drugs and dietary supplements under the statute, it creates a safe harbor from designation as a "drug" for certain dietary supplements whose labels or labeling advertise a beneficial relationship to a disease or health-related condition: If the FDA authorizes a label claim under [FFDCA § 403](r), the product is not considered a drug under [FFDCA § 201](g)(1). The FDA authorizes a claim only when it determines, based on the totality of publicly available scientific evidence (including evidence from well-designed studies conducted in a manner which is consistent with generally recognized scientific procedures and principles), that there is significant scientific agreement among experts qualified by scientific training and experience to evaluate such claims, that the claim is supported by such evidence.

. . . .

The requirement that health claims be approved before being added to the label of a dietary supplement constitutes the primary regulatory hurdle faced by marketers of dietary supplements. The actual sale of dietary supplements is regulated only when the supplement contains a "new dietary ingredient," [FFDCA § 413], or poses a safety risk [FFDCA § 402].

Against this background, and in light of the further concern that the FDA might lack statutory authority to permit health claims on foods without also requiring that the claim meet the premarket approval requirements applicable to drugs, Congress enacted the Nutrition Labeling and Education Act of 1990 (NLEA). The NLEA addressed foods and dietary supplements separately. A health claim on a food may be made without FDA approval as a new drug, or the risk of sanctions for issuing a "misbranded" product, if it has been certified by the FDA as supported by "significant scientific agreement." [FFDCA § 403](r)(3)(B)(i). Congress created a similar safe harbor for health claims on dietary supplements, but delegated to the FDA the task of establishing "procedure and standard respecting the validity of [the health] claim." [FFDCA § 403](r)(5)(D).

The FDA has since promulgated 21 C.F.R. § 101.14—the "significant scientific agreement" "standard" (quoted above)—and 21 C.F.R. § 101.70—a "procedure" (not particularly relevant to this case)—for evaluating the validity of health claims on dietary supplements. In doing so, the agency rejected arguments asserted by commenters—including appellants—that the "significant scientific agreement" standard violates the First Amendment because it precludes the approval of less-well supported claims accompanied by a disclaimer and because it is impermissibly vague. The FDA explained that, in its view, the disclaimer approach would be ineffective because "there would be a question as to whether consumers would be able to ascertain which claims were preliminary [and accompanied by a disclaimer] and which were not," and concluded that its prophylactic approach is consistent with applicable commercial speech doctrine. The agency, responding to the comment that "significant scientific agreement" is impermissibly vague, asserted that the standard is "based on objective factors" and that its procedures for approving health claims, including the notice and comment procedure, sufficiently circumscribe its discretion.

. . . .

The problem with these claims, according to the FDA, was not a dearth of supporting evidence; rather, the agency concluded that the evidence was inconclusive for one reason or another and thus failed to give rise to "significant scientific agreement." But the FDA never explained just how it measured "significant" or otherwise defined the phrase. The agency refused to approve the dietary fiber-cancer claim because "a supplement would contain only fiber, and there is no evidence that any specific fiber itself caused the effects that were seen in studies involving fiber rich [foods]." The FDA gave similar reasons for rejecting the antioxidant vitamins-cancer claim and the omega-3 fatty acids-coronary heart disease claim. As for the claim that 0.8 mg of folic acid in a dietary supplement is more effective in reducing the risk of neural tube defects than a lower amount in foods in common form, the FDA merely stated that "the scientific literature does not support the superiority of any one source over others." The FDA declined to consider appellants' suggested alternative of permitting the claim while requiring a corrective disclaimer such as "The FDA has determined that the evidence supporting this claim is inconclusive."

. . . .

II.

Appellants raise a host of challenges to the agency's action. But the most important are that their First Amendment rights have been impaired and that under the Administrative Procedure Act the FDA was obliged, at some point, to articulate a standard a good deal more concrete than the undefined "significant scientific agreement." Normally we would discuss the nonconstitutional argument first, particularly because we believe it has merit. We invert the normal order here to discuss first appellants' most powerful constitutional claim, that the government has violated the First Amendment by declining to employ a less draconian method—the use of disclaimers—to serve the government's interests, because the requested remedy stands apart from appellants' request under the APA that the FDA flesh out its standards. That is to say, even if "significant scientific agreement" were given a more concrete meaning, appellants might be entitled to make health claims that do not meet that standard—with proper disclaimers.

Appellants also claim that the agency's "non-definition" runs afoul of Fifth Amendment concerns for vagueness. This contention is, however, closely connected to appellants' APA challenge and may well not be implicated if appellants' APA challenge affords ultimate relief. Therefore we will defer it until our APA analysis.

**A. Disclaimers**

It is undisputed that FDA's restrictions on appellants' health claims are evaluated under the commercial speech doctrine. It seems also undisputed that the FDA has unequivocally rejected the notion of requiring disclaimers to cure "misleading" health claims for dietary supplements. Although the general regulation does not *in haec verba* preclude authorization of qualified claims, the government implied in its statement of basis and purpose that disclaimers were not adequate, and did not consider their use in the four sub-regulations before us. The government makes two alternative arguments in response to appellants' claim that it is unconstitutional for the government to refuse to entertain a disclaimer requirement for the proposed health claims: first, that health claims lacking "significant scientific agreement" are inherently misleading and thus entirely outside the protection of the First Amendment; and second, that even if the claims are only potentially misleading, under *Central Hudson*, the government is not obliged to consider requiring disclaimers in lieu of an outright ban on all claims that lack significant scientific agreement.

If such health claims could be thought inherently misleading, that would be the end of the inquiry.

> Truthful advertising related to lawful activities is entitled to the protections of the First Amendment. But when the particular content or method of the advertising suggests that it is inherently misleading or when experience has proved that in fact such advertising is subject to abuse, the States may impose appropriate restrictions. Inherently misleading advertising may be prohibited entirely. But the States may not place an absolute prohibition on . . . potentially misleading information . . . if the information also may be presented in a way that is not deceptive.

*In re R.M.J.*, 455 U.S. 191, 203 (1982). As best we understand the government, its first argument runs along the following lines: that health claims lacking "significant scientific agreement" are inherently misleading because they have such an awesome impact on consumers as to make it virtually impossible for them to exercise any judgment at the point of sale. It would be as if the consumers were asked to buy something while hypnotized, and therefore they are bound to be misled. We think this contention is almost frivolous. We reject it. But the government's alternative argument is more substantial. It is asserted that health claims on dietary supplements should be thought at least potentially misleading because the consumer would have difficulty in independently verifying these claims. We are told, in addition, that consumers might actually assume that the government has approved such claims.

Under *Central Hudson*, we are obliged to evaluate a government scheme to regulate potentially misleading commercial speech by applying a three-part test. First, we ask whether the asserted government interest is substantial. The FDA advanced two general concerns: protection of public health and prevention of consumer fraud. The Supreme Court has said "there is no question that [the government's] interest in ensuring the accuracy of commercial information in the marketplace is substantial," and that government has a substantial interest in "promoting the health, safety, and welfare of its citizens." At this level of generality, therefore, a substantial governmental interest is undeniable.

The more significant questions under *Central Hudson* are the next two factors: "whether the regulation directly advances the governmental interest asserted," and whether the fit between the government's ends and the means chosen to accomplish those ends "is not necessarily perfect, but reasonable," We think that the government's regulatory approach encounters difficulty with both factors.

It is important to recognize that the government does not assert that appellants' dietary supplements in any fashion threaten consumer's health and safety. The government simply asserts its "common sense judgment" that the health of consumers is advanced directly by barring any health claims not approved by the FDA. Because it is not claimed that the product is harmful, the government's underlying—if unarticulated—premise must be that consumers have a limited amount of either attention or dollars that could be devoted to pursuing health through nutrition, and therefore products that are not indisputably health enhancing should be discouraged as threatening to crowd out more worthy expenditures. We are rather dubious that this simplistic view of human nature or market behavior is sound, but, in any event, it surely cannot be said that this notion—which the government does not even dare openly to set forth—is a direct pursuit of consumer health; it would seem a rather indirect route, to say the least.

. . . .

On the other hand, the government would appear to advance directly its interest in protecting against consumer fraud through its regulatory scheme. If it can be assumed—and we think it can—that some health claims on dietary supplements will mislead consumers, it cannot be denied that requiring FDA pre-approval and setting the standard extremely, perhaps even impossibly, high will surely prevent any confusion among consumers. We also recognize that the government's interest in preventing consumer fraud/confusion may well take on added importance in the context of a product, such as dietary supplements, that can affect the public's health.

The difficulty with the government's consumer fraud justification comes at the final *Central Hudson* factor: Is there a "reasonable" fit between the government's goals and the means chosen to advance those goals? The government insists that it is never obliged to utilize the disclaimer approach, because the commercial speech doctrine does not embody a preference for disclosure over outright suppression. Our understanding of the doctrine is otherwise. In *Bates v. State Bar of Arizona*, 433 U.S. 350 (1977), the Supreme Court addressed an argument similar to the one the government advances. The State Bar had disciplined several attorneys who advertised their fees for certain legal services in violation of the Bar's rule, and sought to justify the rule on the ground that such advertising is inherently misleading "because advertising by attorneys will highlight irrelevant factors and fail to show the relevant factor of skill." The Court observed that the Bar's concern was "not without merit," but refused to credit the notion that "the public is not sophisticated enough to realize the limitations of advertising, and that the public is better kept in ignorance than trusted with correct but incomplete information." Accordingly, the Court held that the "incomplete" attorney advertising was not inherently misleading and that "the preferred remedy is more disclosure rather than less." In more recent cases, the Court has reaffirmed this principle, repeatedly pointing to disclaimers as constitutionally preferable to outright suppression.

The government suggests that the Supreme Court's guidance on this issue is not so consistent. It points to *Friedman v. Rogers*, 440 U.S. 1 (1979), where the Court, in the course of upholding a ban on the use of trade names by optometrists, stated that "there is no First Amendment rule . . . requiring a State to allow deceptive or misleading commercial speech whenever the publication of additional information can clarify or offset the effects of the spurious communication." To be sure, this language cuts against the notion that government must, where possible, regulate misleading commercial speech by requiring disclaimers rather than by imposing an outright ban. But the Court in *Friedman* made clear the narrowness of its holding as limited to the special status of trade names:

> We emphasize . . . that the restriction on the use of trade names has only the most incidental effect on the content of the commercial speech of Texas optometrists. . . . [A] trade name conveys information only because of the associations that grow up over time between the name and a certain level of price and quality of service. . . . Since the [Texas Optometry] Act does not prohibit or limit the type of informational advertising held to be protected in . . . *Bates*, the factual information associated with trade names may be communicated freely and explicitly to the public.

The government does not assert here that appellants' health claims convey no factual information, only that the factual information conveyed is misleading.

. . . .

Our rejection of the government's position that there is no general First Amendment preference for disclosure over suppression, of course, does not determine that any supposed weaknesses in the claims at issue can be remedied by disclaimers and thus does not answer whether the subregulations, 21 C.F.R. § 101.71(a), (c), (e); id. § 101-79(c)(2)(i)(G), are valid. The FDA deemed the first three claims—(1) "Consumption of antioxidant vitamins may reduce the risk of certain kinds of cancers," (2) "Consumption of fiber may reduce the risk of colorectal cancer," and (3) "Consumption of omega-3 fatty acids may reduce the risk of coronary heart disease"—to lack significant scientific agreement because existing research had examined only the relationship between consumption of foods containing these components and the risk of these diseases. The FDA logically determined that the specific effect of the component of the food constituting the dietary supplement could not be determined with certainty. But certainly this concern could be accommodated, in the first claim for example, by adding a prominent disclaimer to the label along the following lines: "The evidence is inconclusive because existing studies have been performed with foods containing antioxidant vitamins, and the effect of those foods on reducing the risk of cancer may result from other components in those foods." A similar disclaimer would be equally effective for the latter two claims.

The FDA's concern regarding the fourth claim—"0.8 mg of folic acid in a dietary supplement is more effective in reducing the risk of neural tube defects than a lower amount in foods in common form"—is different from its reservations regarding the first three claims; the agency simply concluded that "the scientific literature does not support the superiority of any one source [of folic acid] over others." But it appears that credible evidence did support this claim, and we suspect that a clarifying disclaimer could be added to the effect that "The evidence in support of this claim is inconclusive."[3]

---

3. In general, the FDA appears quite reluctant to approve health claims on dietary supplements; only two are currently authorized. See 21 C.F.R. § 101.72(c)(2)(ii)(C) (calcium-osteoporosis);

The government's general concern that, given the extensiveness of government regulation of the sale of drugs, consumers might assume that a claim on a supplement's label is approved by the government, suggests an obvious answer: The agency could require the label to state that "The FDA does not approve this claim." Similarly, the government's interest in preventing the use of labels that are true but do not mention adverse effects would seem to be satisfied—at least ordinarily—by inclusion of prominent disclaimer setting forth those adverse effects.

The government disputes that consumers would be able to comprehend appellants' proposed health claims in conjunction with the disclaimers we have suggested—this mix of information would, in the government's view, create confusion among consumers. But all the government offers in support is the FDA's pronouncement that "consumers would be considerably confused by a multitude of claims with differing degrees of reliability." Although the government may have more leeway in choosing suppression over disclosure as a response to the problem of consumer confusion where the product affects health, it must still meet its burden of justifying a restriction on speech—here the FDA's conclusory assertion falls far short.

We do not presume to draft precise disclaimers for each of appellants' four claims; we leave that task to the agency in the first instance. Nor do we rule out the possibility that where evidence in support of a claim is outweighed by evidence against the claim, the FDA could deem it incurable by a disclaimer and ban it outright.[10] For example, if the weight of the evidence were against the hypothetical claim that "Consumption of Vitamin E reduces the risk of Alzheimer's disease," the agency might reasonably determine that adding a disclaimer such as "The FDA has determined that no evidence supports this claim" would not suffice to mitigate the claim's misleadingness. Finally, while we are skeptical that the government could demonstrate with empirical evidence that disclaimers similar to the ones we suggested above would bewilder consumers and fail to correct for deceptiveness, we do not rule out that possibility.

### B. The Unarticulated Standard

Wholly apart from the question whether the FDA is obliged to consider appropriate disclaimers is appellants' claim that the agency is obliged to give some content to the phrase "significant scientific agreement." Appellants contend that the agency's failure to do so independently violates their constitutional rights under the First and Fifth Amendments. The First, because producers of dietary supplements are assertedly subject to a "prior restraint" on their protected speech—the labeling

---

*id.* § 101.79(c)(2)(ii)(B) (folate-neural tube defects). The FDA has, however, approved several health claims on foods. *See, e.g., id.* § 101.72(c)(2)(ii) (calcium-osteoporosis); *id.* § 101.76 (fiber-containing products-cancer); *id.* § 101.78 (fruits and vegetables-cancer); *id.* § 101.79 (folate-neural tube defects); *id.* § 101.81 (soluble fiber-coronary heart disease).

10. Similarly, we see no problem with the FDA imposing an outright ban on a claim where evidence in support of the claim is qualitatively weaker than evidence against the claim—for example, where the claim rests on only one or two old studies

of products. The Fifth, because the agency's approach is so vague as to deprive the producers of liberty without due process.

Appellants do not challenge the concept of a pre-screening system per se; their complaint is with the FDA's lack of guidance on which health claims will survive the prescreening process. But appellants never connected their vagueness concern with their oblique First Amendment prior restraint argument, and for that reason we need not decide whether prior restraint analysis applies to commercial speech. On the other hand, appellants' Fifth Amendment vagueness argument is squarely presented. Still, by prevailing on their APA claim appellants would seem to gain the same relief—invalidation of the FDA's interpretation of the general standard and a remand for more guidance—as they would through a successful Fifth Amendment claim (or indeed a First Amendment prior restraint claim, if it had been properly presented and assuming arguendo that prior restraint analysis applies in the commercial speech context).[12]

Consideration of this constitutional claim seems unnecessary because we agree with appellants that the APA requires the agency to explain why it rejects their proposed health claims—to do so adequately necessarily implies giving some definitional content to the phrase "significant scientific agreement." We think this proposition is squarely rooted in the prohibition under the APA that an agency not engage in arbitrary and capricious action. See 5 U.S.C. § 706(2)(A) (1994). It simply will not do for a government agency to declare—without explanation—that a proposed course of private action is not approved. To refuse to define the criteria it is applying is equivalent to simply saying no without explanation. Indeed, appellants' suspicions as to the agency's real reason for its volte-face on the general folate-neural tube defect claim highlight the importance of providing a governing rationale for approving or rejecting proposed health claims.

To be sure, Justice Stewart once said, in declining to define obscenity, "I know it when I see it," *Jacobellis v. Ohio*, 378 U.S. 184, 197 (1964) (Stewart, J., concurring), which is basically the approach the FDA takes to the term "significant scientific agreement." But the Supreme Court is not subject to the Administrative Procedure Act. Nor for that matter is the Congress. That is why we are quite unimpressed with the government's argument that the agency is justified in employing this standard without definition because Congress used the same standard in [FFDCA § 403](r)(3)(B)(i). Presumably—we do not decide—the FDA in applying that statutory standard would similarly be obliged under the APA to give it content.

12. To be sure, there could be some differences between an APA analysis and a First or Fifth Amendment analysis. It is possible that a standard may be sufficiently well-delineated to satisfy the APA but not the First or Fifth Amendment. And, the APA may allow the agency to provide guidance in implementation, whereas the First or Fifth Amendment may require the agency to define its standard up front. Neither of these issues is presently before us (they could only conceivably arise after remand to the agency), and we leave them for another day.

That is not to say that the agency was necessarily required to define the term in its initial general regulation—or indeed that it is obliged to issue a comprehensive definition all at once. The agency is entitled to proceed case by case or, more accurately, sub-regulation by subregulation, but it must be possible for the regulated class to perceive the principles which are guiding agency action. Accordingly, on remand, the FDA must explain what it means by significant scientific agreement or, at minimum, what it does not mean.

* * * *

For the foregoing reasons, we hold invalid the four sub-regulations, 21 C.F.R. § 101.71(a), (c), (e); § 101.79(c)(2)(i)(G), and the FDA's interpretation of its general regulation, id. § 101.14. The decision of the district court is reversed, and the case is remanded to the district court with instructions to remand in turn to the FDA for reconsideration of appellants' health claims.

So ordered.

## Whitaker v. Thompson

248 F. Supp. 2d 1 (D.D.C. 2002)

**Kessler, District Judge.**

Plaintiffs are individuals and companies with a direct financial interest in dietary supplements containing vitamins C and E ("antioxidant vitamins") as well as a non-profit therapeutic health organization composed of physician members who sell dietary supplements containing antioxidant vitamins. They bring this action against Defendants Tommy F. Thompson, Secretary, United States Department of Health and Human Services ("HHS"), [various other HHS officials], and the United States of America.

Plaintiffs challenge the FDA decision prohibiting dietary supplements' labels from including the health claim that "Consumption of antioxidant vitamins may reduce the risk of certain kinds of cancers" ("Antioxidant Vitamin Claim" or "Claim"). Plaintiffs contend that the FDA's decision violates the First Amendment, the Fifth Amendment, the Defendants' oaths of office to uphold the Constitution, 5 U.S.C. § 3331, the Food, Drug and Cosmetic Act ("FDCA"), [FFDCA § 403](r)(1)(B), and the Administrative Procedure Act ("APA"), 5 U.S.C. § 706. Plaintiffs seek a preliminary injunction enjoining the FDA from taking any action which would prevent the use of the desired antioxidant vitamin health claim as proffered or with reasonable disclaimers.

This matter is before the Court on Plaintiffs' Motion for a Preliminary Injunction. [F]or the reasons discussed below, Plaintiffs' Motion for a Preliminary Injunction is granted.

## I. Background

### A. Statutory Framework

*[The court's discussion of the statutory framework is omitted.]*

### B. Procedural History

After a lengthy rule-making procedure under the APA, the FDA adopted a final rule prohibiting claims associating antioxidant vitamins with cancer on January 6, 1993. The FDA found significant scientific agreement that there was evidence supporting the relationship between a decreased risk of several types of cancer and "*diets* rich in fruits and vegetables, which are generally low in fat and high in vitamin A (as beta-carotene), vitamin C, and dietary fiber." However, the FDA did not find that such evidence was "sufficient to attribute the reduction in risk specifically to . . . vitamin C, or vitamin E, alone or in combination, or to other components of these diets." Nine months later, the FDA reiterated its refusal to authorize health claims associating antioxidant vitamins with cancer.

#### 1. The Pearson Plaintiffs

On November 16, 1995, Plaintiffs Durk Pearson, Sandy Shaw, and the American Preventive Medical Association ("Pearson Plaintiffs") brought suit arguing that the FDA had violated the First Amendment, the APA, and other laws through its unlawful suppression of four health claims, including the Antioxidant Vitamin Claim and requesting that the court invalidate the FDA's decision. On January 12, 1998, this Court upheld the FDA's decision and granted summary judgment in its favor.

On January 15, 1999, the Court of Appeals for the District of Columbia Circuit reversed and remanded the case with instructions to remand it in turn to the FDA for reconsideration of the prohibited health claims, including Plaintiffs' Antioxidant Vitamin Claim, in light of its discussion of the relevant legal issues.

The Court of Appeals in *Pearson I* strongly suggested, without explicitly holding, that Plaintiffs' Antioxidant Vitamin Claim was only "potentially misleading," not "inherently misleading," and therefore the FDA's refusal to authorize the Antioxidant Vitamin Claim (or to propose a disclaimer to accompany the Claim) violated the First Amendment. Specifically, while *Pearson I* recognized the FDA's concern that the antioxidant health claim lacked "significant scientific agreement because existing research had examined only the relationship between consumption of foods containing these components and the risk of these diseases," the Court stated that the FDA's concern "could be accommodated . . . by adding a prominent disclaimer to the label."

*Pearson I* left the task of drafting precise disclaimers to the agency and acknowledged that in some circumstances a complete ban of a claim might be appropriate. While recognizing the possibility that a disclaimer could be an inadequate guard against deceptiveness, the Court was "skeptical that the government could demonstrate with empirical evidence that disclaimers similar to the ones [suggested by the Court] would bewilder consumers and fail to correct for deceptiveness."

In addition, *Pearson I* held that the FDA acted arbitrarily and capriciously in violation of the APA by failing to adequately define the "significant scientific agreement" standard for reviewing health claims that it had adopted pursuant to [FFDCA § 403](r)(5)(D). Accordingly, the Court of Appeals directed the FDA on remand: (1) to determine whether a disclaimer could be added to the Antioxidant Vitamin Claim and other health claims to cure them of potentially misleading connotations, and (2) to explain "what it means by significant scientific agreement or, at minimum, what it does not mean."

### 2. Remand to the FDA

As directed by the Court of Appeals, this Court remanded the case to the FDA on April 20, 1999. In response to the first order in *Pearson I*, the FDA published a notice requesting that interested parties submit scientific data concerning the four substance-disease relationships at issue in *Pearson I*, including the antioxidant vitamin/cancer relationship. The FDA also contracted with a non-government entity "to conduct a literature search to identify for each of the four claims relevant scientific information that became available after the agency's initial review of these claims." As a result of these two information-gathering measures, the FDA received a large number of post-1992 scientific studies describing the relationship between antioxidant vitamins and cancer that had been published since its 1993 rulemaking. Among these were six submissions from Plaintiff that included 136 scientific references.

In response to the second order in *Pearson I* that the FDA further define the "significant scientific agreement" standard for evaluating dietary supplement health claims, the FDA issued "Guidance for the Industry: Significant Scientific Agreement in the Review of Health Claims for Conventional Foods and Dietary Supplements" ("Guidance Report" or "Report") and announce its availability in the Federal Register. The Guidance Report stated that significant scientific agreement meant that "the validity of the relationship is not likely to be reversed by new and evolving science, although the exact nature of the relationship may need to be refined." The FDA further explained that:

> Although significant scientific agreement is not consensus in the sense of unanimity, it represents considerably more than an initial body of emerging evidence. Because each situation may differ with the nature of the claimed substance/disease relationship, it is necessary to consider both the extent of agreement and the nature of the disagreement on a case-by-case basis.

In the Guidance Report, the agency also outlined the various aspects of its assessment of proposed health claims. For example, the FDA divided its analysis of studies on humans into interventional and observational studies and noted that "[i]n general, interventional studies provide the strongest evidence for [a supplement's] effect." However, the agency stated that "[b]ecause of the limitations of various research methods that can be used to study substance/disease relationships" it would not be able to "specify the type or number of studies needed to support a health claim."

On October 3, 2000, over 18 months after the *Pearson I* decision, the FDA published a notice revoking the four rules held unconstitutional by the Court of Appeals. However, the FDA continued to refuse to authorize the health claims at issue in *Pearson I*, including Plaintiffs' Antioxidant Vitamin Claim.

. . . .

#### 4. Final FDA Action on the Antioxidant Vitamin Claim

On May 4, 2001, the FDA issued a letter decision in which it declared that it would not authorize Plaintiffs' Antioxidant Vitamin Claim given the agency's review of new antioxidant vitamin/cancer relationship studies under the "significant scientific agreement" standard described in the Guidance Report. The FDA found a lack of significant scientific agreement as to the relationship between antioxidant vitamin intake and reduction in the risk of developing cancer. The FDA also found that the weight of the scientific evidence against the relationship was greater than the weight of evidence in favor of the relationship, and therefore concluded that Plaintiffs' Antioxidant Vitamin Claim was "inherently misleading and cannot be made non-misleading with a disclaimer or other qualifying language."

On July 17, 2001, Plaintiffs filed the present lawsuit.

### II. Analysis

Plaintiffs contend that the FDA's Antioxidant Vitamin Decision fundamentally misread and misapplied the legal standard articulated by the Court of Appeals in *Pearson I*, in violation of the First Amendment. Plaintiffs further contend that the FDA's continued refusal to authorize the Antioxidant Vitamin Claim, even with disclaimers, causes them irreparable harm, thus necessitating the issuance of a preliminary injunction. Defendants respond that denial of the Antioxidant Vitamin Claim was based on the agency's conclusion that the scientific evidence weighed more heavily against than in favor of the antioxidant vitamin/cancer relationship, and therefore Plaintiffs' proposed health claim was misleading and incurable by disclaimer. The FDA contends that the Antioxidant Vitamin Claim is not protected speech because it is misleading and that the agency's decision to prohibit Plaintiffs' health claim was neither arbitrary nor capricious under the APA.

To obtain a preliminary injunction, Plaintiffs must show (1) a substantial likelihood of success on the merits; (2) a substantial threat that they will suffer irreparable injury if the injunction is not granted; (3) that the threatened irreparable injury outweighs the threatened harm that the injunction would cause Defendants and third parties; and (4) that granting the preliminary injunction would be in the public interest.

Applying these four criteria, the Court concludes that a preliminary injunction is warranted in this case. Upon reviewing the FDA's Antioxidant Vitamin Decision conclusion that the Claim is "misleading and incurable by a disclaimer," the Court concludes that the FDA has failed to comply with the Court of Appeals decision in *Pearson I* and that Plaintiffs have demonstrated a substantial likelihood of success on the merits of their First Amendment claim.

The Court finds, as a matter of law, that Plaintiffs' Antioxidant Vitamin Claim is not "inherently misleading," and that the FDA therefore erred in not considering disclaimers to accompany the Claim. The FDA has failed to carry its burden of showing that suppression of Plaintiffs' Antioxidant Vitamin Claim is the least restrictive means of protecting consumers against the potential of being misled by the Claim. As explained below, it is clear that the FDA has once again failed to comply with the constitutional guidelines outlined in *Pearson I.*

However, as it is not the Court's institutional role to draft accurate, adequate, and succinct health claim disclaimers, the Court will require the FDA to draft and submit one or more alternative disclaimers, one of which may be selected by designers, sellers, and manufacturers of dietary supplements containing antioxidant vitamins. Because the Court is granting only limited relief to Plaintiffs at this time, Plaintiffs will not be authorized to design, sell, or manufacture their dietary supplements without an approved disclaimer.

. . . .

### III. Conclusion

For the reasons stated, the Court finds that the FDA's decision to completely prohibit Plaintiffs' Antioxidant Vitamin Claim as "inherently misleading" was unconstitutional and "not in accordance with law" under the APA, 5 U.S.C. §706(2)(A). Plaintiffs' proposed Claim is only potentially misleading and therefore subject to First Amendment protection. Accordingly, the Court concludes that the FDA has acted in violation of the Court of Appeals decision in *Pearson I* by suppressing Plaintiffs' Claim rather than proposing a clarifying disclaimer to accompany the Claim. Accordingly, the Court grants Plaintiffs' Motion for a Preliminary Injunction insofar as it requests a declaration that the FDA's refusal to authorize the Antioxidant Vitamin Claim violates the First Amendment.

However, because it is the FDA's, rather than the Court's, institutional role to draft accurate, adequate, and succinct health claim disclaimers, the Court hereby remands this case to the FDA, instructing the agency to draft and submit one or more such appropriately short, succinct, and accurate disclaimers. The Court strongly suggests that, at a minimum, the agency consider the two disclaimers suggested by the Court of Appeals in *Pearson I* ("The evidence in support of this claim is inconclusive" and "The FDA does not approve this claim").

### ORDER

**ORDERED**, that Plaintiffs' Motion for a Preliminary Injunction is granted, insofar as it requests a declaration that the Food and Drug Administration's May 4, 2001, denial of Plaintiffs' Antioxidant Vitamin Claim ("Consumption of antioxidant vitamins may reduce the risk of certain kinds of cancers.") violates the First Amendment of the U.S. Constitution; and it is further

**ORDERED**, that this case is remanded, effective immediately, to the Food and Drug Administration, for the purpose of drafting one or more short, succinct, and accurate alternative disclaimers, which may be chosen by Plaintiffs to accompany their Antioxidant Vitamin Claim, consistent with the accompanying Memorandum Opinion.

## E. FDA Label-Claim Guidance

The two documents excerpted below are the primary documents setting out FDA's current policy on qualified health claims. The first addresses qualified health claims generally; the second discusses the way FDA will evaluate evidence for both SSA health claims and qualified health claims.

### FDA, Guidance for Industry: FDA's Implementation of Qualified Health Claims (May 2006)

#### Background

**1. Why is FDA providing for "qualified" health claims?**

Through the Better Nutrition Information for Consumer Health Initiative (see Consumer Health Information for Better Nutrition Initiative, issued July 10, 2003), FDA acknowledged that consumers benefit from more information on food labels concerning diet and health. As part of this initiative, the agency established interim procedures whereby "qualified" health claims can be made not only for dietary supplements but for conventional foods as well. . . . Moreover, past court decisions have clarified the need to provide for health claims based on less scien[tific] evidence rather than just on the standard of significant scientific agreement (SSA), as long as the claims do not mislead the consumers. . . .

**2. What are the similarities and differences between SSA health claims established under the 1993 regulations and the newer "qualified" health claims?**

Both types of health claims characterize a relationship between a substance (specific food component or a specific food) and a disease (e.g., lung cancer or heart disease) or health-related condition (e.g., high blood pressure), and are supported by scientific evidence (see 21 CFR 101.14). Health claims generally undergo review by FDA through a petition process. All SSA health claims as provided for by Congress in 1990 . . . must meet the SSA standard. Past court decisions resulting in qualified health claims on dietary supplements focused on whether a manufacturer could make statements about diet/disease relationships when the science supporting the claim did not meet the significant scientific agreement standard, provided that the claim about the relationship was stated or "qualified" in such a way as to not mislead consumers. Thus, qualified health claims differ from SSA health claims in that they must be accompanied by a disclaimer or otherwise qualified.

**3. Why are the procedures for qualified health claims "interim"?**

FDA believes that more information is needed before the agency can establish final procedures to provide for qualified health claims. . . .

**4. Will rulemaking for qualified health claims take place?**

FDA is currently considering various options regarding the development of proposed regulations related to qualified health claims. In the meantime, the agency plans to review qualified health claim petitions on a case-by-case basis to determine whether to issue a letter concerning the use of enforcement discretion for a qualified health claim or to deny the qualified health claim....

**5. What is a letter of enforcement discretion?**

A letter of enforcement discretion is a letter issued by FDA to the petitioner specifying the nature of the qualified health claim for which FDA intends to consider the exercise of its enforcement discretion. If a letter of enforcement discretion has been issued, FDA does not intend to object to the use of the claim specified in the letter, provided that the products that bear the claim are consistent with the stated criteria.

All letters of enforcement discretion will be posted on the FDA website. Once the letter is posted on the website, all manufacturers will have notice about how the agency intends to exercise its enforcement discretion on the use of the qualified health claim.

**6. How are health claims different from structure/function claims?**

Both SSA and qualified health claims characterize the relationship between a substance and its ability to reduce the risk of a disease or health-related condition (see 21 CFR 101.14). Structure/function claims describe the effect that a substance has on the structure or function of the body and do not make reference to a disease. An example of a structure/function claim is "Calcium builds strong bones." Structure/function claims must be truthful and not misleading and are not pre-reviewed or authorized by FDA. [[FFDCA 403](r)(6); 21 CFR 101.93]

**7. How are health claims different from statements about dietary guidance?**

Health claims characterize a relationship between a substance (specific food or food component) and a disease or health-related condition (see 21 CFR 101.14). Both elements of 1) a substance and 2) a disease are present in a health claim. Dietary guidance does not contain both elements (and therefore does not constitute a health claim (see 58 FR 2478 at 2487; January 6, 1993), but may contain one element or another. Typically, dietary guidance statements make reference to a category of foods (i.e., a grouping that is not readily characterized compositionally) and not to a specific substance. The following illustrations may be helpful:

> Two examples of an authorized health claim, which by definition must contain the elements of a substance and a disease or health-related condition, are: "Diets low in sodium may reduce the risk of high blood pressure, a disease associated with many factors" and "Diets low in saturated fat and cholesterol that include 25 grams of soy protein a day may reduce the risk of heart disease".
>
> An example of dietary guidance, which does not refer to a specific substance but rather refers to a broad class of foods without an expressed or implied

> connection to a specific substance that is present the class of foods is: "Diets rich in fruits and vegetables may reduce the risk of some types of cancer." One element is present, but not both. It is not a health claim because it cannot reasonably be understood to be about a specific substance.
>
> A dietary guidance statement that refers to a specific food or food component but not a disease or health-related condition is: "Carrots are good for your health," or "Calcium is good for you." Again, one element is present, but not both.

**8. How is dietary guidance provided for on food labels?**

Truthful, non-misleading dietary guidance statements may be used on food labels, and do not undergo pre-review by FDA. However, once the food is marketed with the statement, FDA can consider whether the statement meets the requirement to be truthful and not misleading (see 21 CFR 101.14).

....

**Procedures for Qualified Health Claims**

**9. What are the regulatory procedures associated with qualified health claims?**

All health claims, whether SSA or qualified, require that a petition be submitted to FDA. The requirements for health claim petitions are specified in 21 CFR 101.70, and the general requirements for health claims are in 21 CFR 101.14. Both types of health claims can be applicable to conventional foods and dietary supplements, must characterize the substance's ability to reduce the risk of disease, and cannot be about mitigating or treating disease.

Qualified health claims have differences that relate to scientific support, wording of the claim, use of enforcement discretion, and timelines.

**10. How is the science supporting a qualified health claim different from that for an SSA health claim?**

SSA health claims require significant scientific agreement based on the totality of publicly available scientific evidence (see 21 CFR 101.14). Qualified health claims are still based on the totality of publicly available evidence but the scientific support does not have to be as strong as that for significant scientific agreement. Under its interim guidance . . . , FDA is tentatively providing for 3 levels of science below the Significant Scientific Agreement standard: good to moderate level of scientific agreement, low level of scientific agreement, and very low level of scientific agreement. The criteria for the scientific review are described in the interim guidance.

**11. How the language for qualified health claims is different?**

Qualified health claims language must be worded ("qualified") in such a way that consumers are not misled about the nature of the supporting science. As part of its interim guidance . . . , FDA has specified qualifying language for the 3 levels of scientific support below the Significant Scientific Agreement standard. FDA also notes that it may consider other qualifying language on a case-by-case basis.

**12. How do the regulatory procedures for qualified health claims differ from SSA health claims?**

Petitions requesting an SSA health claim are evaluated under the Significant Scientific Agreement standard (see Significant Scientific Agreement in the Review of Health Claims for Conventional Foods and Dietary Supplements). If FDA decides that standard is met, it authorizes the claim through notice-and-comment rulemaking.

Petitions requesting a qualified health claim are posted on the FDA web page for a 60-day public comment period. Qualified health claims meeting the interim procedures criteria are provided for by letters of enforcement discretion (as described above). The letter of enforcement discretion will be posted on the FDA web page. Petitions for a qualified health claim that have no credible scientific evidence for the claim may be denied. These letters will be posted on FDA's website.

**What is the procedural timeline for qualified health claims?**

- Within 15 days of receipt, FDA will acknowledge the petition.
- Within 45 days of receipt, FDA will file the petition and a docket number will be assigned. Note: Petitions that do not meet content requirements as specified in 21 CFR 101.70 will not be filed and will be returned to the petitioner.
- At the time of filing, FDA will post the petition on the FDA webpage for a 60-day public comment period. During this time, written comments may be submitted to the docket.
- On or before 270 days after receipt of the petition, a final decision will be sent to the petitioner in the form of a letter as to whether FDA intends to exercise enforcement discretion with respect to a qualified health claim or deny the petition. The letter will be posted on FDA's website.
- Extensions beyond 270 days can be granted upon mutual agreement between the petitioner and the agency.

## FDA, Guidance for Industry: Evidence-Based Review System for the Scientific Evaluation of Health Claims (Jan. 2009)

### I. Introduction

This guidance document is for industry. It represents the agency's current thinking on 1) the process for evaluating the scientific evidence for a health claim, 2) the meaning of the significant scientific agreement (SSA) standard in section 403(r)(3) of the [FFDCA] and 21 CFR 101.14(c), and 3) credible scientific evidence to support a qualified health claim.

This guidance document describes the evidence-based review system that FDA intends to use to evaluate the publicly available scientific evidence for SSA health claims or qualified health claims on the relationship between a substance and a disease or health-related condition. This guidance document explains the agency's current thinking on the scientific review approach FDA should use and is intended to provide guidance to health claim petitioners.

The specific topics addressed in this guidance document are: (1) identifying studies that evaluate the substance/disease relationship, (2) identifying surrogate endpoints for disease risk, (3) evaluating the human studies to determine whether scientific conclusions can be drawn from them about the substance/disease relationship, (4) assessing the methodological quality of each human study from which scientific conclusions about the substance/disease relationship can be drawn, (5) evaluating the totality of scientific evidence, (6) assessing significant scientific agreement, (7) specificity of claim language for qualified health claims, and (8) reevaluation of existing SSA or qualified health claims.

. . . .

### II. Background

The Nutrition Labeling and Education Act of 1990 (NLEA) was designed to give consumers more scientifically valid information about foods they eat. Among other provisions, the NLEA directed FDA to issue regulations providing for the use of statements that describe the relationship between a substance and a disease ("health claims") in the labeling of foods, including dietary supplements, after such statements have been reviewed and authorized by FDA. For these health claims, that is, statements about substance/disease relationships, FDA has defined the term "substance" by regulation as a specific food or food component (21 CFR 101.14(a)(2)). An authorized health claim may be used on both conventional foods and dietary supplements, provided that the substance in the product and the product itself meet the appropriate standards in the authorizing regulation. Health claims are directed to the general population or designated subgroups (e.g., the elderly) and are intended to assist the consumer in maintaining healthful dietary practices.

In evaluating a petition for an authorized health claim, FDA considers whether the evidence supporting the relationship that is the subject of the claim meets the SSA standard. This standard derives from [FFDCA § 403] (r)(3)(B)(i), which provides that FDA shall authorize a health claim to be used on conventional foods if the agency "determines based on the totality of the publicly available evidence (including evidence from well-designed studies conducted in a manner which is consistent with generally recognized scientific procedures and principles), that there is significant scientific agreement among experts qualified by scientific training and experience to evaluate such claims, that the claim is supported by such evidence." This scientific standard was prescribed by statute for conventional food health claims; by regulation, FDA adopted the same standard for dietary supplement health claims. See 21 CFR 101.14(c).

The genesis of qualified health claims was the court of appeals decision in *Pearson v. Shalala* (*Pearson*). In that case, the plaintiffs challenged FDA's decision not to authorize health claims for four specific substance-disease relationships in the labeling of dietary supplements. Although the district court ruled for FDA, the U.S. Court of Appeals for the D.C. Circuit reversed the lower court's decision. The appeals court held that the First Amendment does not permit FDA to reject health claims that the agency determines to be potentially misleading unless the agency also reasonably determines that a disclaimer would not eliminate the potential deception. The appeals court also held that the Administrative Procedure Act (APA) required FDA to clarify the "significant scientific agreement" (SSA) standard for authorizing health claims.

On December 22, 1999, FDA announced the issuance of its Guidance for Industry: Significant Scientific Agreement in the Review of Health Claims for Conventional Foods and Dietary Supplements. This guidance document was issued to clarify FDA's interpretation of the SSA standard in response to the court of appeals' second holding in *Pearson*.

On December 20, 2002, the agency announced its intention to extend its approach to implementing the Pearson decision to include health claims for conventional foods. . . .

Because of the similarity between the scientific reviews for SSA and qualified health claims, FDA intends to use the approach set out in this guidance for evaluating the scientific evidence in petitions that are submitted for an SSA health claim or qualified health claim. The evidence-based review system set out in this guidance will assist the agency in determining whether the scientific evidence meets the SSA standard or, if not, whether the evidence supports a qualified health claim. In addition to a science review, health claims undergo a regulatory review. Health claims that meet the SSA standard are authorized by publication of a final rule or an interim final rule in the Federal Register. For qualified health claims supported by credible evidence, FDA issues a letter regarding its intent to consider enforcement discretion.

Although this guidance replaces the Guidance for Industry: Significant Scientific Agreement in the Review of Health Claims for Conventional Foods and Dietary Supplements, issued to clarify FDA's interpretation of the SSA standard in response to the court of appeals' second holding in *Pearson*, FDA believes this guidance continues to be consistent with the court's holding. The basic principles of SSA articulated in the 1999 guidance have not changed. A finding of SSA still requires the agency's best judgment as to whether qualified experts would likely agree that the scientific evidence supports the substance/disease relationship that is the subject of a proposed health claim. In fact, many of the explanations of SSA in this guidance are taken verbatim from the 1999 guidance. This guidance represents further scientific developments in the agency's approach to the review of scientific evidence rather than a change in its understanding of what constitutes SSA.

## F. Key Points

- Congress's decision to permit explicit health and structure/function claims for dietary supplements presents a fundamental challenge to the traditional definition of "drug."

  - FDA's reluctance to approve dietary supplement label claims can be understood as an agency effort to preserve, to the extent possible, the traditional food/drug distinction.
- The five primary types of label claims are SSA health claims; qualified health claims; structure/function claims; nutrient content claims; and dietary guidance. All five of these primary types of claims are available for both conventional foods and dietary supplements.
  - See the chart in Part C of this chapter for a summary of each of these types of claims.
- Courts have held that the First Amendment Commercial Speech doctrine sets some limits on FDA's ability to regulate label claims for foods and dietary supplements. One concrete result of these court decisions was FDA's development of interim procedures to permit a new type of "qualified" health claim.

Part Four

# FFDCA Chapter V Products—Drugs, Animal Drugs, Devices, and Combination Products

## Chapter 10

# Drugs

## A. Introduction

Please read (or review) the following excerpts in the statutory supplement:

- FFDCA § 201. Definitions, generally. *Subsection (g)(1) and (p) only.*
- FFDCA § 501. Adulterated drugs and devices. *Subsections (a)–(d) only.*
- FFDCA § 502. Misbranded drugs and devices. *Subsections (a)–(c), (f), (o) only.*
- PHSA § 351. Regulation of biological products. *Subsection (j) only.*

Section 201(g)(1) is the "drug" definition, and § 201(p) the "new drug" definition. As you will see when you read further below, the definition of "new drug" is nearly as critical as the definition of "drug" itself, as the new drug definition was the method by which Congress imposed first the premarket safety requirement, and then the premarket efficacy requirement.

Sections 501 and 502 are the drug adulteration and misbranding provisions, respectively. PHSA § 351(j) sets out the relationship between the FFDCA and the PHSA for drugs that also qualify as biologics.

## B. Outline of Regulatory Regime

As in other chapters of this book, this chapter begins with a set of charts. As you read this chapter for the first time, you should do no more than skim these charts to get a general sense of the structure of the applicable statutes and regulations. (For more information on the role of the charts in this casebook, see Chapter 1, Parts A.1 and B).

| Timeline of Key Statutes: Drugs Generally | | | |
|---|---|---|---|
| Year | PL | Stat | Name of Statute |
| 1906 | 59-384 | 34 Stat. 768 | Pure Food and Drug Act |
| 1912 | 62-301 | 37 Stat. 416 | Sherley Amendment |
| 1938 | 75-717 | 52 Stat. 1040 | FFDCA of 1938 |
| 1945 | 79-139 | 59 Stat. 463 | Penicillin Amendment |
| 1962 | 87-781 | 76 Stat. 780 | Kefauver-Harris Amendments of 1962 |

| Year | PL | Stat | Name of Statute |
|---|---|---|---|
| 1983 | 97-414 | 96 Stat. 2049 | Orphan Drug Act |
| 1984 | 98-417 | 98 Stat. 1585 | Hatch-Waxman Act |
| 1988 | 100-293 | 102 Stat. 95 | Prescription Drug Marketing Act of 1987[1] |
| 1992 | 96-660 | 100 Stat. 3748 | Generic Drug Enforcement Act of 1992 |
| 1997 | 105-115 | 111 Stat. 2296 | FDA Modernization Act of 1997 |
| 2002 | 107-188 | 116 Stat. 595 | Public Health Security and Bioterrorism Preparedness and Response Act of 2002 |
| 2003 | 108-173 | 117 Stat. 2003 | Medicare Prescription Drug Improvement and Modernization Act of 2003 |
| 2007 | 110-85 | 121 Stat. 823 | FDA Amendments Act of 2007 |
| | | | Pediatric Research Equity Act of 2007 |
| | | | Best Pharmaceuticals for Children Act of 2007 |
| 2012 | 112-144 | 126 Stat. 993 | FDA Safety and Innovation Act |
| 2013 | 113-54 | 127 Stat. 587 | Drug Quality and Security Act |
| 2014 | 113-195 | 128 Stat. 2035 | Sunscreen Innovation Act |
| 2016 | 114-255 | 130 Stat. 1033 | 21st Century Cures Act |
| 2017 | 115-52 | 131 Stat. 1005 | FDA Reauthorization Act of 2017 |
| 2017 | 115-92 | 131 Stat. 2023 | An Act To amend the Federal Food, Drug, and Cosmetic Act to authorize additional emergency uses for medical products to reduce deaths and severity of injuries caused by agents of war, and for other purposes. |
| 2020 | 116-136 | 134 Stat. 281 | Coronavirus Aid, Relief, and Economic Security Act |

**Timeline of Key Statutes: Statutes Carving Out New Categories from Products Formerly Regulated as Drugs (Some of Which Still Overlap with Drugs)**

| Year | PL | Stat | Name of Statute |
|---|---|---|---|
| 1968 | 90-399 | 82 Stat. 342 | Animal Drug Amendments of 1968 |
| 1976 | 94-295 | 90 Stat. 539 | Medical Devices Amendments of 1976 |
| 1994 | 103-417 | 108 Stat. 4325 | Dietary Supplement Health and Education Act |

1. This is the official short title written into the statute itself. However, the statute did not become law until the following calendar year.

| Key Statutory Provisions: Drugs Generally | | |
|---|---|---|
| **Statute Name or U.S.C. Title** | **§** | **Title of Section or Subsection** |
| FFDCA | 201(g)(1) | [Definition of "drug"] |
| FFDCA | 201(p) | [Definition of "new drug"] |
| FFDCA | 501 | Adulterated drugs and devices |
| FFDCA | 502 | Misbranded drugs and devices |
| FFDCA | 503 | Exemptions and consideration for certain drugs, devices, and biological products |
| FFDCA | 503C | Prereview of television advertisements |
| FFDCA | 505 | New drugs |
| FFDCA | 505D | Pharmaceutical security |
| FFDCA | 505E | Extension of exclusivity period for new qualified infectious disease products |
| FFDCA | 505H | Regulation of certain nonprescription drugs that are marketed without an approved drug application |
| FFDCA | 506 | Expedited approval of drugs for serious or life-threatening diseases or conditions |
| FFDCA | 506H | Competitive generic therapies |
| 21 U.S.C. | 356-1 | Accelerated approval of priority countermeasures |
| FFDCA | 506G | Standards for regenerative medicine and regenerative advanced therapies |
| FFDCA | 508 | Authority to designate official names |
| FFDCA | 509 | Nonapplicability of subchapter to cosmetics |
| FFDCA | 510 | Registration of producers of drugs or devices |
| FFDCA | 525 | Recommendations for investigations of drugs for rare diseases or conditions |
| FFDCA | 526 | Designation of drugs for rare diseases or conditions |
| FFDCA | 527 | Protection for drugs for rare diseases or conditions |
| FFDCA | 529 | Priority review to encourage treatments for rare pediatric diseases |
| FFDCA | 561 | Expanded access to unapproved therapies and diagnostics |
| FFDCA | 561A | Expanded access policy required for investigational drugs |
| FFDCA | 561B | Investigational drugs for use by eligible patients |
| FFDCA | 562 | Dispute resolution |
| FFDCA | 563 | Classification of products [among drug, biological product, device, and combination product] |
| FFDCA | 564 | Authorization for medical products for use in emergencies |

| Statute Name or U.S.C. Title | § | Title of Section or Subsection |
|---|---|---|
| FFDCA | 564A | Emergency use of medical products |
| FFDCA | 564B | Products held for emergency use |
| 21 U.S.C. | 360bbb-3c | Expedited development and review of medical products for emergency uses |
| FFDCA | 565 | Countermeasure development, review, and technical assistance |
| FFDCA | 565A | Priority review to encourage treatments for agents that present national security threats |
| FFDCA | 565B | Medical countermeasure master files |
| FFDCA | 566 | Critical path public-private partnerships |
| FFDCA | 568 | Notification |
| FFDCA | 569A | Optimizing global clinical trials |
| FFDCA | 569B | Use of clinical investigation data from outside the United States |
| FFDCA | 586F | Non-sunscreen time and extent applications |
| 21 U.S.C. | 377 | Revision of United States Pharmacopoeia; development of analysis and mechanical and physical tests |

## Key Regulatory Provisions: Drugs Generally

| 21 C.F.R. Part | Title of Part or Subpart |
|---|---|
| 99 | Dissemination of information on unapproved/new uses for marketed drugs, biologics, and devices |
| 200 | General |
| 201 | Labeling |
| 202 | Prescription drug advertising |
| 203 | Prescription drug marketing |
| 205 | Guidelines for state licensing of wholesale prescription drug distributors |
| 206 | Imprinting of solid oral dosage form drug products for human use |
| 207 | requirements for foreign and domestic establishment registration and listing for human drugs, including drugs that are regulated under a biologics license application, and animal drugs, and the national drug code |
| 208 | Medication guides for prescription drug products |
| 210 | Current good manufacturing practice in manufacturing, processing, packing, or holding of drugs; general |
| 211 | Current good manufacturing practice for finished pharmaceuticals |
| 212 | Current good manufacturing practice for positron emission tomography drugs |

| 21 C.F.R. Part | Title of Part or Subpart |
|---|---|
| 216 | Human drug compounding |
| 250 | Special requirements for specific human drugs |
| 290 | Controlled drugs |
| 299 | Drugs; official names and established names |
| 300 | General |
| 310 | New drugs |
| 312 | Investigational new drug application |
| 314 | Applications for FDA approval to market a new drug |
| 315 | Diagnostic radiopharmaceuticals |
| 316 | Orphan drugs |
| 317 | Qualifying pathogens |
| 320 | Bioavailability and bioequivalence requirements |
| 328 | Over-the-counter drug products intended for oral ingestion that contain alcohol |
| 329 | Nonprescription human drug products subject to section 760 of the Federal Food, Drug, And Cosmetic Act |
| 330 | Over-the-counter (OTC) human drugs which are generally recognized as safe and effective and not misbranded |
| 361 | Prescription drugs for human use generally recognized as safe and effective and not misbranded: drugs used in research |
| 369 | Interpretative statements re warnings on drugs and devices for over-the-counter sale |

**Key Regulatory Provisions: Regulations Authorizing Marketing of Particular Substances as Over-the-Counter Human Drugs (OTC Drug Monographs)**

| 21 C.F.R. Part | Title of Part |
|---|---|
| 331 | Antacid products for over-the-counter (OTC) human use |
| 332. | Antiflatulent products for over-the-counter human use |
| 333 | Topical antimicrobial drug products for over-the-counter human use |
| 335 | Antidiarrheal drug products for over-the-counter human use |
| 336 | Antiemetic drug products for over-the-counter human use |
| 338 | Nighttime sleep-aid drug products for over-the-counter human use |
| 340 | Stimulant drug products for over-the-counter human use |
| 341 | Cold, cough, allergy, bronchodilator, and antiasthmatic drug products for over-the-counter human use |

| 21 C.F.R. Part | Title of Part |
|---|---|
| 343 | Internal analgesic, antipyretic, and antirheumatic drug products for over-the-counter human use |
| 344 | Topical otic drug products for over-the-counter human use |
| 346 | Anorectal drug products for over-the-counter human use |
| 347 | Skin protectant drug products for over-the-counter human use |
| 348 | External analgesic drug products for over-the-counter human use |
| 349 | Ophthalmic drug products for over-the-counter human use |
| 350 | Antiperspirant drug products for over-the-counter human use |
| 352 | Sunscreen drug products for over-the-counter human use [stayed indefinitely] |
| 355 | Anticaries drug products for over-the-counter human use |
| 357 | Miscellaneous internal drug products for over-the-counter human use |
| 358 | Miscellaneous external drug products for over-the-counter human use |

## C. Drug Regulation under the 1906 Statute

The case below was an early setback to FDA in its effort to prohibit fraudulent therapeutic claims. Remember, as you read, that the statutory provisions referenced in this case are those of the Pure Food and Drug Act of 1906—not the FFDCA of 1938.

### United States v. Johnson

221 U.S. 488 (1911)

**Mr. Justice HOLMES delivered the opinion of the court:**

This is an indictment for delivering for shipment from Missouri to Washington, District of Columbia, packages and bottles of medicine bearing labels that stated or implied that the contents were effective in curing cancer, the defendant well knowing that such representations were false. On motion of the defendant, the district judge quashed the indictment, and the United States brought this writ of error. . . .

The question is whether the articles were misbranded within the meaning of § 2 of the food and drugs act of June 30, 1906, making the delivery of misbranded drugs for shipment to any other state or territory or the District of Columbia a punishable offense. By § 6 the term "drug" includes any substance or mixture intended to be used for the cure, mitigation, or prevention of disease. By § 8 the term "misbranded"

> shall apply to all drugs or articles of food, . . . the package or label of which shall bear any statement, design, or device regarding such article, or the ingredients or substances contained therein, which shall be false or misleading in any particular, and to any food or drug product which is falsely branded as to the state, territory, or country in which it is manufactured or produced. . . . An article shall also be deemed to be misbranded: In case of drugs: First. If it be an imitation of, or offered for sale under the name of, another article. Second. [In case of a substitution of contents] . . . or if the package fail to bear a statement on the label of the quantity or proportion of any alcohol, morphine, opium, cocaine, heroin, alpha or beta eucaine, chloroform, cannabis indica, chloral hydrate, or acetanilid, or any derivative or preparation of any such substances contained therein.

It is a postulate, as the case comes before us, that in a certain sense the statement on the label was false, or, at least, misleading. What we have to decide is whether such misleading statements are aimed at and hit by the words of the [Pure Food & Drug] act. It seems to us that the words used convey to an ear trained to the usages of English speech a different aim; and although the meaning of a sentence is to be felt rather than to be proved, generally, and here, the impression may be strengthened by argument, as we shall try to show.

We lay on one side as quite unfounded the argument that the words "statement which shall be misleading in any particular," as used in the statute, do not apply to drugs at all,—that the statements referred to are those "regarding such article," and that "article" means article of food, mentioned by the side of drugs at the beginning of the section. It is enough to say that the beginning of the sentence makes such a reading impossible, and that "article" expressly includes "drugs," a few lines further on in what we have quoted, not to speak of the reason of the thing. But we are of opinion that the phrase is aimed not at all possible false statements, but only at such as determine the identity of the article, possibly including its strength, quality, and purity, dealt within § 7. In support of our interpretation the first thing to be noticed is the second branch of the sentence: "Or the ingredients or substances contained therein." One may say with some confidence that in idiomatic English this half, at least, is confined to identity, and means a false statement as to what the ingredients are. Logically it might mean more, but idiomatically it does not. But if the false statement referred to is a mistatement of identity as applied to a part of its objects, idiom and logic unite in giving it the same limit when applied to the other branch, the article, whether simple or one that the ingredients compose. Again, it is to be noticed that the cases of misbranding, specifically mentioned, and following the general words that we have construed, are all cases analogous to the statement of identity, and not at all to inflated or false commendation of wares. The first is a false statement as to the country where the article is manufactured or produced,—a matter quite unnecessary to specify if the preceding words had a universal scope, yet added as not being within them. The next case is that of imitation and taking the name of another article, of which the same may be said, and so of the next, a substitution of contents. The last is breach of an affirmative requirement to disclose the proportion of alcohol and certain other noxious ingredients in the package,—again a matter of plain past history concerning the nature and amount of the poisons employed, not an estimate or prophecy concerning their effect. In further confirmation, it should be noticed that although the indictment alleges a wilful fraud, the shipment is punished by the statute if the article is misbranded, and that the article may be misbranded without any conscious fraud at all. It was natural enough to throw this risk on shippers with regard to the identity of their wares, but a very different and unlikely step to make them answerable for mistaken praise. It should be noticed still further that by § 4, the determination whether an article is misbranded is left to the Bureau of Chemistry of the Department of Agriculture, which is most natural if the question concerns ingredients and kind, but hardly so as to medical effects.

To avoid misunderstanding, we should add that, for the purposes of this case, at least, we assume that a label might be of such a nature as to import a statement concerning identity, within the statute, although in form only a commendation of the supposed drug. It may be that a label in such form would exclude certain substances so plainly to all common understanding as to amount to an implied statement of what the contents of the package were not; and it may be that such a negation might fall within the prohibitions of the [Pure Food & Drug] act. It may be (we express no opinion upon that matter) that if the present indictment had alleged that the contents of the bottles were water, the label so distinctly implied that they were other than water, as to be a false statement of fact concerning their nature and kind. But such a statement as to contents, undescribed and unknown, is shown to be false only in its commendatory and prophetic aspect, and as such is not within the [Pure Food & Drug] act.

In view of what we have said by way of simple interpretation we think it unnecessary to go into considerations of wider scope. We shall say nothing as to the limits of constitutional power, and but a word as to what Congress was likely to attempt. It was much more likely to regulate commerce in food and drugs with reference to plain matter of fact, so that food and drugs should be what they professed to be, when the kind was stated, than to distort the uses of its constitutional power to establishing criteria in regions where opinions are far apart. As we have said above, the reference of the question of misbranding to the Bureau of Chemistry for determination confirms what would have been our expectation and what is our understanding of the words immediately in point.

Judgment affirmed.

**Mr. Justice HUGHES, dissenting:**

I am unable to concur in the judgment in this case, for the following reasons:

The defendant was charged with delivering for shipment in interstate commerce certain packages and bottles of drugs alleged to have been misbranded in violation of the food and drugs act of June 30, 1906.

The articles were labeled respectively "Cancerine tablets," "Antiseptic tablets," "Blood purifier," "Special No. 4," "Cancerine No. 17," and "Cancerine No. 1,"—the whole constituting what was termed in substance "Dr. Johnson's Mild Combination Treatment for Cancer." There were several counts in the indictment with respect to the different articles. The labels contained the words, "Guaranteed under the Pure Food and Drugs Act, June 30, 1906;" and some of the further statements were as follows:

> Blood Purifier. This is an effective tonic and alternative. It enters the circulation at once, utterly destroying and removing impurities from the blood and entire system. Acts on the bowels, kidneys, and skin, eliminating poisons from the system, and when taken in connection with the Mild Combination Treatment, gives splendid results in the treatment of cancer and other malignant diseases. I always advise that the Blood Purifier be continued some little time after the cancer has been killed and removed and the sore healed.
>
> Special No. 4.... It has a strong stimulative and absorptive power; will remove swelling, arrest development, restore circulation, and remove pain. Is indicated in all cases of malignancy where there is a tendency of the disease to spread, and where there is considerable hardness sur. rounding the sore. Applied thoroughly to a lump or to an enlarged gland will cause it to soften, become smaller, and be absorbed.
>
> Cancerine No. 1.... Tendency is to convert the sore from an unhealthy to a healthy condition and promote healing. Also it destroys and removes dead and unhealthy tissue.

In each case the indictment alleged that the article was "wholly worthless," as the defendant well knew.

In quashing the indictment, the district court construed the statute. The substance of the decision is found in the following words of the opinion:

> Having regard to the intendment of the whole act, which is to protect the public health against adulterated, poisonous, and deleterious food, drugs, etc., the labeling or branding of the bottle or container, as to the quantity or composition of "the ingredients or substances contained therein, which shall be false or misleading," by no possible construction can be extended to an inquiry as to whether or not the prescription be efficacious or worthless to effect the remedy claimed for it.

And question on this writ of error is whether or not this construction is correct.

What, then, is the true meaning of the statute?

Section 8 provides:

> Sec. 8. That the term "misbranded," as used herein, shall apply to all drugs, or articles of food, or articles which enter into the composition of food, the package or label of which shall bear any statement, design, or device regarding such article, or the ingredients or substances contained therein, which

> shall be false or misleading in any particular; and to any food or drug product which is falsely branded as to the state, territory, or country in which it is manufactured or produced.

The words "such article" in this section, as is shown by the immediate context, refer to "drugs" as well as to "food."

"Drugs" are thus defined in § 6:

> Sec. 6. That the term "drug," as used in this act, shall include all medicines and preparations recognized in the United States Pharmacopoeia or National Formulary for internal or external use, *and any substance or mixture of substances intended to be used for the cure, mitigation, or prevention of disease of either man or other animals.*

Articles, then, intended to be used for curative purposes, such as those described in the indictment, are within the statute, though they are not recognized in the United States Pharmacopoeia or the National Formulary. And the offense of misbranding is committed if the package or label of such an article bears any statement regarding it "which shall be false or misleading in any particular."

But it is said that these words refer only to false statements which fix the identity of the article. According to the construction placed upon the statute by the court below in quashing the indictment, if one puts upon the market, in interstate commerce, tablets of inert matter or a liquid wholly worthless for any curative purpose, as he well knows, with the label "Cancer Cure" or "Remedy for Epilepsy," he is not guilty of an offense, for, in the sense attributed by that construction to the words of the statute, he has not made a statement regarding the article which is false or misleading in any particular.

I fail to find a sufficient warrant for this limitation, and, on the contrary, it seems to me to be opposed to the intent of Congress, and to deprive the [Pure Food & Drug] act of a very salutary effect.

It is strongly stated that the clause in § 8—"or the ingredients or substances contained therein"—has reference to identity, and that this controls the interpretation of the entire provision. This, in my judgment, is to ascribe an altogether undue weight to the wording of the clause and to overlook the context. The clause, it will be observed, is disjunctive. If Congress had intended to restrict the offense to misstatements as to identity, it could easily have said so. But it did not say so. To a draftsman with such a purpose, the language used would not naturally occur. Indeed, as will presently be shown, Congress refused, with the question up, so to limit the statute.

Let us look at the context. In the very next sentence, the section provides (referring to drugs) that an article shall "also" be deemed to be misbranded if it be "an imitation of, or offered for sale under the name of, another article;" or in case of substitution of contents, or of failure to disclose the quantity or proportion of certain specified ingredients, if present, such as alcohol, morphine, opium, cocaine, etc.

It is a matter of common knowledge that the "substances" or "mixtures of substances" which are embraced in the [Pure Food & Drug] act, although not recognized by the United States Pharmacopoeia or National Formulary, are sold under trade names without any disclosure of constituents save to the extent necessary to meet the specific requirements of the statute. Are the provisions of the section to which we have referred, introduced by the word "also," and the one relating to the place of manufacture, the only provisions as to descriptive statements which are intended to apply to these medicinal preparations? Was it supposed that, with respect to this large class of compositions, nothing being said as to ingredients except as specifically required, there could be, within the meaning of the [Pure Food & Drug] act, no false or misleading statement in any particular? If false and misleading statements regarding such articles were put upon their labels, was it not the intent of Congress to reach them? And was it not for this very purpose that the general language of § 8 was used?

The legislative history of the section would seem to negative the contention that Congress intended to limit the provision to statements as to identity. The provision in question as to misbranding, as it stood in the original bill in the Senate (then § 9), was as follows:

> If the package containing it, or its label, shall bear any statement regarding the ingredients or the substances contained therein, which statement shall be false or misleading in any particular.

The question arose upon this language whether or not it should be taken as limited strictly to statements with respect to identity. It was insisted that the words had a broader range, and the effort was made to procure an amendment which should be so specific as to afford no basis for the conclusion that anything but false statements as to identity or constituents was intended. An amendment was then adopted in the Senate, making the provision read:

> Any statement as to the constituent ingredients, or the substances contained therein, which statements shall be false or misleading in any particular.

With this amendment the bill was passed by the Senate and went to the House. There the provision was changed by striking out the word "constituent," and inserting the word "regarding," so that it should read:

> Any statement regarding the ingredients or substances contained in such article, which statement shall be false or misleading in any particular.

Finally, it appears, that in conference the bill was amended by inserting the word "design, or device," and also the words "such article, or;" and thus the section became a part of the law in its present form—containing the words:

> Any statement, design, or device regarding such article, or the ingredients or substances contained therein, which shall be false or misleading in any particular.

It is difficult to support that, the question distinctly raised, Congress would have rejected the provision of the Senate bill, and broadened the language in the manner stated, if it had been intended to confine the prohibition to false statements as to identity. Reading the [Pure Food & Drug] act with the sole purpose of giving effect to the intent of Congress, I cannot escape the conclusion that it was designed to cover false and misleading statements of fact on the packages or labels of articles intended for curative purposes, although the statements relate to curative properties.

It is, of course, true, that when Congress used the words "false or misleading statement," it referred to a well defined category in the law, and must be taken to have intended statements of fact, and not mere expressions of opinion.

The argument is that the curative properties of articles purveyed as medicinal preparations are matters of opinion, and the contrariety of views among medical practitioners, and the conflict between the schools of medicine, are impressively described. But, granting the wide domain of opinion, and allowing the broadest range to the conflict of medical views, there still remains a field in which statements as to curative properties are downright falsehoods and in no sense expressions of judgment. This field I believe this statute covers.

The construction which the district court has placed upon this statute is that it cannot be extended to any case where the substance labeled as a cure, with a description of curative properties, is "wholly worthless" and is known by the defendant to be such. That is the charge of the indictment.

The question, then, is whether, if an article is shipped in interstate commerce, bearing on its label a representation that it is a cure for a given disease, when, on a showing of the facts, there would be a unanimous agreement that it was absolutely worthless and an out-and-out cheat, the [Pure Food & Drug] act of Congress can be said to apply to it. To my mind the answer appears clear. One or two hypothetical illustrations have been given above. Others may readily be suggested. The records of actual prosecutions, to which I am about to refer, show the operation the statute has had, and I know of no reason why this should be denied to it in the future.

Our attention has been called to the construction which was immediately placed upon the enactment by the officers charged with its enforcement in the Department of Justice and the Department of Agriculture. It is true that the statute is a recent one, and, of course, the question is one for judicial decision. But it is not amiss to note that the natural meaning or the words used in the statute, reflected in the refusal of Congress to adopt a narrower provision, was the meaning promptly attributed to it in the proceedings that were taken to enforce the law. And this appears to have been acquiesced in by the defendants in many prosecutions in which the defendants pleaded guilty. We have been referred to the records of the Department of Agriculture, showing nearly thirty cases in which either goods had been seized and no defense made, or pleas of guilty had been entered. Among these are found such cases as the following:

> No. 29. Hancock's Liquid Sulphur, falsely represented, among other things, to be "nature's greatest germicide. . . . The great cure for . . . diphtheria." Investigation begun November 22, 1907. Plea of guilty.

> No. 180. Gowan's Pneumonia Cure, falsely represented, among other things, that it "supplies an easily absorbed food for the lungs that quickly effects a permanent cure." Investigation begun November 22, 1907. Criminal information. Plea of guilty.
>
> No. 181. "Eyelin," falsely represented, among other things, that it "repairs and rejuvenates the eye and sight." Investigation begun February 13, 1908. Plea of guilty.
>
> No. 261. "Sure Thing Tonic," falsely represented, among other things, to be "sure thing tonic. . . . Restores nerve energy. Renews vital force." Investigation begun June 3, 1909. Pleaded guilty.
>
> No. 424. "Tuckahoe Lithia Water," falsely represented, among other things, to be "a sure solvent for calculi, either of the kidneys or liver, especially indicated in all diseases due to uric diathesis, such as gout, rheumatism, gravel stone, incipient diabetes, Bright's Disease, inflamed bladder, eczema, stomach, nervous, and malarial disorders." Investigation begun July 9, 1908. Plea of guilty.
>
> No. 427. "Cancerine," falsely represented, among other things, to be "a remarkably curative extract, which, if faithfully adhered to, will entirely eradicate cancerous poison from the system. . . . A specific cure for cancer in all its forms." Investigation begun about April 12, 1909. Criminal information. Plea of guilty.

I find nothing in the language of the statute which requires the conclusion that these persons who have confessed their guilt in making false and misleading statements on their labels should be privileged to conduct their interstate traffic in their so-called medicines, admittedly worthless, because Congress did not intend to reach them.

Nor does it seem to me that any serious question arises in this case as to the power of Congress. I take it to be conceded that misbranding may cover statements as to strength, quality, and purity. But so long as the statement is not as to matter of opinion, but consists of a false representation of fact—in labeling the article as a cure when it is nothing of the sort from any point of view, but wholly worthless—there would appear to be no basis for a constitutional distinction. It is none the less descriptive—and falsely descriptive—of the article. Why should not worthless stuff, purveyed under false labels as cures, be made contraband of interstate commerce, as well as lottery tickets? Lottery Case (*Champion v. Ames*) 188 U.S. 331.

I entirely agree that in any case brought under the [Pure Food & Drug] act for misbranding—by a false or misleading statement as to curative properties of an article—it would be the duty of the court to direct an acquittal when it appeared that the statement concerned a matter of opinion. Conviction would stand only where it had been shown that, apart from any question of opinion, the so-called remedy was absolutely worthless, and hence the label demonstrably false; but in such case it seems to me to be fully authorized by the statute.

Accordingly, I reach the conclusion that the court below erred in the construction that it gave the statute, and hence in quashing the indictment, and that the judgment should be reversed. . . .

### 1. The Sherley Amendment

Congress reacted to *U.S. v. Johnson* by passing the Sherley Amendment. This statute overruled *U.S. v. Johnson* by adding a new paragraph to the Pure Food & Drug Act's misbranding provisions.[2]

This additional paragraph followed the existing text "The term 'misbranded,' as used herein shall apply to all drugs . . . ," and read as follows:

> If its package or label shall bear or contain any statement design, or device regarding the curative or therapeutic effect of such article or any of the ingredients or substances contained therein, which is false and fraudulent.

Sherley Amendment, 37 Stat. 416 (1912).

## D. Drug Regulation under the FFDCA of 1938

The FFDCA repealed the 1906 statute. The new statute introduced a new statutory concept, that of "new drug." It defined a new drug as:

> (p) The term "new drug" means
>
> (1) Any drug the composition of which is such that such drug is not generally recognized, among experts qualified by scientific training and experience to evaluate the safety of drugs, as safe for use under the conditions prescribed, recommended, or suggested in the labeling thereof, except that such a drug not so recognized shall not be deemed to be a "new drug" if at any time prior to the enactment of this Act it was subject to the Food and Drugs Act of June 30, 1906, as amended, and if at such time its labeling contained the same representations concerning the conditions of its use; or
>
> (2) Any drug the composition of which is such that such drug, as a result of investigations to determine its safety for use under such conditions, has become so recognized, but which has not, otherwise than in such investigations, been used to a material extent or for a material time under such conditions.

2. Remember that U.S. Supreme Court decisions are final only on constitutional issues. (Even in that situation, they are final only absent constitutional amendment. But amendment is a difficult process that has been successful only 27 times). On statutory interpretation issues, however, Congress always has the option to "overrule" the U.S. Supreme Court by simply revising the relevant statute.

## 1. The Kefauver-Harris Amendments of 1962

FDA's formal role in evaluating the effectiveness of drugs began with the Kefauver-Harris Amendments (KHA) of 1962. Section 102 of this statute is excerpted below.

**§ 102. Effectiveness and safety of new drugs**

[**KHA § 102(a)(1)**] Section 201(p)(1) of the [FFDCA], defining the term "new drug", is amended by (A) inserting therein, immediately after the words "to evaluate the safety", the words "and effectiveness", and (B) inserting therein, immediately after the words "as safe", the words "and effective".

[**KHA § 102(a)(2)**] Section 201(p)(2) of such Act is amended by inserting therein, immediately after the word "safety", the words "and effectiveness".

[**KHA § 102(b)**] Section 505(b) of such Act (21 U.S.C. 355(b)) is amended by inserting therein, immediately after the words "is safe for use", the words "and whether such drug is effective in use".

[**KHA § 102(c)**] Section 505(d) of such Act (21 U.S.C. 355(d)) is amended to read as follows:

(d) If the Secretary finds, after due notice to the applicant in accordance with subsection (c) and giving him an opportunity for hearing, in accordance with said subsection, that

(1) the investigations, reports of which are required to be submitted to the Secretary pursuant to subsection (b), do not include adequate tests by all methods reasonably applicable to show whether or not such drug is safe for use under the conditions prescribed, recommended, or suggested in the proposed labeling thereof;

(2) the results of such tests show that such drug is unsafe for use under such conditions or do not show that such drug is safe for use under such conditions;

(3) the methods used in, and the facilities and controls used for, the manufacture, processing, and packing of such drug are inadequate to preserve its identity, strength, quality, and purity;

(4) upon the basis of the information submitted to him as part of the application, or upon the basis of any other information before him with respect to such drug, he has insufficient information to determine whether such drug is safe for use under such conditions; or

(5) evaluated on the basis of the information submitted to him as part of the application and any other information before him with respect to such drug, there is a lack of substantial evidence that the drug will have the effect it purports or is represented to have under the conditions of use prescribed, recommended, or suggested in the proposed labeling thereof; or

> (6) based on a fair evaluation of all material facts, such labeling is false or misleading in any particular; he shall issue an order refusing to approve the application.
>
> If, after such notice and opportunity for hearing, the Secretary finds that clauses (1) through (6) do not apply, he shall issue an order approving the application.
>
> As used in this subsection and subsection (e), the term 'substantial evidence' means evidence consisting of adequate and well-controlled investigations, including clinical investigations, by experts qualified by scientific training and experience to evaluate the effectiveness of the drug involved, on the basis of which it could fairly and responsibly be concluded by such experts that the drug will have the effect it purports or is represented to have under the conditions of use prescribed, recommended, or suggested in the labeling or proposed labeling thereof.

This statutory text, however, was only the beginning of efficacy regulation. It was a necessary first step, but it left many decisions about the manner and timeline of its implementation to FDA.

## 2. FDA Implementation of the Kefauver-Harris Amendments

Between 1938 and 1962, many drugs were approved by FDA as "safe" without any formal review for effectiveness. To implement the efficacy requirement of the Kefauver-Harris Amendments, FDA needed to go back through each of these drugs and determine whether each met the new statutory "effectiveness" standard. The Federal Register notice immediately below announces FDA's decision to outsource the initial stages of efficacy review to the National Research Council of the National Academy of Sciences.

### 1966-07-09 FDA Notice, Reports of Information for Drug Effectiveness

31 Fed. Reg. 9426

NEW DRUGS

**Reports of Information for Drug—Effectiveness**

The National Academy of Sciences-National Research Council (NAS-NRC) has agreed to assist the Food and Drug administration in its review of the claims of effectiveness for new drugs cleared through the new-drug procedures from 1938 until October 10, 1962. To facilitate this review and a determination of whether there may be ground for invoking section 505(e) of the [FFDCA], and to provide each holder of such an approved new drug application an opportunity to present for consideration of the reviewing experts the best available data to support the medical claims, this order is entered pursuant to section 505 of the [FFDCA]:

Each holder of a new drug application approved between 1938 and October 10, 1962 shall report the following. . . .

a. New Drug application number, date originally approved, and whether Rx or OTC drug.

b. Brand name of drug or preparation.

c. Applicant's (firm's) name and address.

d. Quantitative formulas using established (nonproprietary) name or active ingredients

e. Dosage form and route of administration. . . .

f. Current labels and package inserts. . . .

g. List of literature references most pertinent to an evaluation of the effectiveness of the drug for the purposes for which it is offered on the label, package insert, or brochure.

h. unpublished articles or other data pertinent to an evaluation of the claims. . . .

---

One of the major decisions FDA had to make in implementing the Kefauver-Harris Amendments was how to define the statutory term "adequate and well-controlled investigations." An excerpt from the preamble to FDA's final rule on this topic is below.

## 1970-05-08 FDA Final Rule, Hearing Regulations and Regulations Describing Scientific Content of Adequate and Well-Controlled Clinical Investigations

35 Fed. Reg. 7250

On February 17, 1970, there was published in the Federal Register . . . a notice of proposed rulemaking to amend §§ 130.12, § 130.14, and 146.1 by describing the scientific content of adequate and well-controlled clinical investigations, by setting forth the procedural requirements for requesting public hearings and demonstrating that there is a genuine and substantial issue of fact that requires a hearing, and stating the Department's rules for summary disposition of requests for hearings which fail to demonstrate that there are genuine and substantial issues of fact.

. . . .

Comments were received from the Proprietary Association, the Pharmaceutical Manufacturer's Association, 15 drug firms, and a professor of pharmacology and internal medicine. . . .

The Commissioner has evaluated all of the comments. The conclusions are:

1. The scientific principles set forth in the regulations, as amended by this order, constitute the essentials of an adequate and well-controlled clinical investigation. Provisions is made in the regulations as amended for any

person to seek exemption from some or all of the criteria by an appropriate showing that, in the case of the particular drug involved, such criteria are not reasonably applicable, what alternative procedures are proposed or have been employed, and with what results, and that there is a reasonable medical basis for concluding that the alternative procedures can and should be accepted as an adequate and well-controlled clinical investigation for that drug. This provides the necessary flexibility in the regulatory scheme. TO make the criteria guidelines only would strip them of any meaningful effect and would be contrary to the legal obligation that all claims of effectiveness for drugs marketed through the new procedures must be supported by "substantial evidence," derived from adequate and well-controlled clinical investigations.

2. Congress has provided that drugs introduced before 1962 shall meet the same standards of proof of effectiveness by substantial evidence as are applicable to newly developed drugs. A different and lesser standard of effectiveness is impermissible legally and would not serve the interest of patient care. Clinical experience with these drugs can and should be considered in evaluating claims of effectiveness, but experience derived from isolated case reports, from random observations, or from clinical reports without details which permit scientific evaluation, or reports of clinical experience derived under circumstances that fall below the standards of appropriate clinical trials are of little or no value. Well documented clinical experience in an uncontrolled or partially controlled situation may be of value in contributing information as to the drug's safety, side effects, contraindication, warnings, and precautionary needs. It can as well be considered as corroborative evidence, along with data derived from adequate and well-controlled clinical investigations, to support claims of effectiveness. But it cannot alone rise to the level of adequate and well-controlled clinical investigations, even when done by an experienced investigator or reported by a number of investigators who have conducted inadequately controlled clinical trials. It is not the agency's intention to require new trials of drugs in accordance with the criteria for claims evaluated by the NAS-NRC as effective, except when the Agency does not concur in the evaluation or when the Agency has reason to draw into question any such claims at a later date based upon new information or a new evaluation.

3. Agency policy provides a period of time after publication of any NAS-NRC evaluation of a drug as "possibly effective" or "probably effective", 6 months in the first case and 12 months in the latter, for development of appropriate proof of effectiveness through clinical investigation which meet the required elements of adequate and well-controlled investigations. When a drug has been evaluated as "ineffective", or "ineffective as a fixed combination", the time frame for action is shorter, 30 days for voluntary corrective action. . . .

4. New testing of drugs for any claim evaluated otherwise than "effective" is necessary in the interest of patient care, as well as to satisfy the requirements of law. If drugs with unsupported claims of effectiveness are to continue in the marketplace, the necessary resources for an appropriate clinical trial must be devoted to the task of producing acceptable clinical data.

5. The regulations have been sustained in *Upjohn v. Finch*, against contentions that they are contrary to law and the Constitution. They are neither. They are an adaption of the summary judgment procedures of the U.S. District Courts; similar procedures are followed by a number of agencies called upon to cope with a very large docket of cases. These regulations are essential to the orderly and timely implementation of the NAS-NRC Drug Efficacy Review; without them the project could not be carried out within the reasonable future. Administrative practices have allowed all drug sponsors to present the best available evidence in support of claims of effectiveness for NAS-NRC review, they allow the sponsor to react to any NAS-NRC evaluation with appropriate medical data before a notice of proposed withdrawal of approval is issued, and they allow the person served with a notice of proposed withdrawal to respond with medical documentation and analysis which establishes that there is a genuine and substantial issue of fact which requires a hearing for its resolution. When all of these steps fail to show a reasonable likelihood that the person requesting a hearing can produce the kind and quality of evidence required by law, i.e., "substantial evidence" derived from adequate and well-controlled clinical investigations, there is no basis for a hearing and delays in implementing the scientific findings of lack of substantial evidence cannot be justified.

6. The Commissioner also has considered the issues discussed in Judge Latchum's opinion. As indicated above, there is no intention to require retesting of drug claims evaluated as effective after NAS-NRC review, except as they may be called into question by future events. The fact that the supply of investigators may be short for at least some drugs cannot justify the continued promotion of these drugs with unsupported claims of effectiveness. The time extensions that the Agency is following are designed to allow as much time as reasonably can be allowed for obtaining support for claims evaluated as "possibly effective" or "probably effective." While it is true that all of the reports of the NAS-NRC evaluations have not been released, the Agency has taken steps to speed the process. There are, nonetheless, many instances where the companies involved know or should know that their claims of effectiveness will be called into question. In these instances, there is no need for any company to wait for the NAS-NRC announcement before developing clinical trials to yield appropriate medical data. The program adopted to related the NAS-NRC evaluations to the needs for future testing has been carefully developed to focus on the claims judged by NAS-NRC and FDA as "possibly" or "probably effective". This, the Commissioner's

judgment, is where future testing of pre-1962 drugs belongs. Ineffective and "ineffective in a fixed combination" claims should be eliminated at the earliest possible times.

....

## 3. Current Text of Some Key Regulations from Kefauver-Harris Implementation

Please read (or review) the following excerpts in the statutory supplement.

From 21 C.F.R. Part 310. New drugs:

- § 310.6. Applicability of "new drug" or safety or effectiveness findings in drug efficacy study implementation notices and notices of opportunity for hearing to identical, related, and similar drug products.
- § 310.100. New drug status opinions; statement of policy.

From 21 C.F.R. Part 314. Applications for FDA approval to market a new drug:

- § 314.126 Adequate and well-controlled studies.

The assigned portions of the two CFR provisions, 21 C.F.R. Parts 310 and 314, are short excerpts from very long regulations. Section 310.6 is the current text of the regulation providing that actions relating to withdrawal of a particular NDA—under the post-Kefauver-Harris efficacy review—also applied to various products "identical to, related to, or similar to" products based on that NDA. Section 310.100 is the current text of the regulation that revoked all of the informal opinions FDA had given, between 1938 and 1962, that a particular article was "not a new drug" or "no longer a new drug." Section 314.126 is the current text of FDA's regulation defining "adequate and well-controlled studies." Earlier versions of these regulations were some of the many subjects addressed in the Federal Register notices, above, and the cases of the 1973 Quartet, below. (Note that the section numbers for these regulations have changed from those referenced in the federal register excerpts, above, and the case excerpts, below).

## 4. Judicial Review of FDA's Kefauver-Harris Implementation

### *a. The 1973 Quartet*

On June 18, 1973, the U.S. Supreme Court issued decisions in four cases challenging FDA's implementation of the Kefauver-Harris Amendments of 1962. This series of decisions has come to be known as the "1973 Quartet." It is these decisions that approved the basic method of drug efficacy regulation FDA still employs today.

The four cases are listed in the order in which they appeared in U.S. Reports. The first case, *Weinberger v. Hynson, Westcott & Dunning, Inc.*, 412 U.S. 609 (1973), involved the drug Lutrexin. The second case, *CIBA Corp. v. Weinberger*, 412 U.S. 640

(1973) involved Ritonic Capsules. The third case, *Weinberger v. Bentax Pharmaceuticals*, 412 U.S. 645 (1973), involved pentylenetetrazol. The fourth case, *USV Pharmaceutical Corp. v. Weinberger*, 412 U.S. 655 (1973), involved citrus bioflavonoid. It is not necessary to be familiar with these substances, but they are listed here to make it easier for you to keep the cases straight. In each case, one or more companies producing the drug failed to provide evidence of efficacy sufficient to satisfy FDA. Two of these four cases—*Hynson* and *Bentax*—are excerpted below.

## Weinberger v. Hynson, Westcott & Dunning, Inc.

412 U.S. 609 (1973)

**Mr. Justice DOUGLAS delivered the opinion of the Court.**

These cases, together with [the other three cases in the 1973 Quartet], all here on certiorari, raise a series of questions under the 1962 amendments to the [FFDCA]. The 1938 Act, which established a system of premarketing clearance for drugs, prohibited the introduction into commerce of any 'new drug' unless a new drug application (NDA) filed with the Food and Drug Administration (FDA) was effective with respect to that drug. § 505(a). Under the 1938 Act a 'new drug' was one not generally recognized by qualified experts as safe for its intended use. § 201(p)(1). The Government could sue to enjoin violations, prosecute criminally, and seize and condemn the articles. §§ 301(d), 302(a), 303, 304. The Act established procedures for filing NDA's, § 505(b), and provided standards under which, after notice and hearing, FDA could refuse to allow an NDA to become effective, § 505(c) and (d), or could suspend an NDA in effect on the basis of new evidence that the drug was unsafe. § 505(e). Orders denying or suspending an NDA could be reviewed in a district court on the administrative record. § 505(h).

The 1962 Act amended § 201(p)(1) of the 1938 Act to define a 'new drug' as a drug not generally recognized among experts as effective as well as safe for its intended use. [FFDCA § 201](p)(1). A new drug, as now defined, still may not be marketed unless an NDA is in effect. FDA is now directed to refuse approval of an NDA and to withdraw any prior approval if 'substantial evidence' that the drug is effective for its intended use is lacking. [FFDCA § 505] (d) and (e). Thus, the basic clearance system, requiring FDA approval of an NDA before a 'new drug' may be lawfully marketed, was continued, except that FDA now either must approve or disapprove an application within 180 days. [FFDCA § 505](c). (Under the 1938 Act an application automatically became effective if it was not disapproved.) Judicial review was transferred to the courts of appeals. [FFDCA § 505](h).

Since the [FFDCA] as amended requires affirmative agency approval, all NDA's 'effective' prior to 1962 were deemed 'approved' under the new definition, and manufacturers were given two years to develop substantial evidence of effectiveness, during which previously approved NDA's could not be withdrawn by FDA for a drug's lack of effectiveness. The 1962 amendments also contain a 'grandfather' clause exempting from the effectiveness requirements any drug which on the day preceding enactment (1) was commercially used or sold in the United States, (2) was not a 'new drug' as defined in the 1938 Act (it being generally recognized as safe), and (3) 'was not covered by an effective application' for a new drug under the 1938 Act.

Between 1938 and 1962 FDA had permitted 9,457 NDA's to become effective. Of these, some 4,000 were still on the market. In addition, there were thousands of drugs which manufacturers had marketed without applying to FDA for clearance. These drugs, known as 'me-toos,' are similar to or identical with drugs with effective NDA's and are marketed in reliance on the 'pioneer' drug application approved by FDA. In some cases, a manufacturer obtained an advisory opinion letter from FDA that its product was generally recognized among experts as safe.

To aid in its task of fulfilling the statutory mandate to review all marketed drugs for their therapeutic efficacy, whether or not previously approved, FDA retained the National Academy of Sciences-National Research Council (NAS-NRC) to create expert panels to review by class the efficacy of each approved drug. Holders of NDA's were invited to furnish the panels with the best available data to establish the effectiveness of their drugs. The panels reported to FDA; and on January 23, 1968, FDA announced its policy of applying the NAS-NRC efficacy findings to all drugs, including the related 'me-too' drugs.[7]

Respondent . . . Hynson, Westcott & Dunning, Inc., had filed an application under the 1938 Act for a drug called Lutrexin, recommended by Hynson for use in the treatment of premature labor, threatened and habitual abortion, and dysmenorrhea. FDA informed Hynson that Hynson's studies submitted with the application were not sufficiently well controlled to justify the claims of effectiveness and urged Hynson not to represent the drug as useful for threatened and habitual abortion. But FDA allowed the application to become effective, since the 1938 Act permitted evaluation of a new drug solely on the grounds of its safety. Before the 1962 amendments Hynson filed an application for a related drug which FDA, again on the basis of the test of safety, allowed to become effective. When the 1962 amendments became effective and NAS-NRC undertook to appraise the efficacy of drugs theretofore approved as safe, Hynson submitted a list of literature references, a copy of an unpublished study, and a representative sample testimonial letter on behalf of Lutrexin. The panel of NAS-NRC working in the relevant field reported to FDA that Hynson's claims for effectiveness of the drug were either inappropriate or unwarranted in the absence of submission of further appropriate documentation. At the invitation of the Commissioner of Food and Drugs, Hynson submitted additional data. But the Commissioner concluded that this additional information was inadequate and published notice of his intention to withdraw approval of the NDA's covering the drug, offering Hynson the opportunity for a prewithdrawal hearing.

---

7. FDA has recently adopted a regulation declaring the manner in which Drug Efficacy Study Implementation Notices and Notices of Opportunity for Hearing apply to identical, related, and similar drugs. Any person with an interest in such drugs is provided an opportunity for hearing on any proposed withdrawal of NDA approval for the basic or pioneer drug.

Before the hearing could take place, Hynson brought suit in the District Court for a declaratory judgment that the drugs in question were exempt from the efficacy review provisions of the 1962 amendments or, alternatively, that there was no lack of substantial evidence of the drug's efficacy. The Government's motion to dismiss was granted, the District Court ruling that FDA had primary jurisdiction and that Hynson had failed to exhaust its administrative remedies.

While the District Court litigation was pending, FDA promulgated new regulations establishing minimal standards for 'adequate and well-controlled investigations' and limiting the right to a hearing to those applicants who could proffer at least some evidence meeting those standards. Although Hynson maintained that it was not subject to the new regulations because its initial request for a hearing predated their issuance, it renewed its request and submitted the material which it claimed constituted 'substantial evidence' of Lutrexin's effectiveness. The Commissioner denied the request for a hearing and withdrew the NDA for Lutrexin. He ruled that Lutrexin is not exempt from the 1962 amendments and that Hynson had not submitted adequate evidence that Lutrexin is not a new drug or is effective. The Court of Appeals reversed, holding that while the drug in question was not exempt, Hynson was entitled to a hearing on the substantial-evidence question.

Section 505(e) directs FDA to withdraw approval of an NDA if the manufacturer fails to carry the burden of showing there is 'substantial evidence' respecting the efficacy of the drug. As the Court of Appeals says, 'substantial evidence' was substituted for 'preponderance' of the evidence. The Act and the Regulations, in their reduction of that standard to detailed guidelines, make FDA's so-called administrative summary judgment procedure appropriate.

The general contours of 'substantial evidence' are defined by § 505(d) of the [FFDCA] to include 'evidence consisting of adequate and well-controlled investigations, including clinical investigations, by experts qualified by scientific training and experience to evaluate the effectiveness of the drug involved, on the basis of which it could fairly and responsibly be concluded by such experts that the drug will have the effect it purports or is represented to have under the conditions of use prescribed, recommended, or suggested in the labeling or proposed labeling thereof.' [FFDCA 505](d). Acting pursuant to his 'authority to promulgate regulations for the efficient enforcement' of the [FFDCA], § 701(a), the Commissioner has detailed the 'principles . . . recognized by the scientific community as the essentials of adequate and well-controlled clinical investigations. They provide the basis for the determination whether there is 'substantial evidence' to support the claims of effectiveness for 'new drugs' . . . .' 21 CFR § 130.12(a)(5)(ii). They include a 'plan or protocol' setting forth the objective of the study and an adequate method for selecting appropriate subjects, explaining the methods of observation and steps taken to minimize bias, providing a comparison by one of four 'recognized' methods of the results of treatment or diagnosis with a control, and summarizing the methods of analysis, including any appropriate statistical methods. No investigation will be considered 'adequate for approval of a new drug' unless the test drug is 'standardized as to identity, strength, quality, purity, and dosage form to give significance to the results of the investigation.' Id., § 130.12(a)(5)(ii)(b). Finally, the regulation provides that '(u)ncontrolled studies or partially controlled studies are not acceptable as the sole basis for the approval of claims of effectiveness. Such studies, carefully conducted and documented, may provide corroborative support.... Isolated case reports, random experience, and reports lacking the details which permit scientific evaluation will not be considered.' Id., § 130.12(a)(5)(ii)(c).

Lower courts have upheld the validity of these regulations, and it is not disputed here that they express well-established principles of scientific investigation. Moreover, their strict and demanding standards, barring anecdotal evidence indicating that doctors 'believe' in the efficacy of a drug, are amply justified by the legislative history. The hearings underlying the 1962 Act show a marked concern that impressions or beliefs of physicians, no matter how fervently held, are treacherous. Congress in its definition of 'substantial evidence' in § 505(d) wrote the requirement of 'evidence consisting of adequate and well-controlled investigations.' The Senate Report makes clear that an abrupt departure was being taken from old norms for marketing drugs. There had been mounting concern over efficacy of drugs we all as their safety. The Report stated:

> '(A) claim could be rejected if it were found (a) that the investigations were not 'adequate'; (b) that they were not 'well controlled'; (c) that they had been conducted by experts not qualified to evaluate the effectiveness of the drug for which the application is made; or (d) that the conclusions drawn by such experts could not fairly and responsibly be derived from their investigations.'

To be sure, the [FFDCA] requires FDA to give 'due notice and opportunity for hearing to the applicant' before it can withdraw its approval of an NDA. § 505(e). FDA, however, by regulation, requires any applicant who desires a hearing to submit reasons 'why the application ... should not be withdrawn, together with a well-organized and full-factual analysis of the clinical and other investigational data he is prepared to prove in support of his opposition to the notice of opportunity for a hearing.... When it clearly appears from the data in the application and from the reasons and factual analysis in the request for the hearing that there is no genuine and substantial issue of fact ..., e.g., no adequate and well-controlled clinical investigations to support the claims of effectiveness,' the Commissioner may deny a hearing and enter an order withdrawing the application based solely on these data. 21 CFR § 130.14(b). What the agency has said, then, is that it will not provide a formal hearing where it is apparent at the threshold that the applicant has not tendered any evidence which on its face meets the statutory standards as particularized by the regulations.

The propriety of such a procedure was decided in *United States v. Storer Broadcasting Co.*, 351 U.S. 192, 205 and *FPC v. Texaco*, 377 U.S. 33, 39. We said in *Texaco*:

> (T)he statutory requirement for a hearing under § 7 (of the Natural Gas Act) does not preclude the Commission from particularizing statutory

> standards through the rulemaking process and barring at the threshold those who neither measure up to them nor show reasons why in the public interest the rule should be waived.

There can be no question that to prevail at a hearing an applicant must furnish evidence stemming from 'adequate and well-controlled investigations.' We cannot impute to Congress the design of requiring, nor does due process demand, a hearing when it appears conclusively from the applicant's 'pleadings' that the application cannot succeed.

The NAS-NRC panels evaluated approximately 16,500 claims made on behalf of the 4,000 drugs marketed pursuant to effective NDA's in 1962. Seventy percent of these claims were found not to be supported by substantial evidence of effectiveness, and only 434 drugs were found effective for all their claimed uses. If FDA were required automatically to hold a hearing for each product whose efficacy was questioned by the NAS-NRC study, even though many hearings would be an exercise in futility, we have no doubt that it could not fulfill its statutory mandate to remove from the market all those drugs which do not meet the effectiveness requirements of the [FFDCA].

If this were a case involving trial by jury as provided in the Seventh Amendment, there would be sharper limitations on the use of summary judgment, as our decisions reveal. *See, e.g., Adickes v. S. H. Kress & Co.*, 398 U.S. 144, 153–161 [(1970)]]. But Congress surely has great leeway in setting standards for releasing on the public, drugs which may well be miracles or, on the other hand, merely easy money-making schemes through use of fraudulent articles labeled in mysterious scientific dress. The standard of 'well-controlled investigations' particularized by the regulations is a protective measure designed to ferret out those drugs for which there is no affirmative, reliable evidence of effectiveness. The drug manufacturers have full and precise notice of the evidence they must present to sustain their NDA's, and under these circumstances we find FDA hearing regulations unexceptionable on any statutory or constitutional ground.

Our conclusion that the summary judgment procedure of FDA is valid does not end the matter, for Hynson argues that its submission to FDA satisfied its threshold burden. In reviewing an order of the Commissioner denying a hearing, a court of appeals must determine whether the Commissioner's findings accurately reflect the study in question and if they do, whether the deficiencies he finds conclusively render the study inadequate or uncontrolled in light of the pertinent regulations.' There is a contrariety of opinion within the Court concerning the adequacy of Hynson's submission. Since a majority are of the view that the submission was sufficient to warrant a hearing, we affirm the Court of Appeals on that phase of the case.

## II

No. 72-414 is a cross-petition by Hynson from the judgment of the Court of Appeals. This cross-petition raises questions concerning the 'new drug' provisions of the 1962 amendments. The Court of Appeals suggested that only a district court has authority to determine whether Lutrexin is a 'new drug.' The Government contends that the Commissioner has authority to determine new drug status in proceedings to withdraw approval of the product's NDA under § 505(e). Although Hynson agrees, some of the manufacturers, parties to other suits in this group of cases, advance the contrary view.

Prior to 1938 there was no machinery for the premarketing approval of drugs sold in commerce. Under the 1906 Act, adulterated and misbranded drugs were narrowly defined, and the [1906] Act provided only criminal sanctions and seizure by libel for condemnation. As previously noted, the 1938 Act provided for regulatory clearance of drugs prior to marketing and for administrative suspension of any clearance if required in interests of public safety. To introduce a new drug an application had to be effective with respect to that drug. The application was to become effective within a fixed period unless the agency after notice and opportunity for hearing refused to permit it to become effective, finding that it could not determine from existing evidence or had not been shown that it was safe. Any NDA could be suspended if clinical experience or new testing showed that the drug was not safe. Orders denying or suspending an NDA were reviewable on the administrative record in a district court. Marketing a new drug without an effective NDA could be enjoined or made the basis of a criminal prosecution, or the drug could be seized in libel and condemnation proceedings.

There was a steady stream of NDA's under that Act supported by voluminous data. Many new drugs claiming 'me-too' status were marketed illegally or were launched with an advisory opinion of FDA that they were recognized as safe. It is estimated that by 1969 there were five identical or similar drugs for every drug with an effective NDA. Enormous administrative problems were created. Each NDA contained about 30 volumes, a stack 10 to 12 feet high; and some contained as many as 400 volumes of data.

It is clear to us that FDA has power to determine whether particular drugs require an approved NDA in order to be sold to the public. FDA is indeed the administrative agency selected by Congress to administer the [FFDCA], and it cannot administer the [FFDCA] intelligently and rationally unless it has authority to determine what drugs are 'new drugs' under § 201(p) and whether they are exempt from the efficacy requirements of the 1962 amendments by the grandfather clause of [KHA] § 107(c)(4).

Regulatory agencies have by the requirements of particular statutes usually proceeded on a case-by-case basis, giving each person subject to regulation separate hearings. But there is not always a constitutional reason why that must be done. *United States v. Storer Broadcasting Co.*, 351 U.S. 192, is one example. We there upheld rules of the Federal Communications Commission limiting the number of broadcasting stations a single individual might own, saying that that was a proper exercise of the agency's 'rule-making authority necessary for the orderly conduct or its business.' The comprehensive, rather than the individual, treatment may indeed be necessary for quick effective relief. A generic drug—which is found to be unsafe and/or lacking in efficacy—may be manufactured by several persons or manufacturers. To require separate judicial proceedings to be brought against each, as if each were the owner of a Black Acre being condemned, would be to create delay where in the interest of public health there should be prompt action. A single administrative proceeding in which each manufacturer may be heard is constitutionally permissible measured by the requirements of procedural due process.

FDA maintains that a withdrawal of any NDA approval covers all 'me-too' drugs. For the reasons stated, that procedure is a permissible one where every manufacturer of a challenged drug has an opportunity to be heard. FDA under § 554 of the Administrative Procedure Act may issue a declaratory order governing all drugs covered by a particular NDA. That section prescribes the procedures an agency must follow 'in every case of adjudication required by statute to be determined on the record after opportunity for an agency hearing.' [APA] § 554(a). The industry maintains that [APA] § 554(e) is of no avail to FDA because in a withdrawal proceeding a common issue is whether a drug is a 'new drug.' That issue, it is argued, can be resolved only in a court proceeding where there is an adjudication 'on the record of (a) hearing.' But that assumes an individualized hearing and adjudication as is common in regulatory proceedings. Section 554(e), however, does not place administrative proceedings in that straitjacket. It provides that an agency 'in its sound discretion, may issue a declaratory order to terminate a controversy or remove uncertainty.' The termination of a controversy over a 'new drug' may often be of prime importance. This is an age of ever-expanding dockets at the administrative as well as at the judicial level. If the administrative controls over drugs are to be efficient, they must be exercised with dispatch. Only paralysis would result if case-by-case battles in the courts were the only way to protect the public against unsafe or ineffective drugs. Moreover, if every 'me-too' drug in a particular generic category had to be put to the test in court actions, great inequities might well result. It might take months to eliminate one 'me-too' drug manufactured by one company from the market. Meanwhile, competitors selling drugs in the same category would go scot-free until the tedious and laborious procedures of litigation reached them. We cannot believe that Congress engaged in such an exercise in futility when it enacted the 1962 amendments. That would in effect restore the enforcement provisions to the status they enjoyed under the rather primitive 1906 Act. We hold that FDA by reasons of § 554(e) of the Administrative Procedure Act may issue a declaratory order to terminate a controversy over a 'new drug' or to remove any uncertainty whether a particular drug is a 'new drug' within the meaning of § 201(p)(1) of the 1938 Act. *See Abbott Laboratories v. Gardner*, 387 U.S. 136 [(1967)].

It is argued, however, that the only lawful purpose of an FDA hearing is to allow it a method for determining which lawsuits it will file in the future. Yet that is only another version of the tactics of delay and procrastination which the industry offers as the way best to serve industry's needs. The public needs are, however, opposed and paramount. We do not accept the invitation to hold that FDA has no jurisdiction to determine whether a particular drug is a 'new drug' and to decide whether an NDA should be withdrawn.

Its determination that a product is a 'new drug' or a 'me-too' drug is, of course, reviewable. But its jurisdiction to determine whether it has jurisdiction is as essential to its effective operation as is a court's like power. The heart of the new procedures designed by Congress is the grant of primary jurisdiction to FDA, the expert agency it created. FDA does not have the final say, for review may be had, not in a district court (except in a limited group of cases we will discuss), but in a court of appeals. FDA does not have unbridled discretion to do what it pleases. Its procedures must satisfy the rudiments of fair play. Judicial relief is available only after administrative remedies have been exhausted.

It is argued that though FDA is empowered to decide the threshold question whether the drug is a "new drug," that power is only an incident to its power to approve or withdraw approval of NDA's. Some manufacturers, however, have no NDA's in effect and are not seeking approval of any drugs. Nevertheless, FDA may make a declaratory order that a drug is a "new drug." While that order is not reviewable in the court of appeals under [FFDCA] § 505(h), it is reviewable by the district court under the Administrative Procedure Act. By analogy an agency order declaring a commodity not exempt from regulation is normally a declaratory order that is reviewable. . . .

The question then presented is whether FDA properly exercised its jurisdiction in this instance. As indicated above, Hynson in requesting an administrative hearing also asked FDA to decide that Lutrexin is not a 'new drug' within the meaning of [FFDCA] § 201(p) as amended. In addition, it asked that Lutrexin be 'grandfathered' under § 107(c)(4) of the 1962 amendments. The Commissioner rejected both claims. Finding that Hynson had failed to present any evidence of adequate and well-controlled investigations in support of Lutrexin's effectiveness, he concluded that 'there is no data base upon which experts can fairly and responsibly conclude that the safety and effectiveness of the drugs has been proven and is so well established that the drugs can be generally recognized among such experts as safe and effective for their intended uses.' The Commissioner also held that Lutrexin is not exempt under [KHA] § 107(c)(4) because its NDA, which had become effective in 1953, had not been withdrawn prior to the enactment of the 1962 amendments and thus was 'covered by an effective application' within the meaning of [KHA] § 107(c)(4)(C). The Court of Appeals affirmed the Commissioner's ruling that Lutrexin is not exempt under [KHA] § 107(c)(4). It did not discuss his holding that Lutrexin currently is a 'new drug.' Although we agree that the Commissioner properly ruled that Lutrexin does not come within [KHA] § 107(c)(4), we conclude that the Commissioner's order with respect to Lutrexin's 'new drug' status must be vacated.

The thrust of § 201(p) is both qualitative and quantitative. The Act, however, nowhere defines what constitutes 'general recognition' among experts. Hynson contends that the 'lack of substantial evidence' is applicable only to proof of the actual effectiveness of drugs that fall within the definition of a new drug and not to the initial determination under § 201(p) whether a drug is 'generally recognized' as effective. It would rely solely on the testimony of physicians and the extant literature, evidence that has been characterized as 'anecdotal.' We agree with FDA, however, that the statutory scheme and overriding purpose of the 1962 amendments compel the conclusion that the hurdle of 'general recognition' of effectiveness requires at least 'substantial evidence' of effectiveness for approval of an NDA. In the absence of any evidence of adequate and well-controlled investigation supporting the efficacy of Lutrexin, a fortiori Lutrexin would be a 'new drug' subject to the provisions of the [FFDCA].

As noted, the 1962 amendments for the first time gave FDA power to scrutinize and evaluate drugs for effectiveness as well as safety. The Act requires the Commissioner to disapprove any application when there is a lack of 'substantial evidence' that the applicant's drug is effective. [FFDCA] § 505(d). Similarly, he may withdraw approval for any drug if he subsequently determines that there is a lack of such evidence. [FFDCA] § 505(e). Evidence may be accepted only if it consists of 'adequate and well-controlled investigations, including clinical investigations, by experts qualified by scientific training and experience to evaluate the effectiveness of the drug involved....' [FFDCA § 505](d). The legislative history of the [FFDCA] indicates that the test was to be a rigorous one. The 'substantial evidence' requirement reflects the conclusion of Congress, based upon hearings, that clinical impressions of practicing physicians and poorly controlled experiments do not constitute an adequate basis for establishing efficacy. This policy underlies the regulations defining the contours of 'substantial evidence': 'Uncontrolled studies or partially controlled studies are not acceptable as the sole basis for the approval of claims of effectiveness. Such studies, carefully conducted and documented, may provide corroborative support of well-controlled studies.... Isolated case reports, random experience, and reports lacking the details which permit scientific evaluation will not be considered.' 21 C.F.R. § 130.12(a)(5)(ii)(c).

These efficacy requirements were not designed to be prospective only. Clearly, after the initial two-year moratorium on existing drugs, FDA has the power to withdraw an application which became effective prior to the adoption of the 1962 amendments, if the applicant has not provided 'substantial evidence' of the drug's efficacy. The Act plainly contemplates that such drugs will be evaluated on the basis of adequate and well-controlled investigations. Hynson would have us hold that withdrawal proceedings can be thwarted by a showing of general recognition of effectiveness based merely on expert testimony and reports with respect to investigations and clinical observation regardless of the controls used. But, we cannot construe § 201(p) to deprive FDA of jurisdiction over a drug which, if subject to

FDA regulation, could not be marketed because it had not passed the 'substantial evidence' test. To do so 'would be to impute to Congress a purpose to paralyze with one hand what it sought to promote with the other.'

Moreover, the interpretation of § 201(p) urged by Hynson is not consistent with the statutory scheme as it operates on a purely prospective basis. Under subsection (2), a drug cannot transcend 'new drug' status until it has been used 'to a material extent or for a material time.' Yet, a drug cannot be marketed lawfully before an NDA has been approved by the Commissioner on the basis of 'substantial evidence.' As the Solicitor General argues, 'the [FFDCA] is designed so that drugs on the market, unless exempt, will have mustered the requisite scientifically reliable evidence of effectiveness long before they are in a position to drop out of active regulation by ceasing to be a "new drug."

It is well established that our task in interpreting separate provisions of a single Act is to give the [FFDCA] 'the most harmonious, comprehensive meaning possible' in light of the legislative policy and purpose. We accordingly have concluded that a drug can be 'generally recognized' by experts as effective for intended use within the meaning of the [FFDCA] only when that expert consensus is founded upon 'substantial evidence' as defined in § 505(d). We have held in No. 72-394, however, that the Commissioner was not justified in withdrawing Hynson's NDA without a prior hearing on whether Hynson had submitted 'substantial evidence' of Lutrexin's effectiveness. Consequently, any ruling as to Lutrexin's 'new drug' status is premature and must await the outcome of this hearing.

Finally, we cannot agree with Hynson that Lutrexin is exempt from the provisions of the [FFDCA] by virtue of [KHA] § 107(c)(4) of the 1962 amendments. That section provides that no drug will be treated as a 'new drug' if, on the day preceding the adoption of the amendments, the drug '(A) was commercially used or sold in the United States, (B) was not a new drug as defined by section 201(p) of the basic Act as then in force, and (C) was not covered by an effective application under section 505 of that Act. . . .' The applicability of this section turns solely on whether Lutrexin was 'covered' by an effective NDA immediately prior to the adoption of the 1962 amendments. Hynson argues that when Lutrexin became generally recognized as safe and was no longer a 'new drug,' its NDA ceased to be effective.

That argument draws no statutory support. The 1938 Act did not provide any mechanism other than the Commissioner's suspension authority under [FFDCA] § 505(e), whereby an NDA once effective could cease to be effective. Indeed, [FFDCA] § 505(e) leads to the conclusion that an NDA remains effective unless it is suspended. That section empowers FDA to withdraw approval of an NDA whenever new evidence comes to light suggesting that the drug has become unsafe, whether or not the drug was generally recognized as safe in the interim.

Moreover, Hynson's argument, as the Court of Appeals recognized, would render clause (C) superfluous. Under Hynson's reasoning, any drug that could satisfy clause (B)—i.e., any drug that had become generally recognized as safe—automatically would satisfy clause (C). This construction, therefore, offends the well-settled rule of statutory construction that all parts of a statute, if at all possible, are to be given effect. The interpretation accorded by the Commissioner and the Court of Appeals, on the other hand, does give clause (C) operative effect. It would limit the exemption to drugs, generally recognized as safe, which had not come under the blanket of an effective NDA. This interpretation accords with the legislative history which suggests that the exemption is afforded only for drugs that never had been subject to new drug regulation.

Except for the modification with respect to Lutrexin's 'new drug' status, the judgment of the Court of Appeals is affirmed.

Judgment affirmed.

**Mr. Justice POWELL, concurring in part, and concurring in the result in part.**

I concur in Part II of the Court's opinion, which disposes of the issues raised by Hynson, Westcott & Dunning, Inc., in its cross-petition (No. 72-414). As to Part I, which addresses issues raised in the petition filed by the Commissioner of FDA (No. 72-394), I concur only in the result and state briefly the limited sense in which I accept the Court's conclusion.

Insofar as the Court today sustains the holding below that Hynson's submission to FDA raised 'a genuine and substantial issue of fact' requiring a hearing on the ultimate issue of efficacy, 21 CFR § 130.14(b), I am in accord. Hynson's presentation in support of the efficacy of Lutrexin clearly justified a hearing as to whether the drug was supported by 'adequate and well-controlled investigations,' [FFDCA 505](d), even as that term is defined in the Commission's regulations. 21 CFR § 130.12(a)(5). For this reason I concur in the result reached in this case. I cannot agree on this record, however, with any implications or conclusions in the Court's opinion to the effect that the regulations—as construed and applied by the Commissioner in this case—are either compatible with the statutory scheme or constitutional under the Due Process Clause. Such questions have not been squarely presented here and, in light of the Court's conclusion that Hynson has complied with the regulations, their resolution is unnecessary to the Court's decision.

Were we required to reach these issues, there might well be serious doubt whether the Commissioner's rigorous threshold specifications as to proof of 'adequate and well-controlled investigations,' coupled with his restrictive summary judgment regulation, go beyond the statutory requirements and in effect frustrate the congressional mandate for a prewithdrawal 'opportunity for hearing.' [FFDCA 505](e). There is also a genuine issue of procedural due process where, as in this case, the Commissioner construes his regulations to deny a hearing as to the efficacy of a drug established and used by the medical profession for two decades, and where its effectiveness is supported by a significant volume of clinical data and the informed opinions of experts whose qualifications are not questioned.

These important and complex questions should await decision in future cases in which the issues are briefed fully and are necessary to the Court's decision.

## Weinberger v. Bentax Pharm.

412 U.S. 645 (1973)

**Mr. Justice DOUGLAS delivered the opinion of the Court.**

In this case Bentex and some 20 other firms that market drugs containing pentylenetetrazol filed this suit for a declaratory judgment that their drugs containing pentylenetetrazol are generally recognized as safe and effective, and thus not "new drugs" within the meaning of § 201 (p)(1) of the [FFDCA]. They also sought exemption from the new effectiveness requirements by reason of § 107(c)(4) of the 1962 amendments to the [FFDCA], known as the "grandfather" clause.

As part of the Food and Drug Administration's (FDA's) Drug Efficacy Study Implementation program, three separate National Academy of Sciences-National Research Council (NAS-NRC) panels reviewed the evidence concerning these drugs, and each concluded that the drug was "ineffective" for the indicated use. The Commissioner concluded there was a lack of substantial evidence that these drugs were effective for their intended uses and gave notice of his intention to initiate proceedings to withdraw approval of the new drug applications (NDA's). FDA had taken the position that withdrawal of approval of an NDA would operate to remove marketing approval for all drugs of similar composition, known as "me-too" drugs, whether or not they were expressly covered by an effective NDA.[3] Accordingly the notice invited the holders of the NDA's for drugs containing pentylenetetrazol, "and any interested person who might be adversely affected by their removal from the market," to submit "adequate and well-controlled studies" to establish the effectiveness of the drugs. Only one NDA holder submitted further evidence, which the Commissioner held did not satisfy the statutory standard. He thereupon gave notice of intent to issue an order withdrawing approval of the NDA's under § 505(e). . . . The Commissioner issued orders withdrawing approval of the three NDA's; no appeal was taken.

The District Court held that although it could determine whether the drugs were "new" or "grandfathered" drugs, its jurisdiction was concurrent with that of FDA and that FDA should resolve the "new drug" issue in an administrative proceeding. . . . The Court of Appeals reversed and remanded with directions that the District Court determine whether the challenged drugs may lawfully be marketed without approved NDA's. . . . In its view the 1962 Act established two forums for the regulation of drugs: an administrative one for premarketing clearances for

3. Volume 37 Fed. Reg. 23187, adding § 130.40 to 21 CFR, defines "identical, related, or similar drug" as used in this Act to include "other brands, potencies, dosage forms, salts, and esters of the same drug moiety as well as of any drug moiety related in chemical structure or known pharmacological properties." It also provides all persons with an interest in such drugs an opportunity for hearing on any proposed withdrawal of NDA approval for the basic drug. A district court order directing FDA to apply the NAS-NRC evaluation to all "me-too" drugs is reproduced in 37 Fed. Reg. 26623–26624.

"new drugs" or withdrawal of previously approved NDA's, with the right of appeal; and, second, a judicial one for enforcement of the requirement that "new drugs" be cleared as safe and effective before marketing by providing the Government with judicial remedies of seizure, injunction, and criminal prosecution available solely in the District Court.

We reverse the Court of Appeals.

FDA, as a result of an NAS-NRC study and after due notice, faced up to the problem of proposing withdrawal of drugs found to be lacking in substantial evidence of effectiveness. One method would be to have 1,000 withdrawal hearings—perhaps as many as 3,500, each one lasting probably for weeks. The cost in time and budget would be enormous. Accordingly, FDA issued regulations, already discussed in *Weinberger v. Hynson, Westcott & Dunning, Inc.*, 412 U.S. 609 (1973), defining the "scientific principles which characterize an adequate and well-controlled clinical investigation," which elaborates on the statutory "substantial evidence" test. And, as we held in *Hynson*, no basis for a hearing under these regulations would be laid unless a party seeking a hearing proffered at least some evidence of that nature and quality.

By May 1972, 102 final orders effecting withdrawal of approval for 452 NDA's had been issued; and they resulted in the removal from the market of an additional 1,473 "me-too" drugs. FDA was still troubled because under the 1962 Act no census of the marketplace was authorized. That is why Congress enacted the Drug Listing Act of 1972. That Act requires manufacturers to submit to FDA a list of all drugs they market, including data showing their composition, labeling, and advertising. The Senate Report stated:

> "The effective enforcement of the drug provisions of the [FFDCA] requires the ready availability of a current inventory of all marketed drugs. The Secretary is just completing a thorough review of the effectiveness of drugs marketed pursuant to new drug applications during the period 1938–1962, as required by the Drug Amendments of 1962. Application of the results of this important review to related drugs would be frustrated if a list of all marketed drugs were not easily obtained."

FDA also realized that it is impossible to apply the 1962 amendments to over-the-counter (OTC) drugs on a case-by-case basis. There are between 100,000 and 500,000 of these products, few of which were previously approved by FDA. In May 1972 FDA adopted a procedure for determining whether particular OTC products, not covered by NDA's are safe products, not ineffective, and not misbranded. The procedure involves the establishment of independent expert panels for different categories of OTC drugs (*e.g.*, antacids, laxatives, analgesics) which would review all available data and prepare monographs prescribing drug composition, labeling, and manufacturing controls. OTC's conforming to the monograph will not be considered either misbranded or a "new drug" requiring an NDA. The regulation provides for a hearing before the expert panel, comments and rebuttal comments on the monograph, and finally a hearing before the Commissioner and judicial review.

This case . . . raises the question whether FDA has authority to decide in an administrative hearing whether a drug satisfies the new effectiveness requirements of the [FFDCA]. . . . The narrow question is whether the FDA may decide whether a drug is a "new drug" on referral from a district court.

As already noted, an order denying an NDA or withdrawing one is reviewable by the Court of Appeals, § 505(h); and we see no reason why Congress could not make one method of review the exclusive one. Certainly an order that does not deny or withdraw an NDA is reviewable under the Administrative Procedure Act, if it declares a "new drug" status. In bolstering that conclusion we should note in passing that *Abbott Laboratories v. Gardner,* 387 U.S. 136, 144 (1967), said that the provisions stated in this Act for judicial review do not manifest "a congressional purpose to eliminate judicial review of other kinds of agency action." While § 505(h) would appear to be the exclusive method of obtaining judicial review of FDA's order withdrawing an NDA covering the instant drugs, the Government apparently did not oppose the District Court's taking jurisdiction, or appeal from its action, and presents no objection to the exercise by the courts of jurisdiction in this case. It does, however, strenuously oppose the conclusions reached by the Court of Appeals.

That court, in holding that FDA has no jurisdiction to determine the "new drug" status of a drug, stated that the question of "new drug" status is never presented when an application of a manufacturer for approval is filed. . . . The FDA, as already stated, may deny an NDA where there is a lack of "substantial evidence" of the drug's effectiveness, based, as we have outlined, on clinical investigation by experts. But the "new drug" definition under § 201(p) encompasses a drug "not generally recognized, among experts qualified by scientific training and experience to evaluate the safety and effectiveness of drugs, as safe and effective for use." Whether a particular drug is a "new drug," depends in part on the expert knowledge and experience of scientists based on controlled clinical experimentation and backed by substantial support in scientific literature. One function is not peculiar to judicial expertise, the other to administrative expertise. The two types of cases overlap and strongly suggest that Congress desired that the administrative agency make both kinds of determination. Even where no such administrative determination has been made and the issue arises in a district court in enforcement proceedings, it would be commonplace for the court to await an appropriate administrative declaration before it acted. It may, of course, be true that in some cases general recognition that a drug is efficacious might be made without the kind of scientific support necessary to obtain approval of an NDA. But, as we indicate in *Hynson, supra*, at 631, the reach of scientific inquiry under both § 505(d) and § 201(p) is precisely the same.

We think that it is implicit in the regulatory scheme, not spelled out *in haec verba*, that FDA has jurisdiction to decide with administrative finality, subject to the types of judicial review provided, the "new drug" status of individual drugs or classes of drugs. The deluge of litigation that would follow if "me-too" drugs and OTC drugs had to receive *de novo* hearings in the courts would inure to the interests of manufacturers and merchants in drugs, but not to the interests of the public that Congress was anxious to protect by the 1962 amendments, as well as OTC drugs and drugs covered by the 1972 Act. We are told that FDA is incapable of handling a caseload of more than perhaps 10 or 15 *de novo* judicial proceedings in a year. Clearly, if FDA were required to litigate, on a case-by-case basis, the "new drug" status of each drug now marketed, the regulatory scheme of the [FFDCA] would be severely undermined, if not totally destroyed. Moreover, a case-by-case approach is inherently unfair because it requires compliance by one manufacturer while his competitors marketing similar drugs remain free to violate the [FFDCA]. . . .

We conclude that the District Court's referral of the "new drug" and the "grandfather" issues to FDA was appropriate, as these are the kinds of issues peculiarly suited to initial determination by the FDA. As the District Court said: "Evaluation of conflicting reports as to the reputation of drugs among experts in the field is not a matter well left to a court without chemical or medical background." The determination whether a drug is generally recognized as safe and effective within the meaning of § 201(p)(1) necessarily implicates complex chemical and pharmacological considerations. Threshold questions within the peculiar expertise of an administrative agency are appropriately routed to the agency, while the court stays its hand. As we stated in *Far Eastern Conference v. United States,* 342 U.S. 570 (1952):

> "In cases raising issues of fact not within the conventional experience of judges or cases requiring the exercise of administrative discretion, agencies created by Congress for regulating the subject matter should not be passed over. This is so even though the facts after they have been appraised by specialized competence serve as a premise for legal consequences to be judicially defined. Uniformity and consistency in the regulation of business entrusted to a particular agency are secured, and the limited functions of review by the judiciary are more rationally exercised, by preliminary resort for ascertaining and interpreting the circumstances underlying legal issues to agencies that are better equipped than courts by specialization, by insight gained through experience, and by more flexible procedure."

*Reversed.*

### *b. "Me-Too" Drugs, the Hatch-Waxman Act, and the Generic Drug Industry*

The next three cases introduce what used to be known as the me-too drug industry and is today known as the generic drug industry. The watershed event in the development of the present-day generic drug industry was the passage of the Hatch-Waxman Act of 1984.

The first two cases below, *Hoffman LaRoche v. Weinberger* (D.D.C. 1975) and *United States v. Generix* (1982), address issues that arose prior the passage of the Hatch-Waxman Act. The third case, *FTC v. Actavis* (2013), presents the basic structure of generic drug regulation today.

## Hoffman-LaRoche, Inc. v. Weinberger

425 F. Supp. 890 (D.D.C. 1975)

**June L. GREEN, District Judge.**

Plaintiff, Hoffmann-LaRoche Inc., has brought suit for declaratory and injunctive relief. It seeks a declaration that the Food and Drug Administration (the FDA) has acted contrary to the statutory requirements of the Food, Drug and Cosmetic Act, and the rulemaking provisions of the Administrative Procedure Act. Specifically, Hoffmann-LaRoche challenges the FDA's policy of permitting the introduction of a new drug in interstate commerce without first approving a new drug application for such drug as required by [FFDCA §§ 301 and 505]....

Plaintiff... is the holder of three approved new drug applications for compounds which contain chlordiazepoxide... [and] markets these drugs under the trademark "Librium"....

On January 20, 1975, plaintiff filed suit in the United States District Court for the District of New Jersey against Zenith Laboratories, Inc. and its subsidiary, Paramount Supply Corp., alleging infringement of plaintiff's patent on chlordiazepoxide. During the course of pretrial discovery in that case, plaintiff learned from officials of the defendant companies that they had begun to ship chlordiazepoxide capsules in interstate commerce. In March 1973, Zenith filed an abbreviated new drug application with the FDA on chlordiazepoxide. On February 27, 1975, plaintiff filed this action in district court. The FDA approved the new drug application submitted by Zenith Laboratories on March 7, 1975.

This action brings before the courts again the troubled administration of the New Drug Amendments of 1962 designed to strengthen the FDA's regulation of new drugs.[2] The Federal Food, Drug and Cosmetic Act of 1938 provided that new drugs introduced after 1938 be subject to regulatory clearance prior to their being sold in interstate commerce... Under the 1938 Act, a new drug was defined as any drug which was not generally recognized by experts as safe. The 1962 New Drug Amendments extended the definition of "new drug" to require that proof of effectiveness, as well as safety... The term "new drug" is defined in [FFDCA § 201(p)] as follows:

> "(1) Any drug... which... is not generally recognized, among experts qualified by scientific training and experience to evaluate the safety and effectiveness of drugs, as safe and effective for use under the conditions prescribed, recommended, or suggested in the labeling thereof... or
>
> (2) Any drug... the composition of which is such that such drug, as a result of investigations to determine its safety and effectiveness for use under such conditions, has become so recognized, but which has not, otherwise than

2. The history of the problems in the early years of implementing these amendments is chronicled in American Public Health Assoc. v. Veneman, 349 F. Supp. 1311 (D.D.C. 1972) and Pharmaceutical Manufacturers Assoc. v. Finch, 307 F. Supp. 858 (D. Del. 1970).

> in such investigations, been used to a material extent or for a material time under such conditions."

The 1962 New Drug Amendments changed the pre-marketing clearance procedures . . . to require the FDA to affirmatively express its approval of new drug applications prior to permitting the marketing of new drugs in interstate commerce.

[FFDCA § 505] prohibits the introduction or delivery for introduction into interstate commerce of any new drug unless approval of an application is effective with respect to such drug. It further provides a scheme for the processing and approval of new drug applications. The required contents of a new drug application are specified. The FDA is required to approve the application within 180 days or give the applicant notice of an opportunity for hearing. After giving notice and opportunity for hearing, the FDA is required to either issue an order refusing to approve the application or issue an order approving the application. [FFDCA § 505(d)]. . . .

The crux of this controversy is the use by the FDA of the new drug application procedure as a sort of administrative holding action to regulate the sale and manufacture of "me-too" drugs. Me-too drugs are drugs which are chemically equivalent to a pioneer drug for which a full new drug application is in effect. It is estimated that five to thirteen me-too drugs exist for every new drug that has a FDA approved new drug application. It is the present policy of the FDA, termed an interim policy, to require the filing of an abbreviated new drug application by the manufacturers of each me-too drug where the pioneer drug has a full new drug application approved pursuant to [FFDCA § 505]. The FDA's position is that marketing of these drugs may be permitted without the approval of each individual new drug application.

The FDA advances two principal arguments to justify its policy. First, it claims that its compliance resources are limited and must be concentrated primarily in those areas where a potential health problem exists. Thus, the FDA has directed its compliance activities toward those drug products which have been found ineffective rather than toward those which have been found effective. Second, for those drugs that the NAS/NRC have found effective and are widely recognized as safe and effective and no bioavailability [5] or special manufacturing problem is known or suspected, the need to police their distribution is minimal. Additionally, the FDA claims that it would have a difficult time in court contending that a specific version is a new drug within the meaning of [FFDCA § 201(p)].

On the contrary, Hoffmann-LaRoche argues that the FDA's action is another example of its failure to follow the 1962 New Drug Amendments. Like the situation condemned in *American Public Health Assoc. v. Veneman,* the FDA is again acting contrary to the clear statutory directives of § 505. Plaintiff contends that the plain meaning of section 355 dictates that once the FDA requires a new drug application to be filed, then the approval process must be completed before such drug can be

5. "Bioavailability" means the rate or extent to which the active ingredient in a drug becomes available to the site of drug action in the human body. See 40 Fed. Reg. 26161 (1975).

marketed. It argues that the Congressionally expressed interest in public health and safety mandates no other choice....

To understand how the present state of affairs has arisen, it is necessary to chronicle some of the administrative actions taken in the implementation of the 1962 amendments with respect to me-too drugs. On January 24, 1968, at a government industry conference, the FDA announced that it would apply the applicable effectiveness findings from the National Academy of Sciences-Natural Research Council studies to all drugs, identical, related, or similar drug products. All opinions previously given to the effect that a drug was no longer a new drug were revoked in regulations published on May 18, 1968. That same day a proposed procedure to determine by rule making those drugs for which a full or abbreviated new drug application would no longer be required was published.... Thus in 1968, virtually all human prescription drugs were regarded as new drugs. Regulations governing the filing and content of abbreviated new drug applications were adopted in February 1969. They provide that an abbreviated new drug application need not contain safety and effectiveness data, except for those drugs for which a drug efficacy study implementation notice, previously published in the Federal Register, requires submission of clinical data adequate to assure the bioavailability of each drug product.

On July 14, 1970, the FDA issued a general notice establishing uniform conditions for the marketing of drugs covered by a drug efficacy study implementation notice. This notice is of central importance to the FDA's view of this litigation. Essentially, it provides that any person who does not hold an approved new drug application and who distributes or intends to distribute a drug covered by a drug efficacy study implementation notice must submit a full or abbreviated new drug application. The notice does not explicitly state that a me-too drug could be marketed prior to approval of an abbreviated or full new drug application. It was implicit, the FDA argues, that such marketing would be permitted. To hold otherwise would be to give an unfair competitive advantage to manufacturers of identical, related or similar drug products marketed prior to a drug efficacy notice by allowing them to remain on the market pending approval of an abbreviated new drug application. Competitors' products would be kept off the market until approval was granted. Of particular importance to this case, by Federal Register notice on July 11, 1972, the FDA declared all compounds containing chlordiazepoxide subject to new drug application requirements. Abbreviated new drug applications were required to be submitted.

On June 18, 1973, the Supreme Court decided four cases interpreting the 1962 amendments. [The court cites the four cases of 1973 Quartet]. These cases sustained the FDA's application of all drug efficacy study implementation notices to me-too drug products and upheld the agency's primary jurisdiction to determine the status of drugs under the [FFDCA].

Preliminarily, the FDA suggests that Count One of plaintiff's complaint is moot because the FDA approved the new drug application of Zenith Labs on March 7, 1975, during the pendency of this litigation. Count One challenges the FDA's policy as violative of [FFDCA § 505]. This general policy continues in operation with respect to whole generic classes of drugs. Voluntary cessation of the alleged wrongful conduct in one instance, while it continues in all other areas, has not conveniently mooted this portion of plaintiff's complaint.

Reaching the merits of plaintiff's statutory argument, the Court holds that the FDA's policy of permitting new drugs to be marketed without an approved new drug application contravenes the clear statutory requirement of preclearance mandated by [FFDCA § 505]. The FDA's choice of policy is not within the intendment of the 1962 New Drug Amendments and the legislative scheme they embody. *American Public Health Assoc. v. Veneman*, 349 F. Supp. 1311 (D.D.C.1972).

Further, the action of the FDA in permitting such marketing of large classes of me-too drugs violates its own regulations. The implication that the FDA seeks to find in the language of the July 14, 1970 notice is an impermissible one. The Court recognizes that the FDA is to be given the administrative flexibility to make regulations and to determine the new drug status of individual drugs or classes of drugs. Certainly it has the power to promulgate regulations that adopt a monograph procedure for human prescription drugs similar to that adopted for over-the-counter drugs whereby a drug or drugs may be declared to be no longer new drugs. The FDA can regulate the bioequivalence and special manufacturing problems through its general rule-making power. However, the argument that the FDA lacks the administrative resources to insure compliance with [FFDCA § 505] cannot be permitted to postpone to some indefinite future date the implementation of the required preclearance approval of new drug applications. . . .

Summary judgment will therefore be entered for the plaintiff.[6] Defendants will be permanently enjoined from implementing its policy which permits the introduction into interstate commerce without an approved new drug application of prescription drugs which the FDA has previously declared to be new drugs within the meaning of [FFDCA § 201(p)].

## United States v. Generix Drug Corp.

460 U.S. 453 (1982)

**Justice STEVENS delivered the opinion of the Court.**

The question presented is whether the statutory prohibition against the marketing of a "new drug" without the prior approval of the Food and Drug Administration (FDA) requires respondent Generix Drug Corp. to have approved new drug applications (NDA's) before it may market its generic drug products. In statutory terms, we are required to determine whether the term "drug" as used in the relevant sections of the [FFDCA] refers only to the active ingredient in a drug product or to the entire product. We hold that Congress intended the word to have the broader meaning.

---

6. Whatever the anticompetitive effects and secondary patent protection judgment for plaintiff will give to manufacturers with approved new drug applications, the overriding interest in insuring the health and safety of the public through compliance with [FFDCA 505] requires the result reached here.

### I

The active ingredients in most prescription drugs constitute less than 10% of the product; inactive "excipients" (such as coatings, binders, and capsules) constitute the rest. The term "generic drug" is used to describe a product that contains the same active ingredients but not necessarily the same excipients as a so-called "pioneer drug" that is marketed under a brand name.[1] Respondent Generix is a distributor of generic drugs manufactured by other firms.

The Government initiated this action to enjoin Generix from distributing in interstate commerce a number of generic drug products that contain eight specified active ingredients. It alleged that the FDA had never approved new drug applications with respect to any of those products.[3]

.... In this case, the District Court found that the Government had established a reasonable possibility that the safety and effectiveness of six of respondent's generic drug products might be affected by differences between their excipients and those found in approved products. Accordingly, it enjoined the defendants from further distribution of products containing the designated active ingredients.

The Court of Appeals for the Fifth Circuit, now the Eleventh Circuit ... held that the statutory prohibition against the sale of a "new drug" without prior approval does not apply to a drug product having the same active ingredients as a previously approved drug product, regardless of any differences in excipients. It based that conclusion on its view that the statutory requirement of evaluating the safety and effectiveness of new drugs must normally relate to active ingredients ... [and] it believed that the legislative history suggested that Congress had not intended to create a product-by-product licensing system ...

Because the question is obviously important and because it has been decided differently in other Circuits, we granted certiorari.

### II

In resolving the narrow issue presented, the Court of Appeals misread the statutory text.

> Section 201(p) of the [FFDCA] defines a "new drug" to be "any drug ... [which] is not generally recognized ... as safe and effective ... or ... which has not, otherwise than in [safety and effectiveness] investigations,

---

1. Generic drugs, also called "copycat" or "me-too" drugs, are usually marketed at relatively low prices because their manufacturers do not incur the research, development, and promotional costs normally associated with the creation and marketing of an original product.

3. Section 505(a) of the [FFDCA], 52 Stat. 1052, as amended, 76 Stat. 784, 21 U. S. C. § 355(a), provides:

> (a) Necessity of effective approval of application
> No person shall introduce or deliver for introduction into interstate commerce any new drug, unless an approval of an application filed pursuant to subsection (b) of this section is effective with respect to such drug.

> been used to a material extent or for a material time. . . ." The Court of Appeals did not rest its decision on a finding that Generix's products are generally recognized as safe and effective; rather, its conclusion rested on the proposition that the statutory phrase "any drug" does not include a complete drug product, but only an active ingredient. That proposition is simply untenable.
>
> The original Federal Food and Drugs Act of June 30, 1906, . . . provided:
>
> That the term 'drug,' as used in this Act, shall include all medicines and preparations recognized in the United States Pharmacopoeia or National Formulary for internal or external use, and any substance or mixture of substances intended to be used for the cure, mitigation, or prevention of disease of either man or other animals.

In 1938, Congress passed the new statute, which requires that an application be submitted to the FDA before any "new drug" may be introduced into interstate commerce. The new Act's definition of the term "drug" is even broader than the old one:

> [201](g)(1) The term 'drug' means (A) articles recognized in the official United States Pharmacopoeia, official Homoeopathic Pharmacopoeia of the United States, or official National Formulary, or any supplement to any of them; and (B) articles intended for use in the diagnosis, cure, mitigation, treatment, or prevention of disease in man or other animals; and (C) articles (other than food) intended to affect the structure or any function of the body of man or other animals; and (D) articles intended for use as a component of any article specified in clauses (A), (B), or (C) of this paragraph; but does not include devices or their components, parts, or accessories.

. . . . The terms of subsections (A), (B), and (C) are plainly broad enough to include more than just active ingredients, and that they *must* do so unless subsection (D) is to be superfluous. Because the definition is disjunctive, generic drug products are quite plainly drugs within the meaning of the [FFDCA].

The natural reading of this definition is corroborated by other sections of the [FFDCA]. Section 501(a) provides that a "drug" is deemed adulterated "if [it is a drug which] bears or contains, for purposes of coloring only, a color additive which is unsafe." Section 502(e) provides that a "drug . . . fabricated from two or more ingredients" shall be deemed to be misbranded unless its label includes, "whether active or not, the established name and quantity or proportion of any bromides, ether, chloroform, [etc.]." And § 505(b) requires that an application for new drug approval contain "a full list of the articles used as components of such drug [and] a full statement of the composition of such drug." The term "drug" is plainly intended throughout the [FFDCA] to include entire drug products, complete with active and inactive ingredients.[9]

Neither the Court of Appeals nor respondents have pointed to anything in the text of the [FFDCA] that is inconsistent with our reading of its plain language....

In this case we are not required to determine what types of differences between drugs would be significant or insignificant under the statute. Respondent Generix argues only that its products are not new drugs under the theory that "drug" means "active ingredient"; it does not argue that its complete products—active ingredients and excipients together—are the same as previously approved products. The latter argument would, of course, have been unavailing on the facts before us; for the respondent has not questioned the District Court's finding of a reasonable possibility that its products are not bioequivalent to any previously approved products. We thus do not reach the issue of whether two demonstrably bioequivalent products, containing the same active ingredients but different excipients, might under some circumstances be the same "drug."

In summary, a generic drug product is a "drug" within the meaning of § 201(g)(1) of the [FFDCA]. Such a product is therefore a "new drug," subject to the requirements of § 505, until the product (and not merely its active ingredient) no longer falls within the terms of § 201(p). The judgment of the Court of Appeals is accordingly

Reversed.

---

The following is complex case involving both antitrust law and generic drug regulation. As you read, try to avoid getting too bogged down in the antitrust issues. Instead, focus on those portions of the case describing the generic drug industry as it exists today.

## FTC v. Actavis, Inc.

570 U.S. 136 (2013)

**Justice BREYER delivered the opinion of the Court.**

Company A sues Company B for patent infringement. The two companies settle under terms that require (1) Company B, the claimed infringer, not to produce the patented product until the patent's term expires, and (2) Company A, the patentee, to pay B many millions of dollars. Because the settlement requires the patentee to pay the alleged infringer, rather than the other way around, this kind of settlement agreement is often called a "reverse payment" settlement agreement. And the basic

9. At oral argument, respondents suggested that it would be nonsensical to understand the word "drug" in § 502(i) of the [FFDCA], to mean "drug product," because any generic drug is "an imitation of another drug." But § 502(i) is intended to prohibit a company from passing an imitation off as the original; if "imitation" is understood with that in mind, it becomes apparent that the word "drug" can and should mean "drug product" in § 502(i), as well.

question here is whether such an agreement can sometimes unreasonably diminish competition in violation of the antitrust laws. *See, e.g.,* 15 U.S.C. § 1 (Sherman Act prohibition of "restraint[s] of trade or commerce").

In this case, the Eleventh Circuit dismissed a Federal Trade Commission (FTC) complaint claiming that a particular reverse payment settlement agreement violated the antitrust laws. In doing so, the Circuit stated that a reverse payment settlement agreement generally is "immune from antitrust attack so long as its anticompetitive effects fall within the scope of the exclusionary potential of the patent." And since the alleged infringer's promise not to enter the patentee's market expired before the patent's term ended, the Circuit found the agreement legal and dismissed the FTC complaint. In our view, however, reverse payment settlements such as the agreement alleged in the complaint before us can sometimes violate the antitrust laws. We consequently hold that the Eleventh Circuit should have allowed the FTC's lawsuit to proceed.

## I

### A

Apparently most if not all reverse payment settlement agreements arise in the context of pharmaceutical drug regulation, and specifically in the context of suits brought under statutory provisions allowing a generic drug manufacturer (seeking speedy marketing approval) to challenge the validity of a patent owned by an already-approved brand-name drug owner. We consequently describe four key features of the relevant drug-regulatory framework established by the Drug Price Competition and Patent Term Restoration Act of 1984, as amended. That Act is commonly known as the Hatch-Waxman Act.

First, a drug manufacturer, wishing to market a new prescription drug, must submit a New Drug Application to the federal Food and Drug Administration (FDA) and undergo a long, comprehensive, and costly testing process, after which, if successful, the manufacturer will receive marketing approval from the FDA. *See* [FFDCA 505](b)(1) (requiring, among other things, "full reports of investigations" into safety and effectiveness; "a full list of the articles used as components"; and a "full description" of how the drug is manufactured, processed, and packed).

Second, once the FDA has approved a brand-name drug for marketing, a manufacturer of a generic drug can obtain similar marketing approval through use of abbreviated procedures. The Hatch-Waxman Act permits a generic manufacturer to file an Abbreviated New Drug Application specifying that the generic has the "same active ingredients as," and is "biologically equivalent" to, the already-approved brand-name drug. In this way the generic manufacturer can obtain approval while avoiding the "costly and time-consuming studies" needed to obtain approval "for a pioneer drug." The Hatch-Waxman process, by allowing the generic to piggy-back on the pioneer's approval efforts, "speed[s] the introduction of low-cost generic drugs to market," thereby furthering drug competition.

Third, the Hatch-Waxman Act sets forth special procedures for identifying, and resolving, related patent disputes. It requires the pioneer brand-name manufacturer to list in its New Drug Application the "number and the expiration date" of any relevant patent. *See* [FFDCA 505](b)(1). And it requires the generic manufacturer in its Abbreviated New Drug Application to "assure the FDA" that the generic "will not infringe" the brand-name's patents.

The generic can provide this assurance in one of several ways. It can certify that the brandname manufacturer has not listed any relevant patents. It can certify that any relevant patents have expired. It can request approval to market beginning when any still-in-force patents expire. Or, it can certify that any listed, relevant patent "is invalid or will not be infringed by the manufacture, use, or sale" of the drug described in the Abbreviated New Drug Application. *See* [FFDCA § 505](j)(2)(A)(vii)(IV). Taking this last-mentioned route (called the "paragraph IV" route), automatically counts as patent infringement, *see* 35 U.S.C. § 271(e)(2)(A) (2006 ed., Supp. V), and often "means provoking litigation." If the brand-name patentee brings an infringement suit within 45 days, the FDA then must withhold approving the generic, usually for a 30-month period, while the parties litigate patent validity (or infringement) in court. If the courts decide the matter within that period, the FDA follows that determination; if they do not, the FDA may go forward and give approval to market the generic product.

Fourth, Hatch-Waxman provides a special incentive for a generic to be the first to file an Abbreviated New Drug Application taking the paragraph IV route. That applicant will enjoy a period of 180 days of exclusivity (from the first commercial marketing of its drug). *See* [FFDCA § 505](j)(5)(B)(iv) (establishing exclusivity period). During that period of exclusivity no other generic can compete with the brand-name drug. If the first-to-file generic manufacturer can overcome any patent obstacle and bring the generic to market, this 180-day period of exclusivity can prove valuable, possibly "worth several hundred million dollars." Indeed, the Generic Pharmaceutical Association said in 2006 that the "'vast majority of potential profits for a generic drug manufacturer materialize during the 180-day exclusivity period.'" The 180-day exclusivity period, however, can belong only to the first generic to file. Should that first-to-file generic forfeit the exclusivity right in one of the ways specified by statute, no other generic can obtain it.

### B

#### 1

In 1999, Solvay Pharmaceuticals, a respondent here, filed a New Drug Application for a brand-name drug called AndroGel. The FDA approved the application in 2000. In 2003, Solvay obtained a relevant patent and disclosed that fact to the FDA, as Hatch-Waxman requires.

Later the same year another respondent, Actavis, Inc. (then known as Watson Pharmaceuticals), filed an Abbreviated New Drug Application for a generic drug modeled after AndroGel. Subsequently, Paddock Laboratories, also a respondent, separately filed an Abbreviated New Drug Application for its own generic product. Both Actavis and Paddock certified under paragraph IV that Solvay's listed patent was invalid and their drugs did not infringe it. A fourth manufacturer, Par Pharmaceutical, likewise a respondent, did not file an application of its own but joined forces with Paddock, agreeing to share the patent litigation costs in return for a share of profits if Paddock obtained approval for its generic drug.

Solvay initiated paragraph IV patent litigation against Actavis and Paddock. Thirty months later the FDA approved Actavis' first-to-file generic product, but, in 2006, the patent-litigation parties all settled. Under the terms of the settlement Actavis agreed that it would not bring its generic to market until August 31, 2015, 65 months before Solvay's patent expired (unless someone else marketed a generic sooner). Actavis also agreed to promote AndroGel to urologists. The other generic manufacturers made roughly similar promises. And Solvay agreed to pay millions of dollars to each generic—$12 million in total to Paddock; $60 million in total to Par; and an estimated $19–$30 million annually, for nine years, to Actavis. The companies described these payments as compensation for other services the generics promised to perform, but the FTC contends the other services had little value. According to the FTC the true point of the payments was to compensate the generics for agreeing not to compete against AndroGel until 2015.

2

On January 29, 2009, the FTC filed this lawsuit against all the settling parties, namely, Solvay, Actavis, Paddock, and Par. The FTC's complaint (as since amended) alleged that respondents violated §5 of the Federal Trade Commission Act, 15 U.S.C. §45, by unlawfully agreeing "to share in Solvay's monopoly profits, abandon their patent challenges, and refrain from launching their low-cost generic products to compete with AndroGel for nine years." The District Court held that these allegations did not set forth an antitrust law violation. It accordingly dismissed the FTC's complaint. The FTC appealed.

The Court of Appeals for the Eleventh Circuit affirmed the District Court. It wrote that "absent sham litigation or fraud in obtaining the patent, a reverse payment settlement is immune from antitrust attack so long as its anticompetitive effects fall within the scope of the exclusionary potential of the patent." The court recognized that "antitrust laws typically prohibit agreements where one company pays a potential competitor not to enter the market." But, the court found that "reverse payment settlements of patent litigation presen[t] atypical cases because one of the parties owns a patent." Patent holders have a "lawful right to exclude others from the market,"; thus a patent "conveys the right to cripple competition." The court recognized that, if the parties to this sort of case do not settle, a court might declare the patent invalid. But, in light of the public policy favoring settlement of disputes (among other considerations) it held that the courts could not require the parties to continue to litigate in order to avoid antitrust liability.

The FTC sought certiorari. Because different courts have reached different conclusions about the application of the antitrust laws to Hatch-Waxman-related patent settlements, we granted the FTC's petition.

## II

### A

Solvay's patent, if valid and infringed, might have permitted it to charge drug prices sufficient to recoup the reverse settlement payments it agreed to make to its potential generic competitors. And we are willing to take this fact as evidence that the agreement's "anticompetitive effects fall within the scope of the exclusionary potential of the patent." But we do not agree that that fact, or characterization, can immunize the agreement from antitrust attack.

For one thing, to refer, as the Circuit referred, simply to what the holder of a valid patent could do does not by itself answer the antitrust question. The patent here may or may not be valid, and may or may not be infringed. "[A] valid patent excludes all except its owner from the use of the protected process or product." And that exclusion may permit the patent owner to charge a higher-than-competitive price for the patented product. But an invalidated patent carries with it no such right. And even a valid patent confers no right to exclude products or processes that do not actually infringe. The paragraph IV litigation in this case put the patent's validity at issue, as well as its actual preclusive scope. The parties' settlement ended that litigation. The FTC alleges that in substance, the plaintiff agreed to pay the defendants many millions of dollars to stay out of its market, even though the defendants did not have any claim that the plaintiff was liable to them for damages. That form of settlement is unusual. And, for reasons discussed in Part II-B, *infra*, there is reason for concern that settlements taking this form tend to have significant adverse effects on competition.

Given these factors, it would be incongruous to determine antitrust legality by measuring the settlement's anticompetitive effects solely against patent law policy, rather than by measuring them against procompetitive antitrust policies as well. And indeed, contrary to the Circuit's view that the only pertinent question is whether "the settlement agreement . . . fall[s] within" the legitimate "scope" of the patent's "exclusionary potential," this Court has indicated that patent and antitrust policies are both relevant in determining the "scope of the patent monopoly"—and consequently antitrust law immunity—that is conferred by a patent.

. . . .

### B

The Eleventh Circuit's conclusion finds some degree of support in a general legal policy favoring the settlement of disputes. The Circuit's related underlying practical concern consists of its fear that antitrust scrutiny of a reverse payment agreement would require the parties to litigate the validity of the patent in order to demonstrate what would have happened to competition in the absence of the settlement.

Any such litigation will prove time consuming, complex, and expensive. The antitrust game, the Circuit may believe, would not be worth that litigation candle.

We recognize the value of settlements and the patent litigation problem. But we nonetheless conclude that this patent-related factor should not determine the result here. Rather, five sets of considerations lead us to conclude that the FTC should have been given the opportunity to prove its antitrust claim.

*First*, the specific restraint at issue has the "potential for genuine adverse effects on competition." The payment in effect amounts to a purchase by the patentee of the exclusive right to sell its product, a right it already claims but would lose if the patent litigation were to continue and the patent were held invalid or not infringed by the generic product. Suppose, for example, that the exclusive right to sell produces $50 million in supracompetitive profits per year for the patentee. And suppose further that the patent has 10 more years to run. Continued litigation, if it results in patent invalidation or a finding of noninfringement, could cost the patentee $500 million in lost revenues, a sum that then would flow in large part to consumers in the form of lower prices.

We concede that settlement on terms permitting the patent challenger to enter the market before the patent expires would also bring about competition, again to the consumer's benefit. But settlement on the terms said by the FTC to be at issue here—payment in return for staying out of the market—simply keeps prices at patentee-set levels, potentially producing the full patent-related $500 million monopoly return while dividing that return between the challenged patentee and the patent challenger. The patentee and the challenger gain; the consumer loses. Indeed, there are indications that patentees sometimes pay a generic challenger a sum even larger than what the generic would gain in profits if it won the paragraph IV litigation and entered the market. The rationale behind a payment of this size cannot in every case be supported by traditional settlement considerations. The payment may instead provide strong evidence that the patentee seeks to induce the generic challenger to abandon its claim with a share of its monopoly profits that would otherwise be lost in the competitive market.

But, one might ask, as a practical matter would the parties be able to enter into such an anticompetitive agreement? Would not a high reverse payment signal to other potential challengers that the patentee lacks confidence in its patent, thereby provoking additional challenges, perhaps too many for the patentee to "buy off?" Two special features of Hatch-Waxman mean that the answer to this question is "not necessarily so." First, under Hatch-Waxman only the first challenger gains the special advantage of 180 days of an exclusive right to sell a generic version of the brand-name product. And as noted, that right has proved valuable—indeed, it can be worth several hundred million dollars.. Subsequent challengers cannot secure that exclusivity period, and thus stand to win significantly less than the first if they bring a successful paragraph IV challenge. That is, if subsequent litigation results in invalidation of the patent, or a ruling that the patent is not infringed, that litigation victory will free not just the challenger to compete, but all other potential competitors too (once they obtain FDA approval). The potential reward available to a subsequent challenger being significantly less, the patentee's payment to the initial challenger (in return for not pressing the patent challenge) will not necessarily provoke subsequent challenges. Second, a generic that files a paragraph IV after learning that the first filer has settled will (if sued by the brand-name) have to wait out a stay period of (roughly) 30 months before the FDA may approve its application, just as the first filer did. These features together mean that a reverse payment settlement with the first filer (or, as in this case, all of the initial filers) "removes from consideration the most motivated challenger, and the one closest to introducing competition." The dissent may doubt these provisions matter, but scholars in the field tell us that "where only one party owns a patent, it is virtually unheard of outside of pharmaceuticals for that party to pay an accused infringer to settle the lawsuit." It may well be that Hatch-Waxman's unique regulatory framework, including the special advantage that the 180-day exclusivity period gives to first filers, does much to explain why in this context, but not others, the patentee's ordinary incentives to resist paying off challengers (i.e., the fear of provoking myriad other challengers) appear to be more frequently overcome.

*Second*, these anticompetitive consequences will at least sometimes prove unjustified. As the FTC admits, offsetting or redeeming virtues are sometimes present. The reverse payment, for example, may amount to no more than a rough approximation of the litigation expenses saved through the settlement. That payment may reflect compensation for other services that the generic has promised to perform—such as distributing the patented item or helping to develop a market for that item. There may be other justifications. Where a reverse payment reflects traditional settlement considerations, such as avoided litigation costs or fair value for services, there is not the same concern that a patentee is using its monopoly profits to avoid the risk of patent invalidation or a finding of noninfringement. In such cases, the parties may have provided for a reverse payment without having sought or brought about the anticompetitive consequences we mentioned above. But that possibility does not justify dismissing the FTC's complaint. An antitrust defendant may show in the antitrust proceeding that legitimate justifications are present, thereby explaining the presence of the challenged term and showing the lawfulness of that term under the rule of reason.

*Third*, where a reverse payment threatens to work unjustified anticompetitive harm, the patentee likely possesses the power to bring that harm about in practice. At least, the "size of the payment from a branded drug manufacturer to a prospective generic is itself a strong indicator of power"—namely, the power to charge prices higher than the competitive level. An important patent itself helps to assure such power. Neither is a firm without that power likely to pay "large sums" to induce "others to stay out of its market." In any event, the Commission has referred to studies showing that reverse payment agreements are associated with the presence of higher-than-competitive profits—a strong indication of market power.

*Fourth*, an antitrust action is likely to prove more feasible administratively than the Eleventh Circuit believed. The Circuit's holding does avoid the need to litigate the patent's validity (and also, any question of infringement). But to do so, it throws the baby out with the bath water, and there is no need to take that drastic step. That is because it is normally not necessary to litigate patent validity to answer the antitrust question (unless, perhaps, to determine whether the patent litigation is a sham). An unexplained large reverse payment itself would normally suggest that the patentee has serious doubts about the patent's survival. And that fact, in turn, suggests that the payment's objective is to maintain supracompetitive prices to be shared among the patentee and the challenger rather than face what might have been a competitive market—the very anticompetitive consequence that underlies the claim of antitrust unlawfulness. The owner of a particularly valuable patent might contend, of course, that even a small risk of invalidity justifies a large payment. But, be that as it may, the payment (if otherwise unexplained) likely seeks to prevent the risk of competition. And, as we have said, that consequence constitutes the relevant anticompetitive harm. In a word, the size of the unexplained reverse payment can provide a workable surrogate for a patent's weakness, all without forcing a court to conduct a detailed exploration of the validity of the patent itself.

*Fifth*, the fact that a large, unjustified reverse payment risks antitrust liability does not prevent litigating parties from settling their lawsuit. They may, as in other industries, settle in other ways, for example, by allowing the generic manufacturer to enter the patentee's market prior to the patent's expiration, without the patentee paying the challenger to stay out prior to that point. Although the parties may have reasons to prefer settlements that include reverse payments, the relevant antitrust question is: What are those reasons? If the basic reason is a desire to maintain and to share patent-generated monopoly profits, then, in the absence of some other justification, the antitrust laws are likely to forbid the arrangement.

In sum, a reverse payment, where large and unjustified, can bring with it the risk of significant anticompetitive effects; one who makes such a payment may be unable to explain and to justify it; such a firm or individual may well possess market power derived from the patent; a court, by examining the size of the payment, may well be able to assess its likely anticompetitive effects along with its potential justifications without litigating the validity of the patent; and parties may well find ways to settle patent disputes without the use of reverse payments. In our view, these considerations, taken together, outweigh the single strong consideration—the desirability of settlements—that led the Eleventh Circuit to provide near-automatic antitrust immunity to reverse payment settlements.

## III

The FTC urges us to hold that reverse payment settlement agreements are presumptively unlawful and that courts reviewing such agreements should proceed via a "quick look" approach, rather than applying a "rule of reason." We decline to do so. In *California Dental*, we held (unanimously) that abandonment of the "rule of reason" in favor of presumptive rules (or a "quick-look" approach) is appropriate only where "an observer with even a rudimentary understanding of economics could conclude that the arrangements in question would have an anticompetitive effect on customers and markets." We do not believe that reverse payment settlements, in the context we here discuss, meet this criterion.

That is because the likelihood of a reverse payment bringing about anticompetitive effects depends upon its size, its scale in relation to the payor's anticipated future litigation costs, its independence from other services for which it might represent payment, and the lack of any other convincing justification. The existence and degree of any anticompetitive consequence may also vary as among industries. These complexities lead us to conclude that the FTC must prove its case as in other rule-of reason cases.

To say this is not to require the courts to insist, contrary to what we have said, that the Commission need litigate the patent's validity, empirically demonstrate the virtues or vices of the patent system, present every possible supporting fact or refute every possible pro-defense theory. As a leading antitrust scholar has pointed out, "'[t]here is always something of a sliding scale in appraising reasonableness,'" and as such "'the quality of proof required should vary with the circumstances.'"

As in other areas of law, trial courts can structure antitrust litigation so as to avoid, on the one hand, the use of antitrust theories too abbreviated to permit proper analysis, and, on the other, consideration of every possible fact or theory irrespective of the minimal light it may shed on the basic question—that of the presence of significant unjustified anticompetitive consequences. We therefore leave to the lower courts the structuring of the present rule-of-reason antitrust litigation. We reverse the judgment of the Eleventh Circuit. And we remand the case for further proceedings consistent with this opinion.

It is so ordered.

**Chief Justice ROBERTS, . . . dissenting.**

Solvay Pharmaceuticals holds a patent. It sued two generic drug manufacturers that it alleged were infringing that patent. Those companies counterclaimed, contending the patent was invalid and that, in any event, their products did not infringe. The parties litigated for three years before settling on these terms: Solvay agreed to pay the generics millions of dollars and to allow them into the market five years before the patent was set to expire; in exchange, the generics agreed to provide certain services (help with marketing and manufacturing) and to honor Solvay's patent. The Federal Trade Commission alleges that such a settlement violates the antitrust laws. The question is how to assess that claim.

A patent carves out an exception to the applicability of antitrust laws. The correct approach should therefore be to ask whether the settlement gives Solvay monopoly power beyond what the patent already gave it. The Court, however, departs from this approach, and would instead use antitrust law's amorphous rule of reason to inquire into the anticompetitive effects of such settlements. This novel approach is without support in any statute, and will discourage the settlement of patent litigation. I respectfully dissent.

I

The point of antitrust law is to encourage competitive markets to promote consumer welfare. The point of patent law is to grant limited monopolies as a way of encouraging innovation. Thus, a patent grants "the right to exclude others from profiting by the patented invention." In doing so it provides an exception to antitrust law, and the scope of the patent—i.e., the rights conferred by the patent—forms the zone within which the patent holder may operate without facing antitrust liability.

This should go without saying, in part because we've said it so many times. Thus, although it is per se unlawful to fix prices under antitrust law, we have long recognized that a patent holder is entitled to license a competitor to sell its product on the condition that the competitor charge a certain, fixed price.

We have never held that it violates antitrust law for a competitor to refrain from challenging a patent. And by extension, we have long recognized that the settlement of patent litigation does not by itself violate the antitrust laws. Like most litigation, patent litigation is settled all the time, and such settlements—which can include agreements that clearly violate antitrust law, such as licenses that fix prices, or agreements among competitors to divide territory—do not ordinarily subject the litigants to antitrust liability.

The key, of course, is that the patent holder—when doing anything, including settling—must act within the scope of the patent. If its actions go beyond the monopoly powers conferred by the patent, we have held that such actions are subject to antitrust scrutiny. If its actions are within the scope of the patent, they are not subject to antitrust scrutiny, with two exceptions concededly not applicable here. . . .

Thus, under our precedent, this is a fairly straight-forward case. Solvay paid a competitor to respect its patent—conduct which did not exceed the scope of its patent. No one alleges that there was sham litigation, or that Solvay's patent was obtained through fraud on the PTO. As in any settlement, Solvay gave its competitors something of value (money) and, in exchange, its competitors gave it something of value (dropping their legal claims). In doing so, they put an end to litigation that had been dragging on for three years. Ordinarily, we would think this a good thing.

II

Today, however, the Court announces a new rule. It is willing to accept that Solvay's actions did not exceed the scope of its patent. But it does not agree that this is enough to "immunize the agreement from antitrust attack." According to the majority, if a patent holder settles litigation by paying an alleged infringer a "large and unjustified" payment, in exchange for having the alleged infringer honor the patent, a court should employ the antitrust rule of reason to determine whether the settlement violates antitrust law.

The Court's justifications for this holding are unpersuasive. . . .

III

The majority's rule will discourage settlement of patent litigation. Simply put, there would be no incentive to settle if, immediately after settling, the parties would have to litigate the same issue—the question of patent validity—as part of a defense against an antitrust suit. In that suit, the alleged infringer would be in the especially awkward position of being for the patent after being against it.

This is unfortunate because patent litigation is particularly complex, and particularly costly. As one treatise noted, "[t]he median patent case that goes to trial costs each side $1.5 million in legal fees" alone. One study found that the cost of litigation in this specific context—a generic challenging a brand name pharmaceutical patent—was about $10 million per suit.

. . . .

The majority seems to think that even if the patent is valid, a patent holder violates the antitrust laws merely because the settlement took away some chance that his patent would be declared invalid by a court. This is flawed for several reasons.

First, a patent is either valid or invalid. The parties of course don't know the answer with certainty at the outset of litigation; hence the litigation. But the same is true of any hard legal question that is yet to be adjudicated. Just because people don't know the answer doesn't mean there is no answer until a court declares one. Yet the majority would impose antitrust liability based on the parties' subjective uncertainty about that legal conclusion.

The Court does so on the assumption that offering a "large" sum is reliable evidence that the patent holder has serious doubts about the patent. Not true. A patent holder may be 95% sure about the validity of its patent, but particularly risk averse or litigation averse, and willing to pay a good deal of money to rid itself of the 5% chance of a finding of invalidity. What is actually motivating a patent holder is apparently a question district courts will have to resolve on a case-by-case basis. The task of trying to discern whether a patent holder is motivated by uncertainty about its patent, or other legitimate factors like risk aversion, will be made all the more difficult by the fact that much of the evidence about the party's motivation may be embedded in legal advice from its attorney, which would presumably be shielded from discovery.

Second, the majority's position leads to absurd results. Let's say in 2005, a patent holder sues a competitor for infringement and faces a counterclaim that its patent is invalid. The patent holder determines that the risk of losing on the question of validity is low, but after a year of litigating, grows increasingly risk averse, tired of litigation, and concerned about the company's image, so it pays the competitor a "large" payment, in exchange for having the competitor honor its patent. Then let's say in 2006, a different competitor, inspired by the first competitor's success, sues the patent holder and seeks a similar payment. The patent holder, recognizing that this dynamic is unsustainable, litigates this suit to conclusion, all the way to the Supreme Court, which unanimously decides the patent was valid. According to the majority, the first settlement would violate the antitrust laws even though the patent was ultimately declared valid, because that first settlement took away some chance that the patent would be invalidated in the first go around. Under this approach, a patent holder may be found liable under antitrust law for doing what its perfectly valid patent allowed it to do in the first place; its sin was to settle, rather than prove the correctness of its position by litigating until the bitter end.

Third, this logic—that taking away any chance that a patent will be invalidated is itself an antitrust problem—cannot possibly be limited to reverse-payment agreements, or those that are "large." The Government's brief acknowledges as much, suggesting that if antitrust scrutiny is invited for such cash payments, it may also be required for "other consideration" and "alternative arrangements." For example, when a patent holder licenses its product to a licensee at a fixed monopoly price, surely it takes away some chance that its patent will be challenged by that licensee. According to the majority's reasoning, that's an antitrust problem that must be analyzed under the rule of reason. Indeed, the Court's own solution—that patent holders should negotiate to allow generics into the market sooner, rather than paying them money—also takes away some chance that the generic would have litigated until the patent was invalidated.

Thus, although the question posed by this case is fundamentally a question of patent law—i.e., whether Solvay's patent was valid and therefore permitted Solvay to pay competitors to honor the scope of its patent—the majority declares that such questions should henceforth be scrutinized by antitrust law's unruly rule of reason. Good luck to the district courts that must, when faced with a patent settlement, weigh the "likely anticompetitive effects, redeeming virtues, market power, and potentially offsetting legal considerations present in the circumstances." *[B]ut see Pacific Bell Telephone Co. v. Linkline Communications, Inc.*, 555 U.S. 438, 452 (2009) ("We have repeatedly emphasized the importance of clear rules in antitrust law").

IV

The majority invokes "procompetitive antitrust policies," but misses the basic point that patent laws promote consumer interests in a different way, by providing protection against competition. As one treatise explains:

> "The purpose of the rule of reason is to determine whether, on balance, a practice is reasonably likely to be anticompetitive or competitively harmless—that is, whether it yields lower or higher marketwide output. By contrast, patent policy encompasses a set of judgments about the proper tradeoff between competition and the incentive to innovate over the long run. Antitrust's rule of reason was not designed for such judgments and is not adept at making them." Hovenkamp § 7.3, at 7–13 (footnote omitted).

The majority recognizes that "a high reverse payment" may "signal to other potential challengers that the patentee lacks confidence in its patent, thereby provoking additional challenges." It brushes this off, however, because of two features of Hatch-Waxman that make it "'not necessarily so.' First, it points out that the first challenger gets a 180-day exclusive period to market a generic version of the brand name drug, and that subsequent challengers cannot secure that exclusivity period—meaning when the patent holder buys off the first challenger, it has bought off its most motivated competitor. There are two problems with this argument. First, according to the Food and Drug Administration, all manufacturers who file on the first day are considered "first applicants" who share the exclusivity period. Thus, if ten generics file an application to market a generic drug on the first day, all will be considered "first applicants." *See* [FFDCA 505](j)(5)(B)(iv)(II)(bb); *see also* FDA, Guidance for Industry: 180-Day Exclusivity When Multiple ANDAs Are Submitted on the Same Day 4 (July 2003). This is not an unusual occurrence. *See* Brief for Generic Pharmaceutical Association as Amicus Curiae 23–24 (citing FTC data indicating that some drugs "have been subject to as many as sixteen first-day" generic applications; that in 2005, the average number of first-day applications per drug was 11; and that between 2002 and 2008, the yearly average never dropped below three first-day applications per drug).

Second, and more fundamentally, the 180 days of exclusivity simply provides more incentive for generic challenges. Even if a subsequent generic would not be entitled to this additional incentive, it will have as much or nearly as much incentive to challenge the patent as a potential challenger would in any other context outside of Hatch-Waxman, where there is no 180-day exclusivity period. And a patent holder who gives away notably large sums of money because it is, as the majority surmises, concerned about the strength of its patent, would be putting blood in water where sharks are always near.

The majority also points to the fact that, under Hatch-Waxman, the FDA is enjoined from approving a generic's application to market a drug for 30 months if the brand name sues the generic for patent infringement within 45 days of that application being filed. According to the majority, this provision will chill subsequent generics from challenging the patent (because they will have to wait 30 months before receiving FDA approval to market their drug). But this overlooks an important feature of the law: the FDA may approve the application before the 30 months are up "if before the expiration of [the 30 months,] the district court decides that the patent is invalid or not infringed." § 355(j)(5)(B)(iii) (I). And even if the FDA did not have to wait 30 months, it is far from clear that a generic would want to market a drug prior to obtaining a judgment of invalidity or noninfringement. Doing so may expose it to ruinous liability for infringement.

The irony of all this is that the majority's decision may very well discourage generics from challenging pharmaceutical patents in the first place. Patent litigation is costly, time consuming, and uncertain. Generics "enter this risky terrain only after careful analysis of the potential gains if they prevail and the potential exposure if they lose." Taking the prospect of settlements off the table—or limiting settlements to an earlier entry date for the generic, which may still be many years in the future—puts a damper on the generic's expected value going into litigation, and decreases its incentive to sue in the first place. The majority assures us, with no support, that everything will be okay because the parties can settle by simply negotiating an earlier entry date for the generic drug manufacturer, rather than settling with money. But it's a matter of common sense, confirmed by experience, that parties are more likely to settle when they have a broader set of valuable things to trade.

V

The majority today departs from the settled approach separating patent and antitrust law, weakens the protections afforded to innovators by patents, frustrates the public policy in favor of settling, and likely undermines the very policy it seeks to promote by forcing generics who step into the litigation ring to do so without the prospect of cash settlements. I would keep things as they were and not subject basic questions of patent law to an unbounded inquiry under antitrust law, with its treble damages and famously burdensome discovery. *See* 15 U.S.C. § 15; *Bell Atlantic Corp. v. Twombly,* 550 U.S. 544, 558–559 (2007). I respectfully dissent.

# E. Additional Issues

## 1. Over the Counter (OTC) Drugs

### 1972-01-05 FDA Proposed Rule, Proposal Establishing Rule-Making Procedures for Classification [of OTC Drugs]

37 Fed. Reg. 85

Because self-medication is essential to the Nation's health care system, it is imperative that over-the-counter (OTC) drugs available for human use be safe and effective and bear fully informative labeling. The Food and Drug Administration is concerned that some formulations presently on the market do not have their claimed effect and/or do not bear adequate labeling for safe and effective use by the laity.

Prior to the enactment in 1938 of the [FFDCA], all drugs were marketed without first undergoing review by the Food and Drug Administration. Under the 1938 act, the Food and Drug Administration was given authority to review, prior to marketing, the safety data on those drugs not generally recognized as safe under their intended uses. Under the Drug Amendments of 1962, which amended the Federal Food, Drug, and Cosmetic Act, the Food and Drug Administration was given authority to review, prior to marketing, the safety and effectiveness of those drugs not generally recognized as safe and effective for their intended use. Pursuant to the 1962 amendments, the Food and Drug Administration was also required to review the efficacy claims of those new drugs introduced into the market between 1938 and 1962. Because of the greater potential for harm of prescription drugs, the review of such drugs was conducted as a matter of first priority and is nearing completion. It is now appropriate to conduct a similar review of OTC drugs.

Cause for concern is illustrated by recent Drug Efficacy Study evaluations of the National Academy of Science-National Research Council. The NAS-NRC reviewed 420 OTC drugs which were broadly representative of the whole range of the OTC market. The NAS-NRC panels' conclusions, which were based upon supporting data submitted by manufacturers, were that approximately 25 percent of the drugs reviewed had an indication that was classifiable as effective. These evaluations, when viewed in the context of the entire OTC drug field, present questions that must be confronted by industry and government.

Estimates of the number of OTC drug products on the market vary from 100,000 to one-half million. Extremely few of these drugs have been approved through the new-drug procedures set forth in section 505 of the [FFDCA]. Some OTC drugs may be excluded from the definition of a new drug by reason of the so-called 1938 grandfather clause in section 201(p)(l) of the [FFDCA], and others may be excluded from application of the Drug Amendments of 1962 by reason of the so-called 1962 grandfather clause in section 107(c) of those amendments. Any OTC drug excluded from new-drug status by reason of the 1938 or 1962 grandfather clause is, however, subject to other requirements for drugs in Chapter V of the [FFDCA], and in particular may not be misbranded under section 502.

The Food and Drug Administration intends to require that all unapproved new drugs and misbranded drugs either be reformulated and/or relabeled to meet all requirements of the [FFDCA] or be removed from the market. In carrying out its responsibilities in this area, the Food and Drug Administration may either initiate a separate court action with respect to each violative OTC drug or deal with an OTC drugs through rulemaking by therapeutic classes on an industrywide basis. It has been determined that the latter approach should be pursued. In making this decision, the following factors were considered:

1. The limited resources of the Food and Drug Administration would be overwhelmed by attempting to review separately the label and the data on the safety and effectiveness for each OTC drug now on the market. This would be further complicated by the almost daily growth in the number of drugs being marketed and the changes in formulation and labeling of previously marketed drugs. In large measure, this is the result of a tendency on the part of some manufacturers to develop new mixtures and adjust formulations and labeling for competitive reasons. The prospects of completing a detailed drug-by-drug review of the OTC market in a reasonable time are extremely remote.
2. Litigation to remove violative OTC preparations from the market would necessarily be on a drug-by-drug basis. Such proceedings would place an enormous burden on the courts which must hear the cases, on the agency which must prepare them, on the community of medical and scientific experts who must testify, and on the members of the pharmaceutical industry who are affected. Such litigation is time-consuming and expensive and is sometimes ineffective because manufacturers may change the formulation of the drug in question

and/ or its labeling claims and reintroduce the product into the market, thus requiring still further litigation.

3. Litigation to delineate the precise scope of the 1938 and 1962 grandfather clauses in order to determine exactly which of the thousands of OTC drugs on the market may validly claim exemption from new-drug status under those clauses and then to determine on a drug-by- rug basis which of those grandfathered claims and formulations are safe and effective under the prescribed, recommended, or suggested conditions of use, and thus not misbranded, would more than exhaust all present resources of the agency. There is no feasible way to determine what formulations and claims may properly be regarded as grandfathered, and in any event the date of entry into the market has no bearing whatever on the safety and effectiveness of the drug and the truthfulness and adequacy of its labeling. It would be unreasonable and unjust to permit grandfathered drugs to remain on the market unchanged while competitive items must be reformulated and/or relabeled or removed from the market. The same scientific and medical determinations involved in reviewing the safety and effectiveness of nongrandfathered OTC drugs are also involved in determining whether grandfathered drugs are misbranded and thus are properly made in a single proceeding that will apply across the board to all products in a single therapeutic class.

4. Of paramount concern is the inadequate consumer protection produced by a product-by-product review and case-by-case litigation against each drug. It is not unreasonable to expect that a very large number of violative drugs would remain on the market for long periods of time because of the limited resources of the agency to evaluate and proceed against such drugs and the delays inherent in complicated litigation through trial and appellate courts.

5. It is impossible to proceed simultaneously by litigation against all manufacturers of similar preparations or their drugs. The situation will arise, as it has before, that preparations similar to those proceeded against will remain on the market long after their less fortunate counterparts have been removed. This situation must be avoided for two reasons. First, and most important, the public is not sufficiently protected when violative drugs remain on the market. Second, equitable enforcement of the law requires that the agency proceed against all manufacturers of similar preparations, since those not proceeded against would have an unfair competitive advantage.

6. Practically all of the thousands of OTC drugs now marketed are compounded from only an estimated 200 active ingredients which are used either alone or in varying combinations. Many thousands of these drugs are readily comparable in that the labeling is similar and the active ingredients are the same, or are essentially the same, but are present in slightly different dosages. Although each is a separate product, the same scientific and medical evidence is relevant in reviewing all OTC drugs within a given therapeutic class.

7. Any approach to the review of the safety and effectiveness of OTC drugs must be consistent with the mandates of the [FFDCA]. In carrying out its responsibilities under the [FFDCA] through administrative proceedings and litigation in Federal courts, the agency has required the presence in published literature of adequate and appropriate medical documentation, consisting at least in part of controlled clinical investigations, as the test of whether a drug is no longer a new drug within the meaning of section 201(p)(1) of the [FFDCA]. Unpublished and uncontrolled studies and data may corroborate published and controlled findings.

Accordingly, the Commissioner proposes to establish procedures for rule making which will result in classifying some OTC drugs as generally recognized among qualified experts as safe and effective and not misbranded under prescribed, recommended, or suggested conditions of use. Any OTC drug not meeting the requirements established for such drugs pursuant to this procedure will have to be the subject of an approved new-drug application prior to marketing. (Since a grandfathered drug that is found to be misbranded would be required to change its formulation and/or labeling and thus lose its grandfathered status, any such product must either meet the applicable monograph or be the subject of an approved new-drug application in order to be legally marketed.) A deviation from a monograph will be approved for an individual manufacturer through approval of a new-drug application justifying such a deviation. Shipment of a nonconforming OTC drug (one neither classified as generally recognized as safe and effective and not misbranded, nor subject to an approved NDA) in interstate commerce will be prohibited. Responsible persons and the manufacturer and distributor will be subject to criminal prosecution and injunctive action, and the drug will be subject to seizure and injunction on the ground that the drug is an unapproved new-drug or is a misbranded drug (if it is exempt from the new-drug definition under the 1938 or 1962 grandfather clause).

. . . .

---

On May 11, 1972, FDA published a final rule based on the proposal immediately above. *See* 1972-05-11 FDA Final Rule, Procedures for Classifying Over-the-Counter Drugs, 37 Fed. Reg. 9464.

---

On March 27, 2020, President Trump signed the Coronavirus Aid, Relief, and Economic Security (CARES) Act. Most press reports naturally focused on the massive economic stimulus included in the statute. In addition to the stimulus money, however, the law contained other important provisions. Subtitle F, "OTC Drug Review," contained major changes to FDA's statutory authority over OTC drugs. A few days later, FDA issued a press release highlighting those statutory changes. That press release is excerpted immediately below.

## 2020-3-30 FDA Press Release on the Signing of the CARES Act

On Friday, the President signed into law a $2 trillion emergency relief bill that will continue to aid the response efforts and ease the economic impact of COVID-19. The legislation will help all of us at the FDA deliver support and guidance to protect and promote public health during this unprecedented pandemic.

Specif[ic]ally, the legislation provided an additional $80 million in funding to continue the Agency's COVID-19 response efforts, including the development of medical countermeasures and vaccines, promoting the advanced manufacturing of medical products and monitoring of the medical product supply chain. The FDA thanks Congress for its continued support of these crucial efforts and looks forward to continuing to work with members of Congress on all legislative efforts to mitigate the impact of COVID-19 on public health.

Add[i]tionally, we want to specifically highlight the portion of the bill that reforms and modernizes the way certain over-the-counter (OTC) drugs are regulated in the United States—a landmark step that will have an impact lasting long after the current public health emergency. The law grants the FDA transformative, new authorities that will meaningfully advance our efforts to modernize the OTC drug development and review process to help advance innovative, safe and effective options for consumers and secure a robust OTC marketplace. The FDA is committed to using these new tools to promote innovation and improve the safety and effectiveness of OTC monograph drugs—including products like hand sanitizers and acetaminophen, which are so critical to the public health emergency we face right now. We look forward to providing updates as we implement this important new law.

## 2. On-Label and Off-Label Use

FDA has not sought to assert authority to regulate the practice of medicine, which has long been regulated at the state level. This has led to an important phenomenon known as *off-label prescribing*. Drugs can be marketed only when approved by FDA, and a drug can be approved only for a specific intended use (or uses). However, once a drug is approved for a single intended use—no matter how narrow or rare—it can be prescribed freely by physicians for *any* intended use. The regulation of physician prescribing activities is seen as an aspect of state-level regulation of the practice of medicine and not within the authority of FDA.

FDA does, however, have authority over the marketing of drugs for off-label uses, and *off-label marketing* is broadly prohibited by FDA. This leads to a situation where health-care providers can prescribe drugs freely for off-label uses in humans, but pharmaceutical companies are largely prohibited from seeking to convince providers to prescribe their drugs off-label. Especially in situations where the potential sales for off-label uses substantially exceed potential sales for on-label uses, the incentive for pharmaceutical companies to violate the off-label marketing prohibition can be significant.

The decision below arose from a commercial speech challenge to an FDA off-label marketing prosecution. Because the decision potentially presented some challenges to the basic structure of FDA's drug regulation program, the decision received significant attention. To the surprise of some, FDA chose not to appeal the Second Circuit's decision.

## United States v. Caronia

703 F.3d 149 (2d Cir. 2012)

**CHIN, Circuit Judge:**

Defendant-appellant Alfred Caronia appeals from a judgment of conviction entered in the United States District Court for the Eastern District of New York on November 30, 2009, following a jury trial at which Caronia was found guilty of conspiracy to introduce a misbranded drug into interstate commerce, a misdemeanor violation of 21 U.S.C. §§ 331(a) and 333(a)(1). Specifically, Caronia, a pharmaceutical sales representative, promoted the drug Xyrem for "off-label use," that is, for a purpose not approved by the U.S. Food and Drug Administration (the "FDA"). Caronia argues that he was convicted for his speech—for promoting an FDA-approved drug for off-label use—in violation of his right of free speech under the First Amendment. We agree. Accordingly, we vacate the judgment of conviction and remand the case to the district court.

### Statement of the Case

### 1. The Regulatory Scheme

Under the Federal Food, Drug and Cosmetic Act (the "FDCA"), before drugs are distributed into interstate commerce, they must be approved by the FDA for specific uses. To obtain FDA approval, drug manufacturers are required to demonstrate, through clinical trials, the safety and efficacy of a new drug for each intended use or indication.

Once FDA-approved, prescription drugs can be prescribed by doctors for both FDA-approved and -unapproved uses; the FDA generally does not regulate how physicians use approved drugs.

Indeed, courts and the FDA have recognized the propriety and potential public value of unapproved or off-label drug use. The FDA itself has observed:

> Once a drug has been approved for marketing, a physician may prescribe it for uses or in treatment regimens or patient populations that are not included in approved labeling. Such "unapproved" or, more precisely, "unlabeled" uses may be appropriate and rational in certain circumstances, and may, in fact, reflect approaches to drug therapy that have been extensively reported in medical literature.

U.S. Food and Drug Administration, FDA Drug Bulletin, 12 FDA Drug Bull. 1, 5 (1982).

The [FFDCA] prohibits "misbranding," or "[t]he introduction or delivery for introduction into interstate commerce of any . . . drug . . . that is . . . misbranded." [FFDCA §301](a). A drug is misbranded if, inter alia, its labeling fails to bear "adequate directions for use," [FFDCA §502](f), which FDA regulations define as "directions under which the lay[person] can use a drug safely and for the purposes for which it is intended," 21 C.F.R. §201.5. FDA regulations define intended use by reference to "the objective intent of the persons legally responsible for the labeling of drugs," which may be demonstrated by, among other evidence, "oral or written statements by such persons or their representatives" and "the circumstances that the article is, with the knowledge of such persons or their representatives, offered and used for a purpose for which it is neither labeled nor advertised." 21 C.F.R. §201.128.

The consequences for misbranding are criminal. Pharmaceutical manufacturers and their representatives can face misdemeanor charges for misbranding or felony charges for fraudulent misbranding. The government has repeatedly prosecuted—and obtained convictions against—pharmaceutical companies and their representatives for misbranding based on their off-label promotion.

The [FFDCA] and its accompanying regulations do not expressly prohibit the "promotion" or "marketing" of drugs for off-label use. The regulations do recognize that promotional statements by a pharmaceutical company or its representatives can serve as proof of a drug's intended use. Off-label promotional statements could thus presumably constitute evidence of an intended use of a drug that the FDA has not approved. The FDA, however, has concluded that "[a]n approved drug that is marketed for an unapproved use (whether in labeling or not) is misbranded because the labeling of such drug does not include 'adequate directions for use.'" See FDA, Draft Guidance, supra, at 2–3 (quoting 21 U.S.C. §352(f)); *see* also Gov't Br. 48 n.18 (contending no set of directions can constitute adequate labeling for drug's off-label use). Thus, the government has treated promotional speech as more than merely evidence of a drug's intended use—it has construed the [FFDCA] to prohibit promotional speech as misbranding itself.

### 2. The Facts

#### a. Orphan Medical and Xyrem

Orphan Medical, Inc. ("Orphan"), now known as Jazz Pharmaceutical, was a Delaware-incorporated pharmaceutical company that primarily developed drugs to treat pain, sleep disorders, and central nervous system disorders. Orphan manufactured the drug Xyrem, a powerful central nervous system depressant. In 2005, after Jazz Pharmaceuticals acquired Orphan, Jazz continued to manufacture and sell Xyrem, grossing $20 million in combined Xyrem sales in 2005.

Xyrem can cause serious side effects, including difficulty breathing while asleep, confusion, abnormal thinking, depression, nausea, vomiting, dizziness, headache, bedwetting, and sleepwalking. If abused, Xyrem can cause additional medical problems, including seizures, dependence, severe withdrawal, coma, and death.

Xyrem's active ingredient is gamma-hydroxybutryate ("GHB"). GHB has been federally classified as the "date rape drug" for its use in the commission of sexual assaults.

#### b. The FDA's Regulation of Xyrem

Despite the risks associated with Xyrem and GHB, the FDA approved Xyrem for two medical indications. In July 2002, the FDA approved Xyrem to treat narcolepsy patients who experience cataplexy, a condition associated with weak or paralyzed muscles. In November 2005, the FDA approved Xyrem to treat narcolepsy patients with excessive daytime sleepiness ("EDS"), a neurological disorder caused by the brain's inability to regulate sleep-wake cycles.

To protect against its serious safety concerns, in 2002, the FDA required a "black box" warning to accompany Xyrem. The black box warning is the most serious warning placed on prescription medication labels. Xyrem's black box labeling stated, among other things, that the drug's safety and efficacy were not established in patients under 16 years of age, and the drug had "very limited" experience among elderly patients.

To identify patients suffering side effects from the drug, the FDA also regulated Xyrem distribution, allowing only one centralized Missouri pharmacy to distribute Xyrem nationally.

#### c. Caronia's Employment with Orphan

In March 2005, Orphan hired Caronia as a Specialty Sales Consultant to promote Xyrem. Caronia primarily worked in Queens, Nassau, and Suffolk counties. Caronia's salary was based on his individual sales.

In July 2005, Caronia started Orphan's "speaker programs" for Xyrem. Speaker programs enlist physicians, for pay, to speak to other physicians about FDA-approved drug use. Orphan's speaker programs for Xyrem presented the benefits of the drug among patients with cataplexy and narcolepsy. Orphan hired Dr. Peter Gleason to promote Xyrem through its speaker programs.

Under Orphan's procedures, if Caronia, as a sales consultant for Xyrem, was asked about the off-label use of Xyrem, he was not permitted to answer; instead, when such questions were posed, Orphan sales consultants would fill out "medical information request forms" and send them to Orphan, and Orphan would send information to the inquiring physician. In contrast, physicians employed by Orphan as promotional speakers for Xyrem were permitted to answer off-label use questions; their responses were often informed by their own experiences with Xyrem.

#### d. Caronia's Participation in the Conspiracy

In the spring of 2005, the federal government launched an investigation of Orphan and Gleason. The investigation focused on the off-label promotion of

Xyrem. Caronia and Gleason were audio-recorded on two occasions as they promoted Xyrem for unapproved uses, including unapproved indications and unapproved subpopulations. The first conversation was recorded on October 26, 2005 between Caronia and Dr. Stephen Charno, a physician who, as a government cooperator, posed as a prospective Xyrem customer. The second conversation was recorded on November 2, 2005; it taped a meeting arranged by Caronia to introduce Charno to Gleason.

On October 26, 2005, Caronia plainly promoted the use of Xyrem in unapproved indications with Charno:

> [Caronia]: And right now the indication is for narcolepsy with cataplexy . . . excessive daytime . . . and fragmented sleep, but because of the properties that . . . it has it's going to insomnia, Fibromyalgia[,] periodic leg movement, restless leg, ahh also looking at ahh Parkinson's and . . . other sleep disorders are underway such as MS.
>
> [Charno]: Okay, so then so then it could be used for muscle disorders and chronic pain and . . .
>
> [Caronia]: Right.
>
> [Charno]: . . . and daytime fatigue and excessive sleepiness and stuff like that?
>
> [Caronia]: Absolutely. Absolutely. Ahh with the Fibromyalgia.

Caronia further directed Charno to list different "diagnosis codes" when prescribing Xyrem, for insurance purposes, including Fibromyalgia, chronic fatigue, or chronic pain.

On separate occasions, Caronia and Gleason each explained to prospective physician-customers that Xyrem could be used with patients under age sixteen, an unapproved Xyrem subpopulation:

> [Caronia]: Um, the youngest patients we have are sixteen in the studies as old as sixty-five. Ahh there have been reports of patients as young as fourteen using it and obviously greater than sixty-five. It's a very safe drug.
>
> [Gleason]: Well, it's actually approved for sixteen and above um, I've had people under thirteen and I've certainly talked to neurologists that have narcoleptics . . . between eight and ten . . . [but] I start at two-thirds the dose, but [if] they're real frail I only start with one-third the dose.

### 3. Proceedings Below

#### a. The Charges

On July 25, 2007, a grand jury returned its first Indictment against Caronia. The charging document at issue on this appeal, however, is the Superseding Information filed by the government on August 19, 2008, which charged Caronia with the following two misdemeanor offenses:

> Count One: Conspiracy to introduce a misbranded drug into interstate commerce in violation of 21 U.S.C. §§ 331(a) and 333(a)(2); and
>
> Count Two: Introducing a misbranded drug, Xyrem, into interstate commerce, in violation of 21 U.S.C. §§ 331(a) and 333(a)(2).

With respect to Count One, the Information alleged a two-prong conspiracy. The first prong charged that between approximately March 2005 and March 2006, Caronia, "together with others, did knowingly and intentionally conspire to" introduce Xyrem and cause the introduction of Xyrem into interstate commerce when Xyrem was misbranded within the meaning of the [FFDCA]. The second prong alleged that "[i]t was part of the conspiracy that [Caronia], together with others, marketed Xyrem for medical indications that were not approved by [the] FDA when, as [they] . . . well knew and believed, Xyrem's labeling lacked adequate directions for and warnings against such uses, where such uses could be dangerous to the user's health."

The Information alleged, in Count One, that Caronia, "together with others, committed and caused to be committed," the following two overt acts.

> a. On or about October 26th, 2005, . . . Caronia promoted Xyrem to [Charno], a physician, so as to cause [Charno] to prescribe Xyrem for fibromyalgia, excessive daytime sleepiness, muscle disorders, chronic pain and fatigue, which were "off-label" indications.
>
> b. On or about November 2, 2005, . . . Caronia introduced [Charno] to [Gleason], a physician, who was paid by Orphan and whom Orphan used to promote Xyrem for "off-label" indications, including fibromyalgia, excessive daytime sleepiness, weight loss and chronic fatigue.

With respect to Count Two, the Information alleged that between approximately March 2005 and March 2006, Caronia "was marketing Xyrem for medical indications that were not approved by [the] FDA when, as the defendant then and there well knew and believed, Xyrem's labeling lacked adequate directions for such uses and adequate warnings against such uses where uses could be dangerous to the user's health."

Additionally, the Information alleged: "A drug that was marketed to the public for an 'off-label' indication or use did not contain 'adequate directions for use' because such an 'off-label' indication or use and related information were not included in the FDA-approved labeling for the drug." The Information further stated: "Xyrem's labeling lacked adequate directions for such uses and adequate warnings against such uses where such uses could be dangerous to the user's health."

Orphan and Gleason were also charged under the misbranding provisions of the [FFDCA]; both pled guilty.

#### b. Caronia's Pre-Trial Motion to Dismiss

On October 9, 2007, before trial, Caronia moved to dismiss the charges against him. In part, Caronia argued that the application of the [FFDCA]'s misbranding provisions to his off-label promotional statements unconstitutionally restricted his right to free speech under the First Amendment and that the provisions were unconstitutionally vague and broad.

On September 11, 2008, the district court denied Caronia's motion, including his First Amendment challenge, which it recognized as raising constitutional issues "very much unsettled, not only in this circuit but nationwide." Although ruling for the government, the district court rejected the government's argument that Caronia was being prosecuted for the unlawful conduct of misbranding and conspiring to misbrand a drug and not for his promotional speech, the latter of which the government contended only constituted proof of Xyrem's intended use. The court observed that "the criminal information ... allege[d] Caronia's promotion of off-label uses of an FDA-approved drug," and concluded that Caronia stood charged with a crime the actus reus of which was First Amendment speech. Nevertheless, the district court held that, to the extent the [FFDCA] criminalizes speech, the law passed constitutional muster under the commercial speech doctrine because the [FFDCA] was not more extensive than necessary to achieve the FDA's objectives.

### c. The Trial

The case was tried before a jury from October 6 to October 16, 2008.

The record makes clear that the government prosecuted Caronia for his off-label promotion, in violation of the [FFDCA]. The government, in its summation and rebuttal, repeatedly asserted that Caronia was guilty because he, with others, conspired to promote and market Xyrem for off-label use. For example, the government argued:

- "[Caronia is] promoting, he's marketing a dangerous drug for use not approved by the FDA";
- "He knew the rules: you can't promote and market Xyrem for uses that have not been approved by the FDA. He admits it";
- "[Caronia] conspired through some act of misbranding, and that act of misbranding ... was the promotion on October 26th and November 2nd[,] marketing [a] drug for unapproved uses";
- "That's misbranding. That's promoting and marketing a drug by a pharmaceutical company representative for muscle disorders, chronic pain, daytime fatigue, excessive sleepiness"; and
- "[Caronia was] promoting, promoting, selling, selling, trying to get Charno to prescribe Xyrem. He tried on the 26th. He tried with Gleason on the 2nd."

Thus, the government's theory of prosecution identified Caronia's speech alone as the proscribed conduct.

The district court, in its jury charge, reinforced the idea that Caronia's promotional speech was enough to support a guilty verdict:

> A misbranded drug may be shown by a promotion of the drug by a distributor for an intended use different from the use for which the drug was approved by the [FDA].

> . . .
>
> The manufacturer, its agents, representatives and employees, are not permitted to promote uses for a drug that have not been cleared by the United States Food and Drug Administration. These non-cleared uses are commonly referred to as 'off-label uses' because they are not included in the drug's labeling.

Prior to jury deliberation, the district court provided a proposed verdict sheet to the parties. With respect to Count One, the verdict sheet read as follows:

> 1. How do you find defendant, ALFRED CARONIA, on Count One of the Information?
>
> (a) Conspiracy to introduce or deliver for introduction into interstate commerce a drug, Xyrem, that was misbranded?
>
> NOT GUILTY ____ GUILTY ____
>
> (b) Conspiracy to do an act with respect to a drug, Xyrem, when such drug was held for sale after shipment in interstate commerce when such act would result in Xyrem being misbranded?
>
> NOT GUILTY ____ GUILTY ____

The district court overruled Caronia's objection that the verdict sheet was erroneous and therefore permitted the jury to reach an inconsistent verdict.

On October 23, 2008, the jury found Caronia guilty as to the first prong of Count One of the Information (Question 1(a)): conspiracy to introduce a misbranded drug into interstate commerce under 18 U.S.C. § 371(a) and 21 U.S.C. § 331(a). As to the second marketing prong of Count One (Question 1(b)), the jury found Caronia not guilty. The jury also found Caronia not guilty of Count Two of the Information.

#### d. Caronia's Post-Trial Motion for Acquittal

After the jury verdict and before judgment was entered, Caronia renewed his Rule 29 motion for acquittal. See Fed.R.Crim.P. 29. On December 13, 2008, after briefing, the district court denied the motion.

#### e. Caronia's Sentence

On November 30, 2009, the district court sentenced Caronia to one year of probation, 100 hours of community service, and a $25 special assessment.

This appeal followed.

### Discussion

On appeal, Caronia principally argues that the misbranding provisions of the [FFDCA] prohibit off-label promotion, and therefore, unconstitutionally restrict speech. Caronia argues that the First Amendment does not permit the government to prohibit and criminalize a pharmaceutical manufacturer's truthful and non-misleading promotion of an FDA-approved drug to physicians for off-label use where such use is not itself illegal and others are permitted to engage in such speech.

We review Caronia's First Amendment challenge to his conspiracy conviction de novo. We agree that Caronia's conviction must be vacated, but for narrower reasons than he urges.

While the [FFDCA] makes it a crime to misbrand or conspire to misbrand a drug, the statute and its accompanying regulations do not expressly prohibit or criminalize off-label promotion. Rather, the [FFDCA] and FDA regulations reference "promotion" only as evidence of a drug's intended use. See 21 C.F.R. § 201.128 (discussing how drug's intended use can be demonstrated). Thus, under the principle of constitutional avoidance, explained *infra,* we construe the [FFDCA] as not criminalizing the simple promotion of a drug's off-label use because such a construction would raise First Amendment concerns. Because we conclude from the record in this case that the government prosecuted Caronia for mere off-label promotion and the district court instructed the jury that it could convict on that theory, we vacate the judgment of conviction.

We begin by addressing the government's contention that Caronia's off-label promotion was used only as evidence of intent in this case. Finding the government's argument unpersuasive, we turn to the principal question on appeal: whether the government's prosecution of Caronia under the [FFDCA] only for promoting an FDA-approved drug for off-label use was constitutionally permissible.

**I. Speech versus Evidence of Intent**

The government contends—and the dissent agrees—that the First Amendment is not implicated in this case. Specifically, the government argues that "[p]romoting an approved drug for off-label uses is not itself a prohibited act under the [FFDCA]" and "the promotion of off-label uses plays an evidentiary role in determining whether a drug is misbranded under [FFDCA § 403](f)(1)." The government contends that Caronia was not prosecuted for his speech, but that Caronia's promotion of Xyrem for off-label use served merely as "evidence of intent," or evidence that the "off-label uses were intended ones[ ] for which Xyrem's labeling failed to provide any directions."

Even assuming the government can offer evidence of a defendant's off-label promotion to prove a drug's intended use and, thus, mislabeling for that intended use, that is not what happened in this case.

First, the government's contention that it did not prosecute Caronia for promoting the off-label use of an FDA-approved drug is belied by its conduct and arguments at trial. The excerpts quoted above demonstrate that the government repeatedly argued that Caronia engaged in criminal conduct by promoting and marketing the off-label use of Xyrem, an FDA-approved drug. The district court record thus confirms overwhelmingly that Caronia was, in fact, prosecuted and convicted for promoting Xyrem off-label. Indeed, in the government's summation and rebuttal at trial, Caronia's off-label promotion of Xyrem is highlighted over forty times.

Second, the government's assertion now that it used Caronia's efforts to promote Xyrem for off-label use only as evidence of intent is simply not true. Even if the government could have used Caronia's speech as evidence of intent, the district court record clearly shows that the government did not so limit its use of that evidence. The government never argued in summation or rebuttal that the promotion was evidence of intent. The government never suggested that Caronia engaged in any form of misbranding other than the promotion of the off-label use of an FDA-approved drug. The government never suggested, for example, that Caronia conspired to place false or deficient labeling on a drug. Rather, the record makes clear that the government prosecuted Caronia for his promotion and marketing efforts.

Third, the government's summation and the district court's instruction left the jury to understand that Caronia's speech was itself the proscribed conduct. Indeed, the district court flatly stated to the jury that pharmaceutical representatives are prohibited from engaging in off-label promotion. Although the district court explained the remaining elements of misbranding and conspiring to misbrand to the jury, this specific instruction—together with the government's summation—would have led the jury to believe that Caronia's promotional speech was, by itself, determinative of his guilt.

Fourth, the government clearly prosecuted Caronia for his words—for his speech. A pharmaceutical representative's promotion of an FDA-approved drug's off-label use is speech. As the Supreme Court has held: "Speech in aid of pharmaceutical marketing . . . is a form of expression protected by the Free Speech Clause of the First Amendment." *Sorrell v. IMS Health*, Inc., 131 S. Ct. 2653 (2011). Here, the proscribed conduct for which Caronia was prosecuted was precisely his speech in aid of pharmaceutical marketing.

Accordingly, we conclude that the government did prosecute Caronia for his speech, and we turn to whether the prosecution was permissible.

### II. The Prosecution of Caronia's Speech

While the government and the FDA have construed the [FFDCA]'s misbranding provisions to prohibit off-label promotion by pharmaceutical manufacturers, as we have observed, the [FFDCA] itself does not expressly prohibit or criminalize off-label promotion. The [FFDCA] defines misbranding in terms of whether a drug's labeling is adequate for its intended use, and permits the government to prove intended use by reference to promotional statements made by drug manufacturers or their representatives. Assuming that this approach to the use of evidence of speech is permissible, it affords little support to the government on this appeal because Caronia was not prosecuted on this basis. Rather, the government's theory of prosecution identified Caronia's speech alone as the proscribed conduct. The district court accepted this theory.

To the extent there is any ambiguity as to whether off-label promotion is tantamount to illegal misbranding, we construe the [FFDCA] narrowly to avoid a serious constitutional question.

As we now explain, we decline the government's invitation to construe the [FFDCA]'s misbranding provisions to criminalize the simple promotion of a drug's off-label use by pharmaceutical manufacturers and their representatives because such a construction—and a conviction obtained under the government's application of the [FFDCA]—would run afoul of the First Amendment.

### A. Applicable First Amendment Doctrine

The First Amendment protects against government regulation and suppression of speech on account of its content. Content-based speech restrictions are subject to "strict scrutiny"—that is, the government must show that the regulation at issue is narrowly tailored to serve or promote a compelling government interest. Meanwhile, non-content-based regulation and regulation of commercial speech—expression solely related to the economic interests of the speaker and its audience—are subject to intermediate scrutiny. Criminal regulatory schemes, moreover, warrant even more careful scrutiny.

In applying these principles, we have a benefit not available to the district court: the Supreme Court's decision in *Sorrell v. IMS Health, Inc.*, a case involving speech restrictions on pharmaceutical marketing. In Sorrell, the Vermont Prescription Confidentiality Law (the "VPCL") prohibited pharmaceutical companies and similar entities from using prescriber-identifying information for marketing purposes; it was challenged on First Amendment grounds.

The *Sorrell* Court held that "[s]peech in aid of pharmaceutical marketing ... is a form of expression protected by the ... First Amendment.... [The] creation and dissemination of information are speech within the meaning of the [Constitution]." The Court held that the Vermont statute set forth content- and speaker-based restrictions, and that the statute was therefore subject to heightened scrutiny. Because the VPCL disfavored speech with a particular content (marketing) when expressed by certain disfavored speakers (pharmaceutical manufacturers), the Court held that it unconstitutionally restricted speech.

In reaching this conclusion, *Sorrell* engaged in a two-step inquiry. First, the Court considered whether the government regulation restricting speech was content- and speaker-based. The Court held that it was; the regulation was therefore subject to heightened scrutiny and was "presumptively invalid." Second, the Court considered whether the government had shown that the restriction on speech was consistent with the First Amendment under the applicable level of heightened scrutiny. The Court did not decide the level of heightened scrutiny to be applied, that is, strict, intermediate, or some other form of heightened scrutiny. Rather, after observing that "[i]n the ordinary case, it is all but dispositive to conclude that a law is content-based," the Court concluded that the Vermont statute was unconstitutional even under the lesser intermediate standard set forth in *Central Hudson*. The Court further observed that the "outcome is the same whether a special commercial speech inquiry or a stricter form of judicial scrutiny is applied."

In considering whether the government had shown that the restriction on speech was consistent with the First Amendment, the Sorrell Court turned to *Central Hudson*. *Central Hudson* sets forth a four-part test to determine whether commercial speech is protected by the First Amendment. First, as a threshold matter, to warrant First Amendment protection, the speech in question must not be misleading and must concern lawful activity. Second, to justify regulations restricting speech, the asserted government interest must be substantial. Third, the regulation must directly advance the governmental interest asserted, "to a material degree," "[A] commercial speech regulation 'may not be sustained if it provides only ineffective or remote support for the government's purpose.'" Fourth, the regulation must be "narrowly drawn," and may not be more extensive than necessary to serve the interest. The government cannot "completely suppress information when narrower restrictions on expression would serve its interests as well." "Under the commercial speech inquiry, it is the [government's] burden to justify its content-based law as consistent with the First Amendment." *Sorrell*, 131 S.Ct. at 2667.

### B. Application

In prosecuting Caronia, the government construed the [FFDCA]'s misbranding provisions to prohibit and criminalize the promotion of off-label drug use. We review the government's theory of prosecution under the *Sorrell* Court's two-step analysis to determine whether it runs afoul of the First Amendment. First, we conclude that the government's construction of the [FFDCA]'s misbranding provisions imposes content- and speaker-based restrictions on speech subject to heightened scrutiny. Second, we conclude the government cannot justify a criminal prohibition of off-label promotion even under *Central Hudson*'s less rigorous intermediate test.

#### 1. Heightened Scrutiny

The government's construction of the [FFDCA]'s misbranding provisions to prohibit and criminalize the promotion of off-label drug use by pharmaceutical manufacturers is content- and speaker-based, and, therefore, subject to heightened scrutiny.

First, the government's interpretation of the [FFDCA]'s misbranding provisions to prohibit off-label promotion is content-based because it distinguishes between "favored speech" and "disfavored speech on the basis of the ideas or views expressed." Under this construction, speech about the government-approved use of drugs is permitted, while certain speech about the off-label use of drugs—that is, uses not approved by the government—is prohibited, even though the off-label use itself is not. Indeed, the content of the regulated speech drives this construction of the [FFDCA]; as in *Sorrell*, the "express purpose and practical effect" of the government's ban on promotion is to "diminish the effectiveness of [off-label drug] marketing by manufacturers."

Second, this construction is speaker-based because it targets one kind of speaker—pharmaceutical manufacturers—while allowing others to speak without restriction. In *Sorrell*, pharmaceutical companies were barred from obtaining and using prescriber-identifying information for marketing purposes, but a wide range of other speakers, including private and academic researchers, could acquire and use the information. Similarly, here, because off-label prescriptions and drug use are legal, the government's application of the [FFDCA] permits physicians and academics, for example, to speak about off-label use without consequence, while the same speech is prohibited when delivered by pharmaceutical manufacturers. This construction "thus has the effect of preventing [pharmaceutical manufacturers]—and only [pharmaceutical manufacturers]—from communicating with physicians in an effective and informative manner."

Additionally, a claim to First Amendment protection here is more compelling than in *Sorrell* because this case involves a criminal regulatory scheme subject to more careful scrutiny.

Accordingly, the government's construction of the [FFDCA]'s misbranding provisions to prohibit and criminalize off-label promotion is content- and speaker-based, and subject to heightened scrutiny under *Sorrell*.

### 2. Central Hudson

The first two prongs of *Central Hudson* are easily satisfied here. First, promoting off-label drug use concerns lawful activity (off-label drug use), and the promotion of off-label drug use is not in and of itself false or misleading. Second, the government's asserted interests in drug safety and public health are substantial. Specifically, the government asserts an interest in preserving the effectiveness and integrity of the [FFDCA]'s drug approval process, and an interest in reducing patient exposure to unsafe and ineffective drugs.

The third and fourth prongs of *Central Hudson* require that the regulation directly advance the government's interests and be narrowly drawn. We turn to the third and fourth prongs below.

#### a. Direct Advancement

The government's construction of the [FFDCA] as prohibiting off-label promotion does not, by itself, withstand scrutiny under *Central Hudson*'s third prong. First, off-label drug usage is not unlawful, and the FDA's drug approval process generally contemplates that approved drugs will be used in off-label ways. In effect, even if pharmaceutical manufacturers are barred from off-label promotion, physicians can prescribe, and patients can use, drugs for off-label purposes. As off-label drug use itself is not prohibited, it does not follow that prohibiting the truthful promotion of off-label drug usage by a particular class of speakers would directly further the government's goals of preserving the efficacy and integrity of the FDA's drug approval process and reducing patient exposure to unsafe and ineffective drugs.

Second, prohibiting off-label promotion by a pharmaceutical manufacturer while simultaneously allowing off-label use "paternalistically" interferes with the ability of physicians and patients to receive potentially relevant treatment information; such barriers to information about off-label use could inhibit, to the public's detriment, informed and intelligent treatment decisions. In fact, in granting safe harbor to manufacturers by permitting the dissemination of off-label information through scientific journals, the FDA itself "recognizes that public health can be served when health care professionals receive truthful and non-misleading scientific and medical information on unapproved uses" of approved drugs.

Here, as the FDA recognizes, it is the physician's role to consider multiple factors, including a drug's FDA-approval status, to determine the best course of action for her patient. While some off-label information could certainly be misleading or unhelpful, this case does not involve false or misleading promotion. Moreover, in the fields of medicine and public health, "where information can save lives," it only furthers the public interest to ensure that decisions about the use of prescription drugs, including off-label usage, are intelligent and well-informed.

The government's construction of the [FFDCA] essentially legalizes the outcome—off-label use—but prohibits the free flow of information that would inform that outcome. If the government's objective is to shepherd physicians to prescribe drugs only on-label, criminalizing manufacturer promotion of off-label use while permitting others to promote such use to physicians is an indirect and questionably effective means to achieve that goal. Thus, the government's construction of the [FFDCA]'s misbranding provisions does not directly advance its interest in reducing patient exposure to off-label drugs or in preserving the efficacy of the FDA drug approval process because the off-label use of such drugs continues to be generally lawful. Accordingly, the government's prohibition of off-label promotion by pharmaceutical manufacturers "provides only ineffective or remote support for the government's purpose."

### b. Narrowly Drawn

The last prong of Central Hudson requires the government's regulation to be narrowly drawn to further the interests served. Here, the government's construction of the [FFDCA] to impose a complete and criminal ban on off-label promotion by pharmaceutical manufacturers is more extensive than necessary to achieve the government's substantial interests. Numerous, less speech-restrictive alternatives are available, as are non-criminal penalties.

To advance the integrity of the FDA's drug approval process and increase the safety of off-label drug use, the government could pursue several alternatives without excessive First Amendment restrictions. For example, if the government is concerned about the use of drugs off-label, it could more directly address the issue. If the government is concerned that off-label promotion may mislead physicians, it could guide physicians and patients in differentiating between misleading and false promotion, exaggerations and embellishments, and truthful or non-misleading information. The government could develop its warning or disclaimer systems, or develop safety tiers within the off-label market, to distinguish between drugs. The government could require pharmaceutical manufacturers to list all applicable or intended indications when they first apply for FDA approval, enabling physicians, the government, and patients to track a drug's development. To minimize off-label use, or manufacturer evasion of the approval process for such use, the government could create other limits, including ceilings or caps on off-label prescriptions. The FDA could further remind physicians and manufacturers of, and even perhaps further regulate, the legal liability surrounding off-label promotion and treatment decisions. Finally, where off-label drug use is exceptionally concerning, the government could prohibit the off-label use altogether. The possibilities are numerous indeed.

"If the First Amendment means anything, it means that regulating speech must be a last—not first—resort." The government has not established a "reasonable fit" among its interests in drug safety and public health, the lawfulness of off-label use, and its construction of the [FFDCA] to prohibit off-label promotion. The government's interests could be served equally well by more limited and targeted restrictions on speech. The government contends that these alternative means of reducing patient exposure to unsafe, untested drugs and maintaining the integrity of the FDA-approval process are "indefensible" because they are not administrable, feasible, or otherwise effective. In the absence of any support, such conclusory assertions are insufficient to sustain the government's burden of demonstrating that the proposed alternatives are less effective than its proposed construction of the [FFDCA] in furthering the government interests identified.

Accordingly, even if speech can be used as evidence of a drug's intended use, we decline to adopt the government's construction of the [FFDCA]'s misbranding provisions to prohibit manufacturer promotion alone as it would unconstitutionally restrict free speech. We construe the misbranding provisions of the [FFDCA] as not prohibiting and criminalizing the truthful off-label promotion of FDA-approved prescription drugs. Our conclusion is limited to FDA-approved drugs for which off-label use is not prohibited, and we do not hold, of course, that the FDA cannot regulate the marketing of prescription drugs. We conclude simply that the government cannot prosecute pharmaceutical manufacturers and their representatives under the [FFDCA] for speech promoting the lawful, off-label use of an FDA-approved drug.

### Conclusion

For the reasons set forth above, we VACATE the judgment of conviction and REMAND the case to the district court.

**DEBRA ANN LIVINGSTON, Circuit Judge, dissenting:**

Alfred Caronia was convicted of conspiring to introduce a prescription drug into interstate commerce with the intent that it be used in ways its labeling neither disclosed nor described. This intent was revealed, inter alia, through his speech. Because the First Amendment has never prohibited the government from using speech as evidence of motive or intent, see *Wisconsin v. Mitchell*, 508 U.S. 476, 489 (1993), I would affirm Caronia's conviction. By holding, instead, that Caronia's conviction must be vacated—and on the theory that whatever the elements of the crime for which he was duly tried, he was in fact convicted for promoting a drug for unapproved uses, in supposed violation of the First Amendment—the majority calls into question the very foundations of our century-old system of drug regulation. I do not believe that the Supreme Court's precedents compel such a result. I therefore respectfully dissent.

. . . .

### I. Intended Uses

Alfred Caronia was convicted of conspiring to introduce a "misbranded" drug into interstate commerce. Under the Federal Food, Drug and Cosmetic Act ("FDCA"), one way in which a drug is misbranded is if its labeling lacks adequate directions for layperson use. Whether a drug's directions are "adequate . . . for use" depends on the drug's intended uses. This is because the Food and Drug Administration ("FDA") defines "adequate directions for use" as "directions under which the layman can use a drug safely and for the purposes for which it is intended." Directions are adequate only if they include, for example, "[s]tatements of all . . . uses for which such drug is intended," and "usual quantities [of dose] for each of the uses for which it is intended." This labeling provision is in part merely a disclosure requirement for the benefit of a drug's lay users. But some uses of drugs are never safe, at least for a layperson; because it is impossible to provide adequate directions for such uses, this provision also effectively prohibits introducing drugs into interstate commerce with the intent that the drugs be used in ways that are unsafe for laypersons.

The labeling on the drug at issue in this case, Xyrem, stated that it was "indicated for the treatment of excessive daytime sleepiness and cataplexy in patients with narcolepsy." At all relevant times, the FDA had not approved Xyrem for any other uses. Xyrem's labeling did not state any other intended uses for the drug, nor provide directions for any other intended uses. Unsurprisingly, then, Caronia did not argue before the jury that Xyrem's labeling included adequate directions for the off-label uses that he was alleged to have promoted. Rather, his trial focused on whether Caronia agreed with his employer, Orphan Medical, Inc. ("Orphan"), and with others associated with Orphan, that Xyrem would be distributed for off-label use.

Determining a product's "intended uses" has long been a central concern of food and drug law. The concept originated in the Pure Food and Drugs Act of 1906, which prohibited introducing any adulterated or misbranded drug into interstate commerce, and which defined "drug" to include "any substance or mixture of substances intended to be used for the cure, mitigation, or prevention of disease,". Courts found violations of that statute where, as in this case, a manufacturer's speech demonstrated an intended use that brought it within the scope of the statute such that its label was required affirmatively to disclose certain information

When Congress expanded the law three decades later in the Food, Drug, and Cosmetic Act of 1938, its revisions remained anchored to the concept of "intended uses." The definition of "drug" was broadened to also include "articles . . . intended to affect the structure or any function of the body and the parallel category of "devices" was created and similarly defined in terms of intended uses. At the same time, Congress broadened the definition of a "misbranded" drug to include any drug with labeling not bearing "adequate directions for use." Under the 1938 Act, courts upheld convictions for introducing drugs into interstate commerce that lacked adequate labeling for their intended uses, and routinely relied on "oral representations made by . . . authorized sales distributors" to determine a product's intended uses.

The modern [FFDCA] continues to define "drugs" (and "devices") on the basis of an article's intended uses. The concept of "intended uses" therefore largely defines the scope of the FDA's regulatory authority. To put the matter in practical terms: it is because of the "intended uses" principle that hardware stores are generally free to sell bottles of turpentine, but may not label those bottles, "Hamlin's Wizard Oil: There is no sore it will not heal, no pain it will not subdue."

According to regulations that have remained essentially unchanged for sixty years, the FDA defines a drug's "intended uses" on an objective, rather than subjective, basis:

> The words intended uses or words of similar import . . . refer to the objective intent of the persons legally responsible for the labeling of drugs. The intent is determined by such persons' expressions or may be shown by the circumstances surrounding the distribution of the article. This objective intent may, for example, be shown by labeling claims, advertising matter, or oral or written statements by such persons or their representatives. It may be shown by the circumstances that the article is, with the knowledge of such persons or their representatives, offered and used for a purpose for which it is neither labeled nor advertised. . . . [I]f a manufacturer knows, or has knowledge of facts that would give him notice, that a drug introduced into interstate commerce by him is to be used for conditions, purposes, or uses other than the ones for which he offers it, he is required to provide adequate labeling for such a drug which accords with such other uses to which the article is to be put.

21 C.F.R. § 201.128. As previously noted, Caronia did not contend at trial that Xyrem's label (which provided dosage and other instructions for Xyrem's use in the treatment of narcolepsy patients who experience cataplexy and excessive daytime sleepiness) provided adequate instructions for any other use. In this case, then, Xyrem was "misbranded" — and Caronia could be guilty of conspiring with others to introduce it into interstate commerce in such a state — if the conduct and statements of the persons legally responsible for labeling the drug (or the conduct and statements of their representatives) demonstrated an objective intent that Xyrem be used for off-label purposes.

## 3. The Rise of Large-Molecule Biologic Drugs

### FDA Website, Frequently Asked Questions About Therapeutic Biological Products*

These frequently asked questions have been developed for the CDER Small Business and Industry Assistance Web site to help small pharmaceutical businesses understand the regulatory process for therapeutic biological products.

**What is a biological product?**

Biological products, like other drugs, are used for the treatment, prevention or cure of disease in humans. In contrast to chemically synthesized small molecular weight drugs, which have a well-defined structure and can be thoroughly characterized, biological products are generally derived from living material—human, animal, or microorganism—are complex in structure, and thus are usually not fully characterized.

Section 351 of the Public Health Service (PHS) Act defines a biological product as a "virus, therapeutic serum, toxin, antitoxin, vaccine, blood, blood component or derivative, allergenic product, or analogous product, . . . applicable to the prevention, treatment, or cure of a disease or condition of human beings." FDA regulations and policies have established that biological products include blood-derived products, vaccines, in vivo diagnostic allergenic products, immunoglobulin products, products containing cells or microorganisms, and most protein products. Biological products subject to the PHS Act also meet the definition of drugs under the Federal Food, Drug and Cosmetic Act (FDC Act). Note that hormones such as insulin, glucagon, and human growth hormone are regulated as drugs under the FDC Act, not biological products under the PHS Act.

**What Center has the regulatory responsibility for therapeutic biological products?**

Both the FDA's Center for Drug Evaluation and Research (CDER) and Center for Biologics Evaluation and Research (CBER) have regulatory responsibility for therapeutic biological products, including premarket review and oversight. The categories of therapeutic biological products regulated by CDER (under the FDC Act and/or the PHS Act, as appropriate) are the following

- Monoclonal antibodies for in vivo use.
- Most proteins intended for therapeutic use, including cytokines (e.g., interferons), enzymes (e.g. thrombolytics), and other novel proteins, except for those that are specifically assigned to the Center for Biologics Evaluation and Research (CBER) (e.g., vaccines and blood products). This category includes therapeutic proteins derived from plants, animals, humans, or microorganisms, and

* From https://www.fda.gov/drugs/therapeutic-biologics-applications-bla/frequently-asked-questions-about-therapeutic-biological-products (last updated 2015-07-07).

recombinant versions of these products. Exceptions to this rule are coagulation factors (both recombinant and human-plasma derived).

- Immunomodulators (non-vaccine and non-allergenic products intended to treat disease by inhibiting or down-regulating a pre-existing, pathological immune response).
- Growth factors, cytokines, and monoclonal antibodies intended to mobilize, stimulate, decrease or otherwise alter the production of hematopoietic cells in vivo.

. . .

**Are the biologic development requirements different than the requirements for a new drug product?**

Biological products are a subset of drugs; therefore both are regulated under provisions of the FDC Act. However, only biological products are licensed under section 351 of the PHS Act. (As previously noted, some therapeutic protein products are approved under section 505 of the FDC Act, not under the PHS Act.)

Following initial laboratory and animal testing that show that investigational use in humans is reasonably safe, biological products (like other drugs), can be studied in clinical trials in humans under an investigational new drug application (IND) in accordance with the regulations at 21 CFR 312. If the data generated by the studies demonstrate that the product is safe and effective for its intended use, the data are submitted as part of a marketing application. Whereas a new drug application (NDA) is used for drugs subject to the drug approval provisions of the FDC Act, a biologics license application (BLA) is required for biological products subject to licensure under the PHS Act. FDA form 356h is used for both NDA and BLA submissions. FDA approval to market a biologic is granted by issuance of a biologics license.

**What are the requirements for licensing a biologic?**

Issuance of a biologics license is a determination that the product, the manufacturing process, and the manufacturing facilities meet applicable requirements to ensure the continued safety, purity and potency of the product.

Among other things, safety and purity assessments must consider the storage and testing of cell substrates that are often used to manufacture biologics. A potency assay is required due to the complexity and heterogeneity of biologics.

The regulations regarding BLAs for therapeutic biological products include 21 CFR parts 600, 601, and 610.

**What does safety mean?**

The word safety means the relative freedom from harmful effects, direct or indirect, when a product is prudently administered, taking into consideration the character of the product in relation to the condition of the recipient at the time.

**What is purity?**

Purity means relative freedom from extraneous matter in the finished product, whether or not harmful to the recipient or deleterious to the product. Purity includes but is not limited to relative freedom from residual moisture or other volatile substances and pyrogenic substances.

**What is potency?**

The word potency is interpreted to mean the specific ability or capacity of the product, as indicated by appropriate laboratory tests, to yield a given result.

**Does FDA issue license certificates upon approval of a BLA?**

Approval to market a biologic is granted by issuance of a biologics license (including US license number) as part of the approval letter. FDA does not issue a license certificate. The US License number must appear on the product labeling.

**Why are biologics regulated under the PHS Act?**

As mentioned above, biologics are subject to provisions of both the [FFDCA] and the PHS Act. Because of the complexity of manufacturing and characterizing a biologic, the PHS Act emphasizes the importance of appropriate manufacturing control for products. The PHS Act provides for a system of controls over all aspects of the manufacturing process. In some cases, manufacturing changes could result in changes to the biological molecule that might not be detected by standard chemical and molecular biology characterization techniques yet could profoundly alter the safety or efficacy profile. Therefore, changes in the manufacturing process, equipment or facilities may require additional clinical studies to demonstrate the product's continued safety, identity, purity and potency.

The PHS Act also provides authority to immediately suspend licenses in situations where there exists a danger to public health.

**10. How is the manufacturing process for a biological product usually different from the process for drugs?**

Because, in many cases, there is limited ability to identify the identity of the clinically active component(s) of a complex biological product, such products are often defined by their manufacturing processes. Changes in the manufacturing process, equipment or facilities could result in changes in the biological product itself and sometimes require additional clinical studies to demonstrate the product's safety, identity, purity and potency. Traditional drug products usually consist of pure chemical substances that are easily analyzed after manufacture. Since there is a significant difference in how biological products are made, the production is monitored by the agency from the early stages to make sure the final product turns out as expected.

**What is comparability testing of biologics?**

A sponsor may be able to demonstrate product comparability between a biological product made after a manufacturing change and a product made before implementation of the change through different types of analytical and functional testing without additional clinical studies. The agency may determine that the two products are comparable if the results of the comparability testing demonstrate that the manufacturing change does not affect safety, identity, purity, or potency. . . .

## 4. Compounded Drugs

### FDA Website, Compounding Laws and Policies*

Compounded drugs are not FDA-approved. This means that FDA does not review these drugs to evaluate their safety, effectiveness, or quality before they reach patients. FDA has investigated many cases of serious patient injury linked to poor quality compounded drugs. In 2012, contaminated drugs compounded by a Massachusetts pharmacy led to more than 750 cases of infection and more than 60 deaths of patients in 20 states.

Congress passed the Drug Quality and Security Act (DQSA) in response to the 2012 fungal meningitis outbreak, as well as numerous other serious adverse events, including deaths, linked to poor quality compounded drugs. The DQSA, which was enacted on November 27, 2013, made important updates to the Federal Food, Drug and Cosmetic Act ([FFDCA]) regarding human drug compounding. Since DQSA enactment, FDA has worked diligently to issue draft and final policy documents to implement the law.

The DQSA eliminated provisions concerning advertising of compounded drugs that had been found to be unconstitutional from existing law addressing compounding—section 503A of the [FFDCA]. This removed uncertainty about the validity of section 503A, which Congress otherwise left intact.

Section 503A describes the conditions under which compounded human drug products are exempt from the [FFDCA] sections on FDA approval prior to marketing, current good manufacturing practice (CGMP) requirements, and labeling with adequate directions for use. One of these conditions is that the drugs must be compounded based on the receipt of valid patient-specific prescriptions.

The DQSA also added a new section 503B to the [FFDCA], which established a new, voluntary category of compounders known as outsourcing facilities. Unlike compounders operating under section 503A, outsourcing facilities are subject to CGMP requirements, and they may distribute compounded drugs either pursuant to a patient-specific prescription or in response to an order from a health care provider, such as a hospital, that is not for an identified individual patient (e.g., for office stock).

---

* From https://www.fda.gov/drugs/human-drug-compounding/compounding-laws-and-policies (content current as of 2018-07-23).

Outsourcing facilities are inspected by FDA according to a risk-based schedule, and must meet certain other conditions, such as reporting adverse events and providing FDA with certain information about the products they compound.

See provisions of federal law that apply to human drug compounding and FDA's policies on other related activities for more information. See also information about the Pharmacy Compounding Advisory Committee, which provides FDA with advice as it implements certain provisions of sections 503A and 503B of the [FFDCA].

Additionally, find information on FDA's work to develop the lists of bulk drug substances that can be used in compounding under sections 503A and 503B of the [FFDCA].

## F. Related Area Not Regulated Primarily by FDA: Federally Controlled Substances

### 1. Controlled Substances

#### Gonzales v. Raich

545 U.S. 1 (2005)

**Justice STEVENS delivered the opinion of the Court.**

California is one of at least nine States that authorize the use of marijuana for medicinal purposes. The question presented in this case is whether the power vested in Congress by Article I, § 8, of the Constitution "[t]o make all Laws which shall be necessary and proper for carrying into Execution" its authority to "regulate Commerce with foreign Nations, and among the several States" includes the power to prohibit the local cultivation and use of marijuana in compliance with California law.

I

California has been a pioneer in the regulation of marijuana. In 1913, California was one of the first States to prohibit the sale and possession of marijuana, and at the end of the century, California became the first State to authorize limited use of the drug for medicinal purposes. In 1996, California voters passed Proposition 215, now codified as the Compassionate Use Act of 1996. The proposition was designed to ensure that "seriously ill" residents of the State have access to marijuana for medical purposes, and to encourage Federal and State Governments to take steps toward ensuring the safe and affordable distribution of the drug to patients in need. The Act creates an exemption from criminal prosecution for physicians, as well as for patients and primary caregivers who possess or cultivate marijuana for medicinal purposes with the recommendation or approval of a physician. A "primary caregiver" is a person who has consistently assumed responsibility for the housing, health, or safety of the patient.

Respondents Angel Raich and Diane Monson are California residents who suffer from a variety of serious medical conditions and have sought to avail themselves of medical marijuana pursuant to the terms of the Compassionate Use Act. They are being treated by licensed, board-certified family practitioners, who have concluded, after prescribing a host of conventional medicines to treat respondents' conditions and to alleviate their associated symptoms, that marijuana is the only drug available that provides effective treatment. Both women have been using marijuana as a medication for several years pursuant to their doctors' recommendation, and both rely heavily on cannabis to function on a daily basis. Indeed, Raich's physician believes that forgoing cannabis treatments would certainly cause Raich excruciating pain and could very well prove fatal.

Respondent Monson cultivates her own marijuana, and ingests the drug in a variety of ways including smoking and using a vaporizer. Respondent Raich, by contrast, is unable to cultivate her own, and thus relies on two caregivers, litigating as "John Does," to provide her with locally grown marijuana at no charge. These caregivers also process the cannabis into hashish or keif, and Raich herself processes some of the marijuana into oils, balms, and foods for consumption.

On August 15, 2002, county deputy sheriffs and agents from the federal Drug Enforcement Administration (DEA) came to Monson's home. After a thorough investigation, the county officials concluded that her use of marijuana was entirely lawful as a matter of California law. Nevertheless, after a 3-hour standoff, the federal agents seized and destroyed all six of her cannabis plants.

Respondents thereafter brought this action against the Attorney General of the United States and the head of the DEA seeking injunctive and declaratory relief prohibiting the enforcement of the federal Controlled Substances Act (CSA), 21 U.S.C. § 801 et seq., to the extent it prevents them from possessing, obtaining, or manufacturing cannabis for their personal medical use. In their complaint and supporting affidavits, Raich and Monson described the severity of their afflictions, their repeatedly futile attempts to obtain relief with conventional medications, and the opinions of their doctors concerning their need to use marijuana. Respondents claimed that enforcing the CSA against them would violate the Commerce Clause, the Due Process Clause of the Fifth Amendment, the Ninth and Tenth Amendments of the Constitution, and the doctrine of medical necessity.

The District Court denied respondents' motion for a preliminary injunction. Although the court found that the federal enforcement interests "wane[d]" when compared to the harm that California residents would suffer if denied access to medically necessary marijuana, it concluded that respondents could not demonstrate a likelihood of success on the merits of their legal claims.

A divided panel of the Court of Appeals for the Ninth Circuit reversed and ordered the District Court to enter a preliminary injunction. The court found that respondents had "demonstrated a strong likelihood of success on their claim that, as applied to them, the CSA is an unconstitutional exercise of Congress' Commerce Clause authority." The Court of Appeals distinguished prior Circuit cases upholding the CSA in the face of Commerce Clause challenges by focusing on what it deemed to be the "separate and distinct class of activities" at issue in this case: "the intrastate, noncommercial cultivation and possession of cannabis for personal medical purposes as recommended by a patient's physician pursuant to valid California state law." The court found the latter class of activities "different in kind from drug trafficking" because interposing a physician's recommendation raises different health and safety concerns, and because "this limited use is clearly distinct from the broader illicit drug market-as well as any broader commercial market for medicinal marijuana-insofar as the medicinal marijuana at issue in this case is not intended for, nor does it enter, the stream of commerce."

The majority placed heavy reliance on our decisions in *United States v. Lopez*, 514 U.S. 549 (1995), and *United States v. Morrison*, 529 U.S. 598 (2000), as interpreted by recent Circuit precedent, to hold that this separate class of purely local activities was beyond the reach of federal power. In contrast, the dissenting judge concluded that the CSA, as applied to respondents, was clearly valid under *Lopez* and *Morrison*; moreover, he thought it "simply impossible to distinguish the relevant conduct surrounding the cultivation and use of the marijuana crop at issue in this case from the cultivation and use of the wheat crop that affected interstate commerce in *Wickard v. Filburn*[, 317 U.S. 111 (1942).]"

The obvious importance of the case prompted our grant of certiorari. The case is made difficult by respondents' strong arguments that they will suffer irreparable harm because, despite a congressional finding to the contrary, marijuana does have valid therapeutic purposes. The question before us, however, is not whether it is wise to enforce the statute in these circumstances; rather, it is whether Congress' power to regulate interstate markets for medicinal substances encompasses the portions of those markets that are supplied with drugs produced and consumed locally. Well-settled law controls our answer. The CSA is a valid exercise of federal power, even as applied to the troubling facts of this case. We accordingly vacate the judgment of the Court of Appeals.

## II

Shortly after taking office in 1969, President Nixon declared a national "war on drugs." As the first campaign of that war, Congress set out to enact legislation that would consolidate various drug laws on the books into a comprehensive statute, provide meaningful regulation over legitimate sources of drugs to prevent diversion into illegal channels, and strengthen law enforcement tools against the traffic in illicit drugs. That effort culminated in the passage of the Comprehensive Drug Abuse Prevention and Control Act of 1970.

This was not, however, Congress' first attempt to regulate the national market in drugs. Rather, as early as 1906 Congress enacted federal legislation imposing labeling regulations on medications and prohibiting the manufacture or shipment of any adulterated or misbranded drug traveling in interstate commerce. Aside from these labeling restrictions, most domestic drug regulations prior to 1970 generally came in the guise of revenue laws, with the Department of the Treasury serving as the Federal Government's primary enforcer. For example, the primary drug control law, before being repealed by the passage of the CSA, was the Harrison Narcotics Act of 1914 (repealed 1970). The Harrison Act sought to exert control over the possession and sale of narcotics, specifically cocaine and opiates, by requiring producers, distributors, and purchasers to register with the Federal Government, by assessing taxes against parties so registered, and by regulating the issuance of prescriptions.

Marijuana itself was not significantly regulated by the Federal Government until 1937 when accounts of marijuana's addictive qualities and physiological effects, paired with dissatisfaction with enforcement efforts at state and local levels, prompted Congress to pass the Marihuana Tax Act (repealed 1970). Like the Harrison Act, the Marihuana Tax Act did not outlaw the possession or sale of marijuana outright. Rather, it imposed registration and reporting requirements for all individuals importing, producing, selling, or dealing in marijuana, and required the payment of annual taxes in addition to transfer taxes whenever the drug changed hands. Moreover, doctors wishing to prescribe marijuana for medical purposes were required to comply with rather burdensome administrative requirements. Noncompliance exposed traffickers to severe federal penalties, whereas compliance would often subject them to prosecution under state law. Thus, while the Marihuana Tax Act did not declare the drug illegal per se, the onerous administrative requirements, the prohibitively expensive taxes, and the risks attendant on compliance practically curtailed the marijuana trade.

Then in 1970, after declaration of the national "war on drugs," federal drug policy underwent a significant transformation. A number of noteworthy events precipitated this policy shift. First, in *Leary v. United States*, 395 U.S. 657 (1969), this Court held certain provisions of the Marihuana Tax Act and other narcotics legislation unconstitutional. Second, at the end of his term, President Johnson fundamentally reorganized the federal drug control agencies. The Bureau of Narcotics, then housed in the Department of the Treasury, merged with the Bureau of Drug Abuse Control, then housed in the Department of Health, Education, and Welfare (HEW), to create the Bureau of Narcotics and Dangerous Drugs, currently housed in the Department of Justice. Finally, prompted by a perceived need to consolidate the growing number of piecemeal drug laws and to enhance federal drug enforcement powers, Congress enacted the Comprehensive Drug Abuse Prevention and Control Act.[19]

---

19. The Comprehensive Drug Abuse Prevention and Control Act of 1970 consists of three titles. Title I relates to the prevention and treatment of narcotic addicts through HEW (now the Department of Health and Human Services). Title II, as discussed in more detail above, addresses drug control and enforcement as administered by the Attorney General and the DEA. Title III concerns the import and export of controlled substances.

Title II of that Act, the CSA, repealed most of the earlier antidrug laws in favor of a comprehensive regime to combat the international and interstate traffic in illicit drugs. The main objectives of the CSA were to conquer drug abuse and to control the legitimate and illegitimate traffic in controlled substances. Congress was particularly concerned with the need to prevent the diversion of drugs from legitimate to illicit channels.

To effectuate these goals, Congress devised a closed regulatory system making it unlawful to manufacture, distribute, dispense, or possess any controlled substance except in a manner authorized by the CSA. 21 U.S.C. §§ 841(a)(1), 844(a). The CSA categorizes all controlled substances into five schedules. § 812. The drugs are grouped together based on their accepted medical uses, the potential for abuse, and their psychological and physical effects on the body. §§ 811, 812. Each schedule is associated with a distinct set of controls regarding the manufacture, distribution, and use of the substances listed therein. §§ 821–830. The CSA and its implementing regulations set forth strict requirements regarding registration, labeling and packaging, production quotas, drug security, and recordkeeping. 21 CFR § 1301 et seq. (2004).

In enacting the CSA, Congress classified marijuana as a Schedule I drug. 21 U.S.C. § 812(c). This preliminary classification was based, in part, on the recommendation of the Assistant Secretary of HEW "that marihuana be retained within schedule I at least until the completion of certain studies now underway." Schedule I drugs are categorized as such because of their high potential for abuse, lack of any accepted medical use, and absence of any accepted safety for use in medically supervised treatment. § 812(b)(1). These three factors, in varying gradations, are also used to categorize drugs in the other four schedules. For example, Schedule II substances also have a high potential for abuse which may lead to severe psychological or physical dependence, but unlike Schedule I drugs, they have a currently accepted medical use. § 812(b)(2). By classifying marijuana as a Schedule I drug, as opposed to listing it on a lesser schedule, the manufacture, distribution, or possession of marijuana became a criminal offense, with the sole exception being use of the drug as part of a Food and Drug Administration preapproved research study. §§ 823(f), 841(a)(1), 844(a); see also *United States v. Oakland Cannabis Buyers' Cooperative*, 532 U.S. 483, 490 (2001).

The CSA provides for the periodic updating of schedules and delegates authority to the Attorney General, after consultation with the Secretary of Health and Human Services, to add, remove, or transfer substances to, from, or between schedules. § 811. Despite considerable efforts to reschedule marijuana, it remains a Schedule I drug.[23]

---

23. Starting in 1972, the National Organization for the Reform of Marijuana Laws began its campaign to reclassify marijuana. After some fleeting success in 1988 when an Administrative Law Judge (ALJ) declared that the DEA would be acting in an "unreasonable, arbitrary, and capricious" manner if it continued to deny marijuana access to seriously ill patients, and concluded that

### III

Respondents in this case do not dispute that passage of the CSA, as part of the Comprehensive Drug Abuse Prevention and Control Act, was well within Congress' commerce power. Nor do they contend that any provision or section of the CSA amounts to an unconstitutional exercise of congressional authority. Rather, respondents' challenge is actually quite limited; they argue that the CSA's categorical prohibition of the manufacture and possession of marijuana as applied to the intrastate manufacture and possession of marijuana for medical purposes pursuant to California law exceeds Congress' authority under the Commerce Clause.

*[An extensive discussion of the commerce clause is here omitted.]*

. . . .

In assessing the scope of Congress' authority under the Commerce Clause, we stress that the task before us is a modest one. We need not determine whether respondents' activities, taken in the aggregate, substantially affect interstate commerce in fact, but only whether a "rational basis" exists for so concluding. Given the enforcement difficulties that attend distinguishing between marijuana cultivated locally and marijuana grown elsewhere, 21 U.S.C. § 801(5), and concerns about diversion into illicit channels, we have no difficulty concluding that Congress had a rational basis for believing that failure to regulate the intrastate manufacture and possession of marijuana would leave a gaping hole in the CSA. Thus, as in *Wickard*, when it enacted comprehensive legislation to regulate the interstate market in a fungible commodity, Congress was acting well within its authority to "make all Laws which shall be necessary and proper" to "regulate Commerce . . . among the several States." U.S. Const., Art. I, § 8. That the regulation ensnares some purely intrastate activity is of no moment. As we have done many times before, we refuse to excise individual components of that larger scheme.

### IV

To support their contrary submission, respondents rely heavily on two of our more recent Commerce Clause cases. In their myopic focus, they overlook the larger context of modern-era Commerce Clause jurisprudence preserved by those cases. Moreover, even in the narrow prism of respondents' creation, they read those cases far too broadly.

Those two cases, of course, are *Lopez* and *Morrison* . . . .

Unlike those at issue in *Lopez* and *Morrison*, the activities regulated by the CSA are quintessentially economic. . . . The CSA is a statute that regulates the production, distribution, and consumption of commodities for which there is an

---

it should be reclassified as a Schedule III substance, the campaign has proved unsuccessful. The DEA Administrator did not endorse the ALJ's findings, and since that time has routinely denied petitions to reschedule the drug, most recently in 2001. The Court of Appeals for the District of Columbia Circuit has reviewed the petition to reschedule marijuana on five separate occasions over the course of 30 years, ultimately upholding the Administrator's final order.

established, and lucrative, interstate market. Prohibiting the intrastate possession or manufacture of an article of commerce is a rational (and commonly utilized) means of regulating commerce in that product.[36] Such prohibitions include specific decisions requiring that a drug be withdrawn from the market as a result of the failure to comply with regulatory requirements as well as decisions excluding Schedule I drugs entirely from the market. Because the CSA is a statute that directly regulates economic, commercial activity, our opinion in Morrison casts no doubt on its constitutionality.

The Court of Appeals was able to conclude otherwise only by isolating a "separate and distinct" class of activities that it held to be beyond the reach of federal power, defined as "the intrastate, noncommercial cultivation, possession and use of marijuana for personal medical purposes on the advice of a physician and in accordance with state law." The court characterized this class as "different in kind from drug trafficking." The differences between the members of a class so defined and the principal traffickers in Schedule I substances might be sufficient to justify a policy decision exempting the narrower class from the coverage of the CSA. The question, however, is whether Congress' contrary policy judgment, i.e., its decision to include this narrower "class of activities" within the larger regulatory scheme, was constitutionally deficient. We have no difficulty concluding that Congress acted rationally in determining that none of the characteristics making up the purported class, whether viewed individually or in the aggregate, compelled an exemption from the CSA; rather, the subdivided class of activities defined by the Court of Appeals was an essential part of the larger regulatory scheme.

First, the fact that marijuana is used "for personal medical purposes on the advice of a physician" cannot itself serve as a distinguishing factor. The CSA designates marijuana as contraband for any purpose; in fact, by characterizing marijuana as a Schedule I drug, Congress expressly found that the drug has no acceptable medical uses. . . .

Second, limiting the activity to marijuana possession and cultivation "in accordance with state law" cannot serve to place respondents' activities beyond congressional reach. The Supremacy Clause unambiguously provides that if there is any conflict between federal and state law, federal law shall prevail. . . .

So, from the "separate and distinct" class of activities identified by the Court of Appeals (and adopted by the dissenters), we are left with "the intrastate, noncommercial cultivation, possession and use of marijuana." Thus the case for the exemption comes down to the claim that a locally cultivated product that is used domestically rather than sold on the open market is not subject to federal regulation. Given the findings in the CSA and the undisputed magnitude of the

36. See 16 U.S.C. § 668(a) (bald and golden eagles); 18 U.S.C. § 175(a) (biological weapons); § 831(a) (nuclear material); § 842(n)(1) (certain plastic explosives); § 2342(a) (contraband cigarettes).

commercial market for marijuana, our decisions in *Wickard v. Filburn* and the later cases endorsing its reasoning foreclose that claim.

V

Respondents also raise a substantive due process claim and seek to avail themselves of the medical necessity defense. These theories of relief were set forth in their complaint but were not reached by the Court of Appeals. We therefore do not address the question whether judicial relief is available to respondents on these alternative bases. We do note, however, the presence of another avenue of relief. As the Solicitor General confirmed during oral argument, the statute authorizes procedures for the reclassification of Schedule I drugs. But perhaps even more important than these legal avenues is the democratic process, in which the voices of voters allied with these respondents may one day be heard in the halls of Congress. Under the present state of the law, however, the judgment of the Court of Appeals must be vacated. The case is remanded for further proceedings consistent with this opinion.

It is so ordered.

**Justice SCALIA, concurring in the judgment.**

I agree with the Court's holding that the Controlled Substances Act (CSA) may validly be applied to respondents' cultivation, distribution, and possession of marijuana for personal, medicinal use. I write separately because my understanding of the doctrinal foundation on which that holding rests is, if not inconsistent with that of the Court, at least more nuanced.

. . . .

I . . . agree with the Court that, however the class of regulated activities is subdivided, Congress could reasonably conclude that its objective of prohibiting marijuana from the interstate market "could be undercut" if those activities were excepted from its general scheme of regulation. That is sufficient to authorize the application of the CSA to respondents.

**Justice O'CONNOR, . . . dissenting.**

We enforce the "outer limits" of Congress' Commerce Clause authority not for their own sake, but to protect historic spheres of state sovereignty from excessive federal encroachment and thereby to maintain the distribution of power fundamental to our federalist system of government. One of federalism's chief virtues, of course, is that it promotes innovation by allowing for the possibility that "a single courageous State may, if its citizens choose, serve as a laboratory; and try novel social and economic experiments without risk to the rest of the country."

This case exemplifies the role of States as laboratories. The States' core police powers have always included authority to define criminal law and to protect the health, safety, and welfare of their citizens. Exercising those powers, California (by ballot initiative and then by legislative codification) has come to its own conclusion about the difficult and sensitive question of whether marijuana should be available to relieve severe pain and suffering. Today the Court sanctions an application of the federal Controlled Substances Act that extinguishes that experiment, without any proof that the personal cultivation, possession, and use of marijuana for medicinal purposes, if economic activity in the first place, has a substantial effect on interstate commerce and is therefore an appropriate subject of federal regulation. In so doing, the Court announces a rule that gives Congress a perverse incentive to legislate broadly pursuant to the Commerce Clause—nestling questionable assertions of its authority into comprehensive regulatory schemes—rather than with precision. That rule and the result it produces in this case are irreconcilable with our decisions in *Lopez*, supra, and *United States v. Morrison*, 529 U.S. 598 (2000). Accordingly I dissent.

....

What is the relevant conduct subject to Commerce Clause analysis in this case? The Court takes its cues from Congress, applying the above considerations to the activity regulated by the Controlled Substances Act (CSA) in general. The Court's decision rests on two facts about the CSA: (1) Congress chose to enact a single statute providing a comprehensive prohibition on the production, distribution, and possession of all controlled substances, and (2) Congress did not distinguish between various forms of intrastate noncommercial cultivation, possession, and use of marijuana. See 21 U.S.C. §§ 841(a)(1), 844(a). Today's decision suggests that the federal regulation of local activity is immune to Commerce Clause challenge because Congress chose to act with an ambitious, all-encompassing statute, rather than piecemeal. In my view, allowing Congress to set the terms of the constitutional debate in this way, i.e., by packaging regulation of local activity in broader schemes, is tantamount to removing meaningful limits on the Commerce Clause.

....

We would do well to recall how James Madison, the father of the Constitution, described our system of joint sovereignty to the people of New York: "The powers delegated by the proposed Constitution to the federal government are few and defined. Those which are to remain in the State governments are numerous and indefinite.... The powers reserved to the several States will extend to all the objects which, in the ordinary course of affairs, concern the lives, liberties, and properties of the people, and the internal order, improvement, and prosperity of the State." The Federalist No. 45, pp. 292–293 (C. Rossiter ed.1961).

Relying on Congress' abstract assertions, the Court has endorsed making it a federal crime to grow small amounts of marijuana in one's own home for one's own medicinal use. This overreaching stifles an express choice by some States, concerned for the lives and liberties of their people, to regulate medical marijuana differently. If I were a California citizen, I would not have voted for the medical marijuana ballot initiative; if I were a California legislator I would not have supported the Compassionate Use Act. But whatever the wisdom of California's experiment with medical marijuana, the federalism principles that have driven our Commerce

Clause cases require that room for experiment be protected in this case. For these reasons I dissent.

**Justice THOMAS, dissenting.**

Respondents Diane Monson and Angel Raich use marijuana that has never been bought or sold, that has never crossed state lines, and that has had no demonstrable effect on the national market for marijuana. If Congress can regulate this under the Commerce Clause, then it can regulate virtually anything-and the Federal Government is no longer one of limited and enumerated powers.

. . . .

The majority prevents States like California from devising drug policies that they have concluded provide much-needed respite to the seriously ill. It does so without any serious inquiry into the necessity for federal regulation or the propriety of "displac[ing] state regulation in areas of traditional state concern." The majority's rush to embrace federal power "is especially unfortunate given the importance of showing respect for the sovereign States that comprise our Federal Union." Our federalist system, properly understood, allows California and a growing number of other States to decide for themselves how to safeguard the health and welfare of their citizens. I would affirm the judgment of the Court of Appeals. I respectfully dissent.

## G. Key Points

- The core element of the FFDCA's "drug" definition is FFDCA 201(g)(1)(B): "articles intended for use in the diagnosis, cure, mitigation, treatment, or prevention of disease in man or other animals."
  - This is a broad definition that FDA reads as including both animal drugs and biologics within the definition of "drug." But this does not operate in reverse. Many products that qualify as drugs are neither animal drugs nor biologics.
- Drugs required no marketing authorization prior to 1938. In that year, Congress required proof of safety for marketing authorization. Congress began requiring proof of efficacy for marketing authorization in 1962.
  - This 1962 mandate required FDA to determine which existing drugs should be withdrawn from the market as ineffective. This was a massive task that plays a major role in FDA's institutional history.
- It is useful to think of the drug industry as divided roughly into pioneers and generics on one hand, and prescription and over-the-counter on the other.
  - Pioneer drugs reach the market through New Drug Applications or Accelerated New Drug Applications. Manufacturers can request, as part of these applications, either prescription or over-the-counter status, and FDA will consider that request as part of its action on the relevant application.

    - Prescription generic drugs reach the market through Abbreviated New Drug Applications or Section 505(b)(2) Applications. Over-the-counter generic drugs reach the market through Abbreviated New Drug Applications, Section 505(b)(2) Applications, or compliance with over-the-counter drug monographs.
    - Pioneer drugs become susceptible to generic competition when their patents and any relevant exclusivity periods expire or when a successful Hatch-Waxman challenge is brought by a generic drug company.
    - There are procedures for requesting that a drug be moved from prescription to over-the-counter status, or vice versa. Prescription status is, as a statutory matter, a question of whether FDA determines that adequate directions can be written to permit a patient to use the drug without the supervision of a physician.
- Any drug that is approved by FDA is approved explicitly for one or more intended uses. Each of those uses is then included in the drug's label.
    - Physicians may prescribe drugs either on-label (for an approved intended use) or off-label (for some use not listed on the label). Drug companies, however, may promote drugs only for on-label uses.
    - Courts have concluded that the commercial speech doctrine places some limits on FDA's ability to regulate drug promotion. The exact scope of those limits is unclear.

## Chapter 11

# Animal Drugs

## A. Introduction

Please read (or review) the following excerpts in the statutory supplement:

- FFDCA 201. Definitions. *Subsections (g)(1) and (v) only.*
- FFDCA 501. Adulterated drugs and devices. *Subsections (a)(5) and (a)(6) only.*
- FFDCA 502. Misbranded drugs and devices. *Subsection (w) only.*
- FFDCA 512. New animal drugs.

## B. Outline of Regulatory Regime

As in other chapters of this book, this chapter begins with a set of charts. As you read this chapter for the first time, you should do no more than skim these charts to get a general sense of the structure of the applicable statutes and regulations. (For more information on the role of the charts in this casebook, see Chapter 1, Parts A.1 and B).

| Timeline of Key Statutes: Animal Drugs | | | |
|---|---|---|---|
| **Year** | **PL** | **Stat** | **Name of Statute** |
| 1968 | 90-399 | 82 Stat. 342 | Animal Drug Amendments of 1968 |
| 1988 | 100-670 | 102 Stat. 3971 | Generic Animal Drug Use and Patent Term Restoration Act |
| 1994 | 103-396 | 108 Stat. 4153 | Animal Drug Use and Patent Term Restoration Act of 1994 |
| 1996 | 104-134 | 110 Stat. 1321 | FDA Export Reform and Enhancement Act |
| 1996 | 104-250 | 110 Stat. 3151 | Animal Drug Availability Act |
| 2004 | 108-282 | 118 Stat. 891 | Minor Use and Minor Species Animal Health Act of 2004 |

| Key Statutory Provisions: Animal Drugs | | |
|---|---|---|
| **Statute Name or U.S.C. Title** | **§** | **Title of Section or Subsection** |
| FFDCA | 201(g)(1) | [Definition of human drug, which includes articles intended to affect disease or structure/function of "man or other animals"] |
| FFDCA | 201(w) | [Definition of "animal feed"] |

| Statute Name or U.S.C. Title | § | Title of Section or Subsection |
|---|---|---|
| FFDCA | 201(v) | [Definition of "new animal drug"] |
| FFDCA | 501(a)(5) | [Adulteration provision specific to new animal drugs] |
| FFDCA | 501(a)(6) | [Adulteration provision specific to animal feed containing new animal drugs] |
| FFDCA | 501(w) | [Misbranding provision specific to new animal drugs] |
| FFDCA | 503(f) | [Veterinary prescription drugs] |
| FFDCA | 504 | Veterinary feed directive drugs |
| FFDCA | 510 | Registration of producers of drugs or devices |
| FFDCA | 512 | New animal drugs |
| FFDCA | 571 | Conditional approval of new animal drugs for minor use and minor species |
| FFDCA | 572 | Index of legally marketed unapproved new animal drugs for minor species |
| FFDCA | 573 | Designated new animal drugs for minor use or minor species |

| Key Regulatory Provisions: Animal Drugs Generally | | |
|---|---|---|
| 21 C.F.R. Part | Subpart | Title of Part or Subpart |
| 225 | — | Current good manufacturing practice for medicated feeds |
| 226 | — | Current good manufacturing practice for type a medicated articles |
| 500 | C | Labeling of animal drugs; misbranding. |
| 500 | E | Regulation of carcinogenic compounds used in food-producing animals |
| 510 | — | New animal drugs |
| 511 | — | New animal drugs for investigational use |
| 514 | — | New animal drug applications |
| 515 | — | Medicated feed mill license |
| 516 | — | New animal drugs for minor use and minor species |
| 530 | — | Extralabel drug use in animals |
| 556 | A | General provisions [from Part titled "Tolerances for Residues of New Animal Drugs In Food"] |
| 558 | A | General provisions (from Part titled "New Animal Drugs for Use in Animal Feeds"] |

| Key Regulatory Provisions: Lists of Approved New Animal Drugs | | |
|---|---|---|
| 21 C.F.R. Part | Subpart | Title of Part or Subpart |
| 520 | — | Oral dosage form new animal drugs |
| 522 | — | Implantation or injectable dosage form new animal drugs |
| 524 | — | Ophthalmic and topical dosage form new animal drugs |
| 526 | — | Intramammary dosage form new animal drugs |
| 528 | — | New animal drugs in genetically engineered animals |
| 529 | — | Certain other dosage form new animal drugs |
| 556 | B | Specific tolerances for residues of approved and conditionally approved new animal drugs |
| 558 | B | Specific new animal drugs for use in animal feeds |

| Key Regulatory Provisions: Animal Drugs in Food and Feed | | |
|---|---|---|
| 21 C.F.R. Part | Subpart | Title of Part or Subpart |
| 556 | — | Tolerances for residues of new animal drugs in food |
| 558 | — | New animal drugs for use in animal feeds |

# C. Overview

## FDA Website, FDA Regulation of Animal Drugs*

### A Brief Overview of FDA's Drug Approval Process

Under the [FFDCA], the term "drug" means articles recognized in the official United States Pharmacopoeia, official Homeopathic Pharmacopoeia of the United States, or official National Formulary; articles intended for use in the diagnosis, cure, mitigation, treatment, or prevention of disease in man or other animals; and articles other than food intended to affect the structure or any function of the body of man or other animals. It also includes articles intended for use as a component of a drug.

Once a product is determined to be a drug for animal use, the next step is to determine whether or not it is a new animal drug. The Act defines a new animal drug (in part) as *any drug intended for use for animals other than man, the composition of which is not generally recognized, among experts qualified by scientific training and experience, as safe and effective for use under the conditions prescribed, recommended, or suggested in its labeling*. By virtue of Supreme Court interpretations of

* From https://www.fda.gov/animal-veterinary/resources-you/fda-regulation-animal-drugs (last updated Nov 19, 2019).

the necessary basis for general recognition, there are, for all practical purposes, no animal drugs which are not also new animal drugs. The Animal Drugs @ FDA, accessible from the CVM Home Page contains a searchable database of all FDA-approved animal drugs.

An unapproved new animal drug may be distributed in accordance with 21 CFR Part 511 if the drug will be used for research, i.e., for the collection of data intended to be submitted in support of an NADA approval. Investigational New Animal Drug (INAD) regulations provide that such drugs may be distributed for use only by experts, qualified by scientific training and expertise, to investigate the safety and effectiveness of animal drugs.

Before a new animal drug may receive FDA approval, the sponsor must establish that the new animal drug is safe and effective.

Safe includes safety to the animal, safety of food products derived from the animal, safety to persons administering the drug or otherwise associated with the animal, and safety in terms of the drug's impact on the environment.

Effective means that the product will consistently and uniformly do what the labeling claims it will do.

Drug sponsors submit a New Animal Drug Application (NADA) along with supporting data, including all adverse effects associated with the drug's use. The NADA must also include information on the drug's chemistry; composition and component ingredients; manufacturing methods, facilities, and controls; proposed labeling; analytical methods for residue detection and analysis if applicable; an environmental assessment; and other information. The sponsor of a new animal drug is responsible for submitting all appropriate data to establish effectiveness and safety. If the drug product is intended for use in a food-producing animal, residues in food products must also be established as safe for human consumption.

FDA review of the NADA submitted by drug sponsors is very detailed and comprehensive. FDA scientists will determine whether the data have been developed in accordance with either Good Laboratory Practice Regulations or clinical trial guidance. If the studies were conducted properly, the data are evaluated with respect to drug safety and effectiveness. The animal safety data for a drug product must relate to the dosage levels and routes of administration proposed in the labeling. The primary objective is to determine the safety of the product relative to labeled usage.

At the conclusion of the animal safety review, a summary is prepared which explains why the product is safe or not shown to be safe. If the product has been shown to be safe but some restrictions or constraints on use are needed, all warning and precaution statements to be placed on the label must be enumerated and included in the summary, as well as any expected side effects.

All effectiveness data submitted must relate either directly or indirectly to the specific label and labeling claims made for the product. The sponsor must demonstrate that the product produces the claimed effect.

With respect to human food safety, it is the responsibility of the producer or sponsor of the animal drug to furnish FDA with the scientific information and experimental data that demonstrate that the presence of residues of the animal drug in the edible food products of the animal are safe for the consumer of the food product. The term "residues" applies to the parent drug and/or its metabolites. Detailed guidance on the studies required for animal drug approval is available from the Center for Veterinary Medicine (CVM). To assure that human food of animal origin can be monitored for the presence of drug residues, FDA requires sponsors of drugs for food animal use to provide acceptable analytical methods capable of determining and confirming the animal drug or its metabolites in the animal tissue.

. . . .

**Classifying RX and OTC Animal Drugs**

FDA is responsible for determining the marketing status (prescription, over-the-counter, or VFD) of animal drug products based on whether or not it is possible to prepare "adequate directions for use" under which a layperson can use the drugs safely and effectively. Prescription (Rx) products can be dispensed only by or upon the lawful written order of a licensed veterinarian. Safe use includes safety to the animal, safety of food products derived from the animal, safety to the persons associated with the animal, and safety in terms of the drug's impact on the environment.

Effective use of a drug product assumes that an accurate diagnosis can be made with a reasonable degree of certainty, that the drug can be properly administered, and that the course of the disease can be followed so that the success or lack of success of the product can be observed.

The same drug substances can be marketed in a number of different dosage forms, intended for use by different routes of administration, and in different species of animals. Thus, these drug products may be appropriately labeled Rx in some cases and OTC in others. Rx products must bear the legend:

*"Caution: Federal law restricts this drug to use by or on the order of a licensed veterinarian."*

**Dispensing Veterinary Prescription Drugs**

Since adequate directions for safe and effective lay use cannot be written for animal prescription drug products, such products can only be sold on the prescription or other order of a licensed veterinarian (Section 503(f)). Prior to being sold or dispensed, they must remain in the possession of a person or firm regularly and lawfully engaged in the manufacture, transportation, storage, or wholesale or retail distribution of animal prescription drug products. The drug products may be distributed only by persons or firms authorized by State and local laws.

Sale (dispensing, shipping, or otherwise making available for use in animals) of an animal prescription drug product to the layperson may be made only by or on the bona fide prescription or other order of a licensed veterinarian. Sale of a[n] animal prescription drug product to a layperson, except on a prescription or on order of a licensed practitioner, causes the product to be misbranded and subjects the seller to civil and/or criminal provisions of the [FFDCA].

A licensed veterinarian may legally use or dispense an animal prescription drug product only within the course of his/her professional practice where a valid veterinarian-client-patient relationship exists. Veterinarians employed by drug manufacturers or distributors may not legally dispense prescription drug products to laypersons unless they meet the above criteria. Similarly, practicing veterinarians or their employees may not legally sell animal prescription drug products to walk-in customers unless the same criteria are met. Federal regulations require that drug manufacturers provide at least the following information on the label of the finished package form of animal prescription drug products:

**What information needs to be on the package label of animal Rx drugs?**

- the statement, "*Caution: Federal law restricts this drug to use by or on the order of a licensed veterinarian;*"
- recommended or usual dosage;
- route of administration, if it is not for oral use;
- quantity or proportion of each active ingredient as well as the information required by section 502(e) of the [FFDCA];
- names of inactive ingredients if it is for other than oral use;
- an identifying lot or control number from which it is possible to determine the complete manufacturing history of the drug.

**What needs to be included in the veterinarian's prescription and included on the label of the dispensed product?**

- name and address of the dispenser;
- serial number and date of the order or its filling;
- name and address of the veterinarian who prescribed or ordered the drug product;
- directions for use; and
- any necessary warning and precautionary statements including withdrawal times.

Any additional requirements of State or local laws for dispensed animal drug products must also be followed.

To protect themselves and their clients, veterinarians should make efforts to ensure their instructions are followed, especially when they prescribe or recommend drugs for food-producing animals that require a withdrawal period.

**Compounding of Animal Drugs**

Under the [FFDCA], new animal drugs must be approved, conditionally approved, or included on the Index of Legally Marketed Unapproved New Animal Drugs for Minor Species to be legally marketed. The [FFDCA] does not generally distinguish between compounding and other methods of animal drug manufacturing.

New animal drugs that are not approved, conditionally approved, or indexed, which includes drugs compounded from bulk drug substances, are considered "unsafe" and "adulterated" under the [FFDCA].

FDA recognizes that in some situations a drug compounded from bulk drug substances may be the only appropriate treatment option for a particular animal. On November 19, 2019, FDA issued draft Guidance for Industry #256, "Compounding Animal Drugs from Bulk Drug Substances," which addresses situations in which, if the guidance is finalized, the FDA does not intend to take action for certain violations of the Food, Drug, & Cosmetic Act when pharmacists and veterinarians compound or oversee the compounding of animal drugs from bulk drug substances:

- to fill patient-specific prescriptions for nonfood-producing animals
- to compound "office stock" (certain drugs kept in veterinarians' supply) for nonfood-producing animals and
- to compound antidotes for food-producing animals.

Animal drugs compounded from bulk drug substances do not undergo review by FDA, meaning that the FDA has not determined that these unapproved products are safe and effective for their intended use. Because of the safety benefits and protections of the pre-market review process and post-market monitoring of FDA-approved, conditionally approved, and indexed drugs, veterinarians should only use drugs compounded from bulk drug substances if FDA-approved, conditionally approved, or indexed drugs are not available to treat the animal.

. . . .

## D. Related Area Not Regulated Primarily by FDA—Veterinary Biologics

FDA regulates animal drugs, human drugs used in animals, medical devices used for animals, and animal feed. However, FDA does not regulate biological products used in animals. Those are instead regulated by the Center for Veterinary Biologics within USDA's Animal and Plant Health Inspection Service.

Please read (or review) the following excerpts in the statutory supplement:

- 21 U.S.C. § 151. Preparation and sale of worthless or harmful products for domestic animals prohibited; preparation to be in compliance with rules at licensed establishments.
- 21 U.S.C. § 152. Importation regulated and prohibited.
- 21 U.S.C. § 153. Inspection of imports; denial of entry and destruction.
- 21 U.S.C. § 154. Regulations for preparation and sale; licenses.
- 9 C.F.R. Part 101. Definitions.
- 9 C.F.R. Part 102. Licenses for biological products.

## 1. Outline of Regulatory Regime

| Timeline of Key Statutes: Veterinary Biologics | | | |
|---|---|---|---|
| Year | PL | Stat | Name of Statute |
| 1913 | 62-430 | 37 Stat. 828, 832-33 | Virus, Serum, and Toxin Act |
| 1985 | 99-198 | 99 Stat 1354,1654 | Food Security Act of 1985<br>[First of two sections 1768 addresses "VIRUSES, SERUMS, TOXINS, AND ANALOGOUS PRODUCTS"] |

| Key Statutory Provisions: Veterinary Biologics | | |
|---|---|---|
| Statute Name or U.S.C. Title | § | Title of Section or Subsection |
| 21 U.S.C. | 151 | Preparation and sale of worthless or harmful products for domestic animals prohibited; preparation to be in compliance with rules at licensed establishments |
| 21 U.S.C. | 152 | Importation regulated and prohibited |
| 21 U.S.C. | 153 | Inspection of imports; denial of entry and destruction |
| 21 U.S.C. | 154 | Regulations for preparation and sale; licenses |

| Key Regulatory Provisions: Veterinary Biologics | | |
|---|---|---|
| 9 C.F.R. Part | Subpart | Title of Part or Subpart |
| 101 | — | Definitions |
| 102 | — | Licenses for biological products |
| 103 | — | Experimental production, distribution, and evaluation of biological products prior to licensing |
| 104 | — | Permits for biological products |
| 105 | — | Suspension, revocation, or termination of biological licenses or permits |
| 106 | — | Exemption for biological products used in department programs or under department control or supervision |
| 107 | — | Exemptions from preparation pursuant to an unsuspended and unrevoked license |
| 108 | — | Facility requirements for licensed establishments |
| 109 | — | Sterilization and pasteurization at licensed establishments |
| 112 | — | Packaging and labeling |
| 113 | — | Standard requirements |
| 114 | — | Production requirements for biological products |

| 9 C.F.R. Part | Subpart | Title of Part or Subpart |
|---|---|---|
| 115 | — | Inspections |
| 116 | — | Records and reports |
| 117 | — | Animals at licensed establishments |
| 118 | — | Detention; seizure and condemnation |
| 121 | — | Possession, use, and transfer of select agents and toxins |
| 122 | — | Organisms and vectors |
| 123 | — | Rules of practice governing proceedings under the virus-serum-toxin act |
| 124 | — | Patent term restoration |

**Key Regulatory Provisions: Regulations Listing Standards for Licensed Veterinary Biologics**

| 9 C.F.R. Part | Subpart | Title of Part or Subpart |
|---|---|---|
| 113 | 113.64–113.71 | Live bacterial vaccines |
| 113 | 113.100–113.123 | Inactivated bacterial vaccines |
| 113 | 113.200–113.216 | Killed virus vaccines |
| 113 | 113.300–113.332 | Live virus vaccines |
| 113 | 113.406–113.409 | Diagnostics and reagents |
| 113 | 113.450–113.499 | Antibody products |

## 2. Overview

### USDA, Veterinary Biologics: Use and Regulation*

Brochure, Revised February 2013

#### VETERINARY BIOLOGICS

Veterinary biologics are products derived from living organisms and biological processes. They are used to prevent, diagnose, or treat animal diseases and function through an immunological process. Immunity is a biological defense mechanism to avoid infection or disease that involves innate and adaptive components. Innate

* From https://www.aphis.usda.gov/publications/animal_health/content/printable_version/vet_biologics.pdf.

immunity is a nonspecific first line of defense against disease-causing organisms that includes physical, chemical, and cellular functions. Adaptive immunity is a specific cellular response that provides long-lasting protective immunity. Biologics generally function through the adaptive immune response, which is further differentiated into two types: active immunity and passive immunity. Active immunity is acquired when the body is exposed by natural infection or vaccination to a disease-causing agent or its derivatives, while passive immunity involves the transfer of protective antibodies from an immune animal to a susceptible or nonimmune animal.

. . . .

## TYPES OF VETERINARY BIOLOGICS

Veterinary biologics are used in a variety of animals, including livestock, pets, fish, birds, and wildlife. There are many types of biologics available, each with a different function and purpose.

**Vaccines, bacterins, bacterial extracts**, and **toxoids** are made from viruses, bacteria, spores, or other disease-causing organisms. These products may contain whole organisms or selected portions of an organism to elicit active immunity. Whole organisms in vaccines may be live or killed. Living organisms in products are modified by cell culture, natural selection, or other processes so that they do not cause disease in animals.

**Antiserums** and **antitoxins** are products containing protective antibodies against a particular organism or a toxic substance that the organism produces. Administering an antibody product to an animal provides passive immunity.

**Diagnostics** are products used to determine the health status of an animal.

**Immunomodulators** are products used to stimulate or suppress the immune system and to treat certain types of tumors or infections.

**Allergenic extracts** are used to diagnose or treat animal allergies to substances like pollen, dust, fleas, and feed ingredients.

About 70 years ago, there were perhaps a half-dozen products available. Today, there are nearly 2,000 licensed veterinary biological products designed to prevent, diagnose, or treat more than 200 different diseases in over 35 animal species. This ever-expanding array of veterinary biologics leads to better animal health care and reinforces the need for strict regulation so that animal and human health and our environment are protected.

## ORIGINS OF VETERINARY BIOLOGICS REGULATION

The regulation of veterinary biologics began soon after the turn of the 20th century because farmers and animal health officials did not have reliable biologics to treat hog cholera, a devastating disease. Many products were ineffective or contaminated with disease-causing organisms. A costly example was an outbreak of foot-and-mouth disease in 1909, caused by a contaminated vaccinia virus imported into the United States to produce a smallpox vaccine. In response to these problems, Congress passed the Virus-Serum-Toxin Act (VSTA) in 1913. VSTA gave the Secretary of Agriculture authority to license and regulate the production and trade of veterinary biologics. After seven decades, Congress amended VSTA in the Food Security Act of 1985, broadening the Secretary's authority to issue regulations, enhancing the Secretary's enforcement powers, and allowing USDA-APHIS to regulate all movement of veterinary biological products within or imported into the United States. In an effort to enhance security at our Nation's borders, the Homeland Security Act of 2002 transferred some import duties to the U.S. Department of Homeland Security. However, USDA continues to have jurisdiction over VSTA regulations and policies. Regulatory activity mandated by these acts is accomplished by CVB in Ames, IA, and Riverdale, MD.

**REGULATORY REQUIREMENTS**

Federal law prohibits the distribution of veterinary biologics unless they are manufactured in compliance with the regulations. Veterinary biologics for commercial use must be produced at a USDA-approved establishment and proven to be pure, safe, potent, and efficacious. APHIS issues an establishment license to acceptable manufacturing facilities and an individual product license for each veterinary biologic that the establishment markets. In addition, APHIS issues permits for importing veterinary biologics for research, transit shipment, or distribution and sale in the United States. APHIS inspects all licensed and permitted manufacturers' facilities to be sure that they are adequate and properly maintained. Agency officials examine production methods and records to ensure that each biological product is made in a consistent manner according to approved methods. Manufacturers test each batch of a biologic, commonly referred to as a serial, to ensure that quality is maintained. APHIS may elect to test selected serials as an independent verification of the test results obtained by the manufacturer. All required quality control tests must be satisfactorily concluded prior to any licensed or permitted veterinary biological product being released to the market. In addition, APHIS works with industry to develop reference standards and validate test methods to improve product evaluation and quality control, and it participates in international efforts to align U.S. regulatory testing requirements with other countries' requirements to facilitate exports

. . . .

## E. Key Points

- Prior to the Animal Drug Amendments of 1968, the FFDCA did not distinguish between human and animal drugs.
- Today, all animal drugs continue to meet the "drug" definition of FFDCA § 201(g)(1). However, animal drugs are explicitly exempted from the "new drug" definition of FFDCA § 201(p). Instead, FFDCA § 201(v) provides a separate definition for "new animal drug." The "new animal drug" definition of FFDCA § 201(v) plays a role in animal drug regulation similar to the role that the FFDCA § 201(p) "new drug" definition plays in human drug regulation.

    - As for food additives and color additives, the FFDCA contains a "Delaney Clause" for new animal drugs. This clause bars FDA approval of a new animal drug if it "induces cancer in man or animal." FFDCA § 512(d)(1)(I). However, there is an exception to the animal drugs Delaney Clause in situations where (among other things) no residue of the drug will be found "in any edible portion of such animals after slaughter or in any food yielded by or derived from the living animals."
    - FDA regulates human biologics, but not veterinary biologics. USDA instead regulates veterinary biologics under the Virus, Serum, and Toxin Act.
- FDA regulates genetically engineered animals under the FFDCA's animal drug provisions. The regulatory program is explained in FDA, Guidance for Industry #187: Regulation of Genetically Engineered Animals Containing Heritable Recombinant DNA Constructs (June 2015). FDA has issued a draft of a revision to this guidance document. *See* FDA, Draft Guidance for Industry: Regulation of Intentionally Altered Genomic DNA in Animals (January 2017). As of October 2020, this revised document had not yet been finalized.

# Chapter 12

# Medical Devices

## A. Introduction

Please read (or review) the following excerpts in the statutory supplement:

- FFDCA § 201. Definitions; generally. *Subsection (h) only.*
- FFDCA § 501. Adulterated drugs and devices. *Subsections (f), (g), (h), (i), and (j) only.*
- FFDCA § 502. Misbranded drugs and devices. *Subsections (a), (b), (c), (e), (f), (j), (o), (q), and (r) only.*
- FFDCA § 520. General provisions respecting control of devices intended for human use.
- 21 C.F.R. Part 868. Anesthesiology devices.
- 21 C.F.R. Part 870. Cardiology devices.
- 21 C.F.R. Part 872. Dental devices.
- 21 C.F.R. Part 878. General and plastic surgery devices.
- 21 C.F.R. Part 880. General hospital and personal use devices.
- 21 C.F.R. Part 890. Physical medicine devices.
- 21 C.F.R. Part 892. Radiology devices.
- 21 C.F.R. Part 895. Banned devices.
- 21 C.F.R. Part 898. Performance standard for electrode lead wires and patient cables.

## B. Outline of Regulatory Regime

As in other chapters of this book, this chapter begins with a set of charts. As you read this chapter for the first time, you should do no more than skim these charts to get a general sense of the structure of the applicable statutes and regulations. (For more information on the role of the charts in this casebook, see Chapter 1, Parts A.1 and B).

| Timeline of Key Statutes: Medical Devices | | | |
|---|---|---|---|
| Year | PL | Stat | Name of Statute |
| 1938 | 75-717 | 52 Stat. 1040 | FFDCA of 1938 |
| 1976 | 94-295 | 90 Stat. 539 | Medical Device Amendments of 1976 |
| 1990 | 101-629 | 104 Stat. 4511 | Safe Medical Devices Act |
| 1992 | 102-300 | 106 Stat. 238 | Medical Device Amendments of 1992 |
| 1997 | 105-115 | 111 Stat. 2296 | FDA Modernization Act of 1997 |
| 2002 | 107-250 | 116 Stat. 1588 | Medical Device User Fee and Modernization Act of 2002 |
| 2012 | 112-144 | 126 Stat. 993 | FDA Safety and Innovation Act |
| 2016 | 114-255 | 130 Stat. 1033 | 21st Century Cures Act |
| 2017 | 115-52 | 131 Stat. 1005 | FDA Reauthorization Act of 2017 |
| 2017 | 115-92 | 131 Stat. 2023 | An Act to Amend the Federal Food, Drug, and Cosmetic Act to authorize additional emergency uses for medical products to reduce deaths and severity of injuries caused by agents of war, and for other purposes. |

| Key Statutory Provisions: Medical Devices | | |
|---|---|---|
| Statute Name or U.S.C. Title | § | Title of Section or Subsection |
| FFDCA | 201(h) | [Definition of "device"] |
| FFDCA | 501 | Adulterated drugs and devices |
| FFDCA | 502 | Misbranded drugs and devices |
| FFDCA | 510 | Registration of producers of drugs or devices |
| FFDCA | 513 | Classification of devices intended for human use |
| FFDCA | 514 | Performance standards |
| FFDCA | 515 | Premarket approval |
| FFDCA | 515C | Breakthrough devices |
| FFDCA | 516 | Banned devices |
| FFDCA | 517 | Judicial review |
| FFDCA | 517A | Agency documentation and review of significant divisions regarding devices |
| FFDCA | 518 | Notification and other remedies |
| FFDCA | 519 | Records and reports on devices |
| FFDCA | 520 | General provisions respecting control of devices intended for human use |
| FFDCA | 521 | State and local requirements respecting devices |

| Statute Name or U.S.C. Title | § | Title of Section or Subsection |
|---|---|---|
| FFDCA | 522 | Postmarket surveillance |
| FFDCA | 523 | Accredited persons |
| FFDCA | 561 | Expanded access to unapproved therapies and diagnostics |
| FFDCA | 562 | Dispute resolution |
| FFDCA | 563 | Classification of products [between drug, biological product, device, and combination product] |
| FFDCA | 564 | Authorization for medical products for use in emergencies |
| FFDCA | 564A | Emergency use of medical products |
| FFDCA | 564B | Products held for emergency use |
| 21 U.S.C. | 360bbb-3c | Expedited development and review of medical products for emergency uses |
| FFDCA | 565 | Countermeasure development, review, and technical assistance |
| FFDCA | 566 | Critical path public-private partnerships |
| FFDCA | 569A | Optimizing global clinical trials |
| FFDCA | 569B | Use of clinical investigation data from outside the United States |
| FFDCA | 569C | Patient participation in medical product discussion |
| FFDCA | 1006 | Practice of medicine |

## Key Regulatory Provisions: Medical Devices Generally

| 21 C.F.R. Part | Subpart | Title of Part or Subpart |
|---|---|---|
| 99 | — | Dissemination of information on unapproved/new uses for marketed drugs, biologics, and devices |
| 800 | — | General |
| 801 | — | Labeling |
| 803 | — | Medical device reporting |
| 806 | — | Medical devices; reports of corrections and removals |
| 807 | — | Establishment registration and device listing for manufacturers and initial importers of devices |
| 808 | — | Exemptions from federal preemption of state and local medical device requirements |
| 809 | — | In vitro diagnostic products for human use |
| 810 | — | Medical device recall authority |
| 812 | — | Investigational device exemptions |

| 21 C.F.R. Part | Subpart | Title of Part or Subpart |
|---|---|---|
| 814 | — | Premarket approval of medical devices |
| 820 | — | Quality system regulation |
| 821 | — | Medical device tracking requirements |
| 822 | — | Postmarket surveillance |
| 830 | — | Unique device identification |
| 860 | — | Medical device classification procedures |
| 861 | — | Procedures for performance standards development |
| 895 | — | Banned devices |
| 898 | — | Performance standard for electrode lead wires and patient cables |
| **Key Regulatory Provisions: Lists of Classified Devices** | | |
| **21 C.F.R. Part** | **Subpart** | **Title of Part or Subpart** |
| 809 | — | In vitro diagnostic products for human use |
| 862 | — | Clinical chemistry and clinical toxicology devices |
| 864 | — | Hematology and pathology devices |
| 866 | — | Immunology and microbiology devices |
| 868 | — | Anesthesiology devices |
| 870 | — | Cardiovascular devices |
| 872 | — | Dental devices |
| 874 | — | Ear, nose, and throat devices |
| 876 | — | Gastroenterology-urology devices |
| 878 | — | General and plastic surgery devices |
| 880 | — | General hospital and personal use devices |
| 882 | — | Neurological devices |
| 884 | — | Obstetrical and gynecological devices |
| 886 | — | Ophthalmic devices |
| 888 | — | Orthopedic devices |
| 890 | — | Physical medicine devices |
| 892 | — | Radiology devices |

# C. Device Misbranding

## United States v. An Article . . . Acu-Dot . . .

483 F. Supp. 1311 (N.D. Ohio 1980)

**LAMBROS, District Judge.**

This action is the result of a libel of information brought by the United States of America for the condemnation of numerous cases of an over-the-counter medical device called an Acu-dot, as provided for in § 304 of the Federal Food Drug and Cosmetics Act (Act). The American firm that markets the seized devices, Acu-dot Corp., was the sole claimant-intervenor responding to the published notice of the in rem action.

. . . .

The sole issue presented to this Court at trial was this: are the Acu-dot devices "misbranded" within the meaning of § 502 of the [FFDCA]?

In simple terms, the Acu-dot is a small, pin-head sized magnet attached to the underside of a circular, adhesive patch. It is sold to the public in sheets of ten, packaged in a flat, cardboard box. Inside the box, in addition to the sheet of ten Acu-dots, can be found a four-page pamphlet, purporting to be instructions for the use of the device.

. . . .

The majority of the evidence presented both by the government and by claimant-intervenor went to the first of the two "misbranding" issues is the labeling "false or misleading in any particular"? § 502(a). Libellant, in presenting its case, specifically attacked the descriptions of the devices as "magnetic analgesic patch(es)" and "for temporary relief of occasional minor aches and pains of muscles and joints".

Libellant offered the testimony of three experts one biophysicist and two medical doctors. These experts were adduced to show that none of the theories offered by claimant-intervenor were valid explanations for the mechanism by which the devices were to achieve their results. Further, each expert testified to his belief that the devices could not achieve the effect alleged by the labeling, other than through a placebo effect.

On behalf of the effectiveness of the res, claimant-intervenor presented several theories for the mechanism of the device. At various times, it was suggested that the magnetic action of the device "drew" blood to the affected area, which action had the therapeutic effect; that the blood, being composed in part of iron-based chemicals, produced an electromotive force within the body when passing through the field of the magnet, much in the way electric generators produce electricity by moving an electric wire through a magnetic field; that the pressure of the device against the skin creates therapeutic effects in a way analogous to acupuncture techniques; that the ionization of molecules in the skin area under the magnet caused the therapeutic effect claimed; and, finally, that the claimed beneficial effect of the device was achieved largely as a result of the psychosomatic placebo response....

The most impressive evidence on behalf of the res was the result of the Antenucci study. That study purported to be a double-blind comparison of the Acu-dots with non-magnetized facsimiles. Of the 70 patients receiving the facsimiles, 10 indicated some degree of pain relief. Of the 152 patients receiving the Acu-dots, 138 reported some degree of pain relief. These figures are impressive and argue strongly for the therapeutic claims.

However, each of the government witnesses was able to suggest major flaws in the conception and execution of the test protocol ... and the Court was finally left with this problem: libellant could demonstrate that the therapeutic claims of the device could not be explained by any reasonable theory that did not rely on a "placebo" explanation, but had no empirical evidence of the lack of efficacy; claimant-intervenor had very weak theoretical support for the mechanism of the device, and vested its claims in unexplained empirical evidence.

....

After careful consideration of all of the evidence, this Court finds that any therapeutic value of the res is the result of its placebo effect, and that this placebo effect is very strong in the case of ailments for which the device is claimed effective. Thus, the device often can achieve its claims of providing "temporary relief of occasional minor aches and pains of muscles and joints"; but this effect is the result of nothing more than sophisticated marketing chicanery.

This Court hastens to affirm here its belief in the right of the American public to seek any treatment it wishes, especially when that treatment is a harmless, if ineffective, drug or device ... There is a difference, however, between the right to use a harmless, ineffective drug or device and a claimed right to promote and profit from the drug or device.

....

This Court resists the impulse to allow claimant to market a product that works only by means of a placebo effect on the basis that it nevertheless often achieves a relief of pain as claimed. The strong placebo effect may save the res from claims of "false labeling" under § 502(a) of the [FFDCA], but it does not protect the device from the charge that the labeling is "misleading" under § 502(a) of the [FFDCA], and that is all that is required to warrant condemnation of the res. The device's label is "misleading" because the device is not inherently effective, its results being attributable to the psychosomatic effect produced by the advertising and marketing of the device. A kiss from mother on the affected area would serve just as well to relieve pain, if mother's kisses were marketed as effectively as the Acu-dot device.

This Court finds that the device is "misbranded" under § 502 of the [FFDCA], and properly subject to seizure and condemnation under § 304 of the [FFDCA], even though the claims are not technically false, because the claims are inherently misleading.

. . . .

The res is properly seized and condemned and this Court must now consider the possibility of salvage of the components of the device. This Court is of the opinion that the claimant-intervenor believed in the efficacy of its product, and, in view of the harmlessness of the device, that destruction of the seized res is not necessary.

. . . . There are a number of uses to which the device or its components might be put that would not violate the provisions of the Food and Drug Act, and there is also the possibility of limited distribution of the device to qualified researchers for further testing of its efficacy.

IT IS SO ORDERED.

## D. Medical Device Classification and Review

Please read (or review) the following excerpts in the statutory supplement:

- FFDCA § 510. Registration of producers of drugs and devices. *Subsections (k), (l), (m), and (n) only.*
- FFDCA § 513. Classification of devices intended for human use.
- FFDCA § 515. Premarket approval.
- 21 C.F.R. Part 807. Establishment registration and device listing for manufacturers and initial importers of devices.
- 21 C.F.R. Part 814. Premarket approval of medical devices.
- 21 C.F.R. Part 860. Medical device classification procedures.

### United States v. An Article of Drug . . . Bacto-Unidisk . . .<br>394 U.S. 784 (1969)

Before reading further, please review the *Bacto-Unidisk* case in Chapter 1, Part D.

## 1992-04-28 FDA Interim Rule, Medical Devices; Substantial Equivalence; 510(k) Summaries and 510(k) Statements; Class III Summaries; Confidentiality of Information

57 Fed. Reg. 18,062

SUMMARY: The Food and Drug Administration (FDA) is issuing an interim rule to implement provisions of the Safe Medical Devices Act of 1990 (SMDA) which require persons who submit a premarket notification to provide to FDA, as part of the submission, an adequate summary of any information respecting safety and effectiveness or a statement that such information will be made available upon request by any person. The interim rule prescribes the content and format of these submissions. The interim rule also implements the requirement that 510(k) submitters, claiming substantial equivalence to a class III preamendments device for which FDA has not yet called for premarket approval, submit a class III summary and certify that they have conducted a search of safety and effectiveness data. In addition, the interim rule amends the medical device regulations governing the confidentiality of certain premarket notification submissions and their summaries to conform to the SMDA. FDA is also requiring that persons who submit a premarket notification (510(k)) certify that the data and information are truthful and accurate and that no material fact has been omitted.

. . . .

SUPPLEMENTARY INFORMATION:

I. Background

A. Statutory Authority and Legislative History

On May 28, 1976, Congress enacted the Medical Device Amendments of 1976 (the amendments), which amended the [FFDCA] to expand FDA's authority to regulate the introduction of medical devices into interstate commerce and thereby ensure their safety and effectiveness. Section 510(k) of the [FFDCA] authorizes FDA to issue regulations to require persons who propose to begin commercial distribution of a device intended for human use into interstate commerce to report to FDA the class in which the device is classified under section 513 of the [FFDCA] or, if such person determines that the device is not classified under such section, a statement of that determination and the basis for the determination that the device is or is not so classified. This premarket notification must be furnished to FDA at least 90 days before introduction of the device into commercial distribution. On August 23, 1977, FDA issued final regulations establishing the requirements for the form and manner in which premarket notifications (510(k) submissions) are to be sent to FDA. These regulations also contained provisions governing public disclosure by FDA of the existence of a 510(k) submission.

On November 28, 1990, the President signed into law the SMDA (Pub. L. 101-629) which amended the [FFDCA]. The SMDA requires that a premarket notification under section 510(k) include an adequate summary of any information on safety and effectiveness (510(k) summary) or a statement (510(k) statement) that such information will be made available upon request by any person. Section 12(a) of the SMDA added section 513(i)(3)(B) of the [FFDCA], which requires FDA to make available to the public any 510(k) summary within 30 days of the issuance of a determination of substantial equivalence. Section 12(b) of the SMDA directs the Secretary to issue regulations establishing the requirements of the summaries under section 513(i)(3)(B) of the [FFDCA].

The SMDA also requires that persons who submit a premarket notification (submitters) claiming substantial equivalence to a class III device introduced into interstate commerce before December 1, 1990, and for which FDA has not required premarket approval under section 515(b) of the [FFDCA], certify that they have conducted a reasonable search of all information known or otherwise available to them about the class III device and other similar legally marketed devices (class III certification.) Submitters are also required under section 513(f)(3) of the [FFDCA] to submit a summary (class III summary) of, and a citation to, all adverse safety and effectiveness data associated with the devices being compared. FDA may require the submitter to submit the safety and effectiveness data described in the class III summary.

B. Section 510(k) Summaries

The regulation prescribes the content and format of the summary of safety and effectiveness information required to be submitted under section 513(i)(3) of the [FFDCA] (510(k) summaries). The regulation defines a 510(k) summary as a summary of the safety and effectiveness information contained in the premarket notification submission upon which a determination of substantial equivalence can be based. This safety and effectiveness information includes data supporting a finding of substantial equivalence and all adverse safety and effectiveness data and information on the device. The decision to submit either a 510(k) summary or a 510(k) statement may not be changed once the premarket notification submission has been received by FDA. FDA's decision regarding the existence of substantial equivalence will be based on all the information contained in the 510(k), not only the information contained in the summary. Indeed, FDA may not review all 510(k) summaries due to resource constraints. Submitters are nevertheless required to prepare an adequate summary.

FDA believes that the intent of the requirement that premarket notification submitters provide either a 510(k) summary or a 510(k) statement is to make available to the public information about a device for which a marketing order has been issued and to provide the public with insight into the basis for an equivalence determination. FDA will make publicly available on a regular basis a list of all premarket notification submissions for which substantial equivalence determinations have been made, and information as to whether a 510(k) summary or a 510(k) statement was included. Summaries will be available to the public in accordance with the requirements of section 12(a) of the SMDA. Because 510(k) summaries submitted in premarket notifications are intended, in part, for public disclosure, they are not subject to predisclosure notification under Executive Order 12600.

The content requirements for 510(k) summaries in this regulation describe the information FDA relies on in determining substantial equivalence. A detailed discussion of FDA's decisionmaking process is contained in FDA's Guidance on the Premarket Notification Review Program. . . . Premarket notification submissions must contain adequate information to permit FDA to conclude whether the new device has the same intended use and technological characteristics as the predicate device. If the device has different technological characteristics, the information in the premarket notification submission must demonstrate that the device is as safe and effective as the predicate device and does not raise any new questions concerning safety and effectiveness. The term different technological characteristics means, with respect to a device being compared to a predicate device, that there is a significant change in the materials, design, energy source, or other features of the predicate device.

Because the content requirements for a 510(k) summary are different depending on the type of supporting data required in a premarket notification submission, it is important to understand the different types of data that may be submitted. All submissions must contain descriptive data and information sufficient to describe clearly the intended use, physical composition, method of operation, specifications, and performance claims of the new device. Any similar information submitted with respect to the predicate or legally marketed device is also considered descriptive data.

Under certain circumstances, FDA requires performance testing information, i.e., data from bench, animal, or clinical tests, to support an assertion that the device performs according to its description. Generally, FDA will not require performance testing data to support substantial equivalence if there are no significant differences in the technological characteristics of the new device and the predicate or legally marketed device, i.e., the new device involves no new materials, methods of operation, etc., and its descriptive characteristics and precise enough to ensure that the devices will perform comparably if the new device is manufactured according to its description.

In contrast, FDA generally will require performance testing data to establish substantial equivalence if a new device has different technological characteristics than a predicate or legally marketed device, or when the descriptive characteristics of the devices are insufficient to ensure that the devices will perform comparably. In these cases, performance testing data are necessary to demonstrate that the new characteristics of the device do not cause it to perform less safely or less effectively than the legally marketed device to which it is being compared.

The regulations delineating the contents of a 510(k) summary are designed to be sufficiently flexible to permit the summary to be as simple or as complex as the supporting information that it is summarizing. In accordance with § 807.92(a), summaries of premarket notification submissions containing only descriptive information to support equivalence would be required to contain only general information about the device and a summary of the descriptive information respecting safety and effectiveness supporting equivalence. FDA believes that these 510(k) summaries should be brief, generally not exceeding one page.

In contrast, when the determination of substantial equivalence is based on an assessment of performance data, the supporting information is generally more voluminous and more complex. Accordingly, § 807.92(a) and (b) require that the 510(k) summaries for these submissions be more comprehensive, and contain descriptions and analyses of the performance data included in the premarket notification submissions. As a result, FDA expects the 510(k) summaries for these submissions to be lengthier than for submissions containing descriptive information only. FDA reminds 510(k) summary preparers that the 510(k) summary is not intended to be a reproduction of the premarket notification. Rather, it should be a clear and concise discussion of the information respecting safety and effectiveness contained in the submission that supports a determination of substantial equivalence.

In determining whether the new device has the same intended use as a predicate device, FDA assesses any differences in indications for use in terms of the safety and effectiveness questions they may raise. The labeling for a new device need not contain the identical therapeutic or diagnostic statements that appear in the labeling of a predicate device in order for FDA to conclude that the devices have the same intended use. FDA may determine that a new device is substantially equivalent to a predicate device even though the indications may differ in certain respects, provided that these differences do not pose new questions concerning safety or effectiveness that were not posed by the intended use of the predicate device. Ordinarily, FDA relies on descriptive information alone in deciding whether any differences in indications preclude a finding of substantial equivalence. However, where the equivalence determination is based on information obtained from limited testing, the summary should include that information, as required in § 807.92(b).

. . . .

---

In the case immediately below, *Medtronic v. Lohr*, the defendant medical device manufacturer asserted that certain state-law tort claims were preempted by the FFDCA and its accompanying regulations. Federal preemption is a complex topic that is addressed in detail in Chapter 20 of this casebook. The *Lohr* case is included here not for its discussion of preemption, but for its discussion of the first two decades of medical device regulation. As you read, focus on the Court's discussion of the tension between the system of medical device regulation envisioned by Congress and the actual system implemented by FDA.

## Medtronic, Inc. v. Lohr

518 U.S. 470 (1996)

**Justice STEVENS announced the judgment of the Court and delivered the opinion of the Court with respect to Parts I, II, III, V, and VII, and an opinion [joined by three other justices] with respect to Parts IV and VI. . . .**

Congress enacted the Medical Device Amendments of 1976, in the words of the statute's preamble, "to provide for the safety and effectiveness of medical devices intended for human use." The question presented is whether that statute pre-empts a state common-law negligence action against the manufacturer of an allegedly defective medical device. Specifically, we must consider whether Lora Lohr, who was injured when her pacemaker failed, may rely on Florida common law to recover damages from Medtronic, Inc., the manufacturer of the device.

I

Throughout our history the several States have exercised their police powers to protect the health and safety of their citizens. Because these are "primarily, and historically, . . . matter[s] of local concern," the "States traditionally have had great latitude under their police powers to legislate as to the protection of the lives, limbs, health, comfort, and quiet of all persons."

Despite the prominence of the States in matters of public health and safety, in recent decades the Federal Government has played an increasingly significant role in the protection of the health of our people. Congress' first significant enactment in the field of public health was the Food and Drug Act of 1906, a broad prohibition against the manufacture or shipment in interstate commerce of any adulterated or misbranded food or drug. Partly in response to an ongoing concern about radio and newspaper advertising making false therapeutic claims for both "quack machines" and legitimate devices such as surgical instruments and orthopedic shoes, in 1938 Congress broadened the coverage of the 1906 Act to include misbranded or adulterated medical devices and cosmetics.

While the [FFDCA] provided for premarket approval of new drugs, it did not authorize any control over the introduction of new medical devices. As technologies advanced and medicine relied to an increasing degree on a vast array of medical equipment "[f]rom bedpans to brainscans," including kidney dialysis units, artificial heart valves, and heart pacemakers, policymakers and the public became concerned about the increasingly severe injuries that resulted from the failure of such devices.

In 1970, for example, the Dalkon Shield, an intrauterine contraceptive device, was introduced to the American public and throughout the world. Touted as a safe and effective contraceptive, the Dalkon Shield resulted in a disturbingly high percentage of inadvertent pregnancies, serious infections, and even, in a few cases, death.

In the early 1970's, several other devices, including catheters, artificial heart valves, defibrillators, and pacemakers (including pacemakers manufactured by petitioner Medtronic), attracted the attention of consumers, the Food and Drug Administration (FDA), and Congress as possible health risks.

In response to the mounting consumer and regulatory concern, Congress enacted the statute at issue here: the Medical Device Amendments of 1976 (MDA or Act). The Act classifies medical devices in three categories based on the risk that they pose to the public. Devices that present no unreasonable risk of illness or injury are designated Class I and are subject only to minimal regulation by "general controls." [FFDCA § 513](a)(1)(A). Devices that are potentially more harmful are designated Class II; although they may be marketed without advance approval, manufacturers of such devices must comply with federal performance regulations known as "special controls." [FFDCA § 513](a)(1)(B). Finally, devices that either "presen[t] a potential unreasonable risk of illness or injury," or which are "purported or represented to be for a use in supporting or sustaining human life or for a use which is of substantial importance in preventing impairment of human health," are designated Class III. [FFDCA § 513](a)(1)(C). Pacemakers are Class III devices. See 21 CFR § 870.3610 (1995).

Before a new Class III device may be introduced to the market, the manufacturer must provide the FDA with a "reasonable assurance" that the device is both safe and effective. See [FFDCA § 515](d)(2). Despite its relatively innocuous phrasing, the process of establishing this "reasonable assurance," which is known as the "premarket approval," or "PMA" process, is a rigorous one. Manufacturers must submit detailed information regarding the safety and efficacy of their devices, which the FDA then reviews, spending an average of 1,200 hours on each submission.

Not all, nor even most, Class III devices on the market today have received premarket approval because of two important exceptions to the PMA requirement. First, Congress realized that existing medical devices could not be withdrawn from the market while the FDA completed its PMA analysis for those devices. The statute therefore includes a "grandfathering" provision which allows pre-1976 devices to remain on the market without FDA approval until such time as the FDA initiates and completes the requisite PMA. See [FFDCA § 515](b)(1)(A); 21 CFR § 814.1(c)(1) (1995).[3] Second, to prevent manufacturers of grandfathered devices from monopolizing the market while new devices clear the PMA hurdle, and to ensure that improvements to existing devices can be rapidly introduced into the market, the

3. The FDA has not yet initiated nor suggested the initiation of a PMA process for pacemakers or most other grandfathered devices. But see 60 Fed.Reg. 41984, 41986 (1995) (pursuant to Safe Medical Devices Act of 1990, 104 Stat. 4511, calling for submission of information by February 1997 which may lead the FDA to reclassify or initiate PMA process at some time in the future for implantable pacemaker pulse generators and lead adapters)

[FFDCA] also permits devices that are "substantially equivalent" to pre-existing devices to avoid the PMA process. See [FFDCA § 515](b)(1)(B).

Although "substantially equivalent" Class III devices may be marketed without the rigorous PMA review, such new devices, as well as all new Class I and Class II devices, are subject to the requirements of [FFDCA § 510](k). That section imposes a limited form of review on every manufacturer intending to market a new device by requiring it to submit a "premarket notification" to the FDA (the process is also known as a "§ 510(k) process," after the number of the section in the original Act). If the FDA concludes on the basis of the § 510(k) notification that the device is "substantially equivalent" to a pre-existing device, it can be marketed without further regulatory analysis (at least until the FDA initiates the PMA process for the underlying pre-1976 device to which the new device is "substantially equivalent"). The § 510(k) notification process is by no means comparable to the PMA process; in contrast to the 1,200 hours necessary to complete a PMA review, the § 510(k) review is completed in an average of only 20 hours. As one commentator noted: "The attraction of substantial equivalence to manufacturers is clear. [Section] 510(k) notification requires little information, rarely elicits a negative response from the FDA, and gets processed very quickly." Adler, *The 1976 Medical Device Amendments: A Step in the Right Direction Needs Another Step in the Right Direction,* 43 Food Drug Cosm. L.J. 511, 516 (1988).

Congress anticipated that the FDA would complete the PMA process for Class III devices relatively swiftly. But because of the substantial investment of time and energy necessary for the resolution of each PMA application, the ever-increasing numbers of medical devices, and internal administrative and resource difficulties, the FDA simply could not keep up with the rigorous PMA process. As a result, the § 510(k) premarket notification process became the means by which most new medical devices—including Class III devices—were approved for the market. In 1983, for instance, a House Report concluded that nearly 1,000 of approximately 1,100 Class III devices that had been introduced to the market since 1976 were admitted as "substantial equivalents" and without any PMA review. This lopsidedness has apparently not evened out; despite an increasing effort by the FDA to consider the safety and efficacy of substantially equivalent devices, the House reported in 1990 that 80% of new Class III devices were being introduced to the market through the § 510(k) process and without PMA review.

*[Numerous sections discussing the main issue in the case, federal preemption, are omitted here.]*

Accordingly, the judgment of the Court of Appeals is reversed insofar as it held that any of the claims were preempted and affirmed insofar as it rejected the preemption defense. The cases are remanded for further proceedings.

## Judith A. Johnson, *Congressional Research Service, FDA Regulation of Medical Devices*

September 14, 2016

. . . .

**The Medical Device Review Process: Premarket Requirements**

FDA requires all medical product manufacturers to register their facilities, list their devices with the agency, and follow general controls requirements. FDA classifies devices according to the risk they pose to consumers. Many medical devices, such as plastic bandages and ice bags, present only minimal risk and can be legally marketed upon registration alone. These low risk devices are deemed exempt from premarket review and manufacturers need not submit an application to FDA prior to marketing. In contrast, most moderate and high risk devices must obtain the agency's permission prior to marketing. FDA grants this permission when a manufacturer meets regulatory premarket requirements and agrees to any necessary postmarket requirements which vary according to the risk that a device presents.

There are two main paths that manufacturers can use to bring moderate and high risk devices to market with FDA's permission. One path consists of conducting clinical studies, submitting a premarket approval (PMA) application, and requires evidence providing reasonable assurance that the device is safe and effective. The PMA process is generally used for novel and high risk devices and results in a type of FDA permission called approval.

The other path is shorter and less costly. It involves submitting a 510(k) notification demonstrating that the device is substantially equivalent to a device already on the market (a predicate device) that does not require a PMA. The 510(k) process is unique to medical devices and results in FDA clearance. Substantial equivalence is determined by comparing the performance characteristics of a new device with those of a predicate device. To be considered substantially equivalent, the new device must have the same intended use and technological characteristics as the predicate; clinical data demonstrating safety and effectiveness are usually not required. The manufacturer selects the predicate device to compare with its new device. However, FDA has the ultimate discretion in determining whether a comparison is appropriate.

Of the unique devices that are listed by manufacturers with FDA in FY2016 . . . about 63% were exempt from premarket review; the remainder entered the market via the 510(k) process (35%), the PMA process (1%), or other means (such as the "Humanitarian Device Exemption (HDE)]")

**Device Classification**

Under the terms of the Medical Device Amendments of 1976 (MDA, P.L. 94 295), FDA classified all medical devices that were on the market at the time of enactment the preamendment devices into one of three classes. Congress provided definitions for the three classes Class I, Class II, and Class III based on the risk (low-, moderate-, and high-risk respectively) to patients posed by the devices. Examples of each class are listed in Table 1.

Device classification determines the type of regulatory requirements that a manufacturer must follow. Regulatory requirements for each class are described below in more detail. General controls apply to all three classes of FDA regulated medical devices, unless exempted by regulation, and are the only level of controls that apply to Class I devices. Examples of general controls include establishment registration, device listing, premarket notification, and good manufacturing practice requirements.

**Class I** devices are those under current law for which general controls "are sufficient to provide reasonable assurance of the safety and effectiveness of the device." Many Class I devices are exempt from the premarket notification and/or the Quality System (QS) regulation requirements, though they still have to comply with the other general controls. A device is exempt if FDA determines that it presents a low risk of illness or injury to patients.

**Class II** devices are those under current law "which cannot be classified as class I because the general controls by themselves are insufficient to provide reasonable assurance of safety and effectiveness of the device." Class II includes devices that pose a moderate risk to patients, and may include new devices for which information or special controls are available to reduce or mitigate risk. Special controls are usually device specific and may include special labeling requirements, mandatory performance standards, and postmarket surveillance. Currently "15% of all device types classified in Class II are subject to special controls." Although most Class II devices require premarket notification via the 510(k) process, a few are exempt by regulation.

**Table 1. Medical Device Classification**

| Device Classification | Examples | Safety/Effectiveness Controls | Required Submission |
|---|---|---|---|
| Class I | elastic bandages, examination gloves, hand-held surgical instruments | General Controls | Registration only unless 510(k) specifically required |
| Class II | powered wheelchairs, infusion pumps, surgical drapes | General Controls & Special Controls | 510(k) notification unless exempt<br>-IDE possible |
| Class III | heart valves, silicone gel-filled breast implants, implanted cerebella stimulators<br><br>*metal-on-metal hip joint, certain dental implants* | General Controls & Premarket Approval<br><br>*General Controls* | PMA application<br>-IDE probable<br><br>*510(k) notification* |

**Note:** IDE means investigational device exemption. Some Class III devices have been cleared via the 510(k) process; these are Class III devices that entered the market prior to regulation calling for a PMA application.

**Class III** devices are those under current law which "cannot be classified as a class I device because insufficient information exists to determine that the application of general controls are sufficient to provide reasonable assurance of the safety and effectiveness of the device," and "cannot be classified as a class II device because insufficient information exists to determine that the special controls . . . would provide reasonable assurance of [their] safety and effectiveness," and are "purported or represented to be for a use in supporting or sustaining human life or for a use which is of substantial importance in preventing impairment of human health," or present "a potential unreasonable risk of illness or injury. . . ."

In other words, general and/or special controls are not sufficient to assure safe and effective use of a Class III device. Class III includes devices which are life supporting or life sustaining, and devices which present a high or potentially unreasonable risk of illness or injury to a patient. New devices that are not Class I or II are automatically designated as Class III unless the manufacturer files a request or petition for reclassification.

Although most Class III devices require premarket approval (PMA), some Class III devices may have been cleared via the 510(k) process. In fact, during the first 10 years following enactment of MDA, over 80% of postamendment Class III devices entered the market on the basis of 510(k) submissions showing substantial equivalence to preamendment devices. These are Class III devices that entered the market prior to regulation calling for a PMA application. FDA explains the situation as follows:

> When FDA's medical device regulation program began in the late 1970s, FDA regulated over 170 Class III device types through the 510(k) program, and those devices were never required to submit PMAs, like a typical Class III device. The intent was that FDA's regulation would be temporary and that, over time, the FDA would reclassify those device types into Class I or II, or sustain the classification in Class III and call for PMA applications. This reclassification process is described in Section 515 of the Federal Food, Drug and Cosmetic Act ([FFDCA]). Over the years, the FDA made significant progress on the original list of 170 devices; however, as of 2009, 26 medical device regulations still required final action.

At the time that the MDA of 1976 was drafted, "relatively few medical devices were permanently implanted or intended to sustain life. The 510(k) process was specifically intended for devices with less need for scientific scrutiny, such as surgical gloves and hearing aids." Over time, FDA's 510(k) review process was "challenged as new devices changed more dramatically and became more complex."

In late 2009, FDA implemented the 515 Program Initiative "to facilitate action on these remaining Class III device types." Examples of Class III devices that were still regulated via the 510(k) program include the metal on metal hip implant, certain dental implants, automated external defibrillator, electroconvulsive therapy device, pedicle screw spinal system, intra aortic balloon and control system, and several device types related to pacemakers. In 2012, FDASIA changed the process for the reclassification of a device from rulemaking to an administrative order. As a result, since 2013 FDA has published a number of final orders in the Federal Register to reclassify many of these remaining Class III device types.

. . . .

## FDA, Guidance for Industry and FDA Staff: De Novo Classification Process (Evaluation of Automatic Class III Designation)(Oct. 2017)

1. Introduction

The purpose of this document is to provide guidance on the process for the submission and review of a De Novo classification request (hereafter a "De Novo request") under section 513(f)(2) of the [FFDCA] (the [FFDCA]), also known as the De Novo classification process. This process provides a pathway to Class I or Class II classification for medical devices for which general controls or general and special controls provide a reasonable assurance of safety and effectiveness, but for which there is no legally marketed predicate device.

. . . .

A device may be classified in class III and be subject to premarket approval (PMA) via several different regulatory vehicles. In accordance with the criteria at section 513(a)(1)(C) of the [FFDCA], FDA may promulgate a regulation classifying, or issue an order reclassifying,[1] a device type into class III based on the risks posed by the device and the inability of general and special controls to provide reasonable assurance of the safety and effectiveness of the device. All particular devices of such a type are considered to be in class III and such devices are not eligible for the De Novo classification process.

Alternatively, devices of a new type that FDA has not previously classified based on the criteria at section 513(a)(1) of the [FFDCA] are "automatically" or "statutorily" classified into class III by operation of section 513(f)(1) of the [FFDCA], regardless of the level of risk they pose or the ability of general and special controls to assure safety and effectiveness. This is because, by definition, a new type of device would not be within a type that was on the market before the 1976 Medical Device Amendments or that has since been classified into class I or class II. Thus, there would be no available predicate device.

This second scenario is what Congress targeted when it enacted section 513(f)(2) of the [FFDCA] as part of the Food and Drug Administration Modernization Act of 1997 (FDAMA). The process created by this provision, which was referred to in FDAMA as the Evaluation of Automatic Class III Designation, will be referred to

1. Prior to the Food and Drug Administration Safety and Innovation Act (FDASIA) enacted in 2012, FDA reclassified devices under section 513(e) of the [FFDCA] through rulemaking; FDASIA changed this to an order process.

as the "De Novo classification process"[2] throughout this guidance document. Congress included this section to limit unnecessary expenditure of FDA and industry resources that could occur if devices for which general controls or general and special controls provide a reasonable assurance of safety and effectiveness were subject to premarket approval under section 515 of the [FFDCA]. Section 513(f)(2) of the [FFDCA] has allowed manufacturers to submit a De Novo request to FDA for devices "automatically" classified into Class III by operation of section 513(f)(1). As enacted by FDAMA, in order to submit a De Novo request, a device first had to be found not substantially equivalent (NSE) to legally-marketed predicate devices through a premarket notification (510(k)). The 21st Century Cures Act removed a requirement that a De Novo request be submitted within 30 days of receiving an NSE determination.

Section 513(f)(2) was modified by section 607 of FDASIA, which created an alternative mechanism for submitting a De Novo request that does not require that a device be reviewed first under a 510(k) and found NSE prior to submission of a De Novo request. If a person believes their device is appropriate for classification into Class I or Class II and determines, based on currently available information, there is no legally marketed predicate device, they may submit a De Novo request without a preceding 510(k) and NSE (hereafter "Direct De Novo").

FDA is issuing this guidance to provide updated recommendations for interactions with FDA related to the De Novo classification process, including what information to submit when seeking a path to market via the De Novo classification process. . . .

## E. Medical Devices and the 2020 Novel Coronavirus

### FDA, Guidance for Industry and FDA Staff: Enforcement Policy for Ventilators and Accessories and Other Respiratory Devices During the Coronavirus Disease 2019 (COVID-19) Public Health Emergency (Mar. 2020)

#### I. Introduction

. . . .

FDA is issuing this guidance to provide a policy to help expand the availability of ventilators as well as other respiratory devices and their accessories during this pandemic.

This policy is intended to remain in effect only for the duration of the public health emergency related to COVID-19 declared by the Department of Health and Human Services (HHS), including any renewals made by the Secretary in accordance with section 319(a)(2) of the PHS Act.

2. The process has been termed "De Novo" because it requires the agency to evaluate novel devices anew, in accordance with the criteria at section 513(a)(1) of the [FFDCA].

Given this public health emergency, this guidance is being implemented without prior public comment because the FDA has determined that prior public participation for this guidance is not feasible or appropriate. . . .

## II. Background

There is currently an outbreak of respiratory disease caused by a novel coronavirus. The virus has been named "severe acute respiratory syndrome coronavirus 2" (SARS-CoV-2) and the disease it causes has been named "Coronavirus Disease 2019" (COVID-19). On January 31, 2020, HHS issued a declaration of a public health emergency related to COVID-19 and mobilized the Operating Divisions of HHS. In addition, on March 13, 2020, the President declared a national emergency in response to COVID-19.

SARS-CoV-2 has demonstrated the capability to spread rapidly, leading to significant impacts on healthcare systems and causing societal disruption. The potential public health threat posed by COVID-19 is high, both globally and to the United States. To respond effectively to the COVID-19 outbreak, appropriate clinical management and infection control in conjunction with implementation of community mitigation efforts are critical.

FDA believes the policy set forth in this guidance may help address these urgent public health concerns by helping to expand the availability of devices that facilitate respiration, including ventilators and their accessories, as well as other respiratory devices.

## III. Scope

The enforcement policy described in this guidance applies to the following devices and their accessories used to provide ventilation and ventilatory support to patients with respiratory failure or respiratory insufficiency during the COVID-19 public health emergency (See Table 1):

**Table 1**

| Classification Regulation | Device Type | Product Code | Device Classification |
|---|---|---|---|
| 21 CFR 868.5895 | Ventilator, Continuous, Facility Use | CBK | II |
| | Ventilator, Continuous, Minimal Ventilatory Support, Facility Use | MNT | II |
| | Continuous, ventilator, home use | NOU | II |
| | Ventilator, continuous, minimal ventilatory support, home use | NQY | II |
| | Ventilator, continuous, non-life-supporting | MNS | II |
| | Mechanical Ventilator | ONZ | II |
| 21 CFR 868.5925 | Ventilator, Emergency, Powered (Resuscitator) | BTL | II |

| Classification Regulation | Device Type | Product Code | Device Classification |
|---|---|---|---|
| 21 CFR 868.5160 | Gas-machine, anesthesia | BSZ | II |
| 21 CFR 868.5905 | Ventilator, non-continuous (respirator) Including masks4 and interfaces under the same product code | BZD | II |
| | Conserver, Oxygen | NFB | II |
| | Device, Positive Pressure Breathing, Intermittent | NHJ | II |
| | Resuscitator, Manual, Non Self-Inflating | NHK | II |
| 21 CFR 868.5454 | High flow/high velocity humidified oxygen delivery device | QAV | II |

### IV. Policy for Modifications to FDA-Cleared Devices

In the context of the COVID-19 public health emergency in which affected patients may develop respiratory illness, it is necessary to maintain an adequate supply of devices to treat patients who develop respiratory failure or respiratory insufficiency. The devices listed above, which include ventilators, anesthesia gas machines, and other respiratory devices, and their accessories, are needed to support patients who develop respiratory compromise from COVID-19 or other respiratory disorders.

Wherever possible, health care facilities should use FDA-cleared conventional/standard full-featured ventilators when necessary to support patients with respiratory failure, or a device subject to an Emergency Use Authorization (EUA), if any. However, to help ensure the availability of the greatest possible number of devices for this purpose, and as described in more detail below, FDA does not intend to object to limited modifications to the indications, claims, functionality, or to the hardware, software, or materials of FDA-cleared devices used to support patients with respiratory failure or respiratory insufficiency, without prior submission of a premarket notification under section 510(k) of the [FFDCA] and 21 CFR 807.81, for the duration of the declared public health emergency. This policy applies where a modification is made to the device that triggers the requirement that a manufacturer submit a new premarket notification (510(k)) to FDA. Examples of such changes could include a significant change or modification in design, material, chemical composition, energy source, or manufacturing process.

More specifically, this policy will create more flexibility for manufacturers that make device modifications to address current manufacturing limitations or supply shortages. Examples may include:

- Changes to the ventilator motor to allow an alternate supplier to meet the required design specifications
- Changes to the material in the ventilator tubing to allow for more flexible material sourcing

We believe this approach will help manufacturers that want to add production lines or manufacture at alternative sites which may have different manufacturing equipment to increase manufacturing capacity and supply and reduce supply change interruptions and manufacturing bottlenecks.

### A. Modifications to FDA-Cleared Indications, Claims, or Functionality

In developing this policy, FDA's intent is to foster the continued availability of safe and effective medical devices while being flexible regarding modifications made to ventilators, anesthesia gas machines and other respiratory devices, and their accessories, in response to the COVID-19 public health emergency.

As noted above, wherever possible, health care facilities should use FDA-cleared conventional/standard full-featured ventilators to treat patients who develop respiratory failure or respiratory insufficiency. However, for the duration of the public health emergency, to help foster the wider availability of devices for patients in need of ventilatory support, FDA does not intend to object to modifications to the FDA-cleared indications, claims, or functionality of these devices, without prior submission of a premarket notification where the modification will not create an undue risk in light of the public health emergency. Examples of circumstances where FDA currently believes a modification would not create such undue risk include:

(1) The use of powered emergency ventilators and anesthesia gas machines for patients needing mechanical ventilation;

(2)The use of ventilators outside their cleared environment of use (for example, use of a ventilator in a health care facility when it is only cleared for use at home or during transport);

(3) The use of devices indicated for sleep apnea (including noncontinuous ventilators delivering continuous positive airway pressure (CPAP) or bilevel positive airway pressure (BiPAP)) to treat patients with respiratory insufficiency, provided that appropriate design mitigations are in place to minimize aerosolization;

(4) The use of oxygen concentrators for primary supply when medically necessary and clinically appropriate.

### B. Hardware, Software, and Material Changes to FDA-cleared Ventilators and Anesthesia Gas Machines

As stated above, wherever possible, health care facilities should use conventional/standard full-featured ventilators to treat patients who develop respiratory failure or respiratory insufficiency. However, for the duration of the public health emergency, in order to help foster the wider availability of devices for patients in need of ventilatory support and to help manufacturers respond to potential device component disruptions in the supply chain, FDA does not intend to object to limited modifications to the FDA-cleared hardware, software, or materials, without prior submission of a premarket notification under section 510(k) of the [FFDCA] and

21 CFR 807.81, where the modification does not create an undue risk in light of the public health emergency. Examples of circumstances where FDA currently believes a modification would not create such undue risk include:

1) Modifications to motors, batteries, or other electrical components;
2) Material changes to components in the gas pathway or with other patient tissue contact;
3) Introduction of filtration to minimize aerosolization.
4) Software modifications intended to modify the ventilation parameters including inspiratory pressure, tidal volumes, flow rates, positive end-expiratory pressure (PEEP) in accordance with any applicable device standard;
5) Software modifications implementing physiological closed loop (automated) algorithms for oxygen titration where the algorithms/devices are the subject of an FDA-approved Investigational Device Exemption (IDE);
6) Hardware and/or software modifications implementing the capability for remote monitoring and remote adjustment of ventilator parameters (i.e., adjustment of parameters by trained health care providers from outside an isolation unit to avoid unnecessary exposures).

Additionally, FDA does not intend to object to firms making modifications or adding to the hardware/software architectures to allow for increased remote monitoring and setting adjustment capability/availability to support additional claims or indications described above. One example is the addition of wireless and/or Bluetooth capability. For any such changes, manufacturers should develop and implement appropriate cybersecurity controls to assure device cybersecurity and maintain device functionality and safety. . . .

**C. Use of Ventilator and Anesthesia Gas Machine Breathing Circuit Devices Beyond Their Indicated Shelf Life and Duration of Use**

Ventilators and anesthesia gas machines are designed to work as a breathing circuit, which is comprised of various ancillary devices such as the tubing that connects the ventilator to the patient, filters, and humidifiers. Constituent parts of the breathing circuit may include, but are not limited to, those identified in Table 2:

**Table 2**

| Classification Regulation | Device Type | Product Code | Device Classification |
|---|---|---|---|
| 21 CFR 868.5240 | Anesthesia breathing circuit | OFP | I |
| | Anesthesia breathing circuit | CAI | I |
| 21 CFR 868.5260 | Filter, Bacterial, Breathing-Circuit | CAH | II |

| Classification Regulation | Device Type | Product Code | Device Classification |
|---|---|---|---|
| 21 CFR 868.5270 | Heated breathing circuit | BZE | II |
| 21 CFR 868.5340 | Cannula, Nasal, Oxygen | CAT | I |
| 21 CFR 868.5440 | Generator, oxygen, portable | CAW | II |
| 21 CFR 868.5450 | Humidifier, Respiratory Gas, (Direct Patient Interface) | BTT | II |
| 21 CFR 868.5580 | Mask, Oxygen | BYG | I |
| 21 CFR 868.5730 | Tube, Tracheal (W/Wo Connector) | BTR | II |
| | Airway Monitoring System | OQU | II |
| 21 CFR 868.5895 | Accessory to Continuous Ventilator (Respirator) | MOD | II |
| 21 CFR 868.5965 | Attachment, Breathing, Positive End Expiratory Pressure | BYE | II |
| 21 CFR 868.5975 | Set, Tubing and Support, Ventilator | BZO | I |

These breathing circuit devices might be labeled with specific durations of use and shelf life. Given the potential for extensive use of ventilators and anesthesia gas machines in response to the COVID-19 pandemic, and to avoid depletion of breathing circuit supplies, for the duration of the public health emergency, FDA does not intend to object to changes in the indicated shelf life and duration of use of these products for treating individual patients, without prior submission of a premarket notification under section 510(k) of the [FFDCA] and 21 CFR 807.81, where the change does not create an undue risk in light of the public health emergency. Examples of circumstances where FDA currently believes a change would not create such an undue risk: the devices are used according to healthcare institutional protocols, or useful life is limited to the occurrence of malfunction or visible soiling.

. . . .

### E. Labeling of Modified Devices

In addition, FDA recommends that the devices described above use labeling that helps users better understand the device modifications such as:

(1) A clear description of the device's new indications, claims, or functions, and information on the device's performance and potential risks.

(2) Adequate instructions for use for the intended user and indicated environment(s) of use. The labeling highlight the differences in design compared to the

unmodified, FDA-cleared version of the device, along with instructions for mitigating any known risks associated with these differences.

(3) A clear distinction delineating FDA-cleared indications and claims from those that are not FDA-cleared. In addition, FDA recommends the labeling include a general statement about changes that have not been cleared by FDA.

## FDA, Guidance for Industry and FDA Staff: Enforcement Policy for Face Masks and Respirators During the Coronavirus Disease (COVID-19) Public Health Emergency (Mar. 2020)

### I. Introduction

The Food and Drug Administration (FDA or Agency) plays a critical role in protecting the United States from threats including emerging infectious diseases, including the Coronavirus Disease 2019 (COVID-19) pandemic. . . .

FDA is issuing this guidance to provide a policy to help expand the availability of general use face masks for the general public and particulate filtering facepiece respirators (including N95 respirators) for health care professionals during this pandemic.

This policy is intended to remain in effect only for the duration of the public health emergency related to COVID-19 . . . .

Given this public health emergency, this guidance is being implemented without prior public comment because the FDA has determined that prior public participation for this guidance is not feasible or appropriate. . . .

### II. Background

*[A discussion of the early 2020 COVID-19 public health emergency and national emergency declarations is omitted here].*

FDA believes the policy set forth in this guidance may help address these urgent public health concerns by clarifying the regulatory landscape of face masks and respirators, helping to expand the availability of general use face masks for use by the general public, and of filtering facepiece respirators (including N95 respirators) for use by health care professionals in healthcare settings.

### III. Scope

There are many products marketed in the United States as "face masks" that offer a range of protection against potential health hazards. Face masks and respirators are regulated by FDA when they meet the definition of a device under section 201(h) of the [FFDCA] ([FFDCA]). Generally, face masks fall within this definition when they are intended for a medical purpose, including for use by health care professionals. Face masks that are not intended for a medical purpose, are not medical devices, as described in further detail below. FDA-regulated face masks and respirators are listed in Table 1:

**Table 1**

| Classification Regulation | Device Type | Product Code |
|---|---|---|
| 21 CFR 878.4040 | Mask, Surgical | FXX |
| | Pediatric/Child Facemask | OXZ |
| | Accessory, Surgical Apparel (Face Shield) | LYU |
| | Surgical mask with antimicrobial/antiviral agent | OUK |
| | Respirator, Surgical | MSH |
| | N95 Respirator with Antimicrobial/Antiviral Agent | ONT |
| 21 CFR 880.6260 | N95 Respirator with Antimicrobial/Antiviral Agent for Use by the General Public in Public Health Medical Emergencies | ORW |
| 21 CFR 880.6260 | Respirator, N95, for Use by the General Public in Public Health Medical Emergencies | NZJ |

This policy does **NOT** apply to other types of masks including but not limited to those in Table 2.

**Table 2**

| Classification Regulation | Device Type | Product Code |
|---|---|---|
| 21 CFR 868.5450 | Humidifier, Respiratory Mask | OBN |
| | Humidifier, Respiratory Gas | BTT |
| 21 CFR 868.5550 | Mask, Anesthetic, Gas | BSJ |
| 21 CFR 868.5580 | Mask, Oxygen | BYG |
| 21 CFR 868.5600 | Mask, Oxygen, Low Concentration, Venturi | BYG |
| 21 CFR 868.5570 | Mask, Oxygen, Non-Rebreathing | KGB |
| 21 CFR 868.5905 | Resuscitator, Manual, Non Self-Inflating | NHK |
| | Mask, Ventilator, Non-Continuous, Reprocessed | NMC |
| 21 CFR 868.5560 | Strap, Head, Gas Mask | BTK |

FDA recognizes that, when alternatives, such as FDA-cleared masks or respirators, are unavailable, individuals, including healthcare professionals, might improvise PPE. FDA does not intend to object to individuals' distribution and use of improvised PPE when no alternatives, such as FDA-cleared masks or respirators, are available.

## IV. Definitions

For the purposes of this guidance, the following definitions are used.

**Face Mask**—A mask that covers the user's nose and mouth and may or may not meet fluid barrier or filtration efficiency levels.

**Surgical Mask**—A mask that covers the user's nose and mouth and provides a physical barrier to fluids and particulate materials. The mask meets certain fluid barrier protection standards and Class I or Class II flammability tests.

**Filtering Facepiece Respirator**—A filtering facepiece respirator (FFR) is a device that is a disposable half-face-piece non-powered air-purifying particulate respirator intended for use to cover the nose and mouth of the wearer to help reduce wearer exposure to pathogenic biological airborne particulates.

**N95 Respirator**—A disposable half-mask filtering facepiece respirator (FFR)that covers the user's airway (nose and mouth) and offers protection from particulate materials at an N95 filtration efficiency level per 42 CFR 84.181. Such an N95 FFR used in a healthcare setting is a class II device, regulated by FDA under 21 CFR 878.4040 (FDA product code MSH).

**NIOSH Approved N95 Respirator**—An N95 respirator, approved by NIOSH that meets filtration efficiency level per 42 CFR 84.181.

**Surgical N95 Respirator**—A disposable FFR used in a healthcare setting that is worn by HCP during procedures to protect both the patient and HCP from the transfer of microorganisms, body fluids, and particulate material at an N95 filtration efficiency level per 42 CFR 84.181. A surgical N95 respirator is a class II device, regulated by FDA under 21 CFR 878.4040 (FDA product code MSH).

## V. Policy

### A. Overview

FDA is taking steps to expand the availability of face masks and respirators and believes the policy set forth in this guidance may help address the urgent public health concerns caused by shortages of such products by taking a risk-based approach and clarifying the policies that FDA intends to apply to masks and respirators, including these products' associated indications and claims.

### B. Face Masks and N95 Respirators Not Intended for a Medical Purpose

Face masks and N95 respirators are devices when they meet the definition of a device set forth in section 201(h) of the [FFDCA]. Under section 201(h) of the [FFDCA], these products are devices when they are intended for use in the diagnosis of disease or other conditions or in the cure, mitigation, treatment, or prevention of disease.

Other face masks and filtering facepiece respirators are marketed to the general public for general, non-medical purposes, such as use in construction and other industrial applications. Because they are not intended for use in the diagnosis of disease or other conditions or in the cure, mitigation, treatment, or prevention of disease, FDA device marketing authorization is not required, and all the other requirements of the [FFDCA] do not apply to manufacturers, importers, and distributors of these products.

Face masks and respirators are devices when they are intended for a medical purpose, such as prevention of infectious disease transmission (including uses related to COVID-19). Face masks and respirators are not devices when they are intended for a non-medical purpose, such as for use in construction. When considering whether these products are intended for a medical purpose, among other considerations, FDA will look at whether:

1) they are labeled or otherwise intended for use by a health care professional;

2) they are labeled or otherwise for use in a health care facility or environment; and

3) they include any drugs, biologics, or anti-microbial/anti-viral agents.

### C. Face Masks Intended for a Medical Purpose that are NOT Intended to Provide Liquid Barrier Protection

In general, FDA recommends that health care providers follow current Centers for Disease Control and Prevention (CDC) guidance regarding personal protective equipment (PPE) that should be used during the COVID-19 outbreak. To ensure the availability of equipment that might offer some benefit to health care providers and the general public during the COVID-19 outbreak, for the duration of the public health emergency FDA does not intend to object to the distribution and use of face masks (not including respirators) that are intended for a medical purpose (whether used by medical personnel or the general public), without compliance with the following regulatory requirements where the face mask does not create an undue risk in light of the public health emergency: prior submission of a premarket notification under section 510(k) of the [FFDCA] and 21 CFR 807.81, Registration and Listing requirements in 21 CFR 807, Quality System Regulation requirements in 21 CFR 820, reports or corrections and removals in 21 CFR Part 806, and Unique Device Identification requirements in 21 CFR Part 830. FDA currently believes such devices would not create an undue risk where:

- The product includes labeling that accurately describes the product as a face mask (as opposed to a surgical mask or FFR) and includes a list of the body contacting materials (which does not include any drugs or biologics);
- The product includes labeling that makes recommendations that would reduce sufficiently the risk of use, for example, recommendations against: use in any surgical setting or where significant exposure to liquid, bodily or other hazardous fluids, may be expected; use in a clinical setting where the infection risk level through inhalation exposure is high; and use in the presence of a high intensity heat source or flammable gas; and
- The product is not intended for any use that would create an undue risk, for example the labeling does not include uses for antimicrobial or antiviral

protection or related uses or uses for infection prevention or reduction or related uses and does not include particulate filtration claims.

### D. Surgical Masks Intended to Provide Liquid Barrier Protection

Surgical masks are class II devices that cover the user's nose and mouth and provide a physical barrier to fluids and particulate materials and are tested for flammability and biocompatibility. FDA does not intend to object where, for the duration of the declared public health emergency, surgical masks are distributed and used without prior submission of a premarket notification under section 510(k) of the [FFDCA] and 21 CFR 807.81, and the surgical masks do not create an undue risk in light of the public health emergency. FDA currently believes such devices would not create an undue risk where:

- The product meets fluid resistance testing (liquid barrier performance) consistent with standard ASTM F186 Standard Test Method for Resistance of Medical Face Masks to Penetration by Synthetic Blood (Horizontal Projection of Fixed Volume at a Known Velocity);
- The product meets Class I or Class II flammability requirement per 16 CFR 1610 (unless labeled with a recommendation against use in the presence of high intensity heat source or flammable gas);
- The product includes labeling that accurately describes the product as a surgical mask and includes a list of the body contacting materials (which does not include any drugs or biologics); and
- The product is not intended for any use that would create an undue risk, for example the labeling does not include uses for antimicrobial or antiviral protection or related uses or uses for infection prevention or reduction or related uses, and does not include particulate filtration claims.

## VI. FDA's Intended Approach for EUAs for Masks and Respirators

### A. EUAs for Reprocessing of Filtering Facepiece Respirators

FDA is responsible for the oversight of reprocessed[8] single use medical devices and generally requires the submission of a 510(k) from entities performing these activities. To facilitate the safe reuse and conservation of PPE for the duration of the public health emergency, FDA is interested in interacting with manufacturers on the reprocessing of otherwise disposable N95 particulate filtering facepiece respirators (and other Filtering Facepiece Respirators) to facilitate marketing authorization

8. The term 'reprocessed', with respect to a single-use device, means an original device that has previously been used on a patient and has been subjected to additional processing and manufacturing for the purpose of an additional single use on a patient. See FDA's Guidance "Medical Device User Fee and Modernization Act of 2002, Validation Data in Premarket Notification Submissions (510(k)s) for Reprocessed Single-Use Medical Devices" available at: https://www.fda.gov/regulatory-information/search-fda-guidance-documents/medical-device-user-fee-and-modernization-act-2002-validation-data-premarket-notification.

through an emergency use authorization (EUA) for reprocessed devices. FDA recommends that firms contact FDA and provide the following information to [web address omitted], if available. FDA will work with reprocessors through its EUA process to facilitate expedited evaluation of the request. . . .

**B. EUAs for Face Masks Intended for a Medical Purpose, Surgical Face Masks and N95 Respirators**

Wherever possible, health care facilities should continue to use FDA-cleared face masks and NIOSH-approved and/or FDA-cleared N95 respirators or better. In response to the COVID-19 pandemic, FDA has also issued EUAs that authorize certain N95 Filtering Facepiece Respirators, including NIOSH-approved disposable FFRs and imported non-NIOSH-approved disposable FFRs, for use in healthcare settings by healthcare personnel and are intended to help increase availability of these devices to front-line personnel during the public health emergency.

For devices that do not fall within the scope of the March 2, 2020 or March 24, 2020 EUAs, FDA is interested in interacting with manufacturers on additional device-specific EUAs. This may include manufacturers of masks and respirators that are not currently legally marketed in the US as well as manufacturers who have not previously manufactured masks or respirators with capabilities to increase supply of these devices. . . .

. . . .

## F. Animal Devices

### FDA Website, How FDA Regulates Animal Devices*

How FDA Regulates Animal Devices

The [FFDCA] defines medical device as "*an instrument, apparatus, implement, machine, contrivance, implant, in-vitro reagent, or other similar or related article, including any component, part, or accessory, which is . . . intended for use in the diagnosis of disease or other conditions, or in the cure, mitigation, treatment, or prevention of disease in man or other animals, or [which is] intended to affect the structure or any function of the body of man or other animals. . . .*" Further, a device "*does not achieve its primary intended purposes through chemical action within or on the body of man or other animals, and . . . is not dependent upon being metabolized for the achievement of its primary intended purposes.*" Examples of devices include such things as needles, syringes, surgical instruments, prosthetic devices, X-ray equipment, certain diagnostic test kits, and dental appliances.

* From https://www.fda.gov/animal-veterinary/animal-health-literacy/how-fda-regulates-animal-devices (last updated July 2, 2019).

FDA does have regulatory oversight over devices intended for animal use and can take appropriate regulatory action if an animal device is misbranded or adulterated.

**Pre-market Approval** is Not Required: The FDA **does not require** submission of a 510(k), PMA, or any pre-market approval for devices intended for animal use.

Device manufacturers who exclusively manufacture or distribute animal devices are not required to register their establishments or list animal devices with FDA and are exempt from post-marketing reporting. It is the responsibility of the manufacturer and/or distributor of these articles to assure that these animal devices are safe, effective, and properly labeled.

The FDA encourages veterinarians and animal owners to report adverse drug experiences and product defects associated with animal devices to FDA using Form FDA 1932a.

An animal device that is also a radiation emitting electronic product, such as an MRI device intended for animal use, must comply with all requirements for animal devices in addition to applicable requirements for radiation-emitting electronic products in 21 CFR 1000–1050. FDA's Center for Devices and Radiological Health (CDRH) is responsible for regulating radiation-emitting electronic products. For further information on CDRH regulations that apply to manufacturers of electronic products, visit FDA's website on Radiation Emitting Products.

Manufacturers and/or distributors of animal medical devices may request a review of their product labeling and promotional literature to ensure that it complies with the [FFDCA] by emailing [address omitted]. This includes devices marketed in another country and offered for importation into the U.S.

## G. Key Points

- There are fundamental differences between medical devices and those medical products that work through chemical action (such as drugs, animal drugs, and biologics).
    - Medical devices are not chemical entities that lose their identity with even a slight molecular modification.
    - Medical devices can frequently be designed in different ways, using very different mechanisms, for achieving the same end.
    - Medical devices can be modified for many reasons. These include safety improvements, efficacy improvements, cost reduction efforts, and changes in available component parts.
    - These differences require a regulatory process that is far more responsive to design variation and design change than the process used for drugs.

  - These differences also have major implications for product liability tort claims. In particular, there are more ways to formulate design defect claims for medical devices than for drugs.
- The FFDCA provides for three classes of medical devices: Class I (general controls); Class II (special controls), and Class III (premarket approval).
  - Many devices were originally placed into Class III. Over time, a large number of these have been reclassified into Class I or Class II.
  - Most medical devices reach the market through the substantial equivalence process of FFDCA 510(k).
    - The more rigorous premarket approval process is the exception, rather than the rule.
- FDA jurisdiction over medical devices began with the FFDCA of 1938. However, FDA did not acquire authority over marketing authorization for medical devices until the Medical Device Amendments of 1976.
  - Between the Kefauver-Harris Amendments of 1962 and the Medical Device Amendments of 1976, FDA regulated a small number of medical devices as "drugs." Later, these came to be known as "transitional devices."

Chapter 13

# Combination Products

## A. Introduction

Please read (or review) the following excerpts in the statutory supplement:

- FFDCA § 503. Exemptions and considerations for certain drugs, devices, and biological products. *Subsection (g) only.*
- FFDCA § 201. Definitions, generally. *Subsection (rr) only.*
- 21 C.F.R. Part 3. Product jurisdiction.
- 21 C.F.R. Part 4. Regulation of combination products.

## B. Outline of Regulatory Regime

As in other chapters of this book, this chapter begins with a set of charts. As you read this chapter for the first time, you should do no more than skim these charts to get a general sense of the structure of the applicable statutes and regulations. (For more information on the role of the charts in this casebook, see Chapter 1, Parts A.1 and B).

| Timeline of Key Statutes: Combination Products | | | |
|---|---|---|---|
| **Year** | **PL** | **Stat** | **Name of Statute** |
| 1990 | 101-629 | 104 Stat. 4511 | Safe Medical Devices Act |
| 1997 | 105-115 | 111 Stat. 2296 | FDA Modernization Act of 1997 |
| 2009 | 111-31 | 123 Stat. 1776 | Family Smoking Prevention and Tobacco Control Act |
| 2016 | 114-255 | 130 Stat. 1033 | 21st Century Cures Act |

| Key Statutory Provisions: Combination Products | | |
|---|---|---|
| Statute Name or U.S.C. Title | § | Title of Section or Subsection |
| FFDCA | 201(rr)(2) | [Exclusion of combination products from tobacco product definition] |
| FFDCA | 503(g) | Regulation of combination products |
| FFDCA | 563 | Classification of products |

| Key Regulatory Provisions: Combination Products | | |
|---|---|---|
| 21 C.F.R. Part | Subpart | Title of Part or Subpart |
| 3 | — | Product jurisdiction |
| 4 | — | Current good manufacturing practice requirements for combination products |

## C. Overview

FDA sets out its definition of "combination product" in its general regulation on product jurisdiction within the agency, 21 C.F.R. Part 3. Product Jurisdiction. FDA then adopts this definition in its general regulation on combination products, 21 C.F.R. Part 4. Regulation of Combination Products. *See* 21 C.F.R. § 4.2, 4.101. Each component of a combination product remains subject to its individual regulatory scheme. FDA's combination product regulations are simply an additional layer of regulations that apply on top of the regulations applicable to each individual component.

These combination product regulations address two main topics. The first is Current Good Manufacturing Practice (cGMP) requirements; the second is postmarket reporting requirements.

### 1991-11-21 FDA Final Rule, Assignment of Agency Component for Review of Premarket Applications

56 Fed. Reg. 58,754

. . . .

SUMMARY: The Food and Drug Administration (FDA) is promulgating a new regulation to describe how the agency will determine which component within FDA will have primary jurisdiction for the premarket review and regulation of: (1) A combination drug, device, or biologic product or (2) any drug, device, or biologic product where the center with primary jurisdiction is unclear or in dispute. This rule describes how to identify the agency's assigned review component which will, in most cases, eliminate the need for a sponsor to obtain approval from more than one FDA component for a combination product.

. . . .

SUPPLEMENTARY INFORMATION:

I. Background

For many years, the agency has been confronted with questions as to which center within FDA should regulate a particular product. For example, in the early 1970's, the agency had to determine where radiopharmaceuticals, radiobiologicals, and in vitro diagnostic products would be regulated. Over time, other products such as medicated wound dressings, bone cement containing an antibiotic, and dental composites with fluoride have raised similar jurisdictional concerns both inside and outside of FDA. The development of new technologies and biotechnological products presents continuing administrative and jurisdictional challenges to the agency.

As the types of products submitted for review have expanded and jurisdictional issues multiplied, FDA has dealt with these questions in a variety of ways. In some cases, review responsibility for the regulation of certain very similar products has been divided or shared between centers. Although these and other solutions developed by the agency answered some jurisdictional questions, others were left unanswered.

II. The Safe Medical Devices Act of 1990

The Safe Medical Devices Act (SMDA) of 1990 (Pub. L. 101-629) has the general purpose of improving the regulation of medical devices. Section 16 of the SMDA, however, addresses product jurisdiction questions involving "combination products," i.e., products containing a combination of drugs, devices, and biological products.

Specifically, this section of the new law requires that the agency designate a component of FDA to have primary jurisdiction for the premarket review and regulation of a product that constitutes a combination of a drug, device, or biological product. The designation is to be made based upon a determination of the "primary mode of action" of the combination product. The new provision explicitly states, however, that FDA can use any agency resources necessary to ensure adequate safety, effectiveness, or (in the case of medical devices) substantial equivalence reviews for the products involved. Section 16 of the SMDA also modifies the definitions of "drug" and "device," and requires the agency to publish regulations implementing this section within a year, or by November 29, 1991.

As part of the process of developing these regulations, the FDA ombudsman chaired a public hearing on September 6, 1991. . . . The hearing panel was comprised of Deputy Directors from the Center for Biologics Evaluation and Research, the Center for Devices and Radiological Health, and the Center for Drug Evaluation and Research. The purpose of the hearing was to give interested persons the opportunity to provide comments and suggestions about the content and scope of this regulation. More than 15 people made oral presentations and over 250 persons attended the hearing. The agency also solicited written comments and suggestions, which were accepted from July 12, 1991 through September 13, 1991 (Docket No. 91N-0257). All comments from the hearing or received in writing have been considered.

III. Highlights of the Final Regulation

This final regulation describes how the agency will determine which component within FDA will have the primary jurisdiction for the premarket review and regulation of a combination product comprised of drugs, devices, or biologics. This regulation, however, is not limited in its scope to the combination products specified in the law. To enhance the efficiency of agency operations, it also applies to any drug, device, or biological product where the jurisdiction is unclear or in dispute. This regulation, however, does not apply to foods, veterinary products, or cosmetics. The agency is aware that such products may present jurisdictional issues, and will further consider whether they should subsequently be included in this rule.

The regulation specifies how a sponsor can obtain an agency determination early in the process, before any required filing, which agency component will have primary jurisdiction for the premarket review and regulation of the product. The regulation also establishes a "product jurisdiction officer" within FDA's Office of the Commissioner to oversee these procedures and processes. The FDA Ombudsman is the Product Jurisdiction Officer.

A. Scope

This regulation applies to two categories: First, any product that constitutes a combination of a drug, device, or biological product under section 503(g)(1) of the [FFDCA]; and, secondly, any drug, device or biological product where the agency component with primary jurisdiction for the premarket review and regulation is unclear or in dispute.

As set forth in § 3.2(e) of this final rule, the term combination product means a product comprised of two or more different regulated entities, e.g., drug, device, or biologic (for example, a syringe prefilled with a drug); or two or more separate products packaged together as one unit (for example, a lumbar puncture kit containing drapes, needles, tubes, a syringe, a local anesthetic and a topical antiseptic). A combination product is also a product that is intended for use only with an approved product where both are required to achieve the intended use, indication, or effect, and the labeling of the approved product needs to be changed to reflect this use (for example, a device to aerosolize medication that works only with a specific drug that when given as an aerosol must be used with this device and that, as a consequence, is labeled for this route of administration using only this device). Finally, a combination product is any investigational product that is intended to be used only with another investigational product where both are required to achieve the intended use, indication, or effect, for example, a novel catecholamine administered by a computerized pump that is to be developed as a pharmacological cardiac stress test.

Thus, the definition of a combination product is intended to exclude most concomitant use of drugs, devices, and biological products. The definition also excludes products comprised exclusively of two or more drugs, two or more devices, or two or more biologicals.

B. Contents of the Regulation

Section 3.4(a) of this rule implements the statutory mandate that the designation of the agency component with primary jurisdiction shall be based on the primary mode of action of the product at issue. Section 3.4(b) of this rule provides that the designation of an agency component does not preclude consultations with other agency components and, where appropriate, does not preclude requiring the approval of a second application, ordinarily by the lead center. In addition, where the agency finds it is necessary, the agency reserves the option to require separate applications to be approved by separate agency components. FDA recognizes that requiring the approval of a second agency component would represent the exception rather than the rule and, in those instances, the reviews will be coordinated to the greatest extent possible.

Section 3.5 of this rule describes how to identify the designated agency component and discusses the intercenter agreements which allocate among the centers primary responsibility for certain products or categories of products. Section 3.6 of this rule identifies a product jurisdiction officer with whom sponsors may file a request for designation of the agency component with primary jurisdiction. Section 3.7 of this rule specifies to whom and when to make a request, and the information to be set forth in the request for designation, including the sponsor's recommendation as to which center should have primary jurisdiction.

Under §3.8 of this rule, the procedures and time periods applicable to FDA actions on requests for designation are set forth, including the procedures to be used if a sponsor disagrees with a designation. Section 3.9 of this rule specifies that once a designation has been made, it can be modified with the written consent of the sponsor or, where necessary, without the sponsor's consent to protect the public health or for other compelling reasons. Section 3.10 of this rule provides that the statutory and regulatory time periods for review of premarket submissions and marketing approval applications is stayed by a filing with or review by the product jurisdiction officer.

This regulation has prospective applicability only. Thus, any marketing application (biologics product license application, premarket approval application, or new drug application), pending on or before the effective date of this regulation is not subject to this regulation. A sponsor of a pending marketing application who wants to use the new procedures will have to withdraw its application and resubmit it. The agency may elect to shift responsibility for investigational products consistent with this rule and the other documents discussed below in section III.D. of this preamble.

C. Authority for This Regulation

This rule provides an administrative mechanism to determine which agency component has responsibility for the review of an application. The agency determined that this is "a matter relating to agency management" and a rule of "agency organization, procedure, or practice" and, as such, it is exempt from notice and comment under the Administrative Procedure Act (5 U.S.C. 553 (a)(2) and (b)(A)). The Commissioner also finds good cause under 5 U.S.C. 553(b)(B) and 21 CFR 10.40(e) to forgo notice and comment as it would be unnecessary and contrary to the public interest to delay implementation of this rule. As provided in FDA's administrative practices and procedures regulation (21 CFR 10.40(e)), FDA is providing an opportunity for public comment on whether the regulation should be modified or revoked.

## 2013-01-22 FDA Final Rule, Current Good Manufacturing Practice Requirements for Combination Products

78 Fed. Reg. 4307

SUMMARY: The Food and Drug Administration (FDA or Agency) is issuing this regulation on the current good manufacturing practice (CGMP) requirements applicable to combination products. This rule is intended to promote the public health by clarifying which CGMP requirements apply when drugs, devices, and biological products are combined to create combination products. In addition, the rule sets forth a transparent and streamlined regulatory framework for firms to use when demonstrating compliance with CGMP requirements for "single-entity" and "co-packaged" combination products.

. . . .

I. Background

A. Rationale for the Rulemaking

*[This section begins by restating the combination product definition from 21 C.F.R. Part 3.]*

The constituent parts of a combination product retain their regulatory status (as a drug or device, for example) after they are combined. Accordingly, the CGMP requirements that apply to each of the constituent parts continue to apply when they are combined to make combination products. To date, however, the Agency has not issued specific regulations clarifying the applicability of the CGMP requirements to combination products. While CGMP regulations are in place that establish requirements for drugs, devices, and biological products, there are currently no regulations that clarify and explain the application of these CGMP requirements when these drugs, devices, and biological products are constituent parts of a combination product. FDA believes that the absence of clear CGMP requirements for combination products could result in inconsistent or differing application of the various CGMP requirements applicable to the constituent parts, which could affect product safety and the public health. In addition, the absence of clear requirements could lead some manufacturers to develop and document manufacturing practices that are redundant and overly burdensome.

In the Federal Register of October 4, 2004, the Agency announced the availability of a Draft Guidance for Industry and FDA entitled "Current Good Manufacturing Practices for Combination Products." The Agency received 15 comments, which were largely supportive of the regulatory approach described in the draft guidance. A common theme that emerged from these comments was the need to develop a clear regulatory framework that takes account of the fact that combination products are made up of drug, device, and biological product constituent parts. At the same time, commenters wanted to ensure that the framework would not lead to unnecessary redundancy in the operating systems used to meet CGMP requirements (CGMP operating systems).

After careful consideration of the comments, and of how best to ensure that CGMPs for combination products are consistent and appropriate, FDA determined that rulemaking was warranted. We concluded that rulemaking would best facilitate the manufacture of safe and effective combination products by providing a clear and transparent regulatory roadmap for the application of CGMP requirements to these products. Accordingly, the Agency published a proposed rule in the Federal Register of September 23, 2009, as part of FDA's ongoing effort to improve the consistency and aid implementation of the regulatory requirements for combination products.

B. The Proposed Rule

The proposed rule addressed CGMP requirements for all combination products. However, for certain types of combination products, the application of CGMP requirements is fairly straightforward. Specifically, the constituent parts of a combination product are each subject only to the CGMP regulations applicable to that type of constituent part (e.g., drug or device) if the constituent parts are manufactured and marketed separately, as may be the case for constituent parts of cross-labeled combination products. Because these constituent parts, while part of a combination product, are separately manufactured and marketed, they remain separate for purposes of applying the CGMP regulations. Therefore, the proposed rule merely provided that all such constituent parts must be manufactured in accordance with the CGMP requirements that would apply to them if they were not part of a combination product.

The application of CGMP requirements to single-entity and co-packaged combination products is less straightforward. Consequently, the proposed rule expressly addressed the practical application of CGMP requirements to these two categories of combination products. The proposed rule reflected Agency recognition that, in most instances, for single-entity and co-packaged combination products, a CGMP operating system that satisfies the CGMP regulations applicable to one constituent part will also satisfy most of the CGMP requirements applicable to the other constituent part. In particular, we explained that compliance with either the CGMP regulations for drugs at parts 210 and 211 (21 CFR parts 210 and 211) (drug CGMPs) or the quality system (QS) regulation for devices at part 820 (21 CFR part 820) will satisfy many, though not all, of the CGMP requirements applicable to both drug and device constituent parts.

In developing the proposed rule, the Agency reviewed the drug CGMPs and QS regulation. We identified specific provisions from the drug CGMPs and QS regulation that a firm would need to satisfy in addition to complying with the other of these two sets of CGMP requirements to demonstrate compliance with both of these sets of requirements. Based on this assessment, the proposed rule offered two options for demonstrating compliance with the CGMP requirements applicable to a co-packaged or single-entity combination product. These options were either: (1) To demonstrate compliance with the specifics of all CGMP regulations applicable to each of the constituent parts included in the combination product or (2) to demonstrate compliance with the specifics of either the drug CGMPs or the QS regulation, rather than both, when the combination contains both a drug and a device, under certain conditions. These conditions included demonstrating compliance with specified provisions from the other of these two sets of CGMP requirements. In addition, for a combination product that included a biological product, the CGMPs requirements for biological products in parts 600 through 680 (21 CFR parts 600 through 680) would apply, and, for a combination product that included any human cell, tissue, and cellular and tissue-based products (HCT/Ps), the regulations in part 1271 (21 CFR part 1271) would apply.

We intended for the proposed rule to help ensure that CGMP requirements that apply to single-entity and co-packaged combination products are clear and consistent, regardless of which Agency component has lead jurisdiction for the combination product, or which type of application is submitted for marketing authorization. The proposed rule was also intended to streamline demonstrating compliance with CGMP requirements for these types of combination products and to help ensure appropriate implementation of these requirements while avoiding unnecessary redundancy in CGMP operating systems for these products.

After publication of the proposed rule, to facilitate development of comments on the rule, FDA co-sponsored a workshop in January 2010. At this workshop, the Agency provided a summary of the proposed rule and stakeholders then worked in groups to identify issues on which it might be helpful to develop comments.

. . . .

C. The Final Rule

The final rule is largely identical to the proposed rule. It is organized in the same four sections addressing scope (§ 4.1), definitions (§ 4.2), the CGMPs that apply to combination products (§ 4.3), and how to comply with these CGMP requirements for a single-entity or co-packaged combination product (§ 4.4).

. . . .

III. Legal Authority

The Agency derives its authority to issue the regulations in 21 CFR part 4, subpart A, from [FFDCA §§ 201, 301, 501, 502, 503, 505, 510, 512–516, 518–520, 522, 531–542, 551–561, 701(a), 702–704, 721, 801, 803, and 1004] and [PHSA §§ 215, 351, 353, 361, and 368].

Most importantly, the provisions at sections 501(a)(2)(B) and (h) of the [FFDCA] require drugs and devices to be manufactured in accordance with CGMPs. Section 520(f) of the [FFDCA] specifically authorizes the issuance of CGMP regulations for devices. Section 501 of the [FFDCA] states that a drug or device is deemed adulterated if it is not manufactured in accordance with CGMPs. This provision applies to biological products including those that are constituent parts of combination products because these products meet the definition of drug or device under section 201 of the [FFDCA]. This provision also applies to HCT/Ps that do not meet the criteria for regulation solely as HCT/Ps under section 361 of the PHS Act, because they meet the definition of a drug, or device under section 201 of the [FFDCA]. In addition, section 351 of the PHS Act authorizes FDA to issue manufacturing standards for biological products. Section 361 of the PHS Act authorizes the issuance of regulations to prevent the introduction, transmission, or spread of communicable diseases.

Under applicable statutory provisions, the following CGMP regulations were previously issued for drugs, devices, biological products, and HCT/Ps that may be included in combination products:

- Drug CGMP regulations for finished pharmaceuticals or drug products set forth at parts 210 and 211). Drug products not subject to these regulations (e.g., bulk drugs or active pharmaceutical ingredients) must still meet the current good manufacturing practice general standard required by the statute.
- QS regulation for devices set forth at part 820.
- Requirements that pertain to manufacturing within the requirements (including standards) for biological products in parts 600 through 680.
- Current good tissue practices for HCT/Ps set forth in part 1271.

There is considerable overlap in the drug CGMPs and QS regulation, and for the most part the overlap is clear. For example, both establish requirements for management, organization, and personnel; both require documentation and recordkeeping; and both allow flexibility in their application to the manufacture of a particular product. FDA considers the drug CGMPs and the QS regulation to be similar, and they are meant to achieve the same general goals.

Nevertheless, these two sets of regulations differ somewhat because each is tailored to the characteristics of the types of products for which it was designed. Each set of regulations contains certain specific requirements for various CGMP concepts that are only more generally addressed in the other regulation. For example, the QS regulation has detailed CAPA requirements (§ 820.100) while CAPA principles are currently more generally addressed in the drug CGMP regulation as part of Subpart J, Records and Reports, specifically at §§ 211.180(e) and 211.192).

This rule clarifies the applicability of these two regulations to combination products and provides a streamlined option for practical implementation for co-packaged and single-entity combination products. Because the drug and device CGMP requirements are so similar, when using this streamlined approach, demonstrating compliance with the requirements of one of these two set of regulations (e.g., drug CGMPs), along with demonstrating compliance with the requirements of the specified provisions from the other set (e.g., QS regulation), would be considered to be demonstrating compliance with all requirements from both.

The CGMP requirements specific to each constituent part of a combination product also apply to the combination product itself because, by definition, combination products consist of drugs, devices, and/or biological products. (See § 3.2(e)). These articles do not lose their discrete regulatory identity when they become constituent parts of a combination product. Therefore, all combination products are subject to at least two sets of CGMP requirements. For example, in the case of a drug-device combination product, the QS regulation in part 820 and the drug CGMP regulations in parts 210 and 211 would apply to the combination product.

Although combination products retain the regulatory identities of their constituent parts, the [FFDCA] also recognizes combination products as a category of products that are distinct from products that are solely drugs, devices, or biological products. For example, section 503(g)(4)(A) of the [FFDCA] requires OCP to "designate" a product as a combination product as well as to ensure "consistent and appropriate postmarket regulation of like products subject to the same statutory requirements." Further, section 563(a) of the [FFDCA] governs the "classification" of products as "drug, biological product, device, or a combination product subject to section 503(g)" (emphasis added). In this respect, the [FFDCA] identifies a combination product as a distinct type of product that could be subject to specialized regulatory controls.

Under the preceding authorities and section 701(a) of the [FFDCA], which authorizes FDA to issue regulations for the efficient enforcement of the [FFDCA], FDA has the authority to issue regulations clarifying the applicability of CGMP requirements to combination products. The Agency is also authorized under these authorities to issue regulations specifying how compliance with CGMP requirements for combination products may be demonstrated.

## 2016-12-20 Final Rule, Postmarket Safety Reporting for Combination Products

81 Fed. Reg. 92,603

SUMMARY: The Food and Drug Administration (FDA or Agency) is issuing regulations to set forth postmarketing safety reporting requirements for combination products. Specifically, this final rule describes the postmarketing safety reporting requirements that apply when two or more different types of regulated medical products (drugs, devices, and/or biological products, which are referred to as "constituent parts" of a combination product) comprise a combination product and the combination product or its constituent parts have received FDA marketing authorization. The rule is intended to promote and protect the public health by setting forth the requirements for postmarketing safety reporting for these combination products, and is part of FDA's ongoing effort to ensure the consistency and appropriateness of the regulatory requirements for combination products.

. . . .

*Executive Summary*

*Purpose of the Final Rule*

The Agency has not previously issued regulations on postmarketing safety reporting specifically for combination products, which are products comprised of: (1) A drug and a device; (2) a device and a biological product; (3) a biological product and a drug; or (4) a drug, a device, and a biological product. Instead, the Agency has applied provisions to combination products from the postmarketing safety reporting regulations applicable to the constituent parts (i.e., reporting requirements specific to drugs, devices, and biological products). These regulations for drugs, devices, and biological products share many similarities; however, each set of regulations has certain unique reporting requirements, standards, and timeframes based in part on the characteristics of the type of product. These variations among the regulations and lack of clarity on how to apply these requirements to combination products can result in inconsistent and incomplete postmarketing safety reporting for combination products and their constituent parts.

The purpose of this final rule is to ensure consistent, complete postmarketing safety reporting requirements for combination products that have received FDA marketing authorization, while avoiding duplicative reporting. The term "postmarketing safety" is used in this rule because this rule concerns certain postmarket events, including manufacturing events, device malfunctions, and events causing injury to users, and the reporting requirements that relate to product and patient safety arising from these events. The final rule supports the underlying purpose of postmarketing safety reporting for all medical products, namely to protect the public health by ensuring continued safety and effectiveness of the product once it is placed on the market.

*Summary of the Major Provisions of the Final Rule*

This final rule requires that a "combination product applicant" (an entity holding the application(s), as the term "application" is defined in 21 CFR 4.101 of this rule, for a combination product) and a "constituent part applicant" (an entity holding the application to market a drug, device, or biological product as a constituent part of a combination product the constituent parts of which are marketed under applications held by different applicants) comply with postmarketing safety reporting requirements applicable to the product based on the application type (e.g., new drug application, premarket approval application, biologics license application) under which the combination product or constituent part received marketing authorization. In addition to these application-type based reporting requirements, the final rule requires combination product applicants to submit additional specified reports based on the constituent parts included in the combination product (e.g., malfunction reports if the combination product includes a device, field alert reports if it includes a drug, and biological product deviation reports if it includes a biological product). The final rule requires constituent part applicants to share certain postmarketing safety information they receive with one another. The rule also specifies how combination product and constituent part applicants must submit postmarketing safety reporting information to the Agency and what records they must maintain.

. . . .

*Legal Authority*

The legal framework underlying this final rule is twofold. The first aspect is that drugs, devices, and biological products do not lose their discrete regulatory identities when they become constituent parts of a combination product. In general, the postmarketing safety reporting requirements specific to each constituent part of a combination product also apply to the combination product itself. Although the constituent parts of combination products retain their regulatory identities, the [FFDCA] also recognizes combination products as a category of products that are distinct from products that are solely drugs, devices, or biological products. FDA has the authority to develop regulations to ensure sufficient and appropriate ongoing assessment of the risks associated with combination products.

The second aspect of the framework is founded on the postmarketing safety reporting regulatory scheme associated with the application under which the combination product received marketing authorization. . . . Although similar in effect to the first aspect of the framework, this aspect is based on the legal authority FDA used to issue each of its existing regulations for postmarketing safety reporting for drugs, devices, and biological products.

. . . .

## 2017-01-09 FDA Final Rule, Clarification of When Products Made or Derived from Tobacco Are Regulated as Drugs, Devices, or Combination Products; Amendments to Regulations Regarding "Intended Uses"

82 Fed. Reg. 2193

SUMMARY:

The Food and Drug Administration (FDA) is issuing this final rule to describe the circumstances in which a product made or derived from tobacco that is intended for human consumption will be subject to regulation as a drug, device, or a combination product under the [FFDCA]. This action is intended to provide direction to regulated industry and to help avoid consumer confusion.

SUPPLEMENTARY INFORMATION:

### Executive Summary

#### Purpose of the Rule

The Family Smoking Prevention and Tobacco Control Act (Tobacco Control Act) amends the [FFDCA] and provides FDA with the authority to regulate tobacco products. Section 201(rr) of the [FFDCA], as amended by the Tobacco Control Act, defines the term "tobacco product" as any product made or derived from tobacco that is intended for human consumption, including any component, part, or accessory of a tobacco product (except for raw materials other than tobacco used in manufacturing a component, part, or accessory of a tobacco product). Excluded from the definition of a tobacco product is any article that is a drug, device, or combination product. Any article that is a drug, device, or combination product will be regulated as such rather than as a tobacco product.

Because some ambiguity surrounds the circumstances under which a product that is made or derived from tobacco would be regulated as a drug, device, or combination product, and the circumstances under which it would be regulated as a tobacco product, FDA is taking this action to provide clarity regarding our interpretation of the drug and device definitions in the [FFDCA] with respect to products made or derived from tobacco. . . . .

#### Summary of the Major Provisions of the Regulatory Action

Conceptually, the final rule follows the disease prong and the structure/function prong (with certain specified limitations) of the statutory definitions of "drug" and "device" (section 201(g) and (h) of the [FFDCA]). Under the final rule, a product made or derived from tobacco and intended for human consumption is regulated as a drug, device, or combination product in two circumstances: (1) If the product is intended for use in the diagnosis of disease or other conditions, or in the cure, mitigation, treatment, or prevention of disease; or (2) if the product is intended to affect the structure or any function of the body in any way that is different from effects related to nicotine that were commonly and legally claimed in the marketing of cigarettes and smokeless tobacco products prior to March 21, 2000. . . .

## D. Key Points

- FDA uses the term "combination product" to refer to combinations of its therapeutic product categories: drugs, devices, and biological products.
- The component parts of combination products remain subject to their individual regulatory schemes. Combination product regulations are simply an overlay of additional cGMP regulations and postmarket reporting requirements.
- Combination products are an emerging area that has become more significant to FDA in recent years.

# Part Five

# PHSA Products — Biologics and HCT/Ps

Chapter 14

# Biologics

## A. Introduction

Please read (or review) the following excerpts in the statutory supplement:

- PHSA § 351. Regulation of biological products.
- PHSA § 361. Regulations to control communicable disease.
- 21 C.F.R. Part 600. General.

PHSA § 351 is the general statutory provision specific to biologics. Pay particular attention to subsections (a), (g), (i), and (k). Subsection (a) sets out the statutory requirements for a biologics license. Subsection (g) sets out the relationship between the PHSA and the FFDCA. Subsection (i) sets out the statutory definition of a biologic. Subsection (k) sets out the procedures FDA can use to license "biosimilar" and "interchangeable" products.

## B. Outline of Regulatory Regime

As in other chapters of this book, this chapter begins with a set of charts. As you read this chapter for the first time, you should do no more than skim these charts to get a general sense of the structure of the applicable statutes and regulations. (For more information on the role of the charts in this casebook, see Chapter 1, Parts A.1 and B).

Note that the charts below list key statutes, and key statutory and regulatory provisions, specific to biologics. However, FDA takes the position that all products meeting the § 351(i) definition of biological products also qualify as drugs under FFDCA § 201(g). Biological products that qualify as drugs are subject to both the biologics provisions and the drug provisions of the statute. Because the system of drug regulation has already been covered in Chapter 10, this chapter limits itself to those aspects of biological products different from those applicable to drugs more generally. Marketing authoriztion for drugs (including biologic drugs) was covered in Chapter 4.

| Timeline of Key Statutes Specific to Biologics | | | |
|---|---|---|---|
| Year | PL | Stat | Name of Statute |
| 1902 | 57-244 | 32 Stat. 728 | Biologics Control Act of 1902 |
| 1941 | 77-366 | 55 Stat. 851 | Insulin Amendment |
| 1944 | 78-410 | 58 Stat. 682 | Public Health Services Act |
| 1986 | 99-660 | 100 Stat. 3755 | Childhood Vaccine Act |
| 2010 | 111-148 | 124 Stat. 119, 804–821 | Biologics Price Competition and Innovation Act of 2009 *[Despite title, passed in 2010 as part of the better-known Affordable Care Act]* |

| Key Statutory Provisions Specific to Biologics | | |
|---|---|---|
| Statute Name or U.S.C. Title | § | Title of Section or Subsection |
| PHSA | 351 | Regulation of biological products |
| PHSA | 361 | Regulations to control communicable diseases |

| Key Regulatory Provisions Specific to Biologics: Generally | | |
|---|---|---|
| 21 C.F.R. Part | Subpart | Title of Part or Subpart |
| 600 | — | Biological products: general |
| 601 | — | Licensing |
| 606 | — | Current good manufacturing practice for blood and blood components |
| 607 | — | Establishment registration and product listing for manufacturers of human blood and blood products and licensed devices |
| 610 | — | General biological products standards |

| Key Regulatory Provisions Specific to Biologics: Lists of Biological Product Standards | | |
|---|---|---|
| 21 C.F.R. Part | Subpart | Title of Part or Subpart |
| 606 | — | Current good manufacturing practice for blood and blood components |
| 607 | — | Establishment registration and product listing for manufacturers of human blood and blood products and licensed devices |
| 610 | — | General biological products standards |
| 630 | — | Requirements for blood and blood components intended for transfusion or for further manufacturing use |

| 21 C.F.R. Part | Subpart | Title of Part or Subpart |
|---|---|---|
| 640 | — | Additional standards for human blood and blood products |
| 660 | — | Additional standards for diagnostic substances for laboratory tests |
| 680 | — | Additional standards for miscellaneous products |

## C. Historical Context

### FDA, Science and the Regulation of Biological Products: From a Rich History to a Challenging Future—Commemorating 100 Years of Biologics Regulation

Brochure, March 2002

The United States Food and Drug Administration's Center for Biologics Evaluation and Research (CBER) is commemorating the Biologics Control Act of 1902 and 100 years of regulating biological products. This law was enacted by Congress to ensure the protection of Americans by providing consistently safe biological products. The Act not only serves as the underpinning for today's regulation of biological products, but also marks a historic turning point in the way America protects the health of its citizens.

Throughout the 20th century, the world witnessed great discoveries in the biological sciences, many of which led to the prevention or eradication of diseases that have devastated populations in the past. For 100 years, what is now known as FDA's Center for Biologics Evaluation and Research or "CBER," has played a significant role in ensuring the safety and efficacy of the fruits of these scientific discoveries. CBER is responsible for the regulation of "biologics," which are medical products such as vaccines, blood and blood derivatives, allergenic patch tests and extracts, HIV and hepatitis tests, gene therapy products, cells and tissues for transplantation, and new treatments for cancers, arthritis, and other serious diseases. CBER reviewed the first vaccines to immunize persons against infectious diseases, such as polio, pertussis ("whooping cough"), and German measles. CBER research led to important discoveries to safely collect, prepare, and transfuse blood and blood plasma.

With continued advancements in medical research and medical technology, CBER will face new challenges—not just scientific and regulatory, but legal and ethical. In the 21st Century, CBER will continue its rich tradition of melding strong scientific research with innovative regulations that ensure timely access to safe and effective biological products.

#### The St. Louis Tragedy and Enactment of the 1902 Biologics Control Act

In 1901, diphtheria patients were routinely treated with antitoxin derived from the blood serum of horses. The horse serum was manufactured in local establishments with no central or uniform controls. In St. Louis, Missouri, the blood of a tetanus-infected retired milk wagon horse named Jim was used for that purpose. By late 1901, this situation erupted into tragedy when 13 children who had been given diphtheria antitoxin died of tetanus.

In 1902, Congress enacted the Biologics Control Act, also known as the Virus-Toxin Law, which gave the government its first control over the processes used for the production of biological products. The first regulations under this Act became effective on August 21, 1903, and mandated that producers of vaccines be licensed annually for the manufacture and sale of vaccines, serum, and antitoxins. Manufacturing facilities also were required to undergo inspections, and licenses could be revoked or suspended when necessary. Production was to be supervised by a qualified scientist. All product labels were required to include the product name, expiration date, and address and license number of the manufacturer. These new controls marked the beginning of a basic change in America's federal public health policy and a steadfast commitment to the protection of public health.

Additional legislation was passed that eventually would provide further protections for recipients of biological products. In 1906 the Federal Food and Drugs Act was passed, which outlawed adulterated and misbranded foods and drugs, but made no reference to biologic products. This Act was later replaced by the 1938 Food, Drug and Cosmetics Act. After 1938, the appropriate provisions of the 1902 and 1938 Acts were used to regulate biologics.

*[A portion omitted here discusses the licensing of the polio, German measles, and pertussis vaccines, the regulation of blood and plasma products, and the CBER response to AIDS.]*

. . . .

**Challenges for the 21st Century**

The discovery of DNA opened the door to a new science—human gene therapy. With the publication of Watson and Crick's pioneering work in 1953 came new hope for sufferers of genetic diseases. The structure that they proposed, the double helix, is the DNA molecule in a human cell that contains genetic information. Understanding DNA allows researchers to manipulate genes and potentially cure inherited diseases. The discovery of recombinant DNA methods led the way to the development of biotechnology. An early outgrowth of biotechnology was the first recombinant DNA vaccine, Hepatitis B (Recombinant), licensed in 1986. Says Philip Noguchi, MD, Director, Division of Cellular and Gene Therapies for CBER, "Gene therapy is either very complicated or very simple. It is a means by which you can actually alter the genetic makeup of a cell. Instead of giving a person interferon—which is a protein used to treat certain cancers and other diseases—why not give the person the gene and then his own body will actually start to make the protein, and might never have to replace it again? That's one of the very intriguing theories of gene therapy."

New therapies such as xenotransplantation (the transplantation of animal cells, tissues or organs into a human) offer hope for an added source of organs. . . .

New vaccines are being developed and modified as new discoveries teach us more about the human immune system. New allergenic products provide relief for Americans who suffer from allergies. Infectious diseases, both new and old, create an urgent demand for the hastened availability of new drugs.

And the genomics and proteomics revolution has scarcely begun. The study of gene structures is leading to potentially effective treatments for a variety of serious diseases and conditions including cancer, diabetes and heart disease. Yet while the genome represents the information archive of the cell, it is the proteins that do all the work. They carry out cellular functions, underpin disease processes, and ultimately dictate cellular growth and death. The main analytical tool being used to study gene structure and proteins is microarray equipment, which is capable of analyzing thousands of genes simultaneously. The joint CBER/NIH Proteomics Program offers molecular imaging of cells and blood, providing early diagnosis of disease and early warning of drug toxicity.

CBER's major challenge for the 21st Century is to expedite approval of biological products for use by the public while, at the same time, maintain high levels of safety and quality. CBER's careful risk management of approved products already in the market also plays an important and essential role in protecting the public health.

Says CBER Director Kathryn C. Zoon, PhD, "This is a moment in time where we are witnessing the exciting and significant progress made in the field of biotechnology. New biological products such as vaccines and therapeutics have already improved the health of the public. The blood supply has never been safer. And, as we move through the 21st century, our strong leadership in science-based regulation, coordinated research, and the use of partnerships will continue to assure that safe and effective new biological products reach the public."

. . . .

## 1972-06-29 Public Health Service and FDA Notice, Statement of Organization, Functions, and Delegations of Authority

37 Fed. Reg. 12,865

Part 6 (Food and Drug Administration) of the Statement of Organization, Functions, and Delegations of Authority of the Department of Health, Education, and Welfare (35 F.R. 3685-92, dated February 25, 1970, as amended) is amended to reflect the transfer of the Division of Biologics Standards, National Institutes of Health, to the Food and Drug Administration, and the elevation of the Division to Bureau status.

Section 6A is amended as follows:

> SEC. 6-A Mission. The mission of the Food and Drug Administration (FDA) is to protect the public health of the Nation as it may be impaired by foods, drugs, biological products, cosmetics, therapeutic devices, hazardous

> household substances, poisons, pesticides, food additives, flammable fabrics and various other types of consumer products. FDA's regulatory functions are geared to insure that: Foods are safe, pure, and wholesome; drugs and biological products are safe and effective; cosmetics are harmless; therapeutic devices are safe and effective; all of the above are honestly and informatively labeled and packaged; dangerous household products carry adequate warnings for safe use and are properly labeled; counterfeiting of drugs is stopped; and that hazards incident to the use of various types of consumer products are reduced.

Section 6B is amended as follows:

> Sec. 6B Organization
>
> ....
>
> (r) Bureau of Biologics. Administers regulation of biological products used in the District of Columbia and in interstate commerce; and prepares biological products for its own use and for use by other Federal and private agencies and organizations engaged in medicine when such products are not available commercially. In carrying out these functions, cooperates with other PHS organizations, governmental and international agencies, volunteer health organizations, universities, individual scientists, nongovemmental laboratories, and manufacturers of biologicals.

## 1972-08-18 FDA Proposed Rule, Procedures for Review of Safety, Effectiveness, and Labeling

37 Fed. Reg. 16,679

The importance to the American public of safe and effective vaccines, serums, blood, and other analogous biological products cannot be understated. As early as 1902, Congress enacted biologics control provisions in the Public Health Service Act. These provisions were revised and codified in section 351 of the Public Health Service Act of 1944. A regulatory program has been developed under this congressional mandate, whereby manufacturers of biological products are licensed to distribute these products with adequate showing that they are pure, potent, and safe for their intended uses.

Section 351 of the Public Health Service Act does not explicitly confer the authority to deny or revoke a license on the ground that the product is ineffective or misbranded. Because all biological products are drugs, and because the [FFDCA] does contain explicit authority to control the effectiveness and misbranding or all drugs, applicable provisions of the [FFDCA] were redelegated, as published in the Federal Register of February 25, 1972, for use to control these aspects of biological products. Shortly thereafter a review of the effectiveness of all licensed biologics was announced, with the first category to consist of certain bacterial vaccines and bacterial antigens, as published in the Federal Register of March 15, 1972. On July 1, 1972, the Division of Biologics Standards, National Institutes or Heath, which has been charged with administering and enforcing section 351 of the Public Health Service Act, was transferred to the Food and Drug Administration, where it is now the Bureau of Biologics. As part of this transfer, the February 25, 1972, redelegation has been rescinded.

The Commissioner of Food and Drugs, in accepting the transfer of responsibilities for the regulation of biological products, concluded that a systematic review of present procedures should be undertaken.

This proposal will establish a procedure under which the safety, effectiveness, and labeling of all biological products presently licensed under section 351 of the Public Health Service Act will be reviewed. Advisory review panels comprised of independent experts will provide their conclusions and recommendations to the Commissioner of Food and Drugs, who then will review and implement them. Although these products have been reviewed for safety in the past, it is concluded that the safety of these products should be reviewed again at this time, not only because a review of effectiveness requires a consideration of safety factors, but also because new safety criteria have been developed relating to the necessity for long term scientific evaluation, in that long periods of time may pass before latent adverse effects become manifest. The use of independent advisory panels to participate in this review will ensure objective review of these past decisions, and thus will assure public confidence in the use of these products.

The review procedure proposed in this notice relies for legal authority on both the [FFDCA] and section 351 of the [PHSA]. To the extent that licensed biological products are presently not required to comply with the provisions of the [FFDCA], these regulations supersede any such exemptions. As the provisions of the [FFDCA] are gradually applied to licensed biological products and new biological products such existing exemptions will be modified or revoked for a biological product or category or products, on a transitional basis.

The Commissioner of Food and Drugs is aware of the unique problems involved in applying the requirement of "substantial evidence of effectiveness" to biological products, under the [FFDCA]. Where adequate and well-controlled studies are not feasible, and acceptable alternative scientific methods of demonstrating effectiveness are available, the latter will be sufficient. The advisory review panels convened under the procedure proposed in this notice will initially develop the standard and methodology for effectiveness for a particular class of biological products, taking into account all of the circumstances involved subject to review by the Commissioner of Food and Drugs.

The review procedure proposed in this notice represents the first amalgamation of the licensing procedure established under section 351 of the Public Health Service Act and the new drug and misbranding provisions established under the [FFDCA]. Each review panel will determine those biological products that are and are not effective, and not misbranded, as well as those for which further study is required. The applicable product licenses will then be confirmed, revoked, or permitted to remain in effect on an interim basis pending further study.

The review procedure proposed in this notice encompasses the overall safety and effectiveness of the biological product. The purity and potency of individual lots of a safe and effective biological product will continue to be handled on a lot-by-lot basis pursuant to the requirements already established in 21 CFR Part 273.

All biological products must be licensed prior to marketing, and there are no exemptions or grandfather clauses. It is possible that some biological products are excluded from the definition of a "new drug" under the 1938 or 1962 grandfather clauses, but no biological product is exempt from the misbranding or adulteration provisions of the [FFDCA]. Accordingly, product licenses for products that are determined by the Commissioner of Food and Drugs on the basis of the recommendation of the applicable advisory review panel, to be either not safe and effective or misbranded, will be revoked.

This notice constitutes only the first step in bringing together the provisions of section 351 of the Public Health Service Act and the requirements of the [FFDCA]. New procedural and substantive regulations governing the licensing of biological products, which will incorporate all applicable provisions of the [FFDCA], are in preparation and will be proposed for comment when they are available. . . .

. . . .

## 1982-06-22 FDA Notice, Statement of Organization, Functions, and Delegations of Authority

47 Fed. Reg. 26,913

Part H, Chapter HF (Food and Drug Administration) of the Statement of Organization, Functions, and Delegations of Authority for the Department of Health and Human Services . . . is amended to reflect the establishment of the National Center for Drugs and Biologics (NCDB) by merging the functions from the Bureau of Biologics (BOB) and the Bureau of Drugs (BD) and abolishing those bureaus, as such. Combining both bureaus will allow the Bureau of Drugs to share in the Bureau of Biologics expertise in laboratory research and build a broader scientific base for making drug decisions. Widening the scope of the Bureau of Biologics research activities will enhance its status and increase its role in the scientific and medical communities. Combining the bureaus will allow FDA to shift additional resources to tasks which are required by law and involve significant public health risks. It will also provide for greater organizational accountability for projects on which the Secretary and the Commissioner place the greatest priority. . . .

## 1987-10-15 FDA Notice, Statement of Organization, Functions, and Delegations of Authority

52 Fed. Reg. 38,275

. . . .

Part H, Chapter HF (Food and Drug Administration) of the Statement of Organization, Functions, and Delegations of Authority for the Department of Health and Human Services . . . is amended to reflect the establishment of the Center for Drug Evaluation and Research and the Center for Biologics Evaluation and Research in place of the current Center for Drugs and Biologics.

Currently, there are two major program concerns within the Center for Drugs and Biologics—Acquired Immune Deficiency Syndrome (AIDS) and the new drug review process. The crises and public pressures generated by these two major programs make them unmanageable in a single organization. FDA believes both programs need more focused leadership on a day-to-day basis and better management of resources than a single center director and deputy can provide. FDA believes that the director of its biologics program, which will focus on the development of AIDS vaccines and diagnostic tests and coordinate all other AIDS activities, needs to continue to report directly to the Commissioner due to the public health significance of the AIDS threat. FDA also believes that the director of the new drug review program needs to continue to report directly to the Commissioner due to the major public health gains that result from the approval of new therapies. Consequently, FDA believes that the establishment of two new centers in place of the current Center for Drugs and Biologics, with the AIDS program as the dominant focus in one and with the new drug review program as the dominant focus in the other, will enable FDA to focus more attention on these two vital programs.

## 1999-10-20 FDA Final Rule, Biological Products Regulated Under Section 351 of the Public Health Service Act; Implementation of Biologics License; Elimination of Establishment License and Product License

64 Fed. Reg. 56,441

### I. Background

In the Federal Register of July 31, 1998, FDA proposed to amend the biologics and other drug regulations to eliminate references to the PLA [(product license application)] and ELA [(establishment license application)] and to replace such references with the BLA. . . .

Prior to the issuance of the proposed rule, FDA had already reviewed its process of licensing biological products and had taken a number of actions to reduce the regulatory burdens imposed by the licensing process and to make the licensing process more consistent with the process for the approval of new drugs. In the Federal Register of May 14, 1996, FDA issued a final rule to amend the biologics regulations by eliminating the ELA requirement for the following specified biotechnology and synthetic biological products licensed under section 351 of the PHS Act: (1) Therapeutic deoxyribonucleic acid (DNA) plasmid products; (2) therapeutic synthetic peptide products of 40 or fewer amino acids; (3) monoclonal antibody products for in vivo use; and (4) therapeutic recombinant DNA-derived products. That provision applied only to those products that FDA determined under principles articulated in the "Intercenter Agreement Between the Center for Drug Evaluation and Research and the Center for Biologics Evaluation and Research" (effective on October 31, 1991) to be subject to licensure under section 351 of the PHS Act. Thus, upon approval, manufacturers of the specified biotechnology and synthetic biological products received a single biologics license instead of a product license and an establishment license (see § 601.2(c) (21 CFR 601.2(c))).

In the Federal Register of July 8, 1997, FDA announced the availability of a revised Form FDA 356h entitled "Application to Market a New Drug, Biologic, or an Antibiotic Drug for Human Use." Form FDA 356h was revised as a "Reinventing Government" initiative to harmonize application procedures between CBER and the Center for Drug Evaluation and Research (CDER) as outlined in the President's November 1995 National Performance Review Report entitled "Reinventing the Regulation of Drugs Made From Biotechnology." In the notice, FDA advised that applicants for biologics licenses for products specified in § 601.2(c) as well as autologous somatic cell therapy products could begin to use Form FDA 356h immediately and were required to do so beginning January 8, 1998. FDA advised applicants for licenses for other biological products that the agency would announce in the future when they can voluntarily begin to use and will be required to use Form FDA 356h. Upon approval of a BLA submitted on Form FDA 356h, FDA will issue a single biologics license. FDA believes that this licensing procedure will greatly simplify the application process, harmonize application procedures with those of CDER, and reduce industry and agency paperwork burdens. As a consequence of this final rule, all manufacturers requesting approval to introduce, or deliver for introduction, a biological product into interstate commerce must use Form FDA 356h to submit a BLA in lieu of separate establishment and product applications.

On November 21, 1997, the President signed into law FDAMA [(the Food and Drug Administration Modernization Act)]. Section 123 of FDAMA, in pertinent part, amended section 351 of the PHS Act to specify that a biologics license shall be in effect for a biological product prior to such product's introduction into interstate commerce. FDAMA thereby statutorily codified FDA's administrative BLA/biologics license "Reinventing Government" initiative. Section 123(a)(1) of FDAMA further states that the Secretary of Health and Human Services (the Secretary) (delegated to the Commissioner of Food and Drugs at 21 CFR 5.10(a)(5)) shall approve a "biologics license application" on the basis of a demonstration that the biological product that is the subject of the application is safe, pure, and potent; and the facility in which the biological product is manufactured, processed, packed, or held meets standards designed to ensure that the biological product continues to be safe, pure, and potent.

With the consolidation of the ELA's and PLA's into a single BLA, the amount of information formerly included in the ELA will be reduced, but not eliminated. Much of the information previously reviewed in an ELA at FDA will be reviewed by FDA investigators at the manufacturing site during a preapproval inspection. Some information formerly included in the ELA will now be submitted as "chemistry, manufacturing, and controls" (CMC) information or under the "establishment description" section of Form FDA 356h. The type and amount of information related to the establishment will vary according to the specific biological product for which licensure is being requested. To describe what information should be included for each type of biological product, CBER has prepared a series of guidance documents. . . .

## 2003-06-26 FDA Notice, Drug and Biological Product Consolidation

68 Fed. Reg. 38,067

SUMMARY: The Food and Drug Administration (FDA) is transferring certain product oversight responsibilities from the Center for Biologics Evaluation and Research (CBER) to the Center for Drug Evaluation and Research (CDER). This consolidation initiative provides the opportunity to further develop and coordinate scientific and regulatory activities between CBER and CDER. FDA believes that as more drug and biological products are developed for a broader range of illnesses, such interaction is necessary for both efficient and consistent agency action.

### I. The Consolidation Initiative

#### A. Therapeutic Biological Products Transferred to CDER

As of June 30, 2003, responsibility for regulating most therapeutic biologics, with certain exceptions (e.g., cell and gene therapy products and therapeutic vaccines) will be transferred from the Office of Therapeutics Research and Review (OTRR), CBER, to the Office of New Drugs (OND), and the Office of Pharmaceutical Science (OPS), CDER. Initially, this transfer of products will take place as the divisions of OTRR within CBER are detailed to offices within CDER. As of June 30, 2003:

- The Division of Therapeutic Proteins and the Division of Monoclonal Antibodies of OTRR, CBER, will be detailed to OPS, CDER.
- The Division of Clinical Trial Design and Analysis, the Division of Application Review and Policy, and the immediate office of the Director, OTRR, CBER, will be detailed to OND, CDER.

FDA anticipates that as of the start of fiscal year 2004 on October 1, 2003, the offices detailed to CDER will be incorporated into CDER's organizational structure, including the creation of a new Office of Drug Evaluation (ODE) in OND, CDER.

#### B. Therapeutic Biological Products Remaining in CBER

Under a previous reorganization, cell and gene therapy products from the Division of Cellular and Gene Therapies, OTRR, CBER were transferred to a new office, the Office of Cellular, Tissue and Gene Therapies (OCTGT).

Overall responsibility for therapeutic vaccines will remain in CBER. The clinical review of therapeutic vaccine-associated investigational new drug applications (INDs) and biologics license applications (BLAs) will be conducted by CBER and coordinated with the consolidated clinical expertise area in CDER.

. . . .

## FDA Website, Transfer of Therapeutic Biological Products to the Center for Drug Evaluation and Research*

On June 30, 2003, FDA transferred some of the therapeutic biological products that had been reviewed and regulated by the Center for Biologics Evaluation and Research (CBER) to the Center for Drug Evaluation and Research (CDER). CDER now has regulatory responsibility, including premarket review and continuing oversight, over the transferred products. In regulating the products assigned to them, CBER and CDER will consult with each other regularly and whenever necessary. On October 1, 2003, the staff comprising CBER's Office of Therapeutics Research and Review also transferred to CDER.

The lists below identify categories of biological products transferred from CBER to CDER, and categories of biological products remaining in CBER. Please note that the CBER list contains only a portion of the products CBER currently regulates; this list contains products that are closely related in chemical structure to products that transferred to CDER, e.g. therapeutic proteins and polysaccharides. Products are included on the CBER list as a means of clarifying the products that transferred and those that did not.

**Categories of Biological Products Transferred to CDER**

Monoclonal antibodies for in vivo use.

Proteins intended for therapeutic use, including cytokines (e.g. interferons), enzymes (e.g. thrombolytics), and other novel proteins, except for those that are specifically assigned to CBER (e.g., vaccines and blood products). This category includes therapeutic proteins derived from plants, animals, or microorganisms, and recombinant versions of these products.

Immunomodulators: proteins or peptides that are not antigen specific (e.g., cytokines, growth factors, chemokines, etc.) that are intended to treat disease by inhibiting or modifying a pre-existing immune response; and proteins or peptides intended to act in antigen-specific fashion to treat or prevent autoimmune diseases by inhibiting or modifying pre-existing immune responses.

Growth factors, cytokines, and monoclonal antibodies intended to mobilize, stimulate, decrease or otherwise alter the production of cells in vivo. This category includes growth factors, cytokines, and monoclonal antibodies, as well

* From https://www.fda.gov/combination-products/jurisdictional-information/transfer-therapeutic-biological-products-center-drug-evaluation-and-research (last updated Feb 16, 2018).

as non-biological agents, administered as mobilizing agents for their direct therapeutic effect on the recipient, as well as growth factors, cytokines, and monoclonal antibodies administered for the purpose of subsequently harvesting the mobilized, stimulated, decreased or otherwise altered cells for use in a human cellular or tissue-based product (HCT/P).

**Categories of Biological Products Remaining in CBER**

Cellular products, including products composed of human, bacterial or animal cells (such as pancreatic islet cells for transplantation), or from physical parts of those cells (such as whole cells, cell fragments, or other components intended for use as preventative or therapeutic vaccines).

Gene therapy products. Human gene therapy/gene transfer is the administration of nucleic acids, viruses, or genetically engineered microorganisms that mediate their effect by transcription and/or translation of the transferred genetic material, and/or by integrating into the host genome. Cells may be modified in these ways ex vivo for subsequent administration to the recipient, or altered in vivo by gene therapy products administered directly to the recipient.

Vaccines and vaccine-associated products: products, regardless of their composition or method of manufacture, intended to induce or enhance a specific immune response to prevent or treat a disease or condition, or to enhance the activity of other therapeutic interventions.

Allergenic extracts used for the diagnosis and treatment of allergic diseases and allergen patch tests.

Antitoxins, antivenins, and venoms

Blood, blood components, plasma derived products (for example, albumin, immunoglobulins, clotting factors, fibrin sealants, proteinase inhibitors), including recombinant and transgenic versions of plasma derivatives (for example clotting factors), blood substitutes, plasma volume expanders, human or animal polyclonal antibody preparations including radiolabeled or conjugated forms, and certain fibrinolytics such as plasma-derived plasmin, and red cell reagents.

Human cells, tissues and cellular and tissue-based products (HCT/P's). This category includes HCT/P's containing cells that have been harvested following in vivo administration of a CDER-regulated growth factor, cytokine, or monoclonal antibody, as well as HCT/P's requiring ex vivo manipulation.

**Combination Products**

The lists above contain some combination products comprised of a biological product component with a device and/or drug component, though such products are not specifically identified. Combination products are assigned to a Center for review and regulation in accordance with the products' primary mode of action. When a product's primary mode of action is attributable to a type of biological product assigned to CDER, the product will be assigned to CDER. Similarly, when a product's primary mode of action is attributable to a type of biological product assigned to CBER, the product will be assigned to CBER. . . .

## 2020-03-23 FDA Press Release, Insulin Gains New Pathway to Increased Competition

Today is a historic day and a landmark moment for patients with diabetes and other serious medical conditions, as insulin and certain other biologic drugs transition to a different regulatory pathway. This regulatory transition, mandated by Congress and implemented by the FDA, is incredibly important for patients. For the first time, a pathway will be open for products that are proposed as biosimilar to, or interchangeable with, the transitioned products. The availability of safe and effective biosimilar and interchangeable versions of these treatments, including insulin, is expected to increase patient access, adding more choices and potentially reducing costs of these vital therapies.

Biologic drugs, including insulin, treat some of the most serious diseases and conditions. The drugs transitioning today are used in the treatment, diagnosis and prevention of many of these conditions, including diabetes, respiratory distress syndrome, fertility conditions, Cushing's syndrome, deep vein thrombosis, Gaucher disease and many more. But these life-saving drugs often also contribute significantly to drug costs. Historically, it was more difficult to develop generic versions of these drugs under the Federal Food, Drug and Cosmetic (FD&C) Act due to scientific challenges and limitations on the scope of data that can be relied upon in a generic drug application. This framework contributed to limited competition for these drugs, resulting in fewer choices and higher prices for patients. Today's transition opens a new pathway for manufacturers to seek FDA approval of and bring biosimilar and interchangeable versions of insulin and other transitioning products to market, facilitating greater competition.

When Congress created the biosimilars pathway in the Biologics Price Competition and Innovation Act of 2009, Congress also created a 10-year timeline for stakeholders to prepare for the regulatory transition of biological products that were historically regulated under the [FFDCA]; now that the day has arrived, the FDA can begin receiving applications for proposed biosimilars to these licensed transition biological products, including insulin products that millions of Americans rely on every day to maintain stable blood glucose. Approved biosimilars will be able to come to market, where there is incredible potential to reduce health care costs, as has been seen with increased generic drug offerings. On the generic drugs side, we know from an FDA analysis that even with one generic on the market, prices are 31 to 39% lower than before the generic competition. Similarly, biosimilars marketed in the U.S. typically have launched with initial list prices 15 to 35% lower than comparative list prices of the reference products.

Over the last 10 years, the FDA has worked hard to establish a strong framework for the biosimilar and interchangeable regulatory pathway, as well as providing clarity to all involved on what the transition means to them and how it may affect our many stakeholders. Our Biosimilars Action Plan was established to improve the efficiency of the biosimilar and interchangeable product development and approval process and to maximize scientific and regulatory clarity for the biosimilar product development community. Through this action plan, we've worked to support robust competition from biosimilars, including supporting market competition and providing clear direction to industry on many relevant topics leading up to the transition.

In just the last six months, we've taken several important actions on biosimilars, and in preparation for this transition, including partnering with the Federal Trade Commission regarding efforts to address false or misleading statements and promotional communications by biologic product manufacturers, deter anti-competitive business practices and support a competitive marketplace for biosimilars; issuing a final rule, draft guidance and final guidances to provide clarity to industry; providing information for patients and health care providers about what the transition means to them; and expanding and digitizing the FDA's database of FDA-licensed biological products, otherwise known as the Purple Book.

These actions, among the many others we've taken in this space, reflect the tireless work of our dedicated workforce to ensure a smooth regulatory transition and provide clarity for biosimilar developers. We stand ready to review incoming applications from industry. We will also continue to work closely with those interested in producing biosimilar and interchangeable products to support efficiency in development, review and approval of these medicines.

Today is a milestone for the future of insulin and other important treatments—potentially a new era of proposed biosimilar and interchangeable insulin products. We expect this regulatory transition to enable a vibrant competitive market for transitioning products, ultimately empowering patients by increasing choices and potentially lowering prices of safe, effective, high-quality medications.

## D. Biologics and the 2020 Novel Coronavirus

### FDA, Guidance for Industry: Investigational COVID-19 Convalescent Plasma (April 2020)

FDA is issuing this guidance to provide recommendations to health care providers and investigators on the administration and study of investigational convalescent plasma collected from individuals who have recovered from COVID-19 (COVID-19 convalescent plasma) during the public health emergency. The guidance also provides recommendations to blood establishments on the collection of COVID-19 convalescent plasma.

. . . .

## II. BACKGROUND

There is currently an outbreak of respiratory disease caused by a novel coronavirus. The virus has been named "SARS-CoV-2" and the disease it causes has been named "Coronavirus Disease 2019" (COVID-19). On January 31, 2020, HHS issued a declaration of a public health emergency related to COVID-19 and mobilized the Operating Divisions of HHS. In addition, on March 13, 2020, the President declared a national emergency in response to COVID-19.

One investigational treatment being explored for COVID-19 is the use of convalescent plasma collected from individuals who have recovered from COVID-19. Convalescent plasma that contains antibodies to severe acute respiratory syndrome coronavirus 2 or SARS-CoV-2 (the virus that causes COVID-19) is being studied for administration to patients with COVID-19. Use of convalescent plasma has been studied in outbreaks of other respiratory infections, including the 2003 SARS-CoV-1 epidemic, the 2009–2010 H1N1 influenza virus pandemic, and the 2012 MERS-CoV epidemic.

Although promising, convalescent plasma has not yet been shown to be safe and effective as a treatment for COVID-19. Therefore, it is important to study the safety and efficacy of COVID-19 convalescent plasma in clinical trials. This guidance provides recommendations to health care providers and investigators on the administration and study of investigational convalescent plasma collected from individuals who have recovered from COVID-19 (COVID-19 convalescent plasma) during the public health emergency. This guidance also provides recommendations to blood establishments on the collection of COVID-19 convalescent plasma.

. . . .

## III. RECOMMENDATIONS

### A. Pathways for Use of Investigational COVID-19 Convalescent Plasma

Because COVID-19 convalescent plasma has not yet been approved for use by FDA,[3] it is regulated as an investigational product. As such, administration of COVID-19 convalescent plasma by a health care provider must be under an investigation new drug application (IND) under the traditional IND regulatory pathway, an expanded access IND, or a single-patient emergency investigational new drug application (eIND). FDA does not collect COVID-19 convalescent plasma or provide COVID-19 convalescent plasma. Health care providers or acute care facilities would instead obtain COVID-19 convalescent plasma from an FDA-registered blood establishment.

The following pathways are available for administering or studying the use of COVID-19 convalescent plasma:

---

3. Convalescent plasma is a biological product subject to licensure under section 351 of the [PHSA].

**1. Clinical Trials**

Investigators wishing to study the use of convalescent plasma in a clinical trial should submit requests to FDA for investigational use under the traditional IND regulatory pathway (21 CFR Part 312). CBER's Office of Blood Research and Review is committed to engaging with sponsors and reviewing such requests expeditiously.

**2. Expanded Access**

An IND application for expanded access is an alternative for use of COVID-19 convalescent plasma for patients with serious or immediately life-threatening COVID-19 disease who are not eligible or who are unable to participate in randomized clinical trials (21 CFR 312.305). FDA has worked with multiple federal partners and academia to open an expanded access protocol to facilitate access to COVID-19 convalescent plasma across the nation. For patients with serious or immediately life-threatening COVID-19 who are not eligible for or who are unable to participate in randomized clinical trials, access to this investigational product may be available through participation of acute care facilities in an investigational expanded access protocol under an IND that is already in place. Currently, the following protocol is in place: National Expanded Access Treatment Protocol.

**3. Single Patient Emergency IND**

Although participation in clinical trials or an expanded access program are ways for patients to obtain access to convalescent plasma, for various reasons these may not be readily available to all patients in potential need. Therefore, given the public health emergency that the COVID-19 pandemic presents, while clinical trials are being conducted and an expanded access protocol is available, FDA also is facilitating access to COVID-19 convalescent plasma for use in patients with serious or immediately life-threatening COVID-19 infections through the process of the patient's physician requesting a single patient eIND for the individual patient under 21 CFR 312.310. This process allows the use of an investigational drug for the treatment of an individual patient by a licensed physician upon FDA authorization, if the applicable regulatory criteria are met. Note, in such case, a licensed physician seeking to administer COVID-19 convalescent plasma to an individual patient must request the eIND.

. . . .

**B. Patient Eligibility**

To facilitate requests for eINDs for use of COVID-19 convalescent plasma to treat patients, health care providers seeking an emergency IND may want to consider the eligibility criteria used for the National Expanded Access Treatment Protocol, discussed in section III.A. of this guidance. These criteria include:

- Laboratory confirmed COVID-19
- Severe or immediately life-threatening COVID-19 . . . .
- Informed consent provided by the patient or healthcare proxy.

### C. Collection of COVID-19 Convalescent Plasma

Under FDA's IND regulations, an IND (including an expanded access or eIND) must provide information with respect to the investigational drug, chemistry, manufacturing, and controls that is adequate to ensure the proper identification, quality, purity, and strength of the investigational drug. For INDs for use of COVID-19 convalescent plasma, the IND would therefore need to contain, among other things, adequate information to demonstrate that the plasma will contain defined SARS-CoV-2 neutralizing antibody titers. Accordingly, health care providers or acute care facilities seeking to use COVID-19 convalescent plasma should include information in the IND submission that the COVID-19 convalescent plasma will be obtained from an FDA-registered blood establishment that follows the donor eligibility criteria and donor qualifications described in section III.C.1. of this guidance in collecting plasma from donors.

. . . .

## E. Related Area Not Regulated Primarily by FDA: Veterinary Biologics

As discussed in Chapter 11, Part D, biologics for animal use ("veterinary biologics") are regulated by USDA rather than FDA.

## F. Key Points

- From 1902 to 1972, biologics were regulated by the National Institutes of Health (and its predecessor, the National Laboratory of Hygiene).
  - NIH regulated biologics first under the Biologics Control Act of 1902, then under the PHSA.
  - In 1972, the Department of Health, Education, and Welfare (predecessor to today's Department of Health and Human Services) transferred NIH's Division of Biologics Standards (the portion of NIH responsible for biologics regulation) to FDA.
    - The transfer followed congressional hearings highly critical of NIH's management of biologics regulation.
- Today, biologics are regulated by FDA under both the PHSA and the FFDCA.
  - FDA takes the position that all products meeting the PHSA definition of "biological product" also meet the FFDCA definition of "drug."
- FDA divides regulatory responsibility for biologics between its Center for Biologics Evaluation and Research (CBER) and its much larger Center for Drug Evaluation and Research (CDER).

  - In 1982, FDA tried merging its drug-regulation and biologics-regulation functions into a single office. In 1987, FDA reversed course and split these functions between two offices again. This created the CBER and CDER offices that still operate today.
  - Today, either CBER or CDER has primary responsibility for each biological product.
    - The exact divisions between CBER-regulated and CDER-regulated biologics is complex, technical, and does not lend itself to summarization.
    - Roughly speaking, most (but not all) therapeutic biologics are regulated by CDER. However, important exceptions remain in CBER, including vaccines and gene therapy products.
- In 2010, Congress created a new pathway for "biosimilar" and "interchangeable" biological products.
  - These are, in effect, "generic" versions of biologics. However, the term "generic" is used only for drugs that do not also qualify as biologics.
- CBER also regulates human cells, tissues, and cellular- and tissue-based products (HCT/Ps).
  - However, these are regulated based on different statutory authority and different regulations than biologics.
  - They are, accordingly, addressed separately in the next chapter.

## Chapter 15

# Human Cells, Tissues, and Cellular and Tissue-Based Products

## A. Introduction

In recent decades, FDA has—by regulation—created a new category of products. This product category is not mentioned explicitly in either FFDCA § 201 or the provision on which FDA relied for the relevant authority, PHSA § 361. The story of FDA's decision to proceed with tissue regulation, and to do so via the PHSA, is told in detail in Richard A. Merrill, *Human Tissue and Reproductive Cloning: New Technologies Challenge FDA*, 3 Hous. J. Health L. & Pol'y (2002).

Please read (or review) the following excerpts in the statutory supplement:

- PHSA § 361. Regulations to control communicable diseases
- 21 C.F.R. Part 1270. Human tissue intended for transplantation.
- 21 C.F.R. Part 1271. Human cells, tissues, and cellular and tissue-based products.

The first item, PHSA 361, is the basic statutory authority on which FDA's regulations of HCT/Ps is based. Focus on subsection (a), which grants broad authority to promulgate regulations relating to communicable disease.

The second item, Part 1270, is the regulatory provision setting out FDA's initial regime for regulation of human tissue. This provision is currently in phase-out—it applies only to human tissue "recovered before May 25, 2005." 21 C.F.R. § 1271.3(j).

The third item, Part 1271, sets out FDA's current regime for the regulation of Human Cells, Tissues, and Cellular and Tissue-Based Products (HCT/Ps). Its establishment registration provisions were promulgated with staggered effective dates; its donor eligibility and cGTP provisions apply to all HCT/Ps recovered on or after May 25, 2005. (These effective dates are listed in the individual federal register notices, rather than the codified regulation).

## B. Outline of Regulatory Regime

As in other chapters of this book, this chapter begins with a set of charts. As you read this chapter for the first time, you should do no more than skim these charts to get a general sense of the structure of the applicable statutes and regulations. (For more information on the role of the charts in this casebook, see Chapter 1, Parts A.1 and B).

| Timeline of Key Statutes: HCT/Ps | | | |
|---|---|---|---|
| Year | PL | Stat | Name of Statute |
| 1944 | 78-410 | 58 Stat. 682 | Public Health Services Act |

| Key Statutory Provisions: HCT/Ps | | |
|---|---|---|
| Statute Name or U.S.C. Title | § | Title of Section or Subsection |
| PHSA | 361 | Regulations to control communicable diseases |

| Key Regulatory Provisions: HCT/Ps | | |
|---|---|---|
| 21 C.F.R. Part | Subpart | Title of Part or Subpart |
| 1270 | — | Human tissue intended for transplantation |
| 1271 | — | Human cells, tissues, and cellular and tissue-based products |

## C. FDA's Implementation of Human Tissue Regulation

### 1997-07-29 FDA Final Rule, Human Tissue Intended for Transplantation

62 Fed. Reg. 40,429

In the Federal Register of December 14, 1993, FDA issued an interim rule on human tissue intended for transplantation (hereinafter referred to as the interim rule). These regulations became effective upon the date of publication in the Federal Register and required human tissue in storage as of that date to be in compliance. The interim rule was issued because of evidence indicating an immediate need to protect the public health from the transmission of HIV infection and hepatitis infection through transplantation of human tissue from known donors infected with or at risk for these diseases. The movement towards regulating human tissue was accelerated by a hearing on appropriate oversight for human tissue banking chaired by Senator (then Representative) Wyden before the Subcommittee on Regulation,

Business Opportunities and Technology of the Committee on Small Business held on October 15, 1993. At the hearing, representatives of persons involved in human tissue banking advocated that legislation setting forth regulatory requirements for human tissue banking be passed. There was testimony that human tissues from foreign sources were being offered for sale in the United States with little documentation as to the source of the human tissue, the cause of death, the medical conditions of the donor, or the results of donor screening and testing. This raised significant concerns about the safety and quality of some of the human tissue available for transplantation. As a result of a number of similar allegations, the agency initiated inquiries into the possibility that human tissues intended for transplantation were being supplied without appropriate infectious disease testing and medical screening. In a relatively brief period of time, the agency was able to confirm the availability for importation and distribution to the United States of human tissue that did not follow adequate screening and testing standards to prevent transmission of infectious disease.

In the early 1990's, prior to the above-mentioned reports of the distribution of imported human tissue not following adequate screening and testing standards, the Centers for Disease Control and Prevention (CDC) reported that HIV had been transmitted through transplantation of human tissue. Based in part on the CDC report, the Assistant Secretary for Health convened a Public Health Service Work Group to evaluate the need for and type of Federal oversight that should be developed for human tissue. In its report on July 18, 1991, the Work Group recommended Federal development and publication of standards or guidance on donor screening, testing, recordkeeping and tracking procedures to reduce the risk of transmission of infectious disease. The Work Group recommended that Federal agencies, including FDA, proceed with pending regulations as "expeditiously as possible." The Work Group charged FDA to "continue to assert its jurisdiction over tissues on a product-by-product basis to ensure adequate oversight." The Work Group noted that investigation into the needed level of mandatory oversight for human tissue transplantation, apart from organ and bone marrow transplantation, should take place and recommended that FDA evaluate this issue. Subsequently, FDA issued the interim rule.

Since the interim rule was issued, FDA has issued 15 orders for retention, recall, and destruction of violative human tissue. In March 1995, following receipt of an order for retention, recall, and destruction that caused shipments of a firm's processed allografts to be held, a processor of human tissue filed a complaint in Federal District Court challenging FDA's interim rule and the application of internal guidance on the interim rule issued to field investigators. The court issued the plaintiff preliminary injunctive relief by enjoining FDA from detaining particular shipments of the plaintiff's tissue. The plaintiff and FDA subsequently entered into an agreement settling their dispute, and the plaintiff's complaint was dismissed.

. . . .

### B. Scientific and Legal Justification

The use of HIV antibody testing on donors of human tissue makes the human tissue inventory safer. However, it does not eliminate the "window" period between the time of infection and the presence of detectable levels of antibodies to HIV. Therefore, as an added safety measure FDA requires screening for behavioral and high risk information in addition to testing for infection with the virus so that the safest product will be made available. Like the HIV virus, evidence of hepatitis B and hepatitis C is determined by screening and testing human tissue donors. Since HIV and hepatitis viruses are transmitted by parenteral and sexual modes, exclusion of potentially infected donations by both screening and testing the human tissue donor has been found to be reliable and widely accepted. These viruses may be transmitted by a wide range of human tissue including solid organs, musculoskeletal and integumentary tissue, and body fluids (e.g., semen and breast milk).

FDA is issuing these regulatory requirements under the legal authority of section 361 of the Public Health Service Act. This section authorizes the Secretary of the Department of Health and Human Services (the Secretary), to make and enforce such regulations as judged necessary to prevent the introduction, transmission, or spread of communicable diseases from foreign countries into the States or from State to State. Intrastate transactions may be regulated under authority of this provision, as appropriate (*see State of Louisiana v. Mathews*, 427 F. Supp. 174 (E. D. La. 1977)). Section 361 of the PHS Act also provides for such inspection and destruction of articles found to be so infected or contaminated as to be sources of dangerous infection to humans, and other measures, as may be deemed by the Secretary to be necessary. Section 361 of the PHS Act has been invoked by FDA to regulate various activities or articles. For example, FDA has invoked this authority to regulate conveyance sanitation, the source and use of potable water, and milk pasteurization. The agency has also acted under section 361 of the PHS Act to prevent the transmission of communicable disease through shellfish, turtles, certain birds, and bristle brushes (see 21 CFR parts 1240 and 1250). FDA has also relied in part on section 361 of the PHS Act in issuing requirements to protect the blood supply.

Authority for the enforcement of section 361 of the PHS Act is provided for in part under section 368 of the PHS Act. Under section 368(a), any person who violates a regulation prescribed under section 361 of the PHS Act may be punished by imprisonment for up to 1 year. Individuals may also be punished for violating such a regulation by a fine of up to $100,000 if death has not resulted from the violation or up to $250,000 if death has resulted. In addition, Federal District Courts have jurisdiction to enjoin individuals and organizations from violating regulations implementing section 361 of the PHS Act.

## 2001-01-19 Final Rule, Human Cells, Tissues, and Cellular and Tissue-Based Products; Establishment Regulation and Listing

66 Fed. Reg. 5447

I. Introduction

We, FDA, are putting in place a comprehensive new system of regulation for human cells, tissues, and cellular and tissue-based products. The goal of the new approach is to improve protection of the public health without imposing unnecessary restrictions on research, development, or the availability of new products. Under the new system, the regulation of different types of human cells, tissues, and cellular and tissue-based products will be commensurate with the public health risks presented, enabling us to use our resources more effectively. Consolidating the regulation of human cells, tissues, and cellular and tissue-based products into one regulatory program is expected to lead to increased consistency and greater efficiency. Together, these planned improvements will increase the safety of human cells, tissues, and cellular and tissue-based products, and public confidence in their safety, while encouraging the development of new products.

A. Background

In 1997, we announced our regulatory plans for human cells, tissues, and cellular and tissue-based products in two documents:

- "A Proposed Approach to the Regulation of Cellular and Tissue-Based Products" and
- "Reinventing the Regulation of Human Tissue."

The proposed approach described a comprehensive plan for regulating human cells, tissues, and cellular and tissue-based products that would include establishment registration and product listing, donor-suitability requirements, good tissue practice regulations, and other requirements. Under this tiered, risk-based approach, we proposed to exert only the type of government regulation necessary to protect the public health. To accomplish this goal, we planned to issue new regulations under the communicable disease provisions of the Public Health Service Act (the PHS Act). Some human cellular and tissue-based products would be regulated only under these new regulations, while other human cellular and tissue-based products would also be regulated as drugs, devices, and/or biological drugs. We requested written comments on the proposed approach and, on March 17, 1997, held a public meeting.

Since 1997, we have published three proposed rules to implement the proposed approach. In 1998, as a first step toward accomplishing these goals, we published the proposed rule, "Establishment Registration and Listing for Manufacturers of Human Cellular and Tissue-Based Products" (the "registration proposed rule"). That rule proposed to require cell and tissue establishments to register with us and submit a list of their human cellular and tissue-based products. We also proposed modifications to current registration and listing requirements for drugs and devices under which cell and tissue establishments already regulated under the [FFDCA] and/or section 351 of the PHS Act would register and list following the new procedures.

In addition to the registration proposed rule, we published two more proposed rules:

- Suitability Determination for Donors of Human Cellular and Tissue-Based Products (September 30, 1999) (the "donor-suitability proposed rule"); and
- Current Good Tissue Practice for Manufacturers of Human Cellular and Tissue-Based Products; Inspection and Enforcement (January 8, 2000) (the "GTP proposed rule").

Together, these three rules when finalized would establish a comprehensive regulatory program for human cellular and tissue-based products, to be contained in part 1271.

In the three proposed rules, we used the term "human cellular and tissue-based products." In this final rule, we have changed the term to "human cells, tissues, and cellular and tissue-based products" (abbreviated "HCT/P's"). This change in terminology is a clarification and does not affect the scope of the definition, which continues to encompass an array of articles containing or consisting of human cells or tissues, and intended for implantation, transplantation, infusion, or transfer into human recipients, including investigational products. The definition of "human cells, tissues, or cellular or tissue-based product" is intended to cover HCT/P's at all stages of their manufacture, from recovery through distribution. Some examples of HCT/P's include skin, tendons, bone, heart valves, corneas, hematopoietic stem cells, manipulated autologous chondrocytes, epithelial cells on a synthetic matrix, and semen or other reproductive tissue.

B. Implementation of the New Regulations

We had intended to finalize the registration proposed rule with the two other rules that would make up part 1271 in its entirety, and to implement all three rules together. However, we are now making the registration rule final, with staggered effective dates, before finalizing the two remaining portions of part 1271. We are taking this action because of recent concerns raised about the safety of tissue, which have led us to believe that accelerating the collection of basic information about the rapidly growing tissue industry is vital. This medical sector has grown rapidly, with a need for clearer standards and improved accountability.... For these reasons, we are going to begin collecting registration and listing information, while continuing to develop the remainder of the final rules that will complete part 1271.... As part of completing the rulemaking for part 1271, we would make any necessary conforming amendments to this regulation to make it consistent with any changes made in the remainder of the rulemaking process, and we would revoke part 1270.

Establishments that engage in the recovery, screening, testing, processing, storage, or distribution of human tissue intended for transplantation currently regulated under section 361 of the PHS Act and the regulations in part 1270 ("Human Tissue Intended for Transplantation") will be required to begin registering with the agency and listing their HCT/P's within 30 days after the effective date of this final rule. The effective date for all other human cells, tissues, and cellular and tissue-based products ... is 2 years after publication, by which time we expect to have completed rulemaking for all the subparts of part 1271. ... Once the entire rulemaking is complete, the new regulatory approach would apply to a broad range of human cells, tissues, and cellular and tissue-based products, including reproductive cells and tissue; hematopoietic stem cells; and tissues and cells regulated as devices, drugs, and/or biological products.

....

C. Legal Authority

We are issuing this final rule under the authority of section 361 of the PHS Act. Under section 361 of the PHS Act, we may make and enforce regulations necessary to prevent the introduction, transmission, or spread of communicable diseases between the States or from foreign countries into the States. (See sec. 1, Reorg. Plan No. 3 of 1966 at 42 U.S.C. 202 for delegation of section 361 of the PHS Act authority from the Surgeon General to the Secretary, Health and Human Services; see 21 CFR 5.10(a)(4) for delegation from the Secretary to FDA.) Intrastate transactions may also be regulated under section 361 of the PHS Act. (See *Louisiana v. Mathews*, 427 F. Supp. 174, 176 (E.D. La. 1977).)

HCT/P's are derivatives of the human body and thus pose a potential risk of transmitting infectious disease. We have determined that some HCT/P's may be effectively regulated solely by controlling the infectious disease risks they present. The regulation now being finalized forms the foundation for a regulatory program that will further the goal of preventing the transmission of communicable disease. To begin implementing this regulatory program, we are publishing the registration final rule, with staggered effective dates so that those HCT/P establishments not currently subject to regulation under section 361 of the PHS Act will have adequate preparation time and FDA can continue working towards finalizing the remainder of the program.

For this regulatory system to be effective in preventing the spread of disease, we must obtain basic information about the human cell and tissue industry and its HCT/P's. The information to be submitted in compliance with the registration and listing requirements in subpart B will provide baseline data on establishments that will be subject to part 1271. This information from the registration rule will assist us in reacting swiftly to newly discovered or understood risks by alerting members of the industry to our concerns and, when appropriate, by conducting establishment inspections. Without this information, we would not be able to effectively monitor compliance with the proposed donor-suitability, GTP, and other regulations that make up the rest of the regulatory program.

Authority for enforcement of section 361 of the PHS Act is provided by section 368 of the PHS Act. Under section 368(a) of the PHS Act, any person who violates a regulation prescribed under section 361 of the PHS Act may be punished by imprisonment for up to 1 year. Individuals may also be punished for violating such a regulation by a fine of up to $100,000 if death has not resulted from the violation or up to $250,000 if death has resulted. In addition, Federal District Courts have jurisdiction to enjoin individuals and organizations from violating regulations implementing section 361 of the PHS Act. The regulations that we have proposed specific to enforcement appear in the GTP proposed rule.

HCT/P's that do not meet FDA's criteria set forth in part 1271 for regulation solely under section 361 of the PHS Act are regulated as drugs, devices, and/or biological products under the [FFDCA] and/or section 351 of the PHS Act, and their manufacturers are required to register with the agency under section 510 of the [FFDCA]. Regulations implementing section 510 of the [FFDCA] are found in parts 207 and 807, among other parts. In order to consolidate our data base on the cell and tissue industry and thus to improve our oversight functions, we are amending parts 207 and 807 to require registering establishments to follow the procedures set out in part 1271 .... Section 510 of the [FFDCA] remains the authority for the substantive registration requirement for products subject to parts 207 and 807. Because harmonizing the registration and listing procedures applicable to the various HCT/P's is intended to further the goal of preventing the spread of communicable disease, we are relying on the additional authority of section 361 of the PHS Act for the proposed amendments to parts 207 and 807.

## 2004-11-24 FDA Final Rule, Current Good Tissue Practice for Human Cell, Tissue, and Cellular and Tissue-Based Product Establishments; Inspection and Enforcement

69 Fed. Reg. 68,612

This rule represents the culmination of FDA's efforts to establish a comprehensive new system for regulating HCT/Ps. The regulations now being issued require certain HCT/Ps to be manufactured in compliance with CGTP. The rule also contains provisions relating to establishment inspection and enforcement, as well as certain labeling and reporting requirements, which are applicable to those HCT/Ps regulated solely under the authority of section 361 of the PHS Act and the regulations in part 1271, and not as drugs, devices, and/or biological products under the [FFDCA].

At this time we (FDA) are not responding to comments submitted on subparts D and E of the proposed rule relating to reproductive HCT/Ps. With two minor exceptions, the regulations in subparts D and E are not being finalized with respect to reproductive HCT/Ps described in § 1271.10 and regulated solely under section 361 of the PHS Act and the regulations in part 1271. The docket will remain open, and we ask that interested parties submit comments on communicable disease risks associated with reproductive HCT/Ps and appropriate regulation to minimize those risks. . . .

The publication of this final rule completes the set of regulations that implements FDA's proposed approach to regulating HCT/Ps. We recognize that over the course of this rulemaking, inadvertent errors or inconsistencies may have been introduced into the regulations. Accordingly, we anticipate that we may need to issue technical corrections in the future.

. . . .

FDA is issuing these new regulations under the authority of section 361 of the PHS Act. Under that section, by delegation from the Surgeon General and the Secretary of Health and Human Services, FDA may make and enforce regulations necessary to prevent the introduction, transmission, or spread of communicable diseases between the States or from foreign countries into the States. It is important to recognize that HCT/P manufacturing inevitably has interstate effects. HCT/Ps recovered in one State may be sent to another for processing, then shipped for use throughout the United States, or beyond. FDA has been involved in many recalls where HCT/Ps processed in a single establishment have been distributed in many States. In any event, intrastate transactions affecting interstate communicable disease transmission may also be regulated under section 361 of the PHS Act. (See Louisiana v. Mathews, 427 F. Supp. 174, 176 (E.D. La. 1977).)

Section 361 of the PHS Act authorizes FDA to issue regulations necessary to prevent the introduction, transmission, or spread of communicable diseases. Certain diseases, such as those caused by the human immunodeficiency virus (HIV) and the hepatitis B and C viruses (HBV and HCV respectively), may be transmitted through the implantation, transplantation, infusion, or transfer of HCT/Ps derived from infected donors. The agency required, in another rule, that most cell and tissue donors be screened and tested for these and other relevant communicable diseases (donor-eligibility final rule. However, donor screening and testing, although crucial, are not sufficient to prevent the transmission of disease by HCT/Ps. Rather, each step in the manufacturing process needs to be appropriately controlled. Errors in labeling, mixups of testing records, failure to adequately clean work areas, and faulty packaging are examples of improper practices that could produce a product capable of transmitting disease to its recipient. Similarly, as noted in the proposed approach document, improper handling of an HCT/P can lead to bacterial or other pathogenic contamination of the HCT/P, or to cross-contamination between HCT/Ps, which in turn can endanger recipients. The agency has determined that the procedural provisions of this rule are necessary to ensure that the important protections created by these regulations are actually effected and are not simply empty promises. Only manufacturing conducted in accordance with established procedures can assure that HCT/Ps meet the standards in these rules. When processes are made up as the manufacturer goes along, mistakes inevitably are made. Moreover, review of procedures can be critical to determining the cause of a disease transmission. Without that analysis, it would be impossible to prevent a future occurrence, with possibly fatal consequences.

The record requirements of this rule are similarly necessary. A single donor may be the source of a large number of HCT/Ps. It may be discovered, long after the donation and transplantations have been completed, that, due to an error in processing, the donor tissue was infected and capable of spreading communicable disease. Although it might be too late to prevent infections in the recipients, it would not be too late for the recipient to obtain treatment and take steps to avoid infecting others, such as close family members. Unless adequate records were maintained, and maintained for the period of time throughout which infections may be identified, it would be impossible to identify the recipients potentially infected by the donor's HCT/Ps. This would be a critical breakdown in the prevention of disease transmission.

Moreover, a single processing error, such as an improper practice that permitted bacterial contamination of all tissue processed at a location during a limited period of time, may also have wide ranging effects. Without reporting and study of adverse events involving the transmission of communicable disease, or involving the release of HCT/Ps presenting an increased risk of such transmission, common causes of seemingly isolated incidents would never come to light. Affected HCT/Ps would continue to place patients at risk of communicable disease. Accordingly, FDA has also determined that HCT/P tracking, maintenance and retention of records, and reporting of adverse reactions and HCT/P deviations are necessary to prevent the transmission of communicable disease through HCT/Ps.

The CGTP regulations govern the methods used in, and the facilities and controls used for, the manufacture of HCT/Ps. CGTP requirements are a fundamental component of FDA's risk-based approach to regulating HCT/Ps. HCT/Ps regulated solely under section 361 of the PHS Act and the regulations in part 1271 are not regulated under the [FFDCA] or section 351 of the PHS Act. By requiring that HCT/Ps meeting the criteria listed in § 1271.10 (361 HCT/Ps) be manufactured in compliance with CGTP, in combination with the other requirements in part 1271, the agency can ensure that 361 HCT/Ps are subject to sufficient regulatory controls to protect the public health.

HCT/Ps regulated as drugs, devices, and/or biological products, and not as [§] 361 HCT/Ps, must be manufactured in accordance with CGTP, in addition to existing requirements. The CGTP regulations supplement the current good manufacturing practice (CGMP) and quality system (QS) regulations applicable to drugs, devices, and biological products in parts 210, 211, and 820. Thus, in keeping with the plan outlined in the proposed approach document, those HCT/Ps regulated as drugs, devices, and/or biological products are subject to CGMP regulations as well as to CGTP regulations. . . .

This final rule is effective May 25, 2005. All HCT/Ps recovered on or after the effective date must be in compliance with applicable requirements in part 1271.

....

The retrospective application of part 1271 to human tissue, defined in § 1270.3(j), recovered before the effective date of the final rule would be overly burdensome and impractical. Therefore, we are not concurrently revoking part 1270 with the effective date of part 1271 as stated in the proposed rule. However, we intend to revoke part 1270 in the future when we are confident that there is no human tissue regulated under 1270 available for use.

Part 1270 applies now only to human tissue defined in § 1270.3(j) and recovered before May 25, 2005. We have amended § 1270.3(j) to implement this provision. Products that meet the definition of HCT/P in § 1271.3(d) that are recovered before May 25, 2005, and that have been regulated as drugs, devices, and/or biological products under section 351 of the PHS Act and/or the [FFDCA] will continue to be subject to the applicable requirements for drugs, devices, and/or biological products.

## D. Related Area Not Regulated Primarily by FDA— Organ Transplantation

While FDA has asserted regulatory authority over HCT/Ps, it has not sought to assert any similar authority over vascularized human organs for transplantation.[1] The excerpt immediately below, from a final rule published by HHS, provides a general overview of the Organ Procurement and Transplantation Network (OPTN). The OPTN is the public-private partnership that regulates organs for transplantation. As you read this, focus on the differences between FDA's approach to HCT/P regulation and the HHS/OPTN approach to regulation of human organs for transplantation.

### 1998-04-02 HHS Final Rule, Organ Procurement and Transplantation Network

63 Fed. Reg. 16,296

SUMMARY: This document sets forth the final rule governing the operation of the Organ Procurement and Transplantation Network (OPTN), which performs a variety of functions related to organ transplantation under contract with HHS. The document also offers a 60 day period for additional public comment. The rule will become effective 30 days following the close of the comment period. If the

1. *See* FDA, Tissue and Tissue Product Questions and Answers, https://www.fda.gov/vaccines-blood-biologics/tissue-tissue-products/tissue-and-tissue-product-questions-and-answers (last visited June 30, 2020) ("FDA does not regulate the transplantation of vascularized human organ transplants such as kidney, liver, heart, lung or pancreas. The Health Resources Services Administration (HRSA) oversees the transplantation of vascularized human organs.").

Department believes that additional time is required to review the comments, we will consider delaying the effective date. In combination with a new National Organ and Tissue Donation Initiative, this rule is intended to improve the effectiveness and equity of the Nation's transplantation system and to further the purposes of the National Organ Transplant Act of 1984, as amended. These purposes include: encouraging organ donation; developing an organ allocation system that functions as much as technologically feasible on a nationwide basis; providing the bases for effective Federal oversight of the OPTN (as well as for implementing related provisions in the Social Security Act); and, providing better information about transplantation to patients, families and health care providers.

. . . .

SUPPLEMENTARY INFORMATION: Over the past two decades, the safety and survival rates for transplantation of human organs have improved markedly, and the number of transplants has increased. In 1996, about 20,000 transplants were performed in the United States. At the same time, the rapid development of transplant techniques and the growth of the Nation's transplant system present new challenges:

1. The demand for organs for transplantation exceeds the supply, and this gap is growing. About 4,000 persons died in 1996 while awaiting transplantation.
2. The Nation's organ allocation system remains heavily weighted to the local use of organs instead of making organs available on a broader regional or national basis for patients with the greatest medical need consistent with sound medical judgment. Technological advances have made it possible to preserve organs longer and share them more widely, but the allocation system does not yet take full advantage of this capacity. Instead, some patients with less urgent medical need receive transplants before other patients with greater medical need whether listed locally or away from home.
3. The criteria used in listing those who need transplantation vary from one transplant center to another, as do the criteria used to determine the medical status of a patient. This lack of uniform, medically objective criteria make it difficult to compare the medical need of patients in different centers.
4. As a result of both the local preference in allocation and the lack of standard medical criteria, waiting times for organs are much longer in some geographic areas than in others. The statute envisions a national allocation system, based on medial criteria, which results in the equitable treatment of transplant patients. But equitable treatment cannot be assured if medical criteria vary from one transplant center to another and if allocation policies prevent suitable organs from being offered first to those with the greatest medical need.
5. Useful, current, transplant-center specific data for patients and health care providers are not available, despite information technology advances that make more current reporting feasible.

Efforts are needed to address these challenges in the areas of both donation and allocation:

In order to bring about substantial increases in the number of organ donors and the number of transplants performed each year, a new National Organ and Tissue Donation Initiative has been launched. Working in partnership with national and local organizations, the Department of Health and Human Services (HHS) seeks to increase donation through encouraging more individuals to cho[o]se to be organ donors and that share that decision with their families; through improved performance by hospitals and organ procurement organizations toward ensuring that the families of potential donors are given the opportunity to allow donation; through higher consent rates by families, especially by encouraging those who elect to be organ donors to inform their families of their decision; and through new research on enhancing donation. Proposed regulations affecting hospitals and organ procurement organizations were published December 19, 1997. The Department expects that the supply of organs may be raised by about 20 percent through this initiative, which would greatly alleviate organ shortages.

In order to improve allocation of organs for transplantation, this final rule establishes performance goals to be achieved by the OPTN. Actions already underway in the OPTN are consistent with several of these goals. The rule does not establish specific allocation policies, but instead looks to the organ transplant community to take action to meet the performance goals. The goals include:

- Minimum Listing Criteria—The OPTN is required to define objective and measurable medical criteria to be used by all transplant centers in determining whether a patient is appropriate to be listed for a transplant. In this way, patients with essentially the same medical need will be listed in the same way at all transplant centers.

- Status Categories—The OPTN is required to determine objective medical criteria to be used nationwide in determining the medical status of those awaiting transplantation. This will provide a common measurement for use by all transplant centers in determining the urgency of an individual's medical condition, and it will facilitate OPTN efforts to direct organs to those with greatest medical need, in accordance with sound medical judgment.

- Equitable Allocation—The OPTN is required to develop equitable allocation policies that provide organs to those with the greatest medical urgency, in accordance with sound medical judgment. This increases the likelihood of patients obtaining matching organs, and gives all patients equal chances to obtain organs compared to other patients of equal medical status, wherever they live or list.

By requiring common criteria for listing eligibility and medical status, and by requiring that organs be directed so as to equalize waiting times, especially for those with greatest medical need, this rule is designed to provide patients awaiting transplants with equal access to organs and to provide organs to sickest patients first, consistent with sound medical judgment. While present OPTN policies give weight to medical need, the "local first" practice thwarts organ allocation over a broad area and thus prevents medical need from being the dominant factor in allocation decisions.

Under the provisions of this rule, it is intended that the area where a person lives or the transplant center where he or she is listed will not be primary factors in how quickly he or she receives a transplant. Instead, organs will be allocated according to objective standards of medical status and need. In this way, suitable organs will reach patients with the greatest medical need, both when they are procured locally and when they are procured outside the listed patients' areas. This objective reflects the views of many commenters on the proposed regulations, as well as the finding of the American Medical Association in its Code of Medical Ethics: "Organs should be considered a national, rather than a local or regional resource. Geographical priorities in the allocation of organs should be prohibited except when transportation of organs would threaten their suitability for transplantation."

The OPTN is required to develop proposals for the new allocation policies (except for livers) within a year of the effective date of the final rule. In the case of liver allocation policies, where policy development work has been underway for several years, the OPTN is required to develop a new proposed allocation policy within 60 days of the effective date.

Other provisions of this rule include requirements that the OPTN make more current data available for the public, including measures of performance of individually identified transplant centers. This information is needed by patients, families, physicians, and payers in choosing a course of action and is needed as a quality measurement instrument.

In addition, the rule defines the governing structure of the OPTN and outlines procedures for the establishment of policies by the OPTN that include appropriate participation by transplant professionals and families, with oversight by HHS. The rule also includes a requirement that the OPTN develop a "grandfathering" proposal for patients currently awaiting liver transplantation so that these patients are treated no less favorably under the new allocation policies than they would have been under current allocation policies. The OPTN also is required to develop proposed transition policies for the initial changes required by this rule to its allocation policies for other organs.

The National Organ and Tissue Donation Initiative and this final rule build on more than a decade of experience, including improving medical technology, to create a national community of organ sharing and to save and improve more lives through transplantation. The rule defines Federal expectations, based on the role given to the Secretary under the statute, but looks to the OPTN to propose policy choices that meet those expectations.

....

## I. Background

### A. Overview

The National Organ Transplant Act of 1984 (NOTA) created the Organ Procurement and Transplantation Network (OPTN). The Act has been the subject of two major sets of amendments. In each instance, the Congress acted to encourage the development of a fair, national system of organ allocation....

Thus, the Congress envisioned an equitable national system that would be operated by the transplant community—including physicians and officials of transplant facilities as well as other specialists and individuals representing transplant patients, their families, and the general public—with oversight by HHS.

....

### B. Legislative and Regulatory History

The OPTN was established under section 372 of the PHS Act, as enacted by the National Organ Transplant Act of 1984 (Pub. L. 98-507), and amended by Pub. L. 100-607 and Pub. L. 101-616. Section 372 requires the Secretary to provide by contract for the establishment and operation of the OPTN to manage the organ allocation system, to increase the supply of donated organs, and to perform related and other activities.

....

### C. DHHS and OPTN Relationships

The public comments indicate that many persons misunderstand the role of the OPTN. The OPTN is sometimes characterized as a voluntary system through which consensus decisions are reached as to how to allocate organs among patients (who may live or die based on these decisions). The underlying statutes, absent Secretarial oversight, give the OPTN authority from which individual patients, physicians, and hospitals have little recourse. If the OPTN changes organ allocation criteria, it may advantage some patients and disadvantage others because there are not enough organs donated to meet the need and no alternative organ allocation entity exists. The unique role of the OPTN thus gives rise to a fundamental question. To what process or remedy can patients, their families, physicians, or members of the general public turn if they wish to question policies, decisions, procedures, or practices of the OPTN? By providing a framework for OPTN policy development and describing the role of the Secretary therein, this rule addresses that question.

The United Network for Organ Sharing (UNOS), a private corporation, operates the OPTN under contract with the Department. The contract is subject to the competitive bidding process. Under recent Requests for Proposals, there have been no effective competitors to the current contractor. The current contract expires September 30, 1999.

As a private organization, UNOS has by-laws, operating procedures, and membership requirements. They apply only to UNOS members and not to OPTN members. Membership in UNOS is not a requirement for membership in the OPTN. Therefore, such procedures are not OPTN procedures, and because they do not bind OPTN members, they are not the subject of this regulation. Because OPTN members are not required to become UNOS members, UNOS procedures are subject to these regulations only if they conflict with OPTN requirements, or if they conflict with the terms of the contract for the operation of the OPTN, or these regulations. For example, UNOS may impose conditions for membership in UNOS, but those conditions may not be substituted for, or used to augment, the regulatory requirements for the UNOS-administered OPTN. In contrast, matters relating to the OPTN are encompassed by these regulations; and UNOS, as the OPTN contractor, is required to comply with these regulations and to issue policies consistent with the requirements of these regulations.

The Department believes that the transplantation network must be operated by professionals in the transplant community, and that both allocation and other policies of the OPTN should be developed by transplant professionals, in an open environment that includes the public, particularly transplant patients and donor families. It is not the desire or intention of the Department to interfere in the practice of medicine. This rule does not alter the role of the OPTN to use its judgment regarding appropriate medical criteria for organ allocation nor is it intended to circumscribe the discretion afforded to doctors who must make the difficult judgments that affect individual patients. At the same time, the Department has an important and constructive role to play, particularly on behalf of patients. Human organs that are given to save lives are a public resource and a public trust.

The process adopted in this rule strikes a balance among these important principles. When the OPTN develops policies, or when complaints are raised concerning OPTN policies, the regulation allows a number of options. The Secretary may approve an OPTN-proposed policy or find that the complaint has no merit. The Secretary also may take another approach depending on the issues presented. For example, the Secretary: may seek broader public input on the issue; may determine whether violations of OPTN-proposed policies should carry any one of a range of consequences—no consequence, loss of membership in the OPTN, or loss of a hospital's ability to participate in Medicare and Medicaid; may provide comments for the OPTN's consideration; may direct the OPTN to adopt a policy; or, may develop a policy that the OPTN must follow. An example of this last option is this regulation's provisions prescribing who the OPTN must admit as members. Instead of an exhaustive listing of these and other options, the regulation, at sections 121.4 (b)(2) and (d) simply provides that the Secretary may "take such other action as the Secretary determines appropriate."

. . . .

## E. Key Points

- Neither the FFDCA nor the PHSA directly addresses regulatory authority over HCT/Ps. However, FDA regulates HCT/Ps under the "communicable diseases" provision of the PHSA.
- FDA created the category "human tissue" when it promulgated 21 C.F.R. Part 1270, and "human cells, tissues, and tissue-related products" when it promulgated 21 C.F.R. Part 1271.
  - Part 1270 applies to human tissue recovered before May 25, 2005.
  - Part 1271 applies to HCT/Ps recovered on or after May 25, 2005.
- FDA has not sought to assert regulatory authority over vascularized human organs for transplantation. These are regulated instead by HHS through a public-private partnership known as the Organ Procurement and Transplantation Network.

Part Six

# FFDCA Chapter VI, VII, and IX Products—Cosmetics, Color Additives, and Tobacco Products

Chapter 16

# Cosmetics

## A. Introduction

Please read (or review) the following excerpts in the statutory supplement:

- FFDCA § 201. Definitions; generally. *Subsection (i) only.*
- FFDCA § 601. Adulterated cosmetics.
- FFDCA § 602. Misbranded cosmetics.
- FFDCA § 603. Regulations making exemptions.
- 15 U.S.C. § 1452. Unfair and deceptive packaging and labeling; scope of prohibition. *Subsection (i) only.*
- 15 U.S.C. § 1454. Rules and regulations. *Subsection (a) only.*
- 15 U.S.C. § 1456. Enforcement. *Subsection (a) only.*
- 15 U.S.C. § 1459. Definitions. *Subsection (a) only.*
- 21 C.F.R. Part 700. General.
- 21 C.F.R. Part 710. Voluntary registration of cosmetic product establishments.
- 21 C.F.R. Part 720. Voluntary filing of cosmetic product ingredient composition statements.
- 21 C.F.R. Part 740. Cosmetic product warning statements.

FFDCA § 201(i) is the statutory definition of "cosmetic." FFDCA §§ 601–603 comprise the entire chapter of the statute dealing specifically with cosmetics. The first item is the adulteration provision, the second is the misbranding provision, and the third is a more technical provision relating to standard industry repackaging practices.

The provisions from Title 15 of the U.S. Code come from the Fair Packaging and Labeling Act (FPLA), 15 U.S.C. §§ 1451 et seq. The Fair Packaging and Labeling Act provides statutory authority to regulate labeling for many FDA-regulated product categories. It is particularly important for cosmetics, however, because it provides an important supplement to the relatively limited authority provided in FFDCA Chapter VI (compared to the authority provided by the FFDCA for many other product categories).

# B. Outline of Regulatory Regime

As in other chapters of this book, this chapter begins with a set of charts. As you read this chapter for the first time, you should do no more than skim these charts to get a general sense of the structure of the applicable statutes and regulations. (For more information on the role of the charts in this casebook, see Chapter 1, Parts A.1 and B).

| Timeline of Key Statutes: Cosmetics | | | |
|---|---|---|---|
| Year | PL | Stat | Name of Statute |
| 1938 | 75-717 | 52 Stat. 1040 | FFDCA of 1938 |
| 1960 | 86-618 | 74 Stat. 397 | Color Additives Amendment of 1960 |
| 1966 | 89-755 | 80 Stat. 1296 | Fair Packaging and Labeling Act |

| Key Statutory Provisions: Cosmetics | | |
|---|---|---|
| Statute Name or U.S.C. Title | § | Title of Section or Subsection |
| FFDCA | 201(i) | [Definition of "cosmetic"] |
| FFDCA | 601 | Adulterated cosmetics |
| FFDCA | 602 | Misbranded cosmetics |
| FFDCA | 603 | Regulations making exemptions |

| Key Regulatory Provisions: Cosmetics | | |
|---|---|---|
| 21 C.F.R. Part | Subpart | Title of Part or Subpart |
| 700 | — | General |
| 701 | — | Cosmetic labeling |
| 710 | — | Voluntary registration of cosmetic product establishments |
| 720 | — | Voluntary filing of cosmetic product ingredient composition statements |
| 740 | — | Cosmetic product warning statements |

## C. The Distinction between Drugs and Cosmetics

### United States v. An Article . . . Sudden Change

409 F.2d 734 (2d Cir. 1969)

ANDERSON, Circuit Judge:

This is an appeal in a seizure action from an order of the United States District Court for the Eastern District of New York entered on July 30, 1968, denying the Government's motion for summary judgment and granting summary judgment for the claimant. The seizure concerned 216 bottles of a cosmetic product called "Sudden Change" which is a clear liquid lotion consisting primarily of two ingredients: bovine albumen (15%) and distilled water (over 84%). It is meant to be applied externally to the surface of the facial skin, and it is claimed, *inter alia*, in its labeling and advertising that it will provide a "Face Lift Without Surgery." The court below described the effects of the product as follows:

> Allowed to dry on the skin, it leaves a film which (1) masks imperfections, making the skin look smoother and (2) acts mechanically to smooth and firm the skin by tightening the surface. Both effects are temporary. There is apparently no absorption by, or changes in, skin tissue resulting from its applications; it washes off.

The central issue presented in this appeal is whether Sudden Change is, within the meaning of the [FFDCA § 201](g)(1) a "drug." That Section, in pertinent part, provides: "The term 'drug' means . . . (C) articles (other than food) intended to affect the structure . . . of the body of man. . . ." The question posed is whether, by reason of its labeling and promotional claims, Sudden Change is to be deemed a drug for purposes of the [FFDCA].

The civil in rem action was instituted by the United States in the United States District Court for the Southern District of Florida, pursuant to the [FFDCA]. The Libel of Information was filed by the Government on May 8, 1964, seeking seizure and condemnation of 216 bottles in individual cartons, allegedly misbranded, labeled in part 'Sudden Change by Lanolin Plus.' The Libel alleges that the article seized is a 'drug' within the meaning of [FFDCA § 201](g)(3) (subsequently redesignated as [FFDCA § 201](g)(1)(C)) and a 'new drug' within the meaning of [FFDCA § 201](p), which had been shipped in interstate commerce without an approved New Drug Application filed pursuant to [FFDCA § 505](b), effective with respect to such drug, in violation of [FFDCA § 505](a). The Libel further alleges that the article was misbranded when introduced into and while in interstate commerce within the meaning of [FFDCA § 502](a), in that the labeling for the article contains false and misleading statements with respect to the effectiveness of the drug for eliminating facial wrinkles and giving a face lift without surgery; and within the meaning of [FFDCA § 502](e)(1)(A)(ii), in that the article is fabricated from two or more ingredients and that the label fails to bear the established name of each active ingredient.

Pursuant to monition issued by the District Court, the United States Marshal for the Southern District of Florida seized the article and labeling material accompanying it. Following the seizure, Hazel Bishop, Inc., now known as Bishop Industries, Inc., intervened, filed a claim to the article and answered the L[i]bel. Claimant's answer admits that the article and its accompanying label were shipped in interstate commerce; that the article was seized within the jurisdiction of the United States District Court for the Southern District of Florida; and that the article has a "temporary cosmetic effect on wrinkles." All other allegations . . . are denied. On September 2, 1964, the action was removed* on claimant's motion to the United States District Court for the Eastern District of New York.

Following discovery proceedings, the Government moved for summary judgment contending, inter alia, that the claims appearing in the article's labeling constituted it a drug under the law and that the product was misbranded as a matter of law since its label failed to bear the established name of each of its active ingredients. To support its motion, the Government relied on claimant's admissions in answers to interrogatories, the deposition of claimant's medical expert, and the affidavits of government experts.

Claimant interposed affidavits in opposition to the Government's motion and in support of its cross-motion for summary judgment, in which it contends that the article is solely a cosmetic which functions simply as a mask for facial lines and wrinkles and that the product's labeling claims were not understood otherwise by cosmetic consumers. It argues that the Government's construction of [FFDCA § 201](g)(1)(C) is so broad that every 'cosmetic' would automatically be a 'drug,' since by definition a cosmetic must have some 'effect' on the human body, even though that effect is only a change of appearance. . . .

The box in which Sudden Change is sold bears the capitalized words " SUDDEN CHANGE" . . . "THE PERFECTED ANTI-WRINKLE FACE LIFT." Another side of the box bears the following description:

> SUDDEN CHANGE by Lanolin Plus is the new and improved, dramatically different wrinkle-smoothing cosmetic. By simple, dynamic contraction, it lifts, firms, tones slack skin . . . smooths out wrinkles, lifts the puffs under eyes, leaving your contours looking beautifully defined. It acts noticeably, visibly . . . and so quickly you will see and feel results minutes after you apply it. Not a hormone or chemical astringent, SUDDEN CHANGE is a concentrated purified natural protein, a clear invisible liquid cosmetic that can be used as often as you like.
>
> Because there never has been a cosmetic exactly like SUDDEN CHANGE before, we suggest you read the directions carefully before applying. For

* *[The court uses the term "removed" here to refer to a procedure relating to consolidation of* in rem *seizure proceedings pursuant to FFDCA § 304. It is* not *a reference to the type of removal from state to federal court—pursuant to 21 U.S.C. § 1441—covered in a standard civil procedure course.]*

> best results, use SUDDEN CHANGE often. The more you use, the longer your wrinkle-free look will last.

The face of the leaflet insert bears the following words, capitalized and displayed prominently: "FACE LIFT WITHOUT SURGERY"—"The Perfected Anti-Wrinkle Face Lift Acts in Minutes Lasts for Hours." It also repeats the descriptive material that appears on the box and contains directions for use.

....

As stated *supra*, the applicable section of the Federal Food, Drug and Cosmetic Act, [FFDCA § 201](g)(1)(C), defines "drug" for purposes of the [FFDCA] in pertinent part as follows:

> "(g)(1) The term 'drug' means ... (C) articles (other than food) intended to affect the structure ... of the body of man. ..."

It is clear that the fact that an article is a cosmetic does not preclude its being a drug for purposes of the [FFDCA].

It is well settled that the intended use of a product may be determined from its label, accompanying labeling, promotional material, advertising and any other relevant source. Thus, Congress has made a judgment that a product is subject to regulation as a drug if certain promotional claims are made for it.

The mere statement of this rule poses a crucial issue: by what standards are these claims to be evaluated? Or to put it another way, what degree of sophistication or vulnerability is to be ascribed to the hypothetical potential consumer in order to understand how these claims are understood by the buying public? The District Court answered this question as follows:

> Such seller's claims [as that of "face lift without surgery"] must be considered in the special context of late twentieth century American mores. The labeling of Sudden Change is directed to women who are potential consumers of the article. Subjected to the incessant advertising campaigns of the cosmetic industry, a potential buyer can be expected to have achieved some immunity to the beautifiers' hyperbole.

And further:

> Against this background of constant exposure to puffing and extravagant claims, we cannot believe that a prospective purchaser of Sudden Change—faced with instructions advising her that she can repeat the process in a few hours—expects anything other than a possibility that she may look better. She would view the promise of 'face lift' with the same skepticism—or lack of it—as she would view other promises offering her beauty, loveliness, rejuvenation or a young look. She would not expect a structural change of the kind available through plastic surgery.

Although this analysis properly focuses on the relevant question by inquiring into the subjective understanding of potential consumers, it appears to us to hypothesize an unduly high level of sophistication and skepticism. A primary purpose of the [FFDCA] is the protection of the ultimate consumer's economic interests. See *Federal Security Administrator v. Quaker Oats Co.*, 318 U.S. 218, 230 (1943). Considering the remedial purposes of the [FFDCA] and particularly of the 1938 amendments, the Supreme Court declared:

> The purposes of this legislation thus touch phases of the lives and health of people which, in the circumstances of modern industrialism, are largely beyond self-protection. Regard for these purposes should infuse construction of the legislation if it is to be treated as a working instrument of government and not merely as a collection of English words.

Accepting this admonition, we conclude that the purposes of the [FFDCA] will best be effected by postulating a consuming public which includes "the ignorant, the unthinking and the credulous. . . ."

While it is not altogether clear what standard the court below applied, the reasoning appears to assume something like a "reasonable woman" standard. Thus, the District Court assumes that the "constant exposure to puffing and extravagant claims" has induced "some immunity to the beautifiers' hyperbole" which is such that the court "cannot believe" that the potential consumer of Sudden Change "expects anything other than a possibility that she may look better." We agree that certain claims which arguably would bring the product within [FFDCA § 201](g)(1)(C) have so drenched the potential consumer that even the "ignorant, the unthinking and the credulous" must be presumed able to discount their promises as typical of cosmetic advertising puffery. We cannot agree, however, with the conclusion that such immunity or skepticism somehow transfers to the promise to "lift out puffs" or give a "face lift without surgery." The references to "face lift" and "surgery" carry distinctly physiological connotations, suggesting, at least to the vulnerable consumer, that the product will "affect the structure . . . of the body . . ." in some way other than merely temporarily altering the appearance. We do not accept the concept that skepticism toward familiar claims necessarily entails skepticism toward unfamiliar claims; the theory of the legislation is that someone might take the claim literally.

In other words, with the exception of those claims which have become so associated with the familiar exaggerations of cosmetics advertising that virtually everyone can be presumed to be capable of discounting them as puffery, the question of whether a product is "intended to affect the structure . . . of the body of man . . ." is to be answered by considering, first, how the claim might be understood by the "ignorant, unthinking or credulous" consumer, and second, whether the claim as so understood may fairly be said to constitute a representation that the product will affect the structure of the body in some medical—or drug-type fashion, i.e., in some way other than merely "altering the appearance."

We agree that the legislative history and the language of the [FFDCA] require rejection of any rule which would convert all cosmetics into drugs. We believe, however, that the test which we have applied draws the necessary line while at the same time protecting the public. For example, promises that a product will "soften" or "moisturize" a woman's skin are so thoroughly familiar that constant exposure can be presumed to have induced sufficient immunity even in our hypothetical vulnerable consumer (this assumes, *arguendo*, that these promises have exactly the same degree of drug-type connotations as the "face lift without surgery" claim—an assumption which we reject).

We hold, therefore, that so long as Sudden Change is claimed to give a "face lift without surgery" and to "lift out puffs" it is to be deemed a drug within the meaning of [FFDCA §](g)(1)(C). It should be understood, however, that if the claimant ceases to employ these promotional claims and avoids any others which may fairly be interpreted as claiming to affect the structure of the skin in some physiological, though temporary, way, then, assuming *arguendo* that no actual physical effect exists, the product will not be deemed a drug for purposes of the [FFDCA]. While there may be merit in the cause of those who seek to require pretesting of new cosmetics, it is not for the courts to legislate such a requirement; rather it must rest in the hands of Congress to decide whether such an amendment to the statute should be enacted or not.

Reversed and remanded for proceedings not inconsistent with this opinion.

---

The excerpt immediately below is a warning letter from FDA to a cosmetics company. FDA warning letters are discussed more generally in Chapter 19. As you read the excerpt, pay attention to the various different violations of the FFDCA alleged in this letter. Note, in particular, the number of allegations in the letter that the products being sold were in fact drugs rather than cosmetics.

## 2011-04-15 FDA Warning Letter to Lifetech Resources

### WARNING LETTER

. . . .

This letter is in reference to your firm's involvement in the manufacturing, distribution, and promotion of RapidLash Eyelash Renewal Serum ("RapidLash"), NeuLash Active Eyelash Technology ("NeuLash"), and NeuveauBrow Active Eyebrow Technology ("NeuveauBrow"). As presently formulated, labeled and promoted, these products violate provisions of the [FFDCA]. As described below, "RapidLash", "NeuLash", and "NeuveauBrow" are unapproved new drugs in violation of sections 505(a) and 301(d) of the [FFDCA] and misbranded drugs in violation of section 502 of the [FFDCA]. Furthermore, because "RapidLash", "NeuLash", and "NeuveauBrow" are intended to be applied to the human body for cleansing, beautifying, promoting attractiveness, or altering the appearance, they also are cosmetics within the meaning of section 201(i) of the [FFDCA] and misbranded under section 602(a) of the [FFDCA]. In addition, "RapidLash" and "NeuLash" are adulterated cosmetics under section 601(a) of the [FFDCA].

**Unapproved New Drug and Misbranded Drug**

"RapidLash", "NeuLash", and "NeuveauBrow" are promoted for growth of eyelashes and eyebrows in labeling on various websites including http://www.RapidLash.com, http://www.NeuLash.com, and http://www.NeaveauBrow.com and in promotional literature about the products. Examples of these claims include, but are not limited to, the following:

RapidLash

- (website) "After 84 days of daily use, RapidLash induced a significant increase in the length of eyelashes"
- (website video) "This formula is designed to lengthen and thicken lashes in 30 days. Your lashes and your eyebrows grow thicker and faster."
- (website video) "RapidLash, which is this eyeliner type stuff that you paint on your eyes, and your lashes grow . . ."
- (website video) "There are brands like RapidLash that really grow your lashes."
- (website) "When I reached about age 50, my eyelashes had seemed to shrink to nothing and wearing mascara was senseless. Then along came Rapid Lash! I began to notice a change with my eyelashes in less th[a]n 4 weeks of using it. In 6 weeks, my eyelashes were back to the original length of my younger days."
- (website audio) ". . . I have been using RapidLash for probably going on three months now, and let me tell you this stuff is awesome. . . . My eyelashes have grown. . . ."
- (promotional pamphlet) "I went to the salon and they asked me if I wanted my eyebrows trimmed. I never had any eyebrows before RapidLash"

NeuLash

- (website) "I lost my eyelashes during chemotherapy and had none for three years. When I heard about products to help lengthen and thicken lashes, I was skeptical but chose to try neuLash because of its great customer reviews. . . . After eight weeks, my lashes were curlier, darker, longer, and thicker than ever before."
- (magazine image from website) "NeuLash®, an active eyelash technology strengthens and lengthens eyelashes in as little as two weeks."
- (website) "Helps promote cell regeneration"

NeuveauBrow

- (promotional pamphlet) "Helps accelerate the length of the hair shaft, while promoting fuller, thicker, and healthier looking brows."
- (promotional pamphlet) "neuveauBrow [sic] features our exclusive (b)(4) which effectively renews and regenerates skin cells. . . ."

- (website) "It took about 6 weeks for me too see anything, but, lo and behold, I looked in the mirror one morning and saw MANY new hairs filling in my brows. I could not believe it."
- (website) "It's easy to apply and you do get growth where you put it."

Based on the labeling and promotional materials described above, "RapidLash", "NeuLash", and "NeuveauBrow" are drugs as defined by sections 201(g)(1)(C) of the [FFDCA] because they are articles intended to affect the structure or function of the body by inducing eyelash and eyebrow growth.

"RapidLash", "NeuLash", and "NeuveauBrow" as currently formulated, contain the active ingredient isopropyl cloprostenate. Isopropyl cloprostenate is a synthetic prostaglandin analog in the same class of compounds as the active ingredients in FDA-approved drugs indicated to lower intraocular pressure in glaucoma patients (e.g., (b)(6) (bimatoprost ophthalmic solution), (b)(6) (travoprost ophthalmic solution) and to treat hypotrichosis of the eyelashes (e.g., (b)(6) (bimatoprost ophthalmic solution)). Prostaglandin analogs are well known to have an effect on the structure or function of the body. The presence of the prostaglandin analog, isopropyl cloprostenate, along with appearance claims such as "enhance the appearance of your lashes and brows," "fuller healthier-looking lashes," and "fuller healthier-looking brows" indicate that your products are intended to affect the structure or function of the body. Accordingly, "RapidLash", "NeuLash", and "NeuveauBrow" are drugs as defined by section 201(g)(1)(C) of the [FFDCA].

Moreover, "RapidLash", "NeuLash", and "NeuveauBrow" are new drugs, as defined by section 201(p) of the [FFDCA], because they are not generally recognized as safe and effective under the conditions prescribed, recommended, or suggested in its labeling. Under sections 301(d) and 505(a) of the [FFDCA], a new drug may not be introduced or delivered for introduction into interstate commerce unless an FDA-approved application is in effect for the drug. Based on our information, you do not have an FDA-approved application on file for these drug products.

"RapidLash" and "NeuLash" are prescription drugs as defined in section 503(b)(1)(A) of the [FFDCA], because, in light of their toxicity or other potentiality for harmful effect, the method of their use, or the collateral measures necessary to their use, they are not safe for use except under the supervision of a practitioner licensed by law to administer them. Specifically, isopropyl cloprostenate, the active ingredient in "RapidLash", and "NeuLash" may lower intraocular pressure. Patients using these products concurrently with intraocular pressure lowering medication should be closely monitored for changes to their intraocular pressure. Other potential adverse events associated with prostaglandin analogs for ophthalmic use include ocular irritation, hyperemia, iris color change, macular edema, ocular inflammation, and interference with glaucoma therapy. In addition, prostaglandin analogs for ophthalmic use are currently classified as Pregnancy Class C.

According to section 502(f)(1) of the [FFDCA], a drug is misbranded if, among other things, it fails to bear adequate directions for its intended uses. "Adequate directions for use" means directions under which a layman can use a drug safely and for the purposes for which it is intended (21 C.F.R. § 201.5). Prescription drugs can only be used safely at the direction, and under the supervision of, a licensed practitioner. Therefore, for prescription drugs, it is not possible to write adequate directions for use by a layperson. FDA-approved prescription drugs that bear their FDA-approved labeling are exempt from the requirement that they bear adequate directions for use by a layperson. Because there is no FDA-approved application for "RapidLash" and "NeuLash", their labeling fails to bear adequate directions for the intended uses, causing them to be misbranded under section 502(f)(1) of the [FFDCA].

Additionally, under section 502(a) of the [FFDCA], a drug is misbranded if its labeling is false or misleading in any particular. Section 201(n) of the [FFDCA] provides that, in determining whether an article's labeling or advertising "is misleading, there shall be taken into account (among other things) not only representations made or suggested . . . but also the extent to which the labeling or advertising fails to reveal facts material in light of such representations or material with respect to consequences which may result from the use of the article to which the labeling or advertising relates under the conditions of use prescribed in the labeling or under such conditions of use as are customary or usual."

"RapidLash", "NeuLash", and "NeuveauBrow" are misbranded under section 502(a) because their labeling makes misleading statements regarding the product's safety and also fails to reveal material facts with respect to consequences that may result from the use of the product. Specifically, your product literature for "RapidLash" states, "Passed the Safety Status in the US and EU," your product literature for "NeuLash" states, "Safety Status in the US and EU—Passed," and your product literature for "NeaveauBrow" states "Safety Status in the US—Passed." However, as stated above, your products have not been approved by FDA based on safety and efficacy. In fact, FDA has determined that drug products in the same class as the active ingredient in "RapidLash", "NeuLash", and "NeuveauBrow" cannot be used safely without the direction, or under the supervision of, a licensed medical practitioner. Despite making a claim regarding safety, your products fail to include warnings about the possible adverse [e]ffects associated with the active ingredients used in your products. Thus, you have failed to reveal consequences that may result from the use of these products as described in the labeling, in violation of section 201(n) of the [FFDCA].

The introduction or delivery for introduction into interstate commerce of a misbranded product violates section 301(a) of the [FFDCA].

### Adulterated and Misbranded Cosmetic

Even if "RapidLash", "NeuLash", and "NeuveauBrow" were cosmetics within the meaning of section 201(i) of the [FFDCA], they could not be lawfully marketed because they would be misbranded under section 602(a) of the [FFDCA] and, in the case of "NeuLash" and "NeuveauBrow" adulterated under section 601(a) of the [FFDCA].

Under section 602(a) of the [FFDCA], a cosmetic is misbranded if its labeling is false or misleading in any particular. "RapidLash", "NeuLash", and "Neuveau-Brow" are misbranded cosmetics under section 602(a) because, as discussed above, their labeling is misleading in that it fails to reveal facts material with respect to consequences that may result from the use of the products under the conditions of use prescribed in the labeling.

In addition, under section 601(a) of the [FFDCA], a cosmetic is adulterated if it bears or contains any poisonous or deleterious substance which may render it injurious to users under the conditions of use prescribed in the labeling thereof, or, under such conditions of use as are customary or usual. "RapidLash" and "Neu-Lash" are adulterated cosmetics under section 601(a) because they bear or contain a deleterious substance that may render them injurious to users under the conditions of use prescribed in their labeling. Specifically, "RapidLash" and "NeuLash" contain isopropyl cloprostenate which, under the conditions of use prescribed in the labeling, may cause the following injuries: ocular irritation, hyperemia, iris color change, macular edema, ocular inflammation, and interference with intraocular pressure reduction therapy. In addition, as mentioned above, prostaglandin analogs for ophthalmic use are currently classified as Pregnancy Class C; women of child-bearing age are considered at risk for injury.

It is a violation of section 301(a) of the [FFDCA] to introduce or deliver for introduction into interstate commerce any cosmetic that is adulterated or misbranded.

* * *

The issues and violations cited in this letter are not intended to be an all-inclusive statement of violations that exist in connection with your product. You are responsible for investigating and determining the causes of the violations identified above and for preventing their recurrence or the occurrence of other violations. Furthermore, please advise what actions you will take to address product that you have already distributed. It is your responsibility to assure that your firm complies with all requirements of federal law and FDA regulations.

You should take prompt action to correct the violations cited in this letter. Failure to promptly correct these violations may result in legal action without further notice, including, without limitation, seizure and injunction. Other federal agencies may take this Warning Letter into account when considering the award of contracts.

Within fifteen working days of receipt of this letter, please notify this office in writing of the specific steps that you have taken to correct violations. Include an explanation of each step being taken to prevent the recurrence of violations, as well as copies of related documentation. If you cannot complete corrective action within fifteen working days, state the reason for the delay and the time within which you will complete the correction.

. . . .

## D. Key Points

- The Pure Food & Drugs Act of 1906 did not cover cosmetics. Congress granted FDA jurisdiction over cosmetics with the FFDCA of 1938.
- The "drug" definition of FFDCA § 201(g)(1) and the "new drug" definition of FFDCA § 201(p) play an important role in policing the boundaries of the "cosmetics" product category.
  - A product positioned in the market as "cosmetic" can become an unapproved "drug" simply by making claims suggesting that it is intended, within the meaning of FFDCA § 201(g)(1), "to affect the structure or any function of the body."
  - A product that is intended "for cleansing, beautifying, promoting attractiveness, or altering the appearance" of the "human body or any part therof" can remain a cosmetic, as these intended uses are all permitted under the "cosmetic" definition of FFDCA § 201(i).
    - However, showing that a product is sold as something "intended to affect the structure . . . of the body" under FFDCA § 201(g)(1), rather than simply intended to "alter the appearance" of the body, under FFDCA § 201(i), can transform a cosmetic into a drug.
- No marketing authorization is required for cosmetics. FDA instead regulates cosmetics primarily through enforcement actions for adulteration and misbranding.
- FDA collects some information about the cosmetics industry through voluntary programs for the submission of establishment registration and ingredient lists.

## Chapter 17

# Color Additives

## A. Introduction

Please read (or review) the following excerpts in the statutory supplement:

- FFDCA § 201. Definitions; generally. *Subsection (t) only.*
- FFDCA § 721. Color additives.
- 21 C.F.R. Part 70. Color additives.
- 21 C.F.R. Part 71. Color additive petitions.

FFDCA § 201(t) sets out the statutory definition of "Color Additive." FFDCA § 721 is the single FFDCA provision specific to color additives. 21 C.F.R. Part 70 is the general regulatory provision on color additives. 21 C.F.R. Part 71 sets out the process for requesting that FDA authorize marketing of ("list") a color additive.

Color additives can be listed as either subject to, or exempt from, certification. Listed color additives exempt from certification are set out in 21 C.F.R. Part 73. Listed color additives subject to certification are set out in 21 C.F.R. Part 74. A limited number of color additives are instead provisionally listed in 21 C.F.R. Part 81. As Parts 73, 74, and 81 read primarily as lists, they are not included in the statutory supplement. However, you should look to them when you need to find what color additives have been granted marketing authorization by FDA.

## B. Outline of Regulatory Regime

As in other chapters of this book, this chapter begins with a set of charts. As you read this chapter for the first time, you should do no more than skim these charts to get a general sense of the structure of the applicable statutes and regulations. (For more information on the role of the charts in this casebook, see Chapter 1, Parts A.1 and B).

| Timeline of Key Statutes: Color Additives | | | |
|---|---|---|---|
| Year | PL | Stat | Name of Statute |
| 1906 | 59-384 | 34 Stat. 768 | Pure Food and Drugs Act |
| 1938 | 75-717 | 52 Stat. 1040 | FFDCA of 1938 |
| 1960 | 86-618 | 74 Stat. 397 | Color Additives Amendment of 1960 |

| Key Statutory Provisions: Color Additives | | |
|---|---|---|
| **Statute Name or U.S.C. Title** | **§** | **Title of Section or Subsection** |
| FFDCA | 201(t) | [Definition of color additive] |
| FFDCA | 721 | Listing and certification of color additives for foods, drugs, devices, and cosmetics |

| Key Regulatory Provisions: Color Additives Generally | | |
|---|---|---|
| **21 C.F.R. Part** | **Subpart** | **Title of Part or Subpart** |
| 70 | — | Color additives |
| 71 | — | Color additive petitions |
| 80 | — | Color additive certification |
| **Key Regulatory Provisions: Listed Color Additives** | | |
| **21 C.F.R. Part** | **Subpart** | **Title of Part or Subpart** |
| 73 | — | Listing of color additives exempt from certification |
| 74 | — | Listing of color additives subject to certification |
| 81 | — | General specifications and general restrictions for provisional color additives for use in foods, drugs, and cosmetics |
| 82 | — | Listing of certified provisionally listed colors and specifications |

## C. Whether Cosmetics Are Color Additives

The case excerpted immediately below is a post-remand stage of one of the three cases in the *Abbott Laboratories* trilogy discussed in Chapter 2.[1] The issue in this pre-*Chevron* case is whether the FFDCA permitted FDA to regulate both finished cosmetic products and their components as "color additives." As you read, recall from Chapter 4 that cosmetics require no marketing authorization from FDA. Color additives, however, require both marketing authorization and—if not determined to be exempt from certification—batch testing. In other words, regulating cosmetic products as color additives would have dramatically altered the regulatory regime applicable to these products.

1. The earlier Supreme Court stage of this case, decided the same day as *Abbott Laboratories v. Gardner* 387 U.S. 136 (1967), was *Gardner v. Toilet Goods*, 387 U.S. 167 (1967).

Please note, as you read this case, that it refers to an earlier statutory location for the Color Additives Amendment and an earlier C.F.R. location for the regulatory definition of color additives. The earlier statutory location was § 706 of the FFDCA, codified at 21 U.S.C. § 376. Today, the relevant statutory provision is FFDCA § 721, codified at 21 U.S.C. § 379e. The earlier C.F.R. location for the regulatory definition of color additives was 21 C.F.R. § 8.1(f). Today, the regulatory definition of color additives is found at 21 C.F.R. § 70.3(f). This regulatory change is a result of a comprehensive recodification of FDA's regulations that took place in the 1970s.

The lead plaintiff, the Toilet Goods Association, Inc., was a cosmetics industry group. The two defendants were Robert H. Finch, Secretary of the Department of Health, Education, and Welfare, and Herbert L. Ley Jr., Commissioner of Food and Drugs. Both defendants were sued in their official capacities.

## Toilet Goods Ass'n v. Finch

419 F.2d 21 (2d Cir. 1969)

**FRIENDLY, Circuit Judge:**

Nine years ago Congress amended the Food, Drug, and Cosmetic Act, by enacting the Color Additive Amendments of 1960. Nearly three years later, after appropriate rule-making proceedings, the Food and Drug Administration (FDA) published its Regulations thereunder. This litigation about the validity of their provisions concerning diluents, finished cosmetics and hair-dyes has continued ever since. An initial effort by the Government to prevent the judicial review of the Regulations sought by the cosmetics industry, on the ground of lack of "ripeness," was rebuffed by Judge Tyler in the District Court for the Southern District of New York. A year later, when the case was nearly ready for trial, the Government renewed its effort to obtain dismissal for lack of ripeness on the basis of an allegedly conflicting decision by another circuit, with no success beyond obtaining a certificate from the district judge for an interlocutory appeal under 28 U.S.C. § 1292(b) which we allowed. We sustained the district court save in one respect no longer material. Both sides successfully sought certiorari but the Supreme Court affirmed. The case then returned to the district court where Judge Tyler rendered a decision favorable to the plaintiffs. This time the defendants were some seventeen months in bringing their appeal to us.

### I.

### Finished Cosmetic Products as Color Additives

The key provision of the Color Additive Amendments is [former FFDCA § 706], providing for what the parties term "premarketing clearance." This begins by saying in subsection (a):

> A color additive shall, whit[h] respect to any particular use (for which it is being used or intended to be used or is represented as suitable) in or on food or drugs or cosmetics, be deemed unsafe for the purposes of the

> application of sections [402](c), [501](a)(4), or [601](e) of [the FFDCA], as the case may be, unless—
>
> (1) (A) there is in effect, and such additive and such use are in conformity with, a regulation issued under subsection (b) of this section listing such additive for such use, including any provision of such regulation prescribing the conditions under which such additive may be safely used, and (B) such additive either (i) is from a batch certified, in accordance with regulations issued pursuant to subsection (c) of this section, for such use, or (ii) has, with respect to such use, been exempted by the Secretary from the requirement of certification; or
>
> (2) such additive and such use thereof conform to the terms of an exemption which is in effect pursuant to subsection (f) of this section.

Subsection (b)(1) directs the Secretary to provide by regulation

> for separately listing color additives for use in or on food, color additives for use in or on drugs, and color additives for use in or on cosmetics, if and to the extent that such additives are suitable and safe for any such use when employed in accordance with such regulations.

Section 8.4(c) of the Regulations sets forth the requirements for a listing application in elaborate detail. These include a complete description of the chemical and physical properties of the color additive, the chemical and physical tests relied on to identify it, and the methods and ingredients used for its production; a description of practical methods to determine the amount of the color additive, and of any substance formed by its use, contained in the final product; full reports of investigation made with respect to its safety; complete data to allow the Commissioner to consider the probable consumption of or other exposure to the additive and any substance formed therefrom; and proposed tolerances. If an exemption from batch certification is requested, supporting data are to be furnished. Each listing application must be accompanied by a fee of $2600 to cover the FDA's costs in processing the application and performing tests. Other provisions of the Regulations, § 8.22–§ 8.30, contain equally detailed requirements with respect to certification, including a provision, § 8.26, that "the person to whom a certificate is issued shall keep complete records showing the disposal of all the color additive from the batch covered by such certificate."

The parties are in basic disagreement concerning what constitutes a color additive requiring the premarketing clearance just described. On this the statute informs us, [FFDCA § 201](t)(1):

> (1) The term 'color additive' means a material which—
>
>> (A) is a dye, pigment, or other substance made by a process of synthesis or similar artifice, or extracted, isolated, or otherwise derived, with or without intermediate or final change of identity, from a vegetable, animal, mineral, or other source, and

> (B) when added or applied to a food drug or cosmetic, or to the human body or any part thereof, is capable (alone or through reaction with any other substance) of imparting color thereto; except that such term does not include any material which the Secretary, by regulation, determines is used (or intended to be used) solely for a purpose or purposes other than coloring.

The disputed Regulation, 21 C.F.R. § 8.1 after repeating this definition, adds two provisions of which the industry complained. One is "This includes all diluents"; the other is:

> A substance that, when applied to the human body results in coloring, is a "color additive," unless the function of coloring is purely incidental to its intended use, such as in the case of deodorants. Lipsticks, rouge, eye makeup colors and related cosmetics intended for coloring the human body are "color additives."

The industry contended, and the district court held, that the Regulation exceeded the statutory authority in requiring premarketing clearance of diluents[1] and of finished cosmetic products. The Government does not claim error in the conclusion that § 8.1(f) is invalid in defining diluents as color additives and thereby making them subject to premarketing clearance. But it vigorously attacks the holding that the section is similarly invalid in so defining finished cosmetic products.

In a valiant effort to overcome the instinctive reaction that when Congress spoke of a "color additive" it scarcely meant the entire product, the Government has developed an ingenious parsing of the definition in [FFDCA § 201](t). A finished cosmetic product, it says, while not a dye or pigment within subdivision (A), is an "other substance." And while such a product is not "added or applied to a food, drug or cosmetic" within subdivision (B), it is applied "to the human body or any part thereof" and "is capable (alone or through reaction with any other substance) of imparting color thereto." Hence the finished cosmetic product is itself a color additive. Indeed, says the Government, any other construction would fail to comply with the canon that every word in a statute must be given effect, since, as it claims, the industry has been unable to point to any "other substance" which, when added or applied to the human body, is capable of imparting color thereto.[2]

The district judge rejected the Government's construction on several grounds. He pointed to the numerous instances where Congress used the word "cosmetics" when that was what it intended. See [FFDCA §§ 301, 704, 801]. He countered

1. Section 8.1(m) defines diluent to mean 'any component of a color additive mixture that is not of itself a color additive and has been intentionally mixed therein to facilitate the use of the mixture in coloring foods, drugs, or cosmetics or in coloring the human body.'

2. The industry argues that 'other substance' was intended to refer to certain ingredients which, in contrast to dyes and pigments, are themselves colorless but nevertheless impart color. However, says the Government, such substances are applied to the human body only through being added to a cosmetic, still leaving 'other substance' applied 'to the human body or any part thereof' a null set.

the defendants' canon with that of *ejusdem generis*; the natural interpretation of "other substance" is a coloring *ingredient* having properties similar to a dye or pigment, see fn. 2. Defendants' reading "other substance" to include a cosmetic would cause the definition to refer to "a dye, pigment, or other substance (including a cosmetic)" which, when added to "a food, drug or cosmetic" is capable of imparting color, a result he deemed absurd. When Congress wished to employ a comprehensive term for finished products, it used the word "articles," [FFDCA § 201], whereas "substance" was used to connote a component or ingredient, [FFDCA §§ 201](s), 406.

The Government answers the last argument rather effectively by pointing to other instances where the word "articles" was used to refer to components, [FFDCA §§ 201](f) and (i) and [FFDCA § 505](b). It also contends that if the industry's construction is right, the exemption for pesticides in [FFDCA § 201](t)(3) was unnecessary, to which the industry responds that this was inserted on the request of pesticide manufacturers out of abundant caution, and that in any case it would have been more logical to call pesticides and fertilizers which might alter the color of plants "color additives" than to apply the term to finished cosmetics. The Government argues from the rejection of many similar requests to limit the definition that it was intended to have broad scope, while the industry asserts that many of these requests stemmed from such absurd fears—for example, that the peas in a can of peas and carrots might be "color additives" because they are not the same color as the carrots—that they reinforce Judge Tyler's restricted reading of the phrase "dye, pigment, or other substance."

Coming closer to the critical issue, the Government points to [FFDCA§ 601](e), hereafter discussed, as showing that the statutory scheme places at least some kinds of finished cosmetic products under the rubric of color additives. It also directs our attention to [FFDCA § 602], which provides that "A cosmetic shall be deemed to be misbranded . . . , (e) if it is a color additive" unless its packaging and labelling accord with prescribed regulations. Although [FFDCA § 201](i) defines "cosmetics" to include the components of finished cosmetics as well as the finished cosmetics themselves, and therefore may make it necessary for "color additives" to be called "cosmetics" even when they are not meant to be used directly by consumers, these provisions scarcely show that all finished cosmetics were thought to be color additives requiring premarketing clearance.

While we consider the industry to be ahead in this exchange of textual volleys, we find more enlightenment in the history and declared purpose of the Color Additive Amendments. The definition of color additives in the 1960 amendment did not spring full-blown from the congressional brain. The Food, Drug, and Cosmetic Act of 1938 had prohibited the sale, § 301(a) (c), of food, § 402(c), drugs, § 501(a)(4) and cosmetics (other than hair dyes), § 601(e), bearing or containing a coal-tar color other than one from a batch certified, in accordance with regulations as authorized for the three categories respectively in §§ 406(b), 504, and 604, to be "harmless and suitable for use."[3] [Another regulation, formerly codified at 21 C.F.R. § 135.1], defined "coaltar color" as meaning "articles which (1) are composed of or contain any substance derived from coal-tar . . . , and (2) when added or applied to a food, drug, cosmetic, or the human body or any part thereof, are capable (alone or through reaction with other substance) of imparting color thereto." There is no indication that the FDA ever considered this definition to require the listing and certification of finished cosmetics as distinguished from the coal-tar colors themselves. The burden thus falls on the Government to show that when, in the Color Additive Amendments, Congress employed words similar to those previously in the FDA's regulations, it meant them to have a different effect. The history seems rather to reinforce the view that it did not.

*[A detailed discussion of legislative history is omitted here.]*

There is still further evidence in favor of the district court's construction. The basic structure of the Color Additive Amendments is to apply the same requirements to foods, drugs and cosmetics which contain coloring materials. Yet the Government's exegesis would result in finished cosmetics with coloring ingredients being subject to listing and certification whereas foods and drugs bearing such ingredients would not be. Yet, if there is a difference in hazard, foods and drugs, which are ingested, would seem to outrank cosmetics; indeed cosmetics were not brought into the regulatory scheme until 32 years after foods and drugs.

We cannot agree with the Government that the district court's invalidation of the portion of § 8(f) which we have quoted frustrates the "safe-for-use" principle which concededly underlay the Color Additive Amendments. Other provisions of [former FFDCA § 706] confer all authority needed to that end. Although the Secretary "may list any color additive for use generally in or on food, or in or on drugs, or in or on cosmetics, if the Secretary finds that such additive is suitable and may safely be employed for such general use," [former FFDCA § 706](b)(2)(A), he also may list an additive "only for any more limited use or uses for which it is suitable and may safely be employed." [former FFDCA § 706](b)(2)(B). He is authorized to prescribe broadly "the conditions under which such additive may be safely employed for such use or uses," including tolerance limitations. [former FFDCA § 706](b)(3). This power and the further directives in [former FFDCA § 706](b)(4) and (5) are ample authority for the Secretary to prescribe that a particular "dye, pigment or other substance" may be used with certain diluents but not with others, or at higher concentrations with some than with others. It may well be that, in some cases, a cosmetics manufacturer might be obliged to supply an amount of information concerning a finished cosmetic equivalent to what would be required for listing. But it does not follow from this that Congress meant to subject the many thousands of cosmetic formulations to premarketing clearance—both listing and certification—at enormous and apparently unnecessary cost both to the industry and to the Government.

---

3. The Food and Drug Act of 1906, 34 Stat. 768 (1906), had contained similar provisions with respect to food and drugs.

"In our anxiety to effectuate the congressional purpose of protecting the public, we must take care not to extend the scope of the statute beyond the point where Congress indicated it would stop." *62 Cases, More or Less, Each Containing Six Jars of Jam v. United States*, 340 U.S. 593, 600 (1951).[5]

. . . .

We therefore affirm the holding of the district court with respect to § 8.1(f) . . . .

## D. Overview and Historical Context

### FDA, Guidance for Industry: Color Additive Petitions—FDA Recommendations for Submission of Chemical and Technological Data on Color Additives for Food, Drugs, Cosmetics, or Medical Devices (Jul. 2009)

I. Introduction

This document provides guidance for the submission of the chemical and technological data that the Food and Drug Administration's Office of Food Additive Safety considers necessary for its evaluation of petitions requesting the listing of color additives for use in food, drugs, cosmetics, or medical devices. These recommendations are provided to assist petitioners who propose to impart color to a food, drug, cosmetic, or medical device that is subject to federal regulation by use of a substance (color additive) that is currently not permitted for that use. These recommendations are not substitutes for the [FFDCA] or Title 21 of the Code of Federal Regulations (CFR), sections which are cited in this document.

. . . .

II. Discussion

As prescribed by law, a color additive must be shown to be safe and be listed in the CFR before it may be used to color foods, drugs, cosmetics, or certain medical devices. An interested person may petition the Food and Drug Administration (FDA) for the proposed use of a color additive and submit data demonstrating its

5. The final paragraph of the form of decree submitted by the defendants would have made entirely clear that the invalidation of portions of § 8.1(f) should not restrain the defendants 'in requiring the presentation of all needed scientific data to support color additive listing regulations which will assure that such listed color additives will be safe for their intended uses, including uses in lipstick, roug[e], eye makeup and related finished cosmetics,' or 'from determining what the relevant factors are in a particular case or from determining the nature, scope and extent of the testing of other data which may be required, and anything else which may be essential in determining that a color is safe for its intended use.' While we see nothing in the decree that would restrain the defendants in these respects, the district court might give further consideration to this on the remand we are directing with respect to the hair-dye exemption.

safety and suitability as described in 21 CFR Part 71. The FDA will, upon written request, advise on the adequacy of experiments planned to yield these data (21 CFR 70.42(c)). If, upon evaluation of the data in the petition, additional data, and public comments, the Agency finds that the petitioned color additive is safe and suitable for the intended use, then a regulation may be issued or an existing regulation altered, thereby listing the color additive for such use. The color additive will be listed in 21 CFR Part 73 if it is exempt from batch certification or in 21 CFR Part 74 if it is subject to batch certification.

The data that are appropriate for approval of a color additive petition depend on the level and type of use and the amount of color additive and its impurities that may enter body tissues. A petition for use of a color additive in externally applied cosmetics generally requires much less data than a petition for use of a color additive in food if it is shown that the color additive, including its impurities, does not penetrate the skin or if the amount used is negligible.

The data and information in a color additive petition that are or are not available for public disclosure are described in 21 CFR 71.15. Questions on the confidentiality of the data and information should be referred to the Office of Food Additive Safety, Division of Petition Review.

III. Statutory and Regulatory Requirements

A. Statutory Requirements

Section 201(t) of the [FFDCA] defines color additive to mean:

> "a material which . . . is a dye, pigment, or other substance made by a process of synthesis or similar artifice, or extracted, isolated, or otherwise derived, with or without intermediate or final change of identity, from a vegetable, animal, mineral, or other source, and . . . [that] when added or applied to a food, drug, or cosmetic, or to the human body or any part thereof, is capable (alone or through reaction with [an]other substance) of imparting color thereto . . . The term 'color' includes black, white, and intermediate grays . . ."

Food (section 402(c) of the [FFDCA]), drugs and devices (section 501(a)(4) of the [FFDCA]), and cosmetics (section 601(e) of the [FFDCA]) are deemed to be adulterated if they contain a color additive that is unsafe within the meaning of section 721(a) of the [FFDCA].

Section 721(a) of the [FFDCA] defines conditions under which a color additive is deemed unsafe. Briefly, a color additive used in or on a food, drug, cosmetic or medical device shall be deemed unsafe unless (1) there is a regulation listing such color additive, (2) the regulation allows that particular use, and (3) the color additive and its use conform to the regulation. A color additive for use in or on a device shall be subject to this section only if the color additive comes in direct contact with the body of man or other animal for a significant period of time.

Coal-tar hair dyes are cosmetic products that have a limited exemption, under section 601(a) of the [FFDCA], from the color additive regulation requirements (section 721(a) of the [FFDCA]). Coal-tar dyes are organic dyes formerly synthesized from coal tar but now synthesized from petroleum or coal sources. Coal-tar dyes used for coloring the hair are not required to be pre-approved by the FDA. Under section 601(a) of the [FFDCA], hair coloring products containing unapproved coal-tar dyes are not considered to be adulterated if the products bear a specified caution statement and adequate directions for a preliminary patch test. Section 601(a) of the [FFDCA] also stipulates that the term "hair dye" does not include eyelash or eyebrow dyes. Currently no color additives are approved for use in dyeing the eyelashes or eyebrows.

Section 721(b) of the [FFDCA] describes the statutory requirements for the listing of color additives. Briefly, when the FDA evaluates safety data, there are four general areas of consideration, of which the most pertinent to these recommendations is:

> "the availability of any needed practicable methods of analysis for determining the identity and quantity of (I) the pure dye and all intermediates and other impurities contained in such color additive, (II) such additive in or on any article of food, drug, device, or cosmetic, and (III) any substance formed in or on such article because of the use of such additive." (Section 721(b)(5)(A)(iv) of the [FFDCA])[.]

Parts 70 and 71 of Title 21 of the Code of Federal Regulations, which were promulgated under the authority of section 706(b) of the [FFDCA], describe in greater detail the format, the administrative requirements, and the information and data required for color additive petitions.

. . . .

An estimate of probable exposure to the petitioned color additive is critical for its safety evaluation. The estimated daily exposure helps to determine the type and extent of animal feeding studies required to establish the safety of the color additive under the proposed conditions of use. If use of color additive lakes is proposed, then the anticipated uses of the lake and the range of total color incorporated into the lake should be appraised, thereby allowing an estimate of probable exposure to the color per se.

### Color Additives Used in Food

A petitioner must provide information sufficient to permit an estimate of chronic daily exposure to a color additive. From analyzed or estimated levels of an additive in food, the concentration of the color additive expected in the daily diet and the estimated daily intake (EDI) can be calculated. The types of information that are needed for the exposure analysis include composition of the color additive, levels of impurities, proposed foods or food categories in which the color additive is intended to be used, and anticipated typical and maximum levels of use.

#### Color Additives Used in Drugs

A petitioner must provide information sufficient to permit an estimate of exposure to the color additive. The composition of the color additive, levels of impurities, proposed drugs or types of drugs that will contain the color additive, and the anticipated typical and maximum levels of use should be provided. The petitioner should note if the drugs in which the color additive would be used will be prescribed for long-term or chronic use or for short-term use (i.e., days, weeks).

#### Color Additives Used in Cosmetics

Migration of color additives from cosmetics to skin will be evaluated on the basis of 100% migration. Skin penetration studies, if submitted, may be used to adjust the results of the 100% migration assumption. Information that is useful for the evaluation includes composition of the color additive, levels of impurities, and anticipated levels of use.

#### Color Additives Used in Medical Devices

For color additives intended for use in medical devices (e.g., sutures, contact lenses), migration of the color additive to tissue is most easily determined by averaging 100% migration over the lifetime of the article. Actual migration studies may also be performed. The types of information that are useful for the exposure analysis include composition of the color additive, levels of impurities, the maximum and typical lifetimes of the device, and typical and maximum anticipated levels of the color additive used in the device. Information on the actual rate of migration of the color additive from the device may also be used in preparation of the exposure estimate. The petitioner may wish to consult the Agency for concurrence with any migration studies that are envisioned.

## E. The Color Additives "Delaney Clause"

Please note, as you read the excerpt immediately below, that (like the *Toilet Goods* case presented earlier in this chapter) it refers to an earlier statutory location for the Color Additives Amendment. This was at § 706 of the FFDCA, codified at 21 U.S.C. § 376. Today, the relevant statutory provision is FFDCA § 721, codified at 21 U.S.C. § 379e. Here, the lead plaintiff was Public Citizen, an advocacy group. The lead defendant was Dr. Frank Young, Commissioner of Food and Drugs, in his official capacity.

### Pub. Citizen v. Young

831 F.2d 1108 (D.C. Cir. 1987)

**WILLIAMS, Circuit Judge:**

The Color Additive Amendments of 1960, part of the [FFDCA], establish an elaborate system for regulation of color additives in the interests of safety. A color additive may be used only after the Food and Drug Administration ("FDA") has published a regulation listing the additive for such uses as are safe. Such listing may occur only if the color additive in question satisfies (among other things) the requirements of the applicable "Delaney Clause," § 706(b)(5)(B) of the [FFDCA], one of three such clauses in the total system for regulation of color additives, food and animal food and drugs.[1] The Clause prohibits the listing of any color additive "found . . . to induce cancer in man or animal."

In [this case], Public Citizen and certain individuals challenge the decision of the FDA to list two color additives, Orange No. 17 and Red No. 19, based on quantitative risk assessments indicating that the cancer risks presented by these dyes were trivial. This case thus requires us to determine whether the Delaney Clause for color additives is subject to an implicit "*de minimis*" exception. We conclude, with some reluctance, that the Clause lacks such an exception.

. . . .

### I. The Delaney Clause and "*De Minimis*" Exceptions

#### A. Factual Background

The FDA listed Orange No. 17 and Red No. 19 for use in externally applied cosmetics on August 7, 1986. In the listing notices, it carefully explained the testing processes for both dyes and praised the processes as "current state-of-the-art toxicological testing." In both notices it specifically rejected industry arguments that the Delaney Clause did not apply because the tests were inappropriate for evaluation of the dyes. It thus concluded that the studies established that the substances caused cancer in the test animals. (Orange No. 17 "induces cancer when tested in laboratory animals"); (Red No. 19 "induces cancer when tested in laboratory animals").

The notices then went on to describe two quantitative risk assessments of the dyes, one by the Cosmetic, Toiletry and Fragrance Association ("CTFA," an intervenor here and the industry proponent of both dyes) and one by a special scientific review panel made up of Public Health Service scientists. Such assessments seek to define the extent of health effects of exposures to particular hazards. As described by the National Research Council, they generally involve four steps: (1) hazard identification, or the determination of whether a substance is causally linked to a health effect; (2) dose-response assessment, or determination of the relation between exposure levels and health effects; (3) exposure assessment, or determination of human exposure; and (4) risk characterization, or description of the nature and magnitude of the risk. All agree that gaps exist in the available information and that the risk estimator must use assumptions to fill those gaps. The choice among possible assumptions is inevitably a matter of policy to some degree.[2]

---

1. The other clauses relate to food additives, [FFDCA § 409](c)(3)(A), and to animal drugs, id. [FFDCA § 512](d)(1)(H). All clauses prohibit carcinogens. The clauses differ slightly in language, more materially in statutory context and legislative history.

2. Agencies have used quantitative risk assessments in a variety of regulatory contexts. For example, the Occupational Safety and Health Administration is under a mandate to establish

The assessments considered the risk to humans from the substances when used in various cosmetics—lipsticks, face powders and rouges, hair cosmetics, nail products, bathwater products, and wash-off products. The scientific review panel found the lifetime cancer risks of the substances extremely small: for Orange No. 17, it calculated them as one in 19 billion at worst, and for Red No. 19 one in nine million at worst. The FDA explained that the panel had used conservative assumptions in deriving these figures, and it characterized the risks as "so trivial as to be effectively no risk." It concluded that the two dyes were safe.

The FDA candidly acknowledged that its safety findings represented a departure from past agency practice: "In the past, because the data and information show that D & C Orange No. 17 is a carcinogen when ingested by laboratory animals, FDA in all likelihood would have terminated the provisional listing and denied CTFA's petition for the externally applied uses . . . without any further discussion." It also acknowledged that "[a] strictly literal application of the Delaney Clause would prohibit FDA from finding [both dyes] safe, and therefore, prohibit FDA from permanently listing [them]. . . ." Because the risks presented by these dyes were so small, however, the agency declared that it had "inherent authority" under the *de minimis* doctrine to list them for use in spite of this language. It indicated that as a general matter any risk lower than a one-in-one-million lifetime risk would meet the requirements for a *de minimis* exception to the Delaney Clause.

Assuming that the quantitative risk assessments are accurate, as we do for these purposes, it seems altogether correct to characterize these risks as trivial. For example, CTFA notes that a consumer would run a one-in-a-million lifetime risk of cancer if he or she ate one peanut with the FDA-permitted level of aflatoxins once every 250 days (liver cancer). Another activity posing a one-in-a-million lifetime risk is spending 1,000 minutes (less than 17 hours) every year in the city of Denver—with its high elevation and cosmic radiation levels—rather than in the District of Columbia. Most of us would not regard these as high-risk activities. Those who indulge in them can hardly be thought of as living dangerously. Indeed, they are risks taken without a second thought by persons whose economic position allows them a broad range of choice.

According to the risk assessments here, the riskier dye poses one ninth as much risk as the peanut or Colorado hypothetical; the less risky one poses only one 19,000th as much.

---

standards "reasonably necessary or appropriate to provide safe or healthful . . . places of employment," 29 U.S.C. § 652(8) (1982) . . . .

In fulfillment of this mandate, OSHA used quantitative risk assessment in promulgating a rule on exposure limits to airborne inorganic arsenic. The FDA itself has used the technique in evaluating safety where the Delaney Clause did not apply. FDA has also used the technique in the face of the Delaney Clause in approving a carcinogenic food additive, methylene chloride. A challenge to the methylene chloride determination is currently pending [separately] before this court.

It may help put the one-in-a-million lifetime risk in perspective to compare it with a concededly dangerous activity, in which millions nonetheless engage, cigarette smoking. Each one-in-a-million risk amounts to less than one 200,000th the lifetime risk incurred by the average male smoker. Thus, a person would have to be exposed to more than 2,000 chemicals bearing the one-in-a-million lifetime risk, at the rates assumed in the risk assessment, in order to reach 100th the risk involved in smoking. To reach that level of risk with chemicals equivalent to the less risky dye (Orange No. 17), he would have to be exposed to more than 40 million such chemicals.

### B. Plain Language and the de minimis Doctrine

The Delaney Clause of the Color Additive Amendments provides as follows:

> a color additive . . . (ii) shall be deemed unsafe, and shall not be listed, for any use which will not result in ingestion of any part of such additive, if, after tests which are appropriate for the evaluation of the safety of additives for such use, or after other relevant exposure of man or animal to such additive, it is found by the Secretary to induce cancer in man or animal. . . . [3]

[former FFDCA § 706](b)(5)(B).

The natural—almost inescapable—reading of this language is that if the Secretary finds the additive to "induce" cancer in animals, he must deny listing. Here, of course, the agency made precisely the finding that Orange No. 17 and Red No. 19 "induce[ ] cancer when tested in laboratory animals." (Below we address later agency pronouncements appearing to back away from these statements.)

The setting of the clause supports this strict reading. Adjacent to it is a section governing safety generally and directing the FDA to consider a variety of factors, including probable exposure, cumulative effects, and detection difficulties. [former FFDCA § 706](b)(5)(A). The contra[s]t in approach seems to us significant. For all safety hazards other than carcinogens, Congress made safety the issue, and authorized the agency to pursue a multifaceted inquiry in arriving at an evaluation. For carcinogens, however, it framed the issue in the simple form, "If A [finding that cancer is induced in man or animals], then B [no listing]." There is language inviting administrative discretion, but it relates only to the process leading to the finding of carcinogenicity: "appropriate" tests or "other relevant exposure," and the agency's "evaluation" of such data. Once the finding is made, the dye "shall be deemed unsafe, and shall not be listed." [former FFDCA § 706](b)(5)(B).

Courts (and agencies) are not, of course, helpless slaves to literalism. One escape hatch, invoked by the government and CTFA here, is the *de minimis* doctrine, shorthand for *de minimis non curat lex* ("the law does not concern itself with trifles"). The doctrine—articulated in recent times in a series of decisions by

---

3. This quotation omits subsection (i), which concerns uses involving ingestion; none of the uses here at issue concerns such a use.

Judge Leventhal—serves a number of purposes. One is to spare agency resources for more important matters. See *Alabama Power Co. v. Costle*, 636 F.2d 323, 360 (D.C.Cir.1979). But that is a goal of dubious relevance here. The finding of trivial risk necessarily followed not only the elaborate animal testing, but also the quantitative risk assessment process itself; indeed, application of the doctrine required additional expenditure of agency resources.

More relevant is the concept that "notwithstanding the 'plain meaning' of a statute, a court must look beyond the words to the purpose of the act where its literal terms lead to 'absurd or futile results.'" *Alabama Power*, 636 F.2d at 360 n. 89 (quoting *United States v. American Trucking Ass'ns*, 310 U.S. 534, 543 (1939)). Imposition of pointless burdens on regulated entities is obviously to be avoided if possible especially as burdens on them almost invariably entail losses for their customers: here, obviously, loss of access to the colors made possible by a broad range of dyes.

We have employed the concept in construing the Clean Air Act's mandate to the Environmental Protection Agency to set standards providing "an ample margin of safety to protect the public health," 42 U.S.C. § 7412(b)(1) (1982). That does not, we said, require limits assuring a "risk-free" environment. Rather, the agency must decide "what risks are acceptable in the world in which we live" and set limits accordingly. Assuming as always the validity of the risk assessments, we believe that the risks posed by the two dyes would have to be characterized as "acceptable." Accordingly, if the statute were to permit a *de minimis* exception, this would appear to be a case for its application.[4]

Moreover, failure to employ a *de minimis* doctrine may lead to regulation that not only is "absurd or futile" in some general cost-benefit sense but also is directly contrary to the primary legislative goal. In a certain sense, precisely that may be the effect here. The primary goal of the [FFDCA] is human safety, but literal application of the Delaney Clause may in some instances increase risk. No one contends that the Color Additive Amendments impose a zero-risk standard for non-carcinogenic substances; if they did, the number of dyes passing muster might prove miniscule. As a result, makers of drugs and cosmetics who are barred from using a carcinogenic dye carrying a one-in-20-million lifetime risk may use instead a noncarcinogenic, but toxic, dye carrying, say, a one-in-10-million lifetime risk. The substitution appears to be a clear loss for safety.

Judge Leventhal articulated the standard for application of *de minimis* as virtually a presumption in its favor: "Unless Congress has been extraordinarily rigid, there is likely a basis for an implication of *de minimis* authority to provide [an] exemption when the burdens of regulation yield a gain of trivial or no value." *Alabama Power*,

4. We do not, of course, purport to decide the appropriate dividing point between de minimis and other risks. FDA's proposed one-in-one-million dividing point has been used by EPA to distinguish acceptable and unacceptable risks. 49 Fed.Reg. 46,294 (1984) (general guidelines); 51 Fed.Reg. 1602, 1635 (1986) (hazardous wastes). FDA has used the same break point to determine whether the general safety clause of the [FFDCA] applies. 47 Fed.Reg. 14,138 (1982).

636 F.2d at 360–61. But the doctrine obviously is not available to thwart a statutory command; it must be interpreted with a view to "implementing the legislative design." Id. at 360. Nor is an agency to apply it on a finding merely that regulatory costs exceed regulatory benefits.

Here, we cannot find that exemption of exceedingly small (but measurable) risks tends to implement the legislative design of the color additive Delaney Clause. The language itself is rigid; the context—an alternative design admitting administrative discretion for all risks other than carcinogens—tends to confirm that rigidity. Below we consider first the legislative history; rather than offering any hint of softening, this only strengthens the inference. Second, we consider a number of factors that make Congress's apparent decision at least a comprehensible policy choice.

**1. Legislative History**

*[An extensive discussion of legislative history is here omitted.]*

**2. Possible Explanations for an Absolute Rule**

Like all legislative history, this is hardly conclusive. But short of an explicit declaration in the statute barring use of a *de minimis* exception, this is perhaps as strong as it is likely to get. Facing the explicit claim that the Clause was "extraordinarily rigid," a claim well supported by the Clause's language in contrast with the bill's grants of discretion elsewhere, Congress persevered.

Moreover, our reading of the legislative history suggests some possible explanations for Congress's apparent rigidity. One is that Congress, and the nation in general (at least as perceived by Congress), appear to have been truly alarmed about the risks of cancer. This concern resulted in a close focus on substances increasing cancer threats and a willingness to take extreme steps to lessen even small risks. Congress hoped to reduce the incidence of cancer by banning carcinogenic dyes, and may also have hoped to lessen public fears by demonstrating strong resolve.

A second possible explanation for Congress's failure to authorize greater administrative discretion is that it perceived color additives as lacking any great value. For example, Congressman Delaney remarked, "Some food additives serve a useful purpose.... However, color additives provide no nutrient value. They have no value at all, except so-called eye appeal." Representative Sullivan said, "we like the bright and light [lipstick] shades but if they cannot safely be produced, then we prefer to do without these particular shades." And Representative King: "The colors which go into our foods and cosmetics are in no way essential to the public interest or the national security.... [C]onsumers will easily get along without [carcinogenic colors]."

It is true that the legislation as a whole implicitly recognizes that color additives are of value, since one of its purposes was to allow tolerances for certain dyes—harmful but not carcinogenic—that would have been banned under the former law. There was also testimony pointing out that in some uses color additives advance health: they can help identify medications and prevent misapplications where a patient must take several. Nevertheless, there is evidence that Congress thought the public could get along without carcinogenic colors, especially in view of the existence of safer substitutes. Thus the legislators may have estimated the costs of an overly protective rule as trivial.

So far as we can determine, no one drew the legislators' attention to the way in which the Delaney Clause, interacting with the flexible standard for determining safety of non-carcinogens, might cause manufacturers to substitute more dangerous toxic chemicals for less dangerous carcinogens. But the obviously more stringent standard for carcinogens may rest on a view that cancer deaths are in some way more to be feared than others.

Finally, as we have already noted, the House committee (or its amanuenses) considered the possibility that its no-threshold assumption might prove false and contemplated a solution: renewed consideration by Congress.

Considering these circumstances—great concern over a specific health risk, the apparently low cost of protection, and the possibility of remedying any mistakes—Congress's enactment of an absolute rule seems less surprising.

### C. Special Arguments for Application of *de minimis*

Apart from their contentions on legislative history, the FDA and CTFA [(Cosmetic, Toiletry, and Fragrance Association)] assert two grounds for a *de minimis* exception: an analysis of two cases applying *de minimis* concepts in the food and drug regulation context, and contentions that, because of scientific advances since enactment, the disallowance of *de minimis* authority would have preposterous results in related areas of food and drug law. (We treat an argument based on a new interpretation of the statutory language separately in section I-D.) We are, ultimately, not persuaded.

#### 1. *De minimis* cases

*Monsanto Co. v. Kennedy*, 613 F.2d 947 (D.C.Cir.1979) (Leventhal, J.), considered whether acrylonitrile in beverage containers was a "food additive" within the meaning of the Food, Drug and Cosmetic Act's definition of that term:

> any substance the intended use of which results or may reasonably be expected to result, directly or indirectly, in its becoming a component or otherwise affecting the characteristics of any food . . . if such substance is not generally recognized . . . to be safe under the conditions of its intended use . . .

[FFDCA § 201](s).

By operation of the second law of thermodynamics, any substance, obviously including acrylonitrile, will migrate in minute amounts from a bottle into a beverage within the bottle. Questions had been raised about its safety. The court found the FDA's decision to ban its use insufficiently well considered. In remanding the case for reconsideration, the court emphasized the FDA Commissioner's discretion to exclude a chemical from the statutory definition of food additives if "the level of migration into food . . . is so negligible as to present no public health or safety concerns."

The opinion makes no suggestion that anyone supposed acrylonitrile to be carcinogenic, or that the Delaney Clause governing food additives, [FFDCA 409](c)(3)(A), was in any way implicated. Thus the case cannot support a view that the food additive Delaney Clause (or, obviously, the color additive one) admits of a *de minimis* exception.[13]

*Scott v. Food and Drug Administration*, 728 F.2d 322 (6th Cir.1984) (per curiam), involves the color additive Delaney Clause, but is nonetheless distinguishable. Petitioner challenged the FDA's listing of Green No. 5, on the grounds that it contained a chemical impurity in minute quantities that had been found to cause cancer in test animals. The dye as a whole, however, had been found not to induce cancer in test animals. The Sixth Circuit upheld the FDA's decision that the Delaney Clause of the Color Additive Amendments did not apply. The court cited *Monsanto* in support of upholding the FDA's view that it had discretion "to find that low-level migration into food of substances in *indirect* additives is so insignificant as to present no public health or safety concerns."

We must evaluate *Scott* in light of the possibility that the carcinogenic impurity in question acted as an "initiating agent" or was a "complete carcinogen," and, accordingly, would be subject to no threshold. If so, it would seem that if the impurity itself were carcinogenic, so would be any substance to which it was added.

Application of a *de minimis* exception for constituents of a color additive, however, seems to us materially different from use of such a doctrine for the color additive itself. As the Scott court noted, the FDA's action was completely consistent with the plain language of the statute, as there was no finding that the dye caused cancer in animals. Here, as we have observed, application of a *de minimis* exception requires putting a gloss on the statute qualifying its literal terms.

*Monsanto* and *Scott* demonstrate that the *de minimis* doctrine is alive and well in the food and drug context, even on the periphery of the Delaney Clauses. But no case has applied it to limit the apparent meaning of any of those Clauses in their core operation.

### 2. Scientific Advance and the Implications for Food Additive Regulation

The CTFA also argues that in a number of respects scientific advance has rendered obsolete any inference of congressional insistence on rigidity. CTFA notes that while in 1958 (date of enactment of the food additive Delaney Clause) there were only four known human carcinogens, by 1978 there were 37 substances known to produce cancer in humans and over 500 in animals. They identify an impressive array of food ingredients now found to be animal carcinogens and that appear in a large number of food products. These include many items normally viewed as essential ingredients in a healthy diet, such as vitamins C and D, calcium, protein,

13. As we note below, the operation of the food additive Delaney Clause raises complex issues distinct from those of this appeal.

and amino acids. If the color additive Delaney Clause has no *de minimis* exception, it follows (they suggest) that the food additive one must be equally rigid. The upshot would be to deny the American people access to a healthy food supply.

As a historical matter, the argument is overdrawn: the House committee was clearly on notice that certain common foods and nutrients were suspected carcinogens.[14]

Beyond that, it is not clear that an interpretation of the food additive Delaney Clause identical with our interpretation of the color additive clause would entail the feared consequences. The food additive definition contains an exception for substances "generally recognized" as safe (known as the "GRAS" exception),[15] an exception that has no parallel in the color additive definition, [FFDCA § 201](t)(1). That definition may permit a *de minimis* exception at a stage that logically precedes the FDA's ever reaching the food additive Delaney Clause. Indeed, *Monsanto* so holds—though, as we have noted, in a case not trenching upon the food additive Delaney Clause. Moreover, the GRAS exception itself builds in special protection for substances used in food prior to January 1, 1958, which may be shown to be safe "through either scientific procedures or experience based on common use in food." Indeed, the Kistiakowsky Report, filed with the House committee, stated that the grandfathering provision of the food additives Delaney Clause "considerably narrows [its] effect . . . on industry and the public."

The relationship of the GRAS exception and the food additive Delaney Clause clearly poses a problem: if the food additive definition allows the FDA to classify as GRAS substances carrying trivial risks (as *Monsanto* and our recent decision in *Natural Resources Defense Council v. EPA* seem to suggest), but the food additive Delaney Clause is absolute, then Congress has adopted inconsistent provisions. On the other

14. See Color Additives Hearings at 270 (statement of vice-president of Eli Lilly) (noting substances implicated in carcinogenicity in animals, including coffee, tea, milk, cream, cocoa, claret, caffeine, whiskey, sulfonamides, fat, cholesterol, vitamins, eggs, sugars, and others); id. at 318, 328 (testimony of Representative of Pharmaceutical Manufacturers' Association) ("so many of our common foods do contain carcinogens"); id. at 337–38 (testimony of representative of Consumers' Union) ("the fact that weak carcinogens are present in natural foods is no justification" for tolerances for carcinogenic additives); id. at 342 (statement of Rep. Nelson) ("we have been told that, for example, hens' eggs, milk, beef, soybeans, corn, lettuce alfalfa, have certain factors in them that create cancer"); id. at 397 (Kistiakowsky Report) ("In foodstuffs, as they occur in nature, one finds traces of chemicals which in larger amounts are generally accepted as carcinogenic. . . ."); id. at 427 (Rep. Flynt) (asking witness whether it was "substantially true that nearly every element of food known at the present time if either injected or ingested in large quantities is capable of producing cancer first or toxicity secondly?").

15. The pertinent part of [FFDCA § 201](s) excepts a substance

> generally recognized, among experts qualified by scientific training and experience to evaluate its safety, as having been adequately shown through scientific procedures (or, in the case as a substance used in food prior to January 1, 1958, through either scientific procedures or experience based on common use in food) to be safe under the conditions of its intended use. . . .

hand, if (1) the GRAS exception does not encompass substances with trivial carcinogenic effect (especially if its special provision for substances used before 1958 does not do so for long-established substances), and (2) the food additive Delaney Clause is as rigid as we find the color additive clause to be, conceivably the consequences identified by the CTFA, or some of them, may follow. All these are difficult questions, but they are neither before us nor is their answer foreordained by our decision here.

Moreover, we deal here only with the color additive Delaney Clause, not the one for food additives. Although the clauses have almost identical wording, the context is clearly different. Without having canvassed the legislative history of the food additive Delaney Clause, we may safely say that its proponents could not have regarded as trivial the social cost of banning those parts of the American diet that CTFA argues are at risk.

Finally, even a court decision construing the food additive provisions to require a ban on dietary essentials would not, in fact, bring about such a ban. As Secretary Flemming noted, in words selected by the House Report for quotation, the FDA could bring critical new discoveries to Congress's attention. If the present law would lead to the consequences predicted, we suppose that the FDA would do so, and that Congress would respond.

### D. The Meaning of "[I]nduce Cancer"

After Public Citizen initiated the litigation in No. 86-5150, the FDA published a notice embellishing the preamble to its initial safety determinations. These notices effectively apply quantitative risk assessment at the stage of determining whether a substance "induce[s] cancer in man or animal." They assert that even where a substance does cause cancer in animals in the conventional sense of the term, the FDA may find that it does not "induce cancer in man or animal" within the meaning of 21 U.S.C. § 376(b)(5)(B). It is not crystal clear whether such a negative finding would flow simply from a quantitative risk assessment finding the risk to be trivial for humans under conditions of intended use, or whether it would require a projection back to the laboratory animals: i.e., an assessment that the risk would be trivial for animals exposed to the substance in quantities proportional to the exposure hypothesized for human risk assessment purposes. (Perhaps the distinction is without a difference.) In any event, the notices argued:

> The words "induce cancer in man or animal" as used in the Delaney Clause are terms of art intended to convey a regulatory judgment that is something more than a scientific observation that an additive is carcinogenic in laboratory animals. To limit this judgment to such a simple observation would be to arbitrarily exclude from FDA's consideration developing sophisticated testing and analytical methodologies, leaving FDA with only the most primitive techniques for its use in this important endeavor to protect public health. Certainly the language of the Delaney Clause itself cannot be read to mandate such a counterproductive limit on FDA's discharge of its responsibilities.

The notices acknowledged that the words "to induce cancer" had not been "rigorously and unambiguously" so limited in the previous notices. This is a considerable understatement. The original determinations were quite unambiguous in concluding that the colors induced cancer in animals in valid tests; the explanations went to some trouble to rebut industry arguments to the contrary. Despite these arguments, FDA concluded that the tests demonstrated that the dyes were responsible for increases in animal tumors.

The plain language of the Delaney Clause covers all animals exposed to color additives, including laboratory animals exposed to high doses. It would be surprising if it did not. High-dose exposures are standard testing procedure, today just as in 1960; such high doses are justified to offset practical limitations on such tests: compared to expected exposure of millions of humans over long periods, the time periods are short and the animals few. Many references in the legislative history reflect awareness of reliance on animal testing, and at least the more sophisticated participants must have been aware that this meant high-dose testing. A few so specified.

. . . .

All this indicates to us that Congress did not intend the FDA to be able to take a finding that a substance causes only trivial risk in humans and work back from that to a finding that the substance does not "induce cancer in . . . animals." This is simply the basic question—is the operation of the clause automatic once the FDA makes a finding of carcinogenicity in animals?—in a new guise. The only new argument offered in the notices is that, without the new interpretation, only "primitive techniques" could be used. In fact, of course, the agency is clearly free to incorporate the latest breakthroughs in animal testing; indeed, here it touted the most recent animal tests as "state of the art." The limitation on techniques is only that the agency may not, once a color additive is found to induce cancer in test animals in the conventional sense of the term, undercut the statutory consequence. As we find the FDA's construction "contrary to clear congressional intent," *Chevron U.S.A. v. Natural Resources Defense Council*, Inc., 467 U.S. 837, 843 n. 9 (1984), we need not defer to it.

* * *

In sum, we hold that the Delaney Clause of the Color Additive Amendments does not contain an implicit *de minimis* exception for carcinogenic dyes with trivial risks to humans. We based this decision on our understanding that Congress adopted an "extraordinarily rigid" position, denying the FDA authority to list a dye once it found it to "induce cancer in . . . animals" in the conventional sense of the term. We believe that, in the color additive context, Congress intended that if this rule produced unexpected or undesirable consequences, the agency should come to it for relief. That moment may well have arrived, but we cannot provide the desired escape.

. . . .

**Conclusion**

In sum, we hold that the agency's *de minimis* interpretation of the Delaney Clause of the Color Additive Amendments is contrary to law. The listing decisions for Orange No. 17 and Red No. 19 based on that interpretation must therefore be corrected.

So ordered.

## F. Key Points

- FDA's statutory authority over color additives is found in FFDCA Chapter VII, "General Authority." The specific provision is FFDCA § 721. FDA's color additive regulations are found in the "General" subchapter of Title 21 of the Code of Federal Regulations. The specific provisions are 21 C.F.R. Parts 70–82.
- The FFDCA defines a color additive as a "dye, pigment, or other substance" that "is capable . . . of imparting color" to "a food, drug, or cosmetic, or to the human body or any part thereof." FFDCA § 201(t)(1).
  - The statute explicitly exempts from this definition "any material which the Secretary, by regulation, determines is used (or intended to be used) solely for a purpose or purposes other than coloring." FFDCA § 201(t)(1).
  - While the statutory definition does not explicitly include use in medical devices, it does include authority over substances "capable . . . of imparting color" to "the human body or any part thereof." FFDCA § 201(t)(1). Other sections of the FFDCA, such as the adulteration provision of FFDCA § 501(a)(4)(B), explicitly contemplate the use of color additives in medical devices.
    - FDA has promulgated regulations listing certain color additives for use in medical devices. These device-specific regulations are found in 21 C.F.R. Part 73, Subpart D and 21 C.F.R. Part 74, Subpart D.

Chapter 18

# Tobacco Products

## A. Introduction

Successful FDA regulation of tobacco products did not begin until President Obama signed the Family Smoking Prevention and Tobacco Control Act (TCA) in 2009. This chapter begins with two excerpts that predate the TCA, then turns to FDA implementation of that statute.

## B. Outline of Regulatory Regime

As in other chapters of this book, this chapter begins with a set of charts. As you read this chapter for the first time, you should do no more than skim these charts to get a general sense of the structure of the applicable statutes and regulations. (For more information on the role of the charts in this casebook, see Chapter 1, Parts A.1 and B).

| Timeline of Key Statutes: FDA Regulation of Tobacco Products | | | |
|---|---|---|---|
| Year | PL | Stat | Name of Statute |
| 2009 | 111-31 | 123 Stat. 1776 | Family Smoking Prevention and Tobacco Control Act |

| Key Statutory Provisions: FDA Regulation of Tobacco Products | | |
|---|---|---|
| Statute Name or U.S.C. Title | § | Title of Section or Subsection |
| FFDCA | 201(rr) | [Definition of "tobacco product"] |
| FFDCA | 900 | Definitions |
| FFDCA | 901 | FDA authority over tobacco products |
| FFDCA | 902 | Adulterated tobacco products |
| FFDCA | 903 | Misbranded tobacco products |
| FFDCA | 904 | Submission of health information to the Secretary |
| FFDCA | 905 | Annual registration |
| FFDCA | 906 | General provisions respecting control of tobacco products |
| FFDCA | 907 | Tobacco product standards |

| Statute Name or U.S.C. Title | § | Title of Section or Subsection |
|---|---|---|
| FFDCA | 908 | Notification and other remedies |
| FFDCA | 909 | Records and reports on tobacco products |
| FFDCA | 910 | Application for review of certain tobacco products |
| FFDCA | 911 | Modified risk tobacco products |
| FFDCA | 920 | Labeling, recordkeeping, records inspection |

| Key Regulatory Provisions Administered by FDA: Tobacco Products | |
|---|---|
| **21 C.F.R. Part** | **Title of Part** |
| 1100 | Tobacco products subject to FDA authority |
| 1107 | Establishment registration, product listing, and substantial equivalence reports |
| 1140 | Cigarettes, smokeless tobacco, and covered tobacco products |
| 1141 | Cigarette package and advertising warnings |
| 1143 | Minimum required warning statements |
| **Key Regulatory Provisions Administered by Treasury: Tobacco Products** | |
| **27 C.F.R. Part** | **Title of Part or Subpart** |
| 40 | Manufacture of tobacco products, cigarette papers and tubes, and processed tobacco |
| 41 | Importation of tobacco products, cigarette papers and tubes, and processed tobacco |
| 44 | Exportation of tobacco products and cigarette papers and tubes, without payment of tax, or with drawback of tax |
| 45 | Removal of tobacco products and cigarette papers and tubes, without payment of tax, for use of the United States |
| 46 | Miscellaneous regulations relating to tobacco products and cigarette papers and tubes |
| **Key Regulatory Provisions Administered by Dept. of Justice: Tobacco Products** | |
| **27 C.F.R. Part** | **Title of Part or Subpart** |
| 646 | Contraband cigarettes |

## C. Nonregulation: 1906–2009

In 1964, the U.S. Surgeon General released a detailed report concluding, based on an extensive review of existing literature, that cigarette smoking had significant harmful effects on smokers. That report, excerpted below, has since become famous as an early milestone in the fight against the public health consequences of tobacco use.

## Smoking and Health: Report of the Advisory Committee to the Surgeon General of the Public Health Service (1964)

. . . .

### The Effects of Smoking: Principal Findings

Cigarette smoking is associated with a 70 percent increase in the age-specific death rates of males, and to a lesser extent with increased death rates of females. The total number of excess deaths causally related to cigarette smoking in the U.S. population cannot be accurately estimated. In view of the continuing and mounting evidence from many sources, it is the judgment of the Committee that cigarette smoking contributes substantially to mortality from certain specific diseases and to the overall death rate.

*Lung Cancer*

Cigarette smoking is causally related to lung cancer in men; the magnitude of the effect of cigarette smoking far outweighs all other factors. The data for women. though less extensive, point in the same direction.

The risk of developing lung cancer increases with duration of smoking and the number of cigarettes smoked per day, and is diminished by discontinuing smoking. In comparison with non-smokers, average male smokers of cigarettes have approximately a 9- to 10-fold risk of developing lung cancer and heavy smokers at least a 20-fold risk.

The risk of developing cancer of the lung for the combined group of pipe smokers, cigar smokers, and pipe and cigar smokers is greater than for non-smokers, but much less than for cigarette smokers. Cigarette smoking is much more important than occupational exposures in the causation of lung cancer in the general population.

*Chronic Bronchitis and Emphysema*

Cigarette smoking is the most important of the causes of chronic bronchitis in the United States, and increases the risk of dying from chronic bronchitis and emphysema. A relationship exists between cigarette smoking and emphysema but it has not been established that the relationship is causal. Studies demonstrate that fatalities from this disease are infrequent among non-smokers.

For the bulk of the population of the United States, the relative importance of cigarette smoking as a cause of chronic broncho-pulmonary disease is much greater than atmospheric pollution or occupational exposures.

*Cardiovascular Diseases*

It is established that male cigarette smokers have a higher death rate from coronary artery disease than non-smoking males. Although the causative role of cigarette smoking in deaths from coronary disease is not proven, the Committee considers it more prudent from the public health viewpoint to assume that the established association has causative meaning than to suspend judgment until no uncertainty remains.

Although a causal relationship has not been established, higher mortality of cigarette smokers is associated with many other cardiovascular diseases, including miscellaneous circulatory diseases, other heart diseases, hypertensive heart disease, and general arteriosclerosis.

*Other Cancer Sites*

Pipe smoking appears to be causally related to lip cancer. Cigarette smoking is a significant factor in the causation of cancer of the larynx. The evidence supports the belief that an association exists between tobacco use and cancer of the esophagus, and between cigarette smoking and cancer of the urinary bladder in men, but the data are not adequate to decide whether these relationships are causal. Data on an association between smoking and cancer of the stomach are contradictory and incomplete.

THE TOBACCO HABIT AND NICOTINE

The habitual use of tobacco is related primarily to psychological and social drives, reinforced and perpetuated by the pharmacological actions of nicotine.

Social stimulation appears to play a major role in a young person's early and first experiments with smoking. No scientific evidence supports the popular hypothesis that smoking among adolescents is an expression rebellion against authority. Individual stress appears to be associated more with fluctuations in the amount of smoking than with the prevalence of smoking. The overwhelming evidence indicates that smoking—its beginning, habituation, and occasional discontinuation—is to a very large extent psychologically and socially determined.

Nicotine is rapidly changed in the body to relatively inactive substances with low toxicity. The chronic toxicity of small doses of nicotine is low in experimental animals. These two facts, when taken in conjunction with the low mortality ratios of pipe and cigar smokers, indicate that the chronic toxicity of nicotine in quantities absorbed from smoking and other methods of tobacco use is very low and probably does not represent an important health hazard.

The significant beneficial effects of smoking occur primarily in the area of mental health, and the habit originates in a search for contentment. Since no means of measuring the quantity of these benefits is apparent, the Committee finds no basis for a judgment which would weigh benefits against hazards of smoking as it may apply to the general population.

THE COMMITTEE'S JUDGMENT IN BRIEF

On the basis of prolonged study and evaluation of many lines of converging evidence, the Committee makes the following judgment:

**Cigarette smoking is a health hazard of sufficient importance in the United States to warrant appropriate remedial action.**

. . . .

---

Despite increasing public acceptance of the negative public health consequences of tobacco use, FDA did not seek to regulate tobacco until the 1990s. In 1996, FDA published a final rule asserting jurisdiction over cigarettes and smokeless tobacco as combination products. It did so by making two major determinations. First, FDA concluded that nicotine was a drug within the meeting of FFDCA § 201(g)(1). Second, FDA concluded that cigarettes and smokeless tobacco were drug delivery devices—and thus combination products—under the FFDCA. Litigation followed. The case eventually reached the U.S. Supreme Court. The Court's decision in that case, *FDA v. Brown & Williamson Tobacco Corp.*, 529 U.S. 120 (2000), is excerpted below.

## FDA v. Brown & Williamson Tobacco Corp.

529 U.S. 120 (2000)

**Justice O'CONNOR delivered the opinion of the Court.**

This case involves one of the most troubling public health problems facing our Nation today: the thousands of premature deaths that occur each year because of tobacco use. In 1996, the Food and Drug Administration (FDA), after having expressly disavowed any such authority since its inception, asserted jurisdiction to regulate tobacco products. The FDA concluded that nicotine is a "drug" within the meaning of the Food, Drug, and Cosmetic Act (FDCA or Act) and that cigarettes and smokeless tobacco are "combination products" that deliver nicotine to the body. Pursuant to this authority, it promulgated regulations intended to reduce tobacco consumption among children and adolescents. The agency believed that, because most tobacco consumers begin their use before reaching the age of 18, curbing tobacco use by minors could substantially reduce the prevalence of addiction in future generations and thus the incidence of tobacco-related death and disease.

Regardless of how serious the problem an administrative agency seeks to address, however, it may not exercise its authority "in a manner that is inconsistent with the administrative structure that Congress enacted into law." And although agencies are generally entitled to deference in the interpretation of statutes that they administer, a reviewing "court, as well as the agency, must give effect to the unambiguously expressed intent of Congress." *Chevron U.S.A. Inc. v. Natural Resources Defense Council, Inc.*, 467 U.S. 837, 842–843 (1984). In this case, we believe that Congress has clearly precluded the FDA from asserting jurisdiction to regulate tobacco products. Such authority is inconsistent with the intent that Congress has expressed in the [FFDCA]'s overall regulatory scheme and in the tobacco-specific legislation that it has enacted subsequent to the [FFDCA]. In light of this clear intent, the FDA's assertion of jurisdiction is impermissible.

### I

The [FFDCA] grants the FDA, as the designee of the Secretary of Health and Human Services (HHS), the authority to regulate, among other items, "drugs" and "devices." The Act defines "drug" to include "articles (other than food) intended to affect the structure or any function of the body." It defines "device," in part, as "an instrument, apparatus, implement, machine, contrivance, . . . or other similar or related article, including any component, part, or accessory, which is . . . intended to affect the structure or any function of the body." The Act also grants the FDA the authority to regulate so-called "combination products," which "constitute a combination of a drug, device, or biological product." The FDA has construed this provision as giving it the discretion to regulate combination products as drugs, as devices, or as both.

On August 11, 1995, the FDA published a proposed rule concerning the sale of cigarettes and smokeless tobacco to children and adolescents. The rule, which included several restrictions on the sale, distribution, and advertisement of tobacco products, was designed to reduce the availability and attractiveness of tobacco products to young people. A public comment period followed, during which the FDA received over 700,000 submissions, more than "at any other time in its history on any other subject."

On August 28, 1996, the FDA issued a final rule entitled "Regulations Restricting the Sale and Distribution of Cigarettes and Smokeless Tobacco to Protect Children and Adolescents." The FDA determined that nicotine is a "drug" and that cigarettes and smokeless tobacco are "drug delivery devices," and therefore it had jurisdiction under the [FFDCA] to regulate tobacco products as customarily marketed—that is, without manufacturer claims of therapeutic benefit. First, the FDA found that tobacco products "affect the structure or any function of the body" because nicotine "has significant pharmacological effects." Specifically, nicotine "exerts psychoactive, or mood-altering, effects on the brain" that cause and sustain addiction, have both tranquilizing and stimulating effects, and control weight. Second, the FDA determined that these effects were "intended" under the [FFDCA] because they "are so widely known and foreseeable that [they] may be deemed to have been intended by the manufacturers,"; consumers use tobacco products "predominantly or nearly exclusively" to obtain these effects; and the statements, research, and actions of manufacturers revealed that they "have designed cigarettes to provide pharmacologically active doses of nicotine to consumers." Finally, the agency concluded that cigarettes and smokeless tobacco are "combination products" because, in addition to containing nicotine, they include device components that deliver a controlled amount of nicotine to the body.

Having resolved the jurisdictional question, the FDA next explained the policy justifications for its regulations, detailing the deleterious health effects associated with tobacco use. It found that tobacco consumption was "the single leading cause of preventable death in the United States." According to the FDA, "[m]ore than 400,000 people die each year from tobacco-related illnesses, such as cancer, respiratory illnesses, and heart disease." The agency also determined that the only way to reduce the amount of tobacco-related illness and mortality was to reduce the level of addiction, a goal that could be accomplished only by preventing children and adolescents from starting to use tobacco. The FDA found that 82% of adult smokers had their first cigarette before the age of 18, and more than half had already become regular smokers by that age. It also found that children were beginning to smoke at a younger age, that the prevalence of youth smoking had recently increased, and that similar problems existed with respect to smokeless tobacco. The FDA accordingly concluded that if "the number of children and adolescents who begin tobacco use can be substantially diminished, tobacco-related illness can be correspondingly reduced because data suggest that anyone who does not begin smoking in childhood or adolescence is unlikely ever to begin."

Based on these findings, the FDA promulgated regulations concerning tobacco products' promotion, labeling, and accessibility to children and adolescents. The access regulations prohibit the sale of cigarettes or smokeless tobacco to persons younger than 18; require retailers to verify through photo identification the age of all purchasers younger than 27; prohibit the sale of cigarettes in quantities smaller than 20; prohibit the distribution of free samples; and prohibit sales through self-service displays and vending machines except in adult-only locations. The promotion regulations require that any print advertising appear in a black-and-white, text-only format unless the publication in which it appears is read almost exclusively by adults; prohibit outdoor advertising within 1,000 feet of any public playground or school; prohibit the distribution of any promotional items, such as T-shirts or hats, bearing the manufacturer's brand name; and prohibit a manufacturer from sponsoring any athletic, musical, artistic, or other social or cultural event using its brand name. The labeling regulation requires that the statement, "A Nicotine-Delivery Device for Persons 18 or Older," appear on all tobacco product packages.

The FDA promulgated these regulations pursuant to its authority to regulate "restricted devices." [FFDCA § 520(e)]. The FDA construed [FFDCA § 503(g)(1)] as giving it the discretion to regulate "combination products" using the [FFDCA]'s drug authorities, device authorities, or both, depending on "how the public health goals of the [FFDCA] can be best accomplished." Given the greater flexibility in the [FFDCA] for the regulation of devices, the FDA determined that "the device authorities provide the most appropriate basis for regulating cigarettes and smokeless tobacco." Under [FFDCA § 520(e)], the agency may "require that a device be restricted to sale, distribution, or use ... upon such other conditions as [the FDA] may prescribe in such regulation, if, because of its potentiality for harmful effect or the collateral measures necessary to its use, [the FDA] determines that there cannot otherwise be reasonable assurance of its safety and effectiveness." The FDA reasoned that its regulations fell within the authority granted by [FFDCA § 520](e) because they related to the sale or distribution of tobacco products and were necessary for providing a reasonable assurance of safety

Respondents, a group of tobacco manufacturers, retailers, and advertisers, filed suit in United States District Court for the Middle District of North Carolina challenging the regulations. They moved for summary judgment on the grounds that the FDA lacked jurisdiction to regulate tobacco products as customarily marketed, the regulations exceeded the FDA's authority under [FFDCA § 520](e), and the advertising restrictions violated the First Amendment. The District Court granted respondents' motion in part and denied it in part. The court held that the [FFDCA] authorizes the FDA to regulate tobacco products as customarily marketed and that the FDA's access and labeling regulations are permissible, but it also found that the agency's advertising and promotion restrictions exceed its authority under [FFDCA § 520](e). The court stayed implementation of the regulations it found valid (except the prohibition on the sale of tobacco products to minors) and certified its order for immediate interlocutory appeal.

The Court of Appeals for the Fourth Circuit reversed, holding that Congress has not granted the FDA jurisdiction to regulate tobacco products. Examining the [FFDCA] as a whole, the court concluded that the FDA's regulation of tobacco products would create a number of internal inconsistencies. Various provisions of the [FFDCA] require the agency to determine that any regulated product is "safe" before it can be sold or allowed to remain on the market, yet the FDA found in its rulemaking proceeding that tobacco products are "dangerous" and "unsafe." Thus, the FDA would apparently have to ban tobacco products, a result the court found clearly contrary to congressional intent. This apparent anomaly, the Court of Appeals concluded, demonstrates that Congress did not intend to give the FDA authority to regulate tobacco. The court also found that evidence external to the [FFDCA] confirms this conclusion. Importantly, the FDA consistently stated before 1995 that it lacked jurisdiction over tobacco, and Congress has enacted several tobacco-specific statutes fully cognizant of the FDA's position. In fact, the court reasoned, Congress has considered and rejected many bills that would have given the agency such authority. This, along with the absence of any intent by the enacting Congress in 1938 to subject tobacco products to regulation under the [FFDCA], demonstrates that Congress intended to withhold such authority from the FDA. Having resolved the jurisdictional question against the agency, the Court of Appeals did not address whether the regulations exceed the FDA's authority under [FFDCA § 520(e)] or violate the First Amendment.

We granted the federal parties' petition for certiorari to determine whether the FDA has authority under the [FFDCA] to regulate tobacco products as customarily marketed.

## II

The FDA's assertion of jurisdiction to regulate tobacco products is founded on its conclusions that nicotine is a "drug" and that cigarettes and smokeless tobacco are "drug delivery devices." Again, the FDA found that tobacco products are "intended" to deliver the pharmacological effects of satisfying addiction, stimulation and tranquilization, and weight control because those effects are foreseeable to any reasonable manufacturer, consumers use tobacco products to obtain those effects, and tobacco manufacturers have designed their products to produce those effects. As an initial matter, respondents take issue with the FDA's reading of "intended," arguing that it is a term of art that refers exclusively to claims made by the manufacturer or vendor about the product. That is, a product is not a drug or device under the [FFDCA] unless the manufacturer or vendor makes some express claim concerning the product's therapeutic benefits. We need not resolve this question, however, because assuming, arguendo, that a product can be "intended to affect the structure or any function of the body" absent claims of therapeutic or medical benefit, the FDA's claim to jurisdiction contravenes the clear intent of Congress.

A threshold issue is the appropriate framework for analyzing the FDA's assertion of authority to regulate tobacco products. Because this case involves an administrative agency's construction of a statute that it administers, our analysis is governed by *Chevron U.S.A. Inc. v. Natural Resources Defense Council, Inc.*, 467 U.S. 837 (1984). Under *Chevron*, a reviewing court must first ask "whether Congress has directly spoken to the precise question at issue." If Congress has done so, the inquiry is at an end; the court "must give effect to the unambiguously expressed intent of Congress." But if Congress has not specifically addressed the question, a reviewing court must respect the agency's construction of the statute so long as it is permissible. Such deference is justified because "[t]he responsibilities for assessing the wisdom of such policy choices and resolving the struggle between competing views of the public interest are not judicial ones," *Chevron*, and because of the agency's greater familiarity with the ever-changing facts and circumstances surrounding the subjects regulated.

In determining whether Congress has specifically addressed the question at issue, a reviewing court should not confine itself to examining a particular statutory provision in isolation. The meaning—or ambiguity—of certain words or phrases may only become evident when placed in context. It is a "fundamental canon of statutory construction that the words of a statute must be read in their context and with a view to their place in the overall statutory scheme." A court must therefore interpret the statute "as a symmetrical and coherent regulatory scheme," and "fit, if possible, all parts into an harmonious whole." Similarly, the meaning of one statute may be affected by other Acts, particularly where Congress has spoken subsequently and more specifically to the topic at hand. In addition, we must be guided to a degree by common sense as to the manner in which Congress is likely to delegate a policy decision of such economic and political magnitude to an administrative agency.

With these principles in mind, we find that Congress has directly spoken to the issue here and precluded the FDA's jurisdiction to regulate tobacco products.

### A

Viewing the [FFDCA] as a whole, it is evident that one of the [FFDCA]'s core objectives is to ensure that any product regulated by the FDA is "safe" and "effective" for its intended use.... The [FFDCA] requires premarket approval of any new drug, with some limited exceptions, and states that the FDA "shall issue an order refusing to approve the application" of a new drug if it is not safe and effective for its intended purpose. If the FDA discovers after approval that a drug is unsafe or ineffective, it "shall, after due notice and opportunity for hearing to the applicant, withdraw approval" of the drug. The Act also requires the FDA to classify all devices into one of three categories. Regardless of which category the FDA chooses, there must be a "reasonable assurance of the safety and effectiveness of the device." Even the "restricted device" provision pursuant to which the FDA promulgated the regulations at issue here authorizes the agency to place conditions on the sale or distribution of a device specifically when "there cannot otherwise be reasonable assurance of its safety and effectiveness." Thus, the [FFDCA] generally requires the FDA to prevent the marketing of any drug or device where the "potential for inflicting death or physical injury is not offset by the possibility of therapeutic benefit."

In its rulemaking proceeding, the FDA quite exhaustively documented that "tobacco products are unsafe," "dangerous," and "cause great pain and suffering from illness." It found that the consumption of tobacco products presents "extraordinary health risks," and that "tobacco use is the single leading cause of preventable death in the United States." It stated that "[m]ore than 400,000 people die each year from tobacco-related illnesses, such as cancer, respiratory illnesses, and heart disease, often suffering long and painful deaths," and that "[t]obacco alone kills more people each year in the United States than acquired immunodeficiency syndrome (AIDS), car accidents, alcohol, homicides, illegal drugs, suicides, and fires, combined." Indeed, the FDA characterized smoking as "a pediatric disease," because "one out of every three young people who become regular smokers . . . will die prematurely as a result."

These findings logically imply that, if tobacco products were "devices" under the [FFDCA], the FDA would be required to remove them from the market. Consider, first, the [FFDCA]'s provisions concerning the misbranding of drugs or devices. The Act prohibits "[t]he introduction or delivery for introduction into interstate commerce of any food, drug, device, or cosmetic that is adulterated or misbranded." In light of the FDA's findings, two distinct [FFDCA] provisions would render cigarettes and smokeless tobacco misbranded devices. First, [FFDCA § 502] deems a drug or device misbranded "[i]f it is dangerous to health when used in the dosage or manner, or with the frequency or duration prescribed, recommended, or suggested in the labeling thereof." The FDA's findings make clear that tobacco products are "dangerous to health" when used in the manner prescribed. Second, a drug or device is misbranded under the [FFDCA] "[u]nless its labeling bears . . . adequate directions for use . . . in such manner and form, as are necessary for the protection of users," except where such directions are "not necessary for the protection of the public health." Given the FDA's conclusions concerning the health consequences of tobacco use, there are no directions that could adequately protect consumers. That is, there are no directions that could make tobacco products safe for obtaining their intended effects. Thus, were tobacco products within the FDA's jurisdiction, the [FFDCA] would deem them misbranded devices that could not be introduced into interstate commerce. Contrary to the dissent's contention, the [FFDCA] admits no remedial discretion once it is evident that the device is misbranded.

Second, the [FFDCA] requires the FDA to place all devices that it regulates into one of three classifications. The agency relies on a device's classification in determining the degree of control and regulation necessary to ensure that there is "a reasonable assurance of safety and effectiveness." The FDA has yet to classify tobacco products. Instead, the regulations at issue here represent so-called "general controls," which the [FFDCA] entitles the agency to impose in advance of classification. Although the [FFDCA] prescribes no deadline for device classification, the FDA has stated that it will classify tobacco products "in a future rulemaking" as required by the [FFDCA]. Given the FDA's findings regarding the health consequences of tobacco use, the agency would have to place cigarettes and smokeless tobacco in Class III because, even after the application of the [FFDCA]'s available controls, they would "presen[t] a potential unreasonable risk of illness or injury." As Class III devices, tobacco products would be subject to the [FFDCA]'s premarket approval process. Under these provisions, the FDA would be prohibited from approving an application for premarket approval without "a showing of reasonable assurance that such device is safe under the conditions of use prescribed, recommended, or suggested in the proposed labeling thereof." In view of the FDA's conclusions regarding the health effects of tobacco use, the agency would have no basis for finding any such reasonable assurance of safety. Thus, once the FDA fulfilled its statutory obligation to classify tobacco products, it could not allow them to be marketed.

The [FFDCA]'s misbranding and device classification provisions therefore make evident that were the FDA to regulate cigarettes and smokeless tobacco, the [FFDCA] would require the agency to ban them. In fact, based on these provisions, the FDA itself has previously taken the position that if tobacco products were within its jurisdiction, "they would have to be removed from the market because it would be impossible to prove they were safe for their intended us[e]." Public Health Cigarette Amendments of 1971: Hearings before the Commerce Subcommittee on S. 1454, 92d Cong., 2d Sess., 239 (1972) (hereinafter 1972 Hearings) (statement of FDA Comm'r Charles Edwards). See also Cigarette Labeling and Advertising: Hearings before the House Committee on Interstate and Foreign Commerce, 88th Cong., 2d Sess., 18 (1964) (hereinafter 1964 Hearings) (statement of Dept. of Health, Education, and Welfare (HEW) Secretary Anthony Celebrezze that proposed amendments to the [FFDCA] that would have given the FDA jurisdiction over "smoking product[s]" "might well completely outlaw at least cigarettes").

. . . .

The dissent contends that our conclusion means that "the [FFDCA] requires the FDA to ban outright 'dangerous' drugs or devices," and that this is a "perverse" reading of the statute. This misunderstands our holding. The FDA, consistent with the [FFDCA], may clearly regulate many "dangerous" products without banning them. Indeed, virtually every drug or device poses dangers under certain conditions. What the FDA may not do is conclude that a drug or device cannot be used safely for any therapeutic purpose and yet, at the same time, allow that product to remain on the market. Such regulation is incompatible with the [FFDCA]'s core objective of ensuring that every drug or device is safe and effective.

Considering the [FFDCA] as a whole, it is clear that Congress intended to exclude tobacco products from the FDA's jurisdiction. A fundamental precept of the [FFDCA] is that any product regulated by the FDA—but not banned—must be safe for its intended use. Various provisions of the [FFDCA] make clear that this refers to the safety of using the product to obtain its intended effects, not the public health ramifications of alternative administrative actions by the FDA. That is, the FDA must determine that there is a reasonable assurance that the product's therapeutic benefits outweigh the risk of harm to the consumer. According to this standard, the FDA has concluded that, although tobacco products might be effective in delivering certain pharmacological effects, they are "unsafe" and "dangerous" when used for these purposes. Consequently, if tobacco products were within the FDA's jurisdiction, the [FFDCA] would require the FDA to remove them from the market entirely. But a ban would contradict Congress' clear intent as expressed in its more recent, tobacco-specific legislation. The inescapable conclusion is that there is no room for tobacco products within the [FFDCA]'s regulatory scheme. If they cannot be used safely for any therapeutic purpose, and yet they cannot be banned, they simply do not fit.

B

In determining whether Congress has spoken directly to the FDA's authority to regulate tobacco, we must also consider in greater detail the tobacco-specific legislation that Congress has enacted over the past 35 years. At the time a statute is enacted, it may have a range of plausible meanings. Over time, however, subsequent acts can shape or focus those meanings. The "classic judicial task of reconciling many laws enacted over time, and getting them to 'make sense' in combination, necessarily assumes that the implications of a statute may be altered by the implications of a later statute." This is particularly so where the scope of the earlier statute is broad but the subsequent statutes more specifically address the topic at hand. . . .

Congress has enacted six separate pieces of legislation since 1965 addressing the problem of tobacco use and human health. Those statutes, among other things, require that health warnings appear on all packaging and in all print and outdoor advertisements, prohibit the advertisement of tobacco products through "any medium of electronic communication" subject to regulation by the Federal Communications Commission (FCC); require the Secretary of HHS to report every three years to Congress on research findings concerning "the addictive property of tobacco"; and make States' receipt of certain federal block grants contingent on their making it unlawful "for any manufacturer, retailer, or distributor of tobacco products to sell or distribute any such product to any individual under the age of 18."

In adopting each statute, Congress has acted against the backdrop of the FDA's consistent and repeated statements that it lacked authority under the [FFDCA] to regulate tobacco absent claims of therapeutic benefit by the manufacturer. In fact, on several occasions over this period, and after the health consequences of tobacco use and nicotine's pharmacological effects had become well known, Congress considered and rejected bills that would have granted the FDA such jurisdiction. Under these circumstances, it is evident that Congress' tobacco-specific statutes have effectively ratified the FDA's long-held position that it lacks jurisdiction under the [FFDCA] to regulate tobacco products. Congress has created a distinct regulatory scheme to address the problem of tobacco and health, and that scheme, as presently constructed, precludes any role for the FDA.

. . . .

The FDA's disavowal of jurisdiction was consistent with the position that it had taken since the agency's inception. As the FDA concedes, it never asserted authority to regulate tobacco products as customarily marketed until it promulgated the regulations at issue here.

. . . .

Taken together, these actions by Congress over the past 35 years preclude an interpretation of the [FFDCA] that grants the FDA jurisdiction to regulate tobacco products. We do not rely on Congress' failure to act—its consideration and rejection of bills that would have given the FDA this authority—in reaching this conclusion. Indeed, this is not a case of simple inaction by Congress that purportedly represents its acquiescence in an agency's position. To the contrary, Congress has enacted several statutes addressing the particular subject of tobacco and health, creating a distinct regulatory scheme for cigarettes and smokeless tobacco. In doing so, Congress has been aware of tobacco's health hazards and its pharmacological effects. It has also enacted this legislation against the background of the FDA repeatedly and consistently asserting that it lacks jurisdiction under the [FFDCA] to regulate tobacco products as customarily marketed. Further, Congress has persistently acted to preclude a meaningful role for any administrative agency in making policy on the subject of tobacco and health. Moreover, the substance of Congress' regulatory scheme is, in an important respect, incompatible with FDA jurisdiction. Although the supervision of product labeling to protect consumer health is a substantial component of the FDA's regulation of drugs and devices, [certain other statutes discussed in the omitted portion above] explicitly prohibit any federal agency from imposing any health-related labeling requirements on cigarettes or smokeless tobacco products.

Under these circumstances, it is clear that Congress' tobacco-specific legislation has effectively ratified the FDA's previous position that it lacks jurisdiction to regulate tobacco. . . . Congress has affirmatively acted to address the issue of tobacco and health, relying on the representations of the FDA that it had no authority to regulate tobacco. It has created a distinct scheme to regulate the sale of tobacco products, focused on labeling and advertising, and premised on the belief that the FDA lacks such jurisdiction under the [FFDCA]. As a result, Congress' tobacco-specific statutes preclude the FDA from regulating tobacco products as customarily marketed.

. . . .

### C

Finally, our inquiry into whether Congress has directly spoken to the precise question at issue is shaped, at least in some measure, by the nature of the question presented. Deference under *Chevron* to an agency's construction of a statute that it administers is premised on the theory that a statute's ambiguity constitutes an implicit delegation from Congress to the agency to fill in the statutory gaps. In extraordinary cases, however, there may be reason to hesitate before concluding that Congress has intended such an implicit delegation.

This is hardly an ordinary case. Contrary to its representations to Congress since 1914, the FDA has now asserted jurisdiction to regulate an industry constituting a significant portion of the American economy. In fact, the FDA contends that, were it to determine that tobacco products provide no "reasonable assurance of safety," it would have the authority to ban cigarettes and smokeless tobacco entirely. Owing to its unique place in American history and society, tobacco has its own unique political history. Congress, for better or for worse, has created a distinct regulatory scheme for tobacco products, squarely rejected proposals to give the FDA jurisdiction over tobacco, and repeatedly acted to preclude any agency from exercising significant policymaking authority in the area. Given this history and the breadth of the authority that the FDA has asserted, we are obliged to defer not to the agency's expansive construction of the statute, but to Congress' consistent judgment to deny the FDA this power.

. . . .

As in [a case discussed in the omitted portion, above], we are confident that Congress could not have intended to delegate a decision of such economic and political significance to an agency in so cryptic a fashion. To find that the FDA has the authority to regulate tobacco products, one must not only adopt an extremely strained understanding of "safety" as it is used throughout the [FFDCA]—a concept central to the [FFDCA]'s regulatory scheme—but also ignore the plain implication of Congress' subsequent tobacco-specific legislation. It is therefore clear, based on the [FFDCA]'s overall regulatory scheme and the subsequent tobacco legislation, that Congress has directly spoken to the question at issue and precluded the FDA from regulating tobacco products.

* * *

By no means do we question the seriousness of the problem that the FDA has sought to address. The agency has amply demonstrated that tobacco use, particularly among children and adolescents, poses perhaps the single most significant threat to public health in the United States. Nonetheless, no matter how "important, conspicuous, and controversial" the issue, and regardless of how likely the public is to hold the Executive Branch politically accountable, an administrative agency's power to regulate in the public interest must always be grounded in a valid grant of authority from Congress. And "[i]n our anxiety to effectuate the congressional purpose of protecting the public, we must take care not to extend the scope of the statute beyond the point where Congress indicated it would stop.' " *United States v. Article of Drug . . . Bacto-Unidisk*, 394 U.S. 784, 800 (1969). Reading the [FFDCA] as a whole, as well as in conjunction with Congress' subsequent tobacco-specific legislation, it is plain that Congress has not given the FDA the authority that it seeks to exercise here. For these reasons, the judgment of the Court of Appeals for the Fourth Circuit is affirmed.

It is so ordered.

**Justice BREYER, . . . dissenting.**

The Food and Drug Administration (FDA) has the authority to regulate "articles (other than food) intended to affect the structure or any function of the body. . . ." [FFDCA § 201] (g)(1)(C). Unlike the majority, I believe that tobacco products fit within this statutory language.

In its own interpretation, the majority nowhere denies the following two salient points. First, tobacco products (including cigarettes) fall within the scope of this statutory definition, read literally. Cigarettes achieve their mood-stabilizing effects through the interaction of the chemical nicotine and the cells of the central nervous system. Both cigarette manufacturers and smokers alike know of, and desire, that chemically induced result. Hence, cigarettes are "intended to affect" the body's "structure" and "function," in the literal sense of these words.

Second, the statute's basic purpose—the protection of public health—supports the inclusion of cigarettes within its scope. See *United States v. Article of Drug . . . Bacto-Unidisk*, 394 U.S. 784, 798 (1969) ([FFDCA] "is to be given *a liberal construction consistent with [its] overriding purpose to protect the public health*" (emphasis added)). Unregulated tobacco use causes "[m]ore than 400,000 people [to] die each year from tobacco-related illnesses, such as cancer, respiratory illnesses, and heart disease." 61 Fed. Reg. 44,398. Indeed, tobacco products kill more people in this country every year "than . . . AIDS . . . , car accidents, alcohol, homicides, illegal drugs, suicides, and fires, *combined*." *Ibid.* (emphasis added).

Despite the [FFDCA]'s literal language and general purpose (both of which support the FDA's finding that cigarettes come within its statutory authority), the majority nonetheless reads the statute as excluding tobacco products for two basic reasons:

(1) the [FFDCA] does not "fit" the case of tobacco because the statute requires the FDA to prohibit dangerous drugs or devices (like cigarettes) outright, and the agency concedes that simply banning the sale of cigarettes is not a proper remedy; and

(2) Congress has enacted other statutes, which, when viewed in light of the FDA's long history of denying tobacco-related jurisdiction and considered together with Congress' failure explicitly to grant the agency tobacco-specific authority, demonstrate that Congress did not intend for the FDA to exercise jurisdiction over tobacco.

In my view, neither of these propositions is valid. Rather, the [FFDCA] does not significantly limit the FDA's remedial alternatives. And the later statutes do not tell the FDA it cannot exercise jurisdiction, but simply leave FDA jurisdictional law where Congress found it. *Cf.* Food and Drug Administration Modernization Act of 1997, 111 Stat. 2380 (statute "shall" not "be construed to affect the question of whether" the FDA "has any authority to regulate any tobacco product").

The bulk of the opinion that follows will explain the basis for these latter conclusions. In short, I believe that the most important indicia of statutory meaning—language and purpose—along with the [FFDCA]'s legislative history . . . are sufficient to establish that the FDA has authority to regulate tobacco. The statute-specific arguments against jurisdiction that the tobacco companies and the majority rely upon . . . are based on erroneous assumptions and, thus, do not defeat the jurisdiction-supporting thrust of the [FFDCA]'s language and purpose. The inferences that the majority draws from later legislative history are not persuasive, since . . . one can just as easily infer from the later laws that Congress did not intend to affect the FDA's tobacco-related authority at all. And the fact that the FDA changed its mind about the scope of its own jurisdiction is legally insignificant because . . . the agency's reasons for changing course are fully justified. Finally, . . . the degree of accountability that likely will attach to the FDA's action in this case should alleviate any concern that Congress, rather than an administrative agency, ought to make this important regulatory decision.

. . . .

According to the FDA, only 2.5% of smokers successfully stop smoking each year, even though 70% say they want to quit and 34% actually make an attempt to do so. The fact that only a handful of those who try to quit smoking actually succeed illustrates a certain reality—the reality that the nicotine in cigarettes creates a powerful physiological addiction flowing from chemically induced changes in the brain. The FDA has found that the makers of cigarettes "intend" these physical effects. Hence, nicotine is a "drug"; the cigarette that delivers nicotine to the body is a "device"; and the [FFDCA]'s language, read in light of its basic purpose, permits the FDA to assert the disease-preventing jurisdiction that the agency now claims.

The majority finds that cigarettes are so dangerous that the [FFDCA] would require them to be banned (a result the majority believes Congress would not have desired); thus, it concludes that the FDA has no tobacco-related authority. I disagree that the statute would require a cigarette ban. But even if I am wrong about the ban, the statute would restrict only the agency's choice of remedies, not its jurisdiction.

. . . .

The upshot is that the Court today holds that a regulatory statute aimed at unsafe drugs and devices does not authorize regulation of a drug (nicotine) and a device (a cigarette) that the Court itself finds unsafe. Far more than most, this particular drug and device risks the life-threatening harms that administrative regulation seeks to rectify. The majority's conclusion is counterintuitive. And, for the reasons set forth, I believe that the law does not require it.

Consequently, I dissent.

# D. 2009–Present: Regulation Under the Tobacco Control Act

The TCA expressly granted FDA direct authority over tobacco, removing any need for FDA to engage in the type of statutory construction that had led to the *Brown & Williamson* decision, above. Congress included extensive findings of fact, which are excerpted below.

## Tobacco Control Act: Findings of Fact

123 Stat. 1776, 1776 (2009)

SEC. 2. FINDINGS.

The Congress finds the following:

(1) The use of tobacco products by the Nation's children is a pediatric disease of considerable proportions that results in new generations of tobacco-dependent children and adults.

(2) A consensus exists within the scientific and medical communities that tobacco products are inherently dangerous and cause cancer, heart disease, and other serious adverse health effects.

(3) Nicotine is an addictive drug.

(4) Virtually all new users of tobacco products are under the minimum legal age to purchase such products.

(5) Tobacco advertising and marketing contribute significantly to the use of nicotine-containing tobacco products by adolescents.

(6) Because past efforts to restrict advertising and marketing of tobacco products have failed adequately to curb tobacco use by adolescents, comprehensive restrictions on the sale, promotion, and distribution of such products are needed.

(7) Federal and State governments have lacked the legal and regulatory authority and resources they need to address comprehensively the public health and societal problems caused by the use of tobacco products.

(8) Federal and State public health officials, the public health community, and the public at large recognize that the tobacco industry should be subject to ongoing oversight.

. . . .

(11) The sale, distribution, marketing, advertising, and use of such products substantially affect interstate commerce through the health care and other costs attributable to the use of tobacco products.

(12) It is in the public interest for Congress to enact legislation that provides the Food and Drug Administration with the authority to regulate tobacco

products and the advertising and promotion of such products. The benefits to the American people from enacting such legislation would be significant in human and economic terms.

(13) Tobacco use is the foremost preventable cause of premature death in America. It causes over 400,000 deaths in the United States each year, and approximately 8,600,000 Americans have chronic illnesses related to smoking.

....

(29) It is in the public interest for Congress to adopt legislation to address the public health crisis created by actions of the tobacco industry.

....

(33) Tobacco dependence is a chronic disease, one that typically requires repeated interventions to achieve long-term or permanent abstinence.

(34) Because the only known safe alternative to smoking is cessation, interventions should target all smokers to help them quit completely.

....

(36) It is essential that the Food and Drug Administration review products sold or distributed for use to reduce risks or exposures associated with tobacco products and that it be empowered to review any advertising and labeling for such products. It is also essential that manufacturers, prior to marketing such products, be required to demonstrate that such products will meet a series of rigorous criteria, and will benefit the health of the population as a whole, taking into account both users of tobacco products and persons who do not currently use tobacco products.

....

---

Congress also included an express statement of purpose in the TCA:

## Tobacco Control Act: Statement of Purpose

123 Stat. 1776, 1781 (2009)

SEC. 3. PURPOSE.

The purposes of [the TCA] are—

(1) to provide authority to the Food and Drug Administration to regulate tobacco products under the [FFDCA], by recognizing it as the primary Federal regulatory authority with respect to the manufacture, marketing, and distribution of tobacco products as provided for in this division;

(2) to ensure that the Food and Drug Administration has the authority to address issues of particular concern to public health officials, especially the use of tobacco by young people and dependence on tobacco;

(3) to authorize the Food and Drug Administration to set national standards controlling the manufacture of tobacco products and the identity, public disclosure, and amount of ingredients used in such products;

(4) to provide new and flexible enforcement authority to ensure that there is effective oversight of the tobacco industry's efforts to develop, introduce, and promote less harmful tobacco products;

(5) to vest the Food and Drug Administration with the authority to regulate the levels of tar, nicotine, and other harmful components of tobacco products;

(6) in order to ensure that consumers are better informed, to require tobacco product manufacturers to disclose research which has not previously been made available, as well as research generated in the future, relating to the health and dependency effects or safety of tobacco products;

(7) to continue to permit the sale of tobacco products to adults in conjunction with measures to ensure that they are not sold or accessible to underage purchasers;

(8) to impose appropriate regulatory controls on the tobacco industry;

(9) to promote cessation to reduce disease risk and the social costs associated with tobacco-related diseases; and

(10) to strengthen legislation against illicit trade in tobacco products.

## 1. Basic Statutory and Regulatory Provisions

Please read (or review) the following excerpts in the statutory supplement:

- FFDCA § 201. Definitions; generally. *Subsection (rr) only.*
- FFDCA § 900. Definitions. *Subsections (1)–(4), (11)–(12), (15), and (17)–(18) only.*
- FFDCA § 901. FDA authority over tobacco products.
- FFDCA § 902. Adulterated tobacco product.
- FFDCA § 903. Misbranded tobacco products.
- 21 C.F.R. Part 1100. Tobacco products subject to FDA authority (the "Tobacco Deeming Rule").
- 21 C.F.R. Part 1140. Cigarettes, smokeless tobacco, and covered tobacco products.

FFDCA § 201(rr) is the statutory definition of "tobacco product." FFDCA § 901 sets out the scope of FDA's authority over tobacco products. FFDCA § 902 is the tobacco-product adulteration provision and FFDCA § 903 is the tobacco-product misbranding provision. 21 C.F.R. Part 1100, discussed in more detail below, is the codified version of the Tobacco Deeming Rule. 21 C.F.R. Part 1140, also discussed further below, sets out restrictions on the sale and distribution of tobacco products.

## 2. Types of Tobacco Products Subject to FDA Authority

Under the FFDCA, FDA authority applies—without any need for further action by FDA—to four types of tobacco products. These are "cigarettes, cigarette tobacco, roll-your-own tobacco, and smokeless tobacco." FFDCA § 901(b). The TCA also authorizes FDA to extend its authority to "any other tobacco products that the Secretary by regulation deems to be subject to this chapter." FFDCA § 901(b).

FDA exercised this deeming authority expansively in 2016. Through notice-and-comment rulemaking, FDA chose to "deem[] all . . . products meeting the definition of tobacco product under section 201(rr) of the [FFDCA], except accessories of such other tobacco products" to be subject to its authority. 2016-05-10 FDA Final Rule, *Deeming Tobacco Products to Be Subject to the Federal Food, Drug, and Cosmetic Act, as Amended by the Family Smoking Prevention and Tobacco Control Act*, 81 Fed. Reg. 28,973 (May 10, 2016) [hereinafter Tobacco Deeming Rule (2016)].[1]

The Tobacco Deeming Rule is the basis for FDA's regulation of tobacco products beyond the four types expressly subjected to FDA authority by FFDCA § 901(b). Several sections of this rule will be excerpted in the latter portions of this chapter.

## 3. Developing a Regulatory Regime: Non-Electronic Tobacco Products

### *a. Reducing Use by Children and Adolescents*

As part of its unsuccessful 1990s effort to regulate cigarettes and smokeless tobacco as drug delivery devices, FDA promulgated a rule restricting distribution of tobacco products. The goal of this rule was to impose restrictions that would reduce the use of tobacco products by children and adolescents. This rule could not be implemented after the U.S. Supreme Court's *Brown & Williamson* decision

1. If you are interested in policy issues relating to tobacco products, the full Tobacco Deeming Rule is essential reading. In the rule's long and detailed preamble, FDA responds to extensive comments submitted by both proponents and opponents of most aspects of FDA's earlier proposed rule. FDA's responses explain the reasons for the agency's decision on each major issue in some detail. They also provide some hints about FDA's thinking, at that time, about regulatory decisions it might make in the future. More generally, the Tobacco Deeming Rule is an excellent example of what notice-and-comment rulemaking currently looks like on a major regulatory issue. Accordingly, it would also be excellent reading if you are interested in administrative law more generally.

(excerpted earlier in this chapter) concluded that FDA could not assert authority over cigarettes and smokeless tobacco as combination products.

Once the TCA granted FDA authority over tobacco products, the *Brown & Williamson* decision no longer prevented FDA from restricting the sale of tobacco products. This gave Congress multiple options to address, in the remainder of the TCA, how to approach restrictions on sale and distribution of cigarettes and smokeless tobacco. These options included imposing those restrictions by statute, directing FDA to engage in new rulemaking, or directing FDA to re-promulgate its earlier rule. Congress chose the third option. Section 102 of the TCA explicitly directed FDA to re-promulgate its earlier rule (with certain relatively minor changes set out in the TCA). The resulting rule, which promulgated 21 C.F.R. Part 1140, is excerpted immediately below.

## 2010-03-19 FDA Final Rule, Regulations Restricting the Sale and Distribution of Cigarettes and Smokeless Tobacco to Protect Children and Adolescents

75 Fed. Reg. 13,225

The Food and Drug Administration (FDA) is reissuing a final rule restricting the sale, distribution, and use of cigarettes and smokeless tobacco. As required by the Family Smoking Prevention and Tobacco Control Act (Tobacco Control Act), FDA is issuing a final rule that is identical to the provisions of the final rule on cigarettes and smokeless tobacco published by FDA in 1996, with certain required exceptions. The rule prohibits the sale of cigarettes and smokeless tobacco to individuals under the age of 18 and imposes specific marketing, labeling, and advertising requirements. . . .

The Tobacco Control Act was enacted on June 22, 2009, amending the [FFDCA] (act) and providing FDA with the authority to regulate tobacco products. Section 102 of the Tobacco Control Act requires FDA to publish a final rule regarding cigarettes and smokeless tobacco identical in its provisions to the regulation issued by FDA in 1996 (61 FR 44396, August 28, 1996) (1996 final rule), with certain specified exceptions.

In enacting the Tobacco Control Act, Congress made extensive legislative findings regarding the lethal and addictive nature of tobacco products, including that tobacco use is the foremost preventable cause of premature death in the United States. . . .

As Congress recognized, the 1996 final rule was "the longest rulemaking proceeding in [FDA] history," with 700,000 comments received in the course of the rulemaking (Congressional Record, S6407, June 10, 2009, Statement of Senator Kennedy). "[I]t makes no sense to require FDA to reinvent the wheel by conducting a new multiyear rulemaking process on the same issues . . . . [T]his legislation will give the youth access and advertising restrictions already developed by FDA the force of law." Both the 1996 final rule and the 1995 proposed rule included extensive discussions of the scientific information available at that time and the final rule included FDA's responses to the more than 700,000 comments on the proposed rule.

....

Consistent with the requirements of section 102 of the Tobacco Control Act, this rule prohibits the sale of cigarettes and smokeless tobacco to any person under age 18 and imposes restrictions on marketing, labeling, and advertising. The rule requires retailers to verify a purchaser's age by photographic identification; prohibits free samples of cigarettes and prohibits free samples of smokeless tobacco, except in qualified adult-only facilities; prohibits the sale of cigarettes and smokeless tobacco products through vending machines and self-service displays, except in facilities where individuals under the age of 18 are not present or permitted at any time; limits the advertising and labeling to which children and adolescents are exposed to a black-and-white, text-only format; prohibits the sale or distribution of brand-identified promotional nontobacco items such as hats and tee shirts; and prohibits sponsorship of sporting and other events, teams, and entries in a brand name of a tobacco product, but permits such sponsorship in a corporate name.

....

In developing its proposed rule and the 1996 final rule, FDA carefully considered the scientific reviews and information available at that time. Although not required to do so by the Tobacco Control Act, FDA reviewed scientific information that has become available since publication of the 1996 final rule and found that, consistent with the evidence in the record for the 1996 final rule, the provisions continue to be overwhelmingly supported by extensive studies on continued youth access to tobacco products, the targeted marketing of tobacco products to youth, and the immense public health harm that results.

....

### *b. Substantial Equivalence*

The final rule excerpted further below sets out FDA's requirements for determining when a tobacco product is sufficiently new to require marketing authorization (in the form of a substantial equivalence determination).

Before reading the final rule, this excerpt from the proposed rule may be helpful:

## 2011-01-06 FDA Proposed Rule, Tobacco Products, Exemptions from Substantial Equivalence Requirements

76 Fed. Reg. 737

SUMMARY:

The Food and Drug Administration (FDA) is issuing this proposed rule to establish procedures for requesting an exemption from the substantial equivalence requirements of the Family Smoking Prevention and Tobacco Control Act (Tobacco

Control Act). The proposed rule would describe the process and statutory criteria for requesting an exemption and explain how FDA would review requests for exemptions. Once finalized, this regulation will satisfy the requirement in the Tobacco Control Act that FDA issue regulations implementing the exemption provision.

. . . .

SUPPLEMENTARY INFORMATION:

I. Background

The Tobacco Control Act . . . amends the [FFDCA] and provides FDA with the authority to regulate tobacco products. Among other things, the Tobacco Control Act requires that, before a new tobacco product may be introduced or delivered for introduction into interstate commerce, one of the following must occur: (1) A premarket application under [FFDCA §] 910(b) must be submitted to FDA, and FDA must issue an order finding that the new product may be introduced or delivered for introduction into interstate commerce under [FFDCA §] 910(c); or (2) a report under [FFDCA §] 905(j) demonstrating the new tobacco product's substantial equivalence to an appropriate predicate product (as defined in the [FFDCA]) must be submitted and FDA must issue an order finding the new product to be substantially equivalent to the predicate product and in compliance with the requirements of [FFDCA §] 910(a)(2). [FFDCA §] 905(j)(3) states that FDA may exempt tobacco products that are modified by adding or deleting a tobacco additive, or increasing or decreasing the quantity of an existing tobacco additive, from the requirement of demonstrating substantial equivalence if the Agency determines that: (1) Such modification would be a minor modification of a tobacco product that can be sold under the [FFDCA], (2) a report demonstrating substantial equivalence is not necessary to ensure that permitting the product to be marketed would be appropriate for the protection of the public health, and (3) an exemption is otherwise appropriate. [FFDCA §] 905(j)(3)(B) requires FDA to issue regulations implementing this provision by July 1, 2011.

"Additive" is defined at [FFDCA §] 900(1), as "any substance the intended use of which results or may reasonably be expected to result, directly or indirectly, in its becoming a component or otherwise affecting the characteristic of any tobacco product (including any substances intended for use as a flavoring or coloring or in producing, manufacturing, packing, processing, preparing, treating, packaging, transporting, or holding), except that such term does not include tobacco or a pesticide chemical residue in or on raw tobacco or a pesticide chemical" ([FFDCA § 906](1)).

The proposed rule, if finalized, would establish a pathway for manufacturers, including importers, to request exemptions from the substantial equivalence requirements of the Tobacco Control Act. It would not establish categories of minor modifications, or identify specific modifications, that meet the statutory criteria for exemptions. As FDA acquires more information about the additives in tobacco products from which to establish such categorical exemptions, it may issue additional regulations or guidance. FDA requests comment on how best to establish categories for these exemptions.

A manufacturer who obtains an exemption under the procedures of this proposed rule is also required to report to FDA under [FFDCA §] 905(j)(1)(A)(ii) (this requirement is not addressed in this proposed rule). [FFDCA §] 905(j)(1)(A)(ii) requires the manufacturer to report at least 90 days prior to introducing or delivering for introduction into interstate commerce the tobacco product that is the subject of the exemption, the basis for the manufacturer's determination that "the tobacco product is modified within the meaning of [section 905(j)(3)], the modifications are to a product that is commercially marketed and in compliance with the requirements of this Act, and all of the modifications are covered by exemptions granted by FDA pursuant to [[FFDCA §] 905(j)(3)]" (section 905(j)(1)(A)(ii) of the [FFDCA]). In addition, this submission must describe "action taken by [the applicant] to comply with the requirements under [FFDCA §] 907 that are applicable to the tobacco product" (section 905(j)(1)(B) of the [FFDCA]).

. . . .

---

In its July 5, 2011 Final Rule (excerpted immediately below), FDA made some changes to the proposed rule (excerpted immediately above). However, these did not affect the explanatory language excerpted above.

## 2011-07-05 FDA Final Rule, Tobacco Products, Exemptions from Substantial Equivalence Requirements

76 Fed. Reg. 38,961

SUMMARY:

The Food and Drug Administration (FDA) is issuing this final rule to establish procedures for requesting an exemption from the substantial equivalence requirements of the Family Smoking Prevention and Tobacco Control Act (Tobacco Control Act). The final rule describes the process and statutory criteria for requesting an exemption and explains how FDA reviews requests for exemptions. This regulation satisfies the requirement in the Tobacco Control Act that FDA issue regulations implementing the exemption provision.

. . . .

SUPPLEMENTARY INFORMATION:

I. Introduction

. . . . This final rule establishes procedures for requesting an exemption under section [FFDCA §] 905(j)(3). . . . The final rule also addresses FDA's review of an exemption request and establishes procedures for rescinding an exemption. The final rule adds these requirements at § 1107.1

The [FFDCA] requires manufacturers to obtain an order under [FFDCA §] 910(c)(1)(A)(i) before they may introduce a new tobacco product into interstate commerce unless either: (1) FDA has issued an order finding the new tobacco product to be substantially equivalent to an appropriate predicate tobacco product and in compliance with the requirements of the [FFDCA] or (2) the tobacco product is exempt from the requirements related to substantial equivalence under a regulation issued under [FFDCA §] 905(j)(3) (see also [FFDCA §] 910(a)(2)(A). This final rule is issued under [FFDCA §] 905(j)(3)(B), which requires that FDA issue regulations to implement the provision on exemptions from the substantial equivalence requirements of the Tobacco Control Act by July 1, 2011. [FFDCA §] 905(j)(3)(A) provides that FDA may exempt from the requirements relating to the demonstration of substantial equivalence, tobacco products that are modified by adding or deleting a tobacco additive, or by increasing or decreasing the quantity of an existing tobacco additive, if FDA determines that: (1) The modification would be a minor modification of a tobacco product that can be sold under the [FFDCA]; (2) a substantial equivalence report is not necessary to ensure that permitting the tobacco product to be marketed would be appropriate for protection of the public health; and (3) an exemption is otherwise appropriate.

. . . .

### c. *The Tobacco Deeming Rule*

As noted earlier in this chapter, the Tobacco Deeming Rule is the basis for FDA's regulation of tobacco products beyond the four types expressly subjected to FDA authority by FFDCA § 901(b) ("cigarettes, cigarette tobacco, roll-your-own tobacco, and smokeless tobacco"). In the excerpt immediately below, FDA relies on additional language in FFDCA § 901(b) to extend its authority to nearly all products meeting the FFDCA § 201(rr) definition of "tobacco product."

The relevant language from 901(b) provides that FFDCA Chapter 9 "shall apply to . . . any other tobacco products that [FDA] by regulation deems to be subject to this chapter." Recall now the "tobacco product" definition in FFDCA § 201(rr). FFDCA § 201(rr) defined "tobacco product" as "means any product made or derived from tobacco that is intended for human consumption, including any component, part, or accessory of a tobacco product." The Tobacco Deeming Rule deems all tobacco products, all components and parts of tobacco products, and almost all accessories of tobacco products to be subject to FDA regulation. Of the products potentially covered by FFDCA § 201(rr), it excludes only a narrowly defined subset of "accessories" set out in 21 C.F.R. § 1000.3.

The core portion of the preamble to the Tobacco Deeming Rule, as it applies to tobacco products generally, is set out immediately below. Later we will look at other portions of this rule relevant to electronic nicotine delivery systems (ENDS).

## 2016-05-10 FDA Final Rule, Deeming Tobacco Products to Be Subject to the Federal Food, Drug, and Cosmetic Act, as Amended by the Family Smoking Prevention and Tobacco Control Act

81 Fed. Reg. 28,974

SUMMARY:

The Food and Drug Administration (FDA) is issuing this final rule to deem products meeting the statutory definition of "tobacco product," except accessories of the newly deemed tobacco products, to be subject to the [FFDCA]. The Tobacco Control Act provides FDA authority to regulate cigarettes, cigarette tobacco, roll-your-own tobacco, smokeless tobacco, and any other tobacco products that the Agency by regulation deems to be subject to the law. With this final rule, FDA is extending the Agency's "tobacco product" authorities in the [FFDCA] to all other categories of products that meet the statutory definition of "tobacco product" in the [FFDCA], except accessories of such newly deemed tobacco products. This final rule also prohibits the sale of "covered tobacco products" to individuals under the age of 18 and requires the display of health warnings on cigarette tobacco, roll-your own tobacco, and covered tobacco product packages and in advertisements. FDA is taking this action to reduce the death and disease from tobacco products. In accordance with the Tobacco Control Act, we consider and intend the extension of our authorities over tobacco products and the various requirements and prohibitions established by this rule to be severable.

. . . .

*Purpose of the Rule*

Cigarettes, cigarette tobacco, roll-your-own tobacco, and smokeless tobacco were immediately covered by FDA's tobacco product authorities in chapter IX of the [FFDCA] when the Tobacco Control Act went into effect. For other kinds of tobacco products, the statute authorizes FDA to issue regulations "deeming" them to be subject to such authorities. Consistent with the statute, once a tobacco product is deemed, FDA may put in place "restrictions on the sale and distribution of a tobacco product," including age-related access restrictions and advertising and promotion restrictions, if FDA determines the restrictions are appropriate for the protection of the public health. This final rule has two purposes: (1) To deem all products that meet the definition of "tobacco product" under the law, except accessories of a newly deemed tobacco product, and subject them to the tobacco control authorities in chapter IX of the [FFDCA] and FDA's implementing regulations; and (2) to establish specific restrictions that are appropriate for the protection of the public health for the newly deemed tobacco products. In accordance with section 5 of the Tobacco Control Act, we consider and intend the extension of our authorities over tobacco products and the various requirements and prohibitions established by this rule to be severable.

FDA is taking this action to reduce the death and disease from tobacco products. Deeming all "tobacco products" (including components and parts but excluding accessories of the newly deemed products) to be subject to the [FFDCA] will result in significant benefits for the public health. The final rule defines "component or part" and "accessory" to provide additional clarity as to which products are subject to FDA's tobacco product authority. With respect to these definitions, FDA notes that "component" and "part" are separate and distinct terms within chapter IX of the [FFDCA]. However, for purposes of this final rule, FDA is using the terms "component" and "part" interchangeably and without emphasizing the distinction between the terms. FDA may clarify the distinctions between 'component' and 'part' in the future. Specifically, "Component or Part" means "any software or assembly of materials intended or reasonably expected: (1) To alter or affect the tobacco product's performance, composition, constituents or characteristics; or (2) to be used with or for the human consumption of a tobacco product. The term excludes anything that is an accessory of a tobacco product." Components and parts of the newly deemed tobacco products, but not their related accessories, are included in the scope of this final rule. The following is a nonexhaustive list of examples of components and parts used with electronic nicotine delivery systems (ENDS) (including e-cigarettes): E-liquids; atomizers; batteries (with or without variable voltage); cartomizers (atomizer plus replaceable fluid-filled cartridge); digital display/lights to adjust settings; clearomisers, tank systems, flavors, vials that contain e-liquids, and programmable software. Similarly, the following is a nonexhaustive list of examples of components and parts used with waterpipe tobacco: Flavor enhancers and the vials in which they are contained; hose cooling attachments; water filtration base additives (including those which are flavored); flavored waterpipe tobacco charcoals and the wrappers or boxes that contain the charcoals; and bowls, valves, hoses, and heads.

FDA is defining "accessory" to mean "any product that is intended or reasonably expected to be used with or for the human consumption of a tobacco product; does not contain tobacco and is not made or derived from tobacco; and meets either of the following: (1) Is not intended or reasonably expected to affect or alter the performance, composition, constituents, or characteristics of a tobacco product or (2) is intended or reasonably expected to affect or maintain the performance, composition, constituents, or characteristics of a tobacco product but (i) solely controls moisture and/or temperature of a stored product or (ii) solely provides an external heat source to initiate but not maintain combustion of a tobacco product." Examples of accessories are ashtrays, spittoons, hookah tongs, cigar clips and stands and pipe pouches, because they do not contain tobacco, are not derived from tobacco, and do not affect or alter the performance, composition, constituents, or characteristics of a tobacco product. Examples of accessories also include humidors or refrigerators that solely control the moisture and/or temperature of a stored product and conventional matches and lighters that solely provide an external heat source to initiate but not maintain combustion of a tobacco product. An electric heater or charcoal used for prolonged heating of waterpipe tobacco is not an accessory because it is maintaining the combustion of the tobacco. Accessories of newly deemed tobacco products are not included within the scope of this final rule, although accessories of cigarettes, cigarette tobacco, roll-your-own tobacco, and smokeless tobacco remain subject to FDA's tobacco product authorities. FDA is not regulating accessories of newly deemed tobacco products because accessories, unlike components or parts, are expected to have little direct impact on the public health.

This final deeming rule affords FDA additional tools to reduce the number of illnesses and premature deaths associated with tobacco product use. For example, FDA will be able to obtain critical information regarding the health risks of newly deemed tobacco products, including information derived from ingredient listing submissions and reporting of harmful and potentially harmful constituents (HPHCs) required under the [FFDCA]. As of the effective date, persons who own or operate a domestic establishment engaged in the manufacture, preparation, compounding, or processing of tobacco products (hereinafter, "manufacturing establishments") will be subject to the registration requirements. FDA will thus receive information on the location and number of manufacturing establishments, which will allow the Agency to establish effective compliance programs. In addition, this rule authorizes FDA to take enforcement action against manufacturers who sell and distribute products with unsubstantiated modified risk tobacco product (MRTP) claims, or false or misleading claims on their labeling or advertising, thus allowing for better-informed consumers and helping to prevent the use of misleading campaigns targeted to youth populations. It will also prevent from entering the market new tobacco products that are not appropriate for the protection of public health, are not substantially equivalent to a valid predicate product, or are not exempt from substantial equivalence (SE). Finally, the newly deemed tobacco products may be subject to future regulations that FDA determines are appropriate for the protection of public health.

### *Summary of the Major Provisions of the Regulatory Action*

The final rule has two main sections: (1) Deeming provisions and (2) additional provisions to protect public health.

*Deeming Provisions*—After thorough review of the comments and the scientific evidence, FDA has concluded that Option 1 (including all cigars, rather than a subset) more effectively protects the public health and, therefore, has made that the scope of the final rule. Accordingly, this final rule deems all products meeting the statutory definition of "tobacco product," except accessories of the newly deemed tobacco products, to be subject to FDA's tobacco product authorities under chapter IX of the [FFDCA]. Section 201(rr) of the [FFDCA], as amended by the Tobacco Control Act, defines the term "tobacco product," to mean "any product made or derived from tobacco that is intended for human consumption, including any component, part, or accessory of a tobacco product (except for raw materials other than tobacco used in manufacturing a component, part, or accessory of a tobacco product)" and does not mean "an article that is a drug under subsection (g)(1), a device under subsection (b), or a combination product described in section 353(g) of this title." Products that meet the statutory definition of "tobacco products" include currently marketed products such as dissolvables not already regulated by FDA, gels, waterpipe tobacco, ENDS (including e-cigarettes, e-hookah, e-cigars, vape pens, advanced refillable personal vaporizers, and electronic pipes), cigars, and pipe tobacco.

In addition, this final rule deems any additional current and future tobacco products that meet the statutory definition of "tobacco product," except accessories of such newly deemed products, to be subject to FDA's authorities under chapter IX of the [FFDCA]. For example, FDA envisions that there could be tobacco products developed in the future that provide nicotine delivery through means (e.g., via dermal absorption or intranasal spray) similar to currently marketed medicinal nicotine products, but which are not drugs or devices. These products would be "tobacco products" and subject to FDA's chapter IX authorities in accordance with this final deeming rule.

Upon the effective date of this final rule (i.e., 90 days from the date of publication), the newly deemed products will be subject to the same [FFDCA] provisions and relevant regulatory requirements to which cigarettes, cigarette tobacco, roll-your-own tobacco, and smokeless tobacco are subject, with respect to the following:

(1) Enforcement action against products determined to be adulterated or misbranded (other than enforcement actions based on lack of a marketing authorization during an applicable compliance period);

(2) Required submission of ingredient listing and reporting of HPHCs;

(3) Required registration of tobacco product manufacturing establishments and product listing;

(4) Prohibition against sale and distribution of products with modified risk descriptors (e.g., "light," "low," and "mild" descriptors) and claims unless FDA issues an order authorizing their marketing;

(5) Prohibition on the distribution of free samples (same as cigarettes); and

(6) Premarket review requirements.

These actions will improve the public health by affording FDA critical information regarding the health risks of such products; preventing new products from entering the market unless such marketing is appropriate for the protection of public health, the products are found substantially equivalent to a valid predicate product, or the products are found exempt from the SE requirements; and preventing the use of unsubstantiated modified risk claims, which may mislead consumers and lead them to initiate tobacco product use or to continue using tobacco when they would otherwise quit.

*Additional Provisions*—In addition to the provisions in the [FFDCA] and implementing regulations that apply automatically to the newly deemed products, FDA has the authority to invoke its other authorities under the Tobacco Control Act in regulating these products. At this time, under section 906(d) of the [FFDCA], FDA is establishing three restrictions for covered tobacco products: (1) Requirement for a minimum age of purchase; (2) requirement for health warnings for product packages and advertisements (which FDA is also applying to cigarette tobacco and roll-your-own tobacco); and (3) prohibition of vending machine sales of such products, unless the vending machine is located in a facility where the retailer ensures that individuals under 18 years of age are prohibited from entering at any time. The term "covered tobacco products" is defined as those products deemed to be subject to the [FFDCA] under section 1100.2 of title 21 of the Code of Federal Regulations (CFR), other than a component or part that is not made or derived from tobacco. We have slightly modified the definition of "covered tobacco products" from the notice of proposed rulemaking (NPRM) to clarify that components or parts that are "covered tobacco products" include not only those that contain tobacco or nicotine, but also those that contain any tobacco derivative (i.e., we have changed the NPRM definition, which excluded "any component or part of a tobacco product that does not contain nicotine or tobacco," to exclude "any component or part of a tobacco product that is not made or derived from tobacco" as stated in this final rule).

. . . .

*Compliance Policy for Premarket Review*—Manufacturers of newly deemed products that are "new tobacco products" as defined in section 910(a)(1) of the [FFDCA] will be required to obtain premarket authorization of their products through one of three pathways—SE., exemption from SE., or premarket tobacco product applications (sections 905 and 910 of the [FFDCA]). As stated in the NPRM, we understand that, for some newly deemed tobacco products, particularly novel products, there may not be appropriate predicate products that were on the market on February 15, 2007, to support a SE claim. Accordingly, in the NPRM, FDA contemplated a compliance period of 24 months after the effective date of the final rule for the submission of applications for all newly deemed, new tobacco products under all three marketing pathways—premarket tobacco applications (PMTAs), SE reports, and SE exemption requests.

FDA carefully considered numerous comments regarding the contemplated compliance period. Many comments expressed concern that newly deemed, new tobacco products would remain available and could continue to be marketed indefinitely without scientific review. Other comments expressed concern, and some submitted data, regarding the effect that flavors have on youth and young adult use of tobacco products. FDA also received comments and data regarding the potential for some net public health benefits that could accrue if flavored ENDS remain available. After carefully considering all of these comments, FDA here announces a revised compliance policy as well as the final rule. . . .

Taking into consideration all of the comments on the compliance period and flavors, we are establishing staggered compliance periods. This approach will enable FDA to balance concerns regarding the extended availability of all newly deemed, new tobacco products without scientific review, concerns regarding flavored tobacco products' appeal to youth, and emerging evidence that some adults may potentially use certain flavored tobacco products to transition away from combusted tobacco use....

According to this revised compliance policy, for newly deemed products that are on the market on the effective date of this final rule and were not on the market on February 15, 2007, FDA is providing a 12-month initial compliance period for manufacturers to submit (and FDA to receive) an SE exemption request, an 18-month initial compliance period for manufacturers to submit (and FDA to receive) SE applications, and a 24-month initial compliance period for manufacturers to submit (and FDA to receive) a PMTA.

....

Regarding concerns as to the inability to use the SE pathway for certain products, FDA notes that an applicant may use as a predicate any tobacco product commercially marketed in the United States as of February 15, 2007, or previously found substantially equivalent (note that we interpret the phrase "as of" February 15, 2007, as meaning that the tobacco product was commercially marketed (other than exclusively in test markets) in the United States on February 15, 2007. If your tobacco product had been commercially marketed in the United States before February 15, 2007, but was not commercially marketed on that date, it is not a grandfathered product and may not be commercially marketed unless you obtain a marketing authorization under section 910 of the [FFDCA]). This may possibly include a predicate that is in a different category or subcategory than the new product that is the subject of the SE report. While FDA currently does not have a policy that limits comparisons to the same category, we do see cross-category comparisons as more challenging for an applicant and we may express limitations on such comparisons in the future, if they become warranted as we gain experience regulating newly deemed products. FDA also is continuing to research e-cigarettes, other ENDS, and heated cigarette products that likely were on the market "as of" (i.e., on) February 15, 2007. Additionally, FDA has determined that some e-cigarettes and other ENDS were manufactured in 2006 and commercially marketed in the United States in early 2007. In particular, we have identified an ENDS product that may have been on the market on February 15, 2007. This product may possibly be able to serve as a valid predicate for purposes of the SE pathway. The burden of demonstrating that a valid predicate exists rests with the manufacturer submitting a SE report.... Regardless of the predicate selected for comparison, manufacturers are responsible for providing scientific data adequate to demonstrate that, in the case of an SE report, the characteristics of the new product are the same as the predicate or, if the characteristics are different, that these differences do not cause the new product to raise different questions of public health....

*Vape Establishments Acting as Manufacturers*—Several comments asked FDA to clarify whether e-cigarette retail stores and vape establishments are considered "tobacco product manufacturers" under the [FFDCA]. In response, FDA has explained that establishments that mix or prepare e-liquids or create or modify aerosolizing apparatus for direct sale to consumers are tobacco product manufacturers under the definition set forth in the [FFDCA] and, accordingly, are subject to the same legal requirements that apply to other tobacco product manufacturers.

. . . .

## 4. Developing a Regulatory Regime: Electronic Nicotine Delivery Systems (ENDS)

FDA is still in the early stages of developing its approach to regulating ENDS products. To give you a sense of the way this regulatory program is developing, three excerpts are included below. The first two excerpts come from the Tobacco Deeming Rule. The first addresses the decision to deem ENDS products; the second addresses the effect of that deeming decision on vape shops. The third excerpt is a press release issued by FDA in late 2019 following a series of sudden deaths by individuals using ENDS products.

### *a. The Decision to Deem ENDS Products*

We looked generally at the Tobacco Deeming Rule earlier in this chapter. The excerpt immediately below, also from the Tobacco Deeming Rule, addresses the specific decision to deem ENDS products to be subject to regulation under the FFDCA.

### 2016-05-10 FDA Final Rule, Deeming Tobacco Products to Be Subject to the Federal Food, Drug, and Cosmetic Act, as Amended by the Family Smoking Prevention and Tobacco Control Act

81 Fed. Reg. 28,974

. . . .

#### Regulation of Electronic Nicotine Delivery Systems (Including E-Cigarettes) and the Continuum of Nicotine-Delivering Products

In the preamble to the NPRM, FDA noted that there are distinctions in the health risks presented by various nicotine-delivering products. FDA requested comment as to how e-cigarettes should be regulated based on this continuum of risk. We explained that some studies have revealed the existence of toxicants in both the e-cigarette liquid and the exhaled aerosol of some e-cigarettes but that we do not have sufficient data to determine what effects e-cigarettes have on public health at the population level. We also noted that some individuals report using e-cigarettes to successfully quit smoking, but we expressed concerns about dual use of e-cigarettes and combusted tobacco products and the possibility that flavored e-liquids are leading children to initiate tobacco use with e-cigarettes.

In this final rule, FDA clarifies that although there are many types of ENDS (including e-cigarettes, e-cigars, e-hookah, vape pens, personal vaporizers, and electronic pipes), all are subject to FDA's chapter IX authorities with this final deeming rule. Comments regarding e-cigarettes, including comments on how the products should be regulated in light of this continuum, and FDA's responses are discussed in the following sections.

. . . .

[E]lectronic nicotine delivery systems or ENDS are sold under several different names including e-cigarettes, e-cigars, e-hookah, vape pens, personal vaporizers, and electronic pipes. These products all meet the definition of "tobacco product" and, therefore, under this rule, all are subject to FDA's tobacco control authorities, regardless of a novel name or heating source. In addition, the definition of tobacco product includes components and parts (the objects intended or reasonably expected to be used with or for the human consumption of a tobacco product that are not accessories) (e.g., e-liquids, tanks, cartridges, pods, wicks, atomizers), which, under this rule, have also been deemed to be subject to FDA's authority under chapter IX of the [FFDCA].

. . . .

FDA agrees with comments stating that the prevalence of use of the newly deemed tobacco products has been increasing, which further substantiates the need for this final rule. FDA remains concerned about the rise in use of newly deemed products by youth and young adults, particularly the increase in use of ENDS. As we stated in the NPRM and throughout this document, long-term studies are not yet available to determine whether these youth and young adults are only experimenting with tobacco use, becoming established ENDS users or dual users, or transitioning to combusted products. In addition, there is not sufficient evidence to conclude that youth and young adults are using ENDS as a means to quit smoking.

. . . .

FDA is concerned that the growth in ENDS use, particularly among youth and young adults, could lead to the re-normalization of cigarette smoking. The Surgeon General recognized that adolescents are particularly vulnerable to visual cues to smoke and to social norms, making this an even greater concern. FDA believes that subjecting ENDS to its tobacco control authorities, and requiring compliance with the various statutory and regulatory requirements (e.g., ingredient listing and others), will help to address the common misunderstanding that these products are safe to use. . . .

### *b. The Implications of the ENDS Deeming Decision for Vape Shops*

The excerpt immediately above focused on FDA's decision to deem vaping products to be subject to FDA authority. The excerpt immediately below, also from the Tobacco Deeming Rule, focuses on the implications of that deeming decision for vape shops. Perhaps the most significant implication is that, following FDA's deeming decision, most vape shops thereby became "tobacco product manufacturer[s]" within the meaning of FFDCA § 900(20).

## 2016-05-10 FDA Final Rule, Deeming Tobacco Products to Be Subject to the Federal Food, Drug, and Cosmetic Act, as Amended by the Family Smoking Prevention and Tobacco Control Act

81 Fed. Reg. 28,974

. . . .

### Effect of Deeming Rule on Vape Shop Manufacturers

Some comments requested clarification regarding the regulatory status of an ENDS retail establishment that sells e-liquids (sometimes known as a vape shop). Such establishments sell a variety of products including ENDS, replacement pieces, hardware, custom mixed e-liquids, and other related accessories.

If an establishment mixes or prepares e-liquids or creates or modifies aerosolizing apparatus for direct sale to consumers for use in ENDS, the establishment fits within the definition of "tobacco product manufacturer" in section 900(20) of the [FFDCA] and the combinations it mixes and/or prepares are new tobacco products within the meaning of section 910(a)(1). . . . As discussed in the Analysis of Impacts, FDA expects that most vape shops will stop mixing e-liquids (and preparing other new tobacco products) to avoid being "manufacturers" under the Tobacco Control Act.

The definition of "tobacco product manufacturer" in section 900(20) includes "any person, including any repacker or relabeler, who manufactures, fabricates, assembles, processes, or labels a tobacco product." Additionally, for purposes of section 905, the [FFDCA] defines "manufacturing, preparation, compounding, or processing" to include "repackaging, or otherwise changing the container, wrapper or labeling of any tobacco product package from the original place of manufacture to the person who makes the final delivery or sale to the ultimate consumer or user." Section 910(a)(1) defines a "new tobacco product" as "any tobacco product (including those products in test markets) that was not commercially marketed in the United States as of February 15, 2007; or any modification (including a change in design, any component, any part, or any constituent, including a smoke constituent, or in the content, delivery or form of nicotine, or any other additive or ingredient) of a tobacco product where the modified product was commercially marketed in the United States after February 15, 2007." Therefore, establishments engaged in mixing or preparing e-liquids or creating or modifying aerosolizing apparatus for direct sale to consumers for use in ENDS are tobacco product manufacturers and, consequently, are subject to all of the statutory and regulatory requirements applicable to manufacturers.

The statute authorizes FDA to regulate the manufacture of all new products, including those manufactured at the retail level. This is important to FDA's ability to protect the public health since products manufactured at the retail level pose many of the same public health risks as those manufactured upstream and possibly additional risks related to the lack of standard manufacturing practices and controls. The introduction of statutory controls and oversight into a historically unregulated market inevitably will lead to some market change and consolidation. FDA recognizes that, with the implementation of this final rule, vape shops that meet the definition of tobacco product manufacturer may cease engaging in manufacturing activities rather than comply with requirements for manufacturers under this final rule. However, FDA notes that such entities will have the option to continue operating solely as retailers, as some vape shops currently do. In addition, as noted earlier, FDA believes that this policy (and the deeming rule as a whole) will not stifle innovation but could, instead, encourage it. Over time, FDA expects that its premarket review authorities will spur creative evolution and help to create a market where available products present a lower risk of user and population harm, provide a more consistent delivery under varying conditions of use, are less likely to lead to initiation of tobacco use, and/or are easier to quit. In recent years, ENDS products have proliferated in the absence of regulation, in some cases resulting in a lack of quality control and consistency, consumer confusion and even availability of acutely toxic products. In this context, we expect that changes in the market in response to regulation will have significant benefits for public health and will be a net benefit overall.

As the ENDS market continues to evolve, it is important that FDA exercise its authority to oversee all establishments engaged in manufacturing activities and their products, in order to protect consumers and to carry out the public health objectives of the Tobacco Control Act.

A. Premarket Requirements (Sections 905 and 910)

As stated throughout the document, manufacturers of newly deemed products that are not grandfathered will be required to obtain premarket authorization of their products through one of three pathways—PMTA, SE or SE exemption (sections 905 and 910 of the [FFDCA]). Therefore, ENDS retailers engaged in mixing or preparing e-liquids or creating or modifying aerosolizing apparatus will be required to obtain premarket authorization for each non-grandfathered product that they prepare for sale or distribution to consumers. However, under the compliance policy laid out in section V.A, FDA does not intend to enforce, during specified compliance periods, the premarket review requirements including for ENDS retailers that mix or prepare the same e-liquids they have been preparing and offering for sale as of the effective date . . . or that create or modify aerosolizing apparatus resulting in the same products they have been creating as of the effective date. An initial compliance period, the length of which is dependent on the type of application to be submitted, is intended to provide additional time to prepare and submit premarket applications. In addition, for the 12 months following this initial compliance period, FDA intends to continue the compliance policy and does not intend to enforce the premarket review requirements if the firm has a pending submission. This means that, during this 12-month continued compliance period of FDA review, FDA expects that ENDS retailers of any kind will sell only those products that are (1) grandfathered; (2) authorized by FDA; or (3) tobacco products for which the ENDS retailer or another (upstream) manufacturer has submitted a marketing application/submission to FDA during the initial compliance period. (For PMTAs, the initial compliance period to submit is 24 months after the final rule effective date.)

FDA expects that this 12-month continued compliance period of FDA review will benefit manufacturers and retailers of newly deemed products, including ENDS retailers, since upstream manufacturers that submit applications will have a significant incentive to make retailers aware of their pending applications/submissions. Specifically, we expect that upstream manufacturer suppliers will inform ENDS retailers selling their products whether the upstream manufacturer has submitted a premarket application for such e-liquids and other ENDS products within the initial compliance period such that the retailers can benefit from the continued compliance period while FDA reviews such applications. FDA expects that manufacturers will have an incentive to make retailers aware of which products are the subject of applications, which will enable retailers to know whether a marketing application has been submitted and whether FDA has acted on an application. In addition, retailers may contact suppliers for relevant product information. Therefore, after 36 months from the effective date (i.e., at the end of the initial compliance period plus 12-month continued compliance period), FDA expects that all ENDS retailers will sell only those products that are either grandfathered or for which they have, or an upstream supplier has, received premarket authorization.

. . . .

In general, the [FFDCA] provides three pathways that manufacturers may use to seek market authorization for a new product: The premarket tobacco product application pathway, the SE pathway, and the exemption from SE pathway. FDA anticipates that most manufacturers of e-liquids and apparatus components/complete delivery systems will seek authorization through the PMTA pathway. To obtain marketing authorization under the PMTA pathway, manufacturers are required to establish, among other things, that permitting their product to be marketed would be appropriate for the protection of the public health. In establishing this, manufacturers should take into account, and FDA will consider, the ways in which the new product is likely to be used. For example, PMTAs for these products should contain information on whether the product is likely to be used alone or together with other legally marketed tobacco products (such as available delivery systems), as well as the type and range of the other products with which it is likely to be used.

While the statutory standard will apply to all products for which a PMTA is filed, FDA expects that different classes of products may have differing likelihoods of success in meeting the standard, by virtue of their expected use. As stated previously, to meet the statutory standard, PMTAs should contain information on whether a product is likely to be used alone or together with other legally marketed products and the public health implications of those likely uses. FDA has issued a draft guidance on PMTAs for ENDS, published concurrently with this final rule, which, when finalized, will explain FDA's current thinking regarding some appropriate means of addressing the premarket authorization requirements for newly deemed e-liquids and hardware/apparatus components. FDA intends to act as expeditiously as possible with respect to all new applications, while ensuring that statutory standards are met.

To reduce research burdens and increase efficiency for ENDS retail establishments that file applications, FDA suggests that ENDS retail establishments use master files whenever possible. By obtaining permission from a master file holder, manufacturers could reference extensive ingredients lists and constituent testing that they otherwise would be required to perform themselves for marketing authorization. To facilitate this process, elsewhere in this issue of the Federal Register, FDA is announcing the availability of a final guidance to provide information on how to establish and reference a TPMF [(Tobacco Product Master File)]. This information will help applicants of newly deemed products prepare premarket and other regulatory submissions because they can reference information in TPMFs rather than develop the information on their own.

Given the anticipated availability and use of master files. . . , which allow[] manufacturers to rely on the data and analysis submitted to FDA by separate entities, FDA anticipates that manufacturers will, over time, benefit from significantly increased efficiencies and reduced costs for complying with the statute. Such a system prevents and reduces duplication and allows for manufacturer reliance on confidential or sensitive non-public information while maintaining its confidentiality, thus saving time and reducing burdens for multiple manufacturers. Because of the nature of upstream supply of many components for ENDS products, especially e-liquids, FDA anticipates that commercial incentives will be sufficient to drive manufacturer reliance on the system of master files. We also note that at present, FDA understands that, based on the Agency's review of publicly available information . . . , the number of entities engaged in upstream production of liquid nicotine and flavors specifically developed for use with e-liquids is small, in the range of seven to thirteen entities. . . . Given the current marketplace, the master file system is likely to prove widely appealing and widely utilized by the ENDS industry, reducing burden significantly.

In addition, FDA intends to open public dockets for uniquely identified compounds likely to be used in an e-liquid product, such as propylene glycol, glycerin, nicotine, colorants, and flavoring agents. FDA intends to invite stakeholders to submit to the docket information regarding specific compounds, including data, studies, or other files, such as data on individual health effects of inhalation exposure, animal study data examining exposure to varying levels of compounds within e-liquids, or testing the impact of temperature on changes to the aerosol constituents. This information could then be used to help support applications for premarket review, for example, generating information on HPHCs in ENDS products that is then submitted as part of a PMTA.

B. Ingredient Listing and HPHC Requirements (Section 904 and 915)

As of the effective date of this rule, the ingredient listing requirements of section 904 of the [FFDCA] will apply to manufacturers of the newly deemed products, including ENDS retail establishments that mix or prepare e-liquids or create or modify aerosolizing apparatus for sale or distribution. At this time, FDA intends to limit enforcement to finished tobacco products. FDA does not at this time intend to enforce these requirements for manufacturers of components and parts of newly deemed products that are sold or distributed solely for further manufacturing into finished tobacco products. This means that FDA generally intends to enforce these requirements with respect to ENDS retail establishments that mix or prepare e-liquids or create or modify aerosolizing apparatus for sale or distribution directly to consumers but not to distributors who sell components for further manufacturing. However, if the upstream distributor submits an ingredient list for a particular product, FDA does not intend to enforce the ingredient listing requirement against an ENDS retailer with respect to that particular product. We note that FDA also intends to issue a guidance regarding HPHC reporting under section 904(a)(3), and later a testing regulation as required by section 915, with enough time for manufacturers to report given the 3-year compliance period for HPHC reporting. Section 904 (a)(3) requires the submission of a report listing all constituents, including smoke constituents, identified as harmful or potentially harmful (HPHC) by the Secretary. Section 915 requires the testing and reporting of the constituents, ingredients, and additives the Secretary determines should be tested to protect the public health. The section 915 testing and reporting requirements apply only after FDA issues a regulation implementing that section, which it has not yet done. Until these testing and reporting requirements have been established, newly deemed tobacco products (and currently regulated tobacco products) are not subject to the testing and reporting provisions found under section 915. As noted elsewhere in this document, FDA does not intend to enforce the reporting requirements under section 904(a)(3) for newly deemed products before the close of the 3-year compliance period, even if the HPHC guidance and the section 915 regulation are issued well in advance of that time.

C. Registration and Product Listing (Section 905)

Section 905 of the [FFDCA] requires every person who owns or operates an establishment engaged in the "manufacture, preparation, compounding, or processing of a tobacco product" to register its establishment with FDA and submit a listing of its tobacco products to the Agency. If an ENDS retail establishment engages in these activities, section 905 requires the establishment to register and list its products with FDA in accordance with this section. These requirements apply under the statute for all distinct products manufactured, and they enable FDA to assess the landscape of products manufactured by these entities. If ENDS retail establishments are mixing or preparing e-liquids or creating or modifying aerosolizing apparatus for direct sale to consumers, then they will have to list each e-liquid combination that they sell. It will be the responsibility of the ENDS retail establishment, as a manufacturer, to determine how many and which products they plan to manufacture. For shops that prepare an expansive array of custom mixes, with many gradations of flavor, nicotine strength or other characteristic, this would mean identifying, listing, and reporting ingredients for a large number of distinct products. In reality, however, we expect that such entities will elect to narrow the list of combinations they sell (with more limited distinctions in strength and flavor, etc.), since such a narrowing will allow them to continue providing custom products and a variety of options while simplifying their reporting. However, since the time and cost of listing each additional mixture is expected to be very low, the reduction will not necessarily be significant. In addition, any narrowing may reflect a reduction in products that are listed but are not actually sold.

. . . .

### c. THC Vaping

Under the Tobacco Deeming Rule, FDA asserted authority over many *components* and *accessories* of tobacco products. These components and accessories include many products that can be used, as a practical matter, for the consumption of either tobacco e-liquids or e-liquids containing other substances. In 2019, a number of severe injuries and deaths were associated with the use of ENDS products. After some investigation, FDA issued the press statement below.

Keep in mind, as you read this, that tetrahydrocannabinol (THC) remains a Schedule I controlled substance under federal law. As a Schedule I substance, it has "no currently accepted medical use in treatment in the United States." 21 U.S.C. § 812(b)(1)(B). Accordingly, it is regulated largely by the Drug Enforcement Administration rather than FDA. FDA's involvement in this investigation results from its role in regulating the components and accessories of tobacco products involved in THC vaping, rather than in regulating THC use itself.

## Press Release, FDA, Statement on Consumer Warning to Stop Using THC Vaping Products Amid Ongoing Investigation Into Lung Illnesses (Oct. 4, 2019)*

Over the past several weeks, the U.S. Food and Drug Administration has been working tirelessly along with the U.S. Centers for Disease Control and Prevention (CDC) and other federal, state and local partners to investigate the distressing incidents of severe lung injuries and deaths associated with the use of vaping products. The latest number of reported cases and deaths, released by the CDC yesterday, continues to underscore the need for us to gather critical information and provide consumers with actionable information to help best protect themselves and their loved ones.

This is why today, we're strengthening our message to the public in an updated consumer alert stating that they should not use vaping products containing tetrahydrocannabinol (THC), the primary psychoactive component of the cannabis plant.

---

* From https://www.fda.gov/news-events/press-announcements/statement-consumer-warning-stop-using-thc-vaping-products-amid-ongoing-investigation-lung-illnesses.

Additionally, consumers who choose to use any vaping products should not modify or add any substances such as THC or other oils to products purchased in stores and should not purchase any vaping products, including those containing THC, off the street or from other illicit channels.

This is a complex, ongoing and evolving investigation. In addition to our own analyses, we are also diligently reviewing published literature of third-party analyses of samples and data, which are beneficial to our ongoing investigation. At this time, the FDA does not have enough data to identify the cause, or causes, of the lung injuries in these cases. Additionally, while no one compound or ingredient has emerged as a singular culprit, we do know that THC is present in most of the samples being tested. Because of this, the agency believes it is prudent to stop using vaping products that contain THC or that have had any substances added to them, including those purchased from retail establishments. Simply put, inhaling harmful contaminants in the lungs could put a patient's health at risk and should be avoided.

For those who choose to continue the use of vaping products, particularly those containing THC, we urge you to monitor for symptoms and promptly seek medical attention if you have concerns about your health. We are also continuing to encourage the public to submit detailed reports of any unexpected tobacco- or vaping-related health or product issues to the FDA via the online Safety Reporting Portal. And, importantly, no youth or women who are pregnant should be using any vaping product, regardless of the substance.

This alert builds on initial recommendations the FDA issued several weeks ago and is based on new information we're continuing to learn from both patients and the samples that have been tested so far. For example, additional testing revealed that a majority of the hundreds of samples of vaping products tested by the states or by the FDA so far have been identified as containing THC. Additionally, according to recent findings, most of the patients impacted by these illnesses reported using THC-containing products, suggesting THC products are playing a role in these illnesses. That said, some patients have reported using both THC products and nicotine products, as well as a smaller number reporting using only nicotine products. Similarly, testing on the samples collected or received by the FDA shows a variety of products, or product components, with different ingredients or delivery systems making this investigation especially challenging.

Federal, state and local agencies will continue to work as quickly as possible to get to the bottom of what's causing people to become ill by following up with patients and doctors to collect important details about the products or substances involved, where they were purchased and how they were being used. In particular, the FDA's work to investigate the illnesses includes sample collections in coordination with states, sample analysis, criminal and civil investigations, and coordination with state and federal partners.

Although these cases present similarly in patients, it is not clear if they have a common cause, or if they have differing pathogenesis with similar presentation.

The investigation has not identified any specific substance or product that is linked to all cases. The FDA is using state-of-the-art methods to assess the presence of a broad range of chemicals, including nicotine, THC and other cannabinoids along with opioids, cutting agents/diluents and other additives, pesticides, poisons and toxins. To date, the agency has collected or received more than 440 samples from 18 states—and that number continues to grow. The FDA is working quickly and thoroughly in testing the samples, prioritizing those associated directly with patient illnesses. More than half of the vaping liquid products have undergone some form of evaluation, with additional testing on these and other samples continuing daily.

We are leaving no stone unturned in following all potential leads regarding any particular product, constituent or compound that may be at issue. In that spirit, the FDA's Office of Criminal Investigations (OCI) began parallel investigative efforts shortly after the emergence of the associated illnesses.

Our OCI agents are focused on identifying the products that are making people ill and following the supply chain to the source. We are not pursuing any enforcement actions associated with personal use of any vaping products; our interest is in the suppliers. And as I previously said, if we determine that someone is manufacturing or distributing illicit, adulterated vaping products that caused illness and death for personal profit, we would consider that to be a criminal act. We are prepared to use our authorities to the fullest extent possible, and will work with other federal, state and local authorities to take appropriate action as the facts emerge in order to protect the public health.

What we've learned so far is that this ongoing investigation is complex and evolving. Every day we're gathering more information, and every day we seek to use that information to better understand the relationship between any specific products or substances and the reported illnesses.

We're committed to working to answer these and other critical questions as quickly as possible, but we also recognize that it will likely take some time. Importantly, the demographic diversity of the patients, as well as the products or substances they've reported using and the samples being tested may mean there are multiple causes of these illnesses—some of which may escape us or may never be fully understood.

As this complex investigation continues, we urge consumers to take heed of our warning and stop using THC vaping products, and to not use vaping products of any kind that are purchased off the street or from unknown sources. And we remain steadfast in our commitment to work with our federal, state and local partners to identify the cause or causes of these illnesses.

The FDA, an agency within the U.S. Department of Health and Human Services, protects the public health by assuring the safety, effectiveness, and security of human and veterinary drugs, vaccines and other biological products for human use, and medical devices. The agency also is responsible for the safety and security of our nation's food supply, cosmetics, dietary supplements, products that give off electronic radiation, and for regulating tobacco products.

## E. Key Points

- In the mid-1990s, FDA sought to exercise jurisdiction over cigarettes and smokeless tobacco under its combination-products authority. However, the U.S. Supreme Court concluded that the FFDCA did not permit FDA to regulate tobacco products.
- In 2009, the Tobacco Control Act amended the FFDCA to give FDA jurisdiction over four categories of tobacco products and the authority to assert jurisdiction over other tobacco products. In 2016, FDA exercised this authority to deem nearly all other tobacco products to be subject to FDA authority.
- FDA is still in the early stages of developing its tobacco-regulation program. Many of its regulatory programs are currently administered based either on statutory language alone, or a combination of statutory language and guidance documents.
    - FDA continues to move gradually toward promulgating regulations implementing its tobacco authority.
    - Many existing regulations are structured in a manner that suggests they will be filled out in later rulemaking.
    - It appears likely that significant additional tobacco regulations will be promulgated by FDA in the coming years.

# Part Seven

# FDA Enforcement, Federal Preemption, and Regulation of Imports

Chapter 19

# FDA Enforcement

## A. Introduction

Most provisions relating to enforcement of the FFDCA are located in two chapters of the statute: Chapter III (Prohibited Acts and Penalties) and Chapter VII (General Authority). The chapter begins by examining this statutory material. It then turns to enforcement discretion, advisory actions, and criminal violations of the FFDCA.

### 1. Chapter III Enforcement Provisions

As you know from the first chapter in this casebook, FFDCA § 301 contains the basic adulteration and misbranding prohibitions that make up the backbone of the statute. Most actions for civil or criminal violation of the FFDCA will allege, as a core claim, violation of FFDCA § 301. In Chapter 1, we focused on the three general prohibitions on adulteration and misbranding set out in FFDCA §§ 301(a)–(c). As you may recall, each of these three subsections prohibits a particular action with respect to "any food, drug, device, tobacco product, or cosmetic." FFDCA § 301(a) prohibits "introduction or delivery" of one of those products "that is adulterated or misbranded." FFDCA § 301(b) prohibits "adulteration or misbranding" of one of those products "in interstate commerce." FFDCA § 301(c) prohibits "receipt in interstate commerce" of one of those products "that is adulterated or misbranded."

It is now time to expand our view of actions prohibited by FFDCA § 301. This statutory provision has well over 50 first-level subsections. These run from (a) through (ddd) and prohibit numerous—and often highly specific—activities. To give you a sense of the range of activities prohibited, seven examples of prohibited acts are listed below:

- "The refusal to permit entry or inspection as authorized by section 704." FFDCA § 301(f).
- "The sale or offering for sale of colored oleomargarine or colored margarine . . . in violation of section 407(b) or 407(c)." FFDCA § 301(m).
- "The failure to register in accordance with section 510 or 905, the failure to provide any information required by section 510(j), 510(k), 905(i), or 905(j), or the failure to provide a notice required by section 510(j)(2) or 905(i)(3)." FFDCA § 301(p).

- "The introduction or delivery for introduction into interstate commerce of a dietary supplement that is unsafe under section 413." FFDCA § 301(v).
- "The failure by . . . any . . . person engaged in the transportation of food to comply with the sanitary transportation practices prescribed by [FDA] under section 416." FFDCA § 301(hh).
- "The charitable distribution of tobacco products." FFDCA § 301(rr).
- "The manufacture or the introduction or delivery for introduction into interstate commerce of a rinse-off cosmetic that contains intentionally added plastic microbeads." FFDCA § 301(ddd)(1).

Moving to the remaining Chapter III enforcement provisions, FFDCA § 303 is the basic penalty provision. It includes both civil and criminal penalties, with criminal penalties including both fines and imprisonment. Fines can go higher than set out in FFDCA § 303 under the alternative fines provision of the U.S. Criminal Code, 18 U.S.C. § 3571. FFDCA § 305 provides for notice and an opportunity to be heard before any violation of the FFDCA is "reported . . . to any United States attorney for institution of a criminal proceeding." FFDCA § 302 sets out FDA's injunction authority, FFDCA § 304 sets out FDA's seizure authority, and FFDCA § 306 sets out FDA's debarment authority. FFDCA § 307 is a separate civil penalty provision for malfeasance relating to generic drugs and FFDCA § 308 provides for withdrawal of generic approvals due to such malfeasance.

FFDCA § 309 emphasizes FDA's enforcement discretion. It provides that formal enforcement action is not necessary for "minor violations" if FDA concludes that "that the public interest will be adequately served by a suitable written notice or warning." FFDCA § 310 provides that, with limited exceptions for actions by state governments, "all . . . proceedings for the enforcement . . . of this chapter shall be by and in the name of the United States."[1]

At this point, please read (or review) the following excerpts in the statutory supplement:

- FFDCA § 301. Prohibited acts. *Please skim full section, but do not get bogged down in the details. The idea is to get an idea of the broad range of actions prohibited.*
- FFDCA § 302. Injunction proceedings.
- FFDCA § 303. Penalties. *Subsections (a), (c)(1),* and *(c)(2) only.*
- 18 U.S.C. § 3571. Sentence of fine.
- FFDCA § 304. Seizure. *Subsections (a)(1), (b), (g)(1), (h)(1).*

1. There is no provision for any private right of action under the FFDCA, and courts have not read a private right of action into the statute.

- FFDCA § 305. Hearing before report of criminal violation.
- FFDCA § 306. Debarment, temporary denial of approval, and suspension. *Subsections (a), (b)(1), (c)(1), and (e) only.*
- FFDCA § 307. Civil penalties. *Subsection (a) only.*
- FFDCA § 309. Report of minor violations.

## 2. Chapter VII Enforcement Provisions

Most of the remaining enforcement provisions are found in FFDCA Chapter VII. FFDCA § 702 gives FDA authority to "conduct examinations and investigations" using three different sets of "officers and employees": those of HHS (which of course includes FDA employees); those of states, territories, and their political subdivisions if "duly commissioned" by the HHS Secretary as "officer[s] of the Department," and, pursuant to an appropriate memorandum of understanding, those of other federal agencies.

FFDCA § 703 requires those involved in transporting or receiving "food, drugs, devices, tobacco products, or cosmetics in interstate commerce" to provide FDA, on its request, with records relating to the movement of such products. However, it prohibits FDA from using "evidence obtained under this section, or any evidence which is directly or indirectly derived from such evidence . . . in a criminal prosecution of the person from whom obtained."

FFDCA § 704 sets out FDA's inspection authority. FFDCA § 704(a)(1)(A) gives FDA general authority "to enter, at reasonable times, any factory, warehouse, or establishment in which food, drugs, devices, tobacco products, or cosmetics are manufactured, processed, packed, or held . . . or to enter any vehicle being used to transport or hold [such products]." FFDCA § 704(a)(1)(B) gives FDA further authority to inspect such places, so long as it is done "at reasonable times and within reasonable limits and in a reasonable manner." FFDCA § 704(a)(2) exempts most state-licensed pharmacies, state-licensed health-care professionals, and producers of drugs or devices for research-related uses from this inspection authority. Most other provisions of FFDCA § 704 provide detailed procedural and record-keeping requirements. FFDCA § 704(g) sets out certain circumstances under which FDA can authorize "accredited persons" to inspect device establishments.

FFDCA § 705 governs publicity. FFDCA § 705(a) governs required disclosure of FDA enforcement proceedings. It requires FDA to publish "reports summarizing all judgments, decrees, and court orders" rendered under the FFDCA. FFDCA § 705(b) governs use of publicity as a way of addressing concerns about FDA-regulated products. It permits FDA to "disseminate[] information regarding food, drugs, devices, tobacco products, or cosmetics" in two situations: those involving "imminent danger to health" and those involving "gross deception of the consumer."

FFDCA § 709 provides that that the necessary "connection with interstate commerce" shall be "presumed to exist" in any "action to enforce the requirements of this chapter respecting a device, tobacco product, food, drug, or cosmetic."

Regulations on FDA enforcement generally are set out in 21 C.F.R. Parts 1 and 7. Procedures relating specifically to recalls are set out in 21 C.F.R. Part 7, Subpart C. Procedures relating specifically to criminal violations of the FFDCA are set out in 21 C.F.R. Part 7, Subpart E. Procedures for regulatory hearings are set out in 21 C.F.R. Part 16, and for hearings on civil monetary penalties in 21 C.F.R. Part 17.

At this point, please read (or review) the following excerpts in the statutory supplement:

- FFDCA § 702. Examinations and investigations. *Subsections (a)(1) and (e).*
- FFDCA § 703. Records.
- FFDCA § 704. Inspection.
- FFDCA § 705. Publicity.
- FFDCA § 709. Presumption of existence of jurisdiction.

## B. Outline of Regulatory Regime

As in other chapters of this book, this chapter begins with a set of charts. As you read this chapter for the first time, you should do no more than skim these charts to get a general sense of the structure of the applicable statutes and regulations. (For more information on the role of the charts in this casebook, see Chapter 1, Parts A.1 and B).

| Timeline of Key Statutes: FDA Enforcement | | | |
|---|---|---|---|
| **Year** | **PL** | **Stat** | **Name of Statute** |
| 1906 | 59-384 | 34 Stat. 768 | Pure Food and Drugs Act |
| 1938 | 75-717 | 52 Stat. 1040 | FFDCA of 1938 |
| 1988 | 100-293 | 102 Stat. 95 | Prescription Drug Marketing Act of 1987 [2] |
| 1990 | 101-629 | 104 Stat. 4511 | Safe Medical Devices Act |
| 1992 | 96-660 | 100 Stat. 3748 | Generic Drug Enforcement Act of 1992 |
| 1997 | 105-115 | 111 Stat. 2296 | FDA Modernization Act |
| 2007 | 110-85 | 121 Stat. 823 | FDA Amendments Act of 2007 |

2. This is the official short title written into the statute itself. However, the statute did not become law until the following calendar year.

| Year | PL | Stat | Name of Statute |
|---|---|---|---|
| 2009 | 111-31 | 123 Stat. 1776 | Family Smoking Prevention and Tobacco Control Act |
| 2011 | 111-353 | 124 Stat. 3885 | FDA Food Safety Modernization Act |
| 2012 | 112-144 | 126 Stat. 993 | FDA Safety and Innovation Act |
| 2013 | 113-54 | 127 Stat. 587 | Drug Quality and Security Act |
| 2017 | 115-52 | 131 Stat. 1005 | FDA Reauthorization Act of 2017 |

| Key Statutory Provisions: FDA Enforcement | | |
|---|---|---|
| **Statute Name or U.S.C. Title** | **§** | **Title of Section or Subsection** |
| FFDCA | 301 | Prohibited acts |
| FFDCA | 302 | Injunction proceedings |
| FFDCA | 303 | Penalties |
| FFDCA | 304 | Seizure |
| FFDCA | 305 | Hearing before report of criminal violation |
| FFDCA | 306 | Debarment, temporary denial of approval, and suspension |
| FFDCA | 307 | Civil penalties |
| FFDCA | 308 | Authority to withdraw approval of abbreviated drug applications |
| FFDCA | 309 | Report of minor violations |
| FFDCA | 310 | Proceedings in name of United States; provision as to subpoenas |
| FFDCA | 311 | Extraterritorial jurisdiction |
| FFDCA | 702 | Examinations and investigations |
| FFDCA | 703 | Records |
| FFDCA | 704 | Inspection |
| FFDCA | 705 | Publicity |
| FFDCA | 708 | Confidential information |
| FFDCA | 709 | Presumption of existence of jurisdiction |
| FFDCA | 710 | Consolidated administrative and laboratory facility |
| FFDCA | 711 | Automation of Food and Drug Administration |

| Key Statutory Provisions: Adulteration and Misbranding | | |
|---|---|---|
| **Statute Name or U.S.C. Title** | **§** | **Title of Section or Subsection** |
| FFDCA | 201 | Definitions |
| FFDCA | 301 | Prohibited acts |

| Statute Name or U.S.C. Title | § | Title of Section or Subsection |
| --- | --- | --- |
| FFDCA | 402, 501, 601, 902 | Chapter-specific *adulteration* provisions<br>402: food<br>501: drugs, devices, biologics, combination products<br>601: cosmetics<br>902: tobacco products |
| FFDCA | 403, 502, 602, 903 | Chapter-specific *misbranding* provisions<br>403: food<br>502: drugs, devices, biologics, combination products<br>602: cosmetics<br>903: tobacco products |

| Key Regulatory Provisions: FDA Enforcement | | |
| --- | --- | --- |
| **21 C.F.R. Part** | **Subpart** | **Title of Part or Subpart** |
| 1 | — | General enforcement regulations |
| 7 | — | Enforcement policy |
| 16 | — | Regulatory hearing before the food and drug administration |
| 17 | — | Civil money penalties hearings |

## C. Enforcement Discretion

The case below is often taught in administrative law classes as a leading case on the topic of agency enforcement discretion in general. It involves a challenge to an FDA decision not to take enforcement action against certain drugs used, without FDA approval for such use, in human execution.

### Heckler v. Chaney

470 U.S. 821 (1985)

**Justice REHNQUIST delivered the opinion of the Court.**

This case presents the question of the extent to which a decision of an administrative agency to exercise its "discretion" not to undertake certain enforcement actions is subject to judicial review under the Administrative Procedure Act, 5 U. S. C. § 501 et seq. (APA). . . . We review here a decision of the Court of Appeals for the District of Columbia Circuit, which held the FDA's refusal to take enforcement actions both reviewable and an abuse of discretion, and remanded the case with directions that the agency be required "to fulfill its statutory function." 718 F.2d 1174, 1191 (1983).

I

Respondents have been sentenced to death by lethal injection of drugs. . . . They alleged that the drugs had not been tested for the purpose for which they were to be used, and that, given that the drugs would likely be administered by untrained personnel, it was also likely that the drugs would not induce the quick and painless death intended. They urged that use of these drugs for human execution was the "unapproved use of an approved drug" and constituted a violation of the [FFDCA]'s prohibitions against "misbranding." They also suggested that the [FFDCA]'s requirements for approval of "new drugs" applied, since these drugs were now being used for a new purpose. Accordingly, respondents claimed that the FDA was required to approve the drugs as "safe and effective" for human execution before they could be distributed in interstate commerce. See FFDCA § 505. . . .

The FDA Commissioner responded, refusing to take the requested actions. The Commissioner first detailed his disagreement with respondents' understanding of the scope of FDA jurisdiction over the unapproved use of approved drugs for human execution, concluding that FDA jurisdiction in the area was generally unclear but in any event should not be exercised to interfere with this particular aspect of state criminal justice systems. . . .

Respondents then filed the instant suit in the United States District Court for the District of Columbia, claiming the same violations of the [FFDCA] and asking that the FDA be required to take the same enforcement actions requested in the prior petition. . . . The District Court granted summary judgment for petitioner. It began with the proposition that "decisions of executive departments and agencies to *refrain* from instituting investigative and enforcement proceedings are essentially unreviewable by the courts." The court then cited case law stating that nothing in the [FFDCA] indicated an intent to circumscribe the FDA's enforcement discretion or to make it reviewable.

A divided panel of the Court of Appeals for the District of Columbia Circuit reversed. The majority began by discussing the FDA's jurisdiction over the unapproved use of approved drugs for human execution, and concluded that the FDA did have jurisdiction over such a use. The court then addressed the Government's assertion of unreviewable discretion to refuse enforcement action. It first discussed this Court's opinions which have held that there is a general presumption that all agency decisions are reviewable under the APA, at least to assess whether the actions were "arbitrary, capricious, or an abuse of discretion." See *Abbott Laboratories v. Gardner*, 387 U.S. 136, 139–141 (1967); 5 U. S. C. § 706(2)(A). It noted that the APA only precludes judicial review of final agency action—including refusals to act, see 5 U. S. C. § 551(13)—when review is precluded by statute, or "committed to agency discretion by law. . . ."

The court found "law to apply" in the form of a FDA policy statement which indicated that the agency was "obligated" to investigate the unapproved use of an approved drug when such use became "widespread" or "[endangered] the public health." The court held that this policy statement constituted a "rule" and was considered binding by the FDA. . . . Citing evidence that the FDA assumed jurisdiction over drugs used to put animals to sleep and the unapproved uses of drugs on prisoners in clinical experiments, the court found that the FDA's refusal, for the reasons given, was irrational, and that respondents' evidence that use of the drugs could lead to a cruel and protracted death was entitled to more searching consideration. The court therefore remanded the case to the District Court, to order the FDA "to fulfill its statutory function."

. . . . A divided Court of Appeals denied the petition for rehearing. We granted certiorari to review the implausible result that the FDA is required to exercise its enforcement power to ensure that States only use drugs that are "safe and effective" for human execution. We reverse.

II

. . . . For us, this case turns on the important question of the extent to which determinations by the FDA *not to exercise* its enforcement authority over the use of drugs in interstate commerce may be judicially reviewed. That decision in turn involves the construction of two separate but necessarily interrelated statutes, the APA and the [FFDCA].

The APA's comprehensive provisions for judicial review of "agency actions" are contained in 5 U. S. C. §§ 701–706. Any person "adversely affected or aggrieved" by agency action, see § 702, including a "failure to act," is entitled to "judicial review thereof," as long as the action is a "final agency action for which there is no other adequate remedy in a court," see § 704. The standards to be applied on review are governed by the provisions of § 706. But before any review at all may be had, a party must first clear the hurdle of § 701(a). That section provides that the chapter on judicial review "applies, according to the provisions thereof, except to the extent that—(1) statutes preclude judicial review; or (2) agency action is committed to agency discretion by law." Petitioner urges that the decision of the FDA to refuse enforcement is an action "committed to agency discretion by law" under § 701(a)(2).

This Court has not had occasion to interpret this second exception in § 701(a) in any great detail. On its face, the section does not obviously lend itself to any particular construction; indeed, one might wonder what difference exists between § (a)(1) and § (a)(2). . . . Mindful, however, of the common-sense principle of statutory construction that sections of a statute generally should be read "to give effect, if possible, to every clause . . . ," see *United States v. Menasche,* 348 U.S. 528, 538–539 (1955), we think there is a proper construction of § (a)(2) which satisfies . . . these concerns.

This Court first discussed § (a)(2) in *Citizens to Preserve Overton Park v. Volpe,* 401 U.S. 402 (1971). . . . Interested citizens challenged the Secretary's approval under the APA, arguing that he had not satisfied the substantive statute's requirements. This Court first addressed the "threshold question" of whether the agency's action was at all reviewable. After setting out the language of § 701(a), the Court stated:

> "In this case, there is no indication that Congress sought to prohibit judicial review and there is most certainly no 'showing of "clear and convincing evidence" of a . . . legislative intent' to restrict access to judicial review. *Abbott Laboratories v. Gardner*, 387 U.S. 136, 141 (1967). . . .
>
> "Similarly, the Secretary's decision here does not fall within the exception for action 'committed to agency discretion.' This is a very narrow exception. . . . The legislative history of the Administrative Procedure Act indicates that it is applicable in those rare instances where 'statutes are drawn in such broad terms that in a given case there is no law to apply.' S. Rep. No. 752, 79th Cong., 1st Sess., 26 (1945)."

*Overton Park, supra, at 410* (footnote omitted).

The above quote . . . clearly separates the exception provided by § (a)(1) from the § (a)(2) exception. The former applies when Congress has expressed an intent to preclude judicial review. The latter applies in different circumstances; even where Congress has not affirmatively precluded review, review is not to be had if the statute is drawn so that a court would have no meaningful standard against which to judge the agency's exercise of discretion. In such a case, the statute ("law") can be taken to have "committed" the decision making to the agency's judgment absolutely. . . .

*Overton Park* did not involve an agency's refusal to take requested enforcement action. It involved an affirmative act of approval under a statute that set clear guidelines for determining when such approval should be given. Refusals to take enforcement steps generally involve precisely the opposite situation, and in that situation we think the presumption is that judicial review is not available. . . . This recognition of the existence of discretion is attributable in no small part to the general unsuitability for judicial review of agency decisions to refuse enforcement.

The reasons for this general unsuitability are many. First, an agency decision not to enforce often involves a complicated balancing of a number of factors which are peculiarly within its expertise. Thus, the agency must not only assess whether a violation has occurred, but whether agency resources are best spent on this violation or another, whether the agency is likely to succeed if it acts, whether the particular enforcement action requested best fits the agency's overall policies, and, indeed, whether the agency has enough resources to undertake the action at all. An agency generally cannot act against each technical violation of the statute it is charged with enforcing. The agency is far better equipped than the courts to deal with the many variables involved in the proper ordering of its priorities. . . .

In addition to these administrative concerns, we note that when an agency refuses to act it generally does not exercise its *coercive* power over an individual's liberty or property rights, and thus does not infringe upon areas that courts often are called upon to protect. . . . Finally, we recognize that an agency's refusal to institute proceedings shares to some extent the characteristics of the decision of a prosecutor in the Executive Branch not to indict—a decision which has long been regarded as the special province of the Executive Branch, inasmuch as it is the Executive who is charged by the Constitution to "take Care that the Laws be faithfully executed." U.S. Const., Art. II, § 3.

We of course only list the above concerns to facilitate understanding of our conclusion that an agency's decision not to take enforcement action should be presumed immune from judicial review under § 701(a)(2). For good reasons, such a decision has traditionally been "committed to agency discretion," and we believe that the Congress enacting the APA did not intend to alter that tradition. In so stating, we emphasize that the decision is only presumptively unreviewable; the presumption may be rebutted where the substantive statute has provided guidelines for the agency to follow in exercising its enforcement powers. Thus, in establishing this presumption in the APA, Congress did not set agencies free to disregard legislative direction in the statutory scheme that the agency administers. Congress may limit an agency's exercise of enforcement power if it wishes, either by setting substantive priorities, or by otherwise circumscribing an agency's power to discriminate among issues or cases it will pursue. . . .

The danger that agencies may not carry out their delegated powers with sufficient vigor does not necessarily lead to the conclusion that courts are the most appropriate body to police this aspect of their performance. That decision is in the first instance for Congress, and we therefore turn to the [FFDCA] to determine whether in this case Congress has provided us with "law to apply." If it has indicated an intent to circumscribe agency enforcement discretion, and has provided meaningful standards for defining the limits of that discretion, there is "law to apply" under *§ 701(a)(2)*, and courts may require that the agency follow that law; if it has not, then an agency refusal to institute proceedings is a decision "committed to agency discretion by law" within the meaning of that section.

### III

To enforce the various substantive prohibitions contained in the [FFDCA], the Act provides for injunctions, [FFDCA § 302], criminal sanctions, [FFDCA §§ 303 and 306], and seizure of any offending food, drug, or cosmetic article, [FFDCA § 304]. The Act's general provision for enforcement, [FFDCA § 702], provides only that "[the] Secretary is *authorized* to conduct examinations and investigations . . ." (emphasis added). Unlike the statute at issue in [a case discussed in an omitted portion of this opinion], [FFDCA § 302] gives no indication of when an injunction should be sought, and [FFDCA § 304], providing for seizures, is framed in the permissive—the offending food, drug, or cosmetic "shall be liable to be proceeded against." The section on criminal sanctions states baldly that any person who violates the [FFDCA]'s substantive prohibitions "shall be imprisoned . . . or fined." Respondents argue that this statement mandates criminal prosecution of every violator of the [FFDCA} but they adduce no indication in case law or legislative history that such was Congress' intention in using this language, which is commonly found in the criminal provisions of Title 18 of the United States Code. We are unwilling to attribute such a sweeping meaning to this language . . . The Act's enforcement provisions thus commit complete discretion to the Secretary to decide how and when they should be exercised.

Respondents nevertheless present three separate authorities that they claim provide the courts with sufficient indicia of an intent to circumscribe enforcement discretion. Two of these may be dealt with summarily. First, we reject respondents' argument that the [FFDCA]'s substantive prohibitions of "misbranding" and the introduction of "new drugs" absent agency approval supply us with "law to apply." These provisions are simply irrelevant to the agency's discretion to refuse to initiate proceedings.

We also find singularly unhelpful the agency "policy statement" on which the Court of Appeals placed great reliance. We would have difficulty with this statement's vague language even if it were a properly adopted agency rule. . . . But in any event the policy statement was attached to a rule that was never adopted. Whatever force such a statement might have, and leaving to one side the problem of whether an agency's rules might under certain circumstances provide courts with adequate guidelines for informed judicial review of decisions not to enforce, we do not think the language of the agency's "policy statement" can plausibly be read to override the agency's express assertion of unreviewable discretion contained in the above rule.

Respondents' third argument, based upon § 309 of the [FFDCA], merits only slightly more consideration. That section provides:

> Nothing in this chapter shall be construed as requiring the Secretary to report for prosecution, or for the institution of libel or injunction proceedings, minor violations of this chapter whenever he believes that the public interest will be adequately served by a suitable written notice or ruling."

Respondents seek to draw from this section the negative implication that the Secretary is *required* to report for prosecution all "major" violations of the [FFDCA], however those might be defined, and that it therefore supplies the needed indication of an intent to limit agency enforcement discretion. We think that this section simply does not give rise to the negative implication which respondents seek to draw from it. The section is not addressed to agency proceedings designed to discover the existence of violations, but applies only to a situation where a violation has already been established to the satisfaction of the agency. We do not believe the section speaks to the criteria which shall be used by the agency for investigating *possible* violations of the [FFDCA].

## IV

We therefore conclude that the presumption that agency decisions not to institute proceedings are unreviewable under 5 U. S. C. § 701(a)(2) is not overcome by the enforcement provisions of the [FFDCA]. The FDA's decision not to take the enforcement actions requested by respondents is therefore not subject to judicial review under the APA. The general exception to reviewability provided by §701(a)(2) for action "committed to agency discretion" remains a narrow one, see *Citizens to Preserve Overton Park v. Volpe*, 401 U.S. 402 (1971), but within that exception are included agency refusals to institute investigative or enforcement proceedings, unless Congress has indicated otherwise. In so holding, we essentially leave to Congress, and not to the courts, the decision as to whether an agency's refusal to institute proceedings should be judicially reviewable. No colorable claim is made in this case that the agency's refusal to institute proceedings violated any constitutional rights of respondents, and we do not address the issue that would be raised in such a case. The fact that the drugs involved in this case are ultimately to be used in imposing the death penalty must not lead this Court or other courts to import profound differences of opinion over the meaning of the Eighth Amendment to the United States Constitution into the domain of administrative law.

The judgment of the Court of Appeals is

*Reversed.*

**Justice MARSHALL, concurring in the judgment.**

. . . .

I write separately to argue for a different basis of decision: that refusals to enforce, like other agency actions, are reviewable in the absence of a "clear and convincing" congressional intent to the contrary, but that such refusals warrant deference when, as in this case, there is nothing to suggest that an agency with enforcement discretion has abused that discretion.

. . . .

First, respondents on summary judgment neither offered nor attempted to offer any evidence that the reasons for the FDA's refusal to act were other than the reasons stated by the agency. Second, as the Court correctly concludes, the [FFDCA] is not a mandatory statute that requires the FDA to prosecute all violations of the [FFDCA]. Thus, the FDA clearly has significant discretion to choose which alleged violations of the [FFDCA] to prosecute. Third, the basis on which the agency chose to exercise this discretion—that other problems were viewed as more pressing—generally will be enough to pass muster. . . .

When a statute does not mandate full enforcement, I agree with the Court that an agency is generally "far better equipped than the courts to deal with the many variables involved in the proper ordering of its priorities." As long as the agency is choosing how to allocate finite enforcement resources, the agency's choice will be entitled to substantial deference, for the choice among valid alternative enforcement policies is precisely the sort of choice over which agencies generally have been left substantial discretion by their enabling statutes. *On the merits*, then, a decision not to enforce that is based on valid resource-allocation decisions will generally not be "arbitrary, capricious, an abuse of discretion, or otherwise not in accordance with law," 5 U.S.C. § 706(2)(A). The decision in this case is no exception to this principle.

The Court, however, is not content to rest on this ground. Instead, the Court transforms the arguments for deferential review on the merits into the wholly different notion that "enforcement" decisions are presumptively unreviewable altogether . . .

This "presumption of unreviewability" is . . . a far cry from prior understandings of the Administrative Procedure Act. As the Court acknowledges, the APA presumptively entitles any person "adversely affected or aggrieved by agency action," 5 U.S.C. § 702—which is defined to include the "failure to act," 5 U.S.C. § 551(13)—to judicial review of that action. That presumption can be defeated if the substantive statute precludes review, [5 U.S.C.] § 701(a)(1), or if the action is committed to agency discretion *by law*, [5 U.S.C.] § 701(a)(2). . . .

Moreover. . . . it is inappropriate to rely on notions of prosecutorial discretion to hold agency inaction unreviewable.

. . . Arguments about prosecutorial discretion do not necessarily translate into the context of agency refusals to act. "In appropriate circumstances the Court has made clear that traditions of prosecutorial discretion do not immunize from judicial scrutiny cases in which the enforcement decisions of an administrator were motivated by improper factors or were otherwise contrary to law." *Marshall v. Jerrico, Inc.*, 446 U.S. 238, 249 (1980). Criminal prosecutorial decisions vindicate only intangible interests, common to society as a whole, in the enforcement of the criminal law. The conduct at issue has already occurred; all that remains is society's general interest in assuring that the guilty are punished. In contrast, requests for administrative enforcement typically seek to prevent concrete and future injuries that Congress has made cognizable—injuries that result, for example, from misbranded drugs, such as alleged in this case, or unsafe nuclear powerplants—or to obtain palpable benefits that Congress has intended to bestow—such as labor union elections free of corruption. Entitlements to receive these benefits or to be free of these injuries often run to specific classes of individuals whom Congress has singled out as statutory beneficiaries. The interests at stake in review of administrative enforcement decisions are thus more focused and in many circumstances more pressing than those at stake in criminal prosecutorial decisions. A request that a nuclear plant be operated safely or that protection be provided against unsafe drugs is quite different from a request that an individual be put in jail or his property confiscated as punishment for past violations of the criminal law. Unlike traditional exercises of prosecutorial discretion, "the decision to enforce—or not to enforce—may itself result in significant burdens on a . . . statutory beneficiary." *Marshall v. Jerrico, Inc., supra*, at 249.

. . . .

To be sure, the Court no doubt takes solace in the view that it has created only a "presumption" of unreviewability, and that this "presumption may be rebutted where the substantive statute has provided guidelines for the agency to follow in exercising its enforcement powers." But this statement implies far too narrow a reliance on positive law, either statutory or constitutional, as the sole source of limitations on agency discretion not to enforce. In my view, enforcement discretion is also channeled by traditional background understandings against which the APA was enacted and which Congress hardly could be thought to have intended to displace in the APA. For example, a refusal to enforce that stems from a conflict of interest, that is the result of a bribe, vindictiveness or retaliation, or that traces to personal or other corrupt motives ought to be judicially remediable. Even in the absence of statutory "guidelines" precluding such factors as bases of decision, Congress should not be presumed to have departed from principles of rationality and fair process in enacting the APA. Moreover, the agency may well narrow its own enforcement discretion through historical practice, from which it should arguably not depart in the absence of explanation, or through regulations and informal action. Traditional principles of rationality and fair process do offer "meaningful standards" and "law to apply" to an agency's decision not to act, and no presumption of unreviewability should be allowed to trump these principles.

.... As Judge Friendly said many years ago, review of even a decision over which substantial administrative discretion exists would then be available to determine whether that discretion had been abused because the decision was "made without a rational explanation, inexplicably departed from established policies, or rested ... on other considerations that Congress could not have intended to make relevant." *Wong Wing Hang v. INS,* 360 F.2d 715, 719 (CA2 1966). In that event, we would not be finding enforcement decisions unreviewable, but rather would be reviewing them on the merits, albeit with due deference, to assure that such decisions did not result from an abuse of discretion.

That is the basis upon which I would decide this case. Under [5 U.S.C.] § 706(A)(2) and *Abbott Laboratories v. Gardner,* 387 U.S. 136 (1967), agency action, including the failure to act, is reviewable to assure that it is not "arbitrary, capricious, or an abuse of discretion," unless Congress has manifested a clear and convincing intent to preclude review. Review of enforcement decisions must be suitably deferential in light of the necessary flexibility the agencies must have in this area, but at least when "enforcement" inaction allegedly deprives citizens of statutory benefits or exposes them to harms against which Congress has sought to provide protection, review must be on the merits to ensure that the agency is exercising its discretion within permissible bounds.

### III

.... Because the Court's approach, if taken literally, would take the courts out of the role of reviewing agency inaction in far too many cases, I join only the judgment today.

## 1. Advisory Actions

As noted earlier in this chapter, FFDCA § 309 explicitly gives FDA discretion to address "minor violations" with "a suitable written notice or warning" as an alternative to formal enforcement action. FDA refers to these generally as *advisory action letters*. FDA has not promulgated regulations governing its use of advisory action letters. Instead, it administers its advisory actions based on a policy set out in Chapter 4 (Advisory Actions) of its *Regulatory Procedures Manual* (RPM). This is a publicly available document setting out some of the agency's internal operating procedures.

In the RPM, FDA provides for agency issuance of two types of advisory action letters: *untitled letters* and *warning letters*. FDA uses untitled letters for less serious violations and warning letters for more serious violations. Warning letters require a response; untitled letters do not.

### *a. Untitled Letters*

The RPM description of untitled letters is below. As you will see, the description is fairly short, and describes untitled letters primarily in relation to a more detailed description of warning letters. The description of untitled letters is below. However, you may find it helpful to look back at this description after you review the more detailed description of warning letters.

### FDA Regulatory Procedures Manual § 4-2-1. Format and Content [of Untitled Letters]

March 2020

An Untitled Letter cites violations that do not meet the threshold . . . of regulatory significance for a Warning Letter. Therefore, the format and content of an Untitled Letter should clearly distinguish it from a Warning Letter. For example:

1. The letter is not titled.
2. The letter does not include a statement that FDA will advise other federal agencies of the issuance of the letter so that they may take this information into account when considering the awarding of contracts.
3. The letter does not include a warning statement that failure to take prompt correction may result in enforcement action.
4. The letter does not evoke a mandated follow-up.
5. The letter requests (rather than requires) a written response from the firm within a reasonable amount of time (e.g., "Please respond within 30 days"), unless more specific instructions are provided in a relevant Compliance Program.

Any appropriate agency compliance official may issue an Untitled Letter.

. . . .

### *b. Warning Letters*

The three excerpts below set out both the RPM description of warning letters and some of the procedures applicable to their issuance. The first, § 4-1-1, sets out warning letter procedures. The second, § 4-1-10, sets out the format and content of warning letters. The third, § 4-1-8, sets out the actions to be taken after FDA receives a response to the warning letter.

## FDA Regulatory Procedures Manual § 4-1-1. Warning Letter Procedures

March 2020

When it is consistent with the public protection responsibilities of the agency and depending on the nature of the violation, it is the Food and Drug Administration's (FDA's) practice to give individuals and firms an opportunity to take voluntary and prompt corrective action before it initiates an enforcement action. Warning Letters are issued to achieve voluntary compliance and to establish prior notice. The use of Warning Letters and prior notice are based on the expectation that most individuals and firms will voluntarily comply with the law.

The agency position is that Warning Letters are issued only for violations of regulatory significance. Significant violations are those violations that may lead to enforcement action if not promptly and adequately corrected. A Warning Letter is the agency's principal means of achieving prompt voluntary compliance with the [FFDCA].

The Warning Letter was developed to correct violations of the statutes or regulations. Also available to the agency are enforcement strategies which are based on the particular set of circumstances at hand and may include sequential or concurrent FDA enforcement actions such as recall, seizure, injunction, administrative detention, civil money penalties and/or prosecution to achieve correction. Despite the significance of the violations, there are some circumstances that may preclude the agency from taking any further enforcement action following the issuance of a Warning Letter. For example, the violation may be serious enough to warrant a Warning Letter and subsequent seizure; however, if the seizable quantity fails to meet the agency's threshold value for seizures, the agency may choose not to pursue a seizure. In this instance, the Warning Letter would document prior warning if adequate corrections are not made and if enforcement action is warranted at a later time.

Responsible officials in positions of authority in regulated firms have a legal duty to implement whatever measures are necessary to ensure that their products, practices, processes, or other activities comply with the law. Under the law such individuals are presumed to be fully aware of their responsibilities. Consequently, responsible individuals should not assume that they would receive a Warning Letter, or other prior notice, before FDA initiates enforcement action.

FDA is under no legal obligation to warn individuals or firms that they or their products are in violation of the law before taking enforcement action, except in a few specifically defined areas. . . .

A Warning Letter is informal and advisory. It communicates the agency's position on a matter, but it does not commit FDA to taking enforcement action. For these reasons, FDA does not consider Warning Letters to be final agency action on which it can be sued.

There are instances when issuing a Warning Letter is not appropriate, and, as previously stated, a Warning Letter is not a prerequisite to taking enforcement action. Examples of situations where the agency will take enforcement action without necessarily issuing a Warning Letter include:

1. The violation reflects a history of repeated or continual conduct of a similar or substantially similar nature during which time the individual and/or firm has been notified of a similar or substantially similar violation;
2. The violation is intentional or flagrant;
3. The violation presents a reasonable possibility of injury or death;
4. The violations, under Title 18 U.S.C. 1001, are intentional and willful acts that once having occurred cannot be retracted. Also, such a felony violation does not require prior notice. Therefore, Title 18 U.S.C. 1001 violations are not suitable for inclusion in Warning Letters; and,
5. When adequate notice has been given by other means and the violations have not been corrected, or are continuing.

. . . .

In certain situations, the agency may also take other actions as an alternative to, or concurrently with, the issuance of a Warning Letter. For example:

1. The product is adulterated under Section 402(a)(3) or 402(a)(4) of the [FFDCA];
2. There is a violation of current good manufacturing practices (CGMP);
3. The product contains illegal pesticide residues; or
4. The product shows short contents, subpotency, or superpotency.

Additional instructions for Warning Letters in specific product areas are found in compliance program guidance and in compliance policy guides.

Also, see Exhibit 4-1, the agency's "Procedures for Clearing FDA Warning Letters and Untitled Letters." All agency components responsible for issuing Warning Letters and Untitled Letters must follow these procedures. Developed to facilitate review of all Warning Letters and Untitled Letters by the Office of Chief Counsel

(OCC), the procedures provide instructions for submitting such letters to OCC, and include timeframes and routing information.

. . . .

## FDA Regulatory Procedures Manual § 4-1-10. Warning Letter Format

March 2020

Warning Letters can vary in form, style, and content to provide the flexibility needed to accurately and effectively state the nature of the violation(s) found and the response expected. However, the elements listed below are common to Warning Letters:

1. Title: "WARNING LETTER."
2. Delivery: Warning Letters should be sent to ensure overnight delivery and receipt of delivery (e.g., return receipt requested, FedEx) should be documented.
3. The Warning Letter should be addressed to the highest known official in the corporation that includes the facility that was inspected, and a copy should be sent to the highest known official at the facility that was inspected. . . .
4. The dates of the inspection and a description of the violative condition, practice, or product in brief but sufficient detail to provide the respondent the opportunity to take corrective action. Include citation of the section of the law and, where applicable, the regulation violated. Cite violations of the law using the appropriate section(s) of both the [FFDCA] and the U.S. Code, e.g., Section 501(a)(2)(B) of the [FFDCA], 21 U.S.C. [§]351(a)(2)(B). Cite violations of other laws (e.g., the Public Health Service Act) in the same manner.
5. Warning Letters not based on inspections and citing violations of statutory requirements for studies such as post marketing requirements (PMRs) and clinical trials should cite the appropriate application number, PMR reference number (if appropriate) and date that the applicant was notified of the PMR.
6. The Warning Letter should appropriately acknowledge corrections promised during the inspection, or annotated on the [Form] 483, or provided to the FDA in a written response. It should reply as to the apparent adequacy of the firm's corrective actions set forth in the response.
7. A request for correction and a written response within a specific period of time after the date of receipt of the letter, usually fifteen (15) working days. At the program office's discretion, the recipient may be offered an opportunity to discuss the letter with program office officials or, when appropriate, with center officials.
8. A warning statement that failure to achieve prompt[] correction may result in enforcement action without further notice. Examples of such actions may be cited. Do not include a commitment to take enforcement action.

. . . .

11. Instructions, as appropriate, that the response include:

    a. each step that has been or will be taken to completely correct the current violations and to prevent similar violations;

    b. the time within which correction will be completed;

    c. any reason the corrective action has not been completed within the response time; and,

    d. any documentation necessary to show that correction has been achieved.

. . . .

## FDA Regulatory Procedures Manual § 4-1-8. Warning Letter Follow-Up

March 2020

The issuing program office or center will evaluate the response to the Warning Letter. If the response is inadequate, or if no response is received, the program office or center will begin follow-up action as necessary to achieve correction. If the Warning Letter contains violations that by their nature are not correctable, then no close-out letter will issue.

If the response appears adequate, the program office or center will verify that commitments have been fulfilled and that correction has been achieved, and will notify other appropriate agency units. Usually, the standard for verifying that corrections have been implemented will be a follow-up inspection. Follow-up inspections should be conducted promptly after the agreed upon date of completion of the promised corrections.

1. Acknowledgment of Response to a Warning Letter

   The program office or center that issued the Warning Letter should acknowledge, in writing, receipt of Warning Letter responses. . . .

2. Warning Letter Close-Out Letter

   A Warning Letter close-out letter ("close-out letter") will not be issued based on representations that some action will or has been taken. The corrective actions must actually have been made and verified by FDA.

   The program office or center that issued the Warning Letter should issue a close-out letter for Warning Letters issued on or after September 1, 2009, if the violations in the Warning Letter have been adequately addressed, and the following conditions have been met:

    a. The firm replied to the Warning Letter with sufficient information to demonstrate that any listed violations have been adequately corrected; or

       A follow-up inspection shows that implementation of the corrective actions was adequate, or, based on other verified, appropriate and reliable information, FDA determines that the follow-up inspection is not needed;

and

b. The follow-up inspection (or other appropriate and reliable information) does not reveal other significant violations.

The issuing office will evaluate the firm's response to the Warning Letter. . . .

Program offices or centers should issue close-out letters within a total of 65 working days of having the necessary information upon which to make a decision. . . .

A close-out letter does not relieve recipients from their responsibility to take all necessary steps to assure sustained compliance with the [FFDCA], and all other applicable requirements. If a subsequent inspection reveals problems with the adequacy or sustainability of the corrections that were taken in response to the Warning Letter, such violations would be considered serious. If FDA observes violations during subsequent inspections or through other means, we may take enforcement action without further notice.

. . . .

3. Follow-Up Enforcement

If a firm has been issued a Warning Letter and has been unable or unwilling to correct the violations, program offices and centers should consider further administrative and/or regulatory actions. . . .

## D. *Mens Rea* for FFDCA Violations

Many criminal violations set out in the FFDCA do not include the type of *mens rea* component that is typical of traditional criminal law. Instead, many FFDCA violations include only an *actus reus* component—they are, or at least approach, strict liability crimes. In the case below, the U.S. Supreme Court affirms a criminal conviction of a company president based on his failure to ensure that lower-level company officials took appropriate action to correct a food safety problem.

### United States v. Park

421 U.S. 658 (1975)

**Mr. Chief Justice BURGER delivered the opinion of the Court.**

. . . .

Acme Markets, Inc., is a national retail food chain. . . . In a five-count information filed in the United States District Court for the District of Maryland, the Government charged Acme and respondent with violations of the [FFDCA]. Each count of the information alleged that the defendants had received food that had been shipped in interstate commerce and that, while the food was being held for sale in Acme's Baltimore warehouse following shipment in interstate commerce, they caused it to be held in a building accessible to rodents and to be exposed to contamination by rodents. These acts were alleged to have resulted in the food's being adulterated within the meaning of FFDCA §§ 402(a)(3) and (4), in violation of FFDCA § 301(k).

Acme pleaded guilty to each count of the information. Respondent pleaded not guilty. The evidence at trial demonstrated that in April 1970 the Food and Drug Administration (FDA) advised respondent by letter of insanitary conditions in Acme's Philadelphia warehouse. In 1971 the FDA found that similar conditions existed in the firm's Baltimore warehouse. An FDA consumer safety officer testified concerning evidence of rodent infestation and other insanitary conditions discovered during a 12-day inspection of the Baltimore warehouse in November and December 1971.[4] He also related that a second inspection of the warehouse had been conducted in March 1972. On that occasion the inspectors found that there had been improvement in the sanitary conditions, but that "there was still evidence of rodent activity in the building and in the warehouses and we found some rodent-contaminated lots of food items."

The Government also presented testimony by the Chief of Compliance of the FDA's Baltimore office ... [and] by Acme's Baltimore division vice president, who had responded to the letter on behalf of Acme and respondent and who described the steps taken to remedy the insanitary conditions discovered by both inspections. The Government's final witness, Acme's vice president for legal affairs and assistant secretary, identified respondent as the president and chief executive officer of the company and read a bylaw prescribing the duties of the chief executive officer.[7]

---

4. The witness testified with respect to the inspection of the basement of the "old building" in the warehouse complex:

> We found extensive evidence of rodent infestation in the form of rat and mouse pellets throughout the entire perimeter area and along the wall.
>
> We also found that the doors leading to the basement area from the rail siding had openings at the bottom or openings beneath part of the door that came down at the bottom large enough to admit rodent entry. There were also roden[t] pellets found on a number of different packages of boxes of various items stored in the basement, and looking at this document, I see there were also broken windows along the rail siding.

On the first floor of the "old building," the inspectors found:

> Thirty mouse pellets on the floor along walls and on the ledge in the hanging meat room. There were at least twenty mouse pellets beside bales of lime Jello and one of the bales had a chewed rodent hole in the product....

7. The bylaw provided in pertinent part:

> The Chairman of the board of directors or the president shall be the chief executive officer of the company as the board of directors may from time to time determine. He shall, subject to the board of directors, have general and active supervision of the affairs, business, offices and employees of the company....
>
> He shall, from time to time, in his discretion or at the order of the board, report the operations and affairs of the company. He shall also perform such other duties and have such other powers as may be assigned to him from time to time by the board of directors.

. . . .

Respondent was the only defense witness. He testified that, although all of Acme's employees were in a sense under his general direction, the company had an "organizational structure for responsibilities for certain functions" according to which different phases of its operation were "assigned to individuals who, in turn, have staff and departments under them." He identified those individuals responsible for sanitation, and related that upon receipt of the January 1972 FDA letter, he had conferred with the vice president for legal affairs, who informed him that the Baltimore division vice president "was investigating the situation immediately and would be taking corrective action and would be preparing a summary of the corrective action to reply to the letter." Respondent stated that he did not "believe there was anything [he] could have done more constructively than what [he] found was being done."

On cross-examination, respondent conceded that providing sanitary conditions for food offered for sale to the public was something that he was "responsible for in the entire operation of the company," and he stated that it was one of many phases of the company that he assigned to "dependable subordinates." Respondent was asked about and, over the objections of his counsel, admitted receiving, the April 1970 letter addressed to him from the FDA regarding insanitary conditions at Acme's Philadelphia warehouse. He acknowledged that, with the exception of the division vice president, the same individuals had responsibility for sanitation in both Baltimore and Philadelphia. Finally, in response to questions concerning the Philadelphia and Baltimore incidents, respondent admitted that the Baltimore problem indicated the system for handling sanitation "wasn't working perfectly" and that as Acme's chief executive officer he was responsible for "any result which occurs in our company."

At the close of the evidence, respondent's renewed motion for a judgment of acquittal was denied. The relevant portion of the trial judge's instructions to the jury challenged by respondent is set out in the margin.[9] Respondent's counsel objected

---

9.

In order to find the Defendant guilty on any count of the Information, you must find beyond a reasonable doubt on each count. . . .

Thirdly, that John R. Park held a position of authority in the operation of the business of Acme Markets, Incorporated.

However, you need not concern yourselves with the first two elements of the case. The main issue for your determination is only with the third element, whether the Defendant held a position of authority and responsibility in the business of Acme Markets.

The statute makes individuals, as well as corporations, liable for violations. An individual is liable if it is clear, beyond a reasonable doubt, that the elements of the adulteration of the food as to travel in interstate commerce are present. As I have instructed you in this case, they are, and that the individual had a responsible relation to the situation, even though he may not have participated personally.

The individual is or could be liable under the statute, even if he did not consciously do wrong. However, the fact that the Defendant is [president] and is a chief executive officer of the Acme Markets does not require a finding of guilt. Though, he need not have personally participated in the situation, he must have had a responsible relationship to

to the instructions on the ground that they failed fairly to reflect our decision in *United States v. Dotterweich, supra*, and to define "'responsible relationship.'" The trial judge overruled the objection. The jury found respondent guilty on all counts of the information, and he was subsequently sentenced to pay a fine of $50 on each count.

The Court of Appeals reversed the conviction and remanded for a new trial....

We granted certiorari because of an apparent conflict among the Courts of Appeals with respect to the standard of liability of corporate officers under the [FFDCA] as construed in *United States v. Dotterweich*, [320 U.S. 277 (1943)], and because of the importance of the question to the Government's enforcement program. We reverse.

I

The question presented by the Government's petition for certiorari in *United States v. Dotterweich*, and the focus of this Court's opinion, was whether "the manager of a corporation, as well as the corporation itself, may be prosecuted under the [FFDCA] for the introduction of misbranded and adulterated articles into interstate commerce"....

In reversing the judgment of the Court of Appeals and reinstating Dotterweich's conviction, this Court looked to the purposes of the [FFDCA] and noted that they "touch phases of the lives and health of people which, in the circumstances of modern industrialism, are largely beyond self-protection." It observed that the [FFDCA] is of "a now familiar type" which "dispenses with the conventional requirement for criminal conduct—awareness of some wrongdoing. In the interest of the larger good it puts the burden of acting at hazard upon a person otherwise innocent but standing in responsible relation to a public danger."

Central to the Court's conclusion that individuals other than proprietors are subject to the criminal provisions of the [FFDCA] was the reality that "the only way in which a corporation can act is through the individuals who act on its behalf."....

At the same time, however, the Court was aware of the concern ... that literal enforcement "might operate too harshly by sweeping within its condemnation any person however remotely entangled in the proscribed shipment.".... In this context, the Court concluded ... that the offense was committed "by all who ... have ... a responsible share in the furtherance of the transaction which the statute outlaws."

The Court recognized that, because the [FFDCA] dispenses with the need to prove "consciousness of wrongdoing," it may result in hardship even as applied to those who share "responsibility in the business process resulting in" a violation. It regarded

the issue. The issue is, in this case, whether the Defendant, John R. Park, by virtue of his position in the company, had a position of authority and responsibility in the situation out of which these charges arose.

as "too treacherous" an attempt "to define or even to indicate by way of illustration the class of employees which stands in such a responsible relation." The question of responsibility, the Court said, depends "on the evidence produced at the trial and its submission—assuming the evidence warrants it—to the jury under appropriate guidance." The Court added: "In such matters the good sense of prosecutors, the wise guidance of trial judges, and the ultimate judgment of juries must be trusted."

II

The rule that corporate employees who have "a responsible share in the furtherance of the transaction which the statute outlaws" are subject to the criminal provisions of the [FFDCA] was not formulated in a vacuum. *Cf. Morissette v. United States*, 342 U.S. 246 (1952). Cases under the Federal Food and Drugs Act of 1906 reflected the view both that knowledge or intent were not required to be proved in prosecutions under its criminal provisions, and that responsible corporate agents could be subjected to the liability thereby imposed. Moreover, the principle had been recognized that a corporate agent, through whose act, default, or omission the corporation committed a crime, was himself guilty individually of that crime. The principle had been applied whether or not the crime required "consciousness of wrongdoing," and it had been applied not only to those corporate agents who themselves committed the criminal act, but also to those who by virtue of their managerial positions or other similar relation to the actor could be deemed responsible for its commission.

In the latter class of cases, the liability of managerial officers did not depend on their knowledge of, or personal participation in, the act made criminal by the statute. Rather, where the statute under which they were prosecuted dispensed with "consciousness of wrongdoing," an omission or failure to act was deemed a sufficient basis for a responsible corporate agent's liability. It was enough in such cases that, by virtue of the relationship he bore to the corporation, the agent had the power to prevent the act complained of.

. . . . The Court has reaffirmed the proposition that "the public interest in the purity of its food is so great as to warrant the imposition of the highest standard of care on distributors." *Smith v. California*, 361 U.S. 147, 152 (1959). In order to make "distributors of food the strictest censors of their merchandise," *ibid.*, the [FFDCA] punishes "neglect where the law requires care, or inaction where it imposes a duty." *Morissette* v. *United States*, 342 *supra*, at 255. "The accused, if he does not will the violation, usually is in a position to prevent it with no more care than society might reasonably expect and no more exertion than it might reasonably exact from one who assumed his responsibilities." *Id., at 256.*

Thus *Dotterweich* and the cases which have followed reveal that in providing sanctions which reach and touch the individuals who execute the corporate mission—and this is by no means necessarily confined to a single corporate agent or employee—the [FFDCA] imposes not only a positive duty to seek out and remedy violations when they occur but also, and primarily, a duty to implement measures that will insure that violations will not occur. . . .

The [FFDCA] does not, as we observed in *Dotterweich,* make criminal liability turn on "awareness of some wrongdoing" or "conscious fraud." The duty imposed by Congress on responsible corporate agents is, we emphasize, one that requires the highest standard of foresight and vigilance, but the [FFDCA], in its criminal aspect, does not require that which is objectively impossible. The theory upon which responsible corporate agents are held criminally accountable for "causing" violations of the [FFDCA] permits a claim that a defendant was "powerless" to prevent or correct the violation to "be raised defensively at a trial on the merits." *United States v. Wiesenfeld Warehouse Co.,* 376 U.S. 86, 91 (1964). If such a claim is made, the defendant has the burden of coming forward with evidence, but this does not alter the Government's ultimate burden of proving beyond a reasonable doubt the defendant's guilt, including his power, in light of the duty imposed by the [FFDCA], to prevent or correct the prohibited condition. Congress has seen fit to enforce the accountability of responsible corporate agents dealing with products which may affect the health of consumers by penal sanctions cast in rigorous terms, and the obligation of the courts is to give them effect so long as they do not violate the Constitution.

III

We cannot agree with the Court of Appeals that it was incumbent upon the District Court to instruct the jury that the Government had the burden of establishing "wrongful action" in the sense in which the Court of Appeals used that phrase. The concept of a "responsible relationship" to, or a "responsible share" in, a violation of the [FFDCA] indeed imports some measure of blameworthiness; but it is equally clear that the Government establishes a prima facie case when it introduces evidence sufficient to warrant a finding by the trier of the facts that the defendant had, by reason of his position in the corporation, responsibility and authority either to prevent in the first instance, or promptly to correct, the violation complained of, and that he failed to do so. The failure thus to fulfill the duty imposed by the interaction of the corporate agent's authority and the statute furnishes a sufficient causal link. The considerations which prompted the imposition of this duty, and the scope of the duty, provide the measure of culpability.

. . . .

Reading the entire charge satisfies us that the jury's attention was adequately focused on the issue of respondent's authority with respect to the conditions that formed the basis of the alleged violations. Viewed as a whole, the charge did not permit the jury to find guilt solely on the basis of respondent's position in the corporation; rather, it fairly advised the jury that to find guilt it must find respondent "had a responsible relation to the situation," and "by virtue of his position . . . had . . . authority and responsibility" to deal with the situation. The situation referred to could only be "food . . . held in unsanitary conditions in a warehouse with the result that it consisted, in part, of filth or . . . may have been contaminated with filth."

. . . .

We conclude that, viewed as a whole and in the context of the trial, the charge was not misleading and contained an adequate statement of the law to guide the jury's determination. . . . Finally, we note that there was no request for an instruction that the Government was required to prove beyond a reasonable doubt that respondent was not without the power or capacity to affect the conditions which founded the charges in the information. In light of the evidence adduced at trial, we find no basis to conclude that the failure of the trial court to give such an instruction *sua sponte* was plain error or a defect affecting substantial rights.

. . . .

*Reversed.*

**Mr. Justice STEWART . . . , dissenting.**

Although agreeing with much of what is said in the Court's opinion, I dissent from the opinion and judgment, because the jury instructions in this case were not consistent with the law as the Court today expounds it.

As I understand the Court's opinion, it holds that in order to sustain a conviction under § 301(k) of the [FFDCA] the prosecution must at least show that by reason of an individual's corporate position and responsibilities, he had a duty to use care to maintain the physical integrity of the corporation's food products. A jury may then draw the inference that when the food is found to be in such condition as to violate the statute's prohibitions, that condition was "caused" by a breach of the standard of care imposed upon the responsible official. This is the language of negligence, and I agree with it.

. . . .

The trial judge instructed the jury to find Park guilty if it found beyond a reasonable doubt that Park "had a responsible relation to the situation. . . . The issue is, in this case, whether the Defendant, John R. Park, by virtue of his position in the company, had a position of authority and responsibility in the situation out of which these charges arose." Requiring, as it did, a verdict of guilty upon a finding of "responsibility," this instruction standing alone could have been construed as a direction to convict if the jury found Park "responsible" for the condition in the sense that his position as chief executive officer gave him formal responsibility within the structure of the corporation. But the trial judge went on specifically to caution the jury not to attach such a meaning to his instruction, saying that "the fact that the Defendant is pres[id]ent and is a chief executive officer of the Acme Markets does not require a finding of guilt." "Responsibility" as used by the trial judge therefore had whatever meaning the jury in its unguided discretion chose to give it.

. . . .

In approving the instructions to the jury in this case—instructions based upon what the Court concedes was a misunderstanding of *Dotterweich*— the Court approves a conspicuous departure from the long and firmly established division of functions between judge and jury in the administration of criminal justice.

. . . .

The *Dotterweich* case stands for two propositions, and I accept them both. First, "any person" within the meaning of [FFDCA § 303] may include any corporate officer or employee "standing in responsible relation" to a condition or transaction forbidden by the [FFDCA]. Second, a person may be convicted of a criminal offense under the [FFDCA] even in the absence of "the conventional requirement for criminal conduct—awareness of some wrongdoing."

But before a person can be convicted of a criminal violation of this [FFDCA], a jury must find—and must be clearly instructed that it must find—evidence beyond a reasonable doubt that he engaged in wrongful conduct amounting at least to common-law negligence. There were no such instructions, and clearly, therefore, no such finding in this case.

For these reasons, I cannot join the Court in affirming Park's criminal conviction.

## E. Key Points

- FDA enforcement is a complex subject; you should consider this chapter to be only a basic introduction.
- FDA's specific enforcement powers vary among the different product categories. When researching an issue relating to FDA enforcement, you should always focus on the agency's specific enforcement powers with respect to the product category of interest.
- FDA, like many other federal agencies, lacks independent litigating authority. Accordingly, to take any enforcement action involving the courts, FDA must convince the Department of Justice to file a lawsuit on its behalf.
- The wide scope of FDA's responsibilities means that the agency cannot possibly take action against all violations of the FFDCA and its implementing regulations.
    - Accordingly, FDA must set enforcement priorities. This necessarily means that, in many areas, enforcement will not be prioritized—and even clear violations will frequently take place without any agency effort to intervene.
- Advisory actions (warning and untitled letters)
    - Warning letters and untitled letters give FDA a less costly (in terms of its own resources) way to pressure companies to comply with regulatory requirements.

- Untitled letters do not carry a threat of future regulatory action.
- Warning letters carry a threat of further regulatory action, but—even after a warning letter—FDA may choose not to pursue further action.

- Advisory action letters can be issued by FDA itself. Unlike enforcement actions, these letters do not require FDA to convince the Department of Justice to take action on FDA's behalf.

# Chapter 20

# Federal Preemption

## A. Introduction

This book has focused primarily on the regulatory programs administered by FDA. However, there is a related topic that arises frequently in legal practice. This is private civil litigation relating to FDA-regulated products. In such litigation, parties (usually defendants) frequently seek to assert that particular state laws are preempted by federal law.[1]

*Federal preemption* is a doctrine based on the Supremacy Clause of the U.S. Constitution. That clause is found in Article VI, Section 2, and reads as follows:

> This Constitution, and the Laws of the United States which shall be made in Pursuance thereof; and all Treaties made, or which shall be made, under the Authority of the United States, shall be the supreme Law of the Land; and the Judges in every State shall be bound thereby, any Thing in the Constitution or Laws of any State to the Contrary notwithstanding.

For purposes of food and drug regulation, the key aspect of this clause is that it makes U.S. federal law supreme over state law.[2] In the language of U.S. Supreme Court jurisprudence, the Supremacy Clause means federal law "preempts" state law in areas where federal and state law are inconsistent.

The U.S. Supreme Court's preemption jurisprudence is complex, and often reflects divisions in the court that are different from the stereotypical left-right splits. They also seem to relate to, but not be full captured by, the individual justices' views of appropriate methods of statutory interpretation. The complex jurisprudence of the U.S. Supreme Court on this issue has resulted in an at-least-equally-complex set of lower court decisions addressing the preemption issue.

---

1. Federal preemption is also relevant outside of private-sector litigation, including in disputes between the federal governments and state (or local) governments with respect to authority over FDA-regulated products.

2. There are, of course, other aspects of this clause. Two are of particular note. First, federal law is supreme over state law only when it is "made in Pursuance" of the Constitution. Second, federal law and "all Treaties made . . . under the Authority of the United States" are given equal rank as the "supreme Law of the Land."

Broadly speaking, U.S. Supreme Court cases appear to distinguish between at least two categories of preemption: *express preemption* and *non-express preemption.*[3] In the situation of express preemption, Congress has adopted a statute directly stating that it preempts certain state laws. The question then becomes one of statutory interpretation: should the express preemption provision be read to cover the situation at issue?

In cases involving non-express preemption, there is less consensus on the proper approach.[4] Terms used by the court, or individual justices, for situations of preemption without express statutory language have included the following (in alphabetical order): "conflict preemption," *Kansas v. Garcia*, 140 S. Ct. 791, 806 (2020); "field preemption," *Kansas*, 140 S. Ct. at 805 (2020); "implied preemption," *Kansas*, 140 S. Ct. at 797 (2020); "impossibility preemption," *Merck Sharp & Dohme Corp. v. Albrecht*, 139 S. Ct. 1668, 1678 (2019); "obstacle preemption," *Virginia Uranium, Inc. v. Warren*, 139 S. Ct. 1894, 1909 (2020) (Ginsburg, J., concurring); "purposes and objectives" preemption, *Kansas*, 140 S. Ct. at 807 (Thomas, J., concurring), and "the purposes-and-objectives branch of conflict preemption." *Virginia Uranium*, 139 S. Ct. at 1908 (2020).[5]

Majority and dissenting opinions frequently disagree about whether express or non-express preemption—and, if so, which type of non-express preemption—is relevant to the particular case. This disagreement about terminology results in part

---

3. This book adopts the term *non-express preemption* to cover all types of preemption not based on express statutory language. This is not an ideal term, but the other potential candidate for a catch-all term—implied preemption—is at times used by courts as synonym for field preemption. Accordingly, the coined term "non-express preemption" allows us to discuss the various types of preemption not based on statutory language more clearly.

4. An older, and still frequently cited, explanation of the different types of preemption comes from *English v. General Electric Co.*, 496 U.S. 72 (1990). This divided preemption into three categories: situations where Congress "made its intent known through explicit statutory language," *id.* at 79; situations where "state law is pre-empted [because] it regulates conduct in a field that Congress intended the Federal Government to occupy exclusively," *id.*; and situations where state law "actually conflicts with federal law." *Id.* After setting out these three categories, the court hedged its explanation with a footnote:

> By referring to these three categories, we should not be taken to mean that they are rigidly distinct. Indeed, field pre-emption may be understood as a species of conflict pre-emption: A state law that falls within a pre-empted field conflicts with Congress' intent (either express or plainly implied) to exclude state regulation. Nevertheless, because we previously have adverted to the three-category framework, we invoke and apply it here.

*English*, 496 U.S. at 79 n.5.

5. Recent decisions—and separate opinions within the same decisions—differ even on whether the word is properly written with, or without, a hyphen. *Compare* Kansas v. Garcia, 140 S. Ct. 791, 797 (2020) (spelling "preemption" without hyphen) *with* Merck Sharp & Dohme Corp. v. Albrecht, 139 S. Ct. 1668, 1678 (2019) (spelling "pre-emption" with a hyphen) and *Garcia,* 140 S. Ct. at 807 (Thomas, J., concurring) (same). For ease of reading, each of the types of preemption in the sentence to which this footnote is added are spelled without a hyphen, regardless of how the word was spelled in the relevant opinion.

from disagreement about principles.[6] Together, they have created a situation where many cases are highly fact-specific, and any discussion arranged around types of preemption risks being at least partially misleading.

Accordingly, this chapter presents cases chronologically, rather than organizing them by type of preemption or by FDA product category. The cases have been chosen both for their importance in preemption jurisprudence and for the degree to which their more detailed discussions will help you to understand the relevant aspects of food and drug regulation more generally.

The first case, *Hillsborough County v. AML, Inc.*, 471 U.S. 707 (1985), involves blood plasma. The second, *Reigel v. Medtronic*, 552 U.S. 312 (2008), involves medical devices. The third, *Wyeth v. Levine*, 555 U.S. 555 (2009), involves a prescription drug. The fourth, *Bruesewitz v. Wyeth LLC*, 562 U.S. 223 (2011), involves a vaccine. The fifth, *Merck Sharp & Dohme Corp. v. Albrecht*, 139 S. Ct. 1668 (2019), is another case involving a prescription drug.

As you read through these cases, do not become discouraged if you do not feel like you can find a single, clear statement of a preemption "test" on which a majority of justices agree, or if you feel that the cases are driven less by a predictable doctrine than by the highly case-specific facts involved. Instead, try to get a sense of the general range of arguments the justices make and the way those arguments interact with the different product categories and case-specific facts. In other words, try to focus less on finding the "right" answer to a preemption case, and more on the range of arguments you can employ in favor of—or against—federal preemption in a particular case.

At this point, please read (or review) the following excerpts in the statutory supplement with respect to federal preemption:

- U.S. Constitution, Article VI, Section 2.
- FFDCA § 521. State and local requirements respecting devices.
- 21 C.F.R. Part 808. Exemptions from federal preemption of state and local medical device requirements.
- 21 C.F.R. § 314.70. Supplements and other changes to an approved NDA.

6. In particular, some justices believe the broader "purposes and objectives" of a statute are relevant to the preemption inquiry, Mutual Pharmaceutical Co., Inc. v. Bartlett, 570 U.S. 472, 502 (Sotomayor J, dissenting, joined by Justice Ginsburg), others do not, *see, e.g.*, *Kansas*, 140 S. Ct. at 807 (Thomas, J., concurring, joined by Justice Gorsuch).

## B. Outline of Regulatory Regime

As in other chapters of this book, this chapter begins with a set of charts. As you read this chapter for the first time, you should do no more than skim these charts to get a general sense of the structure of the applicable statutes and regulations. (For more information on the role of the charts in this casebook, see Chapter 1, Parts A.1 and B).

**Timeline of Key Statutes: Preemption**

| Year | PL | Stat | Name of Statute |
|---|---|---|---|
| 1906 | 59-384 | 34 Stat. 768 | Pure Food and Drugs Act |
| 1938 | 75-717 | 52 Stat. 1040 | FFDCA of 1938 |
| 1990 | 101-535 | 104 Stat. 2353 | Nutrition Labeling and Education Act of 1990 |
| 1997 | 105-115 | 111 Stat. 2296 | FDA Modernization Act |
| 2009 | 111-31 | 123 Stat. 1776 | Family Smoking Prevention and Tobacco Control Act |

**Key Statutory Provisions: Preemption**

| Statute Name or U.S.C. Title | § | Title of Section or Subsection |
|---|---|---|
| FFDCA | 403A | National uniform nutrition labeling |
| FFDCA | 521 | State and local requirements respecting devices |
| FFDCA | 751 | National uniformity for nonprescription drugs |
| FFDCA | 752 | Preemption for labeling or packaging of cosmetics |
| FFDCA | 916 | Preservation of state and local authority |

**Key Regulatory Provisions: Preemption**

| 21 C.F.R. Part | Subpart | Title of Part or Subpart |
|---|---|---|
| 100 | § 100.1 | Petitions requesting exemption from preemption for state or local requirements |
| 314 | § 314.70 | Supplements and other changes to an approved NDA |
| 808 | — | Exemptions from federal preemption of state and local medical device requirement |

## C. Cases

### Hillsborough Cnty. v. Automated Med. Labs. Inc.

471 U.S. 707 (1985)

**Justice MARSHALL delivered the opinion of the Court.**

The question presented is whether the federal regulations governing the collection of blood plasma from paid donors pre-empt certain local ordinances.

I

Appellee Automated Medical Laboratories, Inc., is a Florida corporation that operates, through subsidiaries, eight blood plasma centers in the United States . . . Appellee's plasma centers collect blood plasma from donors by employing a procedure called plasmapheresis. Under this procedure, whole blood removed from the donor is separated into plasma and other components, and "at least the red blood cells are returned to the donor." 21 CFR § 606.3(e) (1984). Appellee sells the plasma to pharmaceutical manufacturers.

Vendors of blood products, such as TPC, are subject to federal supervision. Under [PHSA] § 351(a), such vendors must be licensed by the Secretary of Health and Human Services (HHS). Licenses are issued only on a showing that the vendor's establishment and blood products meet certain safety, purity, and potency standards established by the Secretary. HHS is authorized to inspect such establishments for compliance.

Pursuant to § 351 of the [PHSA], the Food and Drug Administration (FDA), as the designee of the Secretary, has established standards for the collection of plasma. 21 CFR §§ 640.60–640.76 (1984). The regulations require that a licensed physician determine the suitability of a donor before the first donation and thereafter at subsequent intervals of no longer than one year. A physician must also inform the donor of the hazards of the procedure and obtain the donor's consent, and must be on the premises when the procedure is performed. In addition, the regulations establish minimum standards for donor eligibility, specify procedures that must be followed in performing plasmapheresis, and impose labeling requirements.

In 1980, Hillsborough County adopted Ordinances 80-11 and 80-12. Ordinance 80-11 imposes a $ 225 license fee on plasmapheresis centers within the county. It also requires such centers to allow the County Health Department "reasonable and continuing access" to their premises for inspection purposes, and to furnish information deemed relevant by the Department.

Ordinance 80-12 establishes a countywide identification system, which requires all potential donors to obtain from the County Health Department an identification card, valid for six months, that may be used only at the plasmapheresis center specified on the card. The ordinance incorporates by reference the FDA's blood plasma regulations, but also imposes donor testing and recordkeeping requirements beyond those contained in the federal regulations. Specifically, the ordinance requires that donors be tested for hepatitis prior to registration, that they donate at only one center, and that they be given a breath analysis for alcohol content before each plasma donation.

. . . .

In December 1981, appellee filed suit in the United States District Court for the Middle District of Florida, challenging the constitutionality of the ordinances and their implementing regulations. Appellee argued primarily that the ordinances violated the Supremacy Clause, the Commerce Clause, and the Fourteenth Amendment's Equal Protection Clause. Appellee sought a declaration that the ordinances were unlawful and a permanent injunction against their enforcement.

. . . The District Court upheld all portions of the local ordinances and regulations except the requirement that donors be subject to a breath-analysis test. . . .

In addition, the District Court rejected the claim that the ordinances violate the Equal Protection Clause because they regulate only centers that pay donors for plasma, and not centers in which volunteers donate whole blood. . . .

Automated Medical Laboratories appealed to the Court of Appeals for the Eleventh Circuit, which affirmed in part and reversed in part. The Court of Appeals held that the FDA's blood plasma regulations pre-empt all provisions of the county's ordinances and regulations. The court acknowledged the absence of an express indication of congressional intent to pre-empt. Relying on the pervasiveness of the FDA's regulations and on the dominance of the federal interest in plasma regulation, however, it found an implicit intent to pre-empt state and local laws on that subject. . . .

Hillsborough County and the County Health Department appealed to this Court pursuant to 28 U. S. C. § 1254(2). We noted probable jurisdiction, and we now reverse.

## II

It is a familiar and well-established principle that the Supremacy Clause invalidates state laws that "interfere with, or are contrary to," federal law. *Gibbons v. Ogden*, 9 Wheat. 1, 211 (1824) (Marshall, C. J.). Under the Supremacy Clause, federal law may supersede state law in several different ways. First, when acting within constitutional limits, Congress is empowered to pre-empt state law by so stating in express terms. In the absence of express pre-emptive language, Congress' intent to pre-empt all state law in a particular area may be inferred where the scheme of federal regulation is sufficiently comprehensive to make reasonable the inference that Congress "left no room" for supplementary state regulation. *Rice v. Santa Fe Elevator Corp.*, 331 U.S. 218, 230 (1947). Pre-emption of a whole field also will be inferred where the field is one in which "the federal interest is so dominant that the federal system will be assumed to preclude enforcement of state laws on the same subject." Ibid.; see *Hines v. Davidowitz*, 312 U.S. 52 (1941).

Even where Congress has not completely displaced state regulation in a specific area, state law is nullified to the extent that it actually conflicts with federal law. Such a conflict arises when "compliance with both federal and state regulations is a physical impossibility," *Florida Lime & Avocado Growers, Inc. v. Paul*, 373 U.S. 132, 142–143 (1963), or when state law "stands as an obstacle to the accomplishment and execution of the full purposes and objectives of Congress," *Hines v. Davidowitz*, *supra*, at 67.

.... For the purposes of the Supremacy Clause, the constitutionality of local ordinances is analyzed in the same way as that of statewide laws.

III

In arguing that the Hillsborough County ordinances and regulations are preempted, appellee faces an uphill battle. The first hurdle that appellee must overcome is the FDA's statement, when it promulgated the plasmapheresis regulations in 1973, that it did not in-tend its regulations to be exclusive. In response to comments expressing concern that the regulations governing the licensing of plasmapheresis facilities "would pre-empt State and local laws governing plasmapheresis," the FDA explained in a statement accompanying the regulations that "[these] regulations are not intend to usurp the powers of State or local authorities to regulate plasmapheresis procedures in their localities."

The question whether the regulation of an entire field has been reserved by the Federal Government is, essentially, a question of ascertaining the intent underlying the federal scheme. In this case, appellee concedes that neither Congress nor the FDA expressly preempted state and local regulation of plasmapheresis.... According to appellee, two separate factors support the inference of a federal intent to preempt the whole field: the pervasiveness of the FDA's regulations and the dominance of the federal interest in this area. Appellee also argues that the challenged ordinances reduce the number of plasma donors, and that this effect conflicts with the congressional goal of ensuring an adequate supply of plasma.

The FDA's statement is dispositive on the question of implicit intent to pre-empt unless either the agency's position is inconsistent with clearly expressed congressional intent, *see Chevron U. S. A. Inc. v. Natural Resources Defense Council, Inc.*, 467 U.S. 837, 842–845 (1984), or subsequent developments reveal a change in that position. Given appellee's first argument for implicit pre-emption—that the comprehensiveness of the FDA's regulations evinces an intent to pre-empt—any pre-emptive effect must result from the change since 1973 in the comprehensiveness of the federal regulations. To prevail on its second argument for implicit pre-emption—the dominance of the federal interest in plasmapheresis regulation—appellee must show either that this interest became more compelling since 1973, or that, in 1973, the FDA seriously underestimated the federal interest in plasmapheresis regulation.

The second obstacle in appellee's path is the presumption that state or local regulation of matters related to health and safety is not invalidated under the Supremacy

Clause. Through the challenged ordinances, Hillsborough County has attempted to protect the health of its plasma donors by preventing them from donating too frequently. It also has attempted to ensure the quality of the plasma collected so as to protect, in turn, the recipients of such plasma.... Appellee must thus present a showing of implicit pre-emption of the whole field, or of a conflict between a particular local provision and the federal scheme, that is strong enough to overcome the presumption that state and local regulation of health and safety matters can constitutionally coexist with federal regulation.

### IV

Given the clear indication of the FDA's intention not to pre-empt and the deference with which we must review the challenged ordinances, we conclude that these ordinances are not pre-empted by the federal scheme.

### A

We reject the argument that an intent to pre-empt may be inferred from the comprehensiveness of the FDA's regulations at issue here. As we have pointed out, given the FDA's 1973 statement, the relevant inquiry is whether a finding of pre-emption is justified by the increase, since 1973, in the comprehensiveness of the federal regulations....

The FDA has not indicated that the new regulations affected its disavowal in 1973 of any intent to pre-empt state and local regulation, and the fact that the federal scheme was expanded to reach other uses of plasma does not cast doubt on the continued validity of that disavowal. Indeed, even in the absence of the 1973 statement, the comprehensiveness of the FDA's regulations would not justify pre-emption.... But merely because the federal provisions were sufficiently comprehensive to meet the need identified by Congress did not mean that States and localities were barred from identifying additional needs or imposing further requirements in the field.

....

Appellee also relies on the promulgation of the National Blood Policy by the Department of Health, Education, and Welfare (HEW), as an indication that the federal regulatory scheme is now comprehensive enough to justify complete pre-emption. Such reliance is misplaced.

The National Blood Policy was established in 1974 as "a pluralistic and evolutionary approach to the solution of blood collection and distribution problems." The policy contains no regulations; instead, it is a broad statement of goals and a call for cooperation between the Federal Government and the private sector.... The National Blood Policy indicates that federal regulation will be employed only as a last resort: "[If] the private sector is unable to make satisfactory progress toward implementing these policies, a legislative and/or regulatory approach would have to be considered." The adoption of this policy simply does not support the claim that the federal regulations have grown so comprehensive since 1973 as to justify the inference of complete pre-emption.

B

Appellee's second argument for pre-emption of the whole field of plasmapheresis regulation is that an intent to pre-empt can be inferred from the dominant federal interest in this field. We are unpersuaded by the argument. Undoubtedly, every subject that merits congressional legislation is, by definition, a subject of national concern. That cannot mean, however, that every federal statute ousts all related state law. . . .

Instead, we must look for special features warranting pre-emption. Our case law provides us with clear standards to guide our inquiry in this area. For example, in the seminal case of *Hines v. Davidowitz*, 312 U.S. 52 (1941), the Court inferred an intent to pre-empt from the dominance of the federal interest in foreign affairs because "the supremacy of the national power in the general field of foreign affairs . . . is made clear by the Constitution," and the regulation of that field is "intimately blended and intertwined with responsibilities of the national government." Needless to say, those factors are absent here. Rather, as we have stated, the regulation of health and safety matters is primarily, and historically, a matter of local concern.

. . . .

C

Appellee's final argument is that even if the regulations are not comprehensive enough and the federal interest is not dominant enough to pre-empt the entire field of plasmapheresis regulation, the Hillsborough County ordinances must be struck down because they conflict with the federal scheme. Appellee argues principally that the challenged ordinances impose on plasma centers and donors requirements more stringent than those imposed by the federal regulations, and therefore that they present a serious obstacle to the federal goal of ensuring an "adequate supply of plasma." 37 Fed. Reg. 17420 (1972). We find this concern too speculative to support pre-emption.

Appellee claims that "[the] evidence at trial indicated that enforcement of the County ordinances would result in an increase in direct costs of plasma production by $1.50 per litre, and a total increase in production costs (including direct and indirect costs) of $7 per litre of plasma, an increase of approximately 15% in the total cost of production." . . . .

On the basis of the record before it, the District Court rejected each of appellee's factual assertions. The District Court found that appellee's cost-of-compliance estimates "were clouded with speculation." It also found that appellee had presented no facts to support its conclusion that "the vendor population would decrease by twenty-five percent." These findings of fact can be set aside only if they are clearly erroneous, Fed. Rule Civ. Proc. 52(a), and hence come to us with a strong presumption of validity.

. . . .

Finally, the FDA possesses the authority to promulgate regulations pre-empting local legislation that imperils the supply of plasma and can do so with relative ease. Moreover, the agency can be expected to monitor, on a continuing basis, the effects on the federal program of local requirements. Thus, since the agency has not suggested that the county ordinances interfere with federal goals, we are reluctant in the absence of strong evidence to find a threat to the federal goal of ensuring sufficient plasma.

Our analysis would be somewhat different had Congress not delegated to the FDA the administration of the federal program. Congress, unlike an agency, normally does not follow, years after the enactment of federal legislation, the effects of external factors on the goals that the federal legislation sought to promote. Moreover, it is more difficult for Congress to make its intentions known—for example by amending a statute—than it is for an agency to amend its regulations or to otherwise indicate its position.

In summary, given the findings of the District Court, the lack of any evidence in the record of a threat to the "adequacy" of the plasma supply, and the significance that we attach to the lack of a statement by the FDA, we conclude that the Hillsborough County requirements do not imperil the federal goal of ensuring sufficient plasma.

Appellee also argues that the county ordinances conflict with the federal regulations because they prevent individuals with hepatitis from donating their plasma. Such plasma is used for the production of hepatitis vaccines, and the federal regulations provide for its collection pursuant to special authorization and under carefully controlled conditions. To the extent that the Hillsborough County ordinances preclude individuals with hepatitis from donating their plasma, the ordinances are said to stand in the way of the accomplishment of the federal goal of combating hepatitis.

In order to collect plasma from individuals with hepatitis, however, a plasma center must obtain from the FDA, pursuant to [21 C.F.R.] §640.75, an exemption from the good-health requirements of [21 C.F.R.] §640.63(c). The record does not indicate that appellee has received the required exemption. As a result, appellee could not collect plasma from individuals with hepatitis even in the absence of the county ordinances. Thus, appellee lacks standing to challenge the ordinances on this ground.

## V

We hold that Hillsborough County Ordinances 80-11 and 80-12, and their implementing regulations, are not pre-empted by the scheme for federal regulation of plasmapheresis. The judgment of the Court of Appeals for the Eleventh Circuit is therefore reversed, and the case is remanded for further proceedings consistent with this opinion.

It is so ordered.

## Reigel v. Medtronic, Inc.

552 U.S. 312 (2008)

**Justice SCALIA delivered the opinion of the Court.**

We consider whether the pre-emption clause enacted in the Medical Device Amendments of 1976, [FFDCA § 521], bars common-law claims challenging the safety and effectiveness of a medical device given premarket approval by the Food and Drug Administration (FDA).

A

The [FFDCA], has long required FDA approval for the introduction of new drugs into the market. Until the statutory enactment at issue here, however, the introduction of new medical devices was left largely for the States to supervise as they saw fit. See *Medtronic, Inc. v. Lohr*, 518 U.S. 470, 475–476 (1996).

The regulatory landscape changed in the 1960's and 1970's, as complex devices proliferated and some failed. Most notably, the Dalkon Shield intrauterine device, introduced in 1970, was linked to serious infections and several deaths, not to mention a large number of pregnancies. Thousands of tort claims followed. . . . Several States adopted regulatory measures, including California, which in 1970 enacted a law requiring premarket approval of medical devices.

Congress stepped in with passage of the Medical Device Amendments of 1976, which swept back some state obligations and imposed a regime of detailed federal oversight. The MDA includes an express pre-emption provision that states:

> Except as provided in subsection (b) of this section, no State or political subdivision of a State may establish or continue in effect with respect to a device intended for human use any requirement—
>
> (1) which is different from, or in addition to, any requirement applicable under this chapter to the device, and
>
> (2) which relates to the safety or effectiveness of the device or to any other matter included in a requirement applicable to the device under this chapter."
>
> [FFDCA § 521](a).

The exception contained in subsection (b) permits the FDA to exempt some state and local requirements from pre-emption.

The new regulatory regime established various levels of oversight for medical devices, depending on the risks they present. Class I, which includes such devices as elastic bandages and examination gloves, is subject to the lowest level of oversight: "general controls," such as labeling requirements. [FFDCA § 513](a)(1)(A). Class II, which includes such devices as powered wheelchairs and surgical drapes, is subject in addition to "special controls" such as performance standards and postmarket surveillance measures, [FFDCA § 513](a)(1)(B).

The devices receiving the most federal oversight are those in Class III, which include replacement heart valves, implanted cerebella stimulators, and pacemaker pulse generators. In general, a device is assigned to Class III if it cannot be established that a less stringent classification would provide reasonable assurance of safety and effectiveness, and the device is "purported or represented to be for a use in supporting or sustaining human life or for a use which is of substantial importance in preventing impairment of human health," or "presents a potential unreasonable risk of illness or injury." [FFDCA § 513](a)(1)(C)(ii).

Although the MDA established a rigorous regime of premarket approval for new Class III devices, it grandfathered many that were already on the market. Devices sold before the MDA's effective date may remain on the market until the FDA promulgates, after notice and comment, a regulation requiring premarket approval. A related provision seeks to limit the competitive advantage grandfathered devices receive. A new device need not undergo premarket approval if the FDA finds it is "substantially equivalent" to another device exempt from premarket approval. The agency's review of devices for substantial equivalence is known as the § 510(k) process, named after the statutory provision describing the review. Most new Class III devices enter the market through § 510(k). In 2005, for example, the FDA authorized the marketing of 3,148 devices under § 510(k) and granted premarket approval to just 32 devices.

Premarket approval is a "rigorous" process. *Lohr, supra*, at 470. A manufacturer must submit what is typically a multivolume application. It includes, among other things, full reports of all studies and investigations of the device's safety and effectiveness that have been published or should reasonably be known to the applicant; a "full statement" of the device's "components, ingredients, and properties and of the principle or principles of operation"; "a full description of the methods used in, and the facilities and controls used for, the manufacture, processing, and, when relevant, packing and installation of, such device"; samples or device components required by the FDA; and a specimen of the proposed labeling. [FFDCA § 515](c)(1). Before deciding whether to approve the application, the agency may refer it to a panel of outside experts, and may request additional data from the manufacturer.

The FDA spends an average of 1,200 hours reviewing each application, *Lohr*, 518 U.S., at 477, and grants premarket approval only if it finds there is a "reasonable assurance" of the device's "safety and effectiveness," [FFDCA § 515](d). The agency must "weig[h] any probable benefit to health from the use of the device against any probable risk of injury or illness from such use." [FFDCA § 513](a)(2)(C). It may thus approve devices that present great risks if they nonetheless offer great benefits in light of available alternatives. It approved, for example, under its Humanitarian Device Exemption procedures, a ventricular assist device for children with failing hearts, even though the survival rate of children using the device was less than 50 percent.

. . . .

After completing its review, the FDA may grant or deny premarket approval. It may also condition approval on adherence to performance standards, restrictions upon sale or distribution, or compliance with other requirements. The agency is also free to impose device-specific restrictions by regulation.

....

Once a device has received premarket approval, the MDA forbids the manufacturer to make, without FDA permission, changes in design specifications, manufacturing processes, labeling, or any other attribute, that would affect safety or effectiveness. If the applicant wishes to make such a change, it must submit, and the FDA must approve, an application for supplemental premarket approval, to be evaluated under largely the same criteria as an initial application.

After premarket approval, the devices are subject to reporting requirements.... The FDA has the power to withdraw premarket approval based on newly reported data or existing information and must withdraw approval if it determines that a device is unsafe or ineffective under the conditions in its labeling.

**B**

.... The device at issue is an Evergreen Balloon Catheter marketed by defendant-respondent Medtronic, Inc. It is a Class III device that received premarket approval from the FDA in 1994; changes to its label received supplemental approvals in 1995 and 1996.

Charles Riegel underwent coronary angioplasty in 1996, shortly after suffering a myocardial infarction. His right coronary artery was diffusely diseased and heavily calcified. Riegel's doctor inserted the Evergreen Balloon Catheter into his patient's coronary artery in an attempt to dilate the artery, although the device's labeling stated that use was contraindicated for patients with diffuse or calcified stenoses. The label also warned that the catheter should not be inflated beyond its rated burst pressure of eight atmospheres. Riegel's doctor inflated the catheter five times, to a pressure of 10 atmospheres; on its fifth inflation, the catheter ruptured. Riegel developed a heart block, was placed on life support, and underwent emergency coronary bypass surgery.

Riegel and his wife Donna brought this lawsuit in April 1999, in the United States District Court for the Northern District of New York. Their complaint alleged that Medtronic's catheter was designed, labeled, and manufactured in a manner that violated New York common law, and that these defects caused Riegel to suffer severe and permanent injuries. The complaint raised a number of common-law claims. The District Court held that the MDA pre-empted Riegel's claims of strict liability; breach of implied warranty; and negligence in the design, testing, inspection, distribution, labeling, marketing, and sale of the catheter. It also held that the MDA pre-empted a negligent manufacturing claim insofar as it was not premised on the theory that Medtronic violated federal law. Finally, the court concluded that the

MDA pre-empted Donna Riegel's claim for loss of consortium to the extent it was derivative of the pre-empted claims.[2]

The United States Court of Appeals for the Second Circuit affirmed these dismissals. . . . We granted certiorari.

II

Since the MDA expressly pre-empts only state requirements "different from, or in addition to, any requirement applicable . . . to the device" under federal law, [FFDCA § 521](a)(1), we must determine whether the Federal Government has established requirements applicable to Medtronic's catheter. If so, we must then determine whether the Riegels' common-law claims are based upon New York requirements with respect to the device that are "different from, or in addition to," the federal ones, and that relate to safety and effectiveness. [FFDCA § 521](a).

We turn to the first question. In *Lohr*, a majority of this Court interpreted the MDA's pre-emption provision in a manner "substantially informed" by the FDA regulation set forth at 21 CFR § 808.1(d). That regulation says that state requirements are pre-empted "only when the Food and Drug Administration has established specific counterpart regulations or there are other specific requirements applicable to a particular device. . . ." 21 CFR § 808.1(d). Informed by the regulation, we concluded that federal manufacturing and labeling requirements applicable across the board to almost all medical devices did not pre-empt the common-law claims of negligence and strict liability at issue in *Lohr.* The federal requirements, we said, were not requirements specific to the device in question—they reflected "entirely generic concerns about device regulation *generally.*" While we disclaimed a conclusion that general federal requirements could never pre-empt, or general state duties never be pre-empted, we held that no pre-emption occurred in the case at hand based on a careful comparison between the state and federal duties at issue.

Even though substantial-equivalence review under § 510(k) is device specific, *Lohr* also rejected the manufacturer's contention that § 510(k) approval imposed device-specific "requirements." We regarded the fact that products entering the market through § 510(k) may be marketed only so long as they remain substantial equivalents of the relevant pre-1976 devices as a qualification for an exemption rather than a requirement.

Premarket approval, in contrast, imposes "requirements" under the MDA as we interpreted it in *Lohr.* Unlike general labeling duties, premarket approval is specific to individual devices. And it is in no sense an exemption from federal safety review—it *is* federal safety review. Thus, the attributes that *Lohr* found lacking in

2. The District Court later granted summary judgment to Medtronic on those claims of Riegel it had found not pre-empted, viz., that Medtronic breached an express warranty and was negligent in manufacturing because it did not comply with federal standards. It consequently granted summary judgment as well on Donna Riegel's derivative consortium claim. The Court of Appeals affirmed these determinations, and they are not before us.

§ 510(k) review are present here. While § 510(k) is "'focused on *equivalence*, not safety,'" *id.*, at 493 (opinion of the Court), premarket approval is focused on safety, not equivalence. While devices that enter the market through § 510(k) have "never been formally reviewed under the MDA for safety or efficacy," *ibid.*, the FDA may grant premarket approval only after it determines that a device offers a reasonable assurance of safety and effectiveness, [FFDCA § 515](d). And while the FDA does not "'require'" that a device allowed to enter the market as a substantial equivalent "take any particular form for any particular reason," 518 U.S., at 493, the FDA requires a device that has received premarket approval to be made with almost no deviations from the specifications in its approval application, for the reason that the FDA has determined that the approved form provides a reasonable assurance of safety and effectiveness.

### III

We turn, then, to the second question: whether the Riegels' common-law claims rely upon "any requirement" of New York law applicable to the catheter that is "different from, or in addition to," federal requirements and that "relates to the safety or effectiveness of the device or to any other matter included in a requirement applicable to the device." [FFDCA § 521](a). Safety and effectiveness are the very subjects of the Riegels' common-law claims, so the critical issue is whether New York's tort duties constitute "requirements" under the MDA.

#### A

In *Lohr,* five Justices concluded that common-law causes of action for negligence and strict liability do impose "requirement[s]" and would be pre-empted by federal requirements specific to a medical device. We adhere to that view. . . .

Congress is entitled to know what meaning this Court will assign to terms regularly used in its enactments. Absent other indication, reference to a State's "requirements" includes its common-law duties. As the plurality opinion said in *Cipollone [v. Liggett Group, Inc.,* 505 U.S. 504 (1992)], common-law liability is "premised on the existence of a legal duty," and a tort judgment therefore establishes that the defendant has violated a state-law obligation. And while the common-law remedy is limited to damages, a liability award "'can be, indeed is designed to be, a potent method of governing conduct and controlling policy.'"

In the present case, there is nothing to contradict this normal meaning. To the contrary, in the context of this legislation excluding common-law duties from the scope of pre-emption would make little sense. State tort law that requires a manufacturer's catheters to be safer, but hence less effective, than the model the FDA has approved disrupts the federal scheme no less than state regulatory law to the same effect. Indeed, one would think that tort law, applied by juries under a negligence or strict-liability standard, is less deserving of preservation. . . . As Justice Breyer explained in *Lohr,* it is implausible that the MDA was meant to "grant greater power (to set state standards 'different from, or in addition to,' federal standards) to a single state jury than to state officials acting through state administrative or legislative lawmaking processes." That perverse distinction is not required or even suggested by the broad language Congress chose in the MDA,[4] and we will not turn somersaults to create it.

B

The dissent would narrow the pre-emptive scope of the term "requirement" on the grounds that it is "difficult to believe that Congress would, without comment, remove all means of judicial recourse" for consumers injured by FDA-approved devices. *Post,* at 337 (opinion of Ginsburg, J.) (internal quotation marks omitted). But, as we have explained, this is exactly what a pre-emption clause for medical devices does by its terms. The operation of a law enacted by Congress need not be seconded by a committee report on pain of judicial nullification. It is not our job to speculate upon congressional motives. If we were to do so, however, the only indication available—the text of the statute—suggests that the solicitude for those injured by FDA-approved devices, which the dissent finds controlling, was overcome in Congress's estimation by solicitude for those who would suffer without new medical devices if juries were allowed to apply the tort law of 50 States to all innovations.

. . . .

C

The Riegels contend that the duties underlying negligence, strict-liability, and implied-warranty claims are not pre-empted even if they impose "'requirements,'" because general common-law duties are not requirements maintained "'with respect to devices.'" Again, a majority of this Court suggested otherwise in *Lohr.* See 518 U.S., at 504–505 (opinion of Breyer, J.); *id.*, at 514 (opinion of O'Connor, J., joined by Rehnquist, C. J., and Scalia and Thomas, JJ.).[6] And with good reason. The language of the statute does not bear the Riegels' reading. . . . Nothing in the statutory text suggests that the pre-empted state requirement must apply *only* to the relevant device, or only to medical devices and not to all products and all actions in general.

---

4. The Riegels point to [FFDCA § 521](b), which authorizes the FDA to exempt state "requirements" from pre-emption under circumstances that would rarely be met for common-law duties. But a law that permits an agency to exempt certain "requirements" from pre-emption does not suggest that no other "requirements" exist. The Riegels also invoke [FFDCA § 518](d), which provides that compliance with certain FDA orders "shall not relieve any person from liability under Federal or State law." This indicates that some state-law claims are not pre-empted, as we held in *Lohr.* But it could not possibly mean that *all* state-law claims are not pre-empted, since that would deprive the MDA pre-emption clause of all content. And it provides no guidance as to which state-law claims are pre-empted and which are not.

6. The opinions joined by these five Justices dispose of the Riegels' assertion that *Lohr* held common-law duties were too general to qualify as duties "with respect to a device." The majority opinion in *Lohr* also disavowed this conclusion, for it stated that the Court did "not believe that [the MDA's] statutory and regulatory language necessarily precludes . . . 'general' state requirements from ever being pre-empted. . . ." 518 U.S., at 500 (1996).

The Riegels' argument to the contrary rests on the text of an FDA regulation which states that the MDA's pre-emption clause does not extend to certain duties, including "[s]tate or local requirements of general applicability where the purpose of the requirement relates either to other products in addition to devices (e.g., requirements such as general electrical codes, and the Uniform Commercial Code (warranty of fitness)), or to unfair trade practices in which the requirements are not limited to devices." 21 CFR § 808.1(d)(1). . . . [T]he FDA's view put forward in this case is that the regulation does not refer to general tort duties of care . . . That is so, according to the FDA, because the regulation excludes from pre-emption requirements that relate only incidentally to medical devices, but not other requirements. General tort duties of care, unlike fire codes or restrictions on trade practices, "directly regulate" the device itself, including its design. We find the agency's explanation less than compelling, since the same could be said of general requirements imposed by electrical codes, the Uniform Commercial Code, or unfair-trade-practice law, which the regulation specifically excludes from pre-emption.

Other portions of 21 CFR § 808.1, however, support the agency's view that § 808.1(d)(1) has no application to this case . . . Section 808.1(b) states that the MDA sets forth a "general rule" pre-empting state duties "having the force and effect of law (whether established by statute, ordinance, regulation, *or court decision*) . . . ." This sentence is far more comprehensible under the FDA's view that § 808.1(d)(1) has no application here than under the Riegels' view. We are aware of no duties established by court decision other than common-law duties, and we are aware of no common-law duties that relate solely to medical devices.

The Riegels' reading is also in tension with the regulation's statement that adulteration and misbranding claims are pre-empted when they "ha[ve] the effect of establishing a substantive requirement for a specific device, e.g., a specific labeling requirement" that is "different from, or in addition to," a federal requirement. § 808.1(d)(6)(ii). Surely this means that the MDA would pre-empt a jury determination that the FDA-approved labeling for a pacemaker violated a state common-law requirement for additional warnings. The Riegels' reading of § 808.1(d)(1), however, would allow a claim for tortious mislabeling to escape pre-emption so long as such a claim could also be brought against objects other than medical devices.

All in all, we think that § 808.1(d)(1) can add nothing to our analysis but confusion. Neither accepting nor rejecting the proposition that this regulation can properly be consulted to determine the statute's meaning; and neither accepting nor rejecting the FDA's distinction between general requirements that directly regulate and those that regulate only incidentally; the regulation fails to alter our interpretation of the text insofar as the outcome of this case is concerned.

## IV

State requirements are pre-empted under the MDA only to the extent that they are "different from, or in addition to" the requirements imposed by federal law. [FFDCA § 521](a)(1). Thus, [FFDCA § 521] does not prevent a State from providing a damages remedy for claims premised on a violation of FDA regulations; the state duties in such a case "parallel," rather than add to, federal requirements. *Lohr*, 518 U.S., at 495,; see also *id.*, at 513 (O'Connor, J., concurring in part and dissenting in part). The District Court in this case recognized that parallel claims would not be pre-empted, but it interpreted the claims here to assert that Medtronic's device violated state tort law notwithstanding compliance with the relevant federal requirements. Although the Riegels now argue that their lawsuit raises parallel claims, they made no such contention in their briefs before the Second Circuit, nor did they raise this argument in their petition for certiorari. We decline to address that argument in the first instance here.

* * *

For the foregoing reasons, the judgment of the Court of Appeals is affirmed.

## Wyeth v. Levine

555 U.S. 555 (2009)

**Justice STEVENS delivered the opinion of the Court.**

Directly injecting the drug Phenergan into a patient's vein creates a significant risk of catastrophic consequences. A Vermont jury found that petitioner Wyeth, the manufacturer of the drug, had failed to provide an adequate warning of that risk and awarded damages to respondent Diana Levine to compensate her for the amputation of her arm. The warnings on Phenergan's label had been deemed sufficient by the federal Food and Drug Administration (FDA) when it approved Wyeth's new drug application in 1955 and when it later approved changes in the drug's labeling. The question we must decide is whether the FDA's approvals provide Wyeth with a complete defense to Levine's tort claims. We conclude that they do not.

### I

Phenergan is Wyeth's brand name for promethazine hydrochloride, an antihistamine used to treat nausea. The injectable form of Phenergan can be administered intramuscularly or intravenously, and it can be administered intravenously through either the "IV-push" method, whereby the drug is injected directly into a patient's vein, or the "IV-drip" method, whereby the drug is introduced into a saline solution in a hanging intravenous bag and slowly descends through a catheter inserted in a patient's vein. The drug is corrosive and causes irreversible gangrene if it enters a patient's artery.

Levine's injury resulted from an IV-push injection of Phenergan. On April 7, 2000, as on previous visits to her local clinic for treatment of a migraine headache, she received an intramuscular injection of Demerol for her headache and Phenergan for her nausea. Because the combination did not provide relief, she returned later that day and received a second injection of both drugs. This time, the physician assistant administered the drugs by the IV-push method, and Phenergan entered Levine's artery, either because the needle penetrated an artery directly or because the drug escaped from the vein into surrounding tissue (a phenomenon called "perivascular extravasation") where it came in contact with arterial blood. As a result, Levine developed gangrene, and doctors amputated first her right hand and then her entire forearm. In addition to her pain and suffering, Levine incurred substantial medical expenses and the loss of her livelihood as a professional musician.

After settling claims against the health center and clinician, Levine brought an action for damages against Wyeth, relying on common-law negligence and strict-liability theories. Although Phenergan's labeling warned of the danger of gangrene and amputation following inadvertent intra-arterial injection, Levine alleged that the labeling was defective because it failed to instruct clinicians to use the IV-drip method of intravenous administration instead of the higher risk IV-push method. More broadly, she alleged that Phenergan is not reasonably safe for intravenous administration because the foreseeable risks of gangrene and loss of limb are great in relation to the drug's therapeutic benefits.

Wyeth filed a motion for summary judgment, arguing that Levine's failure-to-warn claims were pre-empted by federal law. The court found no merit in either Wyeth's field pre-emption argument, which it has since abandoned, or its conflict pre-emption argument. With respect to the contention that there was an "actual conflict between a specific FDA order," and Levine's failure-to-warn action, the court reviewed the sparse correspondence between Wyeth and the FDA about Phenergan's labeling and found no evidence that Wyeth had "earnestly attempted" to strengthen the intra-arterial injection warning or that the FDA had "specifically disallowed" stronger language . . .

The evidence presented during the 5-day jury trial showed that the risk of intra-arterial injection or perivascular extravasation can be almost entirely eliminated through the use of IV-drip, rather than IV-push, administration. An IV drip is started with saline, which will not flow properly if the catheter is not in the vein and fluid is entering an artery or surrounding tissue. By contrast, even a careful and experienced clinician using the IV-push method will occasionally expose an artery to Phenergan. While Phenergan's labeling warned against intra-arterial injection and perivascular extravasation and advised that "when administering any irritant drug intravenously it is usually preferable to inject it through the tubing of an intravenous infusion set that is known to be functioning satisfactorily," the labeling did not contain a specific warning about the risks of IV-push administration.

The trial record also contains correspondence between Wyeth and the FDA discussing Phenergan's label. The FDA first approved injectable Phenergan in 1955. In 1973 and 1976, Wyeth submitted supplemental new drug applications, which the agency approved after proposing labeling changes. Wyeth submitted a third supplemental application in 1981 in response to a new FDA rule governing drug labels. Over the next 17 years, Wyeth and the FDA intermittently corresponded about Phenergan's label. The most notable activity occurred in 1987, when the FDA suggested different warnings about the risk of arterial exposure, and in 1988, when Wyeth submitted revised labeling incorporating the proposed changes. The FDA did not respond. Instead, in 1996, it requested from Wyeth the labeling then in use and, without addressing Wyeth's 1988 submission, instructed it to "retain verbiage in current label" regarding intra-arterial injection. After a few further changes to the labeling not related to intra-arterial injection, the FDA approved Wyeth's 1981 application in 1998, instructing that Phenergan's final printed label "must be identical" to the approved package insert.

Based on this regulatory history, the trial judge instructed the jury that it could consider evidence of Wyeth's compliance with FDA requirements but that such compliance did not establish that the warnings were adequate. He also instructed, without objection from Wyeth, that FDA regulations "permit a drug manufacturer to change a product label to add or strengthen a warning about its product without prior FDA approval so long as it later submits the revised warning for review and approval."

Answering questions on a special verdict form, the jury found that Wyeth was negligent, that Phenergan was a defective product as a result of inadequate warnings and instructions, and that no intervening cause had broken the causal connection between the product defects and the plaintiff's injury. It awarded total damages of $7,400,000, which the court reduced to account for Levine's earlier settlement with the health center and clinician.

On August 3, 2004, the trial court filed a comprehensive opinion denying Wyeth's motion for judgment as a matter of law. After making findings of fact based on the trial record (supplemented by one letter that Wyeth found after the trial), the court rejected Wyeth's pre-emption arguments. It determined that there was no direct conflict between FDA regulations and Levine's state-law claims because those regulations permit strengthened warnings without FDA approval on an interim basis and the record contained evidence of at least 20 reports of amputations similar to Levine's since the 1960's. The court also found that state tort liability in this case would not obstruct the FDA's work because the agency had paid no more than passing attention to the question whether to warn against IV-push administration of Phenergan. In addition, the court noted that state law serves a compensatory function distinct from federal regulation.

The Vermont Supreme Court affirmed. It held that the jury's verdict "did not conflict with FDA's labeling requirements for Phenergan because Wyeth could have warned against IV-push administration without prior FDA approval, and because federal labeling requirements create a floor, not a ceiling, for state regulation." In dissent, Chief Justice Reiber argued that the jury's verdict conflicted with federal law because it was inconsistent with the FDA's conclusion that intravenous administration of Phenergan was safe and effective.

The importance of the pre-emption issue, coupled with the fact that the FDA has changed its position on state tort law and now endorses the views expressed in Chief Justice Reiber's dissent, persuaded us to grant Wyeth's petition for certiorari. The question presented by the petition is whether the FDA's drug labeling judgments "preempt state law product liability claims premised on the theory that different labeling judgments were necessary to make drugs reasonably safe for use."

II

Wyeth makes two separate pre-emption arguments: first, that it would have been impossible for it to comply with the state-law duty to modify Phenergan's labeling without violating federal law, see *Fidelity Fed. Sav. & Loan Assn. v. De la Cuesta,* 458 U.S. 141 (1982), and second, that recognition of Levine's state tort action creates an unacceptable "obstacle to the accomplishment and execution of the full purposes and objectives of Congress," *Hines v. Davidowitz,* 312 U.S. 52, 67, 61 (1941), because it substitutes a lay jury's decision about drug labeling for the expert judgment of the FDA. As a preface to our evaluation of these arguments, we identify two factual propositions decided during the trial court proceedings, emphasize two legal principles that guide our analysis, and review the history of the controlling federal statute.

The trial court proceedings established that Levine's injury would not have occurred if Phenergan's label had included an adequate warning about the risks of the IV-push method of administering the drug. The record contains evidence that the physician assistant administered a greater dose than the label prescribed, that she may have inadvertently injected the drug into an artery rather than a vein, and that she continued to inject the drug after Levine complained of pain. Nevertheless, the jury rejected Wyeth's argument that the clinician's conduct was an intervening cause that absolved it of liability. In finding Wyeth negligent as well as strictly liable, the jury also determined that Levine's injury was foreseeable. That the inadequate label was both a but-for and proximate cause of Levine's injury is supported by the record and no longer challenged by Wyeth.

The trial court proceedings further established that the critical defect in Phenergan's label was the lack of an adequate warning about the risks of IV-push administration. Levine also offered evidence that the IV-push method should be contraindicated and that Phenergan should never be administered intravenously, even by the IV-drip method. Perhaps for this reason, the dissent incorrectly assumes that the state-law duty at issue is the duty to contraindicate the IV-push method. But, as the Vermont Supreme Court explained, the jury verdict established only that Phenergan's warning was insufficient. It did not mandate a particular replacement warning, nor did it require contraindicating IV-push administration: "There may have been any number of ways for Wyeth to strengthen the Phenergan warning without completely eliminating IV-push administration." We therefore need not decide whether a state rule proscribing intravenous administration would be pre-empted. The narrower question presented is whether federal law pre-empts Levine's claim that Phenergan's label did not contain an adequate warning about using the IV-push method of administration.

. . . .

In order to identify the "purpose of Congress," it is appropriate to briefly review the history of federal regulation of drugs and drug labeling . . .

*[The Court proceeded to go through the history of congressional regulation of drugs and drug labeling.]*

In 2007, after Levine's injury and lawsuit, Congress again amended the [FFDCA]. For the first time, it granted the FDA statutory authority to require a manufacturer to change its drug label based on safety information that becomes available after a drug's initial approval. In doing so, however, Congress did not enact a provision in the Senate bill that would have required the FDA to preapprove all changes to drug labels. Instead, it adopted a rule of construction to make it clear that manufacturers remain responsible for updating their labels.

III

Wyeth first argues that Levine's state-law claims are pre-empted because it is impossible for it to comply with both the state-law duties underlying those claims and its federal labeling duties. See *De la Cuesta*, 458 U.S., at 153. The FDA's premarket approval of a new drug application includes the approval of the exact text in the proposed label. Generally speaking, a manufacturer may only change a drug label after the FDA approves a supplemental application. There is, however, an FDA regulation that permits a manufacturer to make certain changes to its label before receiving the agency's approval. Among other things, this "changes being effected" (CBE) regulation provides that if a manufacturer is changing a label to "add or strengthen a contraindication, warning, precaution, or adverse reaction" or to "add or strengthen an instruction about dosage and administration that is intended to increase the safe use of the drug product," it may make the labeling change upon filing its supplemental application with the FDA; it need not wait for FDA approval.

Wyeth argues that the CBE regulation is not implicated in this case because a 2008 amendment provides that a manufacturer may only change its label "to reflect newly acquired information." Resting on this language (which Wyeth argues simply reaffirmed the interpretation of the regulation in effect when this case was tried), Wyeth contends that it could have changed Phenergan's label only in response to new information that the FDA had not considered. And it maintains that Levine has not pointed to any such information concerning the risks of IV-push administration. Thus, Wyeth insists, it was impossible for it to discharge its state-law obligation to provide a stronger warning about IV-push administration without violating federal law. Wyeth's argument misapprehends both the federal drug regulatory scheme and its burden in establishing a pre-emption defense.

We need not decide whether the 2008 CBE regulation is consistent with the [FFDCA] and the previous version of the regulation, as Wyeth and the United States urge, because Wyeth could have revised Phenergan's label even in accordance with the amended regulation....

Wyeth's cramped reading of the CBE regulation and its broad reading of the [FFDCA]'s misbranding and unauthorized distribution provisions are premised on a more fundamental misunderstanding. Wyeth suggests that the FDA, rather than the manufacturer, bears primary responsibility for drug labeling. Yet through many amendments to the [FFDCA] and to FDA regulations, it has remained a central premise of federal drug regulation that the manufacturer bears responsibility for the content of its label at all times. It is charged both with crafting an adequate label and with ensuring that its warnings remain adequate as long as the drug is on the market.

Indeed, prior to 2007, the FDA lacked the authority to order manufacturers to revise their labels. When Congress granted the FDA this authority, it reaffirmed the manufacturer's obligations and referred specifically to the CBE regulation, which both reflects the manufacturer's ultimate responsibility for its label and provides a mechanism for adding safety information to the label prior to FDA approval. Thus, when the risk of gangrene from IV-push injection of Phenergan became apparent, Wyeth had a duty to provide a warning that adequately described that risk, and the CBE regulation permitted it to provide such a warning before receiving the FDA's approval.

Of course, the FDA retains authority to reject labeling changes made pursuant to the CBE regulation in its review of the manufacturer's supplemental application, just as it retains such authority in reviewing all supplemental applications. But absent clear evidence that the FDA would not have approved a change to Phenergan's label, we will not conclude that it was impossible for Wyeth to comply with both federal and state requirements.

Wyeth has offered no such evidence. It does not argue that it attempted to give the kind of warning required by the Vermont jury but was prohibited from doing so by the FDA. And while it does suggest that the FDA intended to prohibit it from strengthening the warning about IV-push administration because the agency deemed such a warning inappropriate in reviewing Phenergan's drug applications, both the trial court and the Vermont Supreme Court rejected this account as a matter of fact.... We accordingly cannot credit Wyeth's contention that the FDA would have prevented it from adding a stronger warning about the IV-push method of intravenous administration.

Impossibility pre-emption is a demanding defense. On the record before us, Wyeth has failed to demonstrate that it was impossible for it to comply with both federal and state requirements. The CBE regulation permitted Wyeth to unilaterally strengthen its warning, and the mere fact that the FDA approved Phenergan's label does not establish that it would have prohibited such a change.

### IV

Wyeth also argues that requiring it to comply with a state-law duty to provide a stronger warning about IV-push administration would obstruct the purposes and objectives of federal drug labeling regulation. Levine's tort claims, it maintains, are pre-empted because they interfere with "Congress's purpose to entrust an expert agency to make drug labeling decisions that strike a balance between competing objectives." We find no merit in this argument, which relies on an untenable interpretation of congressional intent and an overbroad view of an agency's power to pre-empt state law.

Wyeth contends that the [FFDCA] establishes both a floor and a ceiling for drug regulation: Once the FDA has approved a drug's label, a state-law verdict may not deem the label inadequate, regardless of whether there is any evidence that the FDA has considered the stronger warning at issue. The most glaring problem with this argument is that all evidence of Congress' purposes is to the contrary. Building on its 1906 Act, Congress enacted the [FFDCA] to bolster consumer protection against harmful products. Congress did not provide a federal remedy for consumers harmed by unsafe or ineffective drugs in the 1938 statute or in any subsequent amendment. Evidently, it determined that widely available state rights of action provided appropriate relief for injured consumers. It may also have recognized that state-law remedies further consumer protection by motivating manufacturers to produce safe and effective drugs and to give adequate warnings.

If Congress thought state-law suits posed an obstacle to its objectives, it surely would have enacted an express pre-emption provision at some point during the [FFDCA]'s 70-year history. But despite its 1976 enactment of an express pre-emption provision for medical devices, see § 521, 90 Stat. 574 (codified at [FFDCA § 521](a)), Congress has not enacted such a provision for prescription drugs. See *Riegel*, 552 U.S., at ___ ("Congress could have applied the pre-emption clause to the entire [FFDCA]. It did not do so, but instead wrote a pre-emption clause that applies only to medical devices").[8] Its silence on the issue, coupled with its certain awareness of the prevalence of state tort litigation, is powerful evidence that Congress did not intend FDA oversight to be the exclusive means of ensuring drug safety and effectiveness. . . .

Despite this evidence that Congress did not regard state tort litigation as an obstacle to achieving its purposes, Wyeth nonetheless maintains that, because the [FFDCA] requires the FDA to determine that a drug is safe and effective under the conditions set forth in its labeling, the agency must be presumed to have performed a precise balancing of risks and benefits and to have established a specific labeling standard that leaves no room for different state-law judgments. In advancing this argument, Wyeth relies not on any statement by Congress, but instead on the preamble to a 2006 FDA regulation governing the content and format of prescription drug labels. In that preamble, the FDA declared that the [FFDCA] establishes "both a 'floor' and a 'ceiling,'" so that "FDA approval of labeling . . . preempts conflicting or contrary State law." It further stated that certain state-law actions, such as those involving failure-to-warn claims, "threaten FDA's statutorily prescribed role as the expert Federal agency responsible for evaluating and regulating drugs."

This Court has recognized that an agency regulation with the force of law can pre-empt conflicting state requirements. See, *e.g.*, *Geier v. American Honda Motor Co.*, 529 U.S. 861 (2000); *Hillsborough County v. Automated Medical Laboratories, Inc.*, 471 U.S. 707, 713 (1985). In such cases, the Court has performed its own conflict determination, relying on the substance of state and federal law and not on agency proclamations of pre-emption. We are faced with no such regulation in this case, but rather with an agency's mere assertion that state law is an obstacle to achieving its statutory objectives. Because Congress has not authorized the FDA to pre-empt state law directly, *cf.* [FFDCA § 521] (authorizing the FDA to determine the scope of the Medical Devices Amendments' pre-emption clause) the question is what weight we should accord the FDA's opinion.

In prior cases, we have given "some weight" to an agency's views about the impact of tort law on federal objectives when "the subject matter is technical and the relevant history and background are complex and extensive." *Geier*, 529 U.S., at 883. Even in such cases, however, we have not deferred to an agency's *conclusion* that state law is pre-empted. Rather, we have attended to an agency's explanation of how state law affects the regulatory scheme. While agencies have no special authority to pronounce on pre-emption absent delegation by Congress, they do have a unique understanding of the statutes they administer and an attendant ability to make informed determinations about how state requirements may pose an "obstacle to the accomplishment and execution of the full purposes and objectives of Congress." *Hines*, 312 U.S., at 67. The weight we accord the agency's explanation of state law's impact on the federal scheme depends on its thoroughness, consistency, and persuasiveness. *Cf. United States v. Mead Corp.*, 533 U.S. 218, 234–235 (2001); *Skidmore v. Swift & Co.*, 323 U.S. 134, 140 (1944).

Under this standard, the FDA's 2006 preamble does not merit deference. When the FDA issued its notice of proposed rulemaking in December 2000, it explained that the rule would "not contain policies that have federalism implications or that preempt State law." 65 Fed. Reg. 81103; *see also* 71 *id.*, at 3969 (noting that the "proposed rule did not propose to preempt state law"). In 2006, the agency finalized the rule and, without offering States or other interested parties notice or opportunity for comment, articulated a sweeping position on the [FFDCA]'s pre-emptive effect in the regulatory preamble. The agency's views on state law are inherently suspect in light of this procedural failure.

Further, the preamble is at odds with what evidence we have of Congress' purposes, and it reverses the FDA's own longstanding position without providing a reasoned explanation, including any discussion of how state law has interfered with the FDA's regulation of drug labeling during decades of coexistence. The FDA's 2006 position plainly does not reflect the agency's own view at all times relevant to this litigation. Not once prior to Levine's injury did the FDA suggest that state tort law stood as an obstacle to its statutory mission. To the contrary, it cast federal labeling standards as a floor upon which States could build and repeatedly disclaimed any attempt to pre-empt failure-to-warn claims. For instance, in 1998, the FDA stated that it did "not believe that the evolution of state tort law would cause the development of standards that would be at odds with the agency's regulations." It further noted that, in establishing "minimal standards" for drug labels, it did not intend "to preclude the states from imposing additional labeling requirements."

In keeping with Congress' decision not to pre-empt common-law tort suits, it appears that the FDA traditionally regarded state law as a complementary form of drug regulation. The FDA has limited resources to monitor the 11,000 drugs on the market, and manufacturers have superior access to information about their drugs, especially in the postmarketing phase as new risks emerge. State tort suits uncover unknown drug hazards and provide incentives for drug manufacturers to disclose safety risks promptly. They also serve a distinct compensatory function that may motivate injured persons to come forward with information. Failure-to-warn actions, in particular, lend force to the [FFDCA]'s premise that manufacturers, not the FDA, bear primary responsibility for their drug labeling at all times. Thus, the FDA long maintained that state law offers an additional, and important, layer of consumer protection that complements FDA regulation. The agency's 2006 preamble represents a dramatic change in position.

Largely based on the FDA's new position, Wyeth argues that this case presents a conflict between state and federal law analogous to the one at issue in *Geier*. There, we held that state tort claims premised on Honda's failure to install airbags conflicted with a federal regulation that did not require airbags for all cars. The Department of Transportation (DOT) had promulgated a rule that provided car manufacturers with a range of choices among passive restraint devices. Rejecting an "'all airbag'" standard, the agency had called for a gradual phase-in of a mix of passive restraints in order to spur technological development and win consumer acceptance. Because the plaintiff's claim was that car manufacturers had a duty to install airbags, it presented an obstacle to achieving "the variety and mix of devices that the federal regulation sought."

Wyeth and the dissent contend that the regulatory scheme in this case is nearly identical, but, as we have described, it is quite different. In *Geier*, the DOT conducted a formal rulemaking and then adopted a plan to phase in a mix of passive restraint devices. Examining the rule itself and the DOT's contemporaneous record, which revealed the factors the agency had weighed and the balance it had struck, we determined that state tort suits presented an obstacle to the federal scheme. After conducting our own pre-emption analysis, we considered the agency's explanation of how state law interfered with its regulation, regarding it as further support for our independent conclusion that the plaintiff's tort claim obstructed the federal regime.

By contrast, we have no occasion in this case to consider the pre-emptive effect of a specific agency regulation bearing the force of law. And the FDA's newfound opinion, expressed in its 2006 preamble, that state law "frustrate[s] the agency's implementation of its statutory mandate," does not merit deference for the reasons we have explained. Indeed, the "complex and extensive" regulatory history and background relevant to this case, *Geier*, 529 U.S., at 883, undercut the FDA's recent pronouncements of pre-emption, as they reveal the longstanding coexistence of state and federal law and the FDA's traditional recognition of state-law remedies—a recognition in place each time the agency reviewed Wyeth's Phenergan label.

In short, Wyeth has not persuaded us that failure-to-warn claims like Levine's obstruct the federal regulation of drug labeling. Congress has repeatedly declined to pre-empt state law, and the FDA's recently adopted position that state tort suits interfere with its statutory mandate is entitled to no weight. Although we recognize that some state-law claims might well frustrate the achievement of congressional objectives, this is not such a case.

V

We conclude that it is not impossible for Wyeth to comply with its state and federal law obligations and that Levine's common-law claims do not stand as an obstacle to the accomplishment of Congress' purposes in the [FFDCA]. Accordingly, the judgment of the Vermont Supreme Court is affirmed.

It is so ordered.

**Justice ALITO, . . . dissenting.**

This case illustrates that tragic facts make bad law. The Court holds that a state tort jury, rather than the Food and Drug Administration (FDA), is ultimately responsible for regulating warning labels for prescription drugs. That result cannot be reconciled with *Geier v. American Honda Motor Co.*, 529 U.S. 861 (2000), or general principles of conflict pre-emption. I respectfully dissent.

I

The Court frames the question presented as a "narrow" one—namely, whether Wyeth has a duty to provide "an adequate warning about using the IV-push method" to administer Phenergan. But that ignores the antecedent question of who—the FDA or a jury in Vermont—has the authority and responsibility for determining the "adequacy" of Phenergan's warnings. Moreover, it is unclear how a "stronger" warning could have helped respondent, after all, the physician's assistant who treated her disregarded at least six separate warnings that are already on Phenergan's labeling, so respondent would be hard pressed to prove that a seventh would have made a difference.

More to the point, the question presented by this case is not a "narrow" one, and it does not concern whether Phenergan's label should bear a "stronger" warning. Rather, the real issue is whether a state tort jury can countermand the FDA's considered judgment that Phenergan's FDA-mandated warning label renders its intravenous (IV) use "safe." . . .

Federal law, however, *does* rely on the FDA to make safety determinations like the one it made here. The FDA has long known about the risks associated with IV push in general and its use to administer Phenergan in particular. Whether wisely or not, the FDA has concluded—over the course of extensive, 54-year-long regulatory proceedings—that the drug is "safe" and "effective" when used in accordance with its FDA-mandated labeling. The unfortunate fact that respondent's healthcare providers ignored Phenergan's labeling may make this an ideal medical-malpractice case.

But turning a common-law tort suit into a "frontal assault" on the FDA's regulatory regime for drug labeling upsets the well-settled meaning of the Supremacy Clause and our conflict pre-emption jurisprudence.

. . . .

2

A faithful application of this Court's conflict pre-emption cases compels the conclusion that the FDA's 40-year-long effort to regulate the safety and efficacy of Phenergan pre-empts respondent's tort suit. Indeed, that result follows directly from our conclusion in *Geier.*

*Geier* arose under the National Traffic and Motor Safety Vehicle Act of 1966, which directs the Secretary of the Department of Transportation (DOT) to "establish by order . . . motor vehicle safety standards," 15 U.S.C. § 1392(a), which are defined as "minimum standards for motor vehicle performance, or motor vehicle equipment performance," § 1391(2). Acting pursuant to that statutory mandate, the Secretary of Transportation promulgated Federal Motor Vehicle Safety Standard 208, which required car manufacturers to include passive restraint systems (*i.e.*, devices that work automatically to protect occupants from injury during a collision) in a certain percentage of their cars built in or after 1987. Standard 208 did not require installation of any particular type of passive restraint; instead, it gave manufacturers the option to install automatic seatbelts, airbags, or any other suitable technology that they might develop, provided the restraint(s) met the performance requirements specified in the rule.

Alexis Geier drove her 1987 Honda Accord into a tree, and although she was wearing her seatbelt, she nonetheless suffered serious injuries. She then sued Honda under state tort law, alleging that her car was negligently and defectively designed because it lacked a driver's-side airbag. She argued that Congress had empowered the Secretary to set only "minimum standards" for vehicle safety. 15 U.S.C. § 1391(2). She also emphasized that the National Traffic and Motor Safety Vehicle Act contains a saving clause, which provides that "compliance with any Federal motor vehicle safety standard issued under this subchapter does not exempt any person from any liability under common law." § 1397(k).

Notwithstanding the statute's saving clause, and notwithstanding the fact that Congress gave the Secretary authority to set only "minimum" safety standards, we held Geier's state tort suit pre-empted. In reaching that result, we relied heavily on the view of the Secretary of Transportation—expressed in an *amicus* brief—that Standard 208 "'embodies the Secretary's policy judgment that safety would best be promoted if manufacturers installed *alternative* protection systems in their fleets rather than one particular system in every car.'" Because the Secretary determined that a menu of alternative technologies was "safe," the doctrine of conflict preemption barred Geier's efforts to deem some of those federally approved alternatives "unsafe" under state tort law.

The same rationale applies here. Through Phenergan's label, the FDA offered medical professionals a menu of federally approved, "safe" and "effective" alternatives—including IV push—for administering the drug. Through a state tort suit, respondent attempted to deem IV push "unsafe" and "ineffective." To be sure, federal law does not prohibit Wyeth from contraindicating IV push, just as federal law did not prohibit Honda from installing airbags in all its cars. But just as we held that States may not compel the latter, so, too, are States precluded from compelling the former. If anything, a finding of pre-emption is even more appropriate here because the [FFDCA]—unlike the National Traffic and Motor Safety Vehicle Act—contains no evidence that Congress intended the FDA to set only "minimum standards," and the [FFDCA] does not contain a saving clause.

### III

In its attempt to evade *Geier*'s applicability to this case, the Court commits both factual and legal errors. First, as a factual matter, it is demonstrably untrue that the FDA failed to consider (and strike a "balance" between) the specific costs and benefits associated with IV push. Second, as a legal matter, *Geier* does not stand for the legal propositions espoused by the dissenters (and specifically rejected by the majority) in that case. Third, drug labeling by jury verdict undermines both our broader pre-emption jurisprudence and the broader workability of the federal drug-labeling regime.

### A

Phenergan's warning label has been subject to the FDA's strict regulatory oversight since the 1950's. For at least the last 34 years, the FDA has focused specifically on whether IV-push administration of Phenergan is "safe" and "effective" when performed in accordance with Phenergan's label. The agency's ultimate decision—to retain IV push as one means for administering Phenergan, albeit subject to stringent warnings—is reflected in the plain text of Phenergan's label (sometimes in boldfaced font and all-capital letters). And the record contains ample evidence that the FDA specifically considered and reconsidered the strength of Phenergan's IV-push-related warnings in light of new scientific and medical data. The majority's factual assertions to the contrary are mistaken.

. . .

### 2

When respondent was injured in 2000, Phenergan's label specifically addressed IV push in several passages. For example, the label warned of the risks of intra-arterial injection associated with "aspiration," which is a technique used only in conjunction with IV push. The label also cautioned against the use of "syringes with rigid plungers," which are used only to administer the drug via IV push. As respondent's medical expert testified at trial, "by talking plungers and rigid needles, that's the way you do it, to push it with the plunger." Moreover, Phenergan's 2000 label devoted almost a full page to discussing the "Tubex system," which . . . is used only to administer the drug via IV push.

. . .

Thus, it is demonstrably untrue that, as of 2000, Phenergan's "labeling did not contain a specific warning about the risks of IV-push administration." And whatever else might be said about the extensive medical authorities and case reports that the FDA cited in "support" of its approval of IV-push administration of Phenergan, it cannot be said that the FDA "paid no more than passing attention to" IV push.

3

For her part, respondent does not dispute the FDA's conclusion that IV push has certain benefits. At trial, her medical practitioners testified that they used IV push in order to help her "in a swift and timely way" when she showed up at the hospital for the second time in one day complaining of "intractable" migraines, "terrible pain," inability to "bear light or sound," sleeplessness, hours-long spasms of "retching" and "vomiting," and when "every possible" alternative treatment had "failed.

Rather than disputing the benefits of IV push, respondent complains that the FDA and Wyeth underestimated its costs (and hence did not provide sufficient warnings regarding its risks). But when the FDA mandated that Phenergan's label read, "**INADVERTENT INTRA-ARTERIAL INJECTION CAN RESULT IN GANGRENE OF THE AFFECTED EXTREMITY,**" and when the FDA required Wyeth to warn that "under no circumstances should Phenergan Injection be given by intra-arterial injection", the agency could reasonably assume that medical professionals would take care not to inject Phenergan intra-arterially. Unfortunately, the physician's assistant who treated respondent in this case disregarded Phenergan's label and pushed the drug into the single spot on her arm that is *most* likely to cause an inadvertent intra-arterial injection.

As noted above, when the FDA approved Phenergan's label, it was textbook medical knowledge that the "antecubital fossa" creates a high risk of inadvertent intra-arterial injection, given the close proximity of veins and arteries. According to the physician's assistant who injured respondent, however, "it never crossed my mind" that an antecubital injection of Phenergan could hit an artery. Oblivious to the risks emphasized in Phenergan's warnings, the physician's assistant pushed a double dose of the drug into an antecubital artery over the course of "probably about three to four minutes, notwithstanding respondent's complaints of a "'burning'" sensation that she subsequently described as "'one of the most extreme pains that I've ever felt,'" . . . And when asked why she ignored Phenergan's label and failed to stop pushing the drug after respondent complained of burning pains, the physician's assistant explained that it would have been "just crazy" to "worry about an intra-arterial injection" under the circumstances.

The FDA, however, did not think that the risks associated with IV push—especially in the antecubital space—were "just crazy." That is why Phenergan's label so clearly warns against them.

B

Given the "balance" that the FDA struck between the costs and benefits of administering Phenergan via IV push, *Geier* compels the pre-emption of tort suits (like this one) that would upset that balance. The contrary conclusion requires turning yesterday's dissent into today's majority opinion.

. . . .

*Geier* does not countenance the use of state tort suits to second-guess the FDA's labeling decisions. And the Court's contrary conclusion has potentially far-reaching consequences.

C

By their very nature, juries are ill-equipped to perform the FDA's cost-benefit-balancing function. As we explained in *Riegel*, juries tend to focus on the risk of a particular product's design or warning label that arguably contributed to a particular plaintiff's injury, not on the overall benefits of that design or label; "the patients who reaped those benefits are not represented in court." Indeed, patients like respondent are the only ones whom tort juries ever see, and for a patient like respondent—who has already suffered a tragic accident—Phenergan's risks are no longer a matter of probabilities and potentialities.

In contrast, the FDA has the benefit of the long view. Its drug-approval determinations consider the interests of all potential users of a drug, including "those who would suffer without new medical products" if juries in all 50 States were free to contradict the FDA's expert determinations. And the FDA conveys its warnings with one voice, rather than whipsawing the medical community with 50 (or more) potentially conflicting ones. After today's ruling, however, parochialism may prevail.

. . . .

* * *

To be sure, state tort suits can peacefully coexist with the FDA's labeling regime, and they have done so for decades. But this case is far from peaceful coexistence. The FDA told Wyeth that Phenergan's label renders its use "safe." But the State of Vermont, through its tort law, said: "Not so."

The state-law rule at issue here is squarely pre-empted. Therefore, I would reverse the judgment of the Supreme Court of Vermont.

## Bruesewitz v. Wyeth LLC

562 U.S. 223 (2011)

**Justice SCALIA delivered the opinion of the Court.**

We consider whether a preemption provision enacted in the National Childhood Vaccine Injury Act of 1986 (NCVIA), bars state-law design-defect claims against vaccine manufacturers.

### I

### A

For the last 66 years, vaccines have been subject to the same federal premarket approval process as prescription drugs, and compensation for vaccine-related injuries has been left largely to the States. Under that regime, the elimination of communicable diseases through vaccination became "one of the greatest achievements" of public health in the 20th century. But in the 1970's and 1980's vaccines became, one might say, victims of their own success. They had been so effective in preventing infectious diseases that the public became much less alarmed at the threat of those diseases, and much more concerned with the risk of injury from the vaccines themselves.

Much of the concern centered around vaccines against diphtheria, tetanus, and pertussis (DTP), which were blamed for children's disabilities and developmental delays. This led to a massive increase in vaccine-related tort litigation. Whereas between 1978 and 1981 only nine product-liability suits were filed against DTP manufacturers, by the mid-1980's the suits numbered more than 200 each year. This destabilized the DTP vaccine market, causing two of the three domestic manufacturers to withdraw; and the remaining manufacturer, Lederle Laboratories, estimated that its potential tort liability exceeded its annual sales by a factor of 200. Vaccine shortages arose when Lederle had production problems in 1984.

Despite the large number of suits, there were many complaints that obtaining compensation for legitimate vaccine-inflicted injuries was too costly and difficult.[9] A significant number of parents were already declining vaccination for their children, and concerns about compensation threatened to depress vaccination rates even further. This was a source of concern to public health officials, since vaccines are effective in preventing outbreaks of disease only if a large percentage of the population is vaccinated.

To stabilize the vaccine market and facilitate compensation, Congress enacted the NCVIA in 1986. The Act establishes a no-fault compensation program "designed to work faster and with greater ease than the civil tort system." *Shalala v. Whitecotton,* 514 U.S. 268, 269 (1995). A person injured by a vaccine, or his legal guardian, may file a petition for compensation in the United States Court of Federal Claims, naming the Secretary of Health and Human Services as the respondent. A special master then makes an informal adjudication of the petition within (except for two limited exceptions) 240 days. The Court of Federal Claims must review objections to the special master's decision and enter final judgment under a similarly tight statutory deadline. At that point, a claimant has two options: to accept the court's judgment and forgo a traditional tort suit for damages, or to reject the judgment and seek tort relief from the vaccine manufacturer.

Fast, informal adjudication is made possible by the [NCVIA]'s Vaccine Injury Table, which lists the vaccines covered under the [NCVIA]; describes each vaccine's compensable, adverse side effects; and indicates how soon after vaccination those side effects should first manifest themselves. Claimants who show that a listed injury first manifested itself at the appropriate time are prima facie entitled to compensation. No showing of causation is necessary; the Secretary bears the burden of disproving causation. A claimant may also recover for unlisted side effects, and for listed side effects that occur at times other than those specified in the Table, but for those the claimant must prove causation. Unlike in tort suits, claimants under the [NCVIA] are not required to show that the administered vaccine was defectively manufactured, labeled, or designed.

Successful claimants receive compensation for medical, rehabilitation, counseling, special education, and vocational training expenses; diminished earning capacity; pain and suffering; and $250,000 for vaccine-related deaths. Attorney's fees are provided, not only for successful cases, but even for unsuccessful claims that are not frivolous. These awards are paid out of a fund created by an excise tax on each vaccine dose.

The *quid pro quo* for this, designed to stabilize the vaccine market, was the provision of significant tort-liability protections for vaccine manufacturers. The Act requires claimants to seek relief through the compensation program before filing suit for more than $1,000. Manufacturers are generally immunized from liability for failure to warn if they have complied with all regulatory requirements (including but not limited to warning requirements) and have given the warning either to the claimant or the claimant's physician. They are immunized from liability for punitive damages absent failure to comply with regulatory requirements, "fraud," "intentional and wrongful withholding of information," or other "criminal or illegal activity." And most relevant to the present case, the [NCVIA] expressly eliminates liability for a vaccine's unavoidable, adverse side effects:

> No vaccine manufacturer shall be liable in a civil action for damages arising from a vaccine-related injury or death associated with the administration of a vaccine after October 1, 1988, if the injury or death resulted from side effects that were unavoidable even though the vaccine was properly prepared and was accompanied by proper directions and warnings.

### B

The vaccine at issue here is a DTP vaccine manufactured by Lederle Laboratories. It first received federal approval in 1948 and received supplemental approvals in 1953 and 1970. Respondent Wyeth purchased Lederle in 1994 and stopped manufacturing the vaccine in 1998.

Hannah Bruesewitz was born on October 20, 1991. Her pediatrician administered doses of the DTP vaccine according to the Center for Disease Control's recommended childhood immunization schedule. Within 24 hours of her April 1992 vaccination, Hannah started to experience seizures. She suffered over 100 seizures during the next month, and her doctors eventually diagnosed her with "residual seizure disorder" and "developmental delay." Hannah, now a teenager, is still diagnosed with both conditions.

In April 1995, Hannah's parents, Russell and Robalee Bruesewitz, filed a vaccine injury petition in the United States Court of Federal Claims, alleging that Hannah suffered from on-Table residual seizure disorder and encephalopathy injuries. A Special Master denied their claims on various grounds, though they were awarded $126,800 in attorney's fees and costs. The Bruesewitzes elected to reject the unfavorable judgment, and in October 2005 filed this lawsuit in Pennsylvania state court. Their complaint alleged (as relevant here) that defective design of Lederle's DTP vaccine caused Hannah's disabilities, and that Lederle was subject to strict liability, and liability for negligent design, under Pennsylvania common law.

Wyeth removed the suit to the United States District Court for the Eastern District of Pennsylvania, which granted Wyeth summary judgment on the strict-liability and negligence design-defect claims, holding that the Pennsylvania law providing those causes of action was preempted by 42 U.S.C. § 300aa-22(b)(1) [part of the National Childhood Vaccine Injury Act of 1986]. The United States Court of Appeals for the Third Circuit affirmed. We granted certiorari.

II

A

We set forth again the statutory text at issue:

> "No vaccine manufacturer shall be liable in a civil action for damages arising from a vaccine-related injury or death associated with the administration of a vaccine after October 1, 1988, if the injury or death resulted from side effects that were unavoidable even though the vaccine was properly prepared and was accompanied by proper directions and warnings."

The "even though" clause clarifies the word that precedes it. It delineates the preventative measures that a vaccine manufacturer *must* have taken for a side-effect to be considered "unavoidable" under the statute. Provided that there was proper manufacture and warning, any remaining side effects, including those resulting from design defects, are deemed to have been unavoidable. State-law design-defect claims are therefore preempted.

If a manufacturer could be held liable for failure to use a different design, the word "unavoidable" would do no work. A side effect of a vaccine could *always* have been avoidable by use of a differently designed vaccine not containing the harmful element. The language of the provision thus suggests that the *design* of the vaccine is a given, not subject to question in the tort action. What the statute establishes as a complete defense must be unavoidability (given safe manufacture and warning) *with respect to the particular design*. Which plainly implies that the design itself is not open to question.

A further textual indication leads to the same conclusion. Products-liability law establishes a classic and well known triumvirate of grounds for liability: defective manufacture, inadequate directions or warnings, and defective design. If all three were intended to be preserved, it would be strange to mention specifically only two, and leave the third to implication. It would have been much easier (and much more natural) to provide that manufacturers would be liable for "defective manufacture, defective directions or warning, and defective design." It seems that the statute fails to mention design-defect liability "by deliberate choice, not inadvertence." *Barnhart v. Peabody Coal Co.*, 537 U.S. 149, 168 (2003).

B

The dissent's principal textual argument is mistaken. We agree with its premise that "'side effects that were unavoidable' must refer to side effects caused by a vaccine's *design*." We do not comprehend, however, the second step of its reasoning, which is that the use of the conditional term "if" in the introductory phrase "if the injury or death resulted from side effects that were unavoidable" "plainly implies that some side effects stemming from a vaccine's design are 'unavoidable,' while others are avoidable." That is not so. The "if" clause makes total sense whether the design to which "unavoidable" refers is (as the dissent believes) any feasible design (making the side effects of the design used for the vaccine at issue avoidable), or (as we believe) the particular design used for the vaccine at issue (making its side effects unavoidable). Under the latter view, the condition established by the "if" clause is that the vaccine have been properly labeled and manufactured; and under the former, that it have been properly *designed*, labeled, and manufactured. Neither view renders the "if" clause a nullity. Which of the two variants must be preferred is addressed by our textual analysis, and is in no way determined by the "if" clause.

Petitioners' and the dissent's textual argument also rests upon the proposition that the word "unavoidable" in § 300aa-22(b)(1) is a term of art that incorporates comment *k* to *Restatement (Second) of Torts § 402A* (1963–1964). The Restatement generally holds a manufacturer strictly liable for harm to person or property caused by "any product in a defective condition unreasonably dangerous to the user." Comment *k* exempts from this strict-liability rule "unavoidably unsafe products." An unavoidably unsafe product is defined by a hodge-podge of criteria and a few examples, such as the Pasteur rabies vaccine and experimental pharmaceuticals. Despite this lack of clarity, petitioners seize upon one phrase in the comment *k* analysis, and assert that by 1986 a majority of courts had made this a *sine qua non* requirement for an "unavoidably unsafe product": a case-specific showing that the product was "quite incapable of being made safer for [its] intended . . . use."

We have no need to consider the finer points of comment *k*. Whatever consistent judicial gloss that comment may have been given in 1986, there is no reason to believe that § 300aa-22(b)(1) was invoking it. The comment creates a special category of "unavoidably unsafe products," while the statute refers to "side effects that were unavoidable." That the latter uses the adjective "unavoidable" and the former the adverb "unavoidably" does not establish that Congress had comment *k* in mind. "Unavoidable" is hardly a rarely used word. Even the cases petitioners cite as putting a definitive gloss on comment *k* use the precise phrase "unavoidably unsafe product"; none attaches special significance to the term "unavoidable" standing alone.

The textual problems with petitioners' interpretation do not end there. The phrase "even though" in the clause "even though the vaccine was properly prepared and [labeled]" is meant to signal the unexpected: unavoidable side effects persist *despite* best manufacturing and labeling practices. But petitioners' reading eliminates any opposition between the "even though" clause—called a concessive subordinate clause by grammarians—and the word "unavoidable." Their reading makes preemption turn equally on unavoidability, proper preparation, and proper labeling. Thus, the dissent twice refers to the requirements of proper preparation and proper labeling as "two additional prerequisites" for preemption independent of unavoidability. The primary textual justification for the dissent's position depends on that independence. But linking independent ideas is the job of a coordinating junction like "and," not a subordinating junction like "even though."

Petitioners and the dissent contend that the interpretation we propose would render part of § 300aa-22(b)(1) superfluous: Congress could have more tersely and more clearly preempted design-defect claims by barring liability "if . . . the vaccine was properly prepared and was accompanied by proper directions and warnings." The intervening passage ("the injury or death resulted from side effects that were unavoidable even though") is unnecessary. True enough. But the rule against giving a portion of text an interpretation which renders it superfluous does not prescribe that a passage which could have been more terse does not mean what it says. The rule applies only if verbosity and prolixity can be eliminated by giving the offending passage, or the remainder of the text, a competing interpretation. That is not the case here. To be sure, petitioners' and the dissent's interpretation gives independent meaning to the intervening passage (the supposed meaning of comment *k*); but it does so only at the expense of rendering the remainder of the provision superfluous. Since a vaccine is not "quite incapable of being made safer for [its] intended use" if manufacturing defects could have been eliminated or better warnings provided, the entire "even though" clause is a useless appendage. It would suffice to say "if the injury or death resulted from side effects that were unavoidable"—full stop.

### III

The structure of the NCVIA and of vaccine regulation in general reinforces what the text of § 300aa-22(b)(1) suggests. A vaccine's license spells out the manufacturing method that must be followed and the directions and warnings that must accompany the product. Manufacturers ordinarily must obtain the Food and Drug Administration's (FDA) approval before modifying either. Deviations from the license thus provide objective evidence of manufacturing defects or inadequate warnings. Further objective evidence comes from the FDA's regulations—more than 90 of them—that pervasively regulate the manufacturing process, down to the requirements for plumbing and ventilation systems at each manufacturing facility. Material noncompliance with any one of them, or with any other FDA regulation, could cost the manufacturer its regulatory-compliance defense.

Design defects, in contrast, do not merit a single mention in the NCVIA or the FDA's regulations. Indeed, the FDA has never even spelled out in regulations the criteria it uses to decide whether a vaccine is safe and effective for its intended use. And the decision is surely not an easy one. Drug manufacturers often could trade a little less efficacy for a little more safety, but the safest design is not always the best one. Striking the right balance between safety and efficacy is especially difficult with respect to vaccines, which affect public as well as individual health. Yet the [NCVIA], which in every other respect micromanages manufacturers, is silent on how to evaluate competing designs. Are manufacturers liable only for failing to employ an alternative design that the FDA has approved for distribution (an approval it takes years to obtain)? Or does it suffice that a vaccine design has been approved in other countries? Or could there be liability for failure to use a design that exists only in a lab? Neither [NCVIA] nor the FDA regulations provide an answer, leaving the universe of alternative designs to be limited only by an expert's imagination.

Jurors, of course, often decide similar questions with little guidance, and we do not suggest that the absence of guidance alone suggests preemption. But the lack of guidance for design defects combined with the extensive guidance for the two grounds of liability specifically mentioned in the [NCVIA] strongly suggests that design defects were not mentioned because they are not a basis for liability.

The mandates contained in the [NCVIA] lead to the same conclusion. Design-defect torts, broadly speaking, have two beneficial effects: (1) prompting the development of improved designs, and (2) providing compensation for inflicted injuries. The NCVIA provides other means for achieving both effects. We have already discussed the [NCVIA]'s generous compensation scheme. And the [NCVIA] provides many means of improving vaccine design. It directs the Secretary of Health and Human Services to promote "the development of childhood vaccines that result in fewer and less serious adverse reactions." It establishes a National Vaccine Program, whose Director is "to achieve optimal prevention of human infectious diseases . . . and to achieve optimal prevention against adverse reactions." The Program is to set priorities for federal vaccine research, and to coordinate federal vaccine safety and efficacy testing. The Act requires vaccine manufacturers and health-care providers to report adverse side effects, and provides for monitoring of vaccine safety through a collaboration with eight managed-care organizations. And of course whenever the FDA concludes that a vaccine is unsafe, it may revoke the license.

These provisions for federal agency improvement of vaccine design, and for federally prescribed compensation, once again suggest that § 300aa-22(b)(1)'s silence regarding design-defect liability was not inadvertent. It instead reflects a sensible choice to leave complex epidemiological judgments about vaccine design to the FDA and the National Vaccine Program rather than juries.

And finally, the [NCVIA]'s structural *quid pro quo* leads to the same conclusion: The vaccine manufacturers fund from their sales an informal, efficient compensation program for vaccine injuries; in exchange they avoid costly tort litigation and the occasional disproportionate jury verdict. But design-defect allegations are the most speculative and difficult type of products liability claim to litigate. Taxing vaccine manufacturers' product to fund the compensation program, while leaving their liability for design defect virtually unaltered, would hardly coax manufacturers back into the market.

The dissent believes the [NCVIA]'s mandates are irrelevant because they do not spur innovation in precisely the same way as state-law tort systems. That is a novel suggestion. Although we previously have expressed doubt that Congress would quietly preempt product-liability claims without providing a federal substitute, see *Medtronic, Inc. v. Lohr,* 518 U.S. 470, 486–488 (1996) (plurality opinion), we have never suggested we would be skeptical of preemption unless the congressional substitute operated like the tort system. We decline to adopt that stance today. The dissent's belief that the FDA and the National Vaccine Program cannot alone spur adequate vaccine innovation is probably questionable, but surely beside the point.

### IV

Since our interpretation of § 300aa-22(b)(1) is the only interpretation supported by the text and structure of the NCVIA, even those of us who believe legislative history is a legitimate tool of statutory interpretation have no need to resort to it. In any case, the dissent's contention that it would contradict our conclusion is mistaken.

The dissent's legislative history relies on the following syllogism: A 1986 House Committee Report states that § 300aa-22(b)(1) "sets forth the principle contained in Comment k of Section 402A of the Restatement of Torts (Second);" in 1986 comment k was "commonly understood" to require a case-specific showing that "no feasible alternative design" existed; Congress therefore must have intended § 300aa-22(b)(1) to require that showing. The syllogism ignores unhelpful statements in the Report and relies upon a term of art that did not exist in 1986.

Immediately after the language quoted by the dissent, the 1986 Report notes the difficulty a jury would have in faithfully assessing whether a feasible alternative design exists when an innocent "young child, often badly injured or killed" is the plaintiff. Eliminating that concern is why the Report's authors "strongly believ[e] that Comment *k* is appropriate and necessary as the policy for civil actions seeking damages in tort." The dissent's interpretation of § 300aa-22(b)(1) and its version of "the principle in Comment K" adopted by the 1986 Report leave that concern unaddressed.

The dissent buries another unfavorable piece of legislative history. Because the Report believes that § 300aa-22(b)(1) should incorporate "the principle in Comment K" and because the [NCVIA] provides a generous no-fault compensation scheme, the Report counsels injured parties who cannot prove a manufacturing or labeling defect to "pursue recompense in the compensation system, not the tort system." That counsel echoes our interpretation of § 300aa-22(b)(1).

Not to worry, the dissent retorts, a Committee Report by a later Congress "authoritative[ly]" vindicates its interpretation. Post-enactment legislative history (a contradiction in terms) is not a legitimate tool of statutory interpretation. See *Jones v. United States,* 526 U.S. 227, 238 (1999). Real (pre-enactment) legislative history is persuasive to some because it is thought to shed light on what legislators understood an ambiguous statutory text to mean when they voted to enact it into law. See *Exxon Mobil Corp. v. Allapattah Services, Inc.,* 545 U.S. 546, 568 (2005). But post-enactment legislative history by definition "could have had no effect on the congressional vote," *District of Columbia v. Heller,* 554 U.S. 570, 605 (2008).

It does not matter that § 300aa-22(b)(1) did not take effect until the later Congress passed the excise tax that funds the compensation scheme, and that the supposedly dispositive Committee Report is attached to that funding legislation. Those who voted on the relevant statutory language were not necessarily the same persons who crafted the statements in the later Committee Report; or if they were did not necessarily have the same views at that earlier time; and no one voting at that earlier time could possibly have been informed by those later statements. Permitting the legislative history of subsequent funding legislation to alter the meaning of a statute would set a dangerous precedent. Many provisions of federal law depend on appropriations or include sunset provisions; they cannot be made the device for unenacted statutory revision.

That brings us to the second flaw in the dissent's syllogism: Comment *k* did not have a "commonly understood meaning" in the mid-1980's. Some courts thought it required a case-specific showing that a product was "unavoidably unsafe"; many others thought it categorically exempted certain types of products from strict liability. When all (or nearly all) of the relevant judicial decisions have given a term or concept a consistent judicial gloss, we presume Congress intended the term or concept to have that meaning when it incorporated it into a later-enacted statute. The consistent gloss represents the public understanding of the term. We cannot make the same assumption when widespread disagreement exists among the lower courts. We must make do with giving the term its most plausible meaning using the traditional tools of statutory interpretation. That is what we have done today.

* * *

For the foregoing reasons, we hold that the National Childhood Vaccine Injury Act preempts all design-defect claims against vaccine manufacturers brought by plaintiffs who seek compensation for injury or death caused by vaccine side effects. The judgment of the Court of Appeals is affirmed.

*It is so ordered.*

**Justice SOTOMAYOR, . . . dissenting.**

Vaccine manufacturers have long been subject to a legal duty, rooted in basic principles of products liability law, to improve the designs of their vaccines in light of advances in science and technology. Until today, that duty was enforceable through a traditional state-law tort action for defective design. In holding that § 22(b)(1) of the National Childhood Vaccine Injury Act of 1986 (Vaccine Act or Act), 42 U.S.C. § 300aa-22(b)(1), pre-empts all design defect claims for injuries stemming from vaccines covered under the [NCVIA], the Court imposes its own bare policy preference over the considered judgment of Congress. In doing so, the Court excises 13 words from the statutory text, misconstrues the [NCVIA]'s legislative history, and disturbs the careful balance Congress struck between compensating vaccine-injured children and stabilizing the childhood vaccine market. Its decision leaves a regulatory vacuum in which no one ensures that vaccine manufacturers adequately take account of scientific and technological advancements when designing or distributing their products. Because nothing in the text, structure, or legislative history of the Vaccine Act remotely suggests that Congress intended such a result, I respectfully dissent.

I

A

Section 22 of the Vaccine Act provides "[s]tandards of responsibility" to govern civil actions against vaccine manufacturers. 42 U.S.C. § 300aa-22. Section 22(a) sets forth the "[g]eneral rule" that "State law shall apply to a civil action brought for damages for a vaccine-related injury or death." § 300aa-22(a). This baseline rule that state law applies is subject to three narrow exceptions, one of which, § 22(b)(1), is at issue in this case. Section 22(b)(1) provides:

> No vaccine manufacturer shall be liable in a civil action for damages arising from a vaccine-related injury or death associated with the administration of a vaccine after October 1, 1988, if the injury or death resulted from side effects that were unavoidable even though the vaccine was properly prepared and was accompanied by proper directions and warnings.

The provision contains two key clauses: "if the injury or death resulted from side effects that were unavoidable" (the "if" clause), and "even though the vaccine was properly prepared and was accompanied by proper directions and warnings" (the "even though" clause).

Blackletter products liability law generally recognizes three different types of product defects: design defects, manufacturing defects, and labeling defects (*e.g.*, failure to warn). The reference in the "even though" clause to a "properly prepared" vaccine "accompanied by proper directions and warnings" is an obvious reference to two such defects—manufacturing and labeling defects. The plain terms of the "even though" clause thus indicate that § 22(b)(1) applies only where neither kind of defect is present. Because § 22(b)(1) is invoked by vaccine manufacturers as a defense to tort liability, it follows that the "even though" clause requires a vaccine manufacturer in each civil action to demonstrate that its vaccine is free from manufacturing and labeling defects to fall within the liability exemption of § 22(b)(1).

Given that the "even though" clause requires the absence of manufacturing and labeling defects, the "if " clause's reference to "side effects that were unavoidable" must refer to side effects caused by something other than manufacturing and labeling defects. The only remaining kind of product defect recognized under traditional products liability law is a design defect. Thus, "side effects that were unavoidable" must refer to side effects caused by a vaccine's *design* that were "unavoidable." Because § 22(b)(1) uses the conditional term "if," moreover, the text plainly implies that some side effects stemming from a vaccine's design are "unavoidable," while others are avoidable. Accordingly, because the "if" clause (like the "even though" clause) sets forth a condition to invoke § 22(b)(1)'s defense to tort liability, Congress must also have intended a vaccine manufacturer to demonstrate in each civil action that the particular side effects of a vaccine's design were "unavoidable."

Congress' use of conditional "if" clauses in two other provisions of the Vaccine Act supports the conclusion that § 22(b)(1) requires an inquiry in each case in which a manufacturer seeks to invoke the provision's exception to state tort liability. In § 22(b)(2), Congress created a presumption that, for purposes of § 22(b)(1), "a vaccine shall be presumed to be accompanied by proper directions and warnings if the vaccine manufacturer shows that it complied in all material respects with" federal labeling requirements. 42 U.S.C. § 300aa-22(b)(2). Similarly, in § 23(d)(2), Congress created an exemption from punitive damages "[i]f . . . the manufacturer shows that it complied, in all material respects," with applicable federal laws, unless it engages in "fraud," "intentional and wrongful withholding of information" from federal regulators, or "other criminal or illegal activity." § 300aa-23(d)(2). It would be highly anomalous for Congress to use a conditional "if" clause in §§ 22(b)(2) and 23(d)(2) to require a specific inquiry in each case while using the same conditional "if" clause in § 22(b)(1) to denote a categorical exemption from liability.

. . .

The plain text and structure of the Vaccine Act thus compel the conclusion that § 22(b)(1) pre-empts some—but not all—design defect claims. Contrary to the majority's and respondent's categorical reading, petitioners correctly contend that, where a plaintiff has proved that she has suffered an injury resulting from a side effect caused by a vaccine's design, a vaccine manufacturer may invoke § 22(b)(1)'s liability exemption only if it demonstrates that the side effect stemming from the particular vaccine's design is "unavoidable," and that the vaccine is otherwise free from manufacturing and labeling defects.

**B**

The legislative history confirms petitioners' interpretation of § 22(b)(1) and sheds further light on its pre-emptive scope. The House Energy and Commerce Committee Report accompanying the Vaccine Act, H. R. Rep. No. 99-908, pt. 1 (1986) (hereinafter 1986 Report), explains in relevant part:

> *Subsection (b)—Unavoidable Adverse Side Effects; Direct Warnings.*—This provision sets forth the principle contained in Comment K of Section 402A

> of the Restatement of Torts (Second) that a vaccine manufacturer should not be liable for injuries or deaths resulting from unavoidable side effects even though the vaccine was properly prepared and accompanied by proper directions and warnings.
>
> The Committee has set forth Comment K in this bill because it intends that the principle in Comment K regarding 'unavoidably unsafe' products, i.e., those products which in the present state of human skill and knowledge cannot be made safe, apply to the vaccines covered in the bill and that such products not be the subject of liability in the tort system.

The Report expressly adopts comment *k* of §402A of the Restatement of Torts (Second) (1963–1964) (hereinafter Restatement), which provides that "unavoidably unsafe" products—i.e., those that "in the present state of human knowledge, are quite incapable of being made safe for their intended and ordinary use"—are not defective. As "[a]n outstanding example" of an "[u]navoidably unsafe" product, comment k cites "the vaccine for the Pasteur treatment of rabies, which not uncommonly leads to very serious and damaging consequences when it is injected"; "[s]ince the disease itself invariably leads to a dreadful death, both the marketing and the use of the vaccine are fully justified, notwithstanding the unavoidable high degree of risk which they involve." Comment k thus provides that "seller[s]" of "[u]navoidably unsafe" products are "not to be held to strict liability" provided that such products "are properly prepared and marketed, and proper warning is given."

As the 1986 Report explains, Congress intended that the "principle in Comment K regarding 'unavoidably unsafe' products" apply to the vaccines covered in the bill. That intent, in turn, is manifested in the plain text of §22(b)(1)—in particular, Congress' use of the word "unavoidable," as well as the phrases "properly prepared" and "accompanied by proper directions and warnings," which were taken nearly verbatim from comment *k*. 42 U.S.C. §300aa-22(b)(1); see Restatement 353–354 ("Such a[n unavoidably unsafe] product, properly prepared, and accompanied by proper directions and warning, is not defective"). By the time of the Vaccine Act's enactment in 1986, numerous state and federal courts had interpreted comment k to mean that a product is "unavoidably unsafe" when, given proper manufacture and labeling, no feasible alternative design would reduce the safety risks without compromising the product's cost and utility. Given Congress' expressed intent to codify the "principle in Comment K," 1986 Report 26, the term "unavoidable" in §22(b)(1) is best understood as a term of art, which incorporates the commonly understood meaning of "unavoidably unsafe" products under comment k at the time of the [NCVIA]'s enactment in 1986. See *McDermott Int'l, Inc. v. Wilander*, 498 U.S. 337, 342 (1991) ("[W]e assume that when a statute uses . . . a term [of art], Congress intended it to have its established meaning") Similarly, courts applying comment *k* had long required manufacturers invoking the defense to demonstrate that their products were not only "unavoidably unsafe" but also properly manufactured and labeled. By requiring "prope[r] prepar[ation]" and "proper directions and warnings" in § 22(b)(1), Congress plainly intended to incorporate these additional comment *k* requirements.

. . .

In addition to the 1986 Report, one other piece of the [NCVIA]'s legislative history provides further confirmation of the petitioners' textual reading of *§ 22(b)(1)*. When Congress enacted the Vaccine Act in 1986, it did not initially include a source of payment for the no-fault compensation program the [NCVIA] established. The Act thus "made the compensation program and accompanying tort reforms contingent on the enactment of a tax to provide funding for the compensation." 1987 Report 690. In 1987, Congress passed legislation to fund the compensation program. The House Energy and Commerce Committee Report accompanying that legislation specifically stated that "the codification of Comment *(k)* of The Restatement (Second) of Torts was not intended to decide as a matter of law the circumstances in which a vaccine should be deemed unavoidably unsafe." The Committee noted that "[a]n amendment to establish . . . that a manufacturer's failure to develop [a] safer vaccine was not grounds for liability was rejected by the Committee during its original consideration of the [NCVIA]." In light of that rejection, the Committee emphasized that "there should be no misunderstanding that the [NCVIA] undertook to decide as a matter of law whether vaccines were unavoidably unsafe or not," and that "[t]his question is left to the courts to determine in accordance with applicable law."

. . .

In sum, the text, structure, and legislative history of the Vaccine Act are fully consistent with petitioners' reading of § 22(b)(1). Accordingly, I believe § 22(b)(1) exempts vaccine manufacturers from tort liability only upon a showing by the manufacturer in each case that the vaccine was properly manufactured and labeled, and that the side effects stemming from the vaccine's design could not have been prevented by a feasible alternative design that would have eliminated the adverse side effects without compromising the vaccine's cost and utility.

. . .

The majority's decision today disturbs that careful balance based on a bare policy preference that it is better "to leave complex epidemiological judgments about vaccine design to the FDA and the National Vaccine Program rather than juries." To be sure, reasonable minds can disagree about the wisdom of having juries weigh the relative costs and benefits of a particular vaccine design. But whatever the merits of the majority's policy preference, the decision to bar all design defect claims against vaccine manufacturers is one that Congress must make, not this Court. By construing § 22(b)(1) to pre-empt all design defect claims against vaccine manufacturers for covered vaccines, the majority's decision leaves a regulatory vacuum in which no one—neither the FDA nor any other federal agency, nor state and federal juries—ensures that vaccine manufacturers adequately take account of scientific and technological advancements. This concern is especially acute with respect to vaccines that have already been released and marketed to the public. Manufacturers, given the lack of robust competition in the vaccine market, will often have little or no incentive to improve the designs of vaccines that are already generating significant profit margins. Nothing in the text, structure, or legislative history remotely suggests that Congress intended that result.

I respectfully dissent.

## Merck Sharp & Dohme Corp. v. Albrecht

139 S. Ct. 1668 (2019)

**Justice BREYER delivered the opinion of the Court.**

When Congress enacted the [FFDCA], it charged the Food and Drug Administration with ensuring that prescription drugs are "safe for use under the conditions prescribed, recommended, or suggested" in the drug's "labeling." [FFDCA § 505](d). When the FDA exercises this authority, it makes careful judgments about what warnings should appear on a drug's label for the safety of consumers.

For that reason, we have previously held that "clear evidence" that the FDA would not have approved a change to the drug's label pre-empts a claim, grounded in state law, that a drug manufacturer failed to warn consumers of the change-related risks associated with using the drug. See *Wyeth v. Levine*, 555 U. S. 555, 571 (2009). We here determine that this question of pre-emption is one for a judge to decide, not a jury. We also hold that "clear evidence" is evidence that shows the court that the drug manufacturer fully informed the FDA of the justifications for the warning required by state law and that the FDA, in turn, informed the drug manufacturer that the FDA would not approve a change to the drug's label to include that warning.

### I

The central issue in this case concerns federal pre-emption, which as relevant here, takes place when it is "'impossible for a private party to comply with both state and federal requirements.'" *Mutual Pharmaceutical Co. v. Bartlett*, 570 U. S. 472, 480 (2013). The state law that we consider is state common law or state statutes that require drug manufacturers to warn drug consumers of the risks associated with drugs. The federal law that we consider is the statutory and regulatory scheme through which the FDA regulates the information that appears on brand-name prescription drug labels. The alleged conflict between state and federal law in this case has to do with a drug that was manufactured by petitioner Merck Sharp & Dohme and was administered to respondents without a warning of certain associated risks.

### A

The FDA regulates the safety information that appears on the labels of prescription drugs that are marketed in the United States. [FFDCA 505](b)(1)(F); 21 C.F.R. § 201.57(a) (2018). Although we commonly understand a drug's "label" to refer to the sticker affixed to a prescription bottle, in this context the term refers more broadly to the written material that is sent to the physician who prescribes the drug and the written material that comes with the prescription bottle when the drug is handed to the patient at the pharmacy. [FFDCA § 201](m). These (often lengthy) package inserts contain detailed information about the drug's medical uses and health risks. [FFDCA § 505](b)(1)(F); 21 C.F.R. § 201.57(a).

FDA regulations set out requirements for the content, the format, and the order of the safety information on the drug label. § 201.57(c). Those regulations require drug labels to include, among other things: (1) prominent "boxed" warnings about risks that may lead to death or serious injury; (2) contraindications describing any situation in which the drug should not be used because the risk of use outweighs any therapeutic benefit; (3) warnings and precautions about other potential safety hazards; and (4) any adverse reactions for which there is some basis to believe a causal relationship exists between the drug and the occurrence of the adverse event.

As those requirements make clear, the category in which a particular risk appears on a drug label is an indicator of the likelihood and severity of the risk. The hierarchy of label information is designed to "prevent overwarning" so that less important information does not "overshadow" more important information. 73 Fed. Reg. 49605–49606 (2008). It is also designed to exclude "[e]xaggeration of risk, or inclusion of speculative or hypothetical risks," that "could discourage appropriate use of a beneficial drug."

Prospective drug manufacturers work with the FDA to develop an appropriate label when they apply for FDA approval of a new drug. [FFDCA §§ 505](a), [505](b), [505](d)(7); 21 C.F.R. § 314.125(b)(6). But FDA regulations also acknowledge that information about drug safety may change over time, and that new information may require changes to the drug label. [21 C.F.R.] §§ 314.80(c), 314.81(b)(2)(i). Drug manufacturers generally seek advance permission from the FDA to make substantive changes to their drug labels. However, an FDA regulation called the "changes being effected" or "CBE" regulation permits drug manufacturers to change a label without prior FDA approval if the change is designed to "add or strengthen a . . . warning" where there is "newly acquired information" about the "evidence of a causal association" between the drug and a risk of harm. 21 C.F.R. § 314.70(c)(6)(iii)(A).

### B

Petitioner Merck Sharp & Dohme manufactures Fosamax, a drug that treats and prevents osteoporosis in postmenopausal women. Fosamax belongs to a class of drugs called "bisphosphonates." Fosamax and other bisphosphonates work by affecting the "bone remodeling process," that is, the process through which bones are continuously broken down and built back up again. For some postmenopausal women, the two parts of the bone remodeling process fall out of sync; the body removes old bone cells faster than it can replace them. That imbalance can lead to osteoporosis, a disease that is characterized by low bone mass and an increased risk of bone fractures. Fosamax (like other bisphosphonates) slows the breakdown of old bone cells and thereby helps postmenopausal women avoid osteoporotic fractures.

However, the mechanism through which Fosamax decreases the risk of osteoporotic fractures may increase the risk of a different type of fracture. That is because all bones—healthy and osteoporotic alike—sometimes develop microscopic cracks that are not due to any trauma, but are instead caused by the mechanical stress of everyday activity. Those so-called "stress fractures" ordinarily heal on their own through the bone remodeling process. But, by slowing the breakdown of old bone cells, Fosamax and other bisphosphonates may cause stress fractures to progress to complete breaks that cause great pain and require surgical intervention to repair. When that rare type of complete, low-energy fracture affects the thigh bone, it is called an "atypical femoral fracture."

The Fosamax label that the FDA approved in 1995 did not warn of the risk of atypical femoral fractures. At that time, Merck's scientists were aware of at least a theoretical risk of those fractures. Indeed, as far back as 1990 and 1991, when Fosamax was undergoing preapproval clinical trials, Merck scientists expressed concern in internal discussions that Fosamax could inhibit bone remodeling to such a "'profound'" degree that "inadequate repair may take place" and "'micro-fractures would not heal.'" When Merck applied to the FDA for approval of Fosamax, Merck brought those theoretical considerations to the FDA's attention. But, perhaps because the concerns were only theoretical, the FDA approved Fosamax's label without requiring any mention of this risk.

Evidence connecting Fosamax to atypical femoral fractures developed after 1995. Merck began receiving adverse event reports from the medical community indicating that long-term Fosamax users were suffering atypical femoral fractures. For example, Merck received a report from a doctor who said that hospital staff had begun calling atypical femoral fractures the "'Fosamax Fracture' " because "'100% of patients in his practice who have experienced femoral fractures (without being hit by a taxicab), were taking Fosamax . . . for over 5 years.'" Merck performed a statistical analysis of Fosamax adverse event reports, concluding that these reports revealed a statistically significant incidence of femur fractures. And about the same time, Merck began to see numerous scholarly articles and case studies documenting possible connections between long-term Fosamax use and atypical femoral fractures.

In 2008, Merck applied to the FDA for preapproval to change Fosamax's label to add language to both the "Adverse Reaction[s]" and the "Precaution[s]" sections of the label. In particular, Merck proposed adding a reference to "'low-energy femoral shaft fracture'" in the Adverse Reactions section, and cross-referencing a longer discussion in the Precautions section that focused on the risk of stress fractures associated with Fosamax. The FDA approved the addition to the Adverse Reactions section, but rejected Merck's proposal to warn of a risk of "stress fractures." The FDA explained that Merck's "justification" for the proposed change to the Precautions section was "inadequate," because "[i]dentification of 'stress fractures' may not be clearly related to the atypical subtrochanteric fractures that have been reported in the literature." The FDA invited Merck to "resubmit" its application and to "fully address all the deficiencies listed." But Merck instead withdrew its application and decided to make the changes to the Adverse Reactions section through the CBE process. Merck made no changes to the Precautions section at issue here.

A warning about "atypical femoral fractures" did not appear on the Fosamax label until 2011, when the FDA ordered that change based on its own analyses. Merck was initially resistant to the change, proposing revised language that, once again, referred to the risk of "stress fractures." But the FDA, once again, rejected that language. And this time, the FDA explained that "the term 'stress fracture' was considered and was not accepted" because, "for most practitioners, the term 'stress fracture' represents a minor fracture and this would contradict the seriousness of the atypical femoral fractures associated with bisphosphonate use." In January 2011, Merck and the FDA ultimately agreed upon adding a three-paragraph discussion of atypical femoral fractures to the Warnings and Precautions section of the Fosamax label. The label now refers to the fractures five times as "atypical" without using the term "stress fracture."

C

The respondents here are more than 500 individuals who took Fosamax and who suffered atypical femoral fractures between 1999 and 2010. Respondents, invoking federal diversity jurisdiction, filed separate actions seeking tort damages on the ground that, during the relevant period, state law imposed upon Merck a legal duty to warn them and their doctors about the risk of atypical femoral fractures associated with using Fosamax. One respondent, for example, filed a complaint alleging that she took Fosamax for roughly 10 years and suffered an atypical femoral fracture. One day in 2009, when the respondent was 70 years old, she turned to unlock the front door of her house, heard a popping sound, and suddenly felt her left leg give out beneath her. She needed surgery, in which doctors repaired her leg with a rod and screws. She explained she would not have used Fosamax for so many years if she had known that she might suffer an atypical femoral fracture as a result.

Merck, in defense, argued that respondents' state-law failure-to-warn claims should be dismissed as pre-empted by federal law. Both Merck and the FDA have long been aware that Fosamax could theoretically increase the risk of atypical femoral fractures. But for some period of time between 1995 (when the FDA first approved a drug label for Fosamax) and 2010 (when the FDA decided to require Merck to add a warning about atypical femoral fractures to Fosamax's label), both Merck and the FDA were unsure whether the developing evidence of a causal link between Fosamax and atypical femoral fractures was strong enough to require adding a warning to the Fosamax drug label. Merck conceded that the FDA's CBE regulation would have permitted Merck to try to change the label to add a warning before 2010, but Merck asserted that the FDA would have rejected that attempt. In particular, Merck pointed to the FDA's rejection of Merck's 2008 attempt to amend the Fosamax label to warn of the risk of "stress fractures" associated with Fosamax. On that basis, Merck claimed that federal law prevented Merck from complying with any state-law duty to warn the respondents of the risk of atypical femoral fractures associated with Fosamax.

The District Court agreed with Merck's pre-emption argument and granted summary judgment to Merck, but the Court of Appeals vacated and remanded. The Court of Appeals concluded that its pre-emption analysis was controlled by this Court's decision in *Wyeth*. The Court of Appeals understood that case as making clear that a failure-to-warn claim grounded in state law is pre-empted where there is "'clear evidence that the FDA would not have approved a change to the . . . label.'" The Court of Appeals, however, suggested that this statement had led to varying lower court applications and that it would be helpful for this Court to "clarif[y] or buil[d] out the doctrine."

In attempting to do so itself, the Court of Appeals held that "the Supreme Court intended to announce a standard of proof when it used the term 'clear evidence' in *Wyeth*." That is, the Court of Appeals believed that "[t]he term 'clear evidence' . . . does not refer directly to the *type* of facts that a manufacturer must show, or to the circumstances in which preemption will be appropriate." "Rather, it specifies how *difficult* it will be for the manufacturer to convince the factfinder that the FDA would have rejected a proposed label change." And in the Court of Appeals' view, "for a defendant to establish a preemption defense under *Wyeth*, the factfinder must conclude that it is highly probable that the FDA would not have approved a change to the drug's label." Moreover and importantly, the Court of Appeals also held that "whether the FDA would have rejected a proposed label change is a question of fact that must be answered by a jury."

Merck filed a petition for a writ of certiorari. Merck's petition asked the Court to decide whether Merck's case and others like it "must . . . go to a jury" to determine whether the FDA, in effect, has disapproved a state-law-required labeling change. In light of differences and uncertainties among the courts of appeals and state supreme courts in respect to the application of *Wyeth*, we granted certiorari.

## II

We stated in *Wyeth v. Levine* that state law failure-to-warn claims are pre-empted by the [FFDCA] and related labeling regulations when there is "clear evidence" that the FDA would not have approved the warning that state law requires. We here decide that a judge, not the jury, must decide the pre-emption question. And we elaborate *Wyeth*'s requirements along the way.

### A

We begin by describing *Wyeth*. [The court's extensive description of *Wyeth v. Levine* is here omitted].

### B

The underlying question for this type of impossibility pre-emption defense is whether federal law (including appropriate FDA actions) prohibited the drug manufacturer from adding any and all warnings to the drug label that would satisfy state law. And, of course, in order to succeed with that defense the manufacturer must show that the answer to this question is yes. But in *Wyeth*, we confronted that question in the context of a particular set of circumstances. Accordingly, for purposes of this case, we assume—but do not decide—that, as was true of the warning at issue in *Wyeth*, there is sufficient evidence to find that Merck violated state law by failing to add a warning about atypical femoral fractures to the Fosamax label. In a case like *Wyeth*, showing that federal law prohibited the drug manufacturer from adding a warning that would satisfy state law requires the drug manufacturer to show that it fully informed the FDA of the justifications for the warning required by state law and that the FDA, in turn, informed the drug manufacturer that the FDA would not approve changing the drug's label to include that warning.

These conclusions flow from our precedents on impossibility pre-emption and the statutory and regulatory scheme that we reviewed in *Wyeth*. In particular, "it has long been settled that state laws that conflict with federal law are without effect." *Mutual Pharmaceutical Co.*, 570 U. S. at 480. But as we have cautioned many times before, the "possibility of impossibility [is] not enough." *PLIVA, Inc. v. Mensing*, 564 U. S. 604, 625, n. 8 (2011) (internal quotation marks omitted). Consequently, we have refused to find clear evidence of such impossibility where the laws of one sovereign permit an activity that the laws of the other sovereign restrict or even prohibit.

And, as we explained in *Wyeth*, 555 U.S. at 571–573 federal law—the FDA's CBE regulation—permits drug manufacturers to change a label to "reflect newly acquired information" if the changes "add or strengthen a . . . warning" for which there is "evidence of a causal association," without prior approval from the FDA. 21 C.F.R. § 314.70(c)(6)(iii)(A). Of course, the FDA reviews CBE submissions and can reject label changes even after the manufacturer has made them. And manufacturers cannot propose a change that is not based on reasonable evidence. But in the interim, the CBE regulation permits changes, so a drug manufacturer will not ordinarily be able to show that there is an actual conflict between state and federal law such that it was impossible to comply with both.

We do not further define *Wyeth*'s use of the words "clear evidence" in terms of evidentiary standards, such as "preponderance of the evidence" or "clear and convincing evidence" and so forth, because, as we shall discuss, courts should treat the critical question not as a matter of fact for a jury but as a matter of law for the judge to decide. And where that is so, the judge must simply ask himself or herself whether the relevant federal and state laws "irreconcilably conflic[t]." *Rice v. Norman Williams Co.*, 458 U. S. 654, 659 (1982).

We do note, however, that the only agency actions that can determine the answer to the pre-emption question, of course, are agency actions taken pursuant to the FDA's congressionally delegated authority. The Supremacy Clause grants "supreme" status only to the "the *Laws* of the United States." U. S. Const., Art. VI, cl. 2. And pre-emption takes place "'only when and if [the agency] is acting within the scope of its congressionally delegated authority, . . . for an agency literally has no power to act, let alone pre-empt the validly enacted legislation of a sovereign State, unless and until Congress confers power upon it.' " *New York v. FERC*, 535 U. S. 1, 18 (2002) (some alterations omitted). Federal law permits the FDA to communicate its disapproval of a warning by means of notice-and-comment rulemaking setting forth labeling standards; by formally rejecting a warning label that would have been adequate under state law; or with other agency action carrying the force of law. The question of disapproval "method" is not now before us. And we make only the obvious point that, whatever the means the FDA uses to exercise its authority, those means must lie within the scope of the authority Congress has lawfully delegated.

## III

We turn now to what is the determinative question before us: Is the question of agency disapproval primarily one of fact, normally for juries to decide, or is it a question of law, normally for a judge to decide without a jury?

The complexity of the preceding discussion of the law helps to illustrate why we answer this question by concluding that the question is a legal one for the judge, not a jury. The question often involves the use of legal skills to determine whether agency disapproval fits facts that are not in dispute. Moreover, judges, rather than lay juries, are better equipped to evaluate the nature and scope of an agency's determination. Judges are experienced in "[t]he construction of written instruments," such as those normally produced by a federal agency to memorialize its considered judgments. And judges are better suited than are juries to understand and to interpret agency decisions in light of the governing statutory and regulatory context. To understand the question as a legal question for judges makes sense given the fact that judges are normally familiar with principles of administrative law. Doing so should produce greater uniformity among courts; and greater uniformity is normally a virtue when a question requires a determination concerning the scope and effect of federal agency action.

We understand that sometimes contested brute facts will prove relevant to a court's legal determination about the meaning and effect of an agency decision. For example, if the FDA rejected a drug manufacturer's supplemental application to change a drug label on the ground that the information supporting the application was insufficient to warrant a labeling change, the meaning and scope of that decision might depend on what information the FDA had before it. Yet in litigation between a drug consumer and a drug manufacturer (which will ordinarily lack an official administrative record for an FDA decision), the litigants may dispute whether the drug manufacturer submitted all material information to the FDA.

But we consider these factual questions to be subsumed within an already tightly circumscribed legal analysis. And we do not believe that they warrant submission alone or together with the larger pre-emption question to a jury. Rather, in those contexts where we have determined that the question is "for the judge and not the jury," we have also held that "courts may have to resolve subsidiary factual disputes" that are part and parcel of the broader legal question. And, as in contexts as diverse as the proper construction of patent claims and the voluntariness of criminal confessions, they create a question that "'falls somewhere between a pristine legal standard and a simple historical fact.'" In those circumstances, "'the fact/law distinction at times has turned on a determination that, as a matter of the sound administration of justice, one judicial actor is better positioned than another to decide the issue in question.' " In this context, that "better positioned" decisionmaker is the judge.

### IV

Because the Court of Appeals treated the pre-emption question as one of fact, not law, and because it did not have an opportunity to consider fully the standards we have described in Part II of our opinion, we vacate its judgment and remand the case to that court for further proceedings consistent with this opinion.

It is so ordered.

**Justice THOMAS, concurring.**

I join the Court's opinion and write separately to explain my understanding of the relevant pre-emption principles and how they apply to this case. [Here, Justice Thomas quotes the Supremacy Clause].

Under this Clause, "[w]here state and federal law 'directly conflict,' state law must give way." Although the Court has articulated several theories of pre-emption, Merck's sole argument here is that state law is pre-empted because it is impossible for Merck to comply with federal and state law. I remain skeptical that "physical impossibility" is a proper test for deciding whether a direct conflict exists between federal and state law. But even under our impossibility precedents, Merck's pre-emption defense fails.

### I

As I have explained before, it is not obvious that the "'physical impossibility' standard is the best proxy for determining when state and federal laws 'directly conflict' for purposes of the Supremacy Clause." *Wyeth v. Levine*, 555 U. S. 555, 590 (2009) (opinion concurring in judgment). Evidence from the founding suggests that, under the original meaning of the Supremacy Clause, federal law pre-empts state law only if the two are in logical contradiction. Sometimes, federal law will logically contradict state law even if it is possible for a person to comply with both. For instance, "if federal law gives an individual the right to engage in certain behavior that state law prohibits, the laws would give contradictory commands notwithstanding the fact that an individual could comply with both by electing to refrain from the covered behavior." (opinion of THOMAS, J.).

Merck does not advance this logical-contradiction standard, and it is doubtful that a pre-emption defense along these lines would succeed here. "To say, as the statute does, that [Merck] may not market a drug without federal approval (*i.e.*, without [a Food and Drug Administration (FDA)] approved label) is not to say that federal approval gives [Merck] the unfettered right, for all time, to market its drug with the specific label that was federally approved." Nothing in the federal brand-name-drug "statutory or regulatory scheme necessarily insulates [Merck] from liability under state law simply because the FDA has approved a particular label." The relevant question would be whether federal law gives Merck "an unconditional right to market [a] federally approved drug at all times with the precise label initially approved by the FDA," or whether it instead provides a federal floor that can be supplemented by different state standards. Absent a federal statutory right to sell a brand-name drug with an FDA-approved label, FDA approval "does not represent a finding that the drug, as labeled, can never be deemed unsafe by later federal action, or as in this case, the application of state law."

II

Applying the Court's impossibility precedents leads to the same conclusion. . . .

Here, Merck's impossibility pre-emption defense fails because it does not identify any federal law that "prohibited [it] from adding any and all warnings . . . that would satisfy state law." By its reference to "the Laws of the United States," the Supremacy Clause "requires that pre-emptive effect be given only to those federal standards and policies that are set forth in, or necessarily follow from, the statutory text that was produced through the constitutionally required bicameral and presentment procedures." *Wyeth*, at 586 (opinion of THOMAS, J.). Merck's primary argument, based on various agency communications, is that the FDA would have rejected a hypothetical labeling change submitted via the CBE process. But neither agency musings nor hypothetical future rejections constitute pre-emptive "Laws" under the Supremacy Clause.

. . . .

Because Merck points to no statute, regulation, or other agency action with the force of law that would have prohibited it from complying with its alleged state-law duties, its pre-emption defense should fail as a matter of law.

**Justice ALITO, . . . concurring in the judgment.**

I concur in the judgment because I agree with the Court's decision on the only question that it actually decides, namely, that whether federal law allowed Merck to include in the Fosamax label the warning alleged to be required by state law is a question of law to be decided by the courts, not a question of fact. I do not, however, join the opinion of the Court because I am concerned that its discussion of the law and the facts may be misleading on remand.

I

I begin with the law. The Court correctly notes that a drug manufacturer may prove impossibility pre-emption by showing that "federal law (including appropriate [Food and Drug Administration (FDA)] actions) prohibited the drug manufacturer from adding any and all warnings to the drug label that would satisfy state law." But in expounding further on the pre-emption analysis, the Court provides a skewed summary. While dwelling on our decision in *Wyeth*, the Court barely notes a statutory provision enacted after the underlying events in that case that may have an important bearing on the ultimate pre-emption analysis in this case.

Under [FFDCA 505](*o*)(4)(A), which was enacted in 2007, Congress has imposed on the FDA a duty to initiate a label change "[i]f the Secretary becomes aware of new information, including any new safety information . . . that the Secretary determines should be included in the labeling of the drug." This provision does not relieve drug manufacturers of their own responsibility to maintain their drug labels, see [FFDCA § 505](*o*)(4)(I), but the FDA's "actions," taken pursuant to this duty arguably affect the pre-emption analysis. This is so because, if the FDA declines to require a label change despite having received and considered information regarding a new risk, the logical conclusion is that the FDA determined that a label change was unjustified. The FDA's duty does not depend on whether the relevant drug manufacturer, as opposed to some other entity or individual, brought the new information to the FDA's attention. Nor does [FFDCA § 505](*o*)(4)(A) require the FDA to communicate to the relevant drug manufacturer that a label change is unwarranted; instead, the FDA could simply consider the new information and decide not to act.

[FFDCA § 505](*o*)(4)(A) is thus highly relevant to the pre-emption analysis, which turns on whether "federal law (*including appropriate FDA actions*) prohibited the drug manufacturer from adding any and all warnings to the drug label that would satisfy state law." *Ante,* at 1678 (emphasis added). On remand, I assume that the Court of Appeals will consider the effect of [FFDCA § 505](*o*)(4)(A) on the pre-emption issue in this case.

Two other aspects of the Court's discussion of the legal background must also be mentioned. First, although the Court's discussion of the point is a bit opaque, the Court holds—correctly, in my view—that *Wyeth*'s use of the phrase "clear evidence" was merely a rhetorical flourish. . . . Standards of proof, such as preponderance of the evidence and clear and convincing evidence, have no place in the resolution of this question of law.

Second, for reasons that entirely escape me, the Court refuses to acknowledge that there are two ways in which a drug manufacturer may attempt to alter a drug's label. The Court notes that a manufacturer may proceed under the FDA's "'changes being effected' " or "'CBE' " regulation, which permits a manufacturer to change a label without prior FDA approval under some circumstances. But the Court refuses to note that a manufacturer may (and, in many circumstances, must) submit a Prior Approval Supplement (PAS). 21 C.F.R. § 314.70(b) (2018). As the name suggests, changes proposed in a PAS must receive FDA approval before drug manufacturers may make the changes. § 314.70(b)(3). And "[h]istorically," the FDA has "accepted PAS applications instead of CBE supplements, as occurred in this case, particularly where significant questions exist on whether to revise or how to modify existing drug labeling." Brief for United States as *Amicus Curiae.*

## II

I now turn to the facts. Resolution of the legal question that the Court decides does not require much discussion of the facts, but if the Court wishes to include such a summary, its presentation should be balanced. Instead, the Court provides a one-sided account. For example, it highlights historical accounts dating back to the 1990s that purportedly linked atypical femoral fractures with Fosamax use, but it omits any mention of the extensive communication between Merck and the FDA during the relevant period.

A reader of the Court's opinion will inevitably be left with the impression that, once the FDA rejected Merck's proposed warning in 2009, neither the FDA nor Merck took any other actions related to atypical femoral fractures "until 2011." But that is simply not true.

While Merck's 2008 proposal was pending, the FDA remained in contact with Merck about the issue of atypical femoral fractures, which Merck, at the time, labeled as a type of stress fracture. An internal Merck memorandum describes a phone call in which an FDA official allegedly told Merck that "[t]he conflicting nature of the literature does not provide a clear path forward, and more time will be need[ed] for FDA to formulate a formal opinion on the issue of a precaution around these data." In an e-mail about a week later, another FDA official told Merck that the FDA would "close out" Merck's applications if Merck "agree[d] to hold off on the [Precautions] language at this time." The official went on to say that the FDA "would then work with . . . Merck to decide on language for a [Precautions] atypical fracture language, if it is warranted."

Then, months after the FDA rejected Merck's proposed warning, the FDA issued a Safety Announcement regarding its "[o]ngoing safety review of oral bisphosphonates and atypical subtrochanteric femur fractures." The Safety Announcement stated that, "[a]t this point, the data that FDA has reviewed have not shown a clear connection between bisphosphonate use and a risk of atypical subtrochanteric femur fractures." Nonetheless, the Safety Announcement announced the FDA's intent to further study the issue alongside a task force formed to address the atypical fractures. And the Safety Announcement concluded by admonishing healthcare professionals to "continue to follow the recommendations in the drug label when prescribing oral bisphosphonates" and patients to "not stop taking their medication unless told to do so by their healthcare professional."

In September 2010, the task force published its report, which concluded that, although there was no established "causal association" between bisphosphonates and atypical femoral fractures, "recent observations suggest that the risk rises with increasing duration of exposure, and there is concern that lack of awareness and underreporting may mask the true incidence of the problem." The same day, the FDA issued a statement acknowledging the task force report and committing to "considering label revisions." And in October 2010, the FDA issued another Safety Announcement in which the FDA stated that it would initiate changes in the

Precautions section of bisphosphonate drug labels to warn of atypical femoral fractures. It was not until then that, pursuant to its [FFDCA § 505](*o*)(4)(A) obligations, the FDA instructed Merck to include a warning about such fractures in its Fosamax drug labels.

Thus, for years the FDA was: aware of this issue, communicating with drug manufacturers, studying all relevant information, and instructing healthcare professionals and patients alike to continue to use Fosamax as directed. For this reason, the FDA itself, speaking through the Solicitor General, takes the position that the FDA's decision not to require a label change prior to October 2010 reflected the FDA's "determin[ation]" that a new warning "should [not] be included in the labeling of the drug," [FFDCA § 505](*o*)(4)(A).

For these reasons, I concur in the judgment only.

## D. Key Points

- Federal preemption arises from the Supremacy Clause of the U.S. Constitution.
- There has long been, and remains, significant dispute on the U.S. Supreme Court over the basic structure of preemption doctrine.
  - All justices agree that Congress can, by express statutory language, preempt state law in any area where Congress has legislative power.
  - There is substantial dispute, however, about three other things:
    - how to determine *what language counts* as expressly preemptive
    - how to determine the *scope* of language determined to be expressly preemptive of at least some things
    - how to determine when a statute should be read as *preemptive despite a lack of expressly preemptive language*
  - These disputes have led to a set of highly fact-specific preemption cases. These cases tend to mix broad statements about preemption with detailed reliance on the facts of the relevant case.
    - These disputes at the U.S. Supreme Court are naturally mirrored in lower-court precedents.
    - The fact-specific holdings of these cases make it relatively easy for courts to distinguish even closely related precedents.
- In product liability litigation, the core preemption issue frequently comes down to a question about the relationship between the safety aspect of FDA marketing authorization decisions and state law.
  - Plaintiffs typically assert that FDA marketing authorization decisions set a minimum level of safety, but that individual states—through either statutes or common-law decisions—can require higher levels of safety.

- Defendants typically assert that FDA marketing authorization decisions are intended to balance risks and benefits, setting both a minimum level of safety permitted and a maximum level of safely that can be required. This is based on the idea that many products have some inherent risks and cannot be made safer without imposing other tradeoffs, such as reduced efficacy or reduced product availability. They take the position that individual states accordingly cannot require more safety (with the attendant risk of reduced efficacy or product availability) than FDA requires.
- In more colloquial terms, plaintiffs typically take the position that FDA marketing authorization decisions set a floor for safety requirements, but not a ceiling. Defendants, by contrast, typically take the position that FDA marketing authorization decisions set both a floor and a ceiling for safety requirements.

# Chapter 21

# Regulation of Imports

## A. Introduction

FFDCA § 801(a) sets out FDA's core statutory authority authority over imports. Upon FDA request, FFDCA § 801(a) requires U.S. Customs & Border Protection (CBP) to provide FDA with "samples of food, drugs, devices, tobacco products, and cosmetics which are being imported or offered for import into the United States."[1] FFDCA § 801(a) then sets out numerous circumstances under which such articles "shall be refused admission" to the United States. If a product is refused admission, FFDCA § 801(a) requires CBP to "cause the destruction of any such article refused admission" unless the article "is exported" in a timely manner under applicable regulations. The remainder of FFDCA § 801, which runs from §§ 801(a) to 801(u), contains additional detailed requirements relating to import and export of FDA-regulated products.

FFDCA § 803 establishes FDA's Office of International Relations, gives FDA authority to enter into certain international agreements, and directs FDA to work with other agencies on international regulatory harmonization efforts. FFDCA § 804 sets out specific requirements governing importation of prescription drugs from Canada, including importation for personal use.

FFDCA §§ 805–809 all relate to import safety; the first four focusing on food, the last on drugs and devices. FFDCA § 805 requires each importer of food to "perform risk-based foreign supplier verification activities" to ensure compliance with various statutory requirements, including FFDCA §§ 402 (food adulteration), 418 (hazard analysis and risk-based preventative controls), 419 (produce safety), and 403(w) (food allergen labeling). FFDCA § 806 provides for a *voluntary qualified*

1. The statutory text requires these duties to be undertaken by the "Secretary of the Treasury" and the "Secretary of Health and Human Services." This reference to the "Secretary of the Treasury" is legacy text that is unchanged from the time that the U.S. Customs Service—a predecessor to U.S. Customs and Border Protection—was part of the Department of the Treasury. As the U.S. District Court for the District of Columbia has observed about this provision, "[t]here is no dispute that the Secretary of Homeland Security, rather than of the Treasury, currently oversees the actions of the entity now called the U.S. Bureau of Customs and Border Protection, which manages imports generally, or that the actions of the Secretary of Health and Human Services authorized by the statute, which regard monitoring of 'food, drugs, devices, tobacco products, and cosmetics' in particular, [FFDCA § 801(a)], are delegated to the FDA." *Del Monte Fresh Produce N.A., Inc. v. United States*, 706 F. Supp. 2d 116 (2010).

*importer program* "to provide for the expedited review and importation of food" from importers who have "voluntarily agreed to participate" in the program.

FFDCA § 807 gives FDA authority to "enter into arrangements and agreements with foreign governments to facilitate the inspection" of foreign food facilities registered with FDA. It instructs FDA to "direct resources" to these inspections, with a focus on "facilities, suppliers, and food types that present a high risk." FFDCA § 808 gives FDA authority to establish a *third-party auditor accreditation program* to accredit third-party auditors to conduct both "consultative" and "regulatory" audits of foreign food facilities.

FFDCA § 809 gives FDA authority to "enter into arrangements and agreements" with foreign governments and their agencies "to recognize the inspection," by foreign governments meeting certain criteria, "of foreign [drug and device] establishments" that are registered with FDA under FFDCA § 510.

Finally, FFDCA § 311 is a statutory provision that appears designed to respond to a specific statutory interpretation doctrine sometimes applied by the U.S. Supreme Court.[2] This is the *presumption against extraterritoriality.* Under this doctrine, courts presume—unless Congress indicates to the contrary—that statutes are not intended to apply outside of U.S. territory. FFDCA § 311 does this by providing for "extraterritorial jurisdiction" over FFDCA violations in two circumstances. First, it provides for extraterritorial jurisdiction for FFDCA violations relating to any article "intended for import into the United States." Second, it provides for extraterritorial jurisdiction for an FFDCA violation "if any act in furtherance of the violation was committed in the United States."

At this point, please read (or review) the following excerpts in the statutory supplement:

- FFDCA § 311. Extraterritorial jurisdiction.
- FFDCA § 801. Imports and exports. *Subsection (a) only.*
- FFDCA § 803. Office of International Relations.
- FFDCA § 804. Importation of prescription drugs. *Subsections (b) and (j) only.*
- FFDCA § 805. Foreign supplier verification program.
- FFDCA § 806. Voluntary qualified importer program. *Subsection (a) only.*
- FFDCA § 807. Inspection of foreign food facilities.
- FFDCA § 808. Accreditation of third-party auditors. *Subsection (a)* only.
- FFDCA § 809. Recognition of foreign government inspections.

2. The Court issued a prominent decision applying this presumption in 2010, shortly before Congress's 2012 passage of FFDCA § 311. *See Morrison v. National Australia Bank, Ltd.*, 561 U.S. 247 (2010).

## B. Outline of Regulatory Regime

As in other chapters of this book, this chapter begins with a set of charts. As you read this chapter for the first time, you should do no more than skim these charts to get a general sense of the structure of the applicable statutes and regulations. (For more information on the role of the charts in this casebook, see Chapter 1, Parts A.1 and B).

| Timeline of Key Statutes: Regulation of Imports | | | |
|---|---|---|---|
| **Year** | **PL** | **Stat** | **Name of Statute** |
| 1906 | 59-384 | 34 Stat. 768 | Pure Food and Drugs Act |
| 1938 | 75-717 | 52 Stat. 1040 | FFDCA of 1938 |
| 1968 | 90-399 | 82 Stat. 342 | Animal Drug Amendments of 1968 |
| 1970 | 91-513 | 84 Stat. 1236 | Comprehensive Drug Abuse Prevention and Control Act of 1970 |
| 1976 | 94-295 | 90 Stat. 539 | Medical Device Amendments of 1976 |
| 1988 | 100-293 | 102 Stat. 95 | Prescription Drug Marketing Act of 1987[3] |
| 2000 | 106-387 | 114 Stat. 1459 | Agriculture, Rural Development, Food and Drug Administration, and Related Agencies—Appropriations |
| 2002 | 107-188 | 116 Stat. 595 | Public Health Security and Bioterrorism Preparedness and Response Act of 2002 |
| 2009 | 111-31 | 123 Stat. 1776 | Family Smoking Prevention and Tobacco Control Act |
| 2011 | 111-353 | 124 Stat. 3885 | FDA Food Safety Modernization Act |
| 2012 | 112-144 | 126 Stat. 993 | FDA Safety and Innovation Act |
| 2017 | 115-52 | 131 Stat. 1005 | FDA Reauthorization Act of 2017 |

| Key Statutory Provisions: Regulation of Imports | | |
|---|---|---|
| **Statute Name or U.S.C. Title** | **§** | **Title of Section or Subsection** |
| FFDCA | 311 | Extraterritorial jurisdiction |
| FFDCA | 801 | Imports and exports |
| FFDCA | 802 | Exports of certain unapproved products |
| FFDCA | 803 | Office of International Relations |
| FFDCA | 804 | Importation of prescription drugs |
| FFDCA | 805 | Foreign supplier verification program |

3. This is the official short title written into the statute itself. However, the statute did not become law until the following calendar year.

| Statute Name or U.S.C. Title | § | Title of Section or Subsection |
|---|---|---|
| FFDCA | 806 | Voluntary qualified importer program |
| FFDCA | 807 | Inspection of foreign food facilities |
| FFDCA | 808 | Accreditation of third-party auditors |
| FFDCA | 809 | Recognition of foreign government inspections |

**Key Regulatory Provisions: Regulation of Imports**

| 21 C.F.R. Part | Subpart | Title of Part or Subpart |
|---|---|---|
| 1 | D | Electronic import entries |
| 1 | E | Imports and exports |
| 1 | I | Prior notice of imported food |
| 1 | L | Foreign supplier verification programs for food importers |
| 1 | M | Accreditation of third-party certification bodies to conduct food safety audits and to issue certifications |
| 1 | O | Sanitary transportation of human and animal food |
| 26 | — | Mutual recognition of pharmaceutical good manufacturing practice reports, medical device quality system audit reports, and certain medical device product evaluation reports: United States and the European Community |

## 1998-11-06 FDA Final Rule, Mutual Recognition of Pharmaceutical Good Manufacturing Practice Inspection Reports, Medical Device Quality System Audit Reports, and Certain Medical Device Product Evaluation Reports Between the United States and the European Community

63 Fed. Reg. 60,122

ACTION: Final rule.

SUMMARY: The Food and Drug Administration (FDA) is amending its regulations pursuant to an international agreement between the United States and the European Community (EC). The agreement is entitled "Agreement on Mutual Recognition Between the United States of America and the European Community" (MRA). Under the terms of that agreement, the importing country authority may normally endorse good manufacturing practice (GMP) inspection reports for pharmaceuticals provided by the exporting authority determined by the importing authority to have an equivalent regulatory system. Likewise, the importing country authority may normally endorse medical device quality system evaluation reports and certain medical device product evaluation reports provided by conformity assessment bodies (CAB's) determined by the importing country authority to have equivalent assessment procedures. FDA is taking this action to enhance its ability to ensure the safety and effectiveness of pharmaceuticals and medical devices through more efficient and effective utilization of its regulatory resources. . . .

SUPPLEMENTARY INFORMATION:

**I. Background**

On June 20, 1997, the United States and the EC concluded an agreement on the MRA. The MRA includes two sectoral annexes covering products regulated by FDA. The sectoral annex on medical devices covers medical device quality system-related inspection reports and certain product evaluation reports. The sectoral annex for pharmaceutical GMP's covers pharmaceutical GMP inspection reports. The MRA also includes sectoral annexes covering products regulated by other U.S. regulatory agencies, including telecommunication equipment, electromagnetic compatibility, electrical safety, and recreational craft. Finally, the MRA includes a "framework" agreement that contains general provisions.

At the conclusion of negotiations, the United States and the EC submitted the text of the MRA to their respective authorities to complete the necessary procedures for approval and implementation. For FDA, these procedures included publishing a proposed rule that was published in the Federal Register of April 10, 1998. The proposed rule was based on the provisions contained in the two FDA sectoral annexes and the "framework" agreement of the MRA concluded on June 20, 1997. . . . On May 14, 1998, FDA informed the Office of the U.S. Trade Representative (USTR) that it supported the signing of the MRA. The MRA was signed in London on May 18, 1998. Provisions of the MRA are between the United States and EC, and do not create rights in third parties.

## 2015-11-27 FDA Final Rule, Foreign Supplier Verification Programs for Importers of Food for Humans and Animals

80 Fed. Reg. 74,226

**Executive Summary**

**Purpose and Coverage of the Rule**

This rule is part of FDA's implementation of the FDA Food Safety Modernization Act (FSMA), which intends to better protect public health by, among other things, adopting a modern, preventive, and risk-based approach to food safety regulation. This rule adopts provisions concerning FSVPs [Foreign Supplier Verification Programs] that importers must create and follow to help ensure the safety of imported food. The regulation is designed to be flexible based on risk, and the requirements vary based on the type of food product (such as processed foods, produce, and dietary supplements) and category of importer.

Congress required importers to perform risk-based foreign supplier verification activities and directed FDA to promulgate regulations on the content of FSVPs in section 301 of FSMA, codified in section 805 of the [FFDCA]. The rule requires importers to implement FSVPs to provide adequate assurances that the importer's foreign suppliers produce food in compliance with processes and procedures, including risk-based preventive controls, that provide the same level of public health protection as those required under section 418 (concerning hazard analysis and preventive controls) or 419 (concerning produce safety) of the [FFDCA], as appropriate, and in compliance with sections 402 (concerning adulteration) and 403(w) (concerning misbranding regarding allergen labeling) of the [FFDCA].

This rule is the result of significant stakeholder engagement. We took this approach to help ensure that the rule achieves its public health goal, reflects industry practice, and strikes the right balance between flexibility and accountability.

**Summary of the Major Provisions of the Final Rule**

We are finalizing a flexible, risk-based approach to foreign supplier verification. The FSVP regulation focuses on known or reasonably foreseeable food safety hazards, identified and considered through a hazard analysis and evaluation process, rather than all adulteration covered by the adulteration provisions in section 402 of the [FFDCA]. After considering the comments on the proposed rule and the subsequently revised proposal along with other stakeholder input, we continue to believe that hazard analysis, which is well accepted and understood throughout the international food safety community, provides the most effective way to implement a risk-based framework in which importers can evaluate potential products and suppliers and ensure that appropriate verification activities occur.

The FSVP regulation aligns with key components of the food safety plans that facilities that manufacture, process, pack, or hold must establish and follow under FDA's recently issued regulations on current good manufacturing practice (CGMP) and hazard analysis and risk-based preventive controls for human food and animal food (preventive controls regulations). In particular, the FSVP final rule is consistent with the supply-chain program provisions of those regulations to the extent feasible and appropriate. The general FSVP framework, together with the modified requirements applicable to certain importers and foods, are intended to be sufficiently general and flexible to apply to a variety of circumstances without being unduly burdensome or restrictive of trade.

Although FSVP requirements apply to most imported food under FDA's regulatory jurisdiction, certain categories of imported food are not covered under the FSVP regulation. These exemptions include certain juice, fish, and fishery products (which are already subject to verification under FDA's hazard analysis and critical control point (HACCP) regulations for those products), food for research or evaluation, food for personal consumption, alcoholic beverages, food that is transshipped, food imported for processing and future export, food exported from and returned to the United States without manufacturing/processing in a foreign country, and certain meat, poultry, and egg products regulated by the U.S. Department of Agriculture (USDA).

In the final rule, we have added new provisions to allow greater flexibility with respect to certain requirements to better reflect modern food supply and distribution chains. Under the FSVP regulation, importers are responsible for:

1. Determining the hazards reasonably likely to cause illness or injury with each food. Importers can conduct their own analysis of the potential hazards with a food or review and assess a hazard analysis conducted by another entity.
2. Evaluating the risk posed by a food, using the results of the hazard analysis, and evaluating the foreign supplier's performance. This evaluation informs the approval of foreign suppliers and the determination of appropriate supplier verification activities. An importer may rely on another entity to conduct this evaluation and to determine the appropriate supplier verification activities as long as the importer reviews and assesses the evaluation, determination, or both, as applicable. An importer must approve its own foreign suppliers.
3. Conducting supplier verification activities. In general, importers must establish and follow written procedures to ensure they only import foods from foreign suppliers they have approved. However, importers may import food from unapproved foreign suppliers, on a temporary basis when necessary and appropriate, if they subject the food from these suppliers to adequate verification activities before importing it.

   Importers are responsible for determining and documenting foreign supplier verification activities (as well as the frequency with which those activities must be conducted) that are appropriate to provide assurance that hazards requiring a control in food are significantly minimized or prevented. Importers must conduct supplier verification activities for each foreign supplier before importing a food into the United States and periodically thereafter. An importer may determine, document, and conduct these activities itself or may rely on other entities to perform those tasks, as long as the importer reviews and assesses the relevant documentation, including the results of supplier verification activities.

   The appropriate verification activities and their frequency will vary depending on the food, the foreign supplier, and the nature of the control. Appropriate verification activities include: onsite auditing, sampling and testing of a food, review of the foreign supplier's relevant food safety records, and other activities that are appropriate based on the evaluation of the risk posed by the food and foreign supplier performance.

   When a hazard in a food will be controlled by the foreign supplier and is one for which there is a reasonable probability that exposure to the hazard will result in serious adverse health consequences or death to humans or animals, the default appropriate verification activity under the regulation is an annual onsite audit of the foreign supplier. To provide flexibility even in these circumstances, the rule allows for the performance of a different supplier verification activity and/or less frequent onsite auditing provided an adequate written determination is made that the other approach will meet the public health purpose of supplier verification.

4. Performing appropriate activities in other circumstances. The final rule also adds flexibility and recognizes the reality of modern distribution chains by not requiring an importer to conduct supplier verification (or evaluate the risk posed by a food and the foreign supplier's performance) when the hazard requiring a control in a food will be controlled by a subsequent entity in the distribution chain in the United States. For example, if an importer's customer will control the hazard, the importer can rely on its customer to provide written assurance that the food will be processed for food safety and must disclose that the food has not been processed to control the identified hazard. If the hazard will be controlled by a subsequent entity in the distribution chain, the final rule requires disclosure that the food has not been processed to control the identified hazard as well as a series of written assurances starting with assurances from the customer to the importer and continuing the obligation to provide written assurance of processing for food safety throughout the distribution chain. We also have provided flexibility for an importer to establish, document, and implement an alternative system that ensures adequate control, at a later distribution step, of the hazards in a food product distributed by a manufacturing/processing facility.

5. Conducting corrective actions. An importer must take appropriate corrective actions promptly if it determines that a foreign supplier of a food it imports does not produce the food in compliance with the processes and procedures that provide the same level of public health protection as those required under section 418 or 419 of the [FFDCA], if either is applicable, or produces food that is adulterated under section 402 or misbranded under section 403(w) (if applicable) of the [FFDCA]. This determination could be based on a review of consumer, customer, or other complaints related to food safety, verification activities, or other information. The appropriate corrective actions will depend on the circumstances but could include discontinuing use of the foreign supplier until the problem is resolved.

6. Identifying themselves as the importer of the food for each line of food product offered for importation into the United States.

7. Retaining records of FSVP activities.

### Modified Provisions for Certain Types of Importers

The rule provides several exceptions to the standard FSVP requirements for certain types of importers. First, for dietary supplements and dietary supplement components, importers who establish and verify compliance with certain specifications (concerning dietary supplement components and packaging) under the dietary supplement CGMP regulations will not be required to comply with most of the standard FSVP requirements, including hazard analysis and standard supplier verification activities. The same exception would apply to importers whose customer is required to establish such specifications and verify that they are met, except that the importer would have to obtain written assurance that its customer is complying with those requirements. In contrast, importers of other dietary supplements would be required to comply with most of the standard FSVP requirements but would not have to conduct hazard analyses, and their supplier verification activities would focus on verifying that the supplier is in compliance with the dietary supplement CGMP regulation, rather than verifying that hazards requiring a control are significantly minimized or prevented, as required under the standard supplier verification activity provisions.

Second, the rule establishes modified FSVP requirements for very small importers and importers of food from certain small foreign suppliers. We have aligned the definition of "very small importer" with the definitions of "very small business" under the regulations on preventive controls for human food and animal food. With respect to the importation of human food, the definition of very small importer has an annual sales ceiling of $1,000,000, which is consistent with the $1,000,000 annual sales ceiling for a very small business under the preventive controls for human food regulation. With respect to the importation of animal food, the definition of very small importer has an annual sales ceiling of $2,500,000, which is consistent with the $2,500,000 annual sales ceiling for a very small business under the preventive controls for animal food regulation.

In addition, food from three types of small foreign suppliers is not subject to standard supplier verification requirements. Those foreign suppliers are: (1) Qualified facilities under either of the preventive controls regulations, (2) farms that are not "covered farms" under the produce safety regulation in part 112 (21 CFR part 112) in accordance with § 112.4(a), or in accordance with §§ 112.4(b) and 112.5, and (3) shell egg producers not subject to part 118 (21 CFR part 118) because the shell egg producer has fewer than 3,000 laying hens. Each of these types of producers is either exempt from their underlying FDA food safety regulations or subject to modified requirements, mostly, and in some cases entirely, because of the size of these producers.

The relatively small volume of food imported by and from these entities should reduce consumers' exposure to, and potential risk from, this imported food. Therefore, we are proposing that in these situations the importer would not be required to conduct a hazard analysis and would be able to verify their foreign suppliers by obtaining written assurance of their supplier's compliance with the applicable food safety regulations (or, in some cases, the supplier's acknowledgement that it is subject to the adulteration provisions of the [FFDCA]). This policy is similarly reflected in the supply-chain program provisions of the preventive controls regulations.

Third, the rule excludes from most of the standard FSVP requirements (including hazard analysis and verification that identified hazards are significantly minimized or prevented) certain types of food from a foreign supplier in a country whose food safety system FDA has officially recognized as comparable or determined to be equivalent to that of the United States, provided that:

- The food is within the scope of the relevant official recognition or equivalency determination;
- The importer determines that the foreign supplier of the food is in good compliance standing with the relevant food safety authority; and
- The food is not intended for further processing in the United States, e.g., packaged food products and raw agricultural commodities (RACs) that will not be processed further before consumption.

These provisions are consistent with our risk-based approach to foreign supplier verification because they enable both importers and FDA to leverage the regulatory efforts of food safety authorities in countries the Agency has officially determined to have food safety systems that are comparable or equivalent to that of the United States.

## 2015-11-27 FDA Final Rule, Accreditation of Third-Party Certification Bodies to Conduct Food Safety Audits and to Issue Certifications

80 Fed. Reg. 74,570

### Executive Summary

#### Purpose and Coverage of the Final Rule

This rule is part of FDA's implementation of FSMA, which intends to better protect public health by, among other things, adopting a modern, preventive, and risk-based approach to food safety regulation. In this document, we establish a program for accreditation of third-party certification bodies to conduct food safety audits and issue certifications of foreign food facilities and foods for humans and animals for purposes of sections 801(q) and 806 of the [FFDCA]. We are also codifying certain limited exemptions to mandatory import certification under 801(q) of the [FFDCA].

FSMA added section 808 to the [FFDCA], which directs FDA to establish a new program for accreditation of third-party certification bodies to conduct food safety audits and to certify that eligible foreign entities (including registered foreign food facilities) and food produced by such entities meet applicable FDA requirements for purposes of sections 801(q) and 806 of the [FFDCA]. This rulemaking implements section 808 of the [FFDCA]; we will recognize accreditation bodies to accredit third-party certification bodies, except for limited circumstances in which we may directly accredit third-party certification bodies.

FSMA specifies two uses for the food and facility certifications issued by accredited third-party certification bodies under this program. First, facility certifications will be used by importers to establish eligibility for VQIP under section 806 of the

[FFDCA]. VQIP offers participating importers expedited review and entry of food that is part of VQIP. One condition of participation is importation of food from facilities audited and certified by third-party certification bodies accredited under this subpart. FDA issued draft guidance on VQIP on June 5, 2015.

Second, section 801(q) of the [FFDCA] gives FDA the authority to make a risk-based determination to require, as a condition of admissibility, that a food imported or offered for import into the United States be accompanied by a certification or other assurance that the food meets the applicable requirements of the [FFDCA]. The authority to mandate import certification for food, based on risk, is one of the tools we can use to help prevent potentially harmful food from reaching U.S. consumers. When FDA has determined that a food import is subject to such certification under section 801(q) of the [FFDCA], FDA will require, as a condition of entry, a certification issued either by an accredited third-party certification body under this rule or by an agency or representative of the government of the country from which the food at issue originated, as designated by FDA.

In addition, facilities and importers may choose to use onsite audits conducted by third-party certification bodies accredited under the program set out in this rule in connection with meeting supplier verification requirements under FDA's final rules for Current Good Manufacturing Practice and Hazard Analysis and Risk-Based Preventive Controls for Human Food (final human preventive controls regulation) (80 FR55907, September 17, 2015); Current Good Manufacturing Practice and Hazard Analysis and Risk-Based Preventive Controls for Food for Animals (final animal preventive controls regulation) (80 FR 56169, September 17, 2015); and the Foreign Supplier Verification Programs (FSVP) for Importers of Food for Humans and Animals (published elsewhere in this edition of the Federal Register) (implementing sections 418 and 805 of the [FFDCA], respectively). Under those rules, in circumstances where an onsite audit is the appropriate supplier verification activity, such audit must be conducted by a "qualified auditor." The definitions of "qualified auditor" in those rules make clear that an example of a potential qualified auditor includes, but is not limited to, an audit agent of a certification body that has been accredited in accordance with regulations in part 1, subpart M of this chapter (i.e., this rule implementing section 808 of the [FFDCA]).

**Summary of Major Provisions of the Final Rule**

This rule establishes the framework, procedures, and requirements for accreditation bodies and third-party certification bodies for purposes of section 808 of the [FFDCA]. The rule sets requirements for the legal authority, competency, capacity, conflict of interest safeguards, quality assurance, and records procedures that accreditation bodies must demonstrate to be eligible for recognition. Accreditation bodies also must demonstrate capability to meet the FDA requirements that would apply upon recognition. Additionally, the rule establishes requirements for the legal authority, competency, capacity, conflict of interest safeguards, quality assurance, and records procedures that third-party certification bodies must demonstrate to be eligible for accreditation. Third-party certification bodies also must demonstrate capability to meet the applicable requirements of the rule that would apply upon accreditation.

Pursuant to [FFDCA § 808], the rule requires accredited third-party certification bodies to perform unannounced facility audits, to notify FDA upon discovering a condition that could cause or contribute to a serious risk to the public health, and to submit to FDA reports of regulatory audits conducted for certification purposes. The rule includes stringent requirements to prevent conflicts of interest from influencing the decisions of recognized accreditation bodies and accredited third-party certification bodies. The rule does not, however, establish the audit criteria that accredited third-party certification bodies will use in examining eligible entities for compliance with the applicable food safety requirements of the [FFDCA] and FDA regulations, because those criteria appear elsewhere in FDA regulations and the [FFDCA].

## C. Key Points

- As FDA does not itself have direct authority over shipments into and out of the United States, it must have CBP assistance to carry out its import-regulation role.
- The scale of international trade makes it impracticable for FDA to test even small portions of regulated products entering the country. Accordingly, import regulation must rely on targeted efforts to determine where problems might occur.
- FDA's authority to require facility registration plays an important role in import regulation. Many problems can be managed more easily by inspection of production facilities than by inspection of the products themselves. The list of relevant facilities that can be generated from facility registration is, in other words, an essential precondition to an effective inspection program.
    - This form of regulation is easier for products produced at a small number of facilities (such as drugs and high-end medical devices) than for products produced in a highly dispersed manner (such as basic food commodities).
- With respect to imports, major regulatory concerns vary both by product category and by country of production.
    - For some countries, import regulation is based on a determination that, for a particular product category, the relevant country's internal regulatory system is similar, in overall rigor, to that of the United States. Such a determination may permit FDA to focus its import-regulation resources elsewhere.
    - For other countries and product categories, perceived weaknesses in the relevant country's internal regulatory system may make FDA reluctant to rely on its foreign counterparts.

## Part Eight

# Appendices

Appendix A

# Timeline of All Key Statutes in Casebook

| Timeline of All Key Statutes Listed in Outline of Regulatory Regime Charts | | | |
|---|---|---|---|
| Year | PL | Stat | Name of Statute |
| 1890 | 51-736 | 26 Stat. 313 | An Act to limit the effect of the regulations of commerce between the several States and with foreign countries in certain cases (Wilson Act) |
| 1902 | 57-244 | 32 Stat. 728 | An Act to regulate the sale of viruses, serums, toxins, and analogous products in the District of Columbia, to regulate interstate traffic in said articles, and for other purposes (Biologics Control Act of 1902) |
| 1906 | 59-384 | 34 Stat. 768 | An Act for preventing the manufacture, sale, or transportation of adulterated or misbranded or poisonous or deleterious food, drugs, medicines, and liquors, and for regulating traffic therein, and for other purposes (Pure Food and Drug Act) |
| 1907 | 59-242 | 34 Stat. 1256 | An Act Making appropriations for the Department of Agriculture for the fiscal year ending June thirtieth, nineteen hundred and eight (Meat Inspection Act) |
| 1912 | 62-275 | 37 Stat. 315 | An Act to regulate the importation of nursery stock and other plants and plant products; to enable the Secretary of Agriculture to establish and maintain quarantine districts for plant diseases and insect pests; to permit and regulate the movement of fruits, plants, and vegetables therefrom, and for other purposes (Plant Quarantine Act) |
| 1912 | 62-301 | 37 Stat. 416 | Sherley Amendment |
| 1913 | 62-398 | 37 Stat. 699 | An Act Divesting intoxication liquors of their interstate character in certain cases (Webb-Kenyon Act) |
| 1913 | 62-419 | 37 Stat. 732 | An Act for preventing the manufacture, sale, or transportation of adulterated or misbranded or poisonous or deleterious foods, drugs, medicines, and liquors, and for regulating traffic therein, and for other purposes (Gould Amendment) |

| Year | PL | Stat | Name of Statute |
|---|---|---|---|
| 1913 | 62-430 | 37 Stat. 828 | An Act making appropriations for the Department of Agriculture for the fiscal year ending June thirtieth, nineteen hundred and fourteen (The Virus, Serum, and Toxin Act) |
| 1919 | 66-66 | 41 Stat. 305 | An Act To prohibit intoxicating beverages, and to regulate the manufacture, production, use, and sale of high-proof spirits for other than beverage purposes, and to insure an ample supply of alcohol and promote its use in scientific research and in the development of fuel, dye, and other lawful industries (National Prohibition Act) |
| 1930 | 71-538 | 46 Stat. 1019 | An Act To amend section 8 of the Act entitled: An Act for preventing the manufacture, sale, or transportation of adulterated or misbranded or poisonous or deleterious foods, drugs, medicines, and liquors, and for regulating traffic therein and for other purposes," approved June 30, 1906, as amended (McNary-Mapes Amendment) |
| 1935 | 74-401 | 49 Stat. 977 | An Act To further protect the revenue derived from distilled spirits, wine, and malt beverages, to regulate interstate and foreign commerce and enforce the postal laws with respect thereto, to enforce the twenty-first amendment, and for other purposes (Federal Alcohol Administration Act) |
| 1938 | 75-717 | 52 Stat. 1040 | Federal Food, Drug, and Cosmetic Act (FFDCA of 1938) |
| 1941 | 77-366 | 55 Stat. 851 | An Act To amend the Federal Food, Drug, and Cosmetic Act of June 25, 1938, as amended, by providing for the certification of batches of drugs composed wholly or partly of insulin, and for other purposes (Insulin Amendment) |
| 1944 | 78-410 | 58 Stat. 682 | An Act To consolidate and revise the laws relating to the Public Health Service, and for other purposes (Public Health Services Act) |
| 1945 | 79-139 | 59 Stat. 463 | An Act To amend the Federal Food, Drug, and Cosmetic Act of June 25, 1938, as amended, by providing for the certification of batches of drugs composed wholly or partly of any kind of penicillin or any derivative thereof, and for other purposes (Penicillin Amendment) |
| 1946 | 79-404 | 60 Stat. 237 | An Act To improve the administration of justice by prescribing fair administrative procedure (Administrative Procedure Act) |
| 1950 | 81-459 | 64 Stat. 20 | An Act To regulate oleomargarine, to repeal certain taxes relating to oleomargarine, and for other purposes (Oleomargarine Act) |
| 1954 | 83-518 | 68 Stat. 511 | An Act To amend the Federal Food, Drug, and Cosmetic Act with respect to residues of pesticide chemicals in or on raw agricultural commodities (Miller Pesticide Amendment) |

| Year | PL | Stat | Name of Statute |
|---|---|---|---|
| 1957 | 85-36 | 71 Stat. 31 | An Act To facilitate the regulation, control, and eradication of plant pests (Federal Plant Pest Act) |
| 1957 | 85-172 | 71 Stat. 441 | An Act To provide for the compulsory inspection by the United States Department of Agriculture of poultry and poultry products (Poultry Products Inspection Act) |
| 1958 | 85-765 | 72 Stat. 862 | An Act To Establish the Use of Humane Methods of Slaughter of Livestock as a Policy of the United States, and for other purposes |
| 1958 | 85-929 | 72 Stat. 1784 | Food Additives Amendment of 1958 |
| 1960 | 86-618 | 74 Stat. 397 | Color Additives Amendment of 1960 |
| 1962 | 87-781 | 76 Stat. 780 | Drug Amendments of 1962 (Kefauver-Harris Amendments of 1962) |
| 1966 | 89-755 | 80 Stat. 1296 | Fair Packaging and Labeling Act |
| 1968 | 90-399 | 82 Stat. 342 | Animal Drug Amendments of 1968 |
| 1970 | 91-513 | 84 Stat. 1236 | Comprehensive Drug Abuse Prevention and Control Act of 1970 |
| 1970 | 91-597 | 84 Stat. 1620 | Egg Products Inspection Act |
| 1974 | 93-348 | 88 Stat. 342 | National Research Act |
| 1976 | 94-278 | 90 Stat. 401 | Health Research and Health Services Amendments of 1976 (Vitamin-Mineral Amendments of 1976) |
| 1976 | 94-278 | 90 Stat. 401, 410 | Title V of Vitamin-Mineral Amendments of 1976 (Proxmire Amendment) |
| 1976 | 94-295 | 90 Stat. 539 | Medical Device Amendments of 1976 |
| 1977 | 95-203 | 91 Stat. 1451 | Saccharin Study and Labeling Act |
| 1980 | 96-359 | 94 Stat. 1190 | Infant Formula Act of 1980 |
| 1983 | 97-414 | 96 Stat. 2049 | Orphan Drug Act |
| 1984 | 98-417 | 98 Stat. 1585 | Drug Price Competition and Patent Term Restoration Act of 1984 [Hatch-Waxman Act] |
| 1985 | 99-198 | 99 Stat 1354, 1654 | Food Security Act of 1985, Section 1768, "Viruses, Serums, Toxins, and Analogous Products" |
| 1986 | 99-660 | 100 Stat. 3755 | National Childhood Vaccine Injury Act of 1986 (Childhood Vaccine Act) |
| 1988 | 100-607 | 102 Stat. 3048 | Health Omnibus Programs Extension of 1988 |
| 1988 | 100-607 | 102 Stat. 3048, 3120 | Food and Drug Administration Act of 1988 |
| 1988 | 100-293 | 102 Stat. 95 | Prescription Drug Marketing Act of 1987[1] |

1. This is the official short title written into the statute itself. However, the statute did not become law until the following calendar year.

| Year | PL | Stat | Name of Statute |
|---|---|---|---|
| 1988 | 100-670 | 102 Stat. 3971 | Generic Animal Drug and Patent Term Restoration Act (GADAPTRA) |
| 1990 | 101-535 | 104 Stat. 2353 | Nutrition Labeling and Education Act of 1990 |
| 1990 | 101-629 | 104 Stat. 4511 | Safe Medical Devices Act of 1990 (SMDA) |
| 1992 | 102-282 | 106 Stat. 149 | Generic Drug Enforcement Act of 1992 |
| 1992 | 102-300 | 106 Stat. 238 | Medical Device Amendments of 1992 |
| 1992 | 102-571 | 106 Stat. 4491 | Prescription Drug User Fee Act of 1992 |
| 1992 | 102-571 | 106 Stat. 4491, 4500 | Dietary Supplement Act of 1992 |
| 1993 | 103-80 | 107 Stat. 773 | Nutrition Labeling and Education Act Amendments of 1993 |
| 1994 | 103-396 | 108 Stat. 4153 | Animal Medical Drug Use Clarification Act of 1994 (AMDUCA) |
| 1994 | 103-417 | 108 Stat. 4325 | Dietary Supplement Health and Education Act of 1994 |
| 1996 | 104-134 | 110 Stat. 1321 | FDA Export Reform and Enhancement Act |
| 1996 | 104-170 | 110 Stat. 1489 | Food Quality Protection Act of 1996 |
| 1996 | 104-250 | 110 Stat. 3151 | Animal Drug Availability Act of 1996 (ADAA) |
| 1997 | 105-115 | 111 Stat. 2296 | Food and Drug Administration Modernization Act of 1997 (FDAMA) |
| 2000 | 106-224 | 114 Stat. 358 | Agricultural Risk Protection Act of 2000 (Plant Protection Act) |
| 2000 | 106-387 | 114 Stat. 1549 | Agriculture, Rural Development, Food and Drug Administration, and Related Agencies Appropriations Act |
| 2002 | 107-188 | 116 Stat. 594 | Public Health Security and Bioterrorism Preparedness and Response Act of 2002 |
| 2002 | 107-250 | 116 Stat. 1588 | Medical Device User Fee and Modernization Act of 2002 |
| 2003 | 108-155 | 117 Stat. 1936 | Pediatric Research Equity Act of 2003 |
| 2003 | 108-173 | 117 Stat. 2066 | Medicare Prescription Drug Improvement and Modernization Act of 2003 |
| 2004 | 108-276 | 118 Stat. 835 | Project BioShield Act of 2004 |
| 2004 | 108-282 | 118 Stat. 891 | Minor Use and Minor Species Animal Health Act of 2004 |
| 2004 | 108-282 | 118 Stat. 891, 905 | Food Allergen Labeling and Consumer Protection Act of 2004 |
| 2005 | 109-59 | 114 Stat 1144, 1911–1914 | Sanitary Food Transportation Act of 2005 |
| 2007 | 110-85 | 121 Stat. 823 | Food and Drug Administration Amendments Act of 2007 |

| Year | PL | Stat | Name of Statute |
|---|---|---|---|
| 2007 | 110-85 | 121 Stat. 823, 825 | Prescription Drug User Fee Amendments of 2007 |
| 2007 | 110-85 | 121 Stat. 823, 842 | Medical Device User Fee Amendments of 2007 |
| 2007 | 110-85 | 121 Stat. 823, 866 | Pediatric Research Equity Act of 2007 |
| 2007 | 110-85 | 121 Stat. 823, 876 | Best Pharmaceuticals for Children Act of 2007 |
| 2008 | 110-234 | 122 Stat. 923 | Food, Conservation, and Energy Act of 2008 (2008 Farm Bill) |
| 2008 | 110-316 | 122 Stat. 3509 | Animal Drug User Fee Amendments of 2008, Generic Animal Drug User Fee Act |
| 2009 | 111-31 | 123 Stat. 1776 | Family Smoking Prevention and Tobacco Control and Federal Retirement Reform (Family Smoking Prevention and Tobacco Control Act) |
| 2010 | 111-148 | 124 Stat. 119, 804 | Biologics Price Competition and Innovation Act of 2009[2] |
| 2011 | 111-353 | 124 Stat. 3885 | FDA Food Safety Modernization Act |
| 2012 | 112-144 | 126 Stat. 993 | Food and Drug Administration Safety and Innovation Act |
| 2012 | 112-144 | 126 Stat. 993, 996 | Prescription Drug User Fee Amendments of 2012 |
| 2012 | 112-144 | 126 Stat. 993, 996 | Medical Device User Fee Amendments of 2012 |
| 2012 | 112-144 | 126 Stat. 993, 1008 | Generic Drug User Fee Amendments of 2012 |
| 2012 | 112-144 | 126 Stat. 993, 1026 | Biosimilar User Fee Act of 2012 |
| 2013 | 113-5 | 127 Stat. 161 | Pandemic and All-Hazards Preparedness Reauthorization Act of 2013 |
| 2013 | 113-14 | 127 Stat. 451 | Animal Drug and Animal Generic Drug User Fee Reauthorization Act of 2013 |
| 2013 | 113-54 | 127 Stat. 587 | Drug Quality and Security Act |
| 2014 | 113-79 | 128 Stat. 649 | Agricultural Act of 2014 (2014 Farm Bill) |
| 2014 | 113-195 | 128 Stat. 2035 | Sunscreen Innovation Act |
| 2016 | 114-255 | 130 Stat. 1033 | 21st Century Cures Act |
| 2017 | 115-52 | 131 Stat. 1005 | FDA Reauthorization Act of 2017 |
| 2017 | 115-52 | 131 Stat. 1005, 1006 | Prescription Drug User Fee Amendments of 2017 |
| 2017 | 115-52 | 131 Stat. 1005, 1013 | Medical Device User Fee Amendments of 2017 |
| 2017 | 115-52 | 131 Stat. 1005, 1020 | Generic Drug User Fee Amendments of 2017 |
| 2017 | 115-52 | 131 Stat. 1005, 1028 | Biosimilar User Fee Amendments of 2017 |

2. This is the official short title written into the statute itself. However, the statute did not become law until the following calendar year.

| Year | PL | Stat | Name of Statute |
|---|---|---|---|
| 2017 | 115-92 | 131 Stat. 2023 | An Act to amend the Federal Food, Drug, and Cosmetic Act to authorize additional emergency uses for medical products to reduce deaths and severity of injuries caused by agents of war, and for other purposes. |
| 2018 | 115-234 | 132 Stat. 2427 | Animal Drug and Animal Generic Drug User Fee Amendments of 2018 |
| 2020 | 116-136 | 134 Stat. 281 | Coronavirus Aid, Relief, and Economic Security Act (CARES Act) |

# Appendix B

# Further Reading

**Items marked with two stars are available as audiobooks.

## A. Casebooks and Treatises

BRINGING YOUR PHARMACEUTICAL DRUG TO MARKET (Neil P. DiSpirito ed., 2015)

BARRY R. FURROW ET AL., HEALTH LAW: CASES, MATERIALS, AND PROBLEMS (6th ed. 2008)

MICHELE GOODWIN ET AL., BIOTECHNOLOGY, BIOETHICS, AND THE LAW (2015)

PETER BARTON HUTT ET AL., FOOD AND DRUG LAW: CASES AND MATERIALS (4th ed. 2014)

LUCINDA E. JESSON & STACY TOVINO, COMPLEMENTARY AND ALTERNATIVE MEDICINE AND THE LAW (2010)

WENDY K. MARINER ET AL., PUBLIC HEALTH LAW (3d ed. 2019)

RICHARD MENDELSON, WINE IN AMERICA: LAW AND POLICY (2011)

LARS NOAH, LAW, MEDICINE, AND MEDICAL TECHNOLOGY: CASES AND MATERIALS (3d ed. 2012)

A PRACTICAL GUIDE TO FDA'S FOOD AND DRUG REGULATION (Kenneth W. Piña & Wayne L. Pines eds., 5th ed. 2014)

MAXWELL L. STEARNS & TODD J. ZYWICKI, PUBLIC CHOICE: CONCEPTS AND APPLICATIONS IN LAW (2009)

## B. Food and Drug Regulation Generally (Other Than Casebooks and Treatises)

CHARLES O. JACKSON, FOOD AND DRUG REGULATION IN THE NEW DEAL (1970)

FDA IN THE 21ST CENTURY: THE CHALLENGES OF REGULATING DRUGS AND NEW TECHNOLOGIES (Holly Fernandez Lynch and I. Glenn Cohen eds., 2015)

JAMES HARVEY YOUNG, THE MEDICAL MESSIAHS: A SOCIAL HISTORY OF HEALTH QUACKERY IN TWENTIETH-CENTURY AMERICA (1967)

JAMES HARVEY YOUNG, AMERICAN SELF-DOSAGE MEDICINES: AN HISTORICAL PERSPECTIVE (1974)

## C. Administrative Practice and Procedure

Fred H. Degnan, FDA's Creative Application of Law: Not Merely A Collection of Words, 1–14 (2d. ed. 2006) (Chapter 1, "Groundwork: A Catalog of FDA's Regulatory Tools")

Fred H. Degnan, FDA's Creative Application of Law: Not Merely A Collection of Words, 105–111 (2d. ed. 2006) (Chapter 7, "A Regulatory Masterpiece: The FDA 'Voluntary' Recall")

## D. Food

Fred H. Degnan, FDA's Creative Application of Law: Not Merely A Collection of Words, 47–64 (2d. ed. 2006) (Chapter 4, "Combating Microbial Contamination of Food: The Evolution of FDA's Interpretation and Application of Section 402(a)(4)")

Fred H. Degnan, FDA's Creative Application of Law: Not Merely A Collection of Words, 133–147 (2d. ed. 2006) (Chapter 9, "Section 201(n) and the Food Label: Communicating Essential Information to Consumers")

**Michael Pollan, The Omnivore's Dilemma: A Natural History of Four Meals (2006)

## E. Food Additives

**Deborah Blum, The Poison Squad: One Chemist's Single-Minded Crusade for Food Safety at the Turn of the Twentieth Century (2018)

Fred H. Degnan, FDA's Creative Application of Law: Not Merely A Collection of Words, 15–35 (2d. ed. 2006) (Chapter 2, "The GRAS Concept: Ensuring Food Safety and Fostering Innovation")

## F. Dietary Supplements

Fred H. Degnan, FDA's Creative Application of Law: Not Merely A Collection of Words, 167–192 (2d. ed. 2006) (Chapter 11, "Dietary Supplements: Dealing with Congressional Accommodation to Public Demand")

## G. Food and Drug Classics (Including "Muckraking")

Morris Fishbein, Fads and Quackery in Healing (1932)

Arthur Kallet and F.J. Schlink, 100,000,000 Guinea Pigs: Dangers in Everyday Food, Drugs, and Cosmetics (1933)

Ruth deForest Lamb, American Chamber of Horrors: The Truth about Food and Drugs (1936)

## H. Drugs and Biologics

**John M. Barry, The Great Influenza: The Epic Story of the Deadliest Plague in History (2004)

Fred H. Degnan, FDA's Creative Application of Law: Not Merely A Collection of Words, 36–46 (2d. ed. 2006) (Chapter 3, "DESI Drugs and *Hynson*: The Confirmation of Rulemaking as a Regulatory Tool of Choice")

Fred H. Degnan, FDA's Creative Application of Law: Not Merely A Collection of Words, 70–82 (2d. ed. 2006) (Chapter 5, "New Drug Regulation from Laetrile to AZT: Rigid Enforcement and Accelerated Approval")

Richard A. Epstein, Overdose: How Excessive Government Regulation Stifles Pharmaceutical Innovation (2006)

**Charles Graeber, The Breakthrough: Immunotherapy and the Race to Cure Cancer (2018)

**Thomas Hager, The Demon Under the Microscope: From Battlefield Hospitals to Nazi Labs, One Doctor's Search for the World's First Miracle Drug (2006)

**Thomas Hager, Ten Drugs: How Plants, Powders, and Pills have Shaped the History of Medicine (2019)

**Jeffrey Kluger, Splendid Solution: Jonas Salk and the Conquest of Polio (2004)

**Paul de Kruif, Microbe Hunters (1926, 1954)

Jie Jack Li, Laughing Gas, Viagra, and Lipitor: The Human Stories Behind the Drugs We Use (2006)

Jie Jack Li, Triumph of the Heart: The Story of Statins (2009)

**Jie Jack Li, Blockbuster Drugs: The Rise and Decline of the Pharmaceutical Industry (2014)

**David M. Oshinsky, Polio: An American Story (2005)

**William Rosen, Miracle Cure: The Creation of Antibiotics and the Birth of Modern Medicine (2017)

Peter Temin, Taking Your Medicine: Drug Regulation in the United States (1980)

**Meredith Wadman, The Vaccine Race: Science, Politics, and the Human Costs of Defeating Disease (2017)

## I. Medical Devices

Fred H. Degnan, FDA's Creative Application of Law: Not Merely A Collection of Words, 114–132 (2d. ed. 2006) (Chapter 8, "Sections 510(k) and 513(f)(1): Creative Linkage")

## J. Medicine Generally

Norman Gevitz, The D.O.s: Osteopathic Medicine in America (1982)

**David Oshinsky, Bellevue: Three Centuries of Medicine and Mayhem at America's Most Storied Hospital (2016)

Paul Starr, The Social Transformation of American Medicine (2d ed. 2017)

## K. The Microbiome

**Giulia Enders, Gut: The Inside Story of Our Body's Most Underrated Organ (Revised ed., David Shaw trans., 2018)
**Ed Young, I Contain Multitudes: The Microbiome within Us and a Grander View of Life (2016)

## L. Tobacco Products

Fred H. Degnan, FDA's Creative Application of Law: Not Merely A Collection of Words, 150–166 (2d. ed. 2006) (Chapter 10, "FDA's End-of-Century Effort to Regulate Tobacco: Thinking Outside of the Toolbox?")

## M. Cancer / Carcinogen Regulation

Frank B. Cross, Environmentally Induced Cancer and the Law: Risks, Regulation, and Victim Compensation (1989)

Fred H. Degnan, FDA's Creative Application of Law: Not Merely A Collection of Words, 83–104 (2d. ed. 2006) (Chapter 6, "The Normalization of Avoidance: FDA's Interpretation and Application of the Delaney Clause")

## N. Statutory Interpretation and Administrative Law

Fred H. Degnan, FDA's Creative Application of Law: Not Merely A Collection of Words (2d. ed. 2006)

William N. Eskridge, Jr., Dynamic Statutory Interpretation (1994)

# Index

D

E

## V